The Battle for God

The Battle for God

Fundamentalism in Judaism, Christianity and Islam

KAREN ARMSTRONG

HarperCollins*Publishers*

HarperCollins*Publishers*
77–85 Fulham Palace Road,
Hammersmith, London W6 8JB

www.fireandwater.com

Published by HarperCollins*Publishers* 2000
1 3 5 7 9 8 6 4 2

First published in the USA by
Alfred A. Knopf 2000

A catalogue record for this book
is available from the British Library

ISBN 0 00 255523 9

Printed and bound in Great Britain by
Clays Ltd, St Ives plc

For Jenny Wayman

CONTENTS

INTRODUCTION

ONE OF the most startling developments of the late twentieth century has been the emergence within every major religious tradition of a militant piety popularly known as "fundamentalism." Its manifestations are sometimes shocking. Fundamentalists have gunned down worshippers in a mosque, have killed doctors and nurses who work in abortion clinics, have shot their presidents, and have even toppled a powerful government. It is only a small minority of fundamentalists who commit such acts of terror, but even the most peaceful and law-abiding are perplexing, because they seem so adamantly opposed to many of the most positive values of modern society. Fundamentalists have no time for democracy, pluralism, religious toleration, peacekeeping, free speech, or the separation of church and state. Christian fundamentalists reject the discoveries of biology and physics about the origins of life and insist that the Book of Genesis is scientifically sound in every detail. At a time when many are throwing off the shackles of the past, Jewish fundamentalists observe their revealed Law more stringently than ever before, and Muslim women, repudiating the freedoms of Western women, shroud themselves in veils and chadors. Muslim and Jewish fundamentalists both interpret the Arab-Israeli conflict, which began as defiantly secularist, in an exclusively religious way. Fundamentalism, moreover, is not confined to the great monotheisms. There are Buddhist, Hindu, and even Confucian fundamentalisms, which also cast aside many of the painfully acquired insights of liberal culture, which fight and kill in the name of religion and strive to bring the sacred into the realm of politics and national struggle.

This religious resurgence has taken many observers by surprise. In the middle years of the twentieth century, it was generally taken for granted that secularism was an irreversible trend and that faith would never again play a major part in world events. It was assumed that as human beings became more rational, they either would have no further need for religion or would be content to confine it to the immediately personal and private areas of their lives. But in the late 1970s, fundamentalists began to rebel against this secularist hegemony and started to wrest religion out of its marginal position and back to center stage. In this, at least, they have enjoyed remarkable success. Religion has once again become a force that no government can safely ignore. Fundamentalism has suffered defeats, but it is by no means quiescent. It is now an essential part of the modern scene and will certainly play an important role in the domestic and international affairs of the future. It is crucial, therefore, that we try to understand what this type of religiosity means, how and for what reasons it has developed, what it can tell us about our culture, and how best we should deal with it.

But before we proceed, we must look briefly at the term "fundamentalism" itself, which has been much criticized. American Protestants were the first to use it. In the early decades of the twentieth century, some of them started to call themselves "fundamentalists" to distinguish themselves from the more "liberal" Protestants, who were, in their opinion, entirely distorting the Christian faith. The fundamentalists wanted to go back to basics and reemphasize the "fundamentals" of the Christian tradition, which they identified with a literal interpretation of Scripture and the acceptance of certain core doctrines. The term "fundamentalism" has since been applied to reforming movements in other world faiths in a way that is far from satisfactory. It seems to suggest that fundamentalism is monolithic in all its manifestations. This is not the case. Each "fundamentalism" is a law unto itself and has its own dynamic. The term also gives the impression that fundamentalists are inherently conservative and wedded to the past, whereas their ideas are essentially modern and highly innovative. The American Protestants may have intended to go back to the "fundamentals," but they did so in a peculiarly modern way. It has also been argued that this Christian term cannot be accurately applied to movements that have entirely different priorities. Muslim and Jewish fundamentalisms, for example, are not much concerned with doctrine, which is an essentially Christian preoccupation. A literal translation of "fundamentalism" into Arabic gives us *usuliyyah,* a word that refers to the study of the sources of the various rules and principles of Islamic law.[1] Most of the activists who are dubbed "fundamentalists" in the West are not engaged in this Islamic science, but have quite different concerns. The use of the term "fundamentalism" is, therefore, misleading.

Others, however, argue simply that, like it or not, the word "fundamentalism" is here to stay. And I have come to agree: the term is not perfect, but it is a useful label for movements that, despite their differences, bear a strong family resemblance. At the outset of their monumental six-volume Fundamentalist Project, Martin E. Marty and R. Scott Appleby argue that the "fundamentalisms" all follow a certain pattern. They are embattled forms of spirituality, which have emerged as a response to a perceived crisis. They are engaged in a conflict with enemies whose secularist policies and beliefs seem inimical to religion itself. Fundamentalists do not regard this battle as a conventional political struggle, but experience it as a cosmic war between the forces of good and evil. They fear annihilation, and try to fortify their beleaguered identity by means of a selective retrieval of certain doctrines and practices of the past. To avoid contamination, they often withdraw from mainstream society to create a counterculture; yet fundamentalists are not impractical dreamers. They have absorbed the pragmatic rationalism of modernity, and, under the guidance of their charismatic leaders, they refine these "fundamentals" so as to create an ideology that provides the faithful with a plan of action. Eventually they fight back and attempt to resacralize an increasingly skeptical world.[2]

To explore the implications of this global response to modern culture, I want to concentrate on just a few of the fundamentalist movements that have surfaced in Judaism, Christianity, and Islam, the three monotheistic faiths. Instead of studying them in isolation from one another, I intend to trace their development chronologically, side by side, so that we can see how deeply similar they are. By looking at selected fundamentalisms, I hope to examine the phenomenon in greater depth than would be possible in a more general, comprehensive survey. The movements I have chosen are American Protestant fundamentalism, Jewish fundamentalism in Israel, and Muslim fundamentalism in Egypt, which is a Sunni country, and Iran, which is Shii. I do not claim that my discoveries necessarily apply to other forms of fundamentalism, but hope to show how these particular movements, which have been among the most prominent and influential, have all been motivated by common fears, anxieties, and desires that seem to be a not unusual response to some of the peculiar difficulties of life in the modern secular world.

There have always been people, in every age and in each tradition, who have fought the modernity of their day. But the fundamentalism that we shall be considering is an essentially twentieth-century movement. It is a reaction against the scientific and secular culture that first appeared in the West, but which has since taken root in other parts of the world. The West has developed an entirely unprecedented and wholly different type of civilization, so the religious response to it has been unique. The fundamentalist movements that have evolved in our own day have a symbiotic relationship with modernity. They may reject the scientific rationalism of the West, but they cannot escape it. Western civilization has changed the world. Nothing—including religion—can ever be the same again. All over the globe, people have been struggling with these new conditions and have been forced to reassess their religious traditions, which were designed for an entirely different type of society.

There was a similar transitional period in the ancient world, lasting roughly from 700 to 200 BCE, which historians have called the Axial Age because it was pivotal to the spiritual development of humanity. This age was itself the product and fruition of thousands of years of economic, and therefore social and cultural, evolution, beginning in Sumer in what is now Iraq, and in ancient Egypt. People in the fourth and third millennia BCE, instead of simply growing enough crops to satisfy their immediate needs, became capable of producing an agricultural surplus with which they could trade and thereby acquire additional income. This enabled them to build the first civilizations, develop the arts, and create increasingly powerful polities: cities, city-states, and, eventually, empires. In agrarian society, power no longer lay exclusively with the local king or priest; its locus shifted at least partly to the marketplace, the source of each culture's wealth. In these altered circumstances, people ultimately began to find that the old paganism, which had served their ancestors well, no longer spoke fully to their condition.

In the cities and empires of the Axial Age, citizens were acquiring a wider perspective and broader horizons, which made the old local cults seem limited and parochial. Instead of seeing the divine as embodied in a number of different deities, people increasingly began to worship a single, universal transcendence and source of sacredness. They had more leisure and were thus able to develop a richer interior life; accordingly, they came to desire a spirituality which did not depend entirely upon external forms. The most sensitive were troubled by the social injustice that seemed built into this agrarian society, depending as it did on the labor of peasants who never had the chance to benefit from the high culture. Consequently, prophets and reformers arose who insisted that the virtue of compassion was crucial to the spiritual life: an ability to see sacredness in every single human being, and a willingness to take practical care of the more vulnerable members of society, became the test of authentic piety. In this way, during the Axial Age, the great confessional faiths that have continued to guide human beings sprang up in the civilized world: Buddhism and Hinduism in India, Confucianism and Taoism in the Far East; monotheism in the Middle East; and rationalism in Europe. Despite their major differences, these Axial Age religions had much in common: they all built on the old traditions to evolve the idea of a single, universal transcendence; they cultivated an internalized spirituality, and stressed the importance of practical compassion.

Today, as noted, we are undergoing a similar period of transition. Its roots lie in the sixteenth and seventeenth centuries of the modern era, when the people of Western Europe began to evolve a different type of society, one based not on an agricultural surplus but on a technology that enabled them to reproduce their resources indefinitely. The economic changes over the last four hundred years have been accompanied by immense social, political, and intellectual revolutions, with the development of an entirely different, scientific and rational, concept of the nature of truth; and, once again, a radical religious change has become necessary. All over the world, people are finding that in their dramatically transformed circumstances, the old forms of faith no longer work for them: they cannot provide the enlightenment and consolation that human beings seem to need. As a result, men and women are trying to find new ways of being religious; like the reformers and prophets of the Axial Age, they are attempting to build upon the insights of the past in a way that will take human beings forward into the new world they have created for themselves. One of these modern experiments—however paradoxical it may superficially seem to say so—is fundamentalism.

We tend to assume that the people of the past were (more or less) like us, but in fact their spiritual lives were rather different. In particular, they evolved two ways of thinking, speaking, and acquiring knowledge, which scholars have called *mythos* and *logos*.³ Both were essential; they were regarded as complementary ways of arriving at truth, and each had its special area of competence. Myth was regarded as primary; it was concerned with what was thought to be timeless and constant in our existence. Myth looked back to the origins of life, to the foundations of culture, and to the deepest levels of the human mind. Myth was not concerned with practical matters, but with meaning. Unless we find some significance in our lives, we mortal men and women fall very easily into despair. The *mythos* of a society provided people with a context that made sense of their day-to-day lives; it directed their attention to the eternal and the universal. It was also rooted in what we would call the unconscious mind. The various mythological stories, which were not intended to be taken literally, were an ancient form of psychology. When people told stories about heroes who descended into the underworld, struggled through labyrinths, or fought with monsters, they were bringing to light the obscure regions of the subconscious realm, which is not accessible to purely rational investigation, but which has a profound effect upon our experience and behavior.⁴ Because of the dearth of myth in our modern society, we have had to evolve the science of psychoanalysis to help us to deal with our inner world.

Myth could not be demonstrated by rational proof; its insights were more intuitive, similar to those of art, music, poetry, or sculpture. Myth only became a reality when it was embodied in cult, rituals, and ceremonies which worked aesthetically upon worshippers, evoking within them a sense of sacred significance and enabling them to apprehend the deeper currents of existence. Myth and cult were so inseparable that it is a matter of scholarly debate which came first: the mythical narrative or the rituals attached to it.[5] Myth was also associated with mysticism, the descent into the psyche by means of structured disciplines of focus and concentration which have been evolved in all cultures as a means of acquiring intuitive insight. Without a cult or mystical practice, the myths of religion would make no sense. They would remain abstract and seem incredible, in rather the same way as a musical score remains opaque to most of us and needs to be interpreted instrumentally before we can appreciate its beauty.

In the premodern world, people had a different view of history. They were less interested than we are in what actually happened, but more concerned with the meaning of an event. Historical incidents were not seen as unique occurrences, set in a far-off time, but were thought to be external manifestations of constant, timeless realities. Hence history would tend to repeat itself, because there was nothing new under the sun. Historical narratives tried to bring out this eternal dimension.[6] Thus, we do not know what really occurred when the ancient Israelites escaped from Egypt and passed through the Sea of Reeds. The story has been deliberately written as a myth, and linked with other stories about rites of passage, immersion in the deep, and gods splitting a sea in two to create a new reality. Jews experience this myth every year in the rituals of the Passover Seder, which brings this strange story into their own lives and helps them to make it their own. One could say that unless an historical event is mythologized in this way, and liberated from the past in an inspiring cult, it cannot be religious. To ask whether the Exodus from Egypt took place exactly as recounted in the Bible or to demand historical and scientific evidence to prove that it is factually true is to mistake the nature and purpose of this story. It is to confuse *mythos* with *logos*.

Logos was equally important. *Logos* was the rational, pragmatic, and scientific thought that enabled men and women to function well in the world. We may have lost the sense of *mythos* in the West today, but we are very familiar with *logos*, which is the basis of our society. Unlike myth, *logos* must relate exactly to facts and correspond to external realities if it is to be effective. It must work efficiently in the mundane world. We use this logical, discursive reasoning when we have to make things happen, get something done, or persuade other people to adopt a particular course of action. *Logos* is practical. Unlike myth, which looks back to the beginnings and to the foundations, *logos* forges ahead and tries to find something new: to elaborate on old insights, achieve a greater control over our environment, discover something fresh, and invent something novel.[7]

In the premodern world, both *mythos* and *logos* were regarded as indispensable. Each would be impoverished without the other. Yet the two were essentially distinct, and it was held to be dangerous to confuse mythical and rational discourse. They had separate jobs to do. Myth was not reasonable; its narratives were not supposed to be demonstrated empirically. It provided the context of meaning that made our practical activities worthwhile. You were not supposed to make *mythos* the basis of a pragmatic policy. If you did so, the results could be disastrous, because what worked well in the inner world of the psyche was not readily applicable to the affairs of the external world. When, for example, Pope Urban II summoned the First Crusade in 1095, his plan belonged to the realm of *logos*. He wanted the knights of Europe to stop fighting one another and tearing the fabric of Western Christendom apart, and to expend their energies instead in a war in the Middle East and so extend the power of his church. But when this military expedition became entangled with folk mythology, biblical lore, and apocalyptic fantasies, the result was catastrophic, practically, militarily, and morally. Throughout the long crusading project, it remained true that whenever *logos* was ascendant, the Crusaders prospered. They performed well on the battlefield, created viable colonies in the Middle East, and learned to relate more positively with the local population. When, however, Crusaders started making a mythical or mystical vision the basis of their policies, they were usually defeated and committed terrible atrocities.[8]

Logos had its limitations too. It could not assuage human pain or sorrow. Rational arguments could make no sense of tragedy. *Logos* could not answer questions about the ultimate value of human life. A scientist could make things work more efficiently and discover wonderful new facts about the physical universe, but he could not explain the meaning of life.[9] That was the preserve of myth and cult.

By the eighteenth century, however, the people of Europe and America had achieved such astonishing success in science and technology that they began to think that *logos* was the only means to truth and began to discount *mythos* as false and superstitious. It is also true that the new world they were creating contradicted the dynamic of the old mythical spirituality. Our religious experience in the modern world has changed, and because an increasing number of people regard scientific rationalism alone as true, they have often tried to turn the *mythos* of their faith into *logos*. Fundamentalists have also made this attempt. This confusion has led to more problems.

We need to understand how our world has changed. The first part of this book will, therefore, go back to the late fifteenth and early sixteenth centuries, when the people of Western Europe had begun to develop their new science. We will also examine the mythical piety of the premodern agrarian civilization, so that we can see how the old forms of faith worked. It is becoming very difficult to be conventionally religious in the brave new world. Modernization has always been a painful process. People feel alienated and lost when fundamental changes in their society make the world strange and unrecognizable. We will trace the impact of modernity upon the Christians of Europe and America, upon the Jewish people, and upon the Muslims of Egypt and Iran. We shall then be in a position to see what the fundamentalists were trying to do when they started to create this new form of faith toward the end of the nineteenth century.

Fundamentalists feel that they are battling against forces that threaten their most sacred values. During a war it is very difficult for combatants to appreciate one another's position. We shall find that modernization has led to a polarization of society, but sometimes, to prevent an escalation of the conflict, we must try to understand the pain and perceptions of the other side. Those of us—myself included—who relish the freedoms and achievements of modernity find it hard to comprehend the distress these cause religious fundamentalists. Yet modernization is often experienced not as a liberation but as an aggressive assault. Few have suffered more in the modern world than the Jewish people, so it is fitting to begin with their bruising encounter with the modernizing society of Western Christendom in the late fifteenth century, which led some Jews to anticipate many of the stratagems, postures, and principles that would later become common in the new world.

PART ONE

The Old World and the New

1. Jews: The Precursors
(1492–1700)

IN 1492, three very important things happened in Spain. The events were experienced as extraordinary at the time, but with hindsight we can see that they were characteristic of the new society that was, slowly and painfully, coming to birth in Western Europe during the late-fifteenth, sixteenth, and seventeenth centuries. These years saw the development of our modern Western culture, so 1492 also throws light on some of our own preoccupations and dilemmas. The first of these events occurred on January 2, when the armies of King Ferdinand and Queen Isabella, the Catholic monarchs whose marriage had recently united the old Iberian kingdoms of Aragon and Castile, conquered the city-state of Granada. With deep emotion, the crowd watched the Christian banner raised ceremonially upon the city walls and, as the news broke, bells pealed triumphantly all over Europe, for Granada was the last Muslim stronghold in Christendom. The Crusades against Islam in the Middle East had failed, but at least the Muslims had been flushed out of Europe. In 1499, the Muslim inhabitants of Spain were given the option of conversion to Christianity or deportation, after which, for a few centuries, Europe would become Muslim-free. The second event of this momentous year happened on March 31, when Ferdinand and Isabella signed the Edict of Expulsion, designed to rid Spain of its Jews, who were given the choice of baptism or deportation. Many Jews were so attached to "al-Andalus" (as the old Muslim kingdom had been called) that they converted to Christianity and remained in Spain, but about 80,000 Jews crossed the border into Portugal, while 50,000 fled to the new Muslim Ottoman empire, where they were given a warm welcome.[1] The third event concerned one of the people who had been present at the Christian occupation of Granada. In August, Christopher Columbus, a protégé of Ferdinand and

Isabella, sailed from Spain to find a new trade route to India but discovered the Americas instead.

These events reflect both the glory and the devastation of the early modern period. As the voyage of Columbus showed so powerfully, the people of Europe were on the brink of a new world. Their horizons were broadening, they were entering hitherto uncharted realms, geographically, intellectually, socially, economically, and politically. Their achievements would make them masters of the globe. But modernity had a darker side. Christian Spain was one of the most powerful and advanced kingdoms in Europe. Ferdinand and Isabella were in the process of creating one of the modern centralized states that were also appearing in other parts of Christendom. Such a kingdom could not tolerate the old autonomous, self-governing institutions, such as the guild, the corporation, or the Jewish community, which had characterized the medieval period. The unification of Spain, which was completed by the conquest of Granada, was succeeded by an act of ethnic cleansing, and Jews and Muslims lost their homes. For some people, modernity was empowering, liberating, and enthralling. Others experienced it—and would continue to experience it—as coercive, invasive, and destructive. As Western modernity spread to other parts of the earth, this pattern would continue. The modernizing program was enlightening and would eventually promote humane values, but it was also aggressive. During the twentieth century, some of the people who experienced modernity primarily as an assault would become fundamentalists.

But that was far in the future. In the late fifteenth century, the people of Europe could not have foreseen the enormity of the change they had initiated. In the course of the next three hundred years, Europe would not only transform its society politically and economically, but also achieve an intellectual revolution. Scientific rationalism would become the order of the day, and would gradually oust the older habits of mind and heart. We shall look at the Great Western Transformation, as this period has been called, in more detail in Chapter 3. Before we can appreciate its full implications, however, we must first look at the way that people in the premodern era experienced the world. In the universities of Spain, students and teachers excitedly discussed the new ideas of the Italian Renaissance. The voyage of Columbus would have been impossible without such scientific discoveries as the magnetic compass or the latest insights in astronomy. By 1492, Western scientific rationalism was becoming spectacularly efficient. People were discovering more fully than ever before the potential of what the Greeks had called *logos*, which was always reaching out for something fresh. Thanks to modern science, Europeans had discovered a wholly new world and were achieving unprecedented control over the environment. But they had not yet dismissed *mythos.* Columbus was conversant with science, but he was still at home in the old mythological universe. He seems to have come from a family of converted Jews and to have retained an interest in the Kabbalah, the mystical tradition of Judaism, but he was a devout Christian, and wanted to win the world for Christ. He hoped that when he arrived in India, he would establish a Christian base there for the military conquest of Jerusalem.[2] The people of Europe had started their journey to modernity, but they were not yet fully modern in our sense. For them, the myths of Christianity still gave meaning to their rational and scientific explorations.

Nevertheless, Christianity was changing. Spaniards would become leaders of the Counter-Reformation initiated by the Council of Trent (1545–63), which was a modernizing movement that brought the old Catholicism into line with the streamlined efficiency of the new Europe. The Church, like the modern state, became a more centralized body. The Council reinforced the power of the Pope and the bishops; for the first time a catechism was issued to all the faithful, to ensure doctrinal conformity. The clergy were to be educated to a higher standard, so that they could preach more effectively. The liturgy and devotional practices of the laity were rationalized, and rituals that had been meaningful a century earlier but no longer worked in the new era, were jettisoned. Many Spanish Catholics were inspired by the writings of the Dutch humanist Desiderius Erasmus (1466–1536), who wanted to revitalize Christianity by returning to fundamentals. His slogan was *Ad fontes:* "back to the wellsprings!" Erasmus believed that the authentic Christian faith of the early church had been buried under a mound of lifeless medieval theology. By stripping away these later accretions and going back to the sources—the Bible and the Fathers of the Church—Christians would recover the living kernel of the Gospels and experience new birth.

The chief Spanish contribution to the Counter-Reformation was mystical. The mystics of Iberia became explorers of the spiritual world, in rather the same way as the great navigators were discovering new regions of the physical world. Mysticism belonged to the realm of *mythos;* it functioned in the domain of the unconscious which was inaccessible to the rational faculty and has to be experienced by means of other techniques. Nevertheless, the mystical reformers of Spain wanted to make this form of spirituality less haphazard, and eccentric, less dependent upon the whims of inadequate advisers. John of the Cross (1552–91) weeded out the more dubious and superstitious devotions, and made the mystical process more systematic. The mystics of the new age should know what to expect when they progressed from one stage to another; they must learn how to deal with pitfalls and dangers of the interior life, and husband their spiritual energies productively.

More modern, however, and a sign of things to come was the Society of Jesus, founded by the former soldier Ignatius of Loyola (1491–1555), which embodied the efficiency and effectiveness that would become the hallmark of the modern West. Ignatius was determined to exploit the power of *mythos* practically. His Jesuits did not have time for the lengthy contemplative disciplines evolved by John of the Cross. His *Spiritual Exercises* provided a systematic, time-efficient, thirty-day retreat, which offered every Jesuit a crash course in mysticism. Once the Christian had achieved a full conversion to Christ, he should have his priorities right and be ready for action. This emphasis on method, discipline, and organization was similar to the new science. God was experienced as a dynamic force that propelled Jesuits all over the world, in rather the same way as the explorers. Francis Xavier (1506–52) evangelized Japan, Robert di Nobili (1577–1656) India, and Matteo Ricci (1552–1610) China. Religion had not yet been left behind in early modern Spain. It was able to reform itself and exploit the dawning insights of modernity to further its own reach and vision.

Early modern Spain was, therefore, part of the advance guard of modernity. But Ferdinand and Isabella had to contain all this energy. They were trying to unite kingdoms that had hitherto been independent and separate, and had to be welded together. In 1483 the monarchs had established their own Spanish Inquisition to enforce ideological conformity in their unified realm. They were creating a modern, absolute state, but did not yet have the resources to allow their subjects untrammeled intellectual freedom. The state inquisitors sought out dissidents and forced them to abjure their "heresy," a word whose Greek original meant "to go one's own way." The Spanish Inquisition was not an archaic attempt to preserve a bygone world; it was a modernizing institution, employed by the monarchs to create national unity.[3] They knew very well that religion could be an explosive and revolutionary force. Protestant rulers in such countries as England were equally ruthless to their own Catholic "dissidents," who were seen similarly as enemies of the state. We shall see that this kind of coercion was often part of the modernizing process. In Spain, the chief victims of the Inquisition were the Jews, and it is the reaction of the Jewish people to this aggressive modernity that we shall consider in this chapter. Their experience illustrates many of the ways in which people in other parts of the world would respond to modernization.

The Spanish *reconquista* of the old Muslim territories of al-Andalus was a catastrophe for the Jews of Iberia. In the Islamic state, the three religions of Judaism, Christianity, and Islam had been able to live together in relative harmony for over six hundred years. The Jews in particular had enjoyed a cultural and spiritual renaissance in Spain, and they were not subject to the pogroms that were the lot of the Jewish people in the rest of Europe.⁴ But as the Christian armies gradually advanced through the peninsula, conquering more and more territory from Islam, they brought their anti-Semitism with them. In 1378 and 1391, Jewish communities in both Aragon and Castile were attacked by Christians, who dragged Jews to the baptismal fonts and forced them, on pain of death, to convert to Christianity. In Aragon, the preaching of the Dominican friar Vincent Ferrer (1350–1419) regularly inspired anti-Semitic riots; Ferrer also organized public debates between rabbis and Christians that were designed to discredit Judaism. Some Jews tried to evade persecution by voluntarily converting to Christianity. They were officially known as *conversos* ("converts"), though the Christians called them Marranos ("pigs"), a term of abuse which some of the converts adopted as a badge of pride. The rabbis warned Jews against conversion, but at first the "New Christians," as the *conversos* were called, became wealthy and successful. Some became high-ranking priests, others married into the best families, and many achieved spectacular success in commerce. This brought new problems, since the "Old Christians" resented the upward mobility of the new Jewish Christians. Between 1449 and 1474, there were frequent riots against the Marranos, who were killed, had their property destroyed, or were driven out of town.⁵

Ferdinand and Isabella were alarmed by this development. The conversion of the Jews was not drawing their united kingdom together but instead causing fresh divisions. The monarchs were also disturbed to hear reports that some of the "New Christians" had lapsed, returned to the old faith, and lived as secret Jews. They had, it was said, formed an underground movement to entice other *conversos* back into the Jewish fold. Inquisitors were instructed to hunt out these closet Jews, who, it was thought, could be recognized by such practices as refusing to eat pork or to work on Saturday. Suspects were tortured until they confessed to infidelity, and gave information about other secret "Judaizers." As a result, some 13,000 *conversos* were killed by the Inquisition during the first twelve years of its existence. But in fact many of those who were thus killed or imprisoned, or had their property confiscated, were loyal Catholics who had no Judaizing tendencies at all. The experience not unnaturally made many of the *conversos* bitter and skeptical of their new faith.⁶

When Ferdinand and Isabella conquered Granada in 1492, they inherited a new and substantial Jewish population in that city-state. The situation, they decided, had got out of hand, and as a final solution to the Jewish problem, the monarchs signed the Edict of Expulsion. Spanish Jewry was destroyed. About 70,000 Jews converted to Christianity, and stayed on to be plagued by the Inquisition; the remaining 130,000, as we have seen, went into exile. The

loss of Spanish Jewry was mourned by Jews all over the world as the greatest catastrophe to have befallen their people since the destruction of the
Temple in Jerusalem in 70 CE, when the Jews lost their land and were forced
into exile in scattered communities outside Palestine, known collectively
as the Diaspora. From that time on, exile was a painful leitmotif of Jewish
life. The expulsion from Spain in 1492 came at the end of a century that had
seen the ejection of Jews from one part of Europe after another. They were
deported from Vienna and Linz in 1421, from Cologne in 1424, from Augs-
burg in 1439, from Bavaria in 1442, and from the crown cities of Moravia
in 1454. Jews were expelled from Perugia (1485), Vicenza (1486), Parma
(1488), Milan and Lucca (1489), and Tuscany in 1494. Gradually the Jews
drifted east, establishing, as they thought, a foothold for themselves in
Poland.[7] Exile now seemed an endemic and inescapable part of the Jewish
condition.

This was certainly the conviction of those Spanish Jews who after the
expulsion took refuge in the North African and Balkan provinces of the
Ottoman empire. They were used to Muslim society, but the loss of Spain—
or Sefarad, as they called it—had inflicted a deep psychic wound. These
Sephardic Jews felt that they themselves and everything else were in the
wrong place.[8] Exile is a spiritual as well as a physical dislocation. The world
of the exile is wholly unfamiliar and, therefore, without meaning. A violent
uprooting, which takes away all normal props, breaks up our world, snatches
us forever from places that are saturated in memories crucial to our identity,
and plunges us permanently in an alien environment, can make us feel that
our very existence has been jeopardized. When exile is also associated with
human cruelty, it raises urgent questions about the problem of evil in a
world supposedly created by a just and benevolent God.

The experience of the Sephardic Jews was an extreme form of the
uprooting and displacement that other peoples would later experience when
they were caught up in an aggressive modernizing process. We shall see that
when modern Western civilization took root in a foreign environment, it
transformed the culture so drastically that many people felt alienated and
disoriented. The old world had been swept away, and the new one was
so strange that people could not recognize their once-familiar surroundings and could make no sense of their lives. Many would become convinced,
like the Sephardics, that their very existence was threatened. They would
fear annihilation and extinction. In their confusion and pain, many would do
what some of the Spanish exiles did, and turn to religion. But because
their lives were so utterly changed, they would have to evolve new forms
of faith to make the old traditions speak to them in their radically altered
circumstances.

But this would take time. In the early sixteenth century, the exiled Jews found that traditional Judaism did nothing for them. The disaster seemed unprecedented, and they found that old pieties no longer worked. Some turned to messianism. For centuries, Jews had waited for a Messiah, an anointed king of the house of David, to bring their long exile to an end and return them to the Promised Land. Some Jewish traditions spoke of a period of tribulation immediately before the advent of the Messiah, and it occurred to some of the Sephardic exiles who had taken refuge in the Balkans, that the suffering and persecution that had befallen themselves and so many of their fellow Jews in Europe could only mean one thing: this must be the time of trial foretold by the prophets and sages, and called the "birth pangs of the Messiah," because out of this anguish deliverance and new life would come.⁹ Other peoples who have felt that their world has been destroyed by the onset of modernity would also evolve millennial hopes. But messianism is problematic, because, until now, every single messianic movement that has expected an imminent Redeemer has been disappointed. The Sephardic Jews avoided this dilemma by finding a more satisfying solution. They developed a new *mythos*.

A group of Sephardics had moved from the Balkans to Palestine, where they settled in Safed in Galilee. There was a tradition that when the Messiah came, he would reveal himself in Galilee, and the Spanish exiles wanted to be the first to greet him.¹⁰ Some of them came to believe that they had found him in a saintly, sickly Ashkenazic Jew, Isaac Luria (1534–72), who settled in Safed and was the first to articulate the new myth. He thus founded a form of Kabbalah that still bears his name. We moderns would say that Luria created this myth; that he was so perfectly attuned to the unconscious desires and fears of his people that he was able to evolve an imaginative fiction that brought comfort and hope not only to the exiles in Safed but to Jews all over the world. But we would say this because we think primarily in rational terms and find it hard to enter into the premodern mythical worldview. Luria's disciples did not perceive him as having "made up" his creation myth; instead, as they saw it, the myth had declared itself to him. To an outsider, not involved in the rituals and practices of Lurianic Kabbalah, this creation story seems bizarre. Moreover, it bears no resemblance to the creation story in the Book of Genesis. But to a Kabbalist of Safed—immersed in the rites and meditative exercises prescribed by Luria, and still, a full generation after it had happened, reeling with the shock of exile—the *mythos* made perfect sense. It revealed or "unveiled" a truth that had been evident before but which spoke with such power to the condition of Jews in the early modern period that it acquired instant authority. It illuminated their dark world and made life not only tolerable but joyous.

When confronted with the Lurianic creation myth, a modern person will immediately ask: "Did this really happen?" Because the events seem so improbable and cannot be proved, we will dismiss it as demonstrably false. But that is because we accept only a rational version of truth and have lost the sense that there might be another kind. We have developed, for example, a scientific view of history, which we see as a succession of unique events. In the premodern world, however, the events of history were not seen as singular but as examples of eternal laws, revelations of a timeless, constant reality. A historical occurrence would be likely to happen again and again, because all earthly happenings expressed the fundamental laws of existence. In the Bible, for example, a river parts miraculously on at least two occasions to enable the Israelites to make a rite of passage; the Children of Israel are often "going down" into Egypt and then making a return journey to the Promised Land. One of the most frequently recurring biblical themes was exile, which, after the Spanish catastrophe, seemed to color the whole of Jewish existence and to reflect an imbalance in the very ground of being. Lurianic Kabbalah addressed itself to this problem by going back, as all mythology must, to the beginning in order to examine exile, which seemed one of these fundamental laws, and to reveal its full significance.

In Luria's myth, the creative process begins with an act of voluntary exile. It starts by asking how the world could exist if God is omnipresent. The answer is the doctrine of Zimzum ("withdrawal"): the infinite and inaccessible Godhead, which Kabbalists called Ein Sof ("Without End"), had to shrink into itself, evacuating, as it were, a region within itself in order to make room for the world. Creation had begun, therefore, with an act of divine ruthlessness: in its compassionate desire to make itself known in and by its creatures, Ein Sof had inflicted exile upon a part of itself. Unlike the orderly, peaceful creation described in the first chapter of Genesis, this was a violent process of primal explosions, disasters, and false starts which seemed to the Sephardic exiles a more accurate appraisal of the world they lived in. At an early stage in the Lurianic process, Ein Sof had tried to fill the emptiness it had created by Zimzum with divine light, but the "vessels" or "pipes" which were supposed to channel it shattered under the strain. Sparks of divine light fell into the abyss of all that was not God. After this "breaking of the vessels," some of the sparks returned to the Godhead, but others remained trapped in this Godless realm, which was filled with the evil potential that Ein Sof had purged from itself in the act of Zimzum. After this disaster, creation was awry; things were in the wrong place. When Adam was created, he could have rectified the situation and, had he done so, the divine exile would have ended on the first Sabbath. But Adam sinned and henceforth the divine sparks were trapped in material objects, and the Shekhinah, the Presence that is the closest we come to an apprehension of the divine on earth, wandered through the world, a perpetual exile, yearning to be reunited with the Godhead.[11]

It is a fantastic tale, but if the Kabbalists of Safed had been asked if they believed that this had really occurred, they would have found the question inappropriate. The primordial event described in myth is not simply an incident that happened once in the remote past; it is also an occurrence that happens all the time. We have no concept or word for such an event, because our rational society thinks of time in a strictly chronological way. If the worshippers at Eleusis in ancient Greece had been asked if they could prove that Persephone had been held prisoner by Pluto in the underworld, and that her mother, Demeter, had wandered around mourning the loss of her daughter, they would probably have been bewildered by the query. How could they be certain that Persephone had returned to the earth, as the myth related? Because the fundamental rhythm of life that this *mythos* had revealed was actually taking place. The fields were harvested, seedcorn placed in underground containers was sown at the correct time, and, finally, the corn grew.[12] Both the *mythos* and the phenomenon of the harvest pointed to something fundamental and universal about the world, in rather the same way as the English word "boat" and the French *"bateau"* both point to a reality that is extrinsic and independent of either term. The Sephardic Jews would probably have made a similar reply. Exile was a fundamental law of existence. Wherever you looked, Jews were uprooted aliens. Even the gentiles experienced loss, disappointment, and a sense that they were not quite at home in the world—as witness the universal myths about the first human beings being expelled from a primordial paradise. Luria's complex creation story had revealed this and made it clear in a wholly new way. The exile of the Shekhinah and their own lives as displaced people were not two separate realities but one and the same. Zimzum showed that exile was inscribed in the very ground of being.

Luria was not a writer, and during his lifetime his teachings were known to very few people.[13] But his pupils recorded his teachings for posterity and others spread them in Europe. By 1650, Lurianic Kabbalah had become a mass movement, the only theological system to win such general acceptance among Jews at this time.[14] It did so not because it could be proved rationally or scientifically, since it obviously could not. It clearly contradicted Genesis in almost every particular. But a literal reading of Scripture is, as we shall see, a modern preoccupation, springing from the prevalence of the rational over the mythical consciousness. Before the modern period, Jews, Christians, and Muslims all relished highly allegorical, symbolic, and esoteric interpretations of their sacred texts. Since God's Word was infinite, it was capable of yielding a multitude of meanings. So Jews were not distressed, as many modern religious people would be, by Luria's divergence from the plain meaning of the Bible. His myth spoke to them with authority because it explained their lives and provided them with meaning. Instead of Jews being a marginalized people, thrust out of the modern world that was coming into being, their experience was in tune with the most fundamental laws of existence. Even God suffered exile; everything in creation had been displaced from the very beginning; divine sparks were trapped in matter, and goodness was forced to struggle with evil—an omnipresent fact of life. Further, Jews were not rejects and outcasts, but central actors in the redemptive process. The careful observance of the commandments of the Torah, the Law of Moses, and special rites evolved in Safed could end this universal exile. Jews could thus help to effect the "restoration" *(tikkun)* of the Shekhinah to the Godhead, the Jewish people to the Promised Land, and the rest of the world to its rightful state.[15]

This myth has continued to be important to Jews. Some have found that, after the tragedy of the Holocaust, they can only see God as the suffering, impotent divinity of Zimzum, who is not in control of creation.[16] The imagery of the divine sparks trapped in matter and the restorative mission of *tikkun* still inspires modern and fundamentalist Jewish movements. Lurianic Kabbalah was, like all true myth, a revelation that showed Jews what their lives basically were and what they meant. The myth contained its own truth, and was at some deep level self-evident. It neither could receive nor did it require rational demonstration. Today we should call the Lurianic myth a symbol or a metaphor, but this also is to rationalize it. In the original Greek, the word "symbol" meant to throw two things together so that they became inseparable. As soon as Western people began to say that a rite or an icon was "only a symbol," the modern consciousness, which insists upon such separations, had arrived.

In traditional religion, myth is inseparable from cult, which brings eternal reality into the mundane lives of worshippers by means of ceremonies and meditative practices. Despite the power of its symbolism, Lurianic Kabbalah would not have become so crucial to the Jewish experience had it not been expressed in eloquent rituals that evoked within the exiles a sense of transcendent meaning. In Safed, Kabbalists devised special rites to reenact Luria's theology. They would make night vigils to help them to identify with the Shekhinah, whom they imagined as a woman, wandering in distress through the world, yearning for her divine source. Jews would rise at midnight, remove their shoes, weep, and rub their faces in the dust. These ritual actions served to express their own sense of grief and abandonment, and to link them with the experience of loss endured also by the Divine

Presence. They would lie awake all night, calling out to God like lovers, lamenting the pain of separation that lies at the heart of so much human distress, but which is central to the suffering of exile. There were penitential disciplines—fastings, lashings, rolling in the snow—performed as acts of *tikkun*. Kabbalists would go for long walks through the countryside, wandering like the Shekhinah and acting out their own sense of homelessness. Jewish law insisted that prayer could have its deepest force and meaning only when performed communally, in a group of at least ten males; but in Safed, Jews were instructed to pray alone, to experience fully their very real sense of isolation and vulnerability in the world. This solitary prayer put some distance between the Jew and the rest of society, prepared him for a different type of experience, and helped him to appreciate anew the perilous isolation of the Jewish people in a world that constantly threatened its existence.[17]

But Luria was adamant that there was to be no wallowing; Kabbalists must work through their sorrow in a disciplined, stylized way until they achieved a measure of joy. The midnight rituals always ended at dawn with a meditation upon the final reunion of the Shekhinah with Ein Sof and, consequently, the end of the separation of humanity from the divine. The Kabbalist was instructed to imagine that every one of his limbs was an earthly shrine for the Divine Presence.[18] All the world religions insist that no spirituality is valid unless it results in practical compassion, and Lurianic Kabbalah was true to this insight. There were severe penances for faults that injured others: for sexual exploitation, for malicious gossip, for humiliating one's fellows, and for dishonoring parents.[19]

Finally the Kabbalists were taught the mystical practices that have evolved in most of the world faiths, which help the adept to access the deeper regions of the psyche and gain intuitive insight. In Safed, meditation centered on detailed, skilled reconfigurations of the letters composing God's name. These "concentrations" *(kawwanot)* would help the Kabbalist to become aware of a trace of the divine within himself. He would become, leading Kabbalists believed, a prophet, able to utter a new *mythos*, bring to light a hitherto unknown religious truth, just as Luria had done. These *kawwanot* certainly brought Kabbalists great joy. Haim Vital (1542–1620), one of Luria's disciples, said that in ecstasy he trembled and shook with elation and awe. Kabbalists saw visions and experienced a rapturous transcendence that transfigured the world at a time when it seemed cruel and alien.[20]

Rational thought has achieved astonishing success in the practical sphere, but it cannot assuage our sorrow. After the Spanish disaster, Kabbalists found that the rational disciplines of philosophy, which had been popular among the Jews of al-Andalus, could not address their pain.[21] Life seemed drained of meaning, and without meaning in their lives, human beings can fall into despair. To make life bearable, the exiles turned to *mythos* and mysticism, which enabled them to make contact with the unconscious sources of their pain, loss, and desire, and anchored their lives in a vision that brought them comfort.

It is noticeable, however, that unlike Ignatius of Loyola, Luria and his disciples devised no practical plans for the political salvation of the Jews. Kabbalists had settled in the Land of Israel, but they were not Zionists; Luria did not urge Jews to end their exile by migrating to the Holy Land. He did not use his mythology or his mystical vision to create an ideology that would be a blueprint for action. This was not the job of *mythos;* all such practical planning and political activity were the domain of *logos*—rational, discursive thought. Luria knew that his mission as a mystic was to save Jews from existential and spiritual despair. When these myths were later applied to the practical world of politics, the results could be disastrous, as we shall see later in this chapter.

Without a cult, without prayer and ritual, myths and doctrines have no meaning. Without the special ceremonies and rites that made the myth accessible to the Kabbalists, Luria's creation story would have remained a senseless fiction. It was only in a liturgical context that any religious belief became meaningful. Once people were deprived of that type of spiritual activity, they would lose their faith. This is what happened to some of the Jews who decided to convert to Christianity and remain in the Iberian Peninsula. This has also happened to many modern people who no longer meditate, perform rituals, or take part in any ceremonial liturgy, and then find that the myths of religion mean nothing to them. Many of the *conversos* were able to identify wholly with Catholicism. Some, indeed, such as the reformers Juan de Valdes (1500–41) and Juan Luis Vives (1492–1540), became important leaders of the Counter Reformation and thus made a significant contribution to early modern culture in rather the same way that secularized Jews such as Karl Marx, Sigmund Freud, Emile Durkheim, Albert Einstein, and Ludwig Wittgenstein had a profound impact on later modernism after their assimilation into mainstream society.

One of the most illustrious of these influential *conversos* was Teresa of Avila (1515–82), the mentor and teacher of John of the Cross and the first woman to be declared a Doctor of the Church. She was a pioneer of the reform of spirituality in Spain and was especially concerned that women, who did not have the benefit of a good education and were frequently led into unhealthy mystical practices by inept spiritual directors, receive a proper grounding in religious matters. Hysterical trances, visions, and raptures had nothing to do with holiness, she insisted. Mysticism demanded extreme skill, disciplined concentration, a balanced personality, and a cheerful, sensible disposition, and must be integrated in a controlled and alert manner with normal life. Like John of the Cross, Teresa was a modernizer and a mystic of genius, yet had she remained within Judaism she would not have had the opportunity to develop this gift, since only men were allowed to practice the Kabbalah. Yet, interestingly, her spirituality remained Jewish. In *The Interior Castle,* she charts the soul's journey through seven celestial halls until it reaches God, a scheme which bears a marked resemblance to the Throne Mysticism that flourished in the Jewish world from the first to the twelfth centuries CE. Teresa was a devout and loyal Catholic, but she still prayed like a Jew and taught her nuns to do the same.

In Teresa's case, Judaism and Christianity were able to blend fruitfully, but other, less gifted *conversos* experienced conflict. A case in point: Tomás de Torquemada (1420–98), the first Grand Inquisitor.[22] The zeal with which he attempted to stamp out residual Judaism in Spain may perhaps have been an unconscious attempt to extirpate the old faith from his own heart. Most of the Marranos had accepted Christianity under duress, and many, it seems, had never fully made the transition to the new faith. This was hardly surprising, since, once they had been baptized, they were watched closely by the Inquisition, and lived in constant fear of arrest on the flimsiest of charges. Lighting candles on Friday evening or refusing to eat shellfish could mean imprisonment, torture, death, or, at the very least, the confiscation of one's property. As a result, some became alienated from religion altogether. They could not fully identify with the Catholicism that made their lives a misery, and, over the years, Judaism became an unreal, distant memory. After the Great Expulsion of 1492, there were no practicing Jews left in Spain and, even if Marranos wished to practice their faith in secret, they had no means of learning about Jewish law or ritual practice. In consequence, they had no real allegiance to any faith. Long before secularism, atheism, and religious indifference became common in the rest of Europe, we find instances of these essentially modern attitudes among the Marrano Jews of the Iberian Peninsula.

According to the Israeli scholar Yirmiyahu Yovel, it was quite common for *conversos* to be skeptical about all religion.[23] Even before the Great Expulsion of 1492, some, such as Pedro and Fernando de la Caballeria, members of a great Spanish family, simply immersed themselves in politics, art, and literature, and appeared to have no interest in religion at all. Pedro, indeed, would scoff openly about being a fake Christian, which, he claimed, left him free to do as he wished without bothering about holy rules and regulations.[24] Shortly before 1492, one Alvaro de Montalban was brought before the Inquisition for eating cheese and meat during Lent; he had thereby, significantly, broken not only a Christian fast but also Jewish law, which forbids the consumption of meat and dairy products together. He obviously felt no commitment to either faith. On this occasion, Alvaro escaped with a fine. He was not likely to feel warmly disposed to Catholicism. His parents had been killed by the Inquisition for practicing Judaism secretly; their bodies had been exhumed, their bones burned, and their property confiscated.[25] Unable to retain even a tenuous link with Judaism, Alvaro was forced into a religious limbo. As an old man of seventy, he was finally imprisoned by the Inquisition for a repeated and deliberate denial of the doctrine of the afterlife. "Let me be well off down here," he had said on more than one occasion, "since I don't know if there is anything beyond."[26]

Alvaro's conviction meant that his son-in-law, Fernando de Rojas (c. 1465–1541), author of the tragicomic romance La Celestina, also came under suspicion. He therefore cultivated a careful facade of respectable Christianity, but in La Celestina, first published in 1499, we find a bleak secularism beneath the bawdy exuberance. There is no God; love is the supreme value, but when love dies, the world is revealed as a wasteland. At the end of the play, Pleberio laments the suicide of his daughter, who alone gave meaning to his life. "O world, world," he concludes, "when I was young I thought there was some order governing you and your deeds." But now

> you seem to be a labyrinth of errors, a frightful desert, a den of wild beasts, a game in which men move in circles . . . a stony field, a meadow full of serpents, a flowering but barren orchard, a spring of cares, a river of tears, a sea of suffering, a vain hope.[27]

Unable to practice the old faith, alienated by the cruelty of the Inquisition from the new, Rojas had fallen into a despair that could find no meaning, no order, and no ultimate value.

The last thing that Ferdinand and Isabella had intended was to make Jews skeptical unbelievers. But throughout our story we will find that coercion of the sort they employed is counterproductive. The attempt to force people to accept the prevailing ideology against their will or before they are ready for it often results in ideas and practices which, in the eyes of the persecuting authorities themselves, are highly undesirable. Ferdinand and Isabella were aggressive modernizers who sought to suppress all dissidence; but their inquisitorial methods led to the formation of a secret Jewish underground and to the first declarations of secularism and atheism in Europe. Later some Christians would become so disgusted by this type of religious tyranny that they too would lose faith in all revealed religion. But secularism could be just as ferocious and, during the twentieth century, the imposition of a secularist ethos in the name of progress has been an important factor in the rise of a militant fundamentalism, which has sometimes been fatal to the government concerned.

In 1492, about eighty thousand Jews who had refused to convert to Christianity had been given asylum in Portugal by King João II. It is among these Portuguese Jews and their descendants that we find the most outright and dramatic instances of atheism. Some of these Jews desperately wanted to retain their Jewish faith, yet found it either difficult or impossible to do so because they had no adequate cult. The Jews who fled to Portugal in 1492 were tougher than the Spanish *conversos:* they preferred to be deported rather than abjure their faith. When Manuel I succeeded to the throne in 1495, he was compelled by Ferdinand and Isabella, his parents-in-law, to have the Jews in his domains forcibly baptized, but he compromised by granting them immunity from the Inquisition for a generation. These Portuguese Marranos had almost fifty years to organize an underground in which a dedicated minority continued to practice Judaism in secret and tried to win others back to the old faith.[28]

But these Judaizing Marranos were cut off from the rest of the Jewish world. They had received a Catholic education, and their imaginations were filled with Christian symbols and doctrines. They often thought and spoke about Judaism in Christian terms: they believed, for example, that they had been "saved" by the Law of Moses rather than by Jesus, a concept that has little meaning in Judaism. They had forgotten a great deal of Jewish law, and as the years slipped by, their understanding of Judaism became still more attenuated. Sometimes their only sources of information about the faith were the polemical writings of anti-Semitic Christians. What they ended up practicing was a hybrid faith that was neither truly Jewish nor truly Christian.[29] Their dilemma was not unlike that of many people in the developing world today, who have only a superficial understanding of Western culture but whose traditional way of life has been so undermined by the impact of modernity that they cannot identify with the old ways either. The Marrano Jews of Portugal experienced a similar alienation. They had been forced to assimilate to a modernized culture that did not resonate with their inner selves.

Toward the end of the sixteenth century, some Jews were permitted to leave the Iberian Peninsula. A Marrano diaspora had already formed in some of the Spanish colonies, as well as in southern France, but here Jews were still not allowed to practice their faith. However, during the seventeenth century, Judaizing Marranos migrated to such cities as Venice, Hamburg, and—later—London, where they could openly return to Judaism. Above all, the Iberian refugees from the Inquisition poured into Amsterdam, which became their new Jerusalem. The Netherlands was the most tolerant country in Europe. It was a republic, with a thriving commercial empire which, during its struggle for independence from Spain, had created a liberal identity as a contrast to Iberian values. Jews became full citizens of the republic in 1657; they were not confined to enclosed ghettoes, as they were in most European cities. The Dutch appreciated the Jews' commercial expertise, and Jews became prominent businessmen, mingling freely with gentiles. They had a vigorous social life, an excellent educational system, and a flourishing publishing industry.

Many Jews undoubtedly came to Amsterdam for its social and economic opportunities, but a significant number were eager to return to the full practice of Judaism. This was not easy, however. The "New Jews," who had come from Iberia, had to be reeducated in a faith about which they were largely ignorant. The rabbis had the challenging task of guiding them back, making allowances for their real difficulties without compromising the tradition. It is a tribute to them that most Jews were able to make the transition; despite some initial tension, they found that they enjoyed their return to the ancestral faith.[30] A notable example was Orobio de Castro, a doctor and professor of metaphysics, who had lived in Spain as a secret Judaizer for years. He had been arrested and tortured by the Inquisition, had recanted, and taught medicine in Toulouse as a fake Christian. Finally, weary of deception and a double life, he had arrived in Amsterdam in the 1650s to become a forceful apologist for Judaism and an instructor of other returning Marranos.[31]

Orobio, however, described a whole class of people who found it very difficult to adjust to the laws and customs of traditional Judaism, which seemed senseless and burdensome to them. They had studied modern sciences in Iberia, such as logic, physics, mathematics, and medicine, as Orobio himself had done. But, Orobio reported impatiently, "they are full of vanity, pride and arrogance, confident that they are thoroughly learned in all subjects."

> They think they will lose credit as erudite men if they consent to learn from those who are indeed educated in the sacred laws, and so they feign great science by contradicting what they do not understand.[32]

These Jews, living for decades in religious isolation, had been forced to rely on their own rational powers. They had had no liturgy, no communal religious life, and no experience of the ritual observance of the "sacred laws" of the Torah. When they finally arrived in Amsterdam and, for the first time, found themselves in a fully functioning Jewish community, they were not unnaturally bewildered. To an outsider, the 613 commandments of the Pentateuch seemed arbitrary and arcane. Some of the commandments had become obsolete, because they related to the farming of the Holy Land or the Temple liturgy and were not applicable in the Diaspora. Other injunctions, such as the abstruse dietary rules and the laws of purification, must have seemed barbaric and meaningless to the sophisticated Portuguese Marranos, who found it difficult to accept the explanations of the rabbis because they had become accustomed to thinking things out rationally for themselves. The Halakhah, the codified oral law that had been compiled in the first centuries of the Common Era, seemed even more irrational and arbitrary, because it did not even have biblical sanction.

But the Torah, the Law of Moses, has a *mythos* of its own. Like Lurianic Kabbalah, it had been a response to the dislocation of exile. When the people of Israel had been deported to Babylon in the sixth century BCE, their Temple destroyed and their religious life in ruins, the text of the Law had become a new "shrine" in which the displaced people cultivated a sense of the Divine Presence. The codification of the world into clean and unclean, sacred and profane objects, had been an imaginative reordering of a shattered world. In exile, Jews had found that the study of the Law gave them a profound religious experience. Jews did not peruse the text like moderns, simply for information: it was the process of study—the question and answer, the heated arguments, and immersion in minutiae—that gave them intimations of the divine. The Torah was God's Word; by becoming deeply absorbed in it, committing to memory the words that God himself had spoken to Moses and speaking them aloud, they were bringing the divine into their own beings and entering a sacred realm. The Law had become a symbol, where they found the Shekhinah. The practice of the commandments brought a divine imperative into the smallest details of their lives, when they were eating, washing, praying, or simply relaxing with their families on the Sabbath.

None of this could be immediately perceived by the rational understanding upon which the Marranos had perforce relied all their lives. This type of mythical and cultic observance was alien and unknown. Some of the New Jews, Orobio complained, had become "unspeakable atheists."[33] They were, to be sure, not atheists in our twentieth-century sense, because they still believed in a transcendent deity; but this was not the God of the Bible. The Marranos had developed a wholly rational faith, similar to the deism later fashioned by Enlightenment *philosophes*.[34] This God was the First Cause of all being, whose existence had been logically demonstrated by Aristotle. It always behaved in an entirely rational way. It did not intervene in human history erratically, subvert the laws of nature by working bizarre miracles, or dictate obscure laws on mountaintops. It did not need to reveal a special law code, because the laws of nature were accessible to everybody. This was the sort of God that human reason naturally tends to envisage, and in the past Jewish and Muslim philosophers had in fact produced a very similar deity. But it never went down well with believers generally. It was not religiously useful, since it was doubtful that the First Cause even knew that human beings existed, as it could contemplate nothing short of perfection. Such a God had nothing to say to human pain or sorrow. For that you needed the mythical and cultic spirituality that was unfamiliar to the Marranos.

Most of the Marranos who returned to the faith in Amsterdam were able to one degree or another to learn to appreciate halakhic spirituality. But some found the transition impossible. One of the most tragic cases was that of Uriel da Costa, who had been born into a *converso* family and educated by the Jesuits, but then found Christianity oppressive, cruel, and composed entirely of man-made rules and doctrines that seemed to bear no relation to the Gospels. Da Costa turned to the Jewish scriptures and developed a highly idealized, rationalistic notion of Judaism for himself. When he arrived in Amsterdam in the early seventeenth century, he was shocked, or so he claimed, to discover that contemporary Judaism was just as much a human construct as Catholicism.

Recently scholars have cast doubt on Da Costa's testimony, and have argued that he had almost certainly had a previous encounter, however sketchy, with some form of halakhic Judaism, though he probably had not realized how deeply the Halakhah dominated normal Jewish life. But there is no doubting da Costa's total inability to relate to Judaism in Amsterdam. He wrote a treatise attacking the doctrine of the afterlife and Jewish law, declaring that he believed only in human reason and the laws of nature. The rabbis excommunicated him and for years Da Costa led a miserable, isolated life until he broke down, recanted, and was readmitted to the community. But Da Costa had not actually changed his views. He found it impossible to live according to rituals that made no rational sense to him, and was excommunicated on two further occasions. Finally in 1640, crushed, broken, in despair, he shot himself in the head.

The tragedy of Da Costa showed that there was as yet no secular alternative to the religious life in Europe. You could cross over to another faith, but unless you were a very exceptional human being (which Da Costa was not), you could not live outside a religious community. During his years as an excommunicate, Da Costa had lived utterly alone, shunned by Jews and Christians alike, and jeered at by children in the streets.[35]

An equally telling, if less poignant, case was that of Juan da Prado, who arrived in Amsterdam in 1655 and must often have meditated upon Da Costa's fate. He had been a committed member of the Jewish underground in Portugal for twenty years, but it seems that as early as 1645 he had succumbed to a Marrano form of deism. Prado was neither a brilliant nor a systematic thinker, but his experience shows us that it is impossible to adhere to a confessional religion such as Judaism by relying solely on reason. Without a prayer life, a cult, and a mythical underpinning, Prado could only conclude that "God" was simply identical with the laws of nature. Yet he continued his underground activities for another ten years. For him, "Judaism" seems to have meant fellowship, the close bonding he experienced in a tight-knit group which gave meaning to his life, because when he arrived in Amsterdam and fell afoul of the rabbis there, he still wanted to remain within the Jewish community. Like Da Costa, Prado had for years maintained his right to think and worship as he chose. He had his own idea of "Judaism" and was horrified when he encountered the real thing. Prado voiced his objections loudly. Why did Jews think that God had chosen them alone? What was this God? Was it not more logical to think of God as the First Cause, rather than as a personality who had dictated a set of barbarous, nonsensical laws? Prado became an embarrassment. The rabbis were trying to reeducate the New Jews from Iberia (many of whom shared Prado's opinions) and could not tolerate his deism. On February 14, 1657, he was excommunicated. Yet he refused to leave the community.

It was a clash between two wholly irreconcilable points of view. From their own perspectives, both Prado and the rabbis were correct. Prado could make no sense of traditional Judaism, had lost the mythical cast of mind, and had never had the opportunity to penetrate to the deeper meaning of the faith by means of cult and ritual. He had always had to rely on reason and his own insights, and could not abandon them now. But the rabbis were also right: Prado's deism bore no relation to any form of Judaism that they knew. What Prado wanted to be was a "secular Jew," but in the seventeenth century that category did not exist, and neither Prado nor the rabbis would have been able to formulate it clearly. It was the first of a series of clashes between a modern, wholly rational worldview on the one hand, and the religious mind-set, formed by cult and myth, on the other.

As so often in these principled collisions, neither side behaved very well. Prado was an arrogant man, and he roundly abused the rabbis, threatening at one point to attack them in the synagogue with a drawn sword. The rabbis also acted less than honorably: they set a spy on Prado, who reported that his views had become still more radical. After his excommunication, he maintained that all religion was rubbish and that reason, not so-called "revelation," must always be the sole arbiter of truth. Nobody knows how Prado ended his days. He was forced to leave the community and took refuge in Antwerp. Some said that he even tried to be reconciled with the Catholic church; if so, it was a desperate step which, once again, shows how impossible it was for an ordinarily constituted man to exist outside the confines of religion during the seventeenth century.[36]

Prado and Da Costa were both precursors of the modern spirit. Their stories show that the *mythos* of confessional religion is unsustainable without the spiritual exercises of prayer and ritual, which cultivate the more intuitive parts of the mind. Reason alone can produce only an attenuated deism, which is soon abandoned because it brings us no help when we are faced with sorrow or are in trouble. Prado and Da Costa lost their faith because they were deprived of the opportunity to practice it, but another Marrano Jew from Amsterdam showed that the exercise of reason could become so absorbing and exhilarating in itself that the need for myth receded. This world becomes the sole object of contemplation, and human beings, not God, become the measure of all things. The exercise of reason can itself, in a man or woman of exceptional intellect, lead to some kind of mystical illumination. This has also been part of the modern experience.

At the same time as the rabbis first excommunicated Prado, they also opened proceedings against Baruch Spinoza, who was only twenty-three years old. Unlike Prado, Spinoza had been born in Amsterdam. His parents had lived as Judaizing Marranos in Portugal, and had managed to make the transition to Orthodox Judaism when they arrived in Amsterdam. Spinoza, therefore, had never been hunted or persecuted. He had always lived in liberal Amsterdam, and had access to the intellectual life of the gentile world and the opportunity to practice his faith unmolested. He had received a traditional education at the splendid Keter Torah school, but had also studied modern mathematics, astronomy, and physics. Destined for a life in commerce, Spinoza had seemed devout, but in 1655, shortly after Prado's arrival in Amsterdam, he suddenly stopped attending services in the synagogue and began to voice doubts. He noted that there were contradictions in the biblical text that proved it to be of human not divine origin. He denied the possibility of revelation, and argued that "God" was simply the totality of nature itself. The rabbis eventually, on July 27, 1656, pronounced the sentence of excommunication upon Spinoza, and, unlike Prado, Spinoza did not ask to remain in the community. He was glad to go, and became the first person in Europe to live successfully beyond the reach of established religion.

It was easier for Spinoza to survive in the gentile world than it had been for Prado or Da Costa. He was a genius, able to articulate his position clearly, and, as a genuinely independent man, could sustain the inevitable loneliness it entailed. He was at home in the Netherlands, and had powerful patrons who gave him a reasonable allowance, so that he did not have to live in abject poverty. Spinoza was not, as is often supposed, forced to grind lenses to earn a living; he did it to further his interest in optics. He was able to form friendships with some of the leading gentile scientists, philosophers, and politicians of the day. Yet he remained an isolated figure. Jews and gentiles alike found his irreligion either shocking or disconcerting.[37]

Yet there was spirituality in Spinoza's atheism, since he experienced the world as divine. It was a vision of God immanent within mundane reality which filled Spinoza with awe and wonder. He experienced philosophical study and thought as a form of prayer; as he explained in his *Short Treatise on God* (1661), the deity was not an object to be known but the principle of our thought. It followed that the joy we experience when we attain knowledge *was* the intellectual love of God. A true philosopher, Spinoza believed, would cultivate what he called intuitive knowledge, a flash of insight that fused all the information he had acquired discursively and which was an experience of what Spinoza believed to be God. He called this experience "beatitude": in this state, the philosopher realized that he was inseparable from God, and that God exists through human beings. This was a mystical philosophy, which could be seen as a rational version of the kind of spirituality cultivated by John of the Cross and Teresa of Avila, but Spinoza had no patience with this type of religious insight. He believed that yearning for a transcendent God would alienate human beings from their own nature. Later philosophers would find Spinoza's quest for the ecstasy of beatitude embarrassing, and would dispense with his God altogether. Nevertheless, in his concentration on this world and in his denial of the supernatural, Spinoza became one of the first secularists in Europe.

Like many modern people, Spinoza regarded all formal religion with distaste. Given his experience of excommunication, this was hardly surprising. He dismissed the revealed faiths as a "compound of credulity and prejudices," and "a tissue of meaningless mysteries."[38] He had found ecstasy in the untrammeled use of reason, not by immersing himself in the biblical text, and as a result, he viewed Scripture in an entirely objective way. Instead of experiencing it as a revelation of the divine, Spinoza insisted that the Bible be read like any other text. He was one of the first to study the Bible scientifically, examining the historical background, the literary genres, and the question of authorship.[39] He also used the Bible to explore his political ideas. Spinoza was one of the first people in Europe to promote the ideal of a secular, democratic state which would become one of the hallmarks of Western modernity. He argued that once the priests had acquired more power than the kings of Israel, the laws of the state became punitive and restrictive. Originally, the kingdom of Israel had been theocratic but because, in Spinoza's view, God and the people were one and the same, the voice of the people had been supreme. Once the priests seized control, the voice of God could no longer be heard.[40] But Spinoza was no populist. Like most premodern philosophers, he was an elitist who believed the masses to be incapable of rational thought. They would need some form of religion to give them a modicum of enlightenment, but this religion must be reformed, based not on so-called revealed law but on the natural principles of justice, fraternity, and liberty.[41]

Spinoza was undoubtedly one of the harbingers of the modern spirit, and he would later become somewhat of a hero to secularist Jews, who admired his principled exodus from the shelter of religion. But Spinoza had no Jewish followers in his lifetime, even though it appeared that many Jews were ready for fundamental change. At about the same time as Spinoza was developing his secular rationalism, the Jewish world was engulfed by a messianic ferment that seemed to cast reason to the winds. It was one of the first of the millennial movements of the modern period, which provided men and women with a religious way of breaking with the sacred past and reaching out for something entirely new. We shall often find this in our story. Few people are able to understand the intellectual elite who propounded the secularist philosophies of modernity; most have made the transition to the new world by means of religion, which provides some consoling continuity with the past and grounds the modern *logos* in a mythical framework.

It appears that by the mid-seventeenth century, many Jews had reached a breaking point. None of the other Jews of Europe enjoyed the freedom of the Marrano community in Amsterdam; Spinoza's radical new departure had been possible only because he was able to mix with gentiles and study the new sciences. Elsewhere in Christendom, Jews were excluded from mainstream society. By the sixteenth century, no Jew was permitted to live outside the special Jewish district known as the "ghetto," and this meant that inevitably Jews led an introverted life. Segregation increased anti-Semitic prejudice, and Jews naturally responded to the persecuting gentile world with bitterness and suspicion. The ghetto became a self-contained world. Jews had their own schools, their own social and charitable institutions, their own baths, cemeteries, and slaughterhouses. The ghetto was self-governing and autonomous. The *kehilla* (communal government) of elected rabbis and elders conducted its own courts, according to Jewish law. In effect, the ghetto was a state-within-a-state, a world unto itself, and Jews had little— and, often, little desire for—contact with the gentile society outside. But by the mid-seventeenth century, it seems that many were chafing against these limitations. Ghettoes were usually situated in unhealthy, squalid districts.

They were enclosed by a high wall, which meant that there was overcrowd-ing and no possibility of expansion. There was no room for gardens, even in the larger ghettoes of Rome or Venice. The only way that Jews could pro-vide more accommodation for themselves was to add new floors to existing buildings, often on inadequate foundations, so that everything collapsed. There was constant danger of fire and disease. Jews were forced to wear dis-tinctive dress, they suffered economic restrictions, and were often reduced to peddling and tailoring as the only professions open to them. No large-scale commercial ventures were permitted, and thus a large proportion of the population relied on charity. Deprived of sunlight and contact with nature, Jews deteriorated physically. They were also mentally confined and were out of touch with the arts and sciences of Europe. Their own schools were good, but after the fifteenth century, when the educational curriculum in Christendom was becoming more liberal, Jews continued to study only Torah and Talmud. Immersed as they were solely in their own texts and cultural traditions, there was a tendency for Jewish learning to degenerate into hair-splitting and a concentration on minutiae.[42]

The Jews of the Islamic world were not restricted in this way. Like Chris-tians, they were accorded the status of *dhimmi* ("protected minority"), which gave them civil and military protection, as long as they respected the laws and supremacy of the Islamic state. The Jews of Islam were not perse-cuted, there was no tradition of anti-Semitism, and even though the *dhimmis* were second-class citizens, they were given full religious liberty, were able to run their own affairs according to their own laws, and were more able than the Jews of Europe to participate in mainstream culture and com-merce.[43] But events would show that even the Jews of the Islamic world were growing restless, and dreaming of greater emancipation. Since 1492 they had heard news of one disaster in Europe after another, and in 1648 they were horrified by reports of atrocities in Poland that would remain unequaled in Jewish history until the twentieth century.

Poland had recently annexed much of what is now Ukraine, where peas-ants formed cavalry squads to organize their own defense. These "cossacks" hated both Poles and Jews, who often administered the lands of the Polish nobility as middlemen. In 1648 the cossack leader Boris Chmielnicki led an uprising against the Poles which attacked Polish and Jewish communities alike. When the war finally came to an end in 1667, the chronicles tell us, 100,000 Jews had been killed and 300 Jewish communities destroyed. Even though these numbers were probably exaggerated, the letters and stories of the refugees filled Jews in other parts of the world with terror. They spoke of massacres in which Jews were cut to pieces, of mass graves in which Jewish women and children had been buried alive, of Jews being given rifles and commanded to shoot one another. Many believed that these events must be the long-awaited "birth pangs of the Messiah," and turned in desperation to the rites and penitential disciplines of Lurianic Kabbalah in an attempt to hasten messianic redemption.[44]

When news of the Chmielnicki massacres reached Smyrna in what is now Turkey, a young Jew who was walking and meditating outside the city heard a heavenly voice telling him that he was "the Savior of Israel, the Messiah, the Son of David, the anointed of the God of Jacob."[45] Shabbetai Zevi was a scholarly young man and a Kabbalist (though not, at this point, versed in Lurianic Kabbalah), who would share his insights with a small band of followers. He had an appealing personality, but when he was about twenty he began to exhibit symptoms that we would today call manic-depressive. He used to hide away for days, sunk in misery in a dark little room, but these depressed phases would be succeeded by frenzied periods of "illumination," when he was restless, unable to sleep, and felt that he was in touch with higher powers. Sometimes he would feel impelled to violate the commandments of the Torah, publicly uttering the forbidden Name of God, for example, or eating nonkosher food. He could not explain why he committed these "strange acts," but felt that God had for some reason inspired him to do so.[46] Later he became convinced that these antinomian acts were redemptive: God "would soon give him a new law and new commandments to repair all the worlds."[47] These transgressions were "holy sins"; they were what Lurianic Kabbalists would call acts of *tikkun*. It is likely that they represented an unconscious rebellion against the customary observances of Jewish life and expressed a confused desire for something entirely new.

Eventually Shabbetai's behavior became too much for the Jews of Smyrna, and he had to leave the city in 1650. He then began a fifteen-year period, which he later called his "dark years," during which he wandered through the provinces of the Ottoman empire, going from one city to another. He told nobody about his messianic vocation and may have abandoned the very idea of a special mission. By 1665 he was longing to free himself of his demons and become a rabbi.[48] He had heard about a gifted young Kabbalist in Gaza who had set himself up as a healer, and set off to visit him. This Rabbi Nathan had already heard about Shabbetai, probably when both men, then unknown to each other, had lived in Jerusalem at the same time. Something about Shabbetai's "strange acts" must have lodged in Nathan's imagination, because, shortly before the arrival of his visitor, he had received a revelation about him. He had recently been initiated into Lurianic Kabbalah, and had made a retreat just before Purim, locking himself away, fasting, weeping, and reciting the Psalms. During this vigil, he had seen a vision of Shabbetai and heard his own voice crying aloud in prophecy: "Thus saith the Lord! Behold your Savior cometh. Shabbetai Zevi is his name. He shall cry, yea, roar, he shall prevail against my enemies."[49] When Shabbetai actually turned up on his own doorstep, Nathan could only see this as a miraculous confirmation of his prophetic vision.

How could Nathan, a brilliant thinker, have imagined that this sad, troubled man was his Redeemer? According to Lurianic Kabbalah, the soul of the Messiah had been trapped in the Godless realm created in the original act of Zimzum; from the very beginning, therefore, the Messiah had been forced to struggle with the evil powers of the "other side," but now, Nathan believed, thanks to the penitential disciplines of the Kabbalists, these demonic forces were beginning to lose their hold on the Messiah. From time to time, his soul soared free and he revealed the New Law of the messianic age. But victory was still incomplete, and from time to time the Messiah fell prey once more to the darkness.[50] All this seemed to fit perfectly with Shabbetai's personality and experience. When he arrived, Nathan told him that the End was nigh. Soon his victory over the forces of evil would be complete and he would bring redemption to the Jewish people. The old law would be abrogated, and actions that had once been forbidden and sinful would become holy.

At first, Shabbetai wanted nothing to do with Nathan's fantasy, but gradually he was won over by the power of the young rabbi's eloquence, which, at least, gave him some explanation for his peculiarities. On May 28, 1665, Shabbetai declared himself to be the Messiah, and Nathan immediately dispatched letters to Egypt, Aleppo, and Smyrna announcing that the Redeemer would soon defeat the Ottoman sultan, end the exile of the Jews, and lead them back to the Holy Land. All the gentile nations would submit to his rule.[51] The news spread like wildfire, and by 1666, the messianic ferment had taken root in almost every Jewish community in Europe, the Ottoman empire, and Iran. There were frenzied scenes. Jews started to sell their possessions in preparation for the voyage to Palestine, and business came to a standstill. Periodically, they would hear that the Messiah had abolished one of the traditional fast days, and there would be dancing and processions in the street. Nathan had given orders that Jews were to hasten the End by performing the penitential rituals of Safed, and in Europe, Egypt, Iran, the Balkans, Italy, Amsterdam, Poland, and France Jews fasted, kept vigil, immersed themselves in icy water, rolled in nettles, and gave alms to the poor. It was one of the first of many Great Awakenings of early modernity, when people instinctively sensed the coming of major change. Few people knew much about Shabbetai himself and fewer still were conversant with Nathan's abstruse kabbalistic vision; it was enough that the Messiah had come and that at long last hope was at hand.[52] During these ecstatic months, Jews experienced such hope and vitality that the harsh, constricted world of the ghetto seemed to melt away. They had a taste of something entirely different, and life for many of them would never be the same again. They glimpsed new possibilities, which seemed almost within their grasp. Because they felt free, many Jews were convinced that the old life was over for good.[53]

Those Jews who came under the direct influence of either Shabbetai or Nathan showed that they were ready to jettison the Torah, even though that would mean the end of religious life as they knew it. When Shabbetai visited a synagogue wearing the royal robes of the Messiah, and abolished a fast, uttered the forbidden name of God, ate nonkosher food, or called women to read the Scriptures in the synagogue, people were enraptured. Not everybody succumbed, of course—in each community, there were rabbis and laymen who were appalled by these developments. But people of all classes, rich and poor, accepted Shabbetai and seemed to welcome his antinomianism. The Law had not saved the Jews and seemed unable to do so; Jews were still persecuted, still in exile; people were ready for new freedom.[54]

This was all very dangerous, however. Lurianic Kabbalah was a myth; it was not intended to be translated into practical political programs in this way, but to illuminate the internal life of the spirit. *Mythos* and *logos* were complementary but entirely separate spheres and had different functions. Politics was in the domain of reason and logic; myth gave it meaning but was not intended to be interpreted as literally as Nathan had interpreted the mystical vision of Isaac Luria. Jews may have *felt* powerful, free, and in control of their destiny, but their circumstances had not changed. They were still weak, vulnerable, and dependent upon the goodwill of their rulers. The Lurianic image of the Messiah wrestling with the powers of darkness was a powerful symbol of the universal struggle against evil, but when the attempt was made to give the image concrete embodiment in a real, emotionally unstable human being, the result could only be disastrous.

And so indeed it proved to be. In February 1666, Shabbetai set out, with Nathan's blessing, to confront the sultan, who had understandably been much alarmed by this wild Jewish enthusiasm and, with reason, feared an uprising. When Shabbetai landed near Gallipoli, he was arrested, taken to Istanbul, brought before the sultan, and given the choice of death or conversion to Islam. To the horror of Jews all over the world, Shabbetai chose Islam. The Messiah had become an apostate.

That should have been the end of the matter. The vast majority recoiled in disgust from Shabbetai and, in shame, returned to their normal life and to the full observance of the Torah, anxious to put the whole sorry business behind them. But a significant minority could not give up this dream of freedom. They could not believe that their experience of liberation during those heady months had been an illusion; they were able to come to terms with an apostate Messiah, just as the first Christians had been able to accommodate the equally scandalous idea of a Messiah who had died the death of a common criminal.

Nathan, after a period of intense depression, adapted his theology. The redemption had begun, he explained to his disciples, but there had been a setback, and Shabbetai had been forced to descend still further into the realm of impurity and take the form of evil himself. This was the ultimate "holy sin," the final act of *tikkun*.[55] Shabbateans, those who remained true to Shabbetai, responded to this development in different ways. Nathan's theology was very popular in Amsterdam: now the Messiah had become a Marrano, clinging in secret to the core of Judaism, while conforming outwardly to Islam.[56] Those Marranos who had long had trouble with the Torah looked forward to its imminent demise, once redemption was complete. Other Jews believed that they must continue to observe the Torah until the Messiah brought about full redemption, but that he would then institute a new Law which would contradict the old in every respect. A small minority of radical Shabbateans went further. They could not bring themselves to go back to the old Law, even on a temporary basis; they believed that Jews must follow their Messiah into the realm of evil and become apostates too. They converted to the mainstream faith—Christianity in Europe, and Islam in the Middle East—and remained Jewish in the privacy of their own homes.[57] These radicals also presaged a modern Jewish solution: many Jews would assimilate with gentile culture in most respects, but would privatize their faith, keeping it in a separate sphere.

Shabbateans imagined Shabbetai living his double life in anguish, but in reality he seemed quite content with his Muslim persona. He spent his days studying the Shariah, the sacred law of Islam, and teaching the sultan's spiritual adviser about Judaism. He was permitted visitors, and held court, receiving delegations of Jews from all over the world. They spoke of his great piety. Shabbetai was often to be seen in his home, sitting cradling the Torah scroll in his arms and singing hymns; people marveled at his devotion and his wonderful ability to enter sympathetically into other people's feelings.[58] The ideas in Shabbetai's circle were quite different from those of Nathan's, and far more positive toward gentiles. Shabbetai seems to have seen all faiths as valid; he saw himself as a bridge between Judaism and Islam, and was also fascinated by Christianity and Jesus. Guests reported that sometimes he behaved like a Muslim, sometimes like a rabbi. The Ottomans permitted him to observe the Jewish festivals, and Shabbetai was frequently to be seen with a Koran in one hand and a Torah scroll in the other.[59] In the synagogues, Shabbetai tried to persuade Jews to convert to Islam; only then, he told them, would they return to the Holy Land. In one letter, written in 1669, Shabbetai vehemently denied that he had converted to Islam only under duress; the religion of Islam, he declared, was "the very truth," and he had been sent as the Messiah to the gentiles as well as to the Jews.[60]

Shabbetai's death on September 17, 1676, was a severe blow to Shabbateans, since it seemed to preclude all hope of redemption. Nevertheless, the sect continued its underground existence, showing that the messianic outburst had not been a freak occurrence, but had touched something fundamental in the Jewish experience. For some, this religious movement seems to have been a bridge that would enable them, later, to make the difficult transition to rational modernity. The alacrity with which so many had been ready to jettison the Torah, and the persistence of Shabbateans in dreaming of a new Law, demonstrated that they were ready to envisage change and reform.[61] Gershom Scholem, who has written the definitive study of Shabbetai and Shabbateanism, has argued that many of these closet Shabbateans would become pioneers of the Jewish Enlightenment or of the Reform movement. He points to Joseph Wehte in Prague, who spread the ideas of the Enlightenment in Eastern Europe during the early nineteenth century and had once been a Shabbatean; Aron Chovin, who introduced the Reform movement in Hungary, was also a Shabbatean in his youth.[62] Scholem's theory has been disputed, and cannot be proved definitively one way or the other, but it is generally acknowledged that Shabbateanism did much to undermine traditional rabbinic authority and that it enabled Jews to envisage a change that would once have seemed taboo and impossible.

After Shabbetai's death, two radical Shabbatean movements led to the mass conversion of Jews into the dominant faith. In 1683, about 200 families in Ottoman Turkey converted to Islam. This sect of *donmeh* ("converts") had their own secret synagogues, but also prayed in the mosques. At its peak, in the second half of the nineteenth century, the sect numbered some 115,000 souls.[63] It started to disintegrate in the early nineteenth century, when members began to receive a modern, secular education and no longer felt the need for any religion. Some *donmeh* youth became active in the secularist Young Turk rebellion of 1908. The second of these movements was more sinister and showed the nihilism that can result from a literal translation of myth into practical action. Jacob Frank (1726–91) was initiated into Shabbateanism while visiting the Balkans. When he returned to his native Poland, he formed an underground sect whose members observed Jewish law in public but in secret indulged in forbidden sexual practices. When he was excommunicated in 1756, Frank converted first to Islam (during a visit to Turkey) and then to Catholicism, taking his flock with him.

Frank did not simply cast off the restrictions of the Torah, but positively embraced immorality. In his view, the Torah was not merely outmoded but dangerous and useless. The commandments were the laws of death and must be discarded. Sin and shamelessness were the only ways to achieve redemption and to find God. Frank had come not to build but "only to destroy and annihilate."[64] His followers were engaged in a war against all religious rules: "I say to you that all who would be warriors must be without religion, which means that they must reach freedom under their own power."[65] Like many radical secularists today, Frank regarded all religion as harmful. As the movement progressed, Frankists turned to politics, dreaming of a great revolution that would sweep away the past and save the world. They saw the French Revolution as a sign that their vision was true and that God had intervened on their behalf.[66]

Jews had anticipated many of the postures of the modern period. Their painful brush with the aggressively modernizing society of Europe had led them into secularism, skepticism, atheism, rationalism, nihilism, pluralism, and the privatization of faith. For most Jews, the path to the new world that was developing in the West led through religion, but this religion was very different from the kind of faith we are used to in the twentieth century. It was more mythically based; it did not read the Scriptures literally, and was perfectly prepared to come up with new solutions, some of which seemed shocking in their search for something fresh. To understand the role of religion in premodern society we should turn to the Muslim world, which was undergoing its own upheavals during this early modern period and evolving different forms of spirituality that would continue to influence Muslims well into the modern period.

2. Muslims: The Conservative Spirit
(1492–1799)

IN 1492 the Jews had been one of the first casualties of the new order that was slowly coming to birth in the West. The other victims of that momentous year had been the Muslims of Spain, who had lost their last foothold in Europe. But Islam was by no means a spent force. During the sixteenth century it was still the greatest global power. Even though the Sung dynasty (960–1260) had raised China to a far higher degree of social complexity and might than Islamdom, and the Italian Renaissance had initiated a cultural florescence that would eventually enable the West to pull ahead, the Muslims were at first easily able to contain these challenges and they remained at a political and economic peak. Muslims comprised only about a third of the planet's population, but they were so widely and strategically located throughout the Middle East, Asia, and Africa that at this moment, Islamdom could be seen as a microcosm of world history, expressing the preoccupations of most areas of the civilized world in the early modern period. This was also an exciting and innovative time for Muslims; three new Islamic empires were founded during the early sixteenth century: the Ottoman empire in Asia Minor, Anatolia, Iraq, Syria, and North Africa; the Safavid empire in Iran; and the Moghul empire in the Indian subcontinent. Each reflected a different facet of Islamic spirituality. The Moghul empire represented the tolerant, universalist philosophical rationalism known as Falsafah; the Safavid shahs made Shiism, hitherto the faith of an elite minority, the religion of their state; and the Ottoman Turks, who remained fiercely loyal to Sunni Islam, created a polity based on the Shariah, sacred Muslim law.

These three empires were a new departure. All three were early modern institutions, governed systematically and with bureaucratic and rational precision. In its early years, the Ottoman state was far more efficient and powerful than any kingdom in Europe. Under Suleiman the Magnificent (1520–66), it reached its apogee. Suleiman expanded westward, through Greece, the Balkans, and Hungary, and his advance into Europe was checked only by his failure to take Vienna in 1529. In Safavid Iran, the shahs built roads and caravansaries, rationalized the economy, and put the country in the forefront of international trade. All three empires enjoyed a cultural renewal on a par with the Italian Renaissance. The sixteenth century was the great period of Ottoman architecture, Safavid painting, and the Taj Mahal.

And yet, while these were all modernizing societies, they did not implement radical change. They did not share the revolutionary ethos that would become characteristic of Western culture during the eighteenth century. Instead the three empires expressed what the American scholar Marshall G. S. Hodgson has called "the conservative spirit," which was the hallmark of all premodern society, including that of Europe.[1] Indeed, the empires were the last great political expression of the conservative spirit and, since they were also the most advanced states of the early modern period, they can be said to represent its culmination.[2] Today, conservative society is in trouble. Either it has been effectively taken over by the modern Western ethos, or it is undergoing the difficult transition from the conservative to the modern spirit. Much of fundamentalism is a response to this painful transformation. It is, therefore, important to examine the conservative spirit at its peak in these Muslim empires, so that we can understand its appeal and strengths, as well as its inherent limitations.

Until the West introduced a wholly new kind of civilization (based on a constant reinvestment of capital and technical improvement), which did not come into its own until the nineteenth century, all cultures depended economically upon a surplus of agricultural produce. This meant that there was a limit to the expansion and success of any agrarian-based society, since it would eventually outrun its resources and obligations. There was a limit to the amount of capital available for investment. Any innovation that needed large capital outlay was usually ruled out, since people lacked the means that would enable them to tear everything down, retrain their personnel, and start again. No culture before our own could afford the constant innovation we take for granted in the West today. We now expect to know more than our parents' generation, and are confident that our societies will become ever more technologically advanced. We are future-oriented; our governments and institutions have to look ahead and make detailed plans that will affect the next generation. It will be obvious that this society of ours is the achievement of sustained, single-minded rational thought. It is the child of *logos*, which is always looking forward, seeking to know more and to extend our areas of competence and control of the environment. But no amount of rational thinking could create this aggressively innovative society without a modern economy. It is not impossible for Western societies to keep changing the infrastructure to make new inventions possible, since, by constantly re-investing capital, we can increase our basic resources so that they keep pace with our technological progress. But this was not feasible in an agrarian economy, where people channeled their energies into preserving what had already been achieved. Hence the "conservative" bent of premodern society did not spring from any fundamental timidity but represented a realistic appraisal of the limitations of this type of culture. Education, for example, consisted largely of rote learning and did not encourage originality. Stu-dents were not taught to conceive radically new ideas, because the society could generally not accommodate them; such notions could, therefore, be socially disruptive and endanger a community. In a conservative society, social stability and order were considered more important than freedom of expression.

Instead of looking forward to the future, like moderns, premodern soci-eties turned for inspiration to the past. Instead of expecting continuous improvement, it was assumed that the next generation could easily regress. Instead of advancing to new heights of achievement, societies were believed to have declined from a primordial perfection. This putative Golden Age was held up as a model for governments and individuals. It was by approxi-mating to this past ideal that a society would fulfill its potential. Civilization was experienced as inherently precarious. Everyone knew that a whole soci-ety could easily lapse into barbarism, as Western Europe had done after the collapse of the Roman empire there in the fifth century. During the early modern period in the Islamic world, the memory of the Mongol invasions of the thirteenth century had still not faded. The massacres, the vast uprooting as whole peoples had fled before the approaching hordes, and the destruc-tion of one great Islamic city after another were still recalled with horror. Libraries and institutions of learning had also been destroyed, and with them centuries of painstakingly acquired knowledge had been lost. Muslims had recovered; the Sufi mystics had led a spiritual revival, which had proved to be as healing as Lurianic Kabbalah, and the three new empires were a sign of that recovery. The Ottoman and Safavid dynasties both had their roots in the massive displacement of the Mongol era; both had originated in militant *ghazu* states, led by a chieftain warrior and often linked to a Sufi order, which had sprung up in the wake of the devastation. The power and beauty of these empires and their culture were a reassertion of Islamic values and a proud statement that Muslim history was back on track.

But after such a catastrophe, the natural conservatism of premodern soci-ety was likely to become more pronounced. People concentrated on recovering slowly and painfully what had been lost rather than on striking out for something new. In Sunni Islam, for example—the version of the faith practiced by most Muslims and the established religion of the Ottoman empire—it was agreed that "the gates of *ijtihad* ("independent reasoning") had closed.3 Hitherto, Muslim jurists had been allowed to exercise their own judgment in order to resolve questions that arose in relation to theology and law for which neither the Koran nor established tradition had an explicit answer. But by the early modern period, in an attempt to conserve a tradition that had almost been destroyed, Sunni Muslims believed that there was no need for further independent thought. The answers were all in place; the Shariah was a fixed blueprint for society, and *ijtihad* was neither necessary nor desirable. Instead, Muslims must imitate *(taqlid)* the past. Instead of seeking new solutions, they should submit to the rulings found in the established legal manuals. Innovation *(bidah)* in matters of law and practice was considered as disruptive and dangerous in Sunni Islamdom during the early modern period as was heresy in doctrinal matters in the Christian West.

It would be difficult to imagine an attitude more at odds with the thrusting, iconoclastic spirit of the modern West. The idea of putting a deliberate curb on our reasoning powers is now anathema. As we shall see in the next chapter, modern culture developed only when people began to throw off this type of restraint. If Western modernity is the product of *logos*, it is easy to see how congenial *mythos* was to the conservative spirit of the premodern world. Mythological thinking looks backward, not forward. It directs attention to the sacred beginnings, to a primordial event, or to the foundations of human life. Instead of looking for something fresh, myth focuses on what is constant. It does not bring us "news," but tells us what has always been; everything important has already been achieved and thought. We live on what was said by our ancestors, especially in the sacred texts which tell us everything we need to know. This was the spirituality of the conservative period. The cult, ritual practices, and mythical narratives not only gave individuals a sense of meaning that resonated with their deepest unconscious being, but also reinforced the attitude that was essential for the survival of the agrarian economy and its built-in limitations. As the Shabbetai Zevi fiasco showed so clearly, myth is not meant to initiate practical change. It creates a cast of mind that adapts and conforms to the way things are. This was essential in a society that could not sustain untrammeled innovation.

Just as it is difficult—even impossible—for people living in Western society, which has institutionalized change, to appreciate fully the role of mythology, so too it is extremely difficult—perhaps impossible—for people deeply and powerfully shaped by conservative spirituality to accept the forward-looking dynamic of modern culture. It is also supremely difficult for the modernist to understand people who are still nourished by traditional mythical values. In the Islamic world today, as we shall see, some Muslims are very concerned about two things. First, they abhor the secularism of Western society, which separates religion from politics, church from state. Second, many Muslims would like to see their societies governed according to the Shariah, the sacred law of Islam. This is deeply perplexing to people formed in the modern spirit, who, with reason, fear that a clerical establishment would put a brake on the constant progress that they see as essential to a healthy society. They have experienced the separation of church and state as liberating and shudder at the thought of an inquisitorial body closing the "gates of *ijtihad*." In the same way, the idea of a divinely revealed law is profoundly incompatible with the modern ethos. Modern secularists regard the notion of an unalterable law imposed on humanity by a superhuman being as repellent. They regard law not as the product of *mythos* but of *logos;* it is rational and pragmatic, and must be changed from time to time to meet current conditions. A gulf, therefore, separates the modernist from the Muslim fundamentalist on these key issues.

In its heyday, however, the idea of a Shariah state was deeply satisfying. This was the achievement of the Ottoman empire, which drew legitimacy from its fidelity to Islamic law. The sultan was honored for his defense of the Shariah. Even though the sultan and the governors of the various provinces had their *divans,* the audience-chambers where justice was administered, it was the *qadis* who presided over the Shariah courts (which the Ottomans were the first to organize systematically) who were regarded as the real judges. *Qadis,* their consultants the *muftis,* and the scholars who taught Islamic jurisprudence *(fiqh)* in the *madrasahs* were all state officials in the Ottoman empire. They were as essential to the government as the military and administrative personnel. The inhabitants of the Arab provinces could accept the hegemony of the Turks because the sultan's authority was mediated through the *ulema,* the religious scholars, who had the sacred authority of Islamic law behind them. The *ulema* were thus an important link between the sultan and his subjects, between Istanbul and the distant provinces. They could bring grievances to the sultan's attention and had the power to call even him to order if he violated Islamic norms. The *ulema* could, therefore, feel that the Ottoman state was *their* state, and the sultans for the most part accepted the constraints put upon them by the clergy because the partnership enhanced their authority.[4] Never before had the Shariah played such a prominent role in the daily affairs of state as it did in the Ottoman empire, and the success of the Ottomans during the sixteenth century showed that their fidelity to Islamic law had indeed put them on the right path. They were in tune with the fundamental principles of existence.

All conservative societies (as already noted) looked back to a Golden Age, and for the Sunni Muslims of the Ottoman empire this was the period of the Prophet Muhammad (c. 570–632 CE) and the four *rashidun* ("rightly guided") caliphs who immediately succeeded him. They had governed society according to Islamic law. There had been no separation of religion and the state. Muhammad had been both prophet and political head of the community. The Koran, the revealed scripture that he brought to the Arabs in the early years of the seventh century, insisted that a Muslim's first duty was to create a just, egalitarian society, where poor and vulnerable people were treated with respect. This demanded a *jihad* (a word that should be translated as "struggle" or "effort" rather than as "holy war," as Westerners often assume) on all fronts: spiritual, political, social, personal, military, and economic. By ordering the whole of life so that God was given priority and his plans for humanity were fully implemented, Muslims would achieve a personal and societal integration that would give them intimations of the unity which was God. To fence off one area of life and declare it to be off-limits to this religious "effort" would be a shocking violation of this principle of unification *(tawhid)*, which is the cardinal Islamic virtue. It would be tantamount to a denial of God himself. Hence, for a devout Muslim, politics is what Christians would call a sacrament. It is an activity that must be sacralized so that it becomes a channel of the divine.

Concern for the *ummah,* the Muslim community, is deeply inscribed in the "pillars" *(rukn)*, the five essential practices of Islam, binding on every Muslim, Sunni and Shii alike. Where Christians have come to identify orthodoxy with correct belief, Muslims, like Jews, require orthopraxy, a uniformity of religious practice, and see belief as a secondary issue. The five "pillars" require each Muslim to make the *shehadah* (a brief declaration of faith in the unity of God and the prophethood of Muhammad), to pray five times daily, to pay a tax *(zakat)* to ensure a fair distribution of wealth in the community, to observe the fast of Ramadan as a reminder of the privations suffered by the poor, and to make the *hajj* pilgrimage to Mecca, if circumstances allow. The political health of the *ummah* is clearly central to *zakat* and the Ramadan fast, but it is also strongly present in the *hajj,* an essentially communal event, during which pilgrims wear a uniform white garment to underline the unity of the *ummah* and to obviate the differences between rich and poor.

The focus of the *hajj* is the cube-shaped shrine of the Kabah, situated in the heart of Mecca in the Arabian Hijaz. The Kabah was of extreme antiquity even in Muhammad's day and may originally have been dedicated to Al-Lah, the High God of the Arabian pagan pantheon. Muhammad Islamized the ancient rites of the annual pilgrimage to the Kabah and gave them a monotheistic significance, and the *hajj* to this day gives Muslims a powerful experience of community. The structure of the Kabah conforms to the geometric pattern found by psychologist C. G. Jung (1875–1961) to have archetypal significance. At the heart of most ancient cities, a shrine established a link with the sacred which was regarded as essential to their survival. It brought the primal, more potent reality of the divine world into the fragile and insecure urban communities of mortal men and women. The shrine was described by such classical authors as Plutarch, Ovid, and Dionysius of Halicarnassus as either round or square, and was thought to reproduce the essential structure of the universe. It was a paradigm of the order that had brought the cosmos out of chaos and, by making it viable, had given it reality. Jung believed that it was not necessary to choose between the square and the circle; the geometric figure representing this cosmic order, the foundation of all reality, was, he believed, a square inserted into a circle.[5] The rituals performed at this shrine reminded the worshippers of their duty to bring this divine order into their world of potential chaos and disaster, submitting themselves to the fundamental laws and principles of the universe in order to keep their civilization in being and prevent it from falling prey to illusion. The Kabah in Mecca conformed exactly to this archetype. Pilgrims run in seven ritual circles around the granite cube, whose four corners represent the corners of the world, following the course of the sun around the earth. Only by making an existential surrender *(islam)* of his or her whole being to the basic rhythms of life can a *muslim* (one who makes this submission) live as an authentic human being in the community.

The *hajj*, which is still the peak religious experience of any Muslim who makes the pilgrimage, was thus deeply imbued with the conservative spirit. Rooted in the unconscious world of the mythical archetype, like all true *mythoi*, it directs the attention of Muslims back to a reality that is so fundamental that it is impossible to go beyond it. It helps them at a more profound level than the cerebral, to surrender to the way things essentially are and not to strike out independently for themselves. All the rational work of the community—in politics, economics, commerce, or social relations—takes place in this mythical context. Situated at the heart of the city and, later, at the heart of the Muslim world, the Kabah gave these rational activities meaning and perspective. The Koran also expressed this conservative ethos. It insists repeatedly that it is not bringing a new truth to humanity, but revealing the essential laws of human life. It is a "reminder" of truths known already.[6] Muhammad did not believe that he was creating a new religion, but was bringing the primordial religion of humanity to his Arabian tribe, which had never been sent a prophet before and had no scripture in their own language. From the time of Adam, whom the Koran sees as the first of the prophets, God had sent messengers to every people on the face of the earth to tell them how to live.[7] Unlike animals, fish, or plants, who are natural *muslims*, since they submit instinctively to the divine order, human beings have free will and can choose to disobey it.[8] When they have disregarded these basic laws of existence, creating tyrannical societies that oppress the weak and refuse to share their wealth fairly, their civilizations have collapsed. The Koran tells how all the great prophets of the past— Adam, Noah, Moses, Jesus, and a host of others—have all repeated the same message. Now the Koran gave the same divine message to the Arabs, commanding them to practice the social justice and equity that would bring them into harmony with the basic laws of existence. When Muslims conform to God's will, they feel that they are in tune with the way things ought to be. To violate God's law is regarded as unnatural; it is as though a fish were to try to live on dry land.

The stunning success of the Ottomans during the sixteenth century would have been regarded by their subjects as proof that they were making this surrender to these fundamental principles. That was why their society worked so spectacularly. The unprecedented prominence given to the Shariah in the Ottoman polity would also have been seen in the context of the conservative spirit. Muslims in the early modern period did not experience divine law as a curb on their freedom; it was a ritual and cultic realization of a mythical archetype which, they believed, put them in touch with the sacred. Muslim law had developed gradually in the centuries after Muhammad's death. It was a creative enterprise, since the Koran contained very little legislation and, within a century after the Prophet's demise, Muslims ruled a vast empire stretching from the Himalayas to the Pyrenees which, like any society, needed a complex legal system. Eventually, four schools of Islamic jurisprudence developed, all very similar and regarded as equally valid. The law was based on the person of the Prophet Muhammad, who had made the perfect act of *islam* when he had received the divine revelation. Eyewitness reports *(hadith)* were collected about the Prophet's teaching and behavior, which, during the ninth century, were carefully sifted to ensure that Muslims had an authentic record of his sayings and religious practice *(sunnah)*. The law schools reproduced this Muhammadan paradigm in their legal systems, so that Muslims all over the world could imitate the way the Prophet spoke, ate, washed, loved, and worshipped. By emulating the Prophet in these external ways, they hoped also to acquire his interior submission to the divine.[9] In true conservative style, Muslims were conforming their behavior to a past perfection.

The practice of Muslim law made the historical figure of Muhammad into a myth, releasing him from the period in which he had lived and bringing him to life in the person of every devout Muslim. Similarly, this cultic repetition made Muslim society truly *islamic*, in its approximation to the person of Muhammad; who in his perfect surrender to God was the prime exemplar of what a human being should be. By the time of the Mongol invasions in the thirteenth century, this Shariah spirituality had taken root throughout the Muslim world, Sunni and Shii, not because it was forced on the people by caliphs and *ulema*, but because it did give men and women an experience of the numinous and imbue their lives with meaning. This cultic reference to the past did not, however, imprison Muslims in an archaic devotion to a seventh-century way of life. The Ottoman state was arguably the most up-to-date in the world during the early sixteenth century. It was, for its time, superbly efficient, had developed a new-style bureaucracy, and encouraged a vibrant intellectual life. The Ottomans were open to other cultures. They were genuinely excited by Western navigational science, stirred by the discoveries of the explorers, and eager to adopt such Western military inventions as gunpowder and firearms.[10] It was the job of the *ulema* to see how these innovations could be accommodated to the Muhammadan paradigm in Muslim law. The study of jurisprudence *(fiqh)* did not simply consist in poring over old texts, but also had a challenging dimension. And, at this date, there was no real incompatibility between Islam and the West. Europe was also imbued with the conservative spirit. The Renaissance humanists had tried to renew their culture by a return *ad fontes,* to the sources. We have seen that it was virtually impossible for ordinary mortals to break with religion entirely. Despite their new inventions, Europeans were still ruled by the conservative ethos until the eighteenth century. It was only when Western modernity replaced the backward-looking mythical way of life with a future-oriented rationalism that some Muslims would begin to find Europe alien.

Further, it would be a mistake to imagine that conservative society was entirely static. Throughout Muslim history, there were movements of *islah* ("reform") and *tajdid* ("renewal"), which were often quite revolutionary.[11] A reformer such as Ahmad ibn Taymiyyah of Damascus (1263–1328), for example, refused to accept the closing of the "gates of *ijtihad.*" He lived during and after the Mongol invasions, when Muslims were desperately trying to recover from the trauma and to rebuild their society. Reform movements usually occur at a period of cultural change or in the wake of a great political disaster. At such times, the old answers no longer suffice and reformers, therefore, use the rational powers of *ijtihad* to challenge the status quo. Ibn Taymiyyah wanted to bring the Shariah up to date so that it could meet the real needs of Muslims in these drastically altered circumstances. He was revolutionary, but his program took an essentially conservative form. Ibn Taymiyyah believed that to survive the crisis, Muslims must return to the sources, to the Koran and Sunnah of the Prophet. He wanted to remove later theological accretions and get back to basics. This meant that he overturned much of the medieval jurisprudence *(fiqh)* and philosophy that had come to be considered sacred, in a desire to return to the original Muslim archetype. This iconoclasm enraged the establishment, and Ibn Taymiyyah ended his days in prison. It is said that he died of a broken heart, because his jailers would not allow him pen and paper. But the ordinary people loved him; his legal reforms had been liberal and radical, and they could see that he had their interests at heart.[12] His funeral became a demonstration of popular acclaim. There have been many such reformers in Islamic history. We shall see that some of the Muslim fundamentalists of our own day are working in this tradition of *islah* and *tajdid*.

Other Muslims were able to explore fresh religious ideas and practices in the esoteric movements, which were kept secret from the masses because their practitioners believed that they could be misunderstood. They saw no incompatibility, however, between their version of the faith and that of the majority. They believed that their movements were complementary to the teaching of the Koran and gave them new relevance. The three main forms of esoteric Islam were the mystical discipline of Sufism, the rationalism of Falsafah, and the political piety of the Shiah, which we will explore in detail later in this chapter. But however innovative these esoteric forms of Islam seemed and however radically they appeared to diverge from the Shariah piety of the mainstream, the esoterics believed that they were returning *ad fontes*. The exponents of Falsafah, who tried to apply the principles of Greek philosophy to Koranic religion, wanted to go back to a primordial, universal faith of timeless truths, which, they were convinced, had preceded the various historical religions. Sufis believed that their mystical ecstasy reproduced the spiritual experiences of the Prophet when he had received the Koran; they too were conforming to the Muhammadan archetype. Shiis claimed that they alone cultivated the passion for social justice that informed the Koran, but which had been betrayed by corrupt Muslim rulers. None of the esoterics wanted to be "original" in our sense; all were original in the conservative way of returning to fundamentals, which alone, it was thought, could lead to human perfection and fulfillment.[13]

One of the two Muslim countries we shall be examining in detail in this book is Egypt, which became part of the Ottoman empire in 1517, when Selim I conquered the country in the course of a campaign in Syria. Shariah piety would, therefore, predominate in Egypt. The great university of al-Azhar in Cairo became the most important center for the study of *fiqh* in the Sunni world, but during these centuries of Ottoman rule Egypt fell behind

Istanbul and lapsed into relative obscurity. We know very little about the
country during the early modern period. Since 1250, the region had been
governed by the Mamluks, a crack military corps composed of Circassian
slaves who had been captured as boys and converted to Islam. The Janissaries, a similar slave corps, were the military backbone of the Ottoman
empire. In their prime, the Mamluks led a vibrant society in Egypt and Syria,
and Egypt was one of the most advanced countries in the Muslim world. But
eventually the Mamluk empire succumbed to the inherent limitations of
agrarian civilization and by the late fifteenth century had fallen into decline.
However, the Mamluks were not entirely vanquished in Egypt. The Ottoman
sultan Selim I conquered the country by making an alliance with Khair Bey,
the Mamluk governor of Aleppo. As a result of this deal, Khair Bey was
appointed viceroy when the Ottoman troops left.

At first, the Ottomans were able to keep the Mamluks in check, quashing
two Mamluk uprisings.[14] By the late sixteenth century, however, the Ottomans were just beginning to outrun their own resources. Severe inflation led
to a decline in the administration and, gradually, after several revolts, the
Mamluk commanders *(beys)* reemerged as the real rulers of Egypt, even
though they remained officially subservient to Istanbul. The *beys* formed a
high-ranking military cadre which was able to lead a rebellion of Mamluk
troops in the Ottoman army against the Turkish governor and install one of
their own number in his place. The sultan confirmed this appointment and
the Mamluks were able to retain control of the country, apart from a brief
period toward the end of the seventeenth century when one of the Janissaries seized power. Mamluk rule was unstable, however. The beylicate was
divided between two factions and there was constant unrest and internecine
strife.[15] Throughout this turbulent period, the chief victims were the Egyptian people. During the revolts and factional violence, they had their property confiscated, their homes plundered, and endured crippling taxation.
They felt no affinity with their rulers, Turkish or Circassian, who were foreigners and had no real interest in their welfare. Increasingly, the people
turned to the *ulema*, who were Egyptians, represented the sacred order of
the Shariah, and became the true leaders of the Egyptian masses. As the conflict between the *beys* became more acute during the eighteenth century,
Mamluk leaders found it necessary to appeal to the *ulema* to ensure that their
rule was accepted by the people.[16]

The *ulema* were the teachers, scholars, and intellectuals of Egyptian society. Each town had between one and seven *madrasahs* (colleges for the study
of Islamic law and theology), which provided the country with its teachers.
Intellectual standards were not high. When Selim I conquered Egypt, he
took many of the leading *ulema* back to Istanbul with him together with the

most precious manuscripts. Egypt became a backward province of the Ottoman empire. The Ottomans did not patronize Arab scholars, Egyptians had no contact with the outside world, and Egyptian philosophy, astronomy, medicine, and science, which had flourished under the Mamluk empire, deteriorated.[17]

But because they were a major channel of communication between the rulers and the people, the *ulema* became extremely powerful. Many of them came from the peasant class of *fellahin,* so their influence was considerable in the rural areas. In the Koran schools and *madrasahs,* they controlled the whole educational system; because the Shariah courts were the chief dispensers of justice, the *ulema* also had a monopoly of the legal system. Moreover, they held important political office in the *divan,*[18] and, as the guardians of the Shariah, could also lead a principled opposition to the government. The great *madrasah* of al-Azhar was next to the bazaar, and *ulema* often had family links with the merchant class. If they wished to protest against government policy, a drumroll from the minaret of the Azhar could close the bazaar and bring the crowds onto the street. In 1794, for example, Shaykh al-Sharqawi, the rector of the Azhar, marched at the head of a mob to protest against a new tax, which, he declared, was oppressive and un-Islamic. Three days later, the *beys* were forced to rescind the tax.[19] But there was no real danger of the *ulema* leading an Islamic revolution to replace the government. The *beys* were usually able to keep them in check by confiscating their property, and mob violence could not offer a sustained challenge to the Mamluk army.[20] Nevertheless, the prominence of the *ulema* gave Egyptian society a distinctly religious character. Islam gave the people of Egypt their only real security.[21]

Security was at a premium in the Middle East by the late eighteenth century. The Ottoman state was now in serious disarray. The superb efficiency of its government in the sixteenth century had given way to incompetence, especially on the peripheries of the empire. The West had begun its startling rise to power, and the Ottomans found that they could no longer fight as equals with the powers of Europe. It was difficult for them to respond to the Western challenge, not simply because it occurred at a time of political weakness, but because the new society that was being created in Europe was without precedent in world history.[22] The sultans tried to adapt, but their efforts were superficial. Sultan Selim III (ruled 1789–1807), for example, saw the Western threat in purely military terms. There had been abortive attempts in the 1730s to reform the army along European lines, but when he ascended the throne in 1789 Selim opened a number of military schools with French instructors, where students became acquainted with European languages and Western books on mathematics, navigation, geography, and history.[23] Learning a few military techniques and a smattering of modern sciences, however, would not prove sufficient to contain the Western threat, because Europeans had evolved an entirely new way of life and thought, so that they operated on entirely different norms. To meet them on their own ground, the Ottomans would need to develop a wholly rational culture, dismantle the Islamic structure of society, and be prepared to sever all sacred links with the past. A few members of the elite might be able to achieve this transition, which had taken Europeans almost three hundred years, but how would they persuade the masses, whose minds and hearts were imbued with the conservative ethos, to accept and understand the need for such radical change?

On the margins of the empire, where Ottoman decline was most acutely felt, people responded to the change and unrest as they had always done—in religious terms. In the Arabian Peninsula, Muhammad ibn Abd al-Wahhab (1703–92) managed to break away from Istanbul and create a state of his own in central Arabia and the Persian Gulf region. Abd al-Wahhab was a typical Islamic reformer. He met the current crisis by returning to the Koran and the Sunnah, and by vehemently rejecting medieval jurisprudence, mysticism, and philosophy. Because they diverged from this pristine Islam, as he envisaged it, Abd al-Wahhab declared the Ottoman sultans to be apostates, unworthy of the obedience of the faithful and deserving of death. Their Shariah state was inauthentic. Instead, Abd al-Wahhab tried to create an enclave of pure faith, based on the practice of the first Muslim community in the seventh century. It was an aggressive movement, which imposed itself on the people by force. Some of these violent and rejectionist Wahhabi techniques would be used by some of the fundamentalist Islamist reformers during the twentieth century, a period of even greater change and unrest.[24]

The Moroccan Sufi reformer Ahmad ibn Idris (1780–1836) had quite a different approach, which also has its followers in our own day. His solution to the disintegration of life in the peripheral Ottoman provinces was to educate the people and make them better Muslims. He traveled extensively in North Africa and the Yemen, addressing the people in their own dialect, teaching them how to perform the ritual of communal prayer, and trying to shame them out of immoral practices. This was a grassroots movement. Ibn Idris had no time for Wahhabi methods. In his view, education, not force, was the key. Killing people in the name of religion was obviously wrong. Other reformers worked along similar lines. In Algeria, Ahmad al-Tigrani (d. 1815), in Medina, Muhammad ibn Abd al-Karim Sameem (d. 1775), and in Libya, Muhammad ibn Ali al-Sanusi (d. 1832) all took the faith directly to the people, bypassing the *ulema*. This was a populist reform; they attacked the religious establishment, which they considered to be elitist and out of touch, and, unlike Abd al-Wahhab, were not interested in doctrinal purity. Taking the people back to the basic cult and rituals and persuading them to live morally would cure the ills of society more effectively than complicated *fiqh*.

For centuries, Sufis had taught their disciples to reproduce the Muhammadan paradigm in their own lives; they had also insisted that the way to God lay through the creative and mystical imagination: people had a duty to create their own theophanies with the aid of the contemplative disciplines of Sufism. In the late eighteenth and early nineteenth centuries, these reformers, whom scholars call "Neo-Sufis," went one step further. They taught the common people to rely entirely on their own insights; they should not have to depend upon the scholars and learned clerics. Ibn Idris went so far as to reject the authority of every single Muslim sage and saint, however exalted, except the Prophet. He was thus encouraging Muslims to value what was new and to cast off habits of deference. The goal of the mystical quest was not union with God, but a deep identification with the human figure of the Prophet, who had opened himself so perfectly to the divine. These were incipiently modern attitudes. Even though the Neo-Sufis were still harking back to the archetypal persona of the Prophet, they seem to have been evolving a humanly rather than a transcendently oriented faith and were encouraging their disciples to prize what was novel and innovative as much as the old. Ibn Idris had no contact with the West, never once mentions Europe in his writings, and shows no knowledge of or interest in Western ideas. But the mythical disciplines of Sunni Islam led him to embrace some of the principles of the European Enlightenment.[25]

This was also the case in Iran, whose history during this period is better documented than that of Egypt. When the Safavids conquered Iran in the early sixteenth century, they made Shiism the official religion of the state. Hitherto, the Shiah had been an intellectual and mystical esoteric movement, and Shiis had as a matter of principle refrained from participation in political life. There had always been a few important Shii centers in Iran, but most Shiis were Arabs, not Persians. The Safavid experiment in Iran was, therefore, a startling innovation. There was no doctrinal quarrel between Sunnis and Shiis; the difference was chiefly one of feeling. Sunnis were basically optimistic about Muslim history, whereas the Shii vision was more tragic: the fate of the descendants of the Prophet Muhammad had become a symbol of a cosmic struggle between good and evil, justice and tyranny, in which the wicked always seem to get the upper hand. Where Sunnis have made the life of Muhammad a myth, Shiis have mythologized the lives of his descendants.

In order to understand this Shii faith, without which such events as the Iranian Revolution of 1978–79 are incomprehensible, we must briefly consider the development of the Shiah.

When the Prophet Muhammad died in 632, he had made no arrangements for the succession, and his friend Abu Bakr was elected to the caliphate by a majority of the *ummah*. Some believed, however, that Muhammad would have wished to be succeeded by his closest male relative, Ali ibn Abi Talib, who was his ward, cousin, and son-in-law. But Ali was continually passed over in the elections, until he finally became the fourth caliph in 656. The Shiis, however, do not recognize the rule of the first three caliphs, and call Ali the First Imam ("Leader"). Ali's piety was beyond question, and he wrote inspiring letters to his officers, stressing the importance of just rule. He was, however, tragically assassinated by a Muslim extremist in 661, an event mourned by Sunnis and Shiis alike. His rival, Muawiyyah, seized the caliphate throne, and established the more worldly Umayyad dynasty, based in Damascus. Ali's eldest son, Hasan, whom Shiis call the Second Imam, retired from politics and died in Medina in 669. But in 680, when Caliph Muawiyyah died, there were huge demonstrations in Kufa in Iraq in favor of Ali's second son, Husain. To avoid Umayyad reprisals, Husain sought sanctuary in Mecca, but the new Umayyad caliph, Yazid, sent emissaries to the holy city to assassinate him, violating the sanctity of Mecca. Husain, the Third Shii Imam, decided that he must take a stand against this unjust and unholy ruler. He set out for Kufa with a small band of fifty followers, accompanied by their wives and children, believing that the poignant spectacle of the Prophet's family marching in opposition to tyranny would bring the *ummah* back to a more authentic practice of Islam. But on the holy fast day of Ashura, the tenth of the Arab month of Muharram, Umayyad troops surrounded Husain's little army on the plain of Kerbala outside Kufa and slaughtered them all. Husain was the last to die, with his infant son in his arms.[26]

The Kerbala tragedy would develop its own cult and become a myth, a timeless event in the personal life of every Shii. Yazid has become an emblem of tyranny and injustice; by the tenth century, Shiis mourned the martyrdom of Husain annually on the fast day of Ashura, weeping, beating their bodies, and declaring their undying opposition to the corruption of Muslim political life. Poets sang epic dirges in honor of the martyrs, Ali and Husain. Shiis thus developed a piety of protest, centering on the *mythos* of Kerbala. The cult has kept alive a passionate yearning for social justice that is at the core of the Shii vision. When Shiis walk in solemn procession during the Ashura rituals, they declare their determination to follow Husain and even to die in the struggle against tyranny.[27]

It took some time for the myth and cult to develop. In the first years after Kerbala, Husain's son Ali, who had managed to survive the massacre, and his son Muhammad (known respectively as the Fourth and Fifth Imams) retired to Medina and took no part in politics. But in the meantime, Ali, the First Imam, had become a symbol of righteousness for many people who were dissatisfied with Umayyad rule. When the Abbasid faction managed finally to bring down the Umayyad caliphate in 750, and established their own dynasty (750–1260), they claimed at first to belong to the Shiah-i Ali (the Party of Ali). The Shiah was also associated with some wilder speculations, which most Muslims regarded as "extreme" *(ghuluww)*. In Iraq, Muslims had come into contact with an older and more complex religious world and some were influenced by Christian, Jewish, or Zoroastrian mythology. In some Shii circles, Ali was revered as an incarnation of the divine, like Jesus; Shii rebels believed that their leaders had not died but were in hiding (or "occultation"); they would return one day and lead their followers to victory. Others were fascinated by the idea of the Holy Spirit descending into a human being and imparting divine wisdom to him.[28] All these myths, in a modified form, would become important to the esoteric vision of the Shiah.

The cult in honor of Husain transformed a historical tragedy into a myth that became central to the religious vision of Shii Muslims. It directed their attention to a ceaseless but unseen struggle between Good and Evil at the heart of human existence; the rituals liberated Husain from the particular circumstances of his time and made him a living presence; he became a symbol of a profound truth. But the mythology of Shiism could not be applied practically in the real world. Even when such Shii rulers as the Abbasids managed to seize power, the harsh realities of political life meant that they could not rule according to these lofty ideals. The Abbasid caliphs were highly successful in worldly terms, but once in power they soon dropped their Shii radicalism and became ordinary Sunnis. Their rule seemed no more just than that of the Umayyads, but it was pointless for true Shiis to rebel, since any revolution was of necessity brutally suppressed. Indeed, the myth of Husain seemed to suggest that any attempt to oppose a tyrannical ruler was doomed to failure, no matter how pious and zealous for justice it might be.

The Sixth Shii Imam, Jafar as-Sadiq (d. 765), realized this and formally abandoned armed struggle. He declared that even though he, as the Prophet's descendant, was the only legitimate leader (Imam) of the *ummah*, his true function was not to engage in a fruitless conflict but to guide the Shiah in the mystical interpretation of scripture. Each Imam of Ali's line was, he taught, the spiritual leader of his generation. Each one of the Imams had been designated by his predecessor, who had transmitted to him a secret knowledge *(ilm)* of divine truth. An Imam was, therefore, an infallible spiritual director and a perfect judge. The Shiah thus abjured politics and became a mystical sect, cultivating the techniques of meditation in order to intuit a secret *(batin)* wisdom that lay behind every single word of the Koran. The Shiis were not content with the literal meaning of scripture, but used the text as a basis for new insights. Their symbolism of the divinely inspired Imam reflected the Shii sense of a sacred presence, which a mystic experienced as immanent and accessible in a turbulent, dangerous world. It was not a doctrine for the masses, who might interpret it crudely, so Shiis must keep their spiritual as well as their political views to themselves. The mythology of the Imamate, as developed by Jafar as-Sadiq, was an imaginative vision that looked beyond the literal and factual meaning of scripture and history to the constant, primordial reality of the unseen *(al-ghayb)*. Where the uninitiated could see only a man, the contemplative Shii could discern a trace of the divine in Jafar as-Sadiq.[29]

The Imamate also symbolized the extreme difficulty of incarnating God's will in the flawed and tragic conditions of daily life. Jafar as-Sadiq effectively separated religion from politics, privatizing faith and confining it to the personal realm. He did this to protect religion and enable it to survive in a world that seemed essentially hostile to it. This secularization policy sprang from a profoundly spiritual impulse. Shiis knew that it could be dangerous to mix religion and politics. A century later, this became tragically evident. In 836, the Abbasid caliphs moved their capital to Samarra, some sixty miles south of Baghdad. By this date, Abbasid power was disintegrating, and though the caliph remained the nominal ruler of the whole Muslim world, real authority lay with the local amirs and chieftains throughout the far-flung empire. The caliphs felt that in these disturbed times they could not permit the Imams, the descendants of the Prophet, to remain at large, and in 848, Caliph al-Mutawakkil summoned the Tenth Imam, Ali al-Hadi, from Medina to Samarra, where he was placed under house arrest. He and his son, the Eleventh Imam, Hasan al-Askari, could only maintain contact with the Shiah by means of an agent *(wakil)* who lived in al-Karkh, the mercantile quarter of Baghdad, practicing a trade to deflect the attention of the Abbasid authorities.[30]

In 874, the Eleventh Imam died, probably poisoned at the behest of the caliph. He had been kept in such strict seclusion that Shiis knew very little about him. Did he have a son? If not, what would happen to the succession? Had the line died out, and, if so, did this mean that the Shiah was deprived of mystical guidance? Speculation ran rife, but the most popular theory insisted that Hasan al-Askari indeed had a son, Abu al-Qasim Muhammad, the

Twelfth Imam, who had gone into hiding to save his life. It was an attractive solution, because it suggested that nothing had changed. The last two Imams had been virtually inaccessible. Now the Hidden Imam would continue to make contact with the people through his *wakil,* Uthman al-Amri, who would dispense spiritual advice, collect the *zakat* alms, interpret the scriptures, and deliver legal judgments. But this solution had a limited life span. As time passed beyond the point where the Twelfth Imam seemed likely to be still alive, Shiis became anxious once again, until, in 934, the current agent, Ali ibn Muhammad as-Samarri, brought the Shiah a message from the Hidden Imam. He had not died, but had been miraculously concealed by God; he would return one day shortly before the Last Judgment to inaugurate a reign of justice. He was still the infallible guide of the Shiah and the only legitimate ruler of the *ummah,* but he would no longer be able to commune with the faithful through agents, or have any direct contact with them. Shiis should not expect his speedy return. They would only see him again "after a long time has passed and the earth has become filled with tyranny."[31]

The myth of the "occultation" of the Hidden Imam cannot be explained rationally. It makes sense only in a context of mysticism and ritual practice. If we understand the story as a *logos,* one that should be interpreted literally as a plain statement of fact, all kinds of questions arise. Where in the world had the Imam gone? Was he on earth or in some kind of intermediate realm? What kind of life could he possibly have? Was he getting older and older? How could he guide the faithful, if they could neither see nor hear him? These questions would seem obtuse to a Shii who was involved in a disciplined cultivation of the *batin,* or secret sense of scripture, which bypassed reason and drew on the more intuitive powers of the mind. Shiis did not interpret their scriptures and doctrines literally. Their entire spirituality was now a symbolic quest for the Unseen *(al-ghayb)* that lies beneath the flux of outward *(zahir)* events. Shiis worshipped an invisible, inscrutable God, searched for a concealed meaning in the Koran, took part in a ceaseless but invisible battle for justice, yearned for a Hidden Imam, and cultivated an esoteric version of Islam that had to be secreted from the world.[32] This intense contemplative life was the setting that alone made sense of the Occultation. The Hidden Imam had become a myth; by his removal from normal history, he had been liberated from the confines of space and time and, paradoxically, he became a more vivid presence in the lives of Shiis than when he and the other Imams had lived a normal life in Medina or Samarra. The Occultation is a myth that expresses our sense of the sacred as elusive and tantalizingly absent. It is present in the world but not of it; divine wisdom is inseparable from humanity (for we can only perceive anything, God included, from a human perspective) but takes us beyond the insights of ordinary men and women. Like any myth, the Occultation could not be understood by discursive reason, as though it were a fact that was either self-evident or capable of logical demonstration. But it did express a truth in the religious experience of humanity.

Like any esoteric spirituality, Shiism at this date was only for an elite. It tended to attract the more intellectually adventurous Muslims, who had a talent and a need for mystical contemplation. But Shiis also had a different political outlook from other Muslims. Where the rituals and disciplines of Sunni spirituality helped Sunni Muslims to accept life as it was and to conform to archetypal norms, Shii mysticism expressed a divine discontent. The early traditions that developed shortly after the announcement of the doctrine of the Occultation reveal the frustration and impotence felt by many Shiis during the tenth century.[33] This has been called "the Shii century" because many of the local commanders in the Islamic empire who wielded effective power in a given region had Shii sympathies, but this turned out to make no appreciable difference. For the majority, life was still unjust and inequitable, despite the clear teaching of the Koran. Indeed, the Imams had all been victims of rulers whom Shiis regarded as corrupt and illegitimate: tradition had it that every single one of the Imams after Husain had been poisoned by the Umayyad and Abbasid caliphs. In their longing for a more just and benevolent social order, Shiis developed an eschatology centering on the final appearance *(zuhur)* of the Hidden Imam during the Last Days, when he would return, battle with the forces of evil, and establish a Golden Age of justice and peace before the Final Judgment. But this yearning for the End did not mean that the Shiis had abandoned the conservative ethos and become future-oriented. They were so strongly aware of the archetypal ideal, the way things ought to be, that they found ordinary political life intolerable. The Hidden Imam would not bring something new into the world; he would simply correct human history to make human affairs finally conform to the fundamental principles of existence. Similarly, the Imam's "appearance" would in a profound sense simply make manifest something that had been there all along, for the Hidden Imam is a constant presence in the life of Shiis; he represents the elusive light of God in a dark, tyrannical world and the only source of hope.

The Occultation completed the mythologization of Shii history which had begun when the Sixth Imam gave up political activism and separated religion from politics. Myth does not provide a blueprint for pragmatic political action but supplies the faithful with a way of looking at their society and developing their interior lives. The myth of Occultation depoliticized the Shiah once and for all. There was no sense in Shiis taking useless risks by pitting themselves against the might of temporal rulers. The image of an

Imam, a just political leader who could not exist in the world as it was but had to go into hiding, expressed the Shiis' alienation from their society. From this new perspective, any government had to be viewed as illegitimate, because it usurped the prerogatives of the Hidden Imam, the true Lord of the Age. Nothing could be expected of earthly rulers, therefore, though in order to survive, the Shiis must cooperate with the powers-that-be. They would live a spiritual life, yearning for a justice that could only return to earth in the Last Days "after a long time has passed." The sole authority they would accept was that of the Shii *ulema,* who had taken the place of the former "agents" of the Imams. Because of their learning, their spirituality, and their mastery of the divine law, the *ulema* had become the deputies of the Hidden Imam and spoke in his name. But because all governments were illegitimate, *ulema* must not hold political office.[34]

Shiis thus tacitly condoned a total secularization of politics that could seem to violate the crucial Islamic principle of *tawhid,* which forbade any such separation of state and religion. But the mythology of this seculariza-tion sprang from a religious insight. The legend of the Imams, who had nearly all been assassinated, poisoned, imprisoned, exiled, and, finally, elim-inated by the caliphs, represented the basic incompatibility of religion and politics. Political life belongs to the realm of *logos;* it must be forward-looking, pragmatic, able to compromise, plan, and organize society on a rational basis. It has to balance the absolute demands of religion with the grim reality of life on the ground. Premodern, agrarian society was based on a fundamental inequality; it depended upon the labor of peasants who could not share the fruits of civilization. The great confessional religions of the Axial Age (c. 700–200 BCE) had all been preoccupied with this dilemma and tried to grapple with it. Where there were insufficient resources, and where lack of technology and communications made it harder to impose authority, politics became more brutal and aggressively practical. It was, therefore, extremely difficult for any government to live up to the Islamic ideal or to tolerate the existence of an Imam, an embodiment of divine wis-dom, who made its shortcomings so sadly evident. Religious leaders could admonish, criticize, and protest against flagrant abuses, but in some tragic sense the sacred had to be either marginalized or kept within bounds, as the caliphs had interned the Imams in the Askari fortress in Samarra. But there was nobility in the Shii devotion to an ideal which must be kept alive, even though, like the Hidden Imam, it was concealed and currently unable to operate in a tyrannical and corrupt world.

Even though the Shiah had become a mythological faith, that did not mean that it was irrational. In fact, Shiism became a more rational and intel-lectual version of Islam than the Sunnah. Shiis found that they were in agreement with the Sunni theologians known as the Mutazilites, who tried to rationalize the doctrines of the Koran. In their turn, the Mutazilites gravitated toward the Shiah. Paradoxically, the a-rational doctrine of the Occultation allowed the Shii *ulema* more freedom to exercise their rational powers in the pragmatic world of affairs than the Sunni *ulema*. Because the Hidden Imam was no longer available, they had to rely on their own intellectual powers. In the Shiah, therefore, the "gates of *ijtihad*" were never declared closed, as in the Sunnah.[35] At first, it is true, Shiis did feel mentally hobbled when their Imam vanished, but by the thirteenth century, an eminent and learned Shii cleric was known precisely as a *mujtahid,* one who was deemed capable of the rational activity of *ijtihad.*

Shii rationalism was, however, different from our current secularized rationalism in the West. Shiis were often critical thinkers. The eleventh-century scholars Muhammad al-Mufid and Muhammad al-Tusi, for example, were worried about the authenticity of some of the *hadith* reports about the Prophet and his companions. They felt that it was not sufficient simply to quote one of these unreliable traditions in support of their doctrines but that clerics should use reason and logic instead; yet the rational arguments they produced would not convince a modern skeptic. Tusi, for example, "proved" the doctrine of the Imamate on the grounds that, since God is good and desires our salvation, it is reasonable to believe that he will provide us with an infallible guide. Men and women *can* work out for themselves the necessity for social justice, but a divine sanction makes this imperative more urgent. Even Tusi, however, found himself at a loss when it came to finding a rationale for the Occultation.[36] But this was not disturbing to Shiis. *Mythos* and *logos,* reason and revelation, were not in opposition but simply different from one another and complementary. Where we in the modern West have discounted mythology and mysticism as a source of truth and rely on reason alone, a thinker such as Tusi saw both ways of thinking as valid and necessary. He sought to show that doctrines which made perfect sense while he was engaged in mystical meditation were also reasonable, in an Islamic context. The introspective techniques of contemplation provided insights that were true in their own sphere, but they could not be proved logically, like a mathematical equation that was the product of *logos.*

By the end of the fifteenth century, as we have seen, most Shiis were Arabs and the Shiah was especially strong in Iraq, particularly in the two shrine cities of Najaf and Kerbala, dedicated respectively to Imam Ali and Imam Husain. Most Iranians were Sunni, though the Iranian city of Qum had always been a Shii center, and there were significant numbers of Shiis in Rayy, Kashan, and Khurasan. So there were Iranians who welcomed the arrival of nineteen-year-old Shah Ismail, head of the Safavid order of Sufis, who conquered Tabriz in 1501, subdued the rest of Iran within the next decade, and announced that Shiism would become the official religion of the new Safavid empire. Ismail claimed descent from the Seventh Imam, which, he believed, gave him a legitimacy not enjoyed by other Muslim rulers.[37]

But this was obviously a break with Shii tradition. Most Shiis, known as "Twelvers" (because of their veneration of the twelve Imams), believed that no government could be legitimate in the absence of the Hidden Imam.[38] How, then, could there be a "state Shiism"? This did not trouble Ismail, who knew very little about Twelver orthodoxy. The Safavid order, a mystical fraternity which had been founded in the wake of the Mongol invasions, had originally been Sufi but had absorbed many of the "extreme" *(ghuluww)* ideas of the old Shiah. Ismail believed that Imam Ali had been divine, and that the Shii messiah would return very soon to inaugurate the Golden Age. He may even have told his disciples that he *was* the Hidden Imam, returned from concealment. The Safavid order was a marginal, populist, revolutionary group, far removed from the sophisticated circles of Shii esotericism.[39] Ismail had no qualms about setting up a Shii state, and, instead of trying to find a civilized *modus vivendi* with the Sunni majority, as Shiis had done since the time of Jafar as-Sadiq, he was fanatically opposed to the Sunnah. There was a new sectarian intolerance in both the Ottoman and the Safavid empires that was not dissimilar to the feuds between Catholics and Protestants that were developing in Europe at about this time. In recent centuries, there had been a détente between Sunnis and Shiis. But during the early sixteenth century, the Ottomans were determined to marginalize the Shiah in their domains, and, when Ismail emerged in Iran, he was equally determined to wipe out the Sunnah there.[40]

It did not take the Safavids long, however, to discover that the messianic, "extremist" ideology that had served them well in opposition was no longer suitable once they had become the establishment. Shah Abbas I (1588–1629) was determined to eliminate the old *ghuluww* theology, dismissed "extremists" from his bureaucracy, and imported Arab Shii *ulema* to promote Twelver orthodoxy. He built *madrasahs* for them in Isfahan, his new capital, and Hilla, endowed property *(awqaf)* on their behalf, and gave them generous gifts. This patronage was essential in the early days, since the *ulema* were new immigrants entirely dependent upon the shahs. But it inevitably changed the nature of the Shiah. Shii scholars had always been a minority group. They had never had *madrasahs* of their own but had studied and debated in one another's homes. Now the Shiah was becoming establishment. Isfahan became the official scholastic center of the Shiah.[41] Shiis had always held aloof from government before, but now the *ulema* had taken over the educational and legal system in Iran as well as the more specifically religious duties of government. The administrative bureaucracy was composed of Iranians who were still loyal to the Sunnah, so they were given the more secular tasks. A de facto split between the secular and religious spheres had developed in the government of Iran.[42]

The *ulema*, however, continued to be wary of the Safavid state; they still refused official government posts and preferred to be ranked as subjects. Their position was, therefore, quite unlike that of the Ottoman *ulema*, but was potentially more powerful. The generosity and patronage of the shahs had made the *ulema* financially independent. Where the Ottomans and their successors could always control their *ulema* by threatening to withdraw their subsidies or confiscate their property, the Shii *ulema* could not be cowed in this way.[43] As Shiism spread among the Iranian people, they would also benefit from the fact that they, and not the shahs, were the only authentic spokesmen of the Hidden Imam. The early Safavids were strong enough to keep the *ulema* in check, however, and the clergy would not come fully into their own until the Iranian people as a whole were fully converted to Shiism in the eighteenth century.

But power corrupts. As the *ulema* became more at home in the Safavid empire, they also became more authoritarian and even bigoted. Some of the more attractive traits of the Shiah were submerged. This new hard line was epitomized by Muhammad Baqir Majlisi (d. 1700), who was one of the most powerful and influential *ulema* of all time. For centuries, Shiis had encouraged an innovative approach to scripture. Majlisi, however, was deeply hostile to both mystical spirituality and philosophical speculation, both of which had been the mainstay of the old esoteric Shiah. He began a relentless persecution of the remaining Sufis in Iran and tried to suppress the teaching of both the philosophic rationalism known as Falsafah and mystical philosophy in Isfahan. He thus introduced a profound distrust of both mysticism and philosophy that persists in Iranian Shiism to the present day. Instead of engaging in an esoteric study of the Koran, Shii scholars were encouraged to concentrate on *fiqh*, Islamic jurisprudence.

Majlisi also transformed the meaning of the ritual processions in honor of the martyrdom of Husain.[44] These had become more elaborate: now camels draped in green were ridden by weeping women and children, who represented the Imam's family; soldiers shot rifles in the air, and coffins representing the Imam and his martyred companions were followed by the governor, the notables, and crowds of men who sobbed and wounded themselves with knives.[45] A highly emotional account of the Kerbala story, the *Rawdat ash-Shuhada* by the Iraqi Shii Waiz Kashift (d. 1504), was recited at special meetings known as *rawda-khani* ("recitals of the Rawdat"), while the people wailed and cried aloud. The rituals had always had a revolutionary potential, demonstrating as they did the willingness of the people to fight tyranny to the death. Now, however, instead of encouraging the masses to see Husain as an example, Majlisi and his clergy taught them to see the Imam as a patron who could secure their admission to paradise if they showed their devotion to him by lamenting his death. The rituals now endorsed the status quo, urging the people to curry favor with the powerful, and look only to their own interests.[46] It was an emasculation and a degradation of the old Shii ideal; it also bowdlerized the conservative ethos. Instead of helping people to attune themselves to the basic laws and rhythms of existence, the cult was simply used to keep the masses in line. It was a development that showed in quite a different way how destructive political power could be to religion.

One of Majlisi's chief targets was the school of mystical philosophy developed in Isfahan by Mir Dimad (d. 1631) and his pupil, Mulla Sadra (d. 1640), a thinker who would have a profound influence on future generations of Iranians.[47] Mir Dimad and Mulla Sadra were both utterly opposed to the new intransigence of some of the *ulema*. They saw it as a total perversion of the Shiah, and, indeed, of all religion. In the old days, when the Shiis had searched for hidden meanings in scripture, they had implicitly acknowledged that divine truth was illimitable, fresh insights were always possible, and no single interpretation of the Koran could suffice. For Mir Dimad and Mulla Sadra, true knowledge could never be a matter of intellectual conformity. No sage or religious authority, however eminent, could claim a monopoly of truth.

They also expressed clearly the conservative conviction that mythology and reason were both essential for a full human life: each was diminished unless complemented by the other. Mir Dimad was a natural scientist as well as a theologian. Mulla Sadra criticized both the *ulema,* for belittling the insights of mystical intuition, and the Sufis, for decrying the importance of rational thought. The true philosopher had to become as rational as Aristotle, but must then go beyond him in an ecstatic, imaginative apprehension of truth. Both thinkers emphasized the role of the unconscious, which they depicted as a state existing between the realm of sense perceptions and that of intellectual abstractions. Previously, Sufi philosophers had called this psychic region the *alam al-mithal,* the world of pure images. It was a realm of visions, proceeding from what we would call the subconscious, which rise to the conscious level of the mind in dreams and hypnogogic imagery, but which can also be accessed by some of the exercises and intuitive disciplines of the mystics. Mir Dimad and Mulla Sadra both insisted that these visions were not just subjective fantasies but had objective reality, even if they remained impervious to logical analysis.[48] Instead of discounting them as "imaginary" and, therefore, unreal, as a modern rationalist might do, we should attend to this dimension of our existence. It lies too deep for conscious formulation but has a profound effect upon our behavior and our perceptions. Our dreams *are* real; they tell us something; in our dreams we experience what is imaginary. Mythology was an attempt to organize the experiences of the unconscious into imagery which enabled men and women to relate to these fundamental regions of their own being. Today, people resort to psychoanalysis to gain similar insight into the working of the unconscious mind. The mystical school of Isfahan, spearheaded by Mir Dimad and Mulla Sadra, insisted that truth was not simply that which was logically, publicly, and legally perceived, but had an interior dimension that could not be apprehended by our normal waking consciousness.

This inevitably brought them into conflict with the new hard-line Shiism of some of the *ulema,* who drove Mulla Sadra out of Isfahan. For ten years he was forced to live in a small village near Qum. During this period of solitude, he realized that despite his devotion to mystical philosophy, his approach to religion had still been too cerebral. The study of jurisprudence *(fiqh)* or extrinsic theology could only give us information *about* religion; it could not yield the illumination and personal transformation that is the ultimate goal of the religious quest. It was only when he began seriously to practice the mystical techniques of concentration and descended deeply into the *alam al-mithal* within himself that his heart "caught fire" and "the light of the divine world shone forth upon me . . . and I was able to unravel mysteries that I had not previously understood," he explained later in his great work *al-Asfar al-Arbaah*[49] (The Four Journeys of the Soul).

Sadra's mystical experiences convinced him that human beings could achieve perfection in this world. But, true to the conservative ethos, the perfection that he envisaged was not an evolution to a new and higher state, but a return to the original pure vision of Abraham and the other prophets. It was also a return to God, the Source of all existence. But this did not mean that the mystic abjured the world. In *The Four Journeys of the Soul,* he described the mystical journey of a charismatic political leader. First, he must journey from man to God. Next he travels in the divine sphere, contemplating each of God's attributes until he arrives at an intuitive sense of their indissoluble unity. Gazing thus on the face of God, he is transformed and has a new perception of what monotheism really means and an insight that is not unlike that enjoyed by the Imams. In his third journey, the leader travels back to humankind, and finds that he now sees the world quite differently. His fourth and final quest is to preach God's word in the world and to find new ways to institute the divine law and reorder society in conformity with God's will.[50] It was a vision that linked the perfection of society to a simultaneous spiritual development. The establishment of justice and equity here below could not be achieved without a mystical and religious underpinning. Mulla Sadra's vision fused politics and spirituality, which had become separate in Twelver Shiism, seeing the rational effort that was essential for the transformation of society in the mundane world as inseparable from the mythical and mystical context that gave it meaning. Mulla Sadra had thus proposed a new model of Shii leadership, which would have a profound impact upon Iranian politics in our own day.

The mystical political leader of Mulla Sadra's vision would have divine insight, but that did not mean that he could impose his own opinions and religious practice on others by force. If he did that, in Sadra's view, he denied the essence of religious truth. Sadra was vehemently opposed to the growing power of the *ulema,* and was especially disturbed by a wholly new idea that was gaining ground in Iran during the seventeenth century. Some *ulema* now believed that most Muslims were incapable of interpreting the fundamentals *(usul)* of the faith for themselves; because the *ulema* were the only official spokesmen of the Hidden Imam, ordinary folk must, therefore, select a *mujtahid* who had been deemed capable of exercising *ijtihad* ("independent reasoning") and model their behavior on his legal rulings. Sadra was appalled by these claims of the Usulis, as the proponents of this view were called.[51] In his view, any religion that was based on such servile imitation *(taqlid)* was inherently "polluted."[52] All Shiis were quite capable of understanding the traditions *(akhbar)* of the Prophets and the Imams, and could work out solutions for themselves, based on reason and the spiritual insights they derived from prayer and ritual.

As the seventeenth century progressed, conflict between the Usulis and their opponents became more heated. Safavid power was beginning to decline, and society starting to fragment. People looked to the *ulema* as the only authorities capable of restoring order, but they differed among themselves about the nature of their authority. At this stage, most Iranians opposed the Usulis and followed the so-called Akhbaris, who relied on past tradition. The Akhbaris condemned the use of *ijtihad* and promoted a narrowly literal interpretation of the Koran and the Sunnah. They insisted that all legal decisions must be based on explicit statements of the Koran, the Prophet, or the Imams. If cases arose where there were no inspired rulings, the Muslim jurist must not depend upon his own judgment but should refer the matter to the secular courts.[53] The Usulis wanted a more flexible approach. Jurists could use their own reasoning powers to reach valid decisions, based on legal principles hallowed by Islamic tradition. They thought that the Akhbaris would get so enmeshed in the past that Islamic jurisprudence would be unable to meet new challenges. In the absence of the Hidden Imam, they argued, no jurist could have the last word and no precedent could be binding. Indeed, they went so far as to say that the faithful should always follow the rulings of a living *mujtahid* rather than a revered authority of the past. Both sides were trying to remain true to the conservative spirit at a time of social and political instability, and both were principally concerned with the divine law. Neither the Usulis nor the Akhbaris insisted on intellectual conformity; it was only in matters of behavior or religious practice that the faithful must submit to either a literal reading of scripture or the rulings of a *mujtahid*. Nevertheless, both sides had lost something. The Akhbaris had confused the primordial divine imperative symbolized by the law with the historical traditions of the past; they had become literalists, and were essentially out of touch with the symbolic religion of the old Shiah. In their vision, the faith had become a series of explicit directives. The Usulis had more confidence in human reason, which was still anchored in the *mythos* of their religion. But in demanding that the faithful conform to their judgment, they had lost Mulla Sadra's belief in the sacred freedom of the individual.

By the end of the seventeenth century, it had become crucial to establish a legal authority that could compensate for the weakness of the state. Trade had declined, bringing economic insecurity, and the incompetence of the later shahs made their state vulnerable. When Afghan tribes attacked Isfahan in 1722, the city surrendered ignominiously. Iran entered a period of chaos, and, for a time, it seemed that it might even cease to exist as a separate entity. The Russians invaded from the north, the Ottomans from the west, and the Afghans consolidated their position in the south and east. Tahmasp II, the third son of Sultan-Husain Shah, however, had survived the siege of Isfahan, and, with the help of Nadir Khan, a chieftain of the Iranian Afshar tribe, he succeeded in driving out the invaders. In 1736, Nadir Khan dispensed with Tahmasp Shah and had himself acclaimed as monarch. He ruled the country brutally but effectively until he was assassinated in 1748. A dark anarchic interregnum then ensued, until Aqa Muhammad Khan of the Turcoman Qajar tribe seized control and managed to consolidate his rule in 1794.[54] This new Qajar dynasty would remain in power until the early twentieth century.

During these grim years, there were two important religious developments. Nadir Khan had tried unsuccessfully to reestablish the Sunnah in Iran; as a result, the leading *ulema* left Isfahan and took refuge in the holy shrine cities of Najaf and Kerbala in the Ottoman region of Iraq. At first this seemed a setback, but in the long term it proved a gain for the *ulema*. In Kerbala and Najaf, they achieved still greater autonomy. They were out of the shahs' reach politically, and financially independent, and gradually they became an alternative establishment, superbly placed to challenge the court.[55] The second major change of the period was the victory of the

Usulis, achieved by the somewhat violent methods of the eminent scholar Vahid Bihbehani (1705–92), who defined the role of *ijtihad* with great clarity, and made its use obligatory for jurists. Any Shiis who refused to accept the Usuli position were outlawed as infidels, and opposition was ruthlessly suppressed. There was fighting in Kerbala and Najaf, and some Akhbaris died in the struggle. The mystical philosophy of Isfahan was also banned, and Sufism was suppressed so savagely that Bihbehani's son, Ali, was known as the Sufi-slayer. But, as we have seen, coercion in religious matters is usually counterproductive; mysticism went underground and would continue to shape the ideas of dissidents and intellectuals who fought the status quo. Bihbehani's victory was a political victory for the Iranian *ulema*. The Usuli position was popular with the people during the turbulent years of the interregnum, since it provided them with a source of charismatic authority that brought some measure of order. The *mujtahids* were able to step into the political vacuum and would never lose their power with the people. But Bihbehani's victory, achieved by tyrannical means, was a religious defeat of sorts, since it was far removed from the behavior and ideals of the Imams.[56]

By the end of the eighteenth century, both the Ottoman and Iranian empires were in disarray. They had succumbed to the inevitable fate of an agrarian civilization that had outrun its resources. Ever since the Axial Age, the conservative spirit had helped men and women to accept the limitations of such a society at a profound level. This did not mean that conservative societies were static and fatalistic. This spirituality had inspired great cultural and political achievements in the Islamic world. Until the seventeenth century, Islamdom was the greatest world power. But this political, intellectual, and artistic endeavor had been conducted within a mythological context which would be alien to the values of the new Western culture that had been developing in Europe. Many of the ideals of modern Europe would be congenial to Muslims. We have seen that their faith had encouraged them to form attitudes that would be similar to those promoted by the modern West: social justice, egalitarianism, the freedom of the individual, a humanly based spirituality, a secular polity, a privatized faith, and the cultivation of rational thought. But other aspects of the new Europe would be difficult for people shaped by the conservative ethos to accept. By the end of the eighteenth century, Muslims had fallen behind the West intellectually, and, because the Islamic empires were also politically weak at this date, they would be vulnerable to the European states which were about to make their bid for world hegemony. The British had already established themselves in India, and France was determined to create its own empire. On May 19, 1798, Napoleon Bonaparte set sail for the Middle East from Toulon with 38,000 men and 400 ships to challenge British power in the Orient. The French fleet crossed the Mediterranean and on July 1 Napoleon landed 4300 troops on the beach at Alexandria and took the city shortly after dawn the following day.[57] He thus achieved a base in Egypt. Napoleon had brought with him a corps of scholars, a library of modern European literature, a scientific laboratory, and a printing press with Arabic type. The new scientific, secularist culture of the West had invaded the Muslim world, and it would never be the same again.

3. Christians: Brave New World
(1492–1870)

AT THE SAME TIME as Jews were struggling with the traumatic consequences of their expulsion from Spain and Muslims were establishing their three great empires, the Christians in the West were embarking on a course that would take them far from the certainties and sanctities of the old world. This was an exciting period, but it was also disturbing. During the fourteenth and fifteenth centuries, the Black Death had killed one-third of the population of Christendom, and countries of Europe had been ravaged by such interminable strife as the Hundred Years War between England and France and the internecine Italian wars. Europeans had endured the shock of the Ottoman conquest of Christian Byzantium in 1453, and the papal scandals of the Avignon Captivity and the Great Schism—when as many as three pontiffs had claimed to be the successor of St. Peter at the same time—had caused many to lose faith in the institutional church. People felt obscurely afraid, and found that they could not be religious in the old way. Yet it was also a time of liberation and empowerment. The Iberian explorers had discovered a new world; the astronomers were opening up the heavens, and a new technical efficiency was giving Europeans greater control over their environment than anybody had achieved before. Where the conservative spirit had taught men and women to remain within carefully defined limits, the new culture of Western Christendom showed that it was possible to venture beyond the confines of the known world and not only to survive but to prosper. This would ultimately make the old mythological religion impossible, and it would seem that Western modernity was inherently hostile to faith.

Yet during the early stages of this transformation of Western society this was not the case. Many of the explorers, scientists, and thinkers at the cutting edge of change believed that they were finding new ways of being religious rather than abolishing religion altogether. We shall examine some of their solutions in this chapter and consider their deeper implications. But it is important to be clear that the men who became the spokesmen of the modern spirit did not themselves create it. By the sixteenth century, a complex process was at work in Europe and, later, in its American colonies which was transforming the way that people thought and experienced the world. Change would occur gradually and often unobtrusively. Inventions and innovations, none of which seemed particularly decisive at the time, were occurring simultaneously in many different fields, but their cumulative effect would be conclusive. All these discoveries were characterized by a pragmatic, scientific spirit that slowly undermined the old conservative, mythical ethos and made an increasing number of people receptive to new ideas about God, religion, the state, the individual, and society. Europe and the American colonies would need to accommodate these changes in different political arrangements. Like any other period of far-reaching social change, this was a violent era. There were destructive wars and revolutions, violent uprooting, the despoliation of the countryside, and hideous religious strife. In the course of three hundred years, Europeans and Americans had to employ ruthless methods to modernize their society. There was bloodshed, persecution, inquisition, massacre, exploitation, enslavement, and cruelty. We are witnessing the same bloody upheavals in countries in the developing world which are going through the painful modernizing process today.

The rationalization of agriculture was just one small part of the process, but the increased productivity and healthier livestock affected everybody's life. There were other, more specialized improvements. People started to make precise instruments: the compass, the telescope, the magnifying lens all revealed new worlds and made for better maps, charts, and navigational techniques. The seventeenth-century Dutch microscopist Antony van Leeuwenhoek for the first time observed bacteria, spermatozoa, and other microorganisms, and his observations would one day cast new light on the processes of generation and corruption. This would not only have the pragmatic effect of eliminating disease; it would also divest these basic areas of life and death of much of their mythical content. Medicine began to improve; even though therapy remained a hit-and-miss affair until well into the nineteenth century, there was, during the seventeenth century, a growing concern for sanitation, and some diseases were identified properly for the first time. The earth sciences began to develop, and discussion of such phenomena as earthquakes and volcanoes would push mythological considerations of such events into the background. Mechanical devices improved. Clocks and watches became more reliable and this development would lead to the secularization of time. The application of mathematical and statistical techniques gave people an entirely new sense of the future: in the 1650s and 1660s, the word "probable" began to change its meaning. It would no longer mean that something was "supported by the authorities," as in the conservative period, but "likely in view of all the evidence." This independent attitude and confidence in the future would lead to a new drive for scientific proof and bureaucratic rationalization. The British statisticians William Perry and John Graunt were especially interested in life expectancy, and by the early eighteenth century, people in Europe had begun to insure their lives.[1] All this was potentially subversive to the conservative ethos.

None of these developments seemed conclusive in itself, but, taken together, their effect was radical. By 1600, innovations were occurring on such a scale in Europe that progress seemed irreversible. A discovery in one field would often spark findings in another. The process acquired an unstoppable momentum. Instead of seeing the world as governed by fundamental and unalterable laws, Europeans were discovering that they could explore and manipulate nature to staggering effect. They could manage their environment and satisfy their material wants as never before. But as people became accustomed to this rationalization of their lives, *logos* became ascendant and myth was discredited. People felt more assured about the future. They could institutionalize change without fearful consequences. The wealthy were, for example, now prepared systematically to reinvest capital on the basis of continuing innovation and in the firm expectation that trade would continue to improve. This capitalist economy enabled the West to replace its resources indefinitely, so that it became impervious to the limitations of the old agrarian-based societies. By the time this rationalization and technicalization of society had resulted in the industrial revolution of the nineteenth century, Westerners were so confident of ceaseless progress that they no longer looked back to the past for inspiration, but saw life as a fearless march forward to ever-greater achievement in the future.

The process involved social change. It needed an increasing number of people to take part in the modernization process at quite a humble level. Ordinary folk became printers, machinists, and factory workers, and they too had to acquire, to a degree, modern standards of efficiency. A modicum of education would be required of more and more people. An increasing number of workers became literate, and once that happened they would inevitably demand a greater share in the decision-making processes of their society. A more democratic form of government would be essential. If a nation wanted to use all its human resources to modernize and enhance its productivity, it would be necessary to bring hitherto segregated and marginalized groups, such as the Jews, into mainstream culture. The newly educated working classes would no longer submit to the old hierarchies. The ideals of democracy, toleration, and universal human rights, which have become sacred values in Western secular culture, emerged as part of the intricate modernizing process. They were not simply beautiful ideals dreamed up by statesmen and political scientists, but were, at least in part, dictated by the needs of the modern state. In early modern Europe, social, political, economic, and intellectual change were part of an interlocking process; each element depended upon the others.[2] Democracy was found to be the most efficient and productive way of organizing a modernized society, as became evident when the eastern European states, which did not adopt democratic norms and employed more draconian methods of bringing out-groups into the mainstream, fell behind in the march of progress.[3]

This was an enthralling period, therefore, but also one of wrenching political change, which people tried to absorb religiously. The old medieval forms of faith no longer brought comfort, since they could not function clearly in these altered circumstances. Religion had to be made more efficient and streamlined too, as in the Catholic reformation of the sixteenth century. But the reformations of the early modern period showed that, despite the fact that the modernizing process was well under way in the sixteenth century, Europeans still subscribed to the conservative spirit. The Protestant reformers, like the great Muslim reformers we have considered, were trying to find a new solution during a period of change by going back to the past. Martin Luther (1483–1556), John Calvin (1509–64), and Huldrych Zwingli (1484–1531) all looked back *ad fontes,* to the wellsprings of the Christian tradition. Where Ibn Taymiyyah had rejected medieval theology and *fiqh* in order to return to the pure Islam of the Koran and the Sunnah, Luther likewise attacked the medieval scholastic theologians and sought to return to the pure Christianity of the Bible and the Fathers of the Church. Like the conservative Muslim reformers, therefore, the Protestant reformers were both revolutionary and reactionary. They did not yet belong to the new world that was coming, but were still rooted in the old.

Yet they were also men of their time, and this was a time of transition. Throughout this book, we shall see that the modernizing process can induce great anxiety. As their world changes, people feel disoriented and lost. Living *in medias res,* they cannot see the direction that their society is taking, but experience its slow transformation in incoherent ways. As the old mythology that gave structure and significance to their lives crumbles under the impact of change, they can experience a numbing loss of identity and a paralyzing despair. The most common emotions, as we shall see, are helplessness and a fear of annihilation that can, in extreme circumstances, erupt in violence. We see something of this in Luther. During his early life, he was prey to agonizing depressions. None of the medieval rites and practices of the faith could touch what he called the *tristitia* ("sorrow") that made him terrified of death, which he imagined as total extinction. When this black horror descended upon him, he could not bear to read Psalm 90, which describes the evanescence of human life and portrays men being condemned by the anger and fury of God. Throughout his career, Luther saw death as an expression of God's wrath. His theology of justification by faith depicted human beings as utterly incapable of contributing to their own salvation and wholly reliant on the benevolence of God. It was only by realizing their powerlessness that they could be saved. To escape his depressions, Luther plunged into a frenzy of activity, determined to do what good he could in the world, but consumed also by hatred.4 Luther's rage against the Pope, the Turks, Jews, women, and rebellious peasants—not to mention every single one of his theological opponents—would be typical of other reformers in our own day, who have struggled with the pain of the new world and who have also evolved a religion in which the love of God is often balanced by a hatred of other human beings.

Zwingli and Calvin also experienced utter impotence before they were able to break through to a new religious vision that made them feel born again. They too had been convinced that there was nothing they could contribute to their own salvation and that they were powerless before the trials of human existence. Both stressed the absolute sovereignty of God, as modern fundamentalists would often do.5 Like Luther, Zwingli and Calvin also had to re-create their religious world, sometimes resorting to extreme measures and even to violence in order to make their religion speak to the new conditions of a world that was unobtrusively but irrevocably committed to radical transformation.

As men of their time, the reformers reflected the changes that were taking place. In leaving the Roman Catholic Church, they made one of the earliest of the declarations of independence that would punctuate Western history from this point. As we shall see, the new ethos demanded autonomy and total freedom, and that is what the Protestant reformers demanded for the Christians of this altered world, who must be free to read and interpret their Bibles as they chose, without the punitive control of the Church. (All three could be intransigent, however, about anybody who opposed *their* teaching: Luther believed that "heretical" books should be burned, and both Calvin and Zwingli were prepared to kill dissidents.) All three showed that in this rational age, the old symbolic understanding of religion was beginning to break down. In conservative spirituality, a symbol partook of the reality of the divine; men and women experienced the sacred in earthly objects; the symbol and the sacred were thus inseparable. In the medieval period, Chris-

tians had experienced the divine in the relics of the saints, and had seen the
Eucharistic bread and wine as mystically identical with Christ. Now the
reformers declared that relics were idols, the Eucharist "only" a symbol, and
the Mass no longer a cultic representation of the sacrifice of Calvary that
made it mystically present, but a simple memorial. They were beginning to
speak about the myths of religion as though they were *logoi,* and the alacrity
with which people followed the reformers showed that many of the Christians of Europe were also beginning to lose the mythical sensibility.

Life was slowly becoming secularized in Europe, and the Protestant
Reformation, despite the intensity of its religious drive, was secularizing
too. The reformers claimed to be returning, conservative-wise, to the primary source, the Bible, but they were reading Scripture in a modern way.
The reformed Christian was to stand alone before God, relying simply on
his Bible, but this would not have been possible before the invention of
printing had made it feasible for all Christians to have a Bible of their own
and before the developing literacy of the period enabled them to read it.
Increasingly, Scripture was read literally for the information it imparted, in
much the same way as modernizing Protestants were learning to read other
texts. Silent, solitary reading would help to free Christians from traditional
ways of interpretation and from the supervision of the religious experts.
The stress on individual faith would also help to make truth seem increasingly subjective—a characteristic of the modern Western mentality. But
while he emphasized the importance of faith, Luther rejected reason vehemently. He seemed to sense that reason could, in the coming dispensation, be
inimical to faith. In his writings—though not in Calvin's—we can see that
the old vision of the complementarity of reason and mythology was erod-
ing. In his usual pugnacious way, Luther spoke of Aristotle with hatred, and
loathed Erasmus, whom he regarded as the epitome of reason, which, he
was convinced, could only lead to atheism. In pushing reason out of the religious sphere, Luther was one of the first Europeans to secularize it.[6]

Because, for Luther, God was utterly mysterious and hidden, the world
was empty of the divine. Luther's Deus Absconditus could not be discovered either in human institutions or in physical reality. Medieval Christians
had experienced the sacred in the Church, which Luther now declared to be
Antichrist. Nor was it permissible to reach a knowledge of God by reflecting
on the marvelous order of the universe, as the scholastic theologians (also
objects of Luther's simmering rage) had done.[7] In Luther's writings, God
had begun to retreat from the physical world, which now had no religious
significance at all. Luther also secularized politics. Because mundane reality
was utterly opposed to the spiritual, church and state must operate independently, each respecting the other's proper sphere of activity.[8] Luther's pas-

sionate religious vision had made him one of the first Europeans to advocate the separation of church and state. Yet again, the secularization of politics began as a new way of being religious.

Luther's separation of religion and politics sprang from his disgust with the coercive methods of the Roman Catholic Church, which had used the state to impose its own rules and orthodoxy. Calvin did not share Luther's vision of a Godless world. Like Zwingli, he believed that Christians should express their faith by taking part in political and social life rather than by retreating to a monastery. Calvin helped to baptize the emergent capitalist work ethic by declaring labor to be a sacred calling, not, as the medievals thought, a divine punishment for sin. Nor did Calvin subscribe to Luther's disenchantment of the natural world. He believed that it was possible to see God in his creation, and commended the study of astronomy, geography, and biology. Calvinists of the early modern period would often be good scientists. Calvin saw no contradiction between science and scripture. The Bible, he believed, was not imparting literal information about geography or cosmology, but was trying to express ineffable truth in terms that limited human beings could understand. Biblical language was *balbative* ("baby talk"), a deliberate simplification of a truth that was too complex to be articulated in any other way.[9]

The great scientists of the early modern period shared Calvin's confidence, and also saw their researches and discussions within a mythical, religious framework. The Polish astronomer Nicolaus Copernicus (1473–1543) believed that his science was "more divine than human."[10] Yet his theory of a heliocentric universe was a devastating blow to the old mythical perception. His astounding hypothesis was so radical that in his own day very few people could take it in. He suggested that instead of being located in the center of the universe, the earth and the other planets were actually in rapid motion around the sun. When we looked up at the heavens and thought that we saw the celestial bodies moving, this was simply a projection of the earth's rotation in the opposite direction. Copernicus's theory remained incomplete, but the German physicist Johannes Kepler (1571–1630) was able to provide mathematical evidence in its support, while the Pisan astronomer Galileo Galilei (1564–1642) tested the Copernican hypothesis empirically by observing the planets through the telescope, which he had himself perfected. When Galileo published his findings in 1612, he created a sensation. All over Europe, people made their own telescopes and scanned the heavens for themselves.

Galileo was silenced by the Inquisition and forced to recant, but his own somewhat belligerent temperament had also played a part in his condemnation. Religious people did not instinctively reject science in the early modern period. When Copernicus first presented his hypothesis in the Vatican, the Pope approved it, and Calvin had no problem with the theory. The scientists themselves saw their investigations as essentially religious. Kepler felt himself possessed by "divine frenzy" as he revealed secrets that no human being had ever been privileged to learn before, and Galileo was convinced that his research had been inspired by divine grace.[11] They could still see their scientific rationalism as compatible with religious vision, *logos* as complementary to *mythos*.

Nevertheless, Copernicus had initiated a revolution, and human beings would never be able to see themselves or trust their perceptions in the same way again. Hitherto, people had felt able to rely on the evidence of their senses. They had looked through the outward aspects of the world to find the Unseen, but had been confident that these external appearances corresponded to a reality. The myths they had evolved to express their vision of the fundamental laws of life had been of a piece with what they had experienced as fact. The Greek worshippers at Eleusis had been able to fuse the story of Persephone with the rhythms of the harvest that they could observe for themselves; the Arabs who jogged around the Kabah symbolically aligned themselves with the planetary motions around the earth and hence felt in tune with the basic principles of existence. But after Copernicus a seed of doubt had been sown. It had been proved that the earth, which *seemed* static, was actually moving very fast indeed; that the planets only appeared to be in motion because people were projecting their own vision onto them: what had been assumed to be objective was in fact entirely subjective. Reason and myth were no longer in harmony; indeed, the intensive *logos* produced by the scientists seemed to devalue the perceptions of ordinary human beings and make them increasingly dependent upon learned experts. Where myth had shown that human action was bound up with the essential meaning of life, the new science had suddenly pushed men and women into a marginal position in the cosmos. They were no longer at the center of things, but cast adrift on an undistinguished planet in a universe that no longer revolved around their needs. It was a bleak vision, which, perhaps, needed a myth to make the new cosmology as spiritually meaningful as the old.

But modern science was beginning to discredit mythology. The British scientist Sir Isaac Newton (1642–1727) synthesized the findings of his predecessors by a rigorous use of the evolving scientific methods of experimentation and deduction. Newton posited the idea of gravity as a universal force that held the entire cosmos together and prevented the celestial bodies from colliding with one another. This system, he was convinced, proved the existence of God, the great "Mechanick," since the intricate design of the cos-

mos could not have come about by accident.[12] Like the other early modern
scientists, Newton had brought human beings what he believed to be utterly
new and certain information about the world. He was sure that his "system"
coincided exactly with objective reality and had taken human knowledge
further than before. But his total immersion in the world of *logos* made it
impossible for Newton to appreciate that other, more intuitive forms of perception might also offer human beings a form of truth. In his view, mythology and mystery were primitive and barbaric ways of thought. " 'Tis the
temper of the hot and superstitious part of mankind in matters of religion,"
he wrote irritably, "ever to be fond of mysteries & for that reason to like best
what they understand least."[13]

   Newton became almost obsessed with the desire to purge Christianity of
its mythical doctrines. He became convinced that the a-rational dogmas of
the Trinity and the Incarnation were the result of conspiracy, forgery, and
chicanery. While working on his great book *Philosophiae Naturalis Principia*
(1687), Newton began work on a bizarre treatise entitled *The Philosophical
Origins of Gentile Theology*, which argued that Noah had founded a superstit-
 tion-free religion in which there were no revealed scriptures, no mysteries,
but only a Deity which could be known through the rational contemplation
of the natural world. Later generations had corrupted this pure faith; the
spurious doctrines of the Incarnation and the Trinity had been added to the
creed by unscrupulous theologians in the fourth century. Indeed, the Book
of Revelation had prophesied the rise of Trinitarianism—"this strange religion of ye West," "the cult of three equal Gods"—as the abomination of
desolation.[14] Newton was still a religious man and still, to an extent, in thrall
to the conservative spirit in his quest for a rational primordial religion. But
he could not express his faith in the same way as previous generations. He
was unable to appreciate that the doctrine of the Trinity had been devised by
the Greek Orthodox theologians of the fourth century precisely as *mythos*,
similar to that later created by the Jewish Kabbalists. As Gregory of Nyssa
had explained, the three *hypostases* of Father, Son, and Spirit were not objective facts but simply "terms that we use" to express the way in which the
"unnameable and unspeakable" divine nature *(ousia)* adapts itself to the limitations of our human minds.[15] It made no sense outside the cultic context of
prayer, contemplation, and liturgy. But Newton could only see the Trinity in
rational terms, had no understanding of the role of myth, and was therefore
obliged to jettison the doctrine. The difficulty that many Western Christians
today experience with trinitarian theology shows that they share Newton's
bias in favor of reason. Newton's position was entirely understandable. He
was one of the very first people in the West to master fully the methods and
disciplines of scientific rationalism. His was a towering achievement and the

result was as intoxicating as any religious experience. He used to cry out in the course of his studies: "O God, I think Thy thoughts after Thee!"[16] He had literally no time for the intuitive mystical consciousness, which might actually have impeded his progress. Reason and myth were, for the first time in human history, becoming incompatible because of the intensity and dazzling success of this Western experiment.

By the seventeenth century, progress was so assured that many Europeans were already entirely oriented toward the future. They were discovering that they had to be ready to scrap the past and start again if they wanted to find the truth. This forward momentum was diametrically opposed to the mythical return to the past which was the foundation of the conservative spirit. The new science had to look forward; this was the way it worked. Once Copernicus's theory had been proved satisfactorily, it was no longer possible to bring back the Ptolemaic cosmological system. Later, Newton's own system, though not his methods, would be discounted. Europeans were evolving a new notion of truth. Truth was never absolute, since new discoveries could always replace the old; it had to be demonstrated objectively, and measured by its effectiveness in the practical world. The success of early modern science gave it an authority which was starting to be stronger than that of mythical truth, which met none of these criteria.

This had already been apparent in the *Advancement of Learning* (1605), written by Francis Bacon (1561–1626), counselor to King James I of England. Bacon insisted that all truth, even the most sacred doctrines of religion, must be subjected to the stringent critical methods of empirical science. If they contradicted proven facts and the evidence of our senses, they must be cast aside. None of the great insights of the past could be permitted to impede our creation of a glorious new future for humanity. The inventions of science would end human misery, Bacon believed, and inaugurate here on earth the millennial kingdom foretold by the prophets. In Bacon's writings we sense the excitement of the new age. So confident was he, that he could see no conflict between the Bible and science, and, years before the condemnation of Galileo, he demanded complete intellectual liberty for the men of science, whose work was far too important for the human race to be obstructed by simpleminded clergymen. The *Advancement of Learning* amounted to a declaration of independence on the part of scientific rationalism, which sought emancipation from myth and declared that it alone could give human beings access to truth.

It was an important moment, marking the beginning of science as we know it in the modern West. Hitherto, scientific and rational exploration had always been conducted within a comprehensive mythology which had explained the meaning of these discoveries. The prevailing myth had always controlled these researches and put a brake on their application, as the limitations of conservative society demanded. But by the seventeenth century, European scientists were beginning to liberate themselves from these old constraints. There was no need for them any longer, since the factors that had held agrarian societies back were gradually being overcome. Bacon insisted that science alone was true. His view of science was, admittedly, very different from our own. For Bacon, scientific method consisted chiefly in gathering facts; he did not appreciate the importance of guesswork and hypothesis in scientific research. But Bacon's definition of truth would be extremely influential, especially in the English-speaking countries. He believed that the only information upon which we could safely rely came from our five senses; anything else was pure fantasy. Philosophy, metaphysics, theology, art, imagination, mysticism, and mythology were all dismissed as irrelevant and superstitious because they could not be verified empirically.

People who subscribed to this wholly rational way of life but who wanted to be religious would have to find new ways of thinking about God and spirituality. We see the death of the mythical approach in the philosophy of the French scientist René Descartes (1596–1650), who was able to speak only in *logoi,* in rational language. His was a lonely vision. For Descartes, the universe was a lifeless machine, the physical world inert and dead. It could give us no information about the divine. The single living thing in the cosmos was the human mind, which could find certainty merely by turning in upon itself. We could not even be sure that anything besides our own doubts and thoughts existed. Descartes was a devout Catholic; he wanted to satisfy himself about God's existence, but refused to go back to the primordial, imaginary past of myth and cult. Nor could he rely on the insights of prophets and holy texts. A man of the new age, he would not accept received ideas; the scientist must make his mind a *tabula rasa.* The sole truth was that supplied by mathematics or by such lapidary propositions as "What's done cannot be undone," which was irrefutably correct. Since the way back was closed, Descartes could only inch his way painfully forward.

One evening, sitting beside a wood stove, Descartes evolved the maxim *Cogito, ergo sum:* "I think, therefore I am." This, he believed, was self-evident. The one thing of which we could be certain was our mind's experience of doubt. But this revealed the limitation of the human mind, and the very notion of "limitation" would make no sense if we did not have a prior conception of "perfection." A perfection that did not exist, however, would be a contradiction in terms. *Ergo,* the Ultimate Perfection—God—must be a reality.[17] This so-called proof is unlikely to satisfy a modern unbeliever, and it shows the impotence of pure reason when faced with such issues.

Rational thought is indispensable for our effective functioning in the world. It is at its best when directed toward a pragmatic goal or when, like Descartes, we withdraw from the mundane to consider something as objectively as possible. But when we ask *why* the world exists (if it does!) or whether life has meaning, reason can make little headway, and the object of our thought itself can become strange to us. Descartes beside his stove, in his cold, empty world, locked into his own uncertainty, and uttering a "proof" which is little more than a mental conundrum, embodies the spiritual dilemma of modern humanity.

Thus, at a time when science and unfettered rationality were forging brilliantly ahead, life was becoming meaningless for an increasing number of people, who, for the first time in human history, were having to live without mythology. The British philosopher Thomas Hobbes (1588–1679) believed that there was a God, but for all practical purposes, God might just as well not exist. Like Luther, Hobbes saw the physical world as empty of the divine. God, Hobbes believed, had revealed himself at the dawn of human history and would do so again at its End. But until that time we had to get on without him, waiting, as it were, in the dark.[18] For the French mathematician Blaise Pascal (1623–62), an intensely religious man, the emptiness and the "eternal silence" of the infinite universe opened up by modern science inspired pure dread:

> When I see the blind and wretched state of men, when I survey the whole universe in its deadness and man left to himself with no light, as though lost in this corner of the universe without knowing who put him there, what he has to do, what will become of him when he dies, incapable of knowing anything, I am moved to terror, like a man transported in his sleep to some terrifying desert island, who wakes up quite lost with no means of escape. Then I marvel that so wretched a state does not drive people to despair.[19]

Reason and *logos* were improving the lot of men and women in the modern world in a myriad practical ways, but they were not competent to deal with those ultimate questions that human beings seem forced, by their very nature, to ask and which, hitherto, had been the preserve of *mythos*. As a result, despair and alienation, as described by Pascal, have been a part of the modern experience.

But not for everybody. John Locke (1632–1704), who was one of the first to initiate the philosophical Enlightenment of the eighteenth century, had none of Pascal's existential *angst*. His faith in life and human reason was serene and confident. He had no doubts about God's existence, even though, strictly speaking, he was aware that proving the reality of a deity that lay beyond our sense experience did not pass Bacon's empirical test. Locke's religion, relying entirely on reason, was similar to the deism espoused by some of the Jewish Marranos. He was fully convinced that the natural world gave ample evidence for a Creator and that if reason were allowed to shine forth freely, everybody would discover the truth for himself. False and superstitious ideas had only crept into the world because priests had used cruel and tyrannical methods, such as the Inquisition, to force the people to accept their orthodoxy. For the sake of true religion, therefore, the state must tolerate all manner of beliefs, and must concern itself solely with the practical administration and government of the community. Church and state must be separate, and neither must interfere in the business of the other. This was the Age of Reason, and for the first time in human history, Locke believed, men and women would be free, and, therefore, able to perceive the truth.[20]

This benign vision set the tone for the Enlightenment and the inspiring ideal of the modern, secular, tolerant state. The French and German Enlightenment philosophers also subscribed to the rational religion of deism, and saw the old mythical, revealed religions as outmoded. Since reason was the sole criterion of truth, the older faiths, based on a fictitious notion of "revelation," had simply been naive versions of this natural religion and should be rejected. Faith had to be rational, argued the radical British theologian Matthew Tindal (1655–1733) and the Irish Roman-Catholic-turned-deist John Toland (1670–1722). Our natural reason was the only reliable way to arrive at sacred truth, and Christianity must be purged of the mysterious, the supernatural, and the miraculous. Revelation was unnecessary because it was quite possible for any human being to arrive at the truth by means of his or her unaided reasoning powers.[21] As Newton had pointed out, reflection on the design of the physical universe provided irrefutable evidence for a Creator and First Cause. On the continent, the German historian Hermann Samuel Reimarus (1694–1768) argued that Jesus had never claimed to be divine, and that his ambitions had been entirely political. Jesus should simply be revered as a great teacher, the founder of a "remarkable, simple, exalted and practical religion."[22]

The old truths of *mythos* were now being interpreted as though they were *logoi*, an entirely new development that was, eventually, doomed to disappoint.

For at the same time as these theologians, philosophers, and historians proclaimed the supremacy of reason, the German rationalist Immanuel Kant (1724–1804) undercut the entire Enlightenment project. On the one

hand, Kant issued yet another of the early modern declarations of independence. People must have the courage to throw off their dependence
upon teachers, churches, and authorities and seek the truth for themselves.
"Enlightenment is man's exodus from his self-incurred tutelage," he wrote.
"Tutelage is man's inability to make use of his own understanding, without
direction from another."[23] But on the other hand, in the *Critique of Pure Reason* (1781) Kant argued that it was impossible to be certain that the order we
think we discern in nature bore any relation at all to external reality. This
"order" was simply the creation of our own minds; even the so-called scientific laws of Newton probably tell us more about human psychology than
about the cosmos. When the mind receives information about the physical
world outside itself through the senses, it has to reorganize this data according to its own internal structures in order to make any sense of it. Kant was
wholly confident of the mind's capacity to devise a viable rational vision for
itself, but by showing that it was really impossible for human beings to
escape from their own psychology, he also made it clear that there was no
such thing as absolute truth. All our ideas were essentially subjective and
interpretive. Where Descartes had seen the human mind as the sole, lonely
denizen of a dead universe, Kant severed the link between humanity and the
world altogether and shut us up within our own heads.[24] At the same time as
he had liberated humanity from tutelage, he had enclosed it in a new prison.
As so often, modernity took with one hand what it gave with the other. Reason was enlightening and emancipating, but it could also estrange men and
women from the world they were learning to control so effectively.

    If there was no absolute truth, what became of God? Unlike the other
deists, Kant believed that it was impossible to prove God's existence, since
the deity was beyond the reach of the senses and, therefore, inaccessible
to the human mind.[25] Faced with the ultimate, reason alone had nothing to
say. The only comfort that Kant could offer was that it was, by the same
token, impossible to disprove God's existence either. Kant was himself a
devout man, and did not regard his ideas as hostile to religion. They would,
he thought, liberate faith from a wholly inappropriate reliance upon reason.
He was utterly convinced, he wrote at the end of his *Critique of Practical
Reason* (1788), of the moral law inscribed within each human being, which,
like the grandeur of the heavens, filled him with awe and wonder. But the
only rational grounds he could find for the deist God was the quite dubious
argument that without such a Deity and the possibility of an afterlife, it was
hard to see why we should act morally. This again, as a proof, is highly
unsatisfactory.[26] Kant's God was simply an afterthought, tacked onto the
human condition. Apart from innate conviction, there was no real reason
why a rationalist should bother to believe. As a deist and a man of reason,

Kant had no time for any of the traditional symbols or practices by means of which alone men and women of the past had evoked a sense of the sacred, independently of reason. Kant was deeply opposed to the idea of divine law, which, in his eyes, was a barbarous denial of human autonomy, and he could see no point in mysticism, prayer, or ritual.[27] Without a cult, any notion of religion and the divine would become tenuous, unnecessary, and untenable.

Yet, paradoxically, the emergence of reason as the sole criterion of truth in the West coincided with an eruption of religious irrationality. The great Witch Craze of the sixteenth and seventeenth centuries, which raged through many of the Protestant and Catholic countries of Europe and even made a brief appearance in the American colonies, showed that a cult of scientific rationalism cannot always hold darker forces at bay. Mysticism and mythology had taught men and women to deal with the world of the unconscious. It may not be accidental that at a time when religious faith was beginning to abandon this type of spirituality, the subconscious ran amok. The Witch Craze has been described as a collective fantasy, shared by men, women, and their inquisitors throughout Christendom. People believed that they had sexual intercourse with demons, and flew through the air at night to take part in satanic rituals and perverse orgies. Witches were thought to worship the Devil instead of God in a parody of the Mass—a reversal that could represent a widespread unconscious rebellion against traditional faith. God was beginning to seem so remote, alien, and demanding that for some he was becoming demonic: subconscious fears and desires were projected upon the imaginary figure of Satan, depicted as a monstrous version of humanity.[28] Thousands of men and women convicted of witchcraft were either hanged or burned at the stake before the Craze burned itself out. The new scientific rationalism, which took no cognizance of these deeper levels of the mind, was powerless to control this hysterical outburst. A massive, fearful, and destructive un-reason has also been part of the modern experience.

These were frightening times for the people of the West on both sides of the Atlantic. The Reformation had been a fearful rupture, dividing Europe into viciously hostile camps. Protestants and Catholics had persecuted one another in England; there had been a civil war in France between Protestants and Catholics (1562–63), and a nationwide massacre of Protestants in 1572. The Thirty Years War (1618–48) had devastated Europe, drawing in one nation after another, a power struggle with a strong religious dimension which killed any hope of a reunited Europe. There was political unrest also. In 1642, England was convulsed by a civil war that resulted in the execution of King Charles I (1649) and the establishment of a republic under the Puritan Parliamentarian Oliver Cromwell. When the monarchy was restored in

1660, its powers were curtailed by Parliament. More democratic institutions were painfully and bloodily emerging in the West. Even more catastrophic was the French Revolution of 1789, which was succeeded by a reign of terror and a military dictatorship, before order was restored under Napoleon. The French Revolution's legacy to the modern world was Janus-faced: it promoted the benevolent Enlightenment ideals of liberty, equality, and fraternity, but it also left a memory of malignant state terrorism, which has been equally influential. In the American colonies also, the Seven Years War (1756–63), in which Britain and France fought one another over their imperial possessions, raged down the eastern coast of America with fearful casualties. This led directly to the War of Independence (1775–83) and the creation of the first secular republic of the modern world. A more just and tolerant social order was coming to birth in the West, but this was only achieved after almost two centuries of violence.

In the turmoil, people turned to religion, and some found that in these new circumstances, old forms of faith no longer worked. Antinomian movements, similar to the later Shabbatean revolt in Judaism, attempted a break with the past and reached incoherently for something new. In seventeenth-century England, after the Civil War, Jacob Bauthumely and Lawrence Clarkson (1615–67) preached an incipient atheism. A separate, distant deity was an idolatry, Bauthumely argued in *The Light and Dark Sides of God* (1650); God had been incarnate in men other than Jesus and the divine existed in all things, even in sin. For Clarkson in *The Single Eye*, sin was simply a human fantasy, and evil a revelation of God. Abiezer Coppe (1619–72), a radical Baptist, would flagrantly break sexual taboos and curse in public. Soon, he believed, Christ, the "Mighty Leveller," would return and sweep this present rotten and hypocritical order away.[29] There was antinomianism also in the American colonies of New England. John Cotton (1585–1652), a popular Puritan preacher who arrived in Massachusetts in 1635, insisted that good works were pointless and a good life useless: God could save us without these man-made rules. His disciple Anne Hutchinson (1590–1643) claimed that she received personal revelations from God and felt no need to read her Bible or perform good works.[30] These rebels were, perhaps, trying to express their inchoate sense that old restraints no longer applied in the new world, where life was changing so fundamentally. In a period of constant innovation, it was inevitable that some would strike out for religious and ethical independence and innovation too.

Others tried to express the ideals of the new age in a religious way. George Fox (1624–91), founder of the Society of Friends, preached an enlightenment that was not dissimilar to that later described by Kant. His Quakers should seek a light within their own hearts; Fox taught them to "make use of their own understanding, without direction from another."[31] Religion must, he believed, in this age of science, be "experimental," verified not by an authoritative institution but by personal experience.[32] The Society of Friends espoused the new democratic ideal: all human beings were equal. Quakers should not doff their hats to anybody. Unlearned men and women need not defer to clerics with university degrees, but must make their own views known. Similarly, John Wesley (1703–91) attempted to apply scientific method and system to spirituality. His "Methodists" followed a strict regimen of prayer, Bible-reading, fasting, and philanthropy. Like Kant, Wesley welcomed the emancipation of faith from reason, and declared that religion was not a doctrine in the head but a light in the heart. It could even be a blessing that the rational and historical evidence for Christianity had become "clogged and encumbered" in recent years. This would free men and women, forcing them "to look into themselves and attend to the light shining in their hearts."[33]

Christians were becoming divided: some followed the *philosophes* and tried to demystify and rationalize their faith; others jettisoned reason altogether. This was a worrying development that was especially marked in the American colonies. One of the repercussions of this split would be the development of fundamentalism in the United States at the end of the nineteenth century. In the early years, most of the colonists, except the Puritan New Englanders, had been indifferent toward religion; it seemed as though the colonies were becoming almost entirely secularized by the end of the seventeenth century.[34] But during the early eighteenth century, the Protestant denominations revived, and Christian life became more formal in the new world than in the old. Even such dissenting sects as the Quakers, the Baptists, and the Presbyterians, which had all originally rejected ecclesiastical authority and insisted on the right to follow their own leadings, set up Assemblies in Philadelphia that kept a sharp eye on the local communities, supervised the clergy, vetted the preachers, and snuffed out heresy. All three denominations flourished as a result of this coercive but modernizing centralization, and numbers increased dramatically. At the same time, the Church of England was established in Maryland, and elegant churches transformed the skylines of New York City, Boston, and Charleston.[35]

But while on the one hand there was a move for greater control and discipline, there was also a vehement, grassroots reaction against this rationalized restraint. Conservative religion had always seen mythology and reason as complementary; each would be the poorer without the other. This had also been the case in religious matters, where reason was often allowed to play an important, if subsidiary, role. But the new tendency to sideline or even to jettison reason in some of the new Protestant movements (a development that can be traced back to Luther) led to a disturbing irrationality. The Quakers were so called because, in the early days, they would often express their religious transports so vehemently: they were known to tremble, howl, and yell, making—an observer noted—the dogs bark, the cattle run madly about, and the pigs scream.[36] The Puritans, radical Calvinists who had started by opposing what they deemed the "popery" of the Church of England, also had an extreme, tumultuous spirituality. Their "born-again" conversions were often traumatic; many experienced an agony of guilt, fear, and paralyzing doubt before the breakthrough, when they sank blissfully into the arms of God. Their conversion gave them great energy and enabled them to play leading roles in early modernity. They were good capitalists and often good scientists. But sometimes the effects of grace wore off and Puritans suffered a relapse, falling into chronic depressive states and in a few cases even committing suicide.[37]

Conservative religion had not usually been hysterical in this way. Its rituals and cult had been designed to attune people to reality. Bacchanalian cults and frenzied ecstasy had certainly occurred but had involved the few rather than the majority. Mysticism was not for the masses. At its best, it was a one-to-one process, in which the adept was carefully supervised to make sure that he or she did not fall into unhealthy psychic states. The descent into the unconscious was an enterprise demanding great skill, intelligence, and discipline. When expert guidance was not available, the results could be deplorable. The crazed and neurotic behavior of some of the medieval Christian saints, which was often due to inadequate spiritual direction, showed the dangers of an undisciplined cultivation of alternate states of mind. The reforms of Teresa of Avila and John of the Cross had been designed precisely to correct such abuses. When mystical journeys were undertaken en masse, they could degenerate into crowd hysteria, the nihilism of the Sabbatarians, or the mental imbalance of some of the Puritans.

Emotional excess became a feature of American religious life during the eighteenth century. It was especially evident in the First Great Awakening, which erupted in Northampton, Connecticut, in 1734 and was chronicled by the learned Calvinist minister Jonathan Edwards (1703–58). Before the Awakening, Edwards explained, the people of Northampton had not been particularly religious, but in 1734 two young people died suddenly, and the shock (backed up by Edwards's own emotive preaching) plunged the town into a frenzied religiosity, which spread like a contagion to Massachusetts and Long Island. People stopped work and spent the whole day reading the Bible. Within six months, three hundred people in the town had experienced a wrenching "born-again" conversion. They alternated between soaring highs and devastating lows; sometimes they were quite broken and "sank into an abyss, under a sense of guilt that they were ready to think was beyond the mercy of God." At other times they would "break forth into laughter, tears often at the same time issuing like a flood, and intermingling a loud weeping."[38] The revival was just burning itself out when George Whitefield (1714–70), an English Methodist preacher, toured the colonies and sparked a second wave. During his sermons, people fainted, wept, and shrieked; the churches shook with the cries of those who imagined themselves saved and the groans of the unfortunate who were convinced that they were damned. It was not only the simple and unlearned who were so affected. Whitefield had an ecstatic reception at Harvard and Yale, and finished his tour in 1740 with a mass rally where he preached to 30,000 people on Boston Common.

Edwards showed the dangers of this type of emotionalism in his account of the Awakening. When the revival died down in Northampton, one man was so cast down that he committed suicide, convinced that this loss of ecstatic joy could only mean that he was predestined to Hell. In other towns too, "multitudes . . . seemed to have it strongly suggested to them, and pressed upon them, as if somebody had spoken to them, 'Cut your own throat, now is a good opportunity. Now!' " Two people went mad with "strange enthusiastic delusions."[39] Edwards insisted that most people were calmer and more peaceful than before the Awakening, but his apologia shows how perilous it could be to imagine that religion is purely an affair of the heart. Once faith was conceived as irrational, and the inbuilt constraints of the best conservative spirituality were jettisoned, people could fall prey to all manner of delusions. The rituals of a cult were carefully designed to lead people through a trauma so that they came out healthily on the other side of it. This was clear in the rites of Lurianic Kabbalah, where the mystic was allowed to express his grief and abandonment but made to finish the vigil joyfully. Similarly, the popular Shii processions in honor of Husain gave people an outlet for their frustration and anger, but in a ritualized form: they did not usually run amok after the ceremony was over and vent their rage on the rich and powerful. But in Northampton, there was no stylized cult to help people through their rite of passage. Everything was spontaneous and undisciplined. People were allowed to run the gamut of their emotions and even to indulge them. For a few, this proved fatal.

Nevertheless, Edwards was convinced that the Awakening was the work of God. It revealed that a new age had dawned in America and would spread to the rest of the world. By means of such revivals, Edwards was convinced, Christians would establish God's kingdom on earth; society would reflect the truth and justice of God himself. There was nothing politically radical about the Awakening. Edwards and Whitefield did not urge their audiences to rebel against British rule, campaign for democratic government, or demand an even distribution of wealth, but the experience did help to prepare the way for the American Revolution.[40] The ecstatic experience left many Americans who would be quite unable to relate to the deist Enlightenment ideals of the revolutionary leaders, with the memory of a blissful state of freedom. The word "liberty" was used a great deal to describe the joy of conversion, and a liberation from the pain and sorrow of normal life. Whitefield and Edwards both encouraged their congregations to see their own ecstatic faith as superior to that of the elite, who had not been born again and regarded the frenzy with rationalist disdain. Many who remembered the hauteur of those clerics who condemned the revivals, were left with a strong distrust of institutional authority, which became part of the Christian experience of many American Calvinists. The Awakening had been the first mass movement in American history; it gave the people a heady experience of taking part in earth-shattering events that would, they believed, change the course of history.[41]

But the Awakening also split the Calvinist denominations of the colonies down the middle. People who became known as Old Lights, such as the Boston ministers Jonathan Mayhew (1720–66) and Charles Chauncy (1705–87), believed that Christianity should be a rational, enlightened faith, were appalled by the hysteria of the revivals, and distrusted their anti-intellectual bias.[42] Old Lights tended to come from the more prosperous sectors of society, while the lower classes gravitated toward the emotional piety of the breakaway New Light churches. During the 1740s, over two hundred congregations left existing denominations and founded their own churches.[43] In 1741, the Presbyterian New Lights broke away from the Presbyterian synod, establishing their own colleges for the training of ministers, notably Nassau Hall in Princeton, New Jersey. Later the split was healed, but in the interim the New Lights had acquired a separatist, institutional identity that would be crucial during the emergence of the fundamentalist movement in the late nineteenth century.

The Awakening had shaken everybody up, and henceforth even the Old Lights were ready to ascribe apocalyptic significance to current events. Jonathan Mayhew was convinced that "great revolutions were at hand," when a series of earthquakes occurred simultaneously in various parts of the world in November 1755; he looked forward to "some very remarkable changes in the political and religious state of the world."[44] Mayhew instinctively saw the imperial struggle during the Seven Years War between Protestant Britain and Catholic France over their colonial possessions in America and Canada in eschatalogical terms. It would, he believed, hasten the Second Coming of Christ by weakening the power of the Pope, who was

Antichrist, the Great Pretender of the Last Days.[45] New Lights also saw America as fighting on the front line of a cosmic battle with the forces of evil during the Seven Years War. It was at this time that Pope's Day (November 5) became an annual holiday, during which rowdy crowds burned effigies of the Pontiff.[46] These were frightening and violent times. Americans still looked to the old mythology to give their lives meaning and to explain the tragedies that befell them. But they also seemed to sense impending change and, as they did so, developed a religion of hatred, seeing France and the Roman Catholic Church as satanic and utterly opposed to the righteous American ethos.[47] As they cultivated these apocalyptic fantasies, they seemed to feel that there could be no redemption, no final deliverance, no liberty, and no millennial peace unless popery was destroyed. A bloody purge would be necessary to bring this new world into being. We shall find that a theology of rage would frequently be evolved in response to dawning modernity. Americans could sense that transformation was at hand, but they still belonged to the old world. The economic effects of the Seven Years War led the British government to impose new taxes upon the American colonists, and this provoked the revolutionary crisis that resulted in the outbreak of the American War of Independence in 1775. During this protracted struggle, Americans started the painful process of making that radical break with the past that was central to the modern ethos, and their religion of hatred would play a major role in this development.

The leaders of the Revolution—George Washington, John and Samuel Adams, Thomas Jefferson, and Benjamin Franklin, for example—experienced the revolution as a secular event. They were rationalists, men of the Enlightenment, inspired by the modern ideals of John Locke, Scottish Common Sense philosophy, or Radical Whig ideology. They were deists, and differed from more orthodox Christians in their view of revelation and the divinity of Christ. They conducted a sober, pragmatic struggle against an imperial power, moving only slowly and reluctantly toward revolution. They certainly did not see themselves as fighting a cosmic war against the legions of Antichrist. When the break with Britain became inevitable, their goal was practical and limited to terrestrial objectives: the "united colonies are, and of right ought to be, free and independent states." The Declaration of Independence, drafted by Jefferson, with John Adams and Franklin, and ratified by the Colonial Congress on July 4, 1776, was an Enlightenment document, based on the ideal of self-evident human rights propounded by Locke. These rights were defined as "life, liberty and the pursuit of happiness." The Declaration appealed to the modern ideals of independence, autonomy, and equality in the name of the deist God of Nature. The Declaration was not politically radical, however. There was no utopian talk of redistributing the wealth of society or founding a millennial order. This was practical, rational *logos*, outlining a far-reaching but sustainable program of action.

But the Founding Fathers of the American republic were an aristocratic elite and their ideas were not typical. The vast majority of Americans were Calvinists, and they could not relate to this rationalist ethos. Indeed, many of them regarded deism as a satanic ideology.[48] Initially, most of the colonists were just as reluctant to break with England as their leaders were. Not all joined the revolutionary struggle. Some 30,000 fought on the British side, and after the war between 80,000 and 100,000 left the new states and migrated to Canada, the West Indies, or Britain.[49] Those who elected to fight for independence would be as much motivated by the old myths and millennial dreams of Christianity as by the secularist ideals of the Founders. In fact, it became difficult to separate the religious from the political discourse. Secularist and religious ideology blended creatively to enable the colonists, who had widely divergent hopes for America, to join forces against the imperial might of England. We shall find a similar alliance of religious and secularist idealism in the Islamic Revolution in Iran (1978–79), which was also a declaration of independence against an imperialist power.

During the first decade of the revolutionary struggle, people were loath to make a radical break with the past. Severing relations with Britain seemed unthinkable, and many still hoped that the British government would change its policies. Nobody was straining forward excitedly to the future or dreaming of a new world order. Most Americans still instinctively responded to the crisis in the old, premodern way: they looked back to an idealized past to sustain them in their position. The revolutionary leaders and those who embraced the more secular Radical Whig ideology drew inspiration from the struggle of the Saxons against the invading Normans in 1066, or the more recent struggle of the Puritan Parliamentarians during the English Civil War. The Calvinists harked back to their own Golden Age in New England, recalling the struggle of the Puritans against the tyrannical Anglican establishment in Old England; they had sought liberty and freedom from oppression in the New World, creating a godly society in the American wilderness. The emphasis in the sermons and revolutionary rhetoric of this period (1763–73) was on the desire to conserve the precious achievements of the past. The notion of radical change inspired fears of decline and ruin. The colonists were seeking to preserve their heritage, according to the old conservative spirit. The past was presented as idyllic, the future as potentially horrific. The revolutionary leaders declared that their actions were designed to keep at bay the catastrophe that would inevitably ensue if there was a radical severance from tradition. They spoke of the possible consequences of British policy with fear, using the apocalyptic language of the Bible.[50]

But this changed. As the British clung obstinately to their controversial imperial policies, the colonists burned their boats. After the Boston Tea Party (1773) and the Battles of Lexington and Concord (1775) there could be no going back. The Declaration of Independence expressed a new and courageous determination to break away from the old order and go forward to an unprecedented future. In this respect, the Declaration was a modernizing document, which articulated in political terms the intellectual independence and iconoclasm that had characterized the scientific revolution in Europe. But the majority of the colonists were more inspired by the myths of Christian prophecy than by John Locke. They would need to approach modern political autonomy in a mythological package which was familiar to them, resonated with their deepest beliefs, and enabled them to find the psychological strength to make this difficult transition. As we shall so often find, religion often provides the means that get people through the painful rite of passage to modernity.

Thus, ministers in many of the mainline churches (even the Anglicans) Christianized the revolutionary rhetoric of such populist leaders as Sam Adams. When they spoke of the importance of virtue and responsibility in government, this made sense of Adams's fiery denunciations of the corruption of the British officials.[51] The Great Awakening had already made New Light Calvinists wary of the establishment and confident of their ability to effect major change. When revolutionary leaders spoke of "liberty," they used a term that was already saturated with religious meaning: it carried associations of grace, of the freedom of the Gospel and the Sons of God. It was linked with such themes as the Kingdom of God, in which all oppression would end, and the myth of a Chosen People who would become God's instrument in the transformation of the world.[52] Timothy Dwight (1752–1817), president of Yale University, spoke enthusiastically of the revolution ushering in "Immanuel's Land," and of America becoming "the principal seat of that new, that peculiar Kingdom which shall be given to the saints of the Most High."[53] In 1775, the Connecticut preacher Ebenezer Baldwin insisted that the calamities of the war could only hasten God's plans for the New World. Jesus would establish his glorious Kingdom in America: liberty, religion, and learning had been driven out of Europe and had moved westward, across the Atlantic. The present crisis was preparing the way for the Last Days of the present corrupt order. For Provost William Smith of Philadelphia, the colonies were God's "chosen seat of Freedom, Arts and Heavenly Knowledge."[54]

But if churchmen were sacralizing politics, secularist leaders also used the language of Christian utopianism. John Adams looked back on the settlement of America as God's plan for the enlightenment of the whole of humanity.[55] Thomas Paine was convinced that "we have it in our power to begin the world over again. A situation such as the present hath not happened since the days of Noah until now. The birthday of a new world is at hand."[56] The rational pragmatism of the leaders would not itself have been sufficient to help people make the fearsome journey to an unknown future and break with the motherland. The enthusiasm, imagery, and mythology of Christian eschatology gave meaning to the revolutionary struggle and helped secularists and Calvinists alike to make the decisive, dislocating severance from tradition.

So did the theology of hatred that had erupted during the Seven Years War. In rather the same way as Iranians would later call America "the Great Satan" during their Islamic Revolution, British officials were portrayed as being in league with the devil during the revolutionary crisis. After the passing of the notorious Stamp Act (1765), patriotic poems and songs presented its perpetrators, Lords Bute, Grenville, and North, as the minions of Satan, who were conspiring to lure the Americans into the devil's eternal Kingdom. The Stamp was described as the "mark of the Beast" that, according to the Book of Revelation, would be inscribed on the damned in the Last Days. Effigies depicting the British ministers were carried alongside portraits of Satan in political processions and hung from "liberty trees" throughout the colonies.[57] In 1774, King George III became associated with the Antichrist when he granted religious freedom to the French Catholics in the Canadian territory conquered by England during the Seven Years War. His picture now adorned the liberty trees alongside pictures of the Papal Antichrist and the Devil.[58] Even the more educated colonists fell prey to this fear of hidden cosmic conspiracy. The presidents of Harvard and Yale both believed that the colonists were fighting a war against satanic forces, and looked forward to the imminent defeat of popery, "a religion most favourable to arbitrary power." The War of Independence had become part of God's providential design for the destruction of the Papal Antichrist, which would surely herald the arrival of God's millennial Kingdom in America.[59] This paranoid vision of widespread conspiracy and the tendency to see an ordinary political conflict as a cosmic war between the forces of good and evil seems, unfortunately, to occur frequently when a people is engaged in a revolutionary struggle as it enters the new world. This satanic mythology helped the colonists to separate themselves definitively from the old world, for which they still felt a strong residual affection. The demonizing of England transformed it into the antithetical "other," the polar opposite of America, and thus enabled the colonists to shape a distinct identity for themselves and to articulate the new order they were fighting to bring into being.

Thus, religion played a key role in the creation of the first modern secular republic. After the Revolution, however, when the newly independent states drew up their constitutions, God was mentioned in them only in the most perfunctory manner. In 1786, Thomas Jefferson disestablished the Anglican church in Virginia; his bill declared that coercion in matters of faith was "sinfull and tyrannical," that truth would prevail if people were allowed their own opinions, and that there should be a "wall of separation" between religion and politics.[60] The bill was supported by the Baptists, Methodists, and Presbyterians of Virginia, who resented the privileged position of the Church of England in the state. Later the other states followed Virginia's lead, and disestablished their own churches, Massachusetts being the last to do so, in 1833. In 1787, when the federal Constitution was drafted at the Philadelphia Convention, God was not mentioned at all, and in the Bill of Rights (1789), the First Amendment of the Constitution formally separated religion from the state: "Congress shall make no laws respecting the establishment of religion, or prohibiting the free exercise thereof." Henceforth faith would be a private and voluntary affair in the United States. This was a revolutionary step and has been hailed as one of the great achievements of the Age of Reason. The thinking behind it was indeed inspired by the tolerant philosophy of the Enlightenment, but the Founding Fathers were also moved by more pragmatic considerations. They knew that the federal Constitution was essential to preserve the unity of the states, but they also realized that if the federal government established any single one of the Protestant denominations and made it the official faith of the United States, the Constitution would not be approved. Congregationalist Massachusetts, for example, would never ratify a Constitution that established the Anglican Church. This was also the reason why Article VI, Section 3, of the Constitution abolished religious tests for office in the federal government. There *was* idealism in the Founders' decision to disestablish religion and to secularize politics, but the new nation could not base its identity on any one sectarian option and retain the loyalty of all its subjects. The needs of the modern state demanded that it be tolerant and, therefore, secular.[61]

Paradoxically, however, by the middle of the nineteenth century the new secularist United States had become a passionately Christian nation. During the 1780s, and still more during the 1790s, the churches all experienced new growth[62] and began to counter the Enlightenment ideology of the Founding Fathers. They now sacralized American independence: the new republic, they argued, was God's achievement. The revolutionary battle had been the cause of heaven against hell.[63] Only ancient Israel had experienced such

direct divine intervention in its history. God might not be mentioned in the
Constitution, Timothy Dwight noted wryly, but he urged his students to
"look into the history of your country [and] you will find scarcely less gra-
cious and wonderful proofs of divine protection and deliverance . . . than
that which was shown to the people of Israel in Egypt."[64] The clergy confidently predicted that the American people would become more pious;
they saw the expansion of the frontier as a sign of the coming Kingdom.[65]
Democracy had made the people sovereign, so they must become more
godly if the new states were to escape the dangers inherent in popular rule.
The American people must be saved from the irreligious deism of their
political leaders. Churchmen saw "deism" as the new satanic foe, making it
the scapegoat for all the inevitable failures of the infant nation. Deism, they
insisted, would promote atheism and materialism; it worshipped Nature and
Reason instead of Jesus Christ. A paranoid conspiracy fear developed of
a mysterious cabal called the "Bavarian Illuminati" who were atheists and
Freemasons and were plotting to overthrow Christianity in the United States.
When Thomas Jefferson ran for president in 1800, there was a second anti-
deist campaign which tried to establish a link between Jefferson and the
atheistic "Jacobins" of the godless French Revolution.[66]

The Union of the new states was fragile. Americans nurtured very different hopes for the new nation, secularist and Protestant. Both have proved to
be equally enduring. Americans still revere their Constitution and venerate
the Founding Fathers, but they also see America as "God's own nation"; as
we shall see, some Protestants continue to see "secular humanism" as an evil
of near-satanic proportions. After the revolution, the nation was bitterly
divided and Americans had an internal struggle to determine what their culture should be. They conducted, in effect, a "second revolution" in the early
years of the nineteenth century. With great difficulty and courage, Americans had swept away the past; they had written a groundbreaking Constitution, and brought a new nation to birth. But this involved strain, tension, and
paradox. The people as a whole had still to decide the terms on which they
were to enter the modern world, and many of the less privileged colonists
were prepared to contest the cultural hegemony of the aristocratic Enlightenment elite. After they had vanquished the British, ordinary Americans had
yet to determine what the revolution had meant for them. Were they to
adopt the cool, civilized, polite rationalism of the Founders, or would they
opt for a much rougher and more populist Protestant identity?

The Founding Fathers and the clergy in the mainline churches had cooperated in the creation of a modern, secular republic, but they both still
belonged in many important respects to the old conservative world. They
were aristocrats and elitists. They believed that it was their task, as enlight-

ened statesmen, to lead the nation from above. They did not conceive of the possibility of change coming from below. They still saw historical transformation being effected by great personalities, who acted rather like the prophets of the past as the guides of humanity and who made history happen. They had not yet realized that a society is often pushed forward by impersonal processes; environmental, economic, and social forces can foil the plans and projects of the most coercive leaders.[67] During the 1780s and 1790s, there was much discussion about the nature of democracy. How much power should the people have? John Adams, the second president of the United States, was suspicious of any polity that might lead to mob rule and the impoverishment of the rich.[68] But the more radical Jeffersonians asked how the elite few could speak for the many. They protested against the "tyranny" of Adams's government, and argued that the people's voice must be heard. The success of the revolution had given many Americans a sense of empowerment; it had shown them that established authority was fallible and by no means invincible. The genie could not be put back into the bottle. The Jeffersonians believed that ordinary folk should also enjoy the freedom and autonomy preached by the *philosophes*. In the new newspapers, doctors, lawyers, clergymen, and other specialists were ridiculed. Nobody should have to give total credence to these so-called "experts." The law, medicine, and religion should all be a matter of common sense and within the reach of everyone.[69]

This sentiment was especially rife on the frontiers, where people felt slighted by the republican government. By 1790, some 40 percent of Americans lived in territory that had only been settled by white colonists some thirty years earlier. The frontiersmen felt resentful of the ruling elite, who did not share their hardships, but who taxed them as harshly as the British, and bought land for investment in the territories without any intention of leaving the comforts and refined civilization of the eastern seaboard. They were willing to give ear to a new brand of preacher who helped to stir up the wave of revivals known as the Second Great Awakening. This was more politically radical than the first. These prophets were not simply concerned with saving souls, but worked to shape society and religion in a way that was very different from anything envisaged by the Founders.

The new revivalists were not learned men, like Jonathan Edwards and George Whitefield, who had studied at Yale and Oxford. They hated academia and insisted that all Christians had the right to interpret the Bible for themselves, without submitting to the theological experts. These prophets were not cultivated men; in their preaching they spoke in a way that ordinary people could understand, often using wild gestures along with earthy humor and slang. Their services were not polite and decorous, but noisy, rowdy, and highly emotional. They were recasting Christianity in a popular style that was light-years from the refined ethos of the Age of Reason. They held torchlight processions and mass rallies, and pitched huge tents outside the towns, so that the revivals took on the appearance of a vast campsite. The new genre of the Gospel Song transported the audience to ecstasy, so that they wept, rocked violently backward and forward, and shouted for joy.[70] Instead of making their religion rational, the prophets relied on dreams and visions, signs and wonders—all the things that were deplored by the scientists and philosophers of the Enlightenment. And yet, like the Jeffersonians, they refused to see the past as the repository of wisdom, conservative-wise. They were moderns. People should not be bound by learned traditions. They had the freedom of the sons of God, and, with common sense, relying on the plain facts of scripture, they could figure out the truth for themselves.[71] These new preachers railed against the aristocracy, the establishment, and the learned clergy. They emphasized the egalitarian tendencies of the New Testament, which stated that in the Christian commonwealth the first should be last and the last first. God sent his insights to the poor and unlettered: Jesus and the Apostles had not had college degrees.

Religion and politics were part of a single vision. With his flowing hair and wild, glittering eyes Lorenzo Dow looked like a modern-day John the Baptist. He would see a storm as a direct act of God, and relied on dreams and visions for his insights. A change in the weather could be a "sign" of the approaching End of Days; he claimed the ability to foretell the future. He seemed, in sum, to be the antithesis of the new world of modernity. Yet he was likely to begin a sermon with a quotation from Jefferson or Thomas Paine, and like a true modernist, he urged the people to throw off the shackles of superstition and ignorance, cast off the authority of the learned establishment, and think for themselves. It seemed that in the new United States, religion and politics were two sides of a single coin and spilled easily into each other, whatever the Constitution maintained. Thus Elias Smith first experienced a political conversion during Jefferson's presidential campaign, when he became a radical egalitarian. But he then went on to found a new and more democratic church. Similarly, James O'Kelly had fought in the revolution and been held prisoner by the British. He had been thoroughly politicized, wanted a more equal church, and seceded from mainstream Christianity to found his own "Republican Methodists." When Barton Stone broke with the Presbyterians, he called his secession a "declaration of independence." Alexander Campbell (1788–1866), who had received a university education, cast off his Scottish Presbyterianism when he migrated to America, to found a sect that approximated more closely to the egalitarian Primitive Church.[72] Still more radical was Joseph Smith (1805–44), who was not content to read the Bible, but claimed to have discovered an entirely new scripture. *The Book of Mormon* was one of the most eloquent of all nineteenth-century social protests, and mounted a fierce denunciation of the rich, the powerful, and the learned.[73] Smith and his family had lived for years on the brink of destitution, and felt that there was no place for them in this brave new republic. The first Mormon converts were equally poor, marginalized, and desperate, perfectly ready to follow Smith in an exodus from and symbolic repudiation of the United States. Mormons subsequently founded their own independent kingdoms, first in Illinois and, finally, in Utah.

The establishment looked with disdain upon Dow, Stone, and Joseph Smith, regarding them as mindless demagogues who had nothing to offer the modern world. These preachers seemed to be barbarous anachronisms, relics of a primitive bygone world. The response of the mainline clergy and American aristocrats to these latter-day prophets was not dissimilar to the way in which liberals and secularists regard fundamentalist leaders today. But they were wrong to dismiss them. Men such as Dow or Joseph Smith have been described as folk geniuses.[74] They were able to bring the revolutionary modern ideals of democracy, equality, freedom of speech, and independence to the folk in an idiom that uneducated people could understand and make their own. These new ideals that were going to be essential in the new world that was coming to birth in America were brought to the less privileged majority in a mythological context that gave them meaning, and provided a necessary continuity during this time of turmoil and revolutionary upheaval. These new prophets demanded recognition, and, though they were reviled by the established elite, their reception by the people showed that they answered a real need. They were not content with individual conversions, like the preachers of the First Great Awakening, but wanted to change society. They were able to mobilize the population in nationwide mass movements, using popular music and the new communications media to skilled effect. Instead of trying to impose the modern ethos from above, like the Founding Fathers, they built from the ground up and led what amounted to a grassroots rebellion against the rational establishment. They were highly successful. The sects founded by Elias Smith, O'Kelly, Campbell, and Stone, for example, amalgamated to form the Disciples of Christ. By 1860, the Disciples had some 200,000 members and had become the fifth-largest Protestant denomination in the United States.[75] Like the Mormons, the Disciples had institutionalized a popular discontent that the establishment could not ignore.

But this radical Christian rebellion against the scientific rationalism of the Enlightenment had a still more profound effect. The Second Great Awakening managed to lead many Americans away from the classical republicanism of the Founders to the more vulgar democracy and rugged individualism that characterize much American culture today. They had contested the ruling elite and won a substantial victory. There is a strain in the American spirit that is closer to the populism and anti-intellectualism of the nineteenth-century prophets than to the cool ethos of the Age of Reason. The noisy, spectacular revivals of the Second Great Awakening made a permanent impression on the distinctive political style of the United States, whose mass rallies, unabashed sentiment, and showy charisma are so bewildering to many Europeans. Like many fundamentalist movements today, these prophets of the Second Great Awakening gave people who felt disenfranchised and exploited in the new states a means of making their views and voices heard by the more privileged elite. Their movements gave the people what Martin Luther King called "a sense of somebodiness,"[76] in much the same way as the fundamentalist groups do today. Like the fundamentalist movements, these new sects all looked back to a primitive order, and determined to rebuild the original faith; all relied in an entirely new way upon Scripture, which they interpreted literally and often reductively. All also tended to be dictatorial. It was a paradox in early-nineteenth-century America, as in late-twentieth-century fundamentalist movements, that a desire for independence, autonomy, and equality should lead large numbers of people to obey religious demagogues implicitly. For all his talk about enfranchisement, Joseph Smith created what was virtually a religious dictatorship, and, despite his praise of the egalitarian and communal ideals of the Primitive Church, Alexander Campbell became the richest man in West Virginia, and ruled his flock with a rod of iron.

The Second Great Awakening shows the sort of solutions that many people find attractive when their society is going through the wrenching upheaval of modernization. Like modern fundamentalists, the prophets of the Second Great Awakening mounted a rebellion against the learned rationalism of the ruling classes and insisted on a more religious identity. At the same time, they made the modern ethos accessible to people who had not had the opportunity to study the writings of Descartes, Newton, or John Locke. The prophetic rebellion of these American prophets was both successful and enduring in the United States, and this means that we should not expect modern fundamentalist movements in societies that are currently modernizing to be ephemeral and a passing "madness." The new American sects may have seemed bizarre to the establishment, but they were essentially modern and an integral part of the new world. This was certainly true of the millennial movement founded by the New York farmer William Miller (1782–1849), who pored over the biblical prophecies, and, in a series of careful calculations, "proved" in a pamphlet published in 1831 that the Second Coming of Christ would occur in the year 1843. Miller was reading his Bible in an essentially modern way. Instead of seeing it as a mythical, symbolic account of eternal realities, Miller assumed that such narratives as the Book of Revelation were accurate predictions of imminent events, which could be worked out with scientific and mathematical precision. People now read texts for information. Truth must be capable of logical, scientific demonstration. Miller was treating the *mythos* of Scripture as though it were *logos*, and he and his assistant Joshua Hines constantly stressed the systematic and scientific nature of Miller's investigations.[77] The movement was also democratic: anybody could interpret the Bible for him or herself, and Miller encouraged his followers to challenge his calculations and come up with theories of their own.[78]

Improbable and bizarre as the movement seemed, Millerism had instant appeal. Some 50,000 Americans became confirmed "Millerites," while thousands more sympathized without actually joining up.[79] Inevitably, however, Millerism turned into an object lesson in the danger of interpreting the *mythos* of the Bible literally. Christ failed to return, as promised, in 1843, and Millerites were devastated. Nonetheless, this failure did not mean the end of millennialism, which became and has continued to be a major passion in the United States. Out of the "Great Disappointment" of 1843, other sects, such as the Seventh-Day Adventists, appeared, adjusted the eschatological timetable, and, by eschewing precise predictions, enabled new generations of Americans to look forward to an imminent End of history.

At first this new, rough, and democratic Christianity was confined to the poorer and more uneducated classes. but during the 1840s, Charles Finney (1792–1875), a pivotal figure in American religion, brought it to the middle classes. He thus helped to make this "evangelical" Christianity, based on a literal reading of the Gospels and intent on converting the secular nation to Christ, the dominant faith of the United States by the middle of the nineteenth century.[80] Finney used the uncouth, wild methods of the older prophets, but addressed lawyers, doctors, and merchants, urging them to experience Christ directly, without the mediation of the establishment, to think for themselves and rebel against the hegemony of the learned theologians in the denominations. He also urged his middle-class audiences to join other evangelicals in the social reform of society.[81]

After the Revolution, the state had declared its independence of religion and, at the same time, Christians in all the denominations began to withdraw from the state. There was disillusion and disenchantment with the Revolution, which had not managed to usher in the millennium after all. Protestants began to insist on preserving their own religious "space," apart from the

deist republican government. They were God's community and did not
belong to the federal establishment. Protestants still believed that America
should be a godly nation, and public virtue was increasingly seen as nonpo-
litical[82]; it was better to work for the redemption of society independently of
the state, in churches, schools, and the numerous reform associations which
sprang up in the northern states during the 1820s, after the Second Great
Awakening. Christians started to work for a better world. They campaigned
against slavery and liquor, and to end the oppression of marginalized groups.
Many of the Millerites had been involved in temperance, abolitionist, and
feminist organizations.[83] There was certainly an element of social control in
all this. There was also an unpleasantly nativist motivation in the emphasis
on the Protestant virtues of thrift, sobriety, and clean living. Protestants
were greatly disturbed by the massive flood of Catholic immigrants into the
United States. At the time of the Revolution, America had been a Protestant
country, with Catholics comprising only about one percent of the total
population. But by the 1840s, there were over 2.5 million Catholics in America, and Roman Catholicism was the largest Christian denomination in the
United States.[84] This was an alarming development in a nation that had long
regarded the Pope as Antichrist. Some of the evangelical reform effort was
an obvious attempt to counter this Catholic influence. Temperance, for
example, was promoted to oppose the drinking habits of the new Polish,
Irish, and Italian Americans.[85]

Nevertheless, these evangelical reform movements were also positive and
modernizing. There was an emphasis on the worth of each human being.
They actively promoted an egalitarianism that would help to make slavery, for example, intolerable in the northern states, though not in the South,
which remained virtually untouched by the Second Great Awakening, and
which retained a premodern, elitist social structure until long after the Civil
War.[86] The reform movements helped people to accommodate the modern
ideal of inalienable human rights in a Christian package, at least in the
North. The movements for feminism and for penal and educational reform,
which were spearheaded by evangelical Christians, were also progressive.
The reform groups themselves also helped people to acquire the modern
spirit. Members made a conscious, voluntary decision to join an association,
and learned how to plan, organize, and pursue a clearly defined objective in a
modern, rational way. Eventually evangelical Christians would form the
backbone of the Whig party (to which the later Republican party was in
large measure the successor), while their opponents (the Old Lights and the
Catholics) tended to gravitate to the Democratic party. The Whigs/Repub-
licans wanted to create a "righteous empire" in America, based on Godly
rather than Enlightenment virtues.

By the middle of the nineteenth century, therefore, the evangelicals were no longer marginalized and disenfranchised. They had challenged the secularist establishment and made their voices heard. They were now engaged in a Christian *reconquista* of American society, which they were determined to return to a strictly Protestant ethos. They felt proud of their achievement. They had made an indelible impression upon American culture, which, despite the secular Constitution of the United States, was now more Christian than it had ever been before. Between 1780 and 1860, there was a spectacular rise in the number of Christian congregations in the United States, which far outstripped the national rate of population growth. In 1780, there were only about 2,500 congregations; by 1820 there were 11,000, and by 1860 a phenomenal 52,000—an almost 21-fold increase. In comparison, the population of the United States rose from about four million in 1780 to ten million in 1820, and 31 million in 1860—a less-than-eightfold increase.[87] In Europe, religion was becoming increasingly identified with the establishment, and ordinary people were turning to alternative ideologies, but in America, Protestantism empowered the people against the establishment, and this tendency has continued, so that it is difficult to find a popular movement in America today that is not associated with religion in some way. By the 1850s, Christianity in America was vibrant, and seemed poised for future triumphs.

It was a very different story in Europe. There the chief ideologies taking people into the modern world were not religious but secularist, and, increasingly, people's attention focused on this world rather than the next. This was clear in the work of Georg Wilhelm Friedrich Hegel (1770–1831), who brought the transcendent God down to earth and made it human. Fulfillment was to be found in the mundane, not in the supernatural. In Hegel's *The Phenomenology of Mind* (1807), the universal Spirit could only achieve its full potential if it immersed itself in the limiting conditions of space and time; it was most fully realized in the human mind. So too, human beings had to give up the old idea of a transcendent God in order to understand that they were themselves divine. The myth, a new version of the Christian doctrine of incarnation, can also be seen as a cure for the alienation from the world experienced by many modern people. It was an attempt to resacralize a world that had been emptied of the divine, and to enhance the vision of the human mind whose powers had seemed so curtailed in the philosophy of Descartes and Kant. But above all, Hegel's myth expressed the forward-thrusting dynamic of modernity. There was no harking back to a Golden Age; Hegel's world was continually re-creating itself. Instead of the old conservative conviction that everything had already been said, Hegel envisaged a dialectical process in which human beings were constantly engaged in the destruction of past ideas that had once been sacred and incontrovertible. In this dialectic, every state of being inevitably brings forth its opposite; these opposites clash and are integrated and fulfilled in a more advanced synthesis; then the whole process begins again. In this vision, there was to be no return to fundamentals, but a continuous evolution toward entirely new and unprecedented truth.

Hegel's philosophy expressed the driving optimism of the modern age, which had now irrevocably left the conservative spirit behind. But some could not see why Hegel should even have bothered with God. Religion and mythology were beginning to be viewed by some Europeans as not only outmoded but positively harmful. Instead of curing our sense of alienation, they were thought to compound it. By setting up God as the antithesis of humanity, Hegel's pupil Ludwig Feuerbach (1804–72) argued, religion was bringing about "the disuniting of man from himself. . . . God is perfect, man imperfect; God eternal, man temporal; God almighty, man weak."[88] For Karl Marx (1818–83), religion was a symptom of a sick society, an opiate that made the diseased social system bearable and removed the will to find a cure by directing attention away from this world to the next.[89]

Atheists were beginning to take the high moral ground. This became clear in the aftermath of the publication of *The Origin of Species by Means of Natural Selection* in 1859, by Charles Darwin (1809–82). This represented a new phase of modern science. Instead of collecting facts, as Bacon had prescribed, Darwin put forward a hypothesis: animals, plants, and human beings had not been created fully formed (as the Bible implied), but had developed slowly in a long period of evolutionary adaptation to their environment. In *The Descent of Man* (1871), Darwin proposed that *Homo sapiens* had evolved from the same proto-ape that was the progenitor of the orangutan, gorilla, and chimpanzee. Darwin's name has become a byword for atheism in fundamentalist circles, yet the *Origin* was not intended as an attack upon religion, but was a sober, careful exposition of a scientific theory. Darwin himself was an agnostic but always respectful of religious faith. Nevertheless, the *Origin* was a watershed. It sold 1400 copies on the day of publication. Certainly, it and Darwin's later work dealt another blow to human self-esteem. Copernicus had displaced humanity from the center of the cosmos, Descartes and Kant had alienated humans from the physical world, and now Darwin had suggested that they were simply animals. They had not been specially created by God, but had evolved like everything else. Indeed, there seemed no place for God in the creative process and the world, "red in tooth and claw," had no divine purpose.

Yet in the years immediately following the publication of the *Origin*, the religious reaction was muted. There was much more fuss the following year, when seven Anglican clergymen published *Essays and Reviews,* which made the latest biblical criticism available to the general reader.[90] Since the late eighteenth century, German scholars had applied the new techniques of literary analysis, archaeology, and comparative linguistics to the Bible, subjecting it to a scientifically empirical methodology. They argued that the first five books of the Bible, traditionally attributed to Moses, were in fact written much later and by a number of different authors; the book of Isaiah had at least two different sources, and King David had probably not written the Psalms. Most of the miracles described in the Bible were simply literary tropes and could not be understood literally; many of the biblical events were almost certainly not historical. In *Essays and Reviews,* the British clerics argued that the Bible must not have special treatment, but should be subjected to the same critical rigor as any other text.[91] The new "Higher Criticism" represented the triumph of the rational discourse of *logos* over myth. Rational science had subjected the *mythoi* of the Bible to radical scrutiny and found that some of its claims were "false." The biblical tales were simply "myths," which, in popular parlance, now meant that they were not true. The Higher Criticism would become a bogey of Christian fundamentalists, because it seemed a major assault upon religion, but this was only because Western people had lost the original sense of the mythical, and thought that doctrines and scriptural narratives were *logoi,* narratives that purported to be factually accurate and phenomena that could be investigated scientifically. But in revealing how impossible it was to read the Bible in an entirely literal manner, the Higher Criticism could also have provided a healthy counterbalance to the growing tendency to make modern Christian faith "scientific."

Noting the discrepancy between Darwin's hypothesis and the first chapter of Genesis, some Christians, such as Darwin's American friend and fellow scientist Asa Gray (1810–88), tried to harmonize natural selection with a literal reading of Genesis. Later the project known as Creation Science would go to even greater lengths to make Genesis scientifically respectable. But this was to miss the point, because, as a myth, the biblical creation story was not an historical account of the origins of life but a more spiritual reflection upon the ultimate significance of life itself, about which scientific *logos* has nothing to say.

Even though Darwin had not intended it, the publication of the *Origin* did cause a preliminary skirmish between religion and science, but the first shots were fired not by the religious but by the more aggressive secularists. In England, Thomas H. Huxley (1825–95), and on the Continent, Karl Vogt (1817–95), Ludwig Buchner (1824–99), Jakob Moleschott (1822–93), and Ernst Haeckel (1834–1919), popularized Darwin's theory, touring and lecturing to large audiences to prove that science and religion were incompatible. They were, in fact, preaching a crusade against religion.[92]

Huxley clearly felt that he had a fight on his hands. Reason, he insisted, must be the sole criterion of truth. People would have to choose between mythology and rational science. There could be no compromise: "one or the other would have to succumb after a struggle of unknown duration."[93] Scientific rationalism was, for Huxley, a new secular religion; it demanded conversion and total commitment. "In matters of the intellect, follow your reason as far as it will take you, without regard to any other consideration," he urged his audience. "And negatively, in matters of the intellect, do not pretend that conclusions are certain which are not demonstrated and demonstrable."[94] Huxley was supported by the whole thrust of modern, progressive culture, which had achieved such spectacular results that it could now claim aggressively to be the sole arbiter of truth. But truth had been narrowed to what is "demonstrated and demonstrable," which, religion aside, would exclude the truth told by art or music. For Huxley, there was no other possible path. Reason alone was truthful, and the myths of religion truthless. It was a final declaration of independence from the mythical constraints of the conservative period. Reason no longer had to submit to a higher court. It was not to be restricted by morality but must be pushed to the end "without regard to any other consideration." The continental crusaders went further in their war against religion. Buchner's best-seller, *Force and Matter*, a crude book which Huxley himself despised, argued that the universe had no purpose, that everything in the world had derived from a simple cell, and that only an idiot could believe in God. But the large numbers of people who read this book and the huge crowds who flocked to Haeckel's lectures showed that in Europe a significant number of people wanted to hear that science had disproved religion once and for all.

This was because by treating religious truths as though they were rational *logoi*, modern scientists, critics, and philosophers had made them incredible. In 1882, Friedrich Nietzsche (1844–1900) would proclaim that God was dead. In *The Gay Science*, he told the story of a madman running one morning into the marketplace crying "I seek God!" When the amused and supercilious bystanders asked him if he imagined that God had emigrated or run away, the madman glared. "Where has God gone?" he demanded. "We have killed him—you and I! We are all his murderers!"[95] In an important sense, Nietzsche was right. Without myth, cult, ritual, and prayer, the sense of the sacred inevitably dies. By making "God" a wholly notional truth, struggling to reach the divine by intellect alone, as some modern believers had attempted to do, modern men and women had killed it for themselves. The whole dynamic of their future-oriented culture had made the traditional ways of apprehending the sacred psychologically impossible. Like the Jewish Marranos before them, who had themselves been thrust, for very different reasons, into a religious limbo, many modern men and women were experiencing the truths of religion as tenuous, arbitrary, and incomprehensible.

Nietzsche's madman believed that the death of God had torn humanity from its roots, thrown the earth off course, and cast it adrift in a pathless universe. Everything that had once given human beings a sense of direction had vanished. "Is there still an above and below?" he had asked. "Do we not stray, as though through an infinite nothingness?"[96] A profound terror, a sense of meaninglessness and annihilation, would be part of the modern experience. Nietzsche was writing at a time when the exuberant exhilaration of modernity was beginning to give way to a nameless dread. This would affect not only the Christians of Europe, but Jews and Muslims, who had also been drawn into the modernizing process and found it equally perplexing.

4. Jews and Muslims Modernize
(1700–1870)

IF MODERNIZATION was difficult for the Christians of Europe and America, it was even more problematic for Jews and Muslims. Muslims experienced modernity as an alien, invasive force, inextricably associated with colonization and foreign domination. They would have to adapt to a civilization whose watchword was independence, while themselves suffering political subjugation. The modern ethos was markedly hostile toward Judaism. For all their talk of toleration, Enlightenment thinkers still regarded Jews with contempt. François-Marie Voltaire (1694–1778) had called them "a totally ignorant nation," in his *Dictionnaire philosophique* (1756); they combined "contemptible miserliness and the most revolting superstition with a violent hatred of all the nations which have tolerated them." Baron d'Holbach (1723–89), one of the first avowed atheists of Europe, had called Jews "the enemies of the human race."[1] Kant and Hegel both saw Judaism as a servile, degraded faith, utterly opposed to the rational,[2] while Karl Marx, himself of Jewish descent, argued that the Jews were responsible for capitalism, which, in his view, was the source of all the world's ills.[3] Jews would, therefore, have to adapt to modernity in an atmosphere of hatred.

In America, the developments of the eighteenth and nineteenth centuries had split Protestant Christians into two opposing camps. There had been a similar conflict within Eastern European Jewry at the same time. The Jews of Poland, Galicia, Belorussia, and Lithuania were divided into opposing parties, which would both play a crucial role in the formation of Jewish fundamentalism. The Hasidim, who were not unlike the New Lights, made their appearance at exactly the same time as the American Calvinists were experiencing the First Great Awakening. In 1735, a poor Jewish tavern-keeper called Israel ben Eliezer (1700–60) announced that he had received a revelation that made him a "Master of the Name" *(baal shem),* one of the faith healers and exorcists who roamed through the villages and rural districts of Poland working miracles of healing in the name of God. But Israel soon acquired a special reputation, because he tended to the spiritual as well as to the physical needs of the poor, so he became known as the "Besht," an acronym of the title *Baal Shem Tov*, literally "the Master of the Good Name," a Master of exceptional status. This was a dark time for Polish Jewry. People had still not fully recovered from the Shabbatean scandal, and Jewish communities, which had suffered grave economic problems ever since the massacres of 1648, were now in spiritual crisis. In their struggle for survival, wealthier Jews did not distribute the tax burdens fairly, the social gap between rich and poor widened, strongmen, habitués of the nobles' courts, seized control of the *kehilla,* and the weak were pushed to the wall. Worse, many of the rabbis colluded in this oppression, took no care of the poor, and wasted their intellectual energies on casuistical discussions about minutiae of the Law. The poor felt abandoned, there was a spiritual vacuum, a decline in public morality, and superstition was rife. Popular preachers tried to educate the more needy Jews, took up their cause, and inveighed against the rabbinic establishment for their dereliction of duty. Often these *hasidim* ("pious ones") formed separate cells and prayer groups that were independent of the synagogues. It was to these Hasidic circles that the Besht presented himself in 1735 when he declared himself to be a Baal Shem, and he became their rabbi.[4]

The Besht completely transformed this Hasidism, which sought to wrest control from the corrupt rabbis and to attend to the spiritual needs of the people. By 1750, cells of Hasidim had appeared in most of the towns of Podolia, Volhynia, Galicia, and Ukraine. A contemporary source estimated that by the end of his life, the Besht had about forty thousand followers, who prayed in their own, separate synagogues.[5] By the early nineteenth century, Hasidism dominated most of the Jewish communities of Poland, Ukraine, and East Galicia, it was established in many towns in White Russia and Romania, and it had begun to penetrate Lithuania.

Like New Light Protestantism, Hasidism became a mass movement in opposition to the religious establishment; Hasidim formed their own congregations, just as the New Lights had established their own churches. Both were popular movements with folk elements. Just as the radical Protestants castigated the elite for relying on their learning and theological expertise, the Hasidim reviled the arid Torah scholarship of the rabbis. The Besht declared that prayer must take precedence over the study of Torah, a revolutionary step. For centuries, Jews had accepted the authority of a rabbi based on his Torah learning, but because the rabbis seemed to have retreated from the urgent social problems of the community into the sacred texts, the

Hasidim denounced this trivializing scholarship, even though they studied sacred texts themselves in their own way.

New Light Protestantism had been a modernizing spirituality, however, while Hasidism was a typically conservative reform movement. Its spirituality was mythical, based on the Lurianic symbol of divine sparks that had been trapped in matter during the primal catastrophe, but the Besht transformed this tragic vision into a positive appreciation of the omnipresence of God. A spark of the divine could be found in absolutely everything. There was no place where God was not: the most accomplished Hasidim became aware of this hidden divine dimension by means of the practices of concentration and attachment *(devekut)* to God at all times. No activity, however worldly or carnal, was profane. God was always present and available and could be experienced while Hasidim were eating, drinking, making love, or conducting business. Hasidim must show their awareness of this divine presence. From the very first, Hasidic prayer was noisy and ecstatic; Hasidim would combine their worship with strange, violent gestures, designed to help them to put their whole selves into their prayer. They used to clap, throw their heads backward and forward, beat on the walls with their hands, and sway their bodies to and fro. The Hasid was to learn, at a level deeper than the cerebral, that his whole being must be pliable to the divine forces in his immediate environment, as a candle flame responds to every fluctuation of the wind. Some Hasidim would even turn somersaults in the synagogues, to express the overturning of the ego in its total surrender to God.[6]

Hasidism's innovations were rooted in the past, however, and presented as the recovery of an ancient truth. The Besht claimed that he had been instructed in the divine mysteries by Ahijah of Shiloh, the teacher of the Prophet Elijah, and that he himself embodied the spirit of Elijah.[7] The Besht and his followers were still reading scripture in the old mystical way. Instead of reading the Bible critically or to acquire information, Hasidim made their Torah study a spiritual discipline. "I will teach you the way Torah is best taught," the Besht used to tell his disciples; "not to feel [conscious of] oneself at all, but to be like a listening ear that hears the world of sound speaking but does not speak itself."[8] The Hasid had to open his heart to the text, and divest himself of ego. This transcendence of self was a form of ecstasy that demanded a disciplined reining in of a Hasid's mental powers, very different from the wilder transports of the American revivalists. The Besht was not interested in a literal reading but looked beyond the words of the page to the divine, just as he taught his Hasidim to look through the surface of the external world and become aware of the indwelling Presence. There is a story that one day he was visited by Dov Ber (1710–72), a learned Kabbalist who would succeed the Besht as leader of the Hasidic movement. The two men discussed a Lurianic text about angels, and the Besht found Dov Ber's literal exegesis correct but inadequate. He asked him to stand up, out of respect for the angels, and as soon as Dov Ber rose to his feet "the whole house was suffused with light, a fire burned all around, and they [both] sensed the presence of the angels who had been mentioned." "The simple reading is as you say," the Besht told Dov Ber, "but your manner of studying lacked soul."[9] A wholly rational reading, without the attitudes and cultic gestures of prayer, would not bring a Hasid to a vision of the unseen reality to which the text pointed.

In many ways, Hasidism was the antithesis of the spirit of the European Enlightenment that was just beginning to reach Eastern Europe at the end of the Besht's life. Where the *philosophes* and scientists believed that reason alone could lead to truth, the Besht promoted mystical intuition alongside the rational. Hasidism denied the separations of modernity—of religion from politics, the sacred from the profane—and adopted a holistic vision that saw holiness everywhere. Where modern science had disenchanted the world and found the cosmos empty of the divine, Hasidim experienced a sacred immanence. Even though it was a movement of the people, there was nothing democratic about Hasidism. The Besht believed that the ordinary Hasid could not achieve union with God directly. He would find the divine only in the person of a Zaddik ("a righteous man") who had mastered *devekut,* a constant mystical consciousness of God which was beyond the reach of most people.[10] The Hasid was, therefore, wholly dependent upon his Zaddik, an attitude which Kant would have condemned as unworthy tutelage. Hasidism was thus deeply at odds with the Enlightenment, and many Hasidim would reject it when it began to penetrate Eastern Europe.

While the Besht was alive, the rabbinic establishment did not take him seriously, but Dov Ber, the new leader, a learned man, was a very different proposition, and the movement spread under his leadership. When it reached Lithuania, it came to the attention of a powerful figure: Elijah ben Solomon Zalman (1720–97), head *(gaon)* of the Academy of Vilna. The Gaon was appalled by the Hasidic movement, especially its denigration of Torah study, which was his chief passion. His scholarship, however, was very different from the casuistic studies of the corrupt Polish rabbis, and had a deeply mystical cast. His sons tell us that he used to study all night with his feet in icy water to keep himself awake. For the Gaon, Torah study was a more aggressive exercise than it was for the Hasidim. He relished what he called the "effort" of study, and it seems as though this intense mental activity tipped him into a new level of awareness. When he did allow himself to sleep, the Torah penetrated his dreams and he would experience a mystical ascent to the divine. Torah study was thus an encounter with God. As his disciple, Rabbi Hayyim Volozhiner (1749–1821), whom we shall meet later, explained: "he who studies Torah communes with God, for God and the Torah are one."[11] But the Gaon also made time for modern studies; he was proficient in astronomy, anatomy, mathematics, and foreign languages. He found the Hasidim heretical and obscurantist. The conflict became acrimonious. The Gaon's supporters, whom the Hasidim called Misnagdim ("opponents"), would sometimes observe the rites of mourning when one of their number became a Hasid, as though he had died; the Hasidim, for their part, did not regard the Misnagdim as proper Jews. Eventually, in 1772, the Gaon excommunicated the Hasidim of Vilna and Brody; the shock of this expulsion is said to have killed Dov Ber.

Toward the end of the Gaon's life, Rabbi Shneur Zalman (1745–1813), a Hasidic leader in Ukraine and Belorussia, sought to effect a reconciliation, but the Gaon refused to speak with him. Indeed, the publication of Zalman's book the *Tanya* (1791) inspired a new edict of excommunication. This was a pity. Zalman was evolving a new type of Hasidism known as Habad,[12] which was much closer to the spirituality of the Misnagdim, since it made rational thought the starting point of the spiritual quest. Zalman was also open to some of the Enlightenment ideals, which he tried to accommodate within a mystical framework. He believed that our rational powers alone were incapable of finding God; if we relied only upon our senses—as the scientists and philosophers bade us do—the world did indeed seem empty of the divine. But the mystic could use his intuitive powers to break through to a different mode of perception, which revealed the immanent Presence in all phenomena. Zalman was not opposed to reason, but was simply making the old conservative point that rational thinking was not the sole mode of perception; reason and mystical intuition should work hand-in-hand. When Jews engaged in rational speculation and in the study of modern secular subjects, Zalman argued, they became aware of the limitations of their minds and would seek to transcend them by means of ecstatic prayer.[13] Zalman encouraged his Habad Hasidim to propel themselves into a sense of transcendence by the violent gestures that the Besht had introduced. Zalman himself used to roll upon the ground until he entered a tranced state, and would dance wildly like the common people.[14] But this ecstasy was rooted in study and disciplined concentration. Habad Hasidim were taught to manage their unconscious selves by descending ever deeper into their minds until they encountered, like mystics in all the great traditions, a sacred presence in the ground of their being.

The conflict between Hasidim and Misnagdim intensified. Zalman was actually imprisoned in St. Petersburg for some years, when the Misnagdim denounced him to the Russian authorities as a troublemaker. But during the early years of the nineteenth century, the hostility began to abate. Both sides realized that they had more to fear from other quarters than from each other, and should, therefore, join forces to oppose these new threats. The most worrying development was the Haskalah, the Jewish Enlightenment, which had just begun to penetrate Eastern European Jewry and which seemed heretical to Hasidim and Misnagdim alike.

The Haskalah was the creation of Moses Mendelssohn (1729–86), the brilliant son of a poor Torah scholar in Dessau, Germany, who, at the age of fourteen, had followed his favorite teacher to Berlin. There he fell in love with modern secular learning and, at prodigious speed, mastered German, French, English, Latin, mathematics, and philosophy. He longed to take part in the German Enlightenment, became a personal friend of Kant's, and spent all his free time in study. His first book, *Phaedon* (1767), was an attempt to prove the immortality of the soul on rational grounds, and had nothing particularly Jewish about it. Against his will, however, Mendelssohn found himself obliged to defend Judaism when he encountered Enlightenment hostility to the Jewish faith. In 1769, Johan Casper Lavater, a Swiss pastor, challenged Mendelssohn to defend Judaism in public; if he could not refute the rational proofs of Christianity, Lavater declared, he should submit to baptism. Mendelssohn was also disturbed by the anti-Semitic prejudice in a pamphlet written by a Prussian state official, Christian Wilhelm Van Dohm, *On the Civic Improvement of the Condition of the Jews* (1781). In order to function effectively and competitively in the modern world, Van Dohm argued, a nation must mobilize the talents of as many people as possible, so it made sense to emancipate the Jews and integrate them more fully into society, even though they should not be granted citizenship or permitted to hold public office. The underlying assumption was that Jews were objectionable and their religion was barbaric.

Reluctantly, Mendelssohn felt bound to respond, and in 1783 he published *Jerusalem, Concerning Religious Authority and Judaism*. The German Enlightenment was quite positive toward religion, and Mendelssohn himself seemed to share the same serene deist faith as Locke, though it is difficult to recognize it as Judaism. Mendelssohn seemed to find the existence of a benevolent God a matter of common sense, but insisted that reason must precede faith. We could only accept the authority of the Bible after we had demonstrated its truth rationally. This, of course, totally reversed the priorities of traditional, conservative faith, which took it for granted that reason could not demonstrate the truth of the kind of myths found in the scriptures. Mendelssohn also argued for the separation of church and state, and for the privatization of religion—a solution that was very attractive to Jews who longed to shake off the restrictions of the ghetto and become involved in mainstream European culture. By making their faith a purely personal affair, they could both remain Jewish and become good Europeans. Mendelssohn insisted that Judaism was a rational faith that was eminently suited to the temper of the times; its doctrines were based on reason. When God had revealed himself to Moses on Mount Sinai, he had brought the Jewish people a law and not a set of doctrines. Judaism was, therefore, only concerned with morality and human behavior; it left the minds of Jews entirely free. Mendelssohn seemed to have little understanding of the mystical and mythical element in Judaism; his was the first of a number of attempts to make Judaism acceptable to the modern world by forcing it into a rationalistic mold that was alien to it—as it was alien to most religions.

Mendelssohn's ideas were, of course, anathema to the Hasidim and Misnagdim of Eastern Europe, as well as to the more Orthodox Jews of the Western world. He was reviled as a new Spinoza, a heretic who had abandoned the faith and gone over to the gentiles. Yet this would have grieved Mendelssohn; while he clearly found much of traditional Judaism incredible and alien, he did not want to abandon the Jewish God or his Jewish identity. He had a significant number of disciples, however. Ever since the Shabbetai Zevi affair, many Jews had shown that they longed to transcend the strictures of traditional Judaism, which they found confining. They were happy to follow Mendelssohn's example: to mix in gentile society, study the new sciences, and keep their faith a private matter. Mendelssohn was one of the first to devise a way out of the ghetto into modern Europe that did not oblige Jews to reject their people and their own cultural heritage.

Besides engaging in the intellectual life of the Enlightenment, some of these Jewish *maskilim* ("enlightened ones") began to study their own heritage from a more secular standpoint. Some of them, as we shall see, would undertake a modern, scientific exploration of Jewish history; others began to study and to write in Hebrew, the sacred tongue which among Orthodox Jews was reserved for prayer and works of devotion. Now Maskilim began to create a new Hebrew literature, secularizing this holy language. They were trying to find a modern way of being Jewish, to shed what they regarded as the superstitions of the past and to make Judaism acceptable to enlightened society.

Their ability to take part in the life of the mainstream culture, however, was seriously limited by externally imposed restrictions: Jews were given no legal recognition by the state, could not participate in political life, and were still officially a race apart. But the Maskilim had great hopes of the Enlightenment. They noted that after the American Revolution, Jews had been granted citizenship in the secular polity of the United States. When Napoleon Bonaparte, a ruler imbued with the spirit of the Enlightenment, came to power in France and began to build a mighty empire, it seemed for a while that after centuries of persecution Jews would finally be granted equality and respect in Europe as well.

Liberty had been the battle cry of the French Revolution, and was the watchword of Napoleon's government in France. To the incredulous joy of those Jews who longed to escape the ghetto, Napoleon announced that the Jews of France would become full citizens of the republic. On July 29, 1806, Jewish businessmen, bankers, and rabbis were summoned to the Hôtel de Ville in Paris, where they swore fealty to the state. A few weeks later, Napoleon convened a body of Jewish notables he called the "Great Sanhedrin"—the Sanhedrin being the Jewish governing council which had not sat since the destruction of the Temple in Jerusalem in 70 CE. The mandate of this body was to give religious sanction to the resolutions of the previous assembly. Jews were ecstatic. Rabbis declared that the French Revolution was the "second law from Mount Sinai," "our exodus from Egypt, our modern Pesach"; "the Messianic age has arrived with this new society of *liberté, egalité, fraternité.*"[15] As Napoleon's armies swept through Europe, he introduced these egalitarian principles into every country he occupied: the Netherlands, Italy, Spain, Portugal, and Prussia. One principality after another was forced to emancipate its Jews.

But even during the first assembly of 1806, Enlightenment hostility to the Jewish people surfaced in an offensive address by Louis Count Molé, Napoleon's commissioner. He had heard that Jewish moneylenders in Alsace were evading conscription and fleecing the population. The Jewish delegates to the Assembly, therefore, had the task of revitalizing that sense of civic morality which their people had lost during the long centuries of "degrading existence."[16] On March 17, 1808, Napoleon imposed economic strictures on the Jews, which were later called the "Infamous Decrees." During the three years that they were enforced, thousands of Jewish families were ruined. As the American historian Norman Cantor points out, Napoleon offered the Jews a "Faustian bargain": they had to sell their unique Jewish soul in exchange for emancipation.[17] For all its inspiring talk about *liberté,* the modern, centralized state was unable to tolerate autonomous anomalies such as the ghetto. The enlightened polity had to be legally and culturally uniform, and Jews presented a "problem" that must be rationalized away. They must become assimilated, bourgeois Frenchmen, abandon their separate way of life, and privatize their religion: Jews as Jews had to vanish.

The French solution became the pattern of Jewish emancipation in the rest of Europe. The new toleration was an improvement on the old segregation, but it was the result not solely of the noble idealism of the Enlightenment but of the needs of the modern state. A similar pragmatism had, as we have seen, led to the constitutional acceptance of pluralism in the United States. If they were to respond effectively to the challenge of the modern world and build a prosperous society, governments had to use all the human resources at their disposal. Whatever the official religion of the state, Jews, Protestants, Catholics, and secularists were all needed in the new economic and industrial programs. The fabled business acumen of the Jews was particularly desirable, and it was deemed essential to harness this asset to the benefit of the state.[18]

The old prejudices remained, however. Except in France and Holland, the rights granted to the Jews were withdrawn after the defeat of Napoleon at Waterloo (1815) and the collapse of his empire. Jews were herded back into the ghettos, the old restrictions returned, and there were new pogroms. But the needs of the modern state eventually forced one government after another to extend full citizenship to its Jews, provided that they accepted the Faustian bargain. Those states that granted equality and citizenship to Jews, such as Britain, France, Holland, Austria, and Germany, prospered;[19] those eastern European states that did not democratize but tried to confine the benefits of modernity to an elite, fell behind. By 1870, Jewish emancipation had been achieved throughout western Europe; in eastern Europe and Russia, however, where governments used more coercive methods of abolishing Jewish separatism, millions of Jews were alienated from the modern state and clung defiantly to rabbinic and Hasidic traditions.[20]

But in the first years after the original rights granted by Napoleon had been rescinded, many young Jews felt stranded and betrayed. They had received a good secular education, and were ready to take part in modern society, but were now prevented from doing so. Mendelssohn had shown them a way out of the ghetto, Napoleon had promised freedom, and they were unable to return to the traditional way of life. In their frustration, many German Jews converted to Christianity in order to assimilate to the mainstream culture. Others became convinced that if Judaism was to survive, they would have to take drastic action to prevent this stream of conversions. Two related movements developed in Germany, both of which had their roots in the Jewish Enlightenment. The Maskilim believed that they could act as a bridge from the ghetto to the modern world. They could speak good German and had gentile friends, and in public seemed perfectly attuned to the European way of life. Now some of them decided to reform the religion of Judaism itself, to make it fit more easily into the modern world.

This Reform Judaism began as an almost wholly pragmatic movement and, as such, was guided entirely according to the principles of *logos*. Its aim, indeed, was to abolish the *mythos* of Judaism. Israel Jacobson (1768–1828) believed that if Judaism appeared less outlandish to the German people, this would improve the chances of emancipation. A layman and philanthropist, he established a school in Seesen, near the Garz mountains, where students studied secular as well as Jewish subjects. He also opened a synagogue where worship appeared to be more Protestant than Jewish. Prayers were said in the vernacular instead of Hebrew; there was German choral singing, a mixed choir, and a sermon in German, which was much more central to the service than before. The traditional rites were drastically reduced. In 1815, Jacobson and other laymen brought this modernized worship to Berlin, where they opened what they called private "temples" to distinguish them from the regular synagogues. In 1817, Edward Kley founded a new temple in Hamburg, where the reforms were even more revolutionary. Prayers pleading for the coming of the Messiah and the return to Zion were replaced by a prayer celebrating the brotherhood of all humanity: how could Jews pray for the restoration of a messianic state in Palestine when they wanted to become German citizens? By 1822, confirmation services, on the Protestant model, were held for girls and boys; the separate seating of men and women at services was also abandoned. The rabbis of Hamburg condemned this reform movement and even managed, by appealing to the Prussian government, to get the Berlin temples closed down.[21] During the following years, therefore, many young Jews who might have found this reformed Judaism congenial, converted to Christianity. But the Hamburg temple remained open and new ones were established in Leipzig, Vienna, and Denmark. In America, the playwright Isaac Harby founded a reformed temple in Charleston. Reform would become very popular among American Jews, and, by 1870, a substantial proportion of the two hundred synagogues in the United States had adopted at least some Reform practices.[22]

Reform Judaism belonged entirely to the modern world; it was rational, pragmatic, and strongly disposed to privatize faith. Reformers were willing—indeed, eager—to make a radical break with the past and to jettison traditional doctrines and devotions. Instead of seeing the exile as an existential calamity, the Reformers felt perfectly at home in the Diaspora. All promoted Judaism as a religion imbued with all the virtues of modernity: it was rational, liberal, and humane, ready to shed its archaic particularisms and become a universal faith.[23] The Reformers had no time for the irrational, the mystical, or the mysterious. If old beliefs and values were preventing Jews from making a productive contribution to modern life, they must be eliminated. In the early days, their concerns were entirely practical, but by the 1840s, Reform had begun to attract scholars and rabbis who had undertaken a critical study of Jewish history. Leopold Zunz (1794–1886),

Zachariah Frankel (1801–75), Nachman Krochmal (1785–1840), and Abraham Geiger (1810–74) subjected the sacred sources of Judaism to modern scientific methods of inquiry. They formed a school, aptly known as "the Science of Judaism," that was clearly influenced by the philosophies of Kant and Hegel. Judaism, they argued, was not a faith that had been revealed once and for all in the past; it had evolved slowly, becoming ever more rational and self-conscious in the process. Religious experiences, which had hitherto been expressed in visions, could now be conceptualized and apprehended by the critical intelligence.[24] In other words, *mythos* had now been transmuted into *logos*.

The scholars tried to strike a careful balance among the various Jewish positions. Krochmal and Frankel agreed with traditionalists, for example, that the Torah had been revealed to Moses all at once on Mount Sinai, but enraged them by denying the divine origin of the Halakhah, the vast development and elaboration of Jewish law founded upon the Torah. Frankel argued that the Halakhah was entirely man-made, the product of reason, and that it could, therefore, be changed to meet the needs of the age. Krochmal argued that Jewish history showed that Judaism had always borrowed ideas from other cultures; this was how it had managed to survive. There was, therefore, no reason why Jews could not study the modern world and adopt some of its new values. Indeed, this was the only way to stop Jews converting to Christianity in order to enjoy the benefits and challenge of modern society. Geiger believed that Mendelssohn had inaugurated a new Jewish era; Reform Judaism would liberate the faith by giving it a healthy injection of enlightenment philosophy.

But the Science of Judaism was sometimes critical of Reform. Krochmal, for example, was an observant Jew who was faithful to the old rites that the Reformers were abolishing. Frankel and Zunz both believed that there was great danger in such wholesale abolition of tradition. In 1849, Zunz wrote an article that presented Jewish rituals as outer signs of fundamental truths. Dietary laws and the wearing of phylacteries had, over the centuries, become an essential part of the Jewish experience; without these rites, Judaism would degenerate into a system of abstract doctrines. Zunz could appreciate the crucial importance of cult, which alone made the myths and beliefs of religion comprehensible. Frankel could also see the importance of ritual in helping people to create the correct spiritual attitudes. He feared that the Reformers were becoming so rational that they were losing touch with their feelings. Reason alone could not satisfy the emotions or produce the joy and delight that traditional Judaism, at its best, had always been able to inspire. It was wrong to abolish the complex, ancient rites of Yom Kippur or to omit all mention of a messianic return to Zion, because these images had shaped

Jewish consciousness and helped Jews to cultivate a sense of awe and find hope in intolerable circumstances.[25] Some change was certainly necessary, but the Reformers often seemed insensitive to the role of emotion in worship. Zunz and Frankel were alert to the essentially mythical component of religion and did not subscribe wholly to the modern tendency to see reason alone as the gateway to truth. Geiger, for his part, was an out-and-out rationalist, and in favor of sweeping reforms. Yet, over the years, Reform Jews have recognized the wisdom of Zunz's and Frankel's concerns, and have reinstated some of the traditional practices, finding that without an emotive, mystical element, faith and worship lose their soul.

Both the Reformers and the scholars of the Science of Judaism were preoccupied with the survival of their religion in a world that seemed, however benevolently, bent on destroying it. As they watched their fellow Jews rushing to the baptismal font, they were deeply concerned for the future of Judaism and were desperate to find ways of ensuring that it continued to exist. We shall find that many religious people in the modern world have shared this anxiety. In all three of the monotheistic faiths, there has been recurrent alarm that the traditional faith is in deadly danger. The dread of annihilation is one of the most fundamental of human terrors, and many of the religious movements that have arisen in the modern world have sprung from this fear of extinction. As the secular spirit took hold and as the prevailing rationalism became more hostile to faith, religious people became increasingly defensive and their spirituality more embattled.

By the beginning of the nineteenth century, traditional Jews—whom the Reformers called *Altglaubigen,* "old believers"—had certainly begun to feel beleaguered. Even after emancipation, they continued to live as though the ghetto walls were still in place. They immersed themselves totally in the study of Torah and Talmud, and insisted that modernity was to be shunned. gentile studies were, they believed, incompatible with Judaism. One of their leading spokesmen was Rabbi Moses Sofer of Pressburg (1763–1839). He was opposed to any change or accommodation to modernity—God, after all, did not change; he forbade his children to read Mendelssohn's books and refused to allow them a secular education or to participate in modern society in any way.[26] His instinctive response, in sum, was to retreat. But other traditionalists felt it necessary to take a more creative stand against the danger of secularizing, rationalizing influences.

In 1803, Rabbi Hayyim Volozhiner, a disciple of the Gaon of Vilna, took a decisive step that would transform traditional Jewish spirituality, when he founded the Etz Hayyim *yeshiva* in Volozhin, Lithuania. Other new *yeshivot* were founded in the course of the century in other parts of eastern Europe: in Mir, Telz, Slobodka, Lomza, and Novogrudok. In the past, a *yeshiva* (a word that derives from the Hebrew for "to sit") had simply been a series of small rooms behind the synagogue where students studied Torah and Talmud. It had usually been administered by the local community. Volozhin, however, was something entirely different. Here, hundreds of gifted students came from all over Europe to study with internationally famous experts. The curriculum was demanding, the hours were long, and admission to the *yeshiva* far from easy. Rabbi Hayyim taught Talmud according to the method he had learned from the Gaon, analyzing the text and stressing the importance of logical consistency, but in a way that yielded a spiritual encounter with the divine. It was not simply a matter of learning *about* the Talmud; the process of rote learning, preparation, and lively discussion was just as important as any final conclusion reached in class, because it was a form of prayer, a ritual that gave the students a sense of the sacred. It was an intense existence. The young men were isolated in a quasi-monastic community, their spiritual and intellectual lives entirely shaped by the *yeshiva*. They were separated from their families and friends and immersed wholly in the world of Jewish scholarship. Some of the students were permitted to spend a little time on modern philosophy or mathematics, but such secular subjects were secondary, regarded as stealing time from the Torah.[27]

The purpose of the new *yeshivot* had been to counter the threat of Hasidism; the *yeshivot* were distinctively Misnagdic enterprises, designed to reinstate the rigorous study of Torah. But as the century progressed, the Jewish Enlightenment came to be perceived as more of a threat, and Hasidim and Misnagdim began to join forces against the Maskilim, whom they saw as a sort of Trojan Horse, bringing the evils of secular culture within the walls of Jewish communities. Gradually, therefore, the new *yeshivot* became bastions of orthodoxy, whose primary task was to ward off this insidious danger. Only the study of Torah could prevent the extinction of true Judaism.

The *yeshiva* would become the defining institution of the ultra-Orthodox fundamentalism that would develop in the twentieth century. It was one of the first manifestations of this emergent and embattled type of religiosity, and we can learn important lessons from it. Fundamentalism—whether Jewish, Christian, or Muslim—rarely arises as a battle with an external enemy (in the case of Volozhin, this external enemy would have been gentile European culture); it usually begins, instead, as an internal struggle in which traditionalists fight their own coreligionists who, they believe, are making too many concessions to the secular world. The fundamentalist will often instinctively respond to encroaching modernity by creating an enclave of pure faith, such as a *yeshiva*. This marks a withdrawal from the Godless world into a self-contained community where the faithful attempt to reshape existence in defiance of the changes without. It is thus essentially a defensive move. This retreat, however, has within it the potential for a future counter-offensive. The students of such a *yeshiva* are likely to become a cadre, with a shared training and ideology, in their local communities. Such an enclave helps to create a counterculture, an alternative to modern society. The head of the *yeshiva* (the *rosh yeshiva*) became not unlike a Hasidic Zaddik, exert-ing enormous influence over his students. He came to demand absolute obe-dience to the commandments and to tradition, which put a curb on their creativity and capacity for original thought. The *yeshiva* thus evolved an ethos that was directly opposed to the modern spirit and its emphasis on autonomy and innovation.

The principal purpose of the Volozhin and its sister *yeshivot* was not, however, to do battle with the secular culture of Europe but to guard the souls of its young men by steeping them in the traditions of the old world. But herein lies a paradox that would constantly recur in the history of funda-mentalism. Despite its attachment to the conservative spirit, Volozhin and the other new *yeshivot* were essentially modern and modernizing institu-tions. They were committed to the centralization and rationalization of Talmud study. Their creation also implied the possibility of choice. In the ghetto, the traditional way of life had been unchangeable; its values and cus-toms had been experienced as given and beyond question. No other lifestyle had been possible for Jews. But now a Jew had to make a conscious decision to enter an institution such as Volozhin and commit himself to tradition. In a world that had made religion a matter of personal choice, Volozhin was itself a voluntary institution.[28] Even when fundamentalists set their faces against modernity, their faith is, to an extent, modern and innovative.

Other Jews tried to steer a middle course. In 1851, eleven traditionalist members of the Frankfurt community, which was now dominated by Re-form, asked the municipality for permission to form their own religious association. They invited Samuel Raphael Hirsch (1808–88) to become their rabbi. Immediately, Hirsch established secondary and elementary schools in which both Jewish and secular subjects were studied, with financial aid from the Rothschild family. As Hirsch pointed out, it was only in the ghetto that Jews had neglected the study of philosophy, medicine, and mathematics. In the past, Jewish thinkers had sometimes taken a leading role in the intellec-tual life of the mainstream culture, particularly in the Islamic world. In the ghetto, Jews had been separated from nature and they had, perforce, neglected the study of the natural sciences. Judaism, Hirsch was convinced, had nothing to fear from contact with other cultures. Jews should embrace as many modern developments as they could, but without becoming as icono-clastic as the Reformers.[29]

As a young man, Hirsch had published *Nineteen Letters of Ben Uzziel* (1836), which made a moving plea for more orthodox observance, but he blamed the rigid traditionalists, who shunned modernity, for the widespread defections to Christianity and to Reform. He did not subscribe to their fundamentalist literalism either. Jews, he believed, should seek out the hidden, inner meaning of the various commandments by means of careful study and research. Laws that made no rational sense could serve as reminders. The practice of circumcision, for example, called to mind the duty to keep the body pure; the prohibition against mixing meat and milk symbolized the need to preserve the divine order in creation. All the laws must be observed because they built character and, by making Jews holy, enabled them to fulfill their moral mission to humanity. Hirsch's middle road became known as Neo-Orthodoxy. His career shows, yet again, the voluntary nature of religious orthodoxy in the modern world. Where once tradition had been taken for granted, now Jews had to fight and argue in order to become Orthodox.

IN EGYPT AND IRAN, Muslims had an entirely different experience of the modernizing West. When Napoleon invaded Egypt in 1798, he inaugurated a new phase in the relations of East and West. His plan was to establish a base in Suez, whence he could harass Britain's sea-lanes to India and also, perhaps, attack the Ottoman empire from Syria. This meant that Egypt and Palestine became a theater in the war for world domination between England and France. It was a European power game, but Napoleon presented himself to the Egyptians as the bearer of progress and enlightenment. After he defeated the Mamluk cavalry in the Battle of the Pyramids on July 21, 1798, he issued a proclamation in Arabic in which he promised to liberate Egypt from foreign rule. For centuries, Mamluks from Circassia and Georgia had exploited the people of Egypt, but now this tyranny was at an end. He was no latter-day Crusader, he assured the *ulema,* whom he knew to be the representatives of the indigenous Egyptians. Anybody who believed that he had come to destroy their religion should be assured

> that I have come to restore your rights, which have been invaded by usurpers—that I adore God more than the Mamelukes and that I respect the Prophet Muhammad and the Noble Koran. Tell them that all men are equal before God—that intelligence, virtue, and science, are the only distinctions between them.[30]

But this liberation and science had come with a modern army. The Egyptians had just watched this extraordinary fighting machine inflict a devastating defeat upon the Mamluks; only ten French soldiers had been killed and thirty wounded, whereas the Mamluks had lost over two thousand men, four hundred camels, and fifty guns.[31] This liberation obviously had an aggressive edge, as did the modern scientific Institut d'Egypte, whose careful researches into the history of the region had enabled Napoleon to make his proclamation in Arabic and to be reasonably conversant with the ideals and institutions of Islam. Scholarship and science had become a means of promoting European interests in the Middle East and subjecting its peoples to French rule.

The *ulema* were not impressed. "All this is nothing but deceit and trickery, they said, to entice us. Bonaparte is nothing but a Christian, son of a Christian."[32] They were perturbed by the prospect of infidel rule. The Koran taught that as long as men and women organized their societies according to God's will, they could not fail, yet now the Islamic forces had been soundly defeated by a foreign power. Al-Jabarti, a sheikh of the Azhar *madrasah,* saw the invasion as the beginning of

> major battles; formidable happenings; calamitous occurrences; terrible catastrophes; the multiplication of evils, . . . the disruption of time; the inversion of the natural order; the *bouleversement* of manmade conventions.[33]

He was experiencing that sense of the world turned upside down which has so often accompanied the onset of modernization. For all its inflated rhetoric, al-Jabarti's dismay was not entirely misplaced. Napoleon's invasion was the beginning of the Western control of the Middle East, which has indeed been a reversal, causing the people to revise many of their most fundamental beliefs and expectations.

Napoleon gave the *ulema* more power than they had ever had before. He wanted to make them his allies against the Turks and Mamluks, and so gave them the highest positions in government, but the *ulema* could not respond in the way he wished. The Egyptians had been dominated by Mamluks and Turks for so long that direct rule was an entirely alien notion. Some refused to take the posts that he offered them, preferring the consultative role they were used to. They knew nothing about defense or the imposition of law and order, and they preferred to stick to what they knew best: the administration of religious, legal, and Islamic affairs. Most of the *ulema* did cooperate, however; feeling they had little choice, they stepped into the vacuum and helped to restore order, acting as mediators between the government and the people, as they had always done.[34] A few led abortive revolts against the French in October 1798 and March 1800, but these were quickly put down.

They remained bewildered by the French. They could not understand Napoleon's Enlightenment ideology of freedom and autonomy. A world of difference now divided Egyptians and Europeans. When Jabarti visited the Institut d'Egypte, he admired the enthusiasm and scholarship of the French scientists, but did not know what to make of their experiments. He was particularly bemused by the hot-air balloon. There was no place in his mental universe for such a thing and he simply could not see it in the same way as a European, who had two hundred years of empirical science behind him. "They have strange things and objects," he recorded afterwards, "which show effects which our minds are too small to comprehend."[35]

In 1801, the British managed to throw the French out of Egypt; at this point, the British were committed to preserving the integrity of the Ottoman empire and so they returned Egypt to the Turks, making no attempt to establish British rule in Egypt. But the takeover was chaotic. The Mamluks refused to accept the new Turkish governor from Istanbul, and for over two years, Mamluks, Janissaries, and the Albanian garrison sent by the Ottomans fought each other and terrorized the population. During the confusion, a young Albanian officer called Muhammad Ali (1769–1849) seized control. Weary of the confusion and disillusioned by the incompetence of the Mamluks, the *ulema* supported him. Under the remarkable *alim* Umar Makram, the *ulema* led a popular uprising against the Turks and sent a delegation to Istanbul requesting that Muhammad Ali be confirmed as pasha, or governor, of Egypt. The sultan agreed and there was huge excitement in Cairo. A French observer wrote that the enthusiasm of the crowds reminded him of the French Revolution.[36] This was the *ulema*'s finest hour. Muhammad Ali had secured their support by promising that he would make no changes in Egypt without consulting them first. Everybody assumed that the status quo had been restored and that, after the upheavals of the previous few years, life could at last return to normal.

But Muhammad Ali had quite different plans. He had fought the French in Egypt and had been hugely impressed by this modern European army; he wanted an up-to-date and super-efficient army of his own, and he was determined to create a modern state in Egypt that was independent of Istanbul. Muhammad Ali had no interest in the intellectual revolution that had taken place in the West. He was an uneducated man of peasant stock who only learned to read in his forties; all he required of books was that they teach him about government and military science. Like many later reformers, Muhammad Ali simply wanted to acquire the technology and military strength of modernity, and he was perfectly prepared to ignore the effect these changes would have on the cultural and spiritual life of the country. Nevertheless, Muhammad Ali was a remarkable man and his achievement was considerable. When he died in 1849, he had almost single-handedly dragged Egypt, a backward, isolated province of the Ottoman empire, into the modern world. His career provides some illuminating insights into the difficulties of bringing Western modernity to a non-Western society.

First, we must remember that the West had come to modernity gradually, under its own steam. It had taken the people of Europe and America nearly three hundred years to acquire the technology and expertise that would bring them world hegemony. But even so, it had been a wrenching, disturbing process that had involved copious bloodshed as well as spiritual dislocation. Now Muhammad Ali was attempting this highly complex transformation in a mere forty years. To achieve his objectives, he found that he had to declare what amounted to war against the people of Egypt. Egypt was in an appalling state. Pillaging and destruction had taken their toll; the *fellahin* had deserted their lands and fled to Syria; taxes were heavy and arbitrary; the Mamluks threatened to make a comeback. How was it possible to turn this wretched country into a strong, centralized state with a modern administration and a modern army? The West was so far ahead. How could Egypt hope to catch up, beat the West at its own game, and prevent further Western invasion and encroachment?

Muhammad Ali started to build his empire by annihilating the Mamluk leaders. In August 1805, he simply enticed their principal officers into Cairo, ambushed them, and killed all but three. The remaining *beys* were massacred by his son Ibrahim during the next two years, while Muhammad Ali dealt with the British, who were alarmed by this surprisingly effective leadership. Finally, he acceded to pressure from the Ottoman sultan and dispatched an expedition against the Wahhabis in Arabia, who were rebelling against Ottoman hegemony. The army would be under the leadership of his son Tassan, who received his solemn investiture in a grand ceremony in Cairo. As the procession wound through the streets of the city, Muhammad Ali's men trapped the last Mamluk chiefs, killed them, and were then allowed to run amok, looting Mamluk houses and raping their women. One thousand Mamluks were massacred that day, and it was the end of the Mamluk caste in Egypt.[37] Yet again, modernization had begun with an act of ethnic cleansing.

It seems that in order to bring a people into the modern world, a leader must be prepared to wade through blood. In the absence of stable, democratic institutions, violence may be the only way to achieve strong government. Muhammad Ali was equally ruthless regarding the economy. He was astute enough to realize that the real basis of Western power lay in scientific methods of production. Over the years 1805 to 1814, he systematically made himself the personal owner of every acre of land in the country. He had already acquired the estates of the Mamluks; next he appropriated the holdings of the tax farmers, who had long been operating a corrupt system. Finally, he took over all the religiously endowed lands and properties *(awqaf)* that had declined over the years, personally undertaking to pay all outstanding obligations to the foundations. Using similarly arbitrary methods, he achieved the monopoly of every trade and industrial enterprise in the country. In just over a decade, he made himself the sole landlord, merchant, and industrialist in Egypt. The Egyptians put up with this because there were huge compensations. After years of chaos and mismanagement, law and order had been imposed on the country; justice was administered fairly, and everybody had the right to complain directly to Muhammad Ali himself. He was clearly not lining his own pockets with the proceeds, but developing Egypt. His greatest achievement was the cultivation of cotton, which became a valuable export and source of revenue, giving the pasha the foreign currency he needed to buy machinery, weapons, and manufactured goods from Europe.[38]

Yet this itself showed his dependence upon the West. The whole modernizing effort in Europe had been fueled by the need for autonomy and punctuated by declarations of independence in various fields—intellectual, economic, religious, and political. But the only way Muhammad Ali could make himself master of Egypt and independent of Europe was by absolute despotic control. He could not succeed unless he was able to build a strong industrial base. Accordingly, he established a sugar refinery, an arsenal, copper mines, cotton mills, iron foundaries, dyeing works, glass factories, and printing works. But industrialization could not be achieved all at once. Europeans had found that to man their various enterprises, more and more of the ordinary people had to acquire the efficiency and specialized skills that were required by the modern processes. But this took time. The *fellahin* who worked in Muhammad Ali's factories had no technical expertise, no experience, and could not adapt to a life away from their fields. They would need education if they were to contribute to the productivity of the country, and that in itself would mean a vast, almost unthinkable social upheaval. Consequently, most of Muhammad Ali's industrial enterprises failed.[39]

The modernizing process was thus very difficult indeed, the problems almost insuperable. In Europe, the watchword had been innovation. But most Egyptians were still dominated by the premodern conservative spirit. The only way that Muhammad Ali could make Egypt a modern state was not by innovation (as in Europe) but by imitation of the West. He was committed to a program of administrative, technological, and educational emulation (in Islamic terms, *taqlid*), which was the obverse of the modern spirit. Without the independence and creativity which had become prized values of the West, how could a state like Egypt be truly "modern"?

But Muhammad Ali had no choice. He introduced a Western-style administration, manned chiefly by European, Turkish, and Levantine officials, who formed a new class in Egyptian society. Promising young men were sent to study in France and England. A military college for 1200 students, who were clothed and maintained at the pasha's expense, was established at Kasserlyne. Two other artillery schools, staffed by Europeans or by Egyptians who had studied abroad, were founded at Toura and Giza. The boys became the pasha's personal property as soon as they entered college, and studied European languages, mathematics, and the Western art of warfare. These colleges provided the country with a well-educated officer class. But there was no primary education for the *fellahin:* they were more useful to Egypt in the fields, providing the country with its agrarian base.[40] This again would have fateful consequnces. In a non-Western, modernizing country such as Egypt, the people who had the greatest contact with European civilization were in the military. The vast majority of the population were perforce excluded from the process. As a result, army officers would often become the natural leaders and rulers, and modernity would acquire a military emphasis that was different—again—from that of the West.

The army was Muhammad Ali's chief concern. He needed it if he was to achieve his objectives, since throughout his career he had to hold his own against the British on the one hand and the Ottoman Turks on the other. The only way the Turks could tolerate Muhammad Ali's creation of a semi-autonomous state was by calling on his superior fighting machine in Ottoman campaigns: against the Wahhabis in Arabia, or to quell the Greek revolt (1825–28). But in 1832, his son Ibrahim Pasha invaded the Ottoman provinces of Syria and Palestine, inflicting crushing defeats on the Turkish army and creating for his father an impressive *imperium in imperio*. The Egyptian army had, of course, been built on the French model. Muhammad Ali had tried to imitate the discipline and efficiency he had observed in Napoleon's army, and he had indeed created a force that was able to cut through a numerically superior army with ease. But this achievement also involved a brutal assault upon his subjects. At first, Muhammad Ali had recruited and trained some 20,000 conscripts from the Sudan, whom he had housed in a vast barracks in Aswan. But the Sudanese simply could not adapt. Many turned their faces to the wall and died, despite the best efforts of the army doctors (trained in Muhammad Ali's medical school in Abou Zabel) to save them. The pasha was thus forced to conscript the *fellahin*, dragging them from their homes, families, and fields. They usually had no time to make adequate arrangements, and their families were often left destitute, the women forced into prostitution. The possibility of conscription to an utterly alien military life filled many of the *fellahin* with such terror that they frequently resorted to self-mutilation, cutting off their own fingers, pulling out teeth, and even blinding themselves.[41] An efficient fighting force was created, but at a terrible human cost. Not only were the *fellahin* themselves damaged by conscription, but agriculture suffered when the men were torn away from the land.

Every positive reform had a downside. Muhammad Ali's economic policies encouraged European trade to penetrate Egypt, but at the expense of local industry. By becoming the sole monopolist in Egypt, the pasha virtually destroyed the indigenous merchant class.[42] He invested a great deal on much-needed irrigation works and water communications, but the working conditions of the laborers in the *corvée* were so bad that 23,000 are said to have died.[43] The old social systems were being brutally dismantled, yet the premodern, conservative lifestyle and beliefs of the vast majority of Egyptians remained unchanged. Two societies—one, consisting only of the military and administrative personnel, modernized, and the other unmodernized—operating on entirely different norms, were gradually emerging in modern Egypt.

The *ulema* certainly experienced the dawn of modernity as destructive. They had been a power in the land when Muhammad Ali became governor. He wooed them, made them promises, and for three years there was a honeymoon period between the pasha and the clergy. In 1809, however, the *ulema* lost their traditional tax-exempt status, and Umar Makram urged them to oppose Muhammad Ali and force him to rescind the new taxes. But the *ulema* had rarely shown a united front, and the pasha was able to lure a significant number into his own camp. Makram was exiled and with him went the last opportunity for the *ulema* to oppose Muhammad Ali. His departure was also a defeat for the *ulema* as a class. As a Muslim, Muhammad Ali was careful to pay lip service to the religious scholars and the *madrasahs*, but he systematically marginalized them, and divested them of any shred of power. He deposed sheikhs who defied him and, as a result, Jabarti says, most *ulema* acquiesced in the new policies. He also starved them financially. By seizing the revenues of the religiously endowed properties *(awqaf)*, he took away the *ulema*'s principal source of income. By 1815 a large number of the traditional Koran schools were in ruins. Sixty years later, the Islamic establishment was in desperate financial straits. There were no stipends for teachers, and mosques could no longer afford to support their prayer leaders, muezzins, Koran reciters, and caretakers. The great Mamluk buildings had deteriorated, and even the Azhar was in a wretched state.[44]

In the face of this onslaught, the *ulema* of Egypt became cowed and reactionary. Their traditional consultative role in the government was taken by the new foreign elite of administrators, most of whom had little respect for local tradition. The *ulema* were left behind in the march for progress, and the pasha left them alone with their books and manuscripts. Since opposition had become impossible, the *ulema* turned their backs on change, entrenching themselves in their scholarly traditions. This would continue to be the chief *ulema* stance in Egypt. They did not regard modernity as an intellectual challenge but experienced it instead as a series of odious and destructive regulations, as theft of their power and wealth, and as an agonizing loss of prestige and influence.[45] When Muslims in Egypt came into contact with the new Western ideas, therefore, they would find no guidance from the clergy, and would look elsewhere for help.

For centuries, there had been a partnership between the *ulema* and the ruling elite in Egypt. Muhammad Ali had severed that relationship and abruptly inaugurated a new secularism. It had no ideological backing but had been imposed as a political fait accompli. In the West, people had had time to adapt to the gradual separation of church and state, and had even created a spirituality of the mundane. For most Egyptians, however, secularization remained alien, foreign, and incomprehensible.

There had been similar modernizing reforms in the Ottoman empire, but in Istanbul there was a greater awareness of the ideas that lay behind the great Western transformation. Ottomans became diplomats in Europe and mixed with European statesmen in the sultan's court. During the 1820s and 1830s, a generation had grown up conversant with the modern world and committed to the reform of the empire. The father of Ahmed Vefik Pasha, who later became the Grand Vizier, had worked in the Turkish embassy in Paris; Ahmed himself read Gibbon, Hume, Adam Smith, Shakespeare, and Dickens. Mustafa Resid Pasha had also been trained in Paris and studied politics and literature there. He became convinced that the Ottoman empire could not survive in the modern world unless it became a centralized state, with a modern army and a new legal and administrative system, which recognized the equality of all citizens. Christians and Jews must no longer be *dhimmis* ("protected minorities"), but must enjoy the same status as Muslim citizens. The prevalence of these European ideas made it easier for Sultan Mahmud II to inaugurate the Tanzimat ("regulations") in 1826. These abolished the Janissaries, began the modernization of the army, and introduced technical innovations. At first, the sultan thought that this would be enough to halt the accelerating decline of the empire, but the relentless advance of the European powers and their economic and political penetration of Islamic territories gradually made it clear that more fundamental changes were essential.[46]

In 1839, Sultan Abdulhamid, at the instigation of Resid Pasha, issued the Gülhane decree, which ostensibly left Islamic law intact, but made the absolute monarchy of the sultan dependent upon a contractual relationship with his subjects. It looked forward to a fundamental change in the empire's institutions, which must be run more systematically and efficiently. Over the next three decades, central and local government was reorganized, and criminal and commercial codes and courts were established. In 1856, the Hatti Humayun decree granted full citizenship to religious minorities. But this inevitably led to conflict with the *ulema,* who saw these innovations as undermining the Shariah.[47] Those who were committed to reform, therefore, increasingly had to wrestle with the question: how could Muslims become part of the modern world without jettisoning their Islamic heritage? Just as Christianity had changed and was changing under the impact of modernization and enlightened thought, so would Islam in the coming decades.

The question demanded urgent solution, because, as each year passed, the weakness of the Muslim world *vis-à-vis* the West was becoming painfully apparent. Muhammad Ali was able to withstand the sultan, but in 1840 he was forced by the European powers to relinquish his new territories in Syria, Arabia, and Greece. It was a bitter blow, from which he never fully recovered. His grandson Abbas (1813–54), who succeeded him as pasha of Egypt in 1849, hated Europe and all things Western. He was a soldier and, unlike the Ottoman reformers, had not had a liberal education. For him, the West meant exploitation and humiliation: he loathed the privileges European administrators and businessmen had won for themselves in Egypt and deeply resented the way Europeans had urged his grandfather to take on impossible projects, for their own financial advantage. He abolished Muhammad Ali's fleet, reduced the army, and closed the new schools. Abbas was, however, also unpopular with the Egyptians and was assassinated in 1854. He was succeeded by Muhammad Said Pasha (1822–63), the fourth son of Muhammad Ali, who was the complete opposite of Abbas. A Francophile, he adopted a Western lifestyle, relished the company of foreigners, and revived the army. But by the end of his reign, even Said had become disillusioned by the sharp practices and dubious schemes of some European companies and entrepreneurs.

The most spectacular of these European projects was the building of the Suez Canal. Muhammad Ali had consistently opposed any plan to link the Red Sea with the Mediterranean, fearing that it would bring Egypt once more to the attention of the European powers and lead to a new phase of Western invasion and dominance. Said Pasha was fascinated by the idea, however, and only too ready to grant a concession to his old friend the French consul, Ferdinand de Lesseps (1805–94), who convinced him that the Canal would enable Egypt to stand up to England and would cost Egypt nothing, since it would be built with French money. Said was naive; the concession, which was signed on November 30, 1854, was disastrous for Egypt. It was opposed by the sultan and by Lord Palmerston of England, but de Lesseps pushed on, formed his own company, and offered shares to the United States, Britain, Russia, Austria, and the Ottoman empire. When these were not taken up, the pasha guaranteed them, on top of his own investment in the project. Work began in April 1859.

In the event, Egypt provided almost all the money, labor, and materials in addition to donating two hundred square miles of Egyptian territory gratis. In 1863, Said died and was succeeded by his nephew, Ismail (1830–95), who was also in favor of the Canal, but submitted the concession to the arbitration of Emperor Napoleon III of France in the hope of getting a better deal for Egypt. In 1864, the company's right to free Egyptian labor was withdrawn, and some of the territory was returned, but in compensation the company was to receive an indemnity of 84 million francs (over three million pounds) from the Egyptian government. Ismail had no option but to accept, and work resumed on the Canal. The grand opening was a glittering occasion. Visitors were offered a free passage to Egypt and free accommodation; Verdi's opera *Aïda* was commissioned for the new Cairo opera house. A special road was built to take visitors to the Pyramids.[48] The object of this expensive outlay was to convince the international community of Egypt's prosperity and to invite more investment. In fact, however, Egypt was on the verge of bankruptcy.

The Canal certainly helped to ruin the fragile Egyptian economy, but it was not wholly responsible. Yet again, the career of Ismail shows the immense cost of modernization in a non-Western country. Ismail wanted independence; his aim was to liberate Egypt from Ottoman suzerainty. He had the modern vision of autonomy, but all he achieved was a crippling dependency and, eventually, occupation by a European power. Muhammad Ali had been a soldier who tried to fight his way to freedom. Ismail tried to buy his liberty. On June 8, 1867, he bought from the sultan the right to the Persian title *khedive* ("great prince") to distinguish him from the other Ottoman pashas. For this privilege, he paid an extra £350,000 in annual tribute to Istanbul.[49] He also had to deal with the expenses of the Canal, cope with the sudden slump in cotton prices, which had soared during the American Civil War, and fund his own ambitious modernizing projects. These included the building of 900 miles of railways, 430 bridges, and 112 canals, which irrigated some 1,373,000 acres of hitherto uncultivable land.[50] Under the khedive, Egypt advanced more rapidly than under any previous ruler: he also had plans for the education of both sexes, scientific research, and geographical explorations. Cairo became a modern city, with inspiring new buildings, wide boulevards, and pleasure gardens. Unfortunately, Ismail could not pay for any of this. To acquire money, he introduced a system of easy credit and borrowed vast sums, of which a considerable amount vanished into the pockets of European brokers, bankers, and entrepreneurs, who egged him on to further expenditure. The khedive became prey to moneylenders and when Ottoman securities slumped on the London Stock Exchange in October 1875, taking Egyptian securities with them, it was the last straw.

The Suez Canal had given Egypt a wholly new strategic importance, and the European powers could not allow its total ruin. To safeguard their interests, Britain and France imposed financial controls on the khedive, controls which threatened to become political. Muhammad Ali had been correct in his fear that the Canal would jeopardize Egyptian independence. European ministers were appointed to the Egyptian government to supervise its financial dealings, and when Ismail dismissed them in April 1879, the chief powers of Europe—Britain, France, Germany, and Austria—united against him, and put pressure on the sultan to dismiss the khedive. Ismail was succeeded by his son Tewfiq (1852–92), a well-meaning young man, but it was obvious that he was a mere puppet of the powers. Hence he was unpopular with both the people and the army. When the Egyptian officer Ahmad bey Urubi (1840–1911) staged a revolution in 1881, demanding that Egyptians be appointed to more senior posts in the army and government, and managed to gain administrative control of the country, Britain stepped in and established a military occupation. Ismail had dreamed of making Egypt part of Europe; he managed only to make it a virtual European colony.

Muhammad Ali had been cruel and utterly ruthless; his successors were naive, greedy, and shortsighted. But, in fairness, they were pitting themselves against insuperable odds. First, the type of civilization they were attempting to emulate was something entirely new. It was not surprising that these men, with their very limited experience of Europe, were slow to grasp that a few military and technological reforms would not suffice to make them a "modern" nation. The whole of society would have to be reorganized, an independent industrial economy set on a sure footing, and the traditional conservative spirit replaced by a new mentality. Failure would be expensive, because Europe was by this time too powerful. The powers could force Egypt to finance the building of the Suez Canal and yet deny it ownership of a single share. The so-called "Eastern Crisis" (1875–78) had already shown that one of the great powers of Europe (Russia) could penetrate to the heart of Ottoman territory and be checked only by a threat from other European countries, not by the Turks themselves. Even the great Ottoman empire, the last stronghold of Muslim power, no longer controlled its own provinces. This became painfully apparent in 1881 when France occupied Tunis, and in 1882 when Britain occupied Egypt. Europe was invading the Islamic world and beginning to dismantle the empire.

Further, even without the disastrous mistakes of the Egyptian rulers, these weaker Islamic countries could not become "modern" in the same way as the Europeans or the Americans, because the modernizing process in these non-Western lands was fundamentally different. In 1843, the French writer Gérard de Nerval visited Cairo and noted ironically that French bourgeois values were being imposed on the Islamic city. Muhammad Ali's new palaces were built like barracks and furnished with mahogany armchairs and oil portraits of the pasha's sons in their new army uniforms. The exotic, oriental Cairo of Nerval's imagination

> lies under dust and ashes; the modern spirit and its exigencies have triumphed over it like death. In ten years' time, European streets will have cut the dusty and drab old town at right angles. . . . What glitters and expands is the quarter of the Franks, the town of the English, the Maltese and the Marseilles French.[51]

The buildings of the new Cairo, built by Muhammad Ali and Ismail, represented an architecture of domination. This would become even more obvious during the British occupation, as the embassies, banks, villas, and monuments built in parts of Cairo expressed European investment in this Middle Eastern country, exhibiting a jumble of styles, periods, and functions that would have been deemed incoherent in Europe. For, as the British anthropologist Michael Gilsenan points out, Cairo "was *not* passing through the same stages of a unilinear sequence of development that Europe had already passed through on the way to capitalism." It was not becoming an industrial center, not moving purposefully from tradition to modernity, or acquiring a new urban coherence:

> Rather, it was being made into a dependent local metropolis through which a society might be administered and dominated. The spatial forms grew out of a relationship based on force and a world economic order in which in this case Britain played the crucial role.[52]

The whole experience of modernization was crucially different in the Middle East: it was not one of empowerment, autonomy, and innovation, as it had been in Europe, but a process of deprivation, dependence, and patchy, imperfect imitation.

For the vast majority of the people, who were not involved in the process, it was also an experience of alienation. A "modern" city, such as Muhammad Ali's Cairo, was built on entirely different principles from those that gave meaning to the indigenous towns of Egypt. As Gilsenan points out, tourists, colonialists, and travelers have often found Oriental cities confusing and even frightening: the unnamed and unnumbered streets and twisting passages seem to have no order or orientation; Westerners get lost and can make no sense of their surroundings. For most of the colonized peoples of the Middle East and North Africa, the new Westernized cities were equally incomprehensible, and bore no relation to *their* instinctive sense of what a city should be. They frequently felt lost in their own country. Many of these superimposed Westernized cities surrounded the "old town," which, in comparison, looked dark, threatening, and outside the rationally ordered modern world.[53] Egyptians were thus forced to live in a dual world: one modern and Western, the other traditional. This dualism would lead to a grave crisis of identity, and, as in other experiences of modernization, to some surprising religious solutions.

Iran had not yet embarked on the modernizing process, even though the arrival of Napoleon in the Middle East had begun an era of European domination in this country too. Napoleon had intended to invade British India, with the help of the Emperor of Russia; this gave Iran a wholly new strategic importance in the eyes of the European powers. In 1801, Britain signed a treaty with the second Qajar shah, Fath Ali (1798–1834), promising British military equipment and technology in return for Iranian support. Iran had also become a pawn in the power games of Europe, which continued long after Napoleon's downfall. Britain wanted to control the Persian Gulf and the southeast regions of Iran in order to safeguard India, while Russia tried to establish a base in the north. Neither wanted to make Iran a colony, and both worked to preserve Iranian independence, but, in practice, the shahs did not dare to risk offending either power, without the support of one of them. The Europeans presented themselves to the Iranians as the bearers of progress and civilization, but in fact both Britain and Russia promoted only those developments that furthered their own interests, and both blocked the introduction of such innovations as the railway, which could have benefited the Iranian people, lest it endanger their own strategic plans.[54]

In the early nineteenth century, Crown Prince Abbas, governor-general of Azerbaijan, had seen the need for a modern army, and sent young men to study in Europe in order to acquire the requisite expertise. But he died in 1833 before ascending the throne. Thereafter the Qajar shahs made only sporadic attempts to modernize. The shahs were weak and so overshadowed by Britain and Russia that they felt no need for an army of their own: the Europeans would always protect them in an emergency. The sense of urgency that had impelled Muhammad Ali was missing. But it is also fair to say that modernization would be much harder to achieve in Iran than in Egypt. The vast distances and difficult terrain of Iran, as well as the autonomous power of the nomadic tribes in the region, would make centralization well-nigh impossible without sophisticated twentieth-century technology.[55]

Iran could almost be said to have the worst of all worlds. There was debilitating dependence, but none of the advantages of serious investment and colonization. During the first half of the nineteenth century, Russia and Britain established in Iran the "capitulations" which had also undermined the sovereignty of the Ottoman sultans. The capitulations gave special privileges to Russian and British merchants on Iranian soil, exempted them from the law of the land, and fixed tariff concessions for their goods. This was deeply resented. It enabled the Europeans to penetrate Iranian territory, and the consular courts which tried their offenses were often so lenient that a serious crime could go virtually unpunished. The capitulations were also detrimental to local industry, as low-priced Western manufactured goods displaced Iranian crafts. Some goods did benefit from Western trade: cotton, opium, and carpets were exported to Europe. But the silk industry was destroyed when one European firm imported diseased silk worms; the international price of silver, which made up Iranian currency, fell dramatically; and during the 1850s, European economic influence intensified in Iran, as the powers began to demand concessions for particular activities. To improve communications between England and India during the late 1850s, the British got the concessions for all telegraph lines in Iran. In 1847, the British subject Baron Julius de Reuter (1816–99) gained exclusive rights to railway and streetcar construction in Iran, all mineral extraction, all new irrigation works, a national bank, and various industrial projects. This concession had been promoted by Prime Minister Mirza Hosain Khan, who was in favor of reform but probably thought that the shahs were so incompetent that it was better to allow the British to modernize the country. He had miscalculated; a group of concerned officials and *ulema,* led by the shah's wife, protested vociferously against the Reuter concession and Mirza Khan was forced to resign. Nevertheless, by the end of the nineteenth century, both Britain and Russia had won heavy economic concessions in Iran which, in some areas, amounted to political control. Merchants who could see the benefits of modernization, but understandably feared this growth of foreign influence, began to campaign against the regime.[56]

They were supported by the *ulema,* who were in a far stronger position than the *ulema* of Egypt. The Usuli victory at the end of the eighteenth century had given the *mujtahids* a powerful weapon, since, in principle, even the shah was bound by their rulings. They were not cowed and marginalized by the Qajars, who needed their support. The *ulema* had a secure financial base and were centered in the holy cities of Najaf and Kerbala in Ottoman Iraq, beyond the reach of the Qajars. In Iran, the royal capital of Tehran was quite distinct from the Shii shrine city of Qum. There was thus an effective separation of religion and politics. Unlike Muhammad Ali, the Qajar shahs had no modern army and no central bureaucracy capable of enforcing their will on the *ulema* in such matters as education, law, and the administration of religiously endowed land and properties *(awqaf)*, which remained the preserve of the *ulema*. In the early years of the nineteenth century, however, the clergy, faithful to Shii tradition, kept out of politics. When Sheikh Murtada Ansari became in effect the first *mujtahid* to be recognized as the sole and supreme "model for emulation" *(marja-e taqlid)*, the deputy-in-chief of the Hidden Imam, he was preferred to another, more learned candidate who had on his own admission become "involved with the affairs of the people," acting as a legal adviser in commercial and personal matters to the merchants and pilgrims to the shrines. The implication was that the supreme judge of the faithful should be a scholar, not a man of affairs.[57]

But as the Europeans gained more commercial power in Iran, the merchants and artisans turned increasingly for advice to the *ulema*. The clergy and the merchants and artisans of the bazaar, popularly known as the *bazaaris*, were natural allies; they frequently came from the same families, and shared the same religious ideals. During the second half of the nineteenth century, the *ulema* gave the merchants intellectual backing for their objections to foreign penetration: Iran, they argued, would no longer be an Islamic country if the shahs continued to give so much power to the infidels.

The shahs tried to counter these objections by appealing to the popular religion of the masses, especially by associating themselves with the mourning ceremonies for Husain. They had their own *rawda-khans*, who recited the epic accounts of the Kerbala tragedy every day; they built a royal stage in Tehran for the performance of the annual passion play *(taziyeh)* commemorating Husain's death, which took place on five consecutive nights during the sacred month of Muharram in the great court of the royal palace. The battle between Husain and Yazid was enacted, the deaths of the Imam and his sons depicted, and, on the night of the fast-day of Ashura, the anniversary of the Kerbala disaster, there was a grand procession, in which effigies of the martyrs (complete with lifesize representations of their shrines and whole choirs of children) were carried through the streets, while the common people followed, beating their breasts. Throughout Muharram, all the mosques were festooned in black drapery, and in the public squares, booths were erected for the *rawda-khans*, who chanted the dirge mournfully and loudly. By this date, there were a number of celebrated *rawda-khans* in the country who competed with one another for preeminence.

These mourning rites became a major Iranian institution under the Qajars. Besides linking the monarchy with Husain and Kerbala, and thus helping to legitimate Qajar rule, they also served as a safety valve, giving the masses an outlet for their frustration and discontent. The people were not passive spectators; throughout the recitations and performances, they made their presence felt. As a French visitor noted, "the whole auditory responds to them with tears and deep sighs."[58] Throughout the battle scenes, the spectators sobbed and wept, striking their breasts with tears streaming down their cheeks. While the actors expressed their horror and sorrow through the text, it was—and remains—the task of the audience to provide the explicit and violent expressions of grief, completing an essential part of the drama. They were at one and the same time symbolically on the plains of Kerbala and in their own world, weeping for their own tragedies and pain. To this day, the American scholar William Beeman explains, the audience are taught to weep for their sins and their own troubles, and to remind themselves of Husain's even greater suffering.[59] They could thus identify with the Kerbala story, bringing it, by means of these dramatic rituals, into the present, and thus giving the historical tragedy the timeless quality of myth. The flagellants represented the people of Kufa who had abandoned Husain and, therefore, chastised themselves, but they also stood for all Muslims who failed to help the Imams create a just society. Shiis weep for Husain and give him a symbolic funeral, because he did not get one in real life and his ideals were never implemented. To this day, Iranians say that during Muharram, they also recall the sufferings of their friends and relatives. But these personal memories lead them to an emotional apprehension of the problem of evil: *why* do the good suffer and the wicked seem to prevail? As they moan, slap their foreheads, and weep uncontrollably, the participants arouse in themselves that yearning for justice which is at the heart of Shii piety.[60] The dirges and passion plays remind them each year of the persistent evil in the world and reaffirm their belief in the final triumph of goodness.

This popular faith was clearly very different from the legalistic, rationalistic Shiism of the *mujtahids*. It also had an obvious revolutionary potential. It could—and would—be easily used to point to evils in society and to a perceived likeness between the current ruler and Yazid. During the Qajar period, as under the Safavids, however, this rebellious motif was restrained and the emphasis was still on the suffering of Husain, which was seen as a vicarious sacrifice for the sins of the people. During the nineteenth century, it was not through the *taziyeh* that the people rebelled; instead, many expressed their discontent in two popular messianic movements.

The first of these was led by Hajj Muhammad Karim Khan Kirmani (1810–71), a Qajar prince and a cousin and stepson of Fath Ali Shah, whose father was the governor of the turbulent province of Kirman. There, Karim Khan became involved with the Shaikhi sect, a radical mystical movement founded by Shaykh Ahmad al-Ahsai (1753–1826) of Kerbala. He had been deeply influenced by the mysticism of Mulla Sadra and the School of Isfahan, which the Usuli mullahs had tried to suppress. Ahsai and his disciple, Sayyid Kazim Rashti (1759–1843), taught that each of the prophets and imams had perfectly reflected the divine will; their lives and example were gradually drawing the whole of humanity toward a state of perfection. The Hidden Imam was not in hiding in this world; he had been translated to the world of pure archetypes *(alam al-mithal)*, whence, through his earthly representatives, who knew how to penetrate this mystical realm, he continued to guide human beings to the point when they would no longer need the laws of the Shariah; they would internalize God's will and apprehend it directly, instead of following a set of external rules. This, of course, was anathema to the *mujtahids*. Ahsai taught that there always existed in the world a "Perfect Shiah," a group of rare, infallible human beings who were able to get in touch with the Hidden Imam through the intuitive disciplines of contemplation. The implication was that the faith of the *mujtahids* was incomplete, legalistic, and literalistic. It was certainly inferior to the mystical insights of Ahsai and his disciples.[61]

The Shaykhi school, as it was called, was very popular in Iraq and Azerbaijan, but it remained a philosophy, an idea rather than a concrete political program. It was Karim Khan, who became the Shaykhi leader after the death of Rashti, who turned it into a rebellion against the *mujtahids*. He publicly denounced their narrow legalism, their unimaginative literalism, and their lack of interest in new ideas. Muslims must not imagine that their sole duty was *taqlid*, the emulation of a jurist. Anybody was capable of interpreting the scriptures. The *mujtahids* were simply doling out old truths, when the world needed something entirely new. Humanity was constantly changing and evolving, so that each prophet superseded the last. In each generation, the Perfect Shiah unveiled more and more of the esoteric meaning of the Koran and the Shariah, drawing out their hidden depths in an ongoing revelation. The faithful must listen to these mystical teachers, who were appointed by the Imam and whose power had been usurped by the *mujtahids*.

Karim Khan was convinced that this progressive revelation was about to be completed. Human nature would shortly achieve perfection. He was clearly responding to the changes that the Europeans were bringing to Iran. Karim Khan was no democrat; like all premodern philosophers, he was an elitist and an absolutist; impatient with the differences of opinion among the *mujtahids,* he intended to impose his own vision on the people. Nevertheless, he was one of the first Iranian clerics to acquaint himself with the new ideas of Europe. Where the orthodox *ulema* simply opposed the commercial encroachments of the British and Russians, Karim Khan was prescient enough to be more concerned about the new science and secularism of the West. In his spare time, he studied astronomy, optics, chemistry, and linguistics, and prided himself on his knowledge of science. During the 1850s and 1860s, when very few Iranians had firsthand knowledge of Europe, Karim Khan already realized that Western culture posed a grave threat to Iranian civilization. This was a period of transition, and he could see that new solutions must be found to meet this unprecedented challenge. Hence his evolutionary theology, which allowed for the possibility of something fresh, and his intuitive expectation of imminent, radical change.

The Shaykhi movement was, however, rooted in the old world, with its elitist vision of knowledge. Feeling the impact of the industrialized West, it was also defensive. Karim Khan was bitterly opposed to the new Dar al-Funun, the first free high school in Tehran, founded by the reforming minister Amir Kabir. Staffed mainly by Europeans, it taught, with the aid of interpreters, natural science, higher mathematics, foreign languages, and the art of modern warfare. Karim Khan saw the school as part of a plot to extend European influence and destroy Islam. Soon the *ulema* would be silenced, he argued, Muslim children would be educated in Christian schools, and Iranians would become fake Europeans. He could see the dangers of alienation and anomie that lay ahead, and in the face of increasing European encroachment, his stance was rejectionist and separatist. His mystical ideology can be seen as an attempt to open the minds of Iranians to a wholly new solution, but, for better or worse, the Western presence in Iran was a fact of life and no reform movement that was unable to accommodate it could succeed. There were rumors that Karim Khan was about to establish his own religious government; he was summoned to court and kept under surveillance for eighteen months. During the 1850s and 1860s, he gradually retired from public life, kept his opinions to himself, and died, defeated and embittered, on his estate.[62]

The second messianic movement of the period was also rooted in the conservative spirit, but it was also open to some of the new Western values. Its founder, Sayyid Ali Muhammad (1819–50), had been involved in the Shaykhi movement in Najaf and Kerbala, but in 1844 he declared that he was the "gate" *(bab)* to the divine which the *ulema* declared to have been closed at the time of the Occultation of the Hidden Imam.[63] He attracted *ulema,* notables, and wealthy merchants in Isfahan, Tehran, and Khurasan into his movement. In Kerbala, his brilliant woman disciple Qurrat al-Ain

(1814–52) drew huge crowds; his chief male disciples, Mulla Sadiq (known as Muqaddas) and Mirza Muhammad Ali Barfurushi, who was given the title of Quddus (d. 1849), preached what was virtually a new religion: the Bab's name was now mentioned in the call to prayer, and worshippers were instructed to pray facing the direction of his house in Shiraz. When the Bab made the *hajj* pilgrimage to Mecca that year, he stood beside the Kabah and declared that he was the incarnation of the Hidden Imam. Fifteen months later, like Joseph Smith, the Bab produced a newly inspired scripture, the Bayan. All the old holy books had been abrogated. He was the Perfect Man of the age, embodying in his person all the great prophets of the past. Humanity was now approaching perfection and the old faiths would no longer suffice. Like the Book of Mormon, the Bayan called for a new and more just social order, and endorsed the bourgeois values of modernity: it placed a high value on productive work, called for free trade, the reduction of taxes, guarantees for personal property, and an improvement in the position of women. Above all, the Bab had imbibed the nineteenth-century belief that this was the only world we had. Shiis had traditionally focused on tragedies of the past and on the messianic future. The Bab concentrated on the here-and-now. There would be no Last Judgment, no afterlife. Paradise would be found in this world. Instead of waiting passively for redemption, the Bab told the Shiis of Iran, they must work for a better society on earth and seek to achieve salvation in their own lives.[64]

There are many aspects of the Babi movement that recall the career of Shabbetai Zevi. The Bab aroused the same kind of fascination as Shabbetai. When he was imprisoned by the authorities, his transfer from one place of detention to another became a triumphal progress, as huge crowds turned out to meet him. His prisons became places of pilgrimage. While he sat in jail, writing virulent letters to Muhammad Shah, the Qajar "usurper," he was allowed to receive large gatherings of his disciples. Even after the authorities moved him to the remote fortress of Chihrig, outside Urumiyya, there was not enough room in the hall to receive all his visitors, and crowds of people were forced to stand outside in the street. When he visited the public baths, his devotees bought his bathwater. There was huge excitement when he was finally brought to trial in Tabriz in the summer of 1848. Hordes of people thronged to greet him, so that he entered the courtroom in triumph. A mass of supporters stood outside during the trial, expecting the Bab to demolish his enemies and inaugurate a new age of justice, productivity, and peace. But, as with Shabbetai, there ensued a shocking anticlimax. The Bab did not overcome his interrogators. In fact, he appears to have performed very badly.[65] His examiners revealed his deficiency in Arabic, theology, and Falsafah; he had no understanding of the new sciences. How could this man be the Imam, the repository of divine knowledge *(ilm)*? The court sent the Bab back to prison, gravely underestimating the threat he posed to the regime, for by this time, the Babi movement was no longer simply a call for moral and religious reform; it had become a demand for a new socio-political order.

Just as Shabbateanism had appealed to all social classes, the Bab was able to attract the masses with his messianism, the philosophically or esoterically inclined with his mystical theology, and the more secularly minded revolutionaries with his social doctrines. As in the earlier Jewish movement, there was an intuitive sense that the old world was passing away and that traditional sanctities would no longer apply. In June 1848, the Babi leaders held a mass meeting in Budasht, Khurasan. The Koran was formally abrogated, and the Shariah was to remain in place only until the Bab was acknowledged by the world. For the time being, the faithful must follow their own consciences and learn to distinguish good from evil by themselves, instead of relying on the *ulema*. They must feel free to reject the laws of the Shariah if they chose. The charismatic woman preacher Qurrat al-Ain removed her veil as a symbol of the end of female subjection and the end of the old Muslim era. All "impure" objects were henceforth to be regarded as "pure." Truth was not a doctrine revealed all at once, in one moment of time. God's decrees were gradually revealed to the masses through the elect. Like Shabbetai himself, the Babis reached toward a new religious pluralism: in the new order, all previously revealed religions would unite as one.[66]

Many of the Babis who attended the meeting at Budasht were appalled by this radical message, and fled in horror. Other devout Muslims attacked the heretics, and the meeting ended in disorder. But the leaders' work had only just begun. They traveled separately back to Mazanderan, where the Babi leader Mullah Husain Bushrui (d. 1849) gathered two hundred men. He delivered a fiery speech: Babis must sacrifice their worldly possessions and take Imam Husain as their model. Only by martyrdom could they inaugurate the New Day, when the Bab would exalt the downtrodden and enrich the poor. Within a year, the Bab would conquer the world and unify all the religions. Bushrui proved to be a brilliant commander; his little army put the royal troops to flight, so that, we read in the court annals, they ran away "like a herd of sheep escaping from wolves." The Babis raided, looted, plundered, killed, and burned. The religiously inclined believed that their uprising was more important than the Battle of Kerbala, while the poor, who may have joined the movement for more mundane reasons, were the best partisans of all. For the first time, they felt that they counted, and were treated, if not as equals, as valued co-workers.

That revolt was eventually put down by the government, but 1850 saw new uprisings in Yazd, Nairiz, Tehran, and Zanjan. The Babis created an atmosphere of utter terror. Political dissidents joined the revolt, as did local students. Even women, clad in men's clothes, fought valiantly. The movement united all those who were dissatisfied with the regime. Mullahs who felt oppressed by the lofty *mujtahids*, merchants who resented the sale of Iranian resources to foreigners, *bazaaris*, landowners, and impoverished peasants all joined forces with the Babi religious enthusiasts. Shiism had long helped Iranians to cultivate a yearning for social justice, and when the right leader and the right philosophy came along, all kinds of malcontents found it natural to fight under a religious banner.[67]

This time the government was able to quell the insurgents. The Bab was executed on July 9, 1850, the leaders were also put to death, and other suspects rounded up and massacred. Some Babis fled to Ottoman Iraq, and there the movement split in 1863. Some, following Mirza Yahya Nuri Subh-i Azal (1830–1912), the appointed successor of the Bab, remained faithful to the political aims of the rebellion. Later many of these "Azalis" abandoned the old Babi mysticism and became secularists and nationalists. As in the Shabbatean movement, the casting off of taboos, the discarding of old laws, and the taste of rebellion enabled them to break free of religion altogether. Yet again, a messianic movement provided a bridge to a secularist ideology. Most of the surviving Babis, however, followed Subh-i Azal's brother, Mirza Husain Ali Nuri Bahaullah (1817–92), who abjured politics and created the new Bahai religion, which embraced the modern Western ideals of the separation of religion and politics, equal rights, pluralism, and toleration.[68]

The Babi rebellion can be seen as one of the great revolutions of modernity. It set a pattern in Iran. There would be other occasions in the twentieth century when clerics and laymen, secularists and mystics, believers and atheists, would challenge an oppressive Iranian regime together. The battle for justice, which had become a sacred value for Shiis, would encourage later generations of Iranians to brave the armies of the shah to inaugurate a better order. On at least two occasions, a Shii ideology would enable Iranians to establish modern political institutions in their country. Yet again, the Babi revolution had shown that religion could help people to appropriate the ideals and enthusiasms of modernity, by translating them from an alien secular idiom into a language, mythology, and spirituality that they could understand and make their own. If modernity had proved difficult for the Christians of the West, it was even more problematic for Jews and Muslims. It required a struggle—in Islamic terms, a *jihad*, which might sometimes become a holy war.

PART TWO

Fundamentalism

5. Battle Lines
(1870–1900)

BY THE END of the nineteenth century, it was clear that the new society which had finally come to fruition in the West was not quite the universal panacea that some had imagined. The dynamic optimism that had inspired Hegel's philosophy had given way to perplexing doubt and malaise. On the one hand, Europe was going from strength to strength; there was confidence and an exultant sense of mastery as the industrial revolution brought some of the nation-states more wealth and power than they had ever achieved before. But just as characteristic were the isolation, *ennui,* and melancholy explored by Charles Baudelaire in *Les Fleurs du Mal* (1857), the sickening doubt articulated by Alfred Tennyson in *In Memoriam* (1850), and the destructive lassitude and discontent of Flaubert's eponymous heroine in *Madame Bovary* (1856). People felt obscurely afraid. Henceforth, at the same time as they celebrated the achievements of modern society, men and women would also experience an emptiness, a void, that rendered life meaningless; many would crave certainty amid the perplexities of modernity; some would project their fears onto imaginary enemies and dream of universal conspiracy.

We shall find all these elements in the fundamentalist movements that developed in all three of the monotheistic faiths alongside modern culture. Human beings find it almost impossible to live without a sense that, despite the distressing evidence to the contrary, life has ultimate meaning and value. In the old world, mythology and ritual had helped people to evoke a sense of sacred significance that saved them from the void, in rather the same way as did great works of art. But scientific rationalism, the source of Western power and success, had discredited myth and declared that it alone could lead to truth. Yet reason could not address the ultimate questions; that had never been within the competence of *logos.* As a result, traditional faith was no longer possible for a growing number of Western men and women.

The Austrian psychologist Sigmund Freud (1856–1939) would discover that human beings were as strongly motivated by a death wish as by a desire for *eros* and procreation. Increasingly, an apparently perverse yearning for (and terror of) extinction would surface in modern culture. People were beginning to recoil from the civilization they had created, at the same time as they enjoyed the undoubted benefits it conferred. Thanks to modern science, most people in the West lived healthier, longer lives; their democratic institutions meant that, for the most part, life was more equitable. Americans and Europeans were rightly proud of their achievements. But the dream of universal brotherhood that had sustained Enlightenment thinkers was proving to be a chimera. The Franco-Prussian War (1870–71) had revealed the hideous effects of modern weaponry, and there was a dawning realization that science might also have a malignant dimension. There was a sense of anticlimax.[1] During the revolutionary period in the early years of the nineteenth century, a new and better world had seemed finally within the grasp of humanity. But this hope was never fulfilled. Instead, the industrial revolution brought new problems and fresh injustice and exploitation. In *Hard Times* (1854), Charles Dickens presented the industrialized city as an inferno, and showed that modern pragmatic rationalism could be destructive of morality and individuality. The new megacities inspired immense ambivalence. The Romantic poets who denounced the "dark satanic mills"[2] were in flight from urban life, as much as they were inspired by a positive longing for the unspoiled countryside. The British critic George Steiner notes the curious school of painting that developed during the 1830s, which could be seen as a "counter-dream of modernity." The modern cities—London, Paris, and Berlin—which symbolized the great Western achievement, were depicted in ruins, smashed by some unimaginable catastrophe.[3] People were beginning to fantasize about the destruction of civilization and to take practical steps to bring this about.

After the Franco-Prussian War, the nations of Europe began a frantic arms race which led them inexorably to the First World War. They appeared to see war as a Darwinian necessity in which only the fittest would survive. A modern nation must have the biggest army and the most murderous weapons that science could provide, and Europeans dreamed of a war that would purify the nation's soul in a harrowing apotheosis. The British writer I. F. Clarke has shown that between 1871 and 1914 it was unusual to find a single year in which a novel or short story describing a horrific future war did not appear in some European country.[4] The "Next Great War" was imagined as a terrible but inevitable ordeal: out of the destruction, the nation would arise to a new and enhanced life. At the very end of the nineteenth century, however, British novelist H. G. Wells punctured this utopian dream in *The War of the Worlds* (1898) and showed where it was leading. There were terrifying images of London depopulated by biological warfare, and the roads of England crowded with refugees. He could see the dangers of a military technology that had been drawn into the field of the exact sciences. He was right. The arms race led to the Somme and when the Great War broke out in 1914, the people of Europe, who had been dreaming of the war to end all wars for over forty years, entered with enthusiasm upon this conflict, which could be seen as the collective suicide of Europe. Despite the achievements of modernity, there was a nihilistic death wish, as the nations of Europe cultivated a perverse fantasy of self-destruction.

In America, some of the more conservative Protestants were in the grip of a similar vision, but their nightmare scenario took a religious form. The United States had also suffered a terrible conflict and an ensuing anticlimax. Americans had seen the Civil War (1861–65) between the northern and southern states in apocalyptic terms. Northerners believed that the conflict would purge the nation; soldiers sang of the "glory of the coming of the Lord."[5] Preachers spoke of an approaching Armageddon, of a battle between light and darkness, liberty and slavery. They looked forward to a New Man and a New Dispensation emerging, phoenix-like, from this fiery trial.[6] But there was no brave new world in America either. Instead, by the end of the war, whole cities had been destroyed, families had been torn asunder, and there was a white southern backlash. Instead of utopia, the northern states experienced the rapid and painful transition from an agrarian to an industrialized society. New cities were built, old cities exploded in size. Hordes of new immigrants poured into the country from southern and eastern Europe. Capitalists made vast fortunes from the iron, oil, and steel industries, while workers lived below subsistence level. Women and children were exploited in the factories: by 1890, one out of every five children had a job. Conditions were poor, the hours long, and the machinery unsafe. There was also a new gulf between town and countryside, as large parts of the United States, especially the South, remained agrarian. If a void lay beneath the prosperity of Europe, America was becoming a country without a core.[7]

The secular genre of the "future war" which so entranced the people of Europe, did not attract the more religious Americans. Instead, some developed a more consuming interest than ever before in eschatology, dreaming of a Final War between God and Satan, which would bring this evil society to a richly deserved end. The new apocalyptic vision that took root in America during the late nineteenth century is called *pre*millennialism, because it envisaged Christ returning to earth *before* he established his thousand-year

reign. (The older and more optimistic *post*millennialism of the Enlightenment, which was still cultivated by liberal Protestants, imagined human
beings inaugurating God's Kingdom by their own efforts: Christ would
only return to earth *after* the millennium was established.) The new premillennialism was preached in America by the Englishman John Nelson
Darby (1800–82), who found few followers in Britain but toured the
United States to great acclaim six times between 1859 and 1877. His vision
could see nothing good in the modern world, which was hurtling toward
destruction. Instead of becoming more virtuous, as the Enlightenment
thinkers had hoped, humanity was becoming so depraved that God would
soon be forced to intervene and smash their society, inflicting untold misery upon the human race. But out of this fiery ordeal, the faithful Christians would emerge triumphant and enjoy Christ's final victory and glorious
Kingdom.[8]

Darby did not search for mystical meaning in the Bible, which he saw as a
document that told the literal truth. The prophets and the author of the
Book of Revelation were not speaking symbolically but making precise predictions which would shortly come to pass exactly as they had foretold. The
old myths were now seen as factual *logoi,* the only form of truth that many
modern Western people could recognize. Darby divided the whole of salvation history into seven epochs or "dispensations," a scheme derived from a
careful reading of scripture. Each dispensation, he explained, had been
brought to an end when human beings became so wicked that God was
forced to punish them. The previous dispensations had ended with such
catastrophes as the Fall, the Flood, and the crucifixion of Christ. Human
beings were currently living in the sixth, or penultimate, dispensation, which
God would shortly bring to an end in an unprecedentedly terrible disaster. Antichrist, the false redeemer whose coming before the End had been
predicted by St. Paul,[9] would deceive the world with his false allure, take
everybody in, and then inflict a period of Tribulation upon humanity. For
seven years, Antichrist would wage war, massacre untold numbers of people, and persecute all opposition, but eventually Christ would descend to
earth, defeat Antichrist, engage in a final battle with Satan and the forces
of evil on the plain of Armageddon outside Jerusalem, and inaugurate the
Seventh Dispensation. He would rule for a thousand years, before the Last
Judgment brought history to a close. This was a religious version of the
future-war fantasy of Europe. It saw true progress as inseparable from conflict and near-total destruction. Despite its dream of divine redemption and
millennial bliss, it was a nihilistic vision expressive of the modern death
wish. Christians imagined the final extinction of modern society in obses-
sive detail, yearning morbidly toward it.

There was one important difference, however. Where the Europeans imagined everybody enduring the ordeal of the next great war, Darby provided the elect with a way out. On the basis of a chance remark of St. Paul's, who believed that Christians alive at the time of Christ's Second Coming would be "taken up in the clouds . . . to meet the Lord in the air,"[10] Darby maintained that just before the beginning of the Tribulation, there would be a "Rapture," a snatching-up of born-again Christians, who would be taken up to heaven and so would escape the terrible sufferings of the Last Days. Rapture has been imagined in concrete, literal detail by premillennialists. They are convinced that suddenly airplanes, cars, and trains will crash, as born-again pilots and drivers are caught up into the air while their vehicles careen out of control. The stock market will plummet, and governments will fall. Those left behind will realize that they are doomed and that the true believers have been right all along. Not only will these unhappy people have to endure the Tribulation, they will know that they are destined for eternal damnation. Premillennialism was a fantasy of revenge: the elect imagined themselves gazing down upon the sufferings of those who had jeered at their beliefs, ignored, ridiculed, and marginalized their faith, and now, too late, realized their error. A popular picture found in the homes of many Protestant fundamentalists today shows a man cutting the grass outside his house, gazing in astonishment as his born-again wife is raptured out of an upstairs window. Like many concrete depictions of mythical events, the scene looks a little absurd, but the reality it purports to present is cruel, divisive, and tragic.

Ironically, premillennialism had more in common with the secular philosophies it despised than with true religious mythology. Hegel, Marx, and Darwin had all believed that development was the result of conflict. Marx had also divided history into different eras, culminating in a utopia. Geologists had found the successive epochs of the earth's development in the strata of fossilized fauna and flora in rocks and cliffs, and some thought that each had ended in catastrophe. Bizarre as the premillennial program sounds, it was in tune with nineteenth-century scientific thought. It was modern also in its literalism and democracy. There were no hidden or symbolic meanings, accessible only to a mystical elite. All Christians, however rudimentary their education, could discover the truth, which was plainly revealed for all to see in the Bible. Scripture meant exactly what it said: a millennium meant ten centuries; 485 years meant precisely that; if the prophets spoke of "Israel," they were not referring to the Church but to the Jews; when the author of Revelation predicted a battle between Jesus and Satan on the plain of Armageddon outside Jerusalem, that was exactly what would happen.[11] A premillennial reading of the Bible would become even easier for the average Christian after the publication of *The Scofield Reference Bible* (1909), which became an instant best-seller. C. I. Scofield explained this dispensational vision of salvation history in detailed notes accompanying the biblical text, notes that for many fundamentalists have become almost as authoritative as the text itself.

Premillennialism manifests that lust for certainty which is a reaction to a modernity that deliberately leaves questions open and denies the possibility of absolute truth. American Protestants had long been hostile to the expert who alone was deemed capable of understanding the way a modern society worked. By the late nineteenth century, apparently, nothing was as it seemed. The American economy suffered wild fluctuations during this period which were bewildering to people used to the routines of agrarian life. Booms were followed by depressions, which consumed huge fortunes overnight; society seemed controlled by mysterious, unseen "market forces." Sociologists also argued that human life was controlled by an economic dynamic that could not be discerned by the unskilled observer. Darwinists told people that existence was dominated by a biological struggle, unseen by the naked eye. Psychologists talked about the power of the hidden, unconscious mind. The Higher Critics insisted that even the Bible itself was not all that it claimed to be, and that the apparently simple text was actually composed of a bewildering number of different sources and written by authors of whom nobody had ever heard. Many Protestants, who expected their faith to bring them security, felt mental vertigo in this complicated world. They wanted a plain-speaking faith that everybody could understand.

But because by the end of the nineteenth century science and rationalism were the watchwords of the day, religion had to be rational too if it was to be taken seriously. Some Protestants were determined to make their faith logical and scientifically sound. It must be as clear, demonstrable, and objective as any other *logos*. Yet much modern science was too slippery for those in need of total certainty. The discoveries of Darwin and Freud came from unproven hypotheses, which seemed "unscientific" to the more traditional Protestants. Instead, they looked back to the early scientific vision of Francis Bacon, who had had no time for such guesswork. Bacon had believed that we could trust our senses absolutely, because they alone could provide us with sound information. He had been convinced that the world was organized on rational principles by an all-knowing God, and that the task of science was not to make wild conjectures but to catalog phenomena and to organize its findings into theories based on facts that were obvious to everyone. Protestants were also drawn to the philosophy of the eighteenth-century Scottish Enlightenment, which had opposed the subjectivist epistemology of Kant, and claimed that truth was objective and available to any sincere human being of sound "common sense."[12]

This lust for certainty was an attempt to fill the void that lurked at the heart of the modern experience, the God-shaped hole in the consciousness of wholly rational human beings. The American Protestant Arthur Pierson wanted the Bible explained in "a truly impartial and scientific spirit." The very title of his book, *Many Infallible Proofs* (1895), shows the type of certainty that he required from religion:

> I like Biblical theology that . . . does not begin with an hypothesis and then wraps the facts and the philosophy to fit the crook of our dogma, but a Baconian system, which first gathers the teachings of the word of God, and then seeks to deduce some general law upon which the facts can be arranged.[13]

It was an understandable desire, but the *mythoi* of the Bible had never pretended to be factual in the way that Pierson expected. Mythical language could not satisfactorily be translated into rational language without losing its raison d'être. Like poetry, it contained meanings that were too elusive to be expressed in any other way. Once theology tried to turn itself into science, it could only produce a caricature of rational discourse, because these truths are not amenable to scientific demonstration.[14] This spurious religious *logos* would inevitably bring religion into further disrepute.

The New Light Presbyterian seminary at Princeton, New Jersey, became the bastion of this scientific Protestantism.[15] The term "bastion" is appropriate, because the campaign for rational Christianity often used militant imagery, and seemed chronically on the defensive. In 1873, Charles Hodge, who held the chair of theology at Princeton, published the first volume of his two-volume work *Systematic Theology*. Again, the title reveals its scientific bias. The theologian's task was not to look for a meaning *beyond* the words, Hodge insisted, but simply to arrange the clear teachings of scripture into a system of general truths. Every word of the Bible was divinely inspired and must be taken seriously; it should not be distorted by allegorical or symbolic exegesis. Charles's son, Archibald A. Hodge, who took his father's chair in 1878, published a defense of the literal truth of the Bible in *The Princeton Review,* with a young colleague, Benjamin Warfield. The article became a classic. All the stories and statements of the Bible were "absolutely errorless and binding for faith and obedience." Everything the Bible said was absolute "truth to the facts." If the Bible said it was inspired, it *was* inspired,[16] a circular argument that was anything but scientific. Such a view had no rational objectivity, was closed to any alternative, and coherent only within its own terms. The Princeton reliance upon reason alone put it in line with modernity, but its claims were at variance with the facts. "Christianity makes its appeal by right reason," Warfield contended in a later article. "It is solely by reasoning that it has come thus far on its way to its kingship. And it is solely by reasoning that it will put all its enemies under its feet."[17] A cursory glance at Christian history shows that, as in all premodern religion, reason had been exercised only in a mythical context. Christianity had relied on mysticism, intuition, and liturgy rather than "right reason," which had never been the "sole" appeal of Christian faith. Warfield's militant imagery, which looks forward to confounding the "enemies" of the faith by reason, probably reflects a buried insecurity. If Christian truth was really so clear and self-evident, why did so many people refuse to accept it?

There was desperation in Princeton theology. "Religion has to fight for its life against a large class of scientific men," Charles Hodge declared in 1874.[18] It was clearly worrying to Christians who took their stand on scientific reason when the theories of natural scientists seemed to contradict the literal meaning of the Bible. That was why Hodge wrote *What Is Darwinism?* (1874), the first sustained religious attack on the evolutionary hypothesis. For Hodge, the Baconian, Darwinism was simply bad science. He had studied the *Origin* carefully and could not take seriously Darwin's suggestion that the intricate design of nature had come into being by chance, independently of God. He revealed thereby the closed mind-set of the emergent Protestant fundamentalism: Hodge simply could not imagine that any belief that differed from his own was viable. "To any ordinarily constituted mind," he insisted, "it is absolutely impossible to believe that the eye is not the work of design."[19] Human beings had the duty to oppose "all spectacular hypotheses and theories"—such as Darwin's—"which come into conflict with well-established truths." It was a plea for "common sense"; God had given to the human mind "intuitions which are infallible," and if Darwin contradicted these, his hypothesis was untenable and had to be rejected.[20] The scientific Christianity that was being developed at Princeton fell between two stools. Hodge was trying to put a brake on reason in the old conservative way, and refused to allow it the free play that was characteristic of modernity. But in reducing all mythical truth to the level of *logos,* he was flying in the face of the spirituality of the old world. His theology was bad science and inadequate religion.

But Princeton was not typical. Where the Hodges and Warfield were beginning to define faith as correct belief and putting great emphasis upon doctrinal orthodoxy, other Protestants, such as the veteran abolitionist Henry Ward Beecher (1813–87), were taking a more liberal line.[21] Dogma, in Beecher's view, was of secondary importance, and it was unchristian to penalize others for holding different theological opinions. Liberals were open to such modern scientific enterprises as Darwinism or the Higher Criticism of the Bible. For Beecher, God was not a distant, separate reality but was present in natural processes here below, so evolution could be seen as evidence of God's ceaseless concern for his creation. More important than doctrinal correctness was the practice of Christian love. Liberal Protestants continued to emphasize the importance of social work in the slums and cities, convinced that they could, by their dedicated philanthropy, establish God's Kingdom of justice in this world. It was an optimistic theology that appealed to the prosperous middle classes who were in a position to enjoy the fruits of modernity. By the 1880s, this New Theology was taught in many of the main Protestant schools in the northern states. Theologians such as John Bescon in *Evolution and Religion* (1897) and John Fiske in *Through Nature to God* (1899) were convinced that there could be no enmity between science and faith. Both spoke of the divine as immanent in the world; every throb in the pulsing life of the universe revealed God's presence. Throughout history, the spiritual perceptions of human beings had been evolving, and now humanity was on the brink of a new world, in which men and women would finally realize that there was no distinction between the so-called "supernatural" and the mundane. They would realize their profound affinity with God and live in peace with one another.

Like all millennial visions, this liberal theology was doomed to disappoint. Instead of achieving greater harmony, American Protestants were discovering that they were profoundly at odds. Their differences threatened to tear the denominations apart. The chief bone of contention at the end of the nineteenth century was not evolution but the Higher Criticism. Liberals believed that even though the new theories about the Bible might undermine some of the old beliefs, in the long term they would lead to a deeper understanding of scripture. But for the traditionalists, "Higher Criticism" was a scare term. It seemed to symbolize everything that was wrong with the modern industrialized society that was sweeping the old certainties away. By this time, popularizers had brought the new ideas to the general public, and Christians discovered to their considerable confusion that the Pentateuch was not written by Moses, nor the Psalms by King David; the Virgin Birth of Christ was a mere figure of speech, and the Ten Plagues of Egypt were probably natural disasters which had been interpreted later as miracles.[22] In 1888, the British novelist Mrs. Humphry Ward published *Robert Elsmere*, which told the story of a young clergyman whose faith was so undermined by the Higher Criticism that he resigned his orders and devoted his life to social work in the East End of London. The novel became a best-seller, which indicated that many could identify with the hero's doubts. As Robert's wife said, "If the Gospels are not true in fact, as history, I cannot see how they are true at all, or of any value."[23]

The rational bias of the modern world now made it impossible for many Western Christians to understand the role and value of myth. Faith had to be rational, *mythos* had to be *logos*. It was now very difficult to see truth as anything other than factual or scientific. There was a deep fear that these new biblical theories would undermine the basic structure of Christianity and leave nothing at all. Yet again, the void loomed. "If we have no infallible standard," argued the American Methodist clergyman Alexander McAlister, "we may as well have no standard at all."[24] Discount one miracle, and consistency demanded that you reject the lot. If Jonah did not really spend three days in the belly of a whale, did Christ really rise from the tomb? asked the Lutheran pastor James Remensnyder.[25] Once biblical truth had been unraveled in this way, all decent values would disappear. For the Methodist preacher Leander W. Mitchell, the Higher Criticism was to blame for widespread drunkenness, infidelity, and agnosticism.[26] The Presbyterian M. B. Lambdin saw it as the cause of the rising divorce rate, graft, corruption, crime, and murder.[27]

The Higher Criticism could no longer be discussed rationally, since it evoked fundamental fears. When Charles Briggs, a liberal Presbyterian, was charged with heresy and put on trial by the New York Presbytery in 1891 for his public defense of the Higher Criticism, the story hit the front page of the *New York Times*. When he was acquitted, this was hailed by the *New York Tribune* as a victory for the Higher Criticism, but the General Assembly of the denomination overturned the verdict and Briggs was suspended from the ministry. The trial was bitter and acrimonious; the uproar split the denomination down the middle. Out of two hundred presbyteries polled afterward, ninety were opposed to Briggs's views. This was only the most publicized of numerous heresy trials at this time, during which one liberal after another was thrown out of his denomination.

By 1900, the furor seemed to have died down. The ideas of the Higher Criticism appeared to have gained ground everywhere, liberals still held important posts in most of the denominations, and the conservatives seemed stunned but quiescent. Yet this apparent peace was deceptive. Observers at this time were aware that within almost all the denominations— Presbyterian, Methodist, Disciples, Episcopalian, Baptist—there were two distinct "churches," representing the "old" and the "new" ways of looking at the Bible.[28]

Some Christians had already started to mobilize for the struggle that lay ahead. In 1886, the revivalist Dwight Moody (1837–99) founded the Moody Bible Institute in Chicago to combat the teachings of the Higher Criticism.

His aim was to create a cadre of "gap-men," who could stand between the ministers and the laity and combat the false ideas which, he believed, had brought the nation to the brink of destruction. Moody has been called the father of American fundamentalism, and his Bible Institute would, like Princeton, become a bastion of conservative Christianity. But Moody was less interested in dogma than the Hodges and Warfield. His message was simple and primarily emotional: the sinful world could be redeemed by Christ. Moody's priority was the salvation of souls, and he was ready to cooperate with any Christians, whatever their beliefs, in the work of saving sinners. He shared the liberals' concern for social reform: the graduates of his Institute were to become missionaries to the poor. But Moody was a premillennialist, convinced that the Godless ideologies of the age would lead to the destruction of the world. Things were not getting better, as the liberals believed; they were getting worse every day.[29] In 1886, the year he founded his Bible Institute, there was a tragedy in Haymarket Square, Chicago, which shocked the nation. During a trade-union rally, when the demonstrators clashed with the police, a bomb killed seven policemen and injured seventy others. The Haymarket Riot seemed to epitomize all the evils and dangers of industrial society, and Moody could see it only in apocalyptic terms. "Either these people are to be evangelized," he prophesied, "or the leaven of communism and infidelity will assume such enormous proportions that it will break out in a reign of terror such as this country has never known."[30]

The Bible Institute would become a crucial fundamentalist institution. Like the Volozhin *yeshiva*, it represented a safe and sacred enclave in a godless world, which would prepare a cadre for a future counteroffensive against modern society. Other conservative Protestants, who would play a leading role in the coming fundamentalist movement, followed Moody's lead. In 1902, William Bell Riley founded the Northwestern Bible School, and in 1907, the oil magnate Lyman Stewart established the Bible Institute of Los Angeles. Conservatives who felt outmaneuvered by the liberals in the mainline denominations were beginning to band together. The first Prophecy and Bible Conferences were held during the last years of the nineteenth century. Here conservative Protestants could gather to read the Bible in a literal, common-sense manner, cleanse their minds of the Higher Criticism, and discuss their premillennial ideas. They were starting to establish a distinct identity, and during the increasingly crowded conferences became aware of their potential as an independent force.

The creation of a special, unique identity was a natural response to the modern experience. The newly industrialized northern cities were a melting pot. By 1890, four out of every five New Yorkers were either new immigrants or the children of new immigrants.[31] At the time of the Revolution, the United States had been an overwhelmingly Protestant nation. Now the WASP identity seemed about to be obliterated by the "Papist" flood. Unfortunately, the quest for a distinct identity often goes hand-in-hand with the development of a terror of the stereotyped "other" against whom people measure themselves. A paranoid fear of conspiracy would continue to characterize the response to the upheavals of modernization, and would be especially evident in the fundamentalist movements created by Jews, Christians, and Muslims, all of which would cultivate a distorted and often pernicious image of their enemies, who were sometimes depicted as satanically evil. American Protestants had long hated Roman Catholics, and had also feared conspiracies of deists, Freemasons, and Mormons, who were all, at one time or another, believed to be undermining the Christian fabric of society. In the late nineteenth century, these anxieties flared again. In 1887, the American Protective Association was formed and became the nation's largest anti-Catholic body, with a membership that may have reached 2,250,000. It forged "pastoral letters," supposedly from American Catholic bishops, urging their flocks to murder all Protestants and overthrow the heretical government of the United States. In 1885, Josiah Strong published *Our Country: Its Possible Future and Its Present Crisis*, which listed the "Catholic threat" as the most destructive danger faced by the nation. Giving Catholics the vote would make America vulnerable to satanic influence; already the United States had suffered an immigration of Romanists that was twice as large as that of the invasion of the Goths and Vandals which had brought down the Roman empire in the fifth century. Americans were cultivating fantasies of utter ruin; paranoid conspiracy theories enabled them to pin their nameless and amorphous dread onto concrete enemies and thus helped to make it manageable.[32]

IN EUROPE, the conspiracy fears linked to the creation of a distinct identity took the form of a new, "scientific" racism, which would not reach the United States until the 1920s. It centered largely upon the Jewish people, and was a product of the modern scientific culture which had enabled Europeans to control their environment with unprecedented skill. Modern pursuits, such as medicine or landscape gardening, taught people to eliminate things that were harmful, inelegant, or useless. At a time when nationalism was becoming the chief ideology of the European states, Jews seemed inherently and irredeemably cosmopolitan. The scientific theories that were evolved to define the essential biological and genetic characteristics of the *Volk* were too narrow to include the Jews. As the new nations redefined themselves, they needed an "other" against whom they could determine their new selves, and "the Jew" was conveniently at hand. This modern racism, which yearned to eliminate Jews from society as a gardener would root out weeds or a surgeon cut out a cancer, was a form of social engineering, which sprang from a conviction that some people could not be improved or controlled. It drew upon centuries of Christian religious prejudice, and gave it a scientific rationale.

At the same time, however, "the Jew" also became a symbol upon which people could fasten their fears and reservations about the social upheaval of modernization. As Jews moved out of the ghettoes into Christian neighborhoods, and enjoyed extraordinary success in the capitalist economy, they seemed to epitomize the destruction of the old order. Europeans also experienced modernity as a frightening "melting pot." The new industrialized world was breaking down old barriers and some experienced this now apparently formless society, which had no clear boundaries, as anarchic and annihilating. Those Jews who had assimilated to the mainstream seemed especially disturbing. Had they now become "non-Jews" and overcome what many still felt to be an impassable divide?[33] Modern anti-Semitism gave those who were disturbed by the turmoil of modernization and the awesome scale of social confusion a target for their distress and resentment. To "define" was to set limits on these frightening changes; as some Protestants sought certainty by stringent doctrinal definitions, others kept the void at bay by trying to re-erect old social boundaries.

By the 1880s, the tolerance of the Enlightenment was shown to be tragically skin-deep. In Russia, after the assassination of the liberal Tsar Alexander II in 1881, there were fresh restrictions on Jewish entry into the professions. In 1891, over ten thousand Jews were expelled from Moscow, and there were massive expulsions from other regions between 1893 and 1895. There were also pogroms, condoned or even orchestrated by the Ministry of the Interior, in which Jews were robbed and killed, and which culminated in the pogrom at Kishinev (1905) where fifty Jews died and five hundred were injured.[34] Jews began to flee westward, at an average of fifty thousand a year, settling in western Europe, the United States, and Palestine. But the arrival in western Europe of these eastern Jews, with their strange clothes and outlandish customs, stirred old prejudices. In 1886, Germany elected its first parliamentary deputy on an officially anti-Semitic platform; by 1893, there were sixteen. In Austria, the Christian socialist Karl Lueger (1844–1910) built a powerful anti-Semitic movement, and by 1895 he was mayor of Vienna.[35] The new anti-Semitism even struck France, the first modern European nation to emancipate its Jews. On January 5, 1895, Captain Alfred Dreyfus, the only Jewish officer on the general staff, was convicted, on fabricated evidence, of transmitting secrets to the Germans, while an excited mob yelled, "Death to Dreyfus! Death to the Jews!"

Some Jews continued to assimilate, either by converting to Christianity or by living entirely secular lives. Some turned to politics, becoming revolutionary socialists in Russia and other eastern European countries, or leading members of trade unions. Others decided that there was no place for Jews in gentile society; they must return to Zion, to the Holy Land, and build a Jewish state there. Others preferred a modernizing religious solution, such as Reform, Conservative, or Neo-Orthodox Judaism. Some continued to turn their backs on modern society and clung to traditional Orthodoxy. These Haredim ("the trembling ones") were anxious about the future of Judaism in the new world and would try desperately to re-create the old. Even in western Europe or the United States, they continued to wear the fur hats, black knickers, and caftans that their fathers had worn in Russia or Poland. Most were striving to retain a Jewish identity in a hostile world, struggling to fend off annihilation, and to find some absolute security and certainty. Many felt embattled; some became more militant in their determination to survive.

The mood was epitomized by a new development in Habad Hasidism, which was now based in Lubavitch, Russia, and ruled by a hereditary dynasty of the descendants of Rabbi Schneur Zalman. The Fifth Rebbe, R. Shalom Dov Ber (1860–1920), who succeeded to the title in 1893, was deeply worried about the future of Judaism. He had traveled widely, kept in touch with the Misnagdim in Lithuania, and could see the decline in religious observance. In 1897, he established a Habad *yeshiva* modeled on the Misnagdic *yeshivot* of Volozhin, Slobodka, and Mir. He too wanted to create a cadre of young men to fight "the enemies of the Lord." These "enemies" were not the tsar and his officials; Lubavitch Hasidism was becoming a fundamentalist movement, which, in the usual way of such movements, began with a campaign against coreligionists. For the Fifth Rebbe, God's enemies were other Jews: the Maskilim, the Zionists, the Jewish socialists, and the Misnagdim, who were, in his view, gravely endangering the faith. His *yeshiva* students were called the Tamimim: "the pure ones." They were to be "soldiers in the Rebbe's army," who would fight "without concessions or compromise" to ensure that true Judaism would survive. Their struggle would pave the way for the coming of the Messiah.[36]

Zionism, the movement to create a Jewish homeland in Palestine, was the most far-reaching and imaginative of these new Jewish responses to modernity. It was not a monolithic movement. Zionist leaders drew on quite varied currents of modern thought: nationalism, Western imperialism, socialism, and the secularism of the Jewish Enlightenment. Even though the Labor

Zionism of David Ben-Gurion (1886–1973), which sought to establish a socialist community in Palestine, would ultimately become the dominant Zionist ideology, the Zionist enterprise also relied heavily upon capitalism. Between 1880 and 1917, Jewish businessmen invested millions of dollars in the purchase of land from Arab and Turkish absentee landlords who had estates in Palestine. Others, such as Theodor Herzl (1860–1904) and Chaim Weizmann (1874–1952), became political lobbyists. Herzl saw the future Jewish state as a European colony in the Middle East. Still others did not want a nation-state, but saw the new homeland as a cultural center for Jews. Many feared an impending anti-Semitic catastrophe; in order to save the Jewish people from extermination, they must prepare a safe haven and refuge. Their terror of annihilation was not of a moral or psychological void, but a realistic assessment of the murderous potential of modernity.

The Orthodox were appalled by the Zionist movement in all its forms. There had been two attempts to create a form of religious Zionism during the nineteenth century, but neither had received much support. In 1845, Yehuda Hai Alkalai (1798–1878), a Sephardic Jew of Sarajevo, had tried to make the old messianic myth of the return to Zion a program for practical action. The Messiah would not be a person but a process that "will begin with an effort of the Jews themselves; they must organize and unite, choose leaders, and leave the land of exile."[37] Twenty years later, Zvi Hirsch Kallischer (1795–1874), a Polish Jew, made exactly the same point in his *Devishat Zion* ("Seeking Zion," 1862). Alkalai and Kallischer were both attempting to rationalize the ancient mythology and, by bringing it down to earth, were secularizing it. But to the vast majority of devout, observant Jews, any such idea was anathema. As the Zionist movement gained momentum during the last years of the nineteenth century, and achieved an international profile in the big Zionist conferences held in Basel, Switzerland, the Orthodox condemned it in the most extreme terms.[38] In the premodern world, myth was not supposed to be a blueprint for practical action, which was strictly the preserve of *logos*. The function of myth had been to give such action meaning and ground it spiritually. The Shabbetai Zevi affair had shown how disastrous it could be to apply stories and images that belonged to the unseen world of the psyche to the realm of politics. Since the shock of that fiasco, the old prohibition against treating the messianic *mythos* as though it were *logos*, capable of pragmatic application, had acquired in the Jewish imagination the force of a taboo. Any human attempt to achieve redemption or "hasten the end" by taking practical steps to realize the Kingdom in the Holy Land, was abhorrent. Jews were even forbidden to recite too many prayers for the return to Zion. To take any kind of initiative amounted to a rebellion against God, who alone could bring Redemption; anyone who took such action was going over to the "Other Side," the demonic world. Jews *must* remain politically passive. This was a condition of the existential state of Exile.[39] In rather the same way as Shii Muslims, Jews had outlawed political activism, knowing all too well from Jewish history how potentially lethal it could be to incarnate myth in history.

To this day, Zionism and the Jewish state which the movement would create have been more divisive in the Jewish world than modernity itself. A response to Zionism and the State of Israel, for or against, would become the motive power of every form of Jewish fundamentalism.[40] It is largely through Zionism that secular modernity has entered Jewish life and changed it forever. This is because the first Zionists were brilliantly successful in turning the Land of Israel, one of the holiest symbols of Judaism, into a rational, mundane, practical reality. Instead of contemplating it mystically or halakhically, the Zionists settled the Land physically, strategically, and militarily. For the vast majority of the Orthodox, in these early years, this was to trample blasphemously upon a sacred reality. It was a deliberate act of profanation that defied centuries of religious tradition.

For the secular Zionists were quite blatant about their rejection of religion. Their movement was indeed a rebellion against Judaism. Many of them were atheists, socialists, Marxists. Very few of them observed the commandments of the Torah. Some of them positively hated religion, which they thought had failed the Jewish people by encouraging them to sit back passively and wait for the Messiah. Instead of helping them to struggle against persecution and oppression, religion had inspired Jews to retreat from the world in strange mystical exercises or the study of arcane texts. The spectacle of Jews weeping and clinging to the stones of the Western Wall in Jerusalem, the last relic of the ancient Temple, filled many Zionists with dismay. This apparently craven dependence upon the supernatural was the obverse of everything that they were trying to achieve. The Zionists wanted to create a fresh Jewish identity, a New Jew, liberated from the unhealthy, confining life of the ghetto. The New Jew would be autonomous, the controller of his own destiny in his own land. But this quest for roots and self-respect amounted to a declaration of independence from Jewish religion.

The Zionists were, above all else, pragmatists, and this made them men of the modern era. Yet they were all profoundly aware of the explosive "charge" of the symbol of the Land. In the mythical world of Judaism, the Land was inseparable from the two most sacred realities, God and the Torah. In the mystical journey of the Kabbalah, the Land was linked symbolically to the last stage of the interior descent into the self, and was identical with the divine Presence the Kabbalist discovered in the ground of his being. The

Land was thus fundamental to Jewish identity. However practical their approach, Zionists recognized that no other land could really "save" the Jews and bring them psychic healing. Peretz Smolenskin (1842–95), who was bitterly opposed to the rabbinic establishment, was convinced that Palestine was the only possible location for a Jewish state. Leo Pinsker (1821–91) was only converted to this idea slowly, and against his better judgment, but he finally had to admit that the Jewish state had to be in Palestine. Theodor Herzl had nearly lost the leadership of the Zionist movement at the Second Zionist Conference in Basel (1898) when he had suggested a state in Uganda. He was forced to stand before the delegates, raise his hand, and quote the words of the Psalmist: "Jerusalem, if I forget you, may my right hand wither!" Zionists were ready to exploit the power of this *mythos* to make their wholly secular and even Godless campaign a viable reality in the real world. That they succeeded was their triumph. But their endorsement of this mythical, sacred geography would be as problematic as ever when they tried to translate it into hard fact. The first Zionists had very little understanding of the terrestrial history of Palestine during the previous two thousand years; their slogan: "A land without a people for a people without a land!" showed a complete disregard for the fact that the land was inhabited by Palestinian Arabs who had their own aspirations for the country. If Zionism succeeded in its limited, pragmatic, and modern objective of establishing a secular Jewish state, it also embroiled the people of Israel in a conflict which, at this writing, shows little sign of abating.

THE MUSLIMS of Egypt and Iran, as we have seen, had first experienced modernity as aggressive, invasive, and exploitative. Today Western people have become accustomed to hearing Muslim fundamentalists inveighing against their culture, denouncing their policies as satanic, and pouring scorn on such values as secularism, democracy, and human rights. There is an assumption that "Islam" and the West are quite incompatible, their ideals utterly opposed, and that "Islam" is at odds with everything that the West stands for. It is, therefore, important to realize that this is not the case. As we saw in Chapter 2, under the impetus of their own spirituality Muslims arrived at many ideas and values that are similar to our own modern notions. They had evolved an appreciation of the wisdom of separating religion and politics and a vision of the intellectual freedom of the individual, and seen the necessity for the cultivation of rational thought. The Koranic passion for justice and equity is equally sacred in the modern Western ethos. It is not surprising, therefore, that at the end of the nineteenth century, many leading Muslim thinkers were entranced by the West. They could see that Europeans and Muslims held common values, even though the people of Europe had obviously moved on to fashion a much more efficient, dynamic, and creative society, which they longed to reproduce in their own countries.

In Iran, during the second half of the nineteenth century, a circle of intellectual thinkers, politicians, and writers were passionate in their admiration of European culture.[41] Fathadi Akhundzada (1812–78), Malkum Khan (1833–1908), Abdul Rahim Talibzada (1834–1911), and Mirza Aqa Khan Kirmani (1853–96) were in some ways as rebellious as the Zionists. They constantly clashed with the *ulema*, wanted to establish a wholly secular polity, and tried to use religion to effect fundamental change. Like the Zionists, they believed that conventional faith—in their case, Shiism—had held the people back, put a brake on progress, and precluded the free discussion of ideas that had been so crucial to the Great Western Transformation. Kirmani was particularly outspoken. If religion was not practical, in his view, it was useless. What was the point of weeping over Husain, if there was no real justice for the poor?

> While European learned men are busy studying mathematics, sciences, politics and economics, and the rights of man, in this age of socialism and struggle for the improvement of the conditions of the poor, the Iranian ulema are discussing problems of cleanliness and the ascension of the Prophet to heaven.[42]

True religion, Kirmani insisted, meant rational enlightenment and equal rights. It meant "tall buildings, industrial inventions, factories, expansion of the means of communication, promotion of knowledge, general welfare, implementing just laws."[43] But, of course, Kirmani was wrong. Religion did none of these things; it was *logos*, rational thought, which addressed itself to these practical projects. The task of religion had been to provide these pragmatic activities with ultimate meaning. In one way, however, Kirmani was right when he accused Shiism of impeding progress. One of the tasks of conservative, premodern faith had been to help people accept the inherent limitations of their society and, if Iranians wanted to take a full part in the modern world, which was dedicated to progress, religion could no longer be allowed to do that. Islam would have to change. But how?

Like many modern secularists, Kirmani and his friends blamed religion for the disorders of their nation. They believed that the Arabs had foisted Islam upon the Iranian people to their detriment, and so they tried to create a Persian identity based on their sketchy knowledge of pre-Islamic Iran. Their view of the West was equally inadequate and naive, based on an unsystematic reading of European books.[44] These reformers did not fully understand the complex nature of Western modernity, but regarded its institutions as a sort of "machine" (that nineteenth-century symbol of progress, science, and power) which could infallibly and mechanically manufacture the entire European experience. If only Iranians could acquire a Western secular law code (instead of the Shariah) or a European-style education, they would be modern and progressive too. They did not appreciate the importance of industrialization and a modern economy. A European education would certainly open new doors to young Iranians, but if the infrastructure of their society remained unchanged, there would be little they could do with their education. Modernization was not yet even in its infancy in Iran; Iranians would have to undergo the wrenching and distressing process of transforming their agrarian culture into an industrialized, technicalized society. This alone would make it possible for Iranians to have the kind of liberal civilization that these reformers wanted, where everybody could think, write, and explore whatever ideas they chose. An agrarian society could not support this freedom. Western institutions might be beneficial, but they could not by themselves transform the mentality of a people whose horizons were still those of the conservative period.

Indeed, the reformers themselves still had a foot in the old world. This was hardly surprising, given the rudimentary nature of their exposure to modern society. They had come by their progressive ideas through Babism, the mystical philosophy of the school of Isfahan, and Sufism, as well as by reading Western books. These Shii spiritualities had given them the freedom and courage to throw off old restraints, but in a thoroughly conservative manner. Kirmani used to claim that he was a total rationalist: "reason and scientific proofs are the sources of my words and the bases of my deeds,"[45] he insisted. But his rationalism was entirely bound by a mythical and mystical perspective. He had an evolutionary view of history, but identified Darwinism with Mulla Sadra's vision of the progressive development of all beings toward a perfect state. Mulkum Khan did the same. They were simply expanding the ancient Muslim conception of *ilm* ("essential knowledge") to include Western scientific rationalism. The reformers tended to argue more like medieval Faylasufs than modern philosophers. They all promoted the ideal of a constitutional government that would limit the powers of the shahs, and by opening this debate in Iran, they had made an important contribution. But they were as elitist as any premodern philosopher. They certainly did not envisage a government based on the will of the majority. Mulkum Khan's vision was more like the old Falsafah ideal of a philosopher-king guiding the ignorant masses than the democratic vision of a modern political scientist. Talibzada was unable to see the point of a multiparty system; in his view, the role of the opposition was simply to censure the ruling party and to wait in the wings, ready to take over in a crisis.[46] It had taken Western people centuries of economic, political, industrial, and social change to evolve their democratic ideal, so, again, it was not surprising that the reformers had not grasped it fully. They were—and could only be—transitional figures, pointing their people in the direction of change, but unable yet to articulate modernity fully.

Intellectuals like Kirmani and Mulkum Khan would continue to play an important part in the development of Iran, and they would often find themselves in conflict with the *ulema*. But toward the end of the century, the clergy showed that they were not always immersed in old texts but were prepared to intervene in politics if they felt that the shahs had put the people's welfare in jeopardy. In 1891, Nasir ad-Din Shah (1829–96) gave a British company the monopoly on the production and sale of tobacco in Iran. The Qajar shahs had been granting such concessions for years, but hitherto only in areas where Iranians were not involved. But tobacco was a popular crop in Iran, and provided thousands of landowners, shopkeepers, and exporters with their major source of income. There were huge protests all over the country, led by the *bazaaris* and the local *ulema*. But in December, Hajj Mirza Hasan Shirazi, the leading *mujtahid* in Najaf, issued a *fatwa* that banned the sale and use of tobacco in Iran. It was a brilliant move. Everybody stopped smoking, even the non-Muslim Iranians and the shah's wives. The government was forced to climb down and rescind the concession.[47] It was a prophetic moment, and showed the potential power of the Iranian *ulema*, who, as the sole spokesmen of the Hidden Imam, could even command the obedience of the shahs. The *fatwa* was rational, pragmatic, and effective, but made sense only in the old mythical context, deriving as it did from the Imam's authority.

In Egypt too, modern Europe was regarded as exciting and inspiring during the 1870s, It was also seen as congenial to the Islamic spirit, and this despite the difficulties and pain of the modernization process. This enthusiasm is clearly reflected in the work of the Egyptian writer Rifah al-Tahtawi (1801–73),[48] who was a great admirer of Muhammad Ali, had studied at the Azhar, and served as an imam in the new Egyptian army, an institution for which Tahtawi had the deepest respect. But in 1826, Tahtawi became one of the first students sent by Muhammad Ali to study in Paris. It was a revelation to him. For five years, he read French, ancient history, Greek mythology, geography, arithmetic, and logic. He was particularly enthralled by the ideas of the European Enlightenment, whose rational vision he found very similar to Falsafah.[49] Before returning home, Tahtawi published his diary, which gives us a valuable early glimpse of the modern West as seen by an outsider. Tahtawi had his reservations. He found the European view of religion reductive and modern French thinkers arrogant in their lofty assumption that their rational insights were superior to the mystical inspiration of the prophets. But Tahtawi loved the way everything worked properly in Paris. He praised the clean streets, the careful education of French children, the love of work, and the disapproval of laziness. He admired the rational acuity and precision of French culture, noting that the Parisians "are not prisoners of tradition, but always love to know the origin of things and the proofs of them." He was impressed that even the common people could read and write, "and enter like others into important matters, every man according to his capacity." He was also intrigued by the passion for innovation, the essential ingredient of the modern spirit. It could make people changeable and erratic, but not in such serious matters as politics. "Everyone who is master of a craft wishes to invent something which was not known before, or to complete something which has already been invented."[50]

When he returned to Egypt and became director of the new Bureau of Translation, which made European works available to Egyptians, Tahtawi insisted that the people of Egypt must learn from the West. The "gates of *ijtihad*" ("independent reasoning") must be opened, the *ulema* must move with the times, and the Shariah adapt to the modern world. Doctors, engineers, and scientists should have the same status as Muslim religious scholars. Modern science could be no threat to Islam; Europeans had originally learned their science from the Muslims of Spain, so when they studied Western sciences the Arabs would simply be taking back what had originally belonged to them. The government must not stamp down on progress and innovation, but lead the way forward, since change was now the law of life. Education was the key; the common people should be educated as they were in France, girls to the same standard as boys.[51] Tahtawi believed that Egypt stood on the brink of a glorious future. He was intoxicated by the promise of modernity; he wrote a poem in praise of the steam engine, and saw the Suez Canal and the transcontinental railways of the United States as engineering feats that would bring the far-flung peoples of the earth together in brotherhood and peace. Let French and British scientists and engineers come and settle in Egypt! This could only accelerate the rate of progress.[52]

During the 1870s, a new group of writers from what is now Lebanon and Syria came and settled in Cairo.[53] Most of them were Christians who had been educated in the French and American missionary schools and thus had access to Western culture. They were practitioners of the new journalism and found that they had more freedom in Khedive Ismail's Cairo than in the Ottoman territories. They established new journals, which published articles on medicine, philosophy, politics, geography, history, industry, agriculture, ethics, and sociology, bringing crucial modern ideas to the general

Arab reader. Their influence was enormous. In particular, these Christian
Arabs were keen that the Muslim states should become secular, and insisted
that science alone and not religion was the basis of civilization. Like Tahtawi
they were in love with the West, and communicated this enthusiasm to the
people of Egypt.

It is poignant to look back at this early admiration in the light of the
hostility that developed later. Tahtawi and the Syrian journalists were living
in a brief period of harmony between East and West. The old crusading
hatred of Islam seemed to have died in Europe, and Tahtawi clearly did
not see Britain and France as a political threat, even though his sojourn in
Paris coincided with the brutal colonization of Algeria by the French. For
Tahtawi, the British and French were simply bearers of progress. But in
1871, an Iranian arrived in Cairo who had come to fear the West, which, he
realized, was on the way to achieving world hegemony. Even though he
was Iranian and a Shii, Jamal al-Din (1839–97) styled himself "al-Afghani"
(the Afghan), probably because he hoped to attract a wider audience in the
Islamic world by presenting himself as a Sunni.[54] He had had a traditional
madrasah education, which had included both *fiqh* (jurisprudence) and the
esoteric disciplines of Falsafah and mysticism *(irfan)*, yet he had become
convinced, during a visit to British India, that modern science and mathematics were the key to the future. Afghani, however, did not fall in love with
the British as Tahtawi had fallen under the spell of the Parisians. His visit
coincided with the Indian Mutiny against British rule (1857), which left a
lasting bitterness in the subcontinent. Afghani traveled in Arabia, Turkey,
Russia, and Europe, and became acutely anxious about the ubiquity and
power of the West, which, he was convinced, was about to crush the Islamic
world. When he arrived in Cairo in 1871, he was a man with a mission. He
was determined to teach the Muslim world to unite under the banner of
Islam and to use religion to counter the threat of Western imperialism.

Afghani was passionate, eloquent, wild, and quick-tempered. He sometimes made a bad impression, but had undoubted charisma. In Cairo, he
quickly gathered together a circle of disciples and encouraged them to
spread his pan-Islamic ideas. There was much discussion about the form that
modern Egypt should take at this time. Syrian journalists had promoted the
idea of a secular state, and Tahtawi had believed that Egyptians should cultivate a Western-style nationalism. Afghani would have none of this. If religion was weak, in his view, Muslim society was bound to disintegrate. It was
only by reforming Islam and remaining true to their own unique cultural
and religious traditions that the Muslim countries would become strong
again and build their own version of scientific modernity. He was convinced
that unless the Muslims took strong action, the Islamic community *(ummah)*

would soon cease to exist. Time was short. The European imperialists were becoming stronger every day, and in a very short space of time the Islamic world would be overrun by Western culture.

Afghani's religious vision was, therefore, fueled by the fear of annihilation that we have found to be a common response to the difficulties of modernity. He believed that it was not necessary to take on a European lifestyle in order to be modern. Muslims could do it their way. If they merely copied the British and French, superimposing Western values on their own traditions, they would lose themselves. They would simply be bad reproductions, neither one thing nor the other, and thus compound their weakness.[55] They needed modern science and would have to learn it from Europe; however, this was in itself proof, he argued, "of our inferiority and decadence. We civilize ourselves by imitating the Europeans."[56] Afghani had put his finger on a major difficulty. Where Western modernity had succeeded in large part by pursuing innovation and originality, Muslims could only modernize their society by imitation. The modernizing program had an inherent and inescapable flaw.

Afghani had, therefore, perceived a real problem, but his solution, which sounded attractive, was not feasible because it expected too much of religion. He was correct in his prediction that a loss of cultural identity would result in weakness, malaise, and anomie. He was also right to argue that Islam must change in order to deal creatively with these radically new conditions. But a religious reform could not of itself modernize a country and stave off the Western threat. Unless Egypt could industrialize, develop a vibrant modern economy, and transcend the limitations of agrarian civilization, no ideology could bring the country to the same level as Europe. In the West, the modern ideals of autonomy, democracy, intellectual freedom, and toleration had been as much a product of the economy as of the philosophers and political scientists. Events would shortly prove that no matter how free and modern Egyptians might *feel* themselves to be, their economic weakness would make them politically vulnerable and dependent upon the West, and this humiliating subservience would make it even harder for them to cultivate a truly modern spirit.

But despite his hunger for modernity, Afghani, like the Iranian intellectuals with whom he was in touch, still belonged in many respects to the old world. He was a personally devout Muslim, who prayed, observed Islamic rituals, and lived according to Islamic law.[57] He practiced the mysticism of Mulla Sadra, whose vision of evolutionary change was deeply appealing to him. He also taught his disciples the esoteric lore of Falsafah, and often argued like a medieval philosopher. Like other religious thinkers of this period, he tried to prove that his faith was rational and scientific. He pointed out that the Koran taught Muslims to take nothing on trust and to demand proof; it was, therefore, admirably suited to the modern world. Indeed, Afghani went so far as to argue that Islam was identical with modern scientific rationalism, that the Law that the Prophet had received was at one with the laws of Nature, and that all the doctrines of Islam could be demonstrated by logic and natural reason.[58] This was patently false. Like any traditional faith, Islam went beyond the reach of *logos* and depended upon prophetic and mystical insight; and, indeed, that was how Afghani himself experienced religion. In another mood, he could write eloquently of the limitations of science, which "however beautiful, . . . does not completely satisfy humanity, which thirsts for the ideal and which likes to exist in dark and distant regions that the philosophers and the scholars can neither perceive nor explore."[59] Like the Iranian intellectuals, Afghani still had a foot in the old world at the same time as he aspired to the new. He wanted his faith to be wholly rational, but, like any mystic of the conservative period, he knew in his heart that the *mythos* of his religion gave humanity insights that science could not.

This inconsistency was, perhaps, inevitable, because Afghani was a transitional figure. But it also sprang from his anxiety. Time was running out, and Afghani could not wait to iron out all the contradictions in his thought. Muslims must make themselves more rational. This must be their top priority. They had neglected the natural sciences and, as a result, fallen behind Europe. They had been told to close "the gates of *ijtihad*" and to accept the rulings of the *ulema* and the sages of the past. This, Afghani insisted, had nothing to do with authentic Islam. It encouraged a subservience that not only was wholly opposed to the modern spirit but denied the "essential characteristics" of Muslim faith, which were "dominance and superiority."[60] As it was, the West now "owned" science, and the Muslims were weak and vulnerable.[61] Afghani could see that the old conservative ethos, symbolized by the closing of the gates of *ijtihad,* was holding Muslims back. But like any reformer who tries to make the *mythos* of religion sound like *logos,* he ran the risk of producing inadequate religious discourse on the one hand, and faulty science on the other.

The same could be said of his activism. Afghani rightly pointed out that Islam was a faith that expressed itself in action. He liked to quote the Koranic verse: "Verily, God does not change men's condition, unless they change their inner selves."[62] Instead of retreating into the *madrasahs,* Muslims must become involved in the world of politics if they wanted to save Islam. In the modern world, truth was pragmatic; it had to be shown to work in the physical, empirical realm, and Afghani wanted to prove that the truth of Islam could be just as effective as the Western ideologies in the world of

his day. He realized that Europe would soon rule the globe, and was determined to make the Muslim rulers of his day aware of this danger. But
Afghani's revolutionary schemes were often self-destructive and morally
dubious. None of them bore fruit, and they led simply to official curtailment
of his activities. He was expelled from Egypt for anti-government agitation
in 1879, from Iran in 1891, and, though he was subsequently allowed to
reside in Istanbul, he was kept under close surveillance by the Ottoman
authorities. The attempt to convert religious truth into a program for political action runs the risk of nihilism and disaster, and Afghani laid himself
open to the charge of "using" Islam in a superficial way to back up his ill-
thought-out revolutionary activism.[63] He had clearly not integrated the religious imperative with his politics in sufficient depth. When, in 1896, one of
his disciples, at his urging, assassinated Nasir ad-Din Shah, Afghani violated
one of the central tenets of all religion: respect for the absolute sanctity of
human life. He had made Islam look not only inefficient and bizarre but also
immoral.

The obvious defects of his thought sprang from his desperation. Afghani
was convinced that the Islamic world was about to be wiped out by the
imperialistic West. While he was living in Paris during the 1880s, he encountered the new scientific racism in the work of the philologist Ernest Renan
(1823–92), and the two men debated the place of Islam in the modern world.
Renan believed that the Semitic languages Hebrew and Arabic were corrupt and an example of arrested development. They lacked the progressive, developmental qualities inherent in "Aryan" linguistic systems, and
could not regenerate themselves. In the same way, the Semitic races had
produced no real art, commerce, or civilization. Islam was especially incompatible with modernity, as witness the obvious inferiority of the Muslim
countries, the decadence of their governments, and the "intellectual nullity"
of the Muslims themselves. Like the peoples of Africa, the population of the
Islamic world was mentally incapable of scientific rationalism, and unable to
form a single original idea. As European science spread, Renan confidently
predicted, Islam would wither away and would, in the near future, cease to
exist.[64] It is not surprising that Afghani feared for the survival of Islam, or
that he tended to overemphasize the scientific rationality of the Muslim
vision. A new defensiveness had crept into Muslim thought, in response to a
very real threat. The stereotypical and inaccurate view of Islam in the work
of such modern thinkers as Renan would justify the colonial invasion of the
Islamic countries.

Colonialism sprang from the needs of Europe's expanding capitalist
economy. Hegel had argued that an industrialized society would be compelled to expand "in order to search around outside itself among other peo-

ples . . . for consumers and thereby for the necessary means of subsistence."
This quest for new markets would "also provide the soil for colonization
toward which the fully developed bourgeoisie is pushed."[65] By the end of
the century, the colonization of the Middle East was well under way. France
had conquered Algeria in 1830, and Britain, Aden nine years later. Tunisia
was occupied in 1881, the Sudan in 1889, and Libya and Morocco in 1912. In
1915, the Sykes-Picot Agreement divided the territories of the moribund
Ottoman empire between France and England, in anticipation of victory in
the First World War. This colonial penetration was a severe shock, which
meant, in effect, the destruction of the traditional lifestyle of those countries, which were reduced immediately to secondary status.

The colonized country produced raw materials for export, which were
then fed into the European industrial process. In return, it received cheap
manufactured Western goods, which meant that local industry suffered.
In order to ensure that the new colony fit into the modern technicalized
order, the police and military had to be reorganized along European
lines; the financial, commercial, and productive side of the economy also
had to be adapted, and the "natives" had to acquire some familiarity with
modern ideas. This modernization was experienced as intrusive, coercive,
and profoundly unsettling by the subject population.[66] Afghani had wanted
Muslims to modernize themselves and escape this transformation of their
society into an inferior copy of Europe. Colonialism made this impossible. Middle Eastern lands that came under Western domination could
not develop on their own terms. A living civilization had been transformed
by the colonialists into a dependent bloc, and this lack of autonomy induced
an attitude and habit of subservience that was profoundly at odds with
the modern spirit. Inevitably, the earlier love and admiration of Europe,
epitomized by Tahtawi and the Iranian reformers, soured and gave way to
resentment.

During Afghani's residence in Cairo, Egypt was gradually being drawn
into this colonial net, even though it never became a full colony. Khedive
Ismail's costly reforms and modernizing projects had bankrupted the country, which now depended entirely on European loans. In 1875, the khedive had been forced to sell the Suez Canal to the British, and in 1876, as
we have seen, the European shareholders had taken control of the Egyptian economy. When Ismail tried to break free, Britain, acting in concert
with the Ottoman sultan, deposed him, and the khedivate passed to his son,
Tewfiq. In 1881, some of the officers in the Egyptian army staged a coup
under the leadership of one Ahmad bey Urubi. They were joined by some of
Afghani's disciples and others who wanted modern constitutional rule in
Egypt. Urubi managed to impose his government on the new khedive and

after this victory was followed by a popular nationalist uprising, the British government decided to intervene to protect the interests of the shareholders. On July 11, 1882, the British navy attacked Alexandria, and defeated Urubi's forces on September 13 at Tel el-Kebir. The British then established their own military occupation in Egypt, and even though Khedive Tewfiq was officially reinstated, it was clear that the real ruler of Egypt was the British proconsul, Evelyn Baring, Lord Cromer.

Lord Cromer was a typical colonialist. In his view, the Egyptians were an inherently backward people and needed to be colonized for their own good. Like Renan, when he compared the Muslim countries to his own more developed nation, he assumed that Europe had always been in the vanguard of progress. He did not realize that European countries such as Britain and France had once been as "backward" as the Middle East, and that he was simply looking at an imperfectly modernized country. He saw "Orientals" themselves as inherently, genetically flawed. Cromer's achievements in Egypt were considerable. He stabilized the economy, improved irrigation in the country, and increased the market production of cotton. He abolished the *corvée*, the old system of forced labor, and established a competent judicial system. But this progress came at a price. Although the khedive was nominally in charge of his government, each ministry had an English "adviser" whose views invariably carried the day. Cromer believed this to be necessary. He assumed that Europeans had always been rational, efficient, and modern, while the Orientals were naturally illogical, unreliable, and corrupt.[67] Similarly, Islam "as a social system was a complete failure," and incapable of reform or development. It was not possible to resuscitate "a body which is not, indeed, dead, and which may yet linger on for centuries, but which is nevertheless politically and socially moribund, and whose gradual decay cannot be arrested by any modern palliatives."[68] He made it clear that this chronically retarded country would need direct British supervision for some time.

The British occupation created new rifts within Egyptian society. The *ulema* were displaced as the educators and chief guardians of knowledge by those who had received a Western education. The Shariah courts were replaced by the European civil courts established by Lord Cromer. Artisans and small merchants were also adversely affected. A new class of Westernized civil servants and intellectuals formed a new elite, estranged from the vast majority of the people. But most damaging of all, perhaps, was the tendency of Egyptians themselves to internalize the colonialists' negative views of the Egyptian people. Thus, Muhammad Abdu (1849–1905), a disciple of Afghani, was devastated by the British occupation. He described the modern period as a "torrent of science" drowning the traditional men of religion:

It is an age which has formed a bond between ourselves and
the civilized nations, making us aware of their excellent conditions . . . and our mediocre situation: thus revealing their wealth
and our poverty, their pride and our degradation, their strength
and our weakness, their triumphs and our defects.[69]

This corrosive sense of inferiority crept into the religious life of the colonized people, compelling a reformer such as Abdu to answer the charges of
the colonialists and to prove that Islam could be just as rational and modern
as any Western system.[70] For the first time, Muslims were forced to allow
their conquerors to set their intellectual agenda.

Abdu had been involved in the Urubi revolt and was exiled after the
British victory. He joined Afghani in Paris. The two men had much in common. Abdu had been initially drawn into Afghani's circle by his love of mystical religion *(irfan)*, which, he used to say, was "the key to his happiness."[71]
But Afghani had also introduced Abdu to the Western sciences and, later,
Abdu read Guizot, Tolstoy, Renan, Strauss, and Herbert Spencer. Abdu felt
quite at home in Europe and enjoyed the company of Europeans. Like
Afghani, he was convinced that Islam was compatible with modernity and
argued that it was an eminently rational faith, and that the habit of *taqlid* was
corrupting and inauthentic. But, also like Afghani, Abdu was committed to
rational thinking from within a mystical perspective. It was not as yet emancipated from the spirituality of the old world. Eventually, Abdu quarreled
with Afghani about politics. He believed that Egypt needed reform more
than revolution. He was a deeper thinker than his master, and could see that
there could be no shortcut to modernization and independence. Instead of
joining Afghani in his dangerous, pointless schemes, he wanted to rectify
some of Egypt's immense problems by means of education, and in 1888 he
was allowed to return. He became one of the most beloved men in the country, remained on good terms with both Egyptians and British, and became a
personal friend of both Lord Cromer and the khedive.

By this time there was considerable frustration in the country. At first,
many educated Egyptians had been forced to admit that, unwelcome as the
British occupation undoubtedly was, Lord Cromer ruled the country far
more efficiently than Khedive Ismail had done. But by the 1890s, relations
with the British had deteriorated. The British officials were often of lower
caliber than before and made less effort to cement relations with the Egyptians. They created their own privileged colonial enclave in the Gezira district. Egyptian civil servants found that their promotions were blocked by
young Britons, and there was resentment of the privileges accorded the
British and other foreigners by the Capitulations, which exempted them

from the law of the land.[72] More and more people listened to the fiery rhetoric of the nationalist Mustafa Kamil (1874–1908), who called for the immediate evacuation of the British. Abdu regarded Kamil as an empty demagogue. He could see that before Egyptians were able to run a modern independent state, they would have to deal with some serious social problems, which had been exacerbated by the occupation.

In Abdu's view, secularist ideas and institutions were being introduced far too rapidly into a deeply religious country. The people were not being given time to adapt. Abdu greatly respected the political institutions of Europe, but did not think they could be transplanted wholesale into Egypt. The vast mass of the people simply could not understand the new legal system; its spirit and scope were quite alien to them. As a result, Egypt was effectively becoming a country without law.[73] He therefore planned a major revision of Islamic law to meet modern conditions; this program was finally implemented in the 1920s after his death, and it is the system still in use in Egypt today. Abdu could see that Egyptian society was fragmenting; it was, therefore, essential to link modern legal and constitutional developments to traditional Islamic norms. Otherwise, the vast majority of Egyptians, who had not been much exposed to Western ideas, would make no sense of the new institutions. The Islamic principle of *shurah* ("consultation"), for example, could clearly be seen as compatible with democracy; and *ijmah* (the "consensus" of the community, which in Islamic law gave validity to a Muslim doctrine or practice) could now help the people to understand constitutional rule, whereby public opinion limited the power of the ruler.[74]

There was urgent need for educational reform. At present, Abdu noted, there were three entirely separate educational systems in place, which pursued wholly different objectives; this was creating impassable divisions in society. In the religious schools and *madrasahs*, which were still ruled by the conservative ethos, students were discouraged from thinking independently; in the Christian missionary schools, which supported the colonialist venture, young Muslims were alienated from their country and their religion. The state schools had the worst of all worlds: they were inadequate copies of European schools, and taught no religion at all. Those who had been educated by the *ulema* resisted all change, while Western-educated youth accepted any change at all, but were only superficially conversant with European culture and estranged from their own.[75]

In 1899, Abdu became the mufti of Egypt, the country's chief consultant in Islamic law, and was determined to reform traditional religious education. He was convinced that *madrasah* students should study science in order to take a full part in modern society. At the time, the Azhar was, in Abdu's view, an example of everything that was currently wrong with Islam: it had turned its back on the modern world and become a defensive anachronism. But the *ulema* resisted the reforms Abdu tried to implement. Since the time of Muhammad Ali, they had experienced modernization as a destructive assault, which had reduced God's influence in politics, law, education, and the economy. They would continue to resist any attempt to force them into the modern world and, unlike the Iranian *ulema,* fell seriously out of touch with the world outside the *madrasah.* Abdu had little success with them. He managed to modernize the administration of the Azhar and to improve the salaries and working conditions of the teachers. But *ulema* and students alike were fiercely opposed to any attempt to introduce modern secular subjects into the curriculum.[76] Faced with such opposition, Abdu became dispirited. In 1905, he resigned as Mufti, and died shortly afterward.

The struggles of both Abdu and Afghani show how difficult it was to adapt a faith that had come to fruition in the conservative period to the entirely different ethos of the modern world. They were both aware—and rightly so—of the dangers of too rapid secularization. Islam could provide much-needed continuity at a time of dislocating transformation. Egyptians were becoming strangers to one another, and those who had been Westernized were often alienated from their own culture. They were truly at home in neither the East nor the West, and, without the mythical and cultic practices which had once given life meaning, they were beginning to descend into the void that lay at the heart of the modern experience. The old institutions were being destroyed, but the new ones were strange and imperfectly understood. Abdu and Afghani were still nourished personally by the old spirituality. When they insisted that religion must be rational, they were closer to Mulla Sadra than to European rationalists and scientists, who discounted all religiously acquired truth. When they insisted that reason was the sole arbiter of truth and that all doctrines must be capable of rational proof, they spoke as practicing mystics. Shaped by conservative norms, they saw reason and intuition as complementary. But later generations, who had imbibed more of the spirit of Western rationalism, would find that reason alone could not yield a sense of the sacred. This loss of transcendent meaning would not be counter-balanced, as in the West, by the benefits of liberation and independence, because, increasingly, it was the West that set the agenda—even in religious matters.

A telling example of how confusing and damaging this could be occurred in 1899, when Qassim Amin (1865–1908) published *Tahrir al-Mara* ("The Liberation of Women"), which argued that the degraded position of women—in particular, the practice of veiling—was responsible for Egypt's backwardness. The veil was "a huge barrier between woman and her elevation, and consequently a barrier between the nation and its advance."[77] The book caused an uproar, not because it was saying anything new, but because an Egyptian writer had internalized and adopted a colonial prejudice. For years, men and women in Egypt had been agitating for fundamental changes in the position of women. Abdu himself had argued that the Koran presents men and women as equal before God, and that traditional rulings concerning divorce or polygamy were not essential to Islam: they could and should be changed.[78] The lot of women had improved. Muhammad Ali had established a school that trained women in elementary medical procedures; by 1875 about three thousand Egyptian girls attended the mission schools, and in 1873 the government established the first state primary school for girls, and a secondary school the following year. Visitors noted that women were seen more frequently in public; some were discarding the veil, and by the end of the century, women were publishing articles in journals, and becoming doctors and teachers. Change was already under way when the British arrived, and, though there was still a long way to go, a start had been made.

The veiling of women is neither an original nor a fundamental practice in Islam. The Koran does not command all women to cover their heads, and the habit of veiling women and secluding them in harems did not become common in the Islamic world until some three generations after the Prophet's death, when Muslims began to copy the Christians of Byzantium and Zoroastrians of Persia, who had long treated their women in this way. But the veil was not worn by all women; it was a mark of status and worn by women of the upper classes, not by peasants. Qassim Amin's book, however, brought the peripheral practice of veiling right into the heart of the debate about modernization. He insisted that unless the veil were abolished, the Muslim world would remain in a degraded state. Partly as a result of the furor arising from *Tahrir al-Mara,* the veil became for many Muslims a symbol of Islamic authenticity, whereas for many Westerners, the veil was and is "proof" of an ineradicable misogyny in Islam.

Amin was not the first to see the veil as a symbol of everything that was wrong with Islam. When the British arrived, they were appalled by the practice, even though most Western men at this date derided feminism, wanted their own wives securely at home, and opposed the education and enfranchisement of women. Lord Cromer was typical in this respect: he was one of the founders in London of the Men's League for Opposing Women's Suffrage, yet in his monumental book on Egypt, he expressed great concern about the status of Muslim women.[79] Their degraded state was a canker that began its destructive work early in childhood, as infants perceived the oppression of their mothers, and had eaten into the whole system of Islam. The practice of veiling was the "fatal obstacle" that prevented Egyptians from attaining that "elevation of thought and character which should accompany the introduction of Western civilization."[80] Missionaries also lamented the catastrophic influence of the veil, which, they believed, buried a woman alive and reduced her to the status of a prisoner or a slave. It showed how greatly the people of Egypt needed the benevolent supervision of the Western colonialists.[81]

Amin had accepted this somewhat cynical European assessment of veiling at face value. There is nothing feminist about *Tahrir al-Mara*. Amin presented Egyptian women as dirty and ignorant; with such mothers, how could Egypt be anything other than a backward, lazy nation? Did Egyptians imagine that

> the men of Europe, who have attained such completeness of intellect and feeling that they were able to discover the force of steam and electricity, . . . those souls who daily risk their lives in the pursuit of knowledge and honor above the pleasures of life, . . . these intellects and these souls that we so admire, . . . would have abandoned veiling after it had been in use among them if they had seen any good in it?[82]

Not surprisingly, this sickly sycophancy inspired a backlash. Arab writers refused to accept this estimate of their society, and in the course of this heated debate the veil turned into a symbol of resistance to colonialism. And so it has remained. Many Muslims now consider the veil de rigueur for all women, and a sign of true Islam. By using feminist arguments, for which most had little or no sympathy, as part of their propaganda, the colonialists tainted the cause of feminism in the Muslim world, and helped to distort the faith by introducing an imbalance that had not existed before.[83]

The modern ethos was changing religion. By the end of the nineteenth century, there were Jews, Christians, and Muslims who believed that their faith was in danger of being obliterated. To save it from this fate they had resorted to a number of stratagems. Some had retreated from modern society altogether and had built their own militant institutions as a sacred bastion and refuge; some were planning a counteroffensive, others were beginning to create a counterculture and a discourse of their own to challenge the secularist bias of modernity. There was a growing conviction that religion had to become as rational as modern science. In the early years of the twentieth century, a new defensiveness would lead to the first clear manifestation of the embattled religiosity that we now call fundamentalism.

6. Fundamentals
(1900–25)

THE GREAT WAR, which broke out in Europe in 1914 and reduced the landscape of France to a nightmarish inferno, showed the lethal and self-destructive tendency of the modern spirit. By decimating a generation of young men, the war damaged Europe at its core, so that it would, perhaps, never quite recover. After the war, no thinking person could be serenely optimistic about the progress of civilization. The most cultivated and advanced nations in Europe had crippled each other with the new military technology, and the war itself seemed a hideous parody of the mechanization that had brought such wealth and power. Once the intricate apparatus of conscription, transportation of troops, and manufacture of armaments had been set up and switched on, it acquired its own momentum and became difficult to stop. The pointlessness and futility of trench warfare defied the logic and rationalism of the age, and had nothing whatever to do with human need. The people of the West looked straight into the void that some had sensed for decades. The economy of the West had also begun to falter, and in 1910 had begun the decline that would lead to the Great Depression of the 1930s. The world seemed to be hurtling toward some unimaginable catastrophe. The Irish poet W. B. Yeats (1865–1939) saw the "Second Coming" not as a triumph of righteousness and peace, but as the birth of a savage, pitiless era:

> Things fall apart; the centre cannot hold
> Mere anarchy is loosed upon the world,
> The blood-dimmed tide is loosed, and everywhere
> The ceremony of innocence is drowned;
> The best lack all conviction, while the worst
> Are full of passionate intensity.[1]

But these were also years of unparalleled creativity and astonishing achievements in the arts and sciences, revealing the full flowering of the modern spirit. In all fields, the most creative thinkers seemed possessed by the desire to create the world anew, throw away the forms of the past, and break free. Modern people had evolved an entirely different mentality and could no longer look at the world in the same way. The eighteenth- and nineteenth-century novel had developed narratives that expressed an ordered progress of cause and effect; modern narratives splintered, leaving the reader uncertain about what had happened or what to think. Painters such as Pablo Picasso (1881–1973) dismembered their subjects or viewed them from two different perspectives at the same time; they seemed deliberately to flout the expectation of the viewer, and announced that a new vision was necessary. In both the arts and the sciences, there was a desire to go back to first principles, to irreducible fundamentals, and from this zero base to start again. Scientists now searched for the atom or the particle; sociologists and anthropologists reverted to primeval societies or primitive artifacts. This was not like the conservative return *ad fontes,* because the aim was not to re-create the past but to break it asunder, to split the atom, and bring forth something entirely new.

Some of these endeavors were an attempt to create a spirituality, without God or the supernatural. The painting, sculpture, poetry, and drama of the early twentieth century were all quests for meaning in a disordered, changing world; they were trying to create novel modes of perception and modern myths. The psychoanalytical science of Sigmund Freud, which strove to uncover the most fundamental layers of the unconscious, was also a search for new insight and an attempt to access a hidden source of spiritual strength. Freud had no time for conventional religion, which he regarded as the most serious enemy of the *logos* of science.[2] But he tried to revive a modern sense of the old myths of the Greeks and even made up mythical fictions of his own. The horror and fear of much of the modern experience lent new urgency to the search for some intangible significance which could save human beings from despair, but which could not be attained by the normal processes of logical, discursive thought. Freud, indeed, for all his devotion to scientific rationalism, showed that reason represented only the outermost rind of the mind, overlaying a seething cauldron of unconscious, irrational, and primitive impulses that profoundly affect our behavior but over which we have little control.

Religious people too were making similar attempts to build a new vision on fundamentals. The most prescient realized that it was impossible for fully modernized people to be religious in the old way. The conservative spirituality, which had helped people to adjust to essential limitations and to accept things as they were, would not help people in this iconoclastic, future-oriented climate. The whole tenor of their thought and perception had changed. Many in the West, whose education had been entirely rational, were not equipped for the mythical, mystical, and cultic rituals that had evoked a sense of transcendent value in the past. There was no going back. If they wanted to be religious, they would have to develop rites, beliefs, and practices that spoke to them in their radically altered circumstances. In the early twentieth century, people were trying to find new ways to be religious. Just as people in the first Axial Age (c. 700–200 BCE) had found that the old paganism no longer worked in the new conditions of their period and had evolved the great confessional faiths, so too, in this second Axial Age, there was a similar challenge. Like any truly creative enterprise, the search for modern (and, later, for postmodern) faith was supremely difficult. The quest continues; as yet, no definitive or even very satisfactory solution has emerged. The religiosity that we call "fundamentalism" is just one of these attempts.

The Protestants of the United States had been aware for some time of the need for something new. By the end of the nineteenth century, the denominations were polarized, but the crisis of the 1890s, which had seen heresy trials and expulsions, seemed to have passed. Liberals and conservatives in the early years of the century were both involved in the social programs of this so-called Progressive Age (1900–20), which attempted to deal with the problems arising from the rapid and unregulated development of industry and city life. Despite their doctrinal quarrels, Protestants in all the denominations were committed to the progressive ideal, and cooperated together in foreign missions and campaigns for Prohibition or improved education.[3] Despite the immense difficulties they faced, most felt confident. America had been "Christianized," wrote the liberal theologian Walter Rauschenbusch in 1912; it only remained now for business and industry to be transformed by "the thought and spirit of Christ."[4]

Protestants developed what they called the "Social Gospel" to sacralize the Godless cities and factories. It was an attempt to return to what they saw as the basic teachings of the Hebrew prophets and of Christ himself, who had taught his followers to visit prisoners, clothe the naked, and feed the hungry. Social Gospelers set up what they called "institutional churches" to provide services and recreational facilities for the poor and for new immigrants. Liberal Protestants, such as Charles Stelzle, who founded the New York Labor Temple in 1911 in one of the most crowded and desperate neighborhoods in the city, tried to baptize socialism: Christians should study urban and labor problems rather than the minutiae of Bible history, and fight such abuses as child labor.[5] In the early years of the century, conservative

Christians were just as involved in social programs as the liberal Protestants; however, their ideology was different. They might see their social crusades as a war against Satan or as a spiritual challenge to the prevailing materialism, but they were just as concerned about low wages, child labor, and poor working conditions as such liberals as Stelzle.[6] Conservatives would later become very critical of the Social Gospel, and would argue that it was pointless to try to save a world that was doomed. Yet in the early years of the century, even such an arch-conservative as William B. Riley, who had founded the Northwestern Bible College in 1902, was willing to work with social reformers to clean up Minneapolis. He could not approve of the methods of such Social Gospelers as Stelzle, who invited Leon Trotsky and Emma Goldman to lecture in his Temple, but conservatives had not yet moved over to the right of the political spectrum, and led their own welfare campaigns throughout the United States.

But in 1909, Charles Eliot, professor emeritus of Harvard University, delivered an address entitled "The Future of Religion" which struck dismay into the hearts of the more conservative. This was another attempt to return to a simple core value. The new religion, Eliot believed, would have only one commandment: the love of God, expressed in the practical service of others. There would be no churches and no scriptures; no theology of sin, no need for worship. God's presence would be so obvious and overwhelming that there would be no need for liturgy. Christians would not have a monopoly on truth, since the ideas of scientists, secularists, or those who belonged to a different faith would be just as valid. In its care for other human beings, the religion of the future would be no different from such secularist ideals as democracy, education, social reform, or preventative medicine.[7] This extreme version of the Social Gospel was a recoil from the doctrinal disputes of recent decades. In a society that valued only rational or scientifically demonstrable truth, dogma had become a problem. Theology could easily become a fetish, an idol that became a supreme value in itself instead of a symbol of an ineffable and indescribable reality. By seeking to bypass doctrine, Eliot was trying to get back to what he regarded as fundamental: love of God and neighbor. All the world faiths have emphasized the importance of social justice and care for the vulnerable. A disciplined and practically expressed compassion had been found, in all traditions, to yield a sense of the sacred, as long as it did not become a do-gooding ego trip. Eliot was thus attempting to address the real dilemma of Christians in the modern world by building a faith that relied more upon practice than upon orthodox beliefs.

The conservatives, however, were appalled. Faith without infallible doctrine was not Christianity in their view, and they felt obliged to counter this liberal danger. In 1910, the Presbyterians of Princeton, who had formulated the doctrine of the infallibility of Scripture, issued a list of five dogmas which they deemed essential: (1) the inerrancy of Scripture, (2) the Virgin Birth of Christ, (3) Christ's atonement for our sins on the cross, (4) his bodily resurrection, and (5) the objective reality of his miracles. (This last doctrine would later be replaced by the teachings of premillennialism.)[8] Next, the oil millionaires Lyman and Milton Stewart, who had founded the Bible College of Los Angeles to counter the Higher Criticism in 1908, financed a project designed to educate the faithful in the central tenets of the faith. Between 1910 and 1915, they issued a series of twelve paperback pamphlets entitled *The Fundamentals,* in which leading conservative theologians gave accessible accounts of such doctrines as the Trinity, refuted the Higher Criticism, and stressed the importance of spreading the truth of the Gospel. Some three million copies of each of the twelve volumes were dispatched, free of charge, to every pastor, professor, and theology student in America. Later this project would acquire great symbolic significance, since fundamentalists would see it as the germ of their movement. However, at the time, the pamphlets caused little critical interest, and the tone was neither radical nor particularly militant.[9]

But during the Great War, an element of terror entered conservative Protestantism and it became fundamentalist. Americans had always had a tendency to see a conflict as apocalyptic, and the Great War confirmed many of them in their premillennial convictions. The horrific slaughter, they decided, was on such a scale that it could only be the beginning of the End. These must be the battles foretold in the Book of Revelation. Three big Prophecy Conferences were held between 1914 and 1918, where participants combed through the *Scofield Reference Bible* to find more "signs of the times." Everything indicated that these predictions were indeed coming to pass. The Hebrew prophets had foretold that the Jews would return to their own land before the End, so when the British government issued the Balfour Declaration (1917), pledging its support for a Jewish homeland in Palestine, the premillennialists were struck with awe and exultation. Scofield had suggested that Russia was "the power from the North"[10] that would attack Israel shortly before Armageddon; the Bolshevik Revolution (1917), which made atheistic communism the state ideology, seemed to confirm this. The creation of the League of Nations obviously fulfilled the prophecy of Revelation 16:14: it was the revived Roman empire that would shortly be led by Antichrist. As they watched world events, the premillennial Protestants were becoming more politically conscious. What had been in the late nineteenth century a purely doctrinal dispute with the liberals in their denominations, was becoming a struggle for the future of civilization. They saw themselves on the front line against satanic forces that would shortly destroy the world. The wild tales of German atrocities circulating during and immediately after the war seemed to prove to the conservatives how right they had been to reject the nation that had given birth to the Higher Criticism.[11]

Yet this vision was inspired by deep dread. It was xenophobic, fearful of foreign influence seeping into the nation through Catholics, communists, and Higher Critics. This fundamentalist faith shows a profound recoil from the modern world. Conservative Protestants had become extremely ambivalent about democracy: it would lead to "mob rule," to a "red republic," to the "most devilish rule this world has ever seen."[12] Peace-keeping institutions, such as the League of Nations, would henceforth always be imbued with absolute evil in the eyes of the fundamentalists. The League was clearly the abode of Antichrist, who, St. Paul had said, would be a plausible liar whose deceit would take everybody in. The Bible said that there would be war in the End-times, not peace, so the League was dangerously on the wrong track. Indeed, Antichrist himself was likely to be a peacemaker.[13] The fundamentalists' revulsion from the League and other international bodies also revealed a visceral fear of the centralization of modernity and a terror of anything resembling world government. Faced with the universalism of modern society, some people instinctively retreated into tribalism.

This type of conspiracy fear, which makes people feel that they are fighting for their lives, can easily become aggressive. Jesus was no longer the loving savior preached by Dwight Moody. As the leading premillennialist, Isaac M. Haldeman, explained, the Christ of the Book of Revelation "comes forth as one who no longer seeks either friendship or love. . . . His garments are dipped in blood, the blood of others. He descends that he may shed the blood of men."[14] The conservatives were ready for a fight, and, at this crucial moment, the liberal Protestants went on the offensive.

The liberals had their own difficulties with the war, which challenged their vision of a world progressing inexorably toward the Kingdom of God. The only way they could cope was to see this as the war to end all wars, which would make the world safe for democracy. They were horrified by the violence of premillennialism, and its devastating critique of democracy and the League of Nations. These doctrines seemed not only un-American but a denial of Christianity itself. They decided to attack, and, despite their Gospel of love and compassion, their campaign was vicious and unbalanced. In 1917, theologians at the Divinity School of the University of Chicago, the leading scholastic institution of liberal Christianity in the United States, began to attack the Moody Bible Institute on the other side of town.[15] Professor Shirley Jackson Chase accused the premillennialists of being traitors to their country and of taking money from the Germans. Alva S. Taylor compared them to the Bolsheviks, who also wanted to see the world remade in a day. Alfred Dieffenbach, the editor of the *Christian Register,* called premillennialism "the most astounding mental aberration in the field of religious thinking."[16]

By linking the devout teachers of the Moody Bible Institute with foes who were not only their political enemies but whom they regarded as satanic, the liberals had hit below the belt. The conservatives struck back, hard. The editor of the *Moody Bible Institute Monthly* and president of the Institute, James M. Gray, retorted that it was the pacifism of the liberals which had caused the United States to fall behind Germany in the arms race, so it was they who had jeopardized the war effort.[17] In *The King's Business,* a premillennial magazine, Thomas C. Horton argued that it was the liberals who were in league with the Germans, since the Higher Criticism which they taught in their Divinity School had caused the war and was responsible for the collapse of decent values in Germany.[18] Other conservative articles blamed rationalism and evolutionary theory for the alleged German atrocities.[19] Howard W. Kellogg of the Bible Institute of Los Angeles insisted that the philosophy of evolution was responsible for "a monster plotting world domination, the wreck of civilization, and the destruction of Christianity itself."[20] This acrimonious and, on both sides, unchristian dispute had clearly touched a raw nerve, and evoked a deep fear of annihilation. There was no longer any possibility of reconciliation on the subject of the Higher Criticism, which, for the conservatives, now had an aura of absolute evil. The literal truth of scripture was a matter of the life and death of Christianity itself. The critics' attacks on the Bible would result in anarchy and the total collapse of civilization, the Baptist minister John Straton declared in a famous sermon entitled "Will New York City Be Destroyed If It Does Not Repent?"[21] The conflict had got out of hand and it would become almost impossible to heal the rift.

In August 1917, William Bell Riley had sat down with A. C. Dixon (1854–1925), one of the editors of *The Fundamentals,* and the revivalist Reuben Torrey (1856–1928) and decided to form an association to promote the literal interpretation of scripture and the "scientific" doctrines of premillennialism. In 1919 Riley held a massive conference in Philadelphia, attended by six thousand conservative Christians from all the Protestant denominations, and formally established the World's Christian Fundamentals Association (WCFA). Immediately afterward, Riley escorted fourteen speakers with a troupe of Gospel singers on a superbly organized tour of the United States, which visited eighteen cities. The liberals were entirely unprepared for this onslaught, and the response to the fundamentalist speakers was so enthusiastic that Riley believed that he had launched a new Reformation.[22] The fundamentalist campaign was perceived as a battle. Constantly, the leaders used military imagery. "I believe the time has come," wrote E. A. Wollam in the *Christian Workers Magazine*, "when the evangelistic forces of this country, primarily the Bible Institutes, should not only rise up in defense of the faith, but should become a united and offensive power." In the same issue, James M. Gray agreed, calling for the need "for an offensive and defensive alliance in the Church."[23] At a meeting of the Northern Baptist Convention in 1920, Curtis Lee Laws defined the "fundamentalist" as one who was ready to regain territory which had been lost to Antichrist and "to do battle royal for the fundamentals of the faith."[24] Riley went further. This was not just an isolated battle, "it is a war from which there is no discharge."[25]

The fundamentalists' next objective was to expel the liberals from the denominations. Most of the fundamentalists were either Baptists or Presbyterians, and it was here that the fiercest battles were fought. In his celebrated book *Christianity and Liberalism* (1923), the Presbyterian theologian J. Gresham Machen (1881–1937), the most intellectual of the fundamentalists, argued that the liberals were pagans, who, by denying the literal truth of such core doctrines as the Virgin Birth, denied Christianity itself. There were horrific fights in the general assemblies of the denominations, when fundamentalist Presbyterians tried to impose their five-point creed on the church; after a particularly bitter dispute, Riley seceded from the Baptist Assembly to found his own Bible Baptist Union of hard-liners. Some fundamentalist Baptists remained in the mainline denomination, hoping to effect reform from within, only to earn Riley's undying hatred.[26]

The campaigns continued; feeling escalated to such a point that any attempt at mediation only made matters worse. When the liberal preacher Harry Emerson Fosdick (1878–1969), a peaceable man and one of the most influential American clergymen of the time, pleaded for tolerance in a sermon delivered at the Baptist Convention of 1922 (later published in *The Baptist* as "Shall the Fundamentalists Win?"), the rancor of the response showed the visceral disgust that these liberal ideas inspired.[27] It spread to other denominations. After the sermon, there seemed to be a landslide movement toward the fundamentalist camp: the more conservative Disciples of Christ, Seventh-Day Adventists, Pentecostals, Mormons, and the Salvation Army rallied to the fundamentalist cause. Even Methodists and Episcopalians, who had remained aloof from the controversy, were challenged by the conservatives in their ranks to define and make obligatory "the vital and eternal truths of the Christian religion."[28] By 1923, it looked as though the fundamentalists would indeed win and that they would rid the denominations of the liberal danger. But then a new campaign caught the attention of the nation and eventually brought the whole fundamentalist movement into disrepute.

In 1920, the Democratic politician and Presbyterian William Jennings Bryan (1860–1925) had launched a crusade against the teaching of evolution in schools and colleges. In his view, it was not the Higher Criticism but Darwinism that had been responsible for the atrocities of the First World War.[29] Bryan had been impressed by two books which claimed to establish a direct link between evolutionary theory and German militarism: Benjamin Kidd's *The Science of Power* (1918) and Vernon L. Kellogg's *Headquarter Nights* (1917), which included interviews with German officers who described the influence that Darwinism had allegedly played in persuading the Germans to declare war. Not only had the notion that only the strong could or should survive "laid the foundation for the bloodiest war in history," Byran concluded, but "the same science that manufactured poisonous gases to suffocate soldiers is preaching that man has a brutal ancestry and eliminating the miraculous and supernatural from the Bible."[30] At the same time, in his book *Belief in God and Immortality*, Bryn Mawr psychologist James H. Leuba produced statistics that "proved" that a college education endangered religious belief. Darwinism was causing young men and women to lose faith in God, the Bible, and other fundamental doctrines of Christianity. Bryan was not a typical fundamentalist; he was not a premillennialist nor did he read scripture with the new stringent literalism. But his "research" had convinced him that evolutionary theory was incompatible with morality, decency, and the survival of civilization. When he toured the United States with his lecture "The Menace of Darwinism," he drew big audiences and received extensive media coverage.

Bryan's conclusions were superficial, naive, and incorrect, but people were ready to listen to him. The First World War had ended the honeymoon period with science; there was now an uneasiness about its fearsome potential and in some quarters a desire to see it kept within bounds. Darwin's scientific theory was a prime example of the disturbing tendency of some scientific experts to fly in the face of "common sense." People who wanted a plain-speaking religion were all too eager to find a plausible reason— that they could understand—to reject evolution. Bryan gave them this and, single-handedly, pushed the topic of evolution to the top of the fundamentalist agenda. It was a cause that appealed to the new fundamentalist ethos, since Darwinism contradicted the literal truth of scripture, and Bryan's paranoid interpretation of its effect tapped the new fears that had surfaced after the First World War. As Charles Hodge had argued fifty years earlier, the Darwinian hypothesis was repugnant to the Baconian mind-set of the fundamentalists, who still clung to the scientific outlook of early modernity.

Intellectuals and sophisticates might follow these new ideas with enthusiasm in Yale and Harvard and in the big eastern cities, but they were alien to many small-town Americans, who felt that their culture was being taken over by the secularist establishment. Yet the campaign against evolution might still never have replaced the Higher Criticism as the chief fundamentalist bugbear had it not been for a dramatic development in the South, which had hitherto taken little part in the fundamentalist battle.

There had been no need for southerners to become fundamentalists. The southern states were much more conservative than the North at this point, and there were too few liberals in the southern denominations to warrant a fundamentalist campaign. But southerners were worried about the teaching of evolution in the public schools. It was an example of the "colonization" of their society by an alien ideology, and bills were introduced in the state legislatures of Florida, Mississippi, Louisiana, and Arkansas to ban the teaching of Darwinian theory. The anti-evolution laws in Tennessee were particularly severe, and to put them to the test and strike a symbolic blow for freedom of speech and the First Amendment, John Scopes, a young teacher in the small town of Dayton, confessed that he had broken the law when he had once substituted for his school principal in a biology class. In July 1925, he was brought to trial, and the new American Civil Liberties Union (ACLU) sent a team of lawyers to defend him, headed by the rationalist lawyer and campaigner Clarence Darrow (1857–1938). At the request of Riley and other fundamentalist leaders, William Jennings Bryan agreed to support the law. Once Darrow and Bryan became involved, the trial ceased to be simply about civil liberties, and became a contest between God and science.

The Scopes Trial was a clash between two utterly incompatible points of view.[31] Both Darrow and Bryan were defending crucial American values; Darrow was for free speech, and Bryan for the rights of the ordinary people, who had long been leery of the influence of learned experts and specialists. Bryan's political campaigns had all championed the common man. A review of In His Image (1922), Bryan's answer to Darwin, claimed that he was "the spokesman for a numerically large segment of the people who are for the most part inarticulate. In fact, he is almost the only exponent of their ideas who has the public ear. They are part of the body politic and by no means negligible or to be regarded solely with derision as 'lunatic fringe.' "[32] This was undoubtedly true, but unfortunately Bryan was not able to articulate these inchoate and ill-informed anxieties adequately at the trial. Where Darrow was able to argue brilliantly for the freedom that science must have to express itself and advance, Bryan, the Presbyterian and Baconian, insisted that, in the absence of definite proof, people had a right to reject an "unsupported hypothesis" such as Darwinism because of its immoral effects. Where Scopes himself treated the whole trial as a farce, Darrow and Bryan were in deadly earnest, and fighting for values that each considered sacred and inviolable.[33] But when Darrow put Bryan on the stand, his merciless cross-examination exposed the muddle-headed and simplistic nature of Bryan's views. Cornered, Bryan was forced by Darrow to concede that the world was far more than six thousand years old, as a literal reading of the Bible implied, that the six "days" of creation mentioned in Genesis were each longer than twenty-four hours, that he had never read any critical account of the origins of the biblical text, that he had no interest in any other faith, and that, finally, "I do not think about things I don't think about" and only thought about the things he *did* think about "sometimes."[34] It was a rout. Darrow emerged from the trial as the hero of clear rational thought, and the elderly Bryan was discredited as bumbling, incompetent, and obscurantist; he died a few days after the trial, as a result of his exertions.

Scopes was convicted, but the ACLU paid his fine, and Darrow and modern science were the undoubted victors at Dayton. The press gleefully exposed Bryan and his supporters as hopeless anachronisms. In particular, the journalist H. L. Mencken denounced the fundamentalists as the scourge of the nation. It was, he crowed, appropriate that Bryan had ended his days in a "one-horse, Tennessee village," because he loved all country people, including the "gaping primates of the upland valleys." Fundamentalists were everywhere. They

> are thick in the mean streets behind the gas-works. They are everywhere learning is too heavy a burden for mortal minds to carry, even the vague, pathetic learning on tap in the little red schoolhouses.[35]

Fundamentalists belonged to the past; they were the enemies of science and intellectual liberty, and could take no legitimate part in the modern world. As Maynard Shipley argued in *The War on Modern Science* (1927), if the fundamentalists managed to seize power in the denominations and impose their strictures on the people by law, Americans would lose the best part of their culture and be dragged back to the Dark Ages. Liberal secularists felt threatened, and hit back. A culture is always a contested matter, with different groups striving to make their visions prevail. At Dayton, the secularists won the battle and, by pouring scorn on the fundamentalists, seemed to have vanquished them by showing that they could not and should not be taken seriously. The fundamentalists went quiet after the Scopes trial, the liberals gained control of the denominations, and there seemed to be a détente. William Bell Riley and his followers appeared to have given up their struggle; by the end of the decade, Riley was willing to sit on a panel with the liberal Harry Fosdick.

But in fact the fundamentalists had not gone away. Indeed, after the trial their views became more extreme. They felt embittered and nursed a deep grievance against mainstream culture. At Dayton, they had tried—badly—to fight the view of the more radical secularists that religion was an archaic irrelevance, and that only science was important. They could not express this point of view effectively and chose the wrong forum in which to do it. Bryan's anti-German phobia was paranoid, and his demonizing of Darwin inaccurate. But the moral and spiritual imperatives of religion are important for humanity and should not be relegated unthinkingly to the scrap heap of history in the interests of an unfettered rationalism. The relationship between science and ethics has continued to be an issue of pressing concern. But the fundamentalists lost their case at Dayton, and it seemed to them that they had been treated with contempt and pushed to the margins of society. Fifty years earlier, the New Lights had constituted a majority in America; after the Scopes trial, they had become outsiders. But the ridicule of such secularist crusaders as Mencken was counterproductive. Fundamentalist faith was rooted in deep fear and anxiety that could not be assuaged by a purely rational argument. After Dayton, they became more extreme.[36] Before the trial, evolution had not been an important issue for them, and even such literalists as Charles Hodge had accepted that the age of the world was more than six thousand years, whatever it said in the Bible. Few fundamentalists had believed in the so-called "creation science," which argued that Genesis was scientifically sound in every detail. But after Dayton, fundamentalists closed their minds even more, and Creationism and an unswerving biblical literalism became central to the fundamentalist mindset. They also drifted to the far right of the political spectrum. Before the war, fundamentalists like Riley and John R. Straton (1875–1929) had been willing to work for social reform and with people on the left. Now the Social Gospel was tainted by its association with the liberals who had defeated them in the denominations. This will be a constant theme in our story. Fundamentalism exists in a symbiotic relationship with an aggressive liberalism or secularism, and, under attack, invariably becomes more extreme, bitter, and excessive.

Darrow and Mencken were also wrong to assume that fundamentalists belonged entirely to the old world. In their way, fundamentalists were ardent modernists. By attempting to return to "fundamentals," they were in line with other intellectual and scientific currents in the early twentieth century.[37] They were as addicted to scientific rationalism as any other modernists, even though they were Baconians rather than Kantians. As A. C. Dixon explained in 1920, he was a Christian "because I am a Thinker, a Rationalist, a Scientist." Faith was no leap in the dark but depended upon "exact observation and correct thinking."[38] Doctrines were not theological speculations, but facts. This was an entirely modern religious development, which was light-years from the premodern spirituality of the conservative period. Fundamentalists were trying to create a new way of being religious in an age that valued the *logos* of science above all else. Time alone would tell how successful this attempt would be religiously, but Dayton had revealed that fundamentalism was bad science, which could not measure up to the scientific standards of the twentieth century.

At the same time as the fundamentalists were evolving their modern faith, the Pentecostalists were creating a "postmodern" vision that represented a grassroots rejection of the rational modernity of the Enlightenment. Where the fundamentalists were returning to what they regarded as the doctrinal base of Christianity, Pentecostals, who had no interest in dogma, were returning to an even more fundamental level: the nub of raw religiosity that exists beneath the credal formulations of a faith. While fundamentalists put their faith in the written Word of scripture, Pentecostalists bypassed language, which, as the mystics had always insisted, could not adequately express the Reality that lies beyond concepts and reason. Their religious discourse was not the *logos* of the fundamentalists, but went beyond words. Pentecostalists spoke in "tongues," convinced that the Holy Spirit had descended upon them in the same way as it had descended upon Jesus' apostles on the Jewish feast of Pentecost, when the divine presence had manifested itself in tongues of fire, and given the Apostles the ability to speak in strange languages.[39]

The first group of Pentecostalists had experienced the Spirit in a tiny house in Los Angeles on April 9, 1906. The leader of the group was William Joseph Seymour (1870–1915), the son of slaves who had been freed after the Civil War, who had long been searching for a more immediate and uninhibited type of religion than was possible in the more formal white Protestant denominations. By 1900, he had been converted to Holiness spirituality, which believed that, as the prophet Joel had foretold, the gifts of healing, ecstasy, tongues, and prophecy enjoyed by the Primitive Church would be restored to the people of God immediately before the Last Days.[40] When Seymour and his friends experienced the Spirit, the news spread like wildfire. Crowds of African Americans and disadvantaged whites poured into his next service in such huge numbers that they had to move to an old warehouse in Azusa Street. Within four years, there were hundreds of Pentecostal groups all over the United States and the movement had spread to fifty countries.[41] This first Pentecostal upsurge was yet another of the popular

Awakenings that have exploded from time to time during the modern period when people have become convinced at gut level that a great change is at hand. Seymour and the first Pentecostalists were convinced that the Last Days had begun, and that soon Jesus would return and establish a more just social order. But after the First World War, when it seemed that Jesus would not return as quickly as they had expected, Pentecostalists began to interpret their gift of tongues differently. They now saw it as a new way of speaking to God. St. Paul had explained that when Christians found it difficult to pray, "the Spirit itself intercedes for us with groans beyond all utterance."[42] They were reaching out to a God that existed beyond the scope of speech.

In these early years, it did indeed seem that a new world order was coming into being at these Pentecostal services. At a time of economic insecurity and increased xenophobia, blacks and whites prayed together and embraced one another. Seymour became convinced that it was this racial integration rather than the gift of tongues that was the decisive sign of the Last Days.[43] The Pentecostal movement was not entirely idyllic. There were rivalries and factions, and some white Pentecostals set up their own separatist churches.[44] But the extraordinarily rapid spread of the movement among the people reflected a widespread revolt against the status quo. At a Pentecostal service, men and women spoke in tongues, fell into tranced, ecstatic states, were seen to levitate, and felt that their bodies were laughing in unspeakable joy. People saw bright luminous streaks in the air, and sprawled on the ground, felled by what seemed a weight of glory.[45] This wild ecstasy was potentially dangerous, but in these early days, at least, people did not fall into despair and depression, as some had during the Great Awakening. African Americans were more skilled in this ecstatic spirituality, though later, as we shall see, some white Pentecostalists would fall into unhealthy and nihilistic states of mind. In its infancy, the movement emphasized the importance of love and compassion, which provided its own discipline. Seymour used to say: "If you get angry or speak evil, or backbite, I care not how many tongues you have, you have not the baptism with the Holy Spirit."[46] "God sent this latter rain to gather up all the poor and outcast, and make us love everybody," explained D. W. Myland, an early interpreter of Pentecostalism, in 1910. "God is taking the despised things, the base things, and being glorified in them."[47] The stress on inclusiveness and compassionate love was in marked contrast to the divisiveness of fundamentalist Christianity. If charity is the final test of any religiosity, at this point the Pentecostalists were pulling ahead.

As the American scholar Harvey Cox has argued in an illuminating study of Pentecostalism, the movement was an attempt to recover many of the experiences that the modern West had rejected.[48] It can be seen as a grassroots rebellion against the modern cult of reason. Pentecostalism took hold at a time when people were beginning to have doubts about science, and when religious people were becoming uncomfortably aware that a reliance upon reason alone had worrying implications for faith, which had traditionally depended on the more intuitive, imaginative, and aesthetic mental disciplines. While fundamentalists were trying to make their Bible-based religion entirely reasonable and scientific, Pentecostalists were returning to the core of religiousness, defined by Cox as "that largely unprocessed nucleus of the psyche in which the unending struggle for a sense of purpose and significance goes on."[49] Where fundamentalists, by identifying faith with rationally proven dogma, were confining the religious experience to the outermost cerebral rim of the mind, Pentecostalists were delving back into the unconscious source of mythology and religiousness. While fundamentalists stressed the importance of the Word and the literal, Pentecostalists bypassed conventional speech and tried to access the primal spirituality that lies beneath the credal formulations of a tradition. Where the modern ethos insisted that men and women focus pragmatically only upon this world, Pentecostalists demonstrated the human yearning for ecstasy and transcendence. The meteoric explosion of this form of faith showed that by no means everybody was enthralled by the scientific rationalism of modernity. This instinctive recoil from many of the shibboleths of modernity showed that many people felt that something was missing from the brave new world of the West.

We shall often find in our story that the religious behavior of people who have not been major beneficiaries of modernity articulates a strongly felt need for the spiritual, which is so often either excluded or marginalized in a secularist society. The American critic Susan Sontag has noted a "perennial discontent with language," which has surfaced in Eastern and Western civilizations whenever "thought reaches a certain, high *excruciating* order of complexity and spiritual seriousness."[50] At such a moment, people begin to share the mystics' impatience with the capacity of human speech. Mystics in all the faiths have insisted that the ultimate reality is essentially ineffable and inexpressible. Some have developed modes of ecstatic utterance, not dissimilar to the Pentecostal speaking-in-tongues, to help an adept cultivate a sense that, when humans are in the presence of the sacred and the transcendent, words, and the rational concepts they express, fail us: Tibetan monks emit a double-bass drone, for example, and Hindu gurus a nasal whine.[51] The Pentecostalists at Azusa Street had spontaneously hit upon one of the established ways in which the various traditions have sought to prevent the divine from being imprisoned within purely human systems of thought. The fundamentalists, however, were moving in quite the opposite direction.

Yet both Pentecostalists and fundamentalists were reacting, in their different ways, to the fact that by the early decades of the twentieth century, Western discourse had reached an unprecedented complexity. At the Scopes trial, Bryan had fought for the "common sense" of ordinary folk and tried to strike a blow against the tyranny of the experts and the specialists. The Pentecostalists were revolting against the hegemony of reason, but, like the fundamentalists, were insisting on the right of the least educated people to speak out and make their voices heard.

True to their exclusive and condemnatory piety, the fundamentalists hated the Pentecostalists. Warfield argued that the age of miracles had ceased; the Pentecostalists were as bad as the Roman Catholics in their belief that God overturned the laws of nature on a regular basis today. The unreason of the Pentecostalists was an affront to the scientific and verbal control that the fundamentalists were seeking to exert over faith, in their struggle to ensure its survival in a world that seemed hostile to it. Other fundamentalists accused the Pentecostalists of superstition and fanaticism; one went so far as to call the movement "the last vomit of Satan."[52] This vituperative and judgmental strain was one of the most unattractive traits of the new Protestant fundamentalism, and, after the Scopes Trial, this condemnatory attitude, which is so far from the spirit of the Gospels, would become even more marked. But, despite their differences, both the fundamentalists and the Pentecostalists were trying to fill the void left by the victory of reason in the modern Western world. In their emphasis upon love and their wariness of doctrine, the Pentecostalists were closer to the middle-class liberal Protestants at this early stage, though later in the century, as we shall see, some would be drawn into the more extreme, hard-line fundamentalist camp and would lose their sense of the primacy of charity.

IN THE JEWISH WORLD, there were also signs that people were beginning to retreat from the overly rational forms of faith that had developed during the nineteenth century. In Germany, philosophers such as Herman Cohn (1842–1918) and Franz Rosenzweig (1886–1929) attempted to keep alive the values of the Enlightenment, though Rosenzweig also tried to revive the old ideas of mythology and ritual in a way that modernized people could appreciate. He described the various commandments of the Torah, which could not always be explained rationally, as symbols, pointing beyond themselves to the divine. These rites created an interior attitude that opened Jews to the possibility of the sacred, helping them to cultivate a listening, waiting attitude. The biblical stories of creation and revelation were not facts but expressions of spiritual realities in our inner lives. Other scholars, such as

Martin Buber (1878–1965) and Gershom Scholem (1897–1982), directed attention to those forms of faith which had been dismissed by the rationalist historians. Buber revealed the richness of Hasidism and Scholem explored the world of the Kabbalah. But these older spiritualities, which belonged to a different world, were increasingly opaque to Jews who were imbued with the rational spirit.

Zionists often experienced their defiantly secularist ideology in ways that would once have been called religious. People had to fill the spiritual vacuum somehow, in order to avoid nihilistic despair. If conventional religion no longer worked, they would create a secularist spirituality that filled their lives with transcendent meaning. Zionism was, like other modern movements, a return to a single, fundamental value that represented a new way of being Jewish. By going back to the Land, Jews would not only save themselves from the anti-Semitic catastrophe that some felt to be imminent, but they would also find psychic healing without God, the Torah, or the Kabbalah. The Zionist writer Asher Ginsberg (1856–1927), who wrote under the pseudonym Ahad Ha-Am ("One of the People"), was convinced that Jews had to develop a more rational and scientific way of looking at the world. But, like a true modern, he wanted to return to the irreducible *essence* of Judaism, which could only be found when Jews returned to their roots and took up residence in Palestine. Religion, he believed, was only the outer shell of Judaism. The new national spirit that Jews would create in the Holy Land would do what God had once done for them. It would become "a guide to all the affairs of life," would reach "to the depths of the heart" and "connect with all one's feelings."[53] The return to Zion would thus become the sort of interior journey once undertaken by Kabbalists: a descent to the depths of the psyche to achieve integration.

Zionists, who often hated religion, instinctively spoke of their movement in Orthodox terminology. *Aliyah,* the Hebrew word they used for "immigration," was originally a term used to describe an ascent to a higher state of being. They called immigrants *olim* ("those who ascend," or "pilgrims"). A "pioneer" who joined one of the new agricultural settlements was called a *chalutz,* a word with strong religious connotations of salvation, liberation, and rescue.[54] When they arrived at the port of Jaffa, Zionists would often kiss the ground; they experienced their immigration as a new birth, and, like the biblical patriarchs, sometimes changed their names to express their sense of empowerment.

The spirituality of Labor Zionism was most eloquently and powerfully expressed by Aharon David Gordon (1856–1922), who arrived in Palestine in 1904 and worked in the new cooperative settlement in Degania in the Galilee. There he experienced what religious Jews would have called an experience of the Shekhinah. Gordon was an Orthodox Jew and Kabbalist, but he was also a student of Kant, Schopenhauer, Nietzsche, Marx, and Tolstoy. He had come to believe that modern industrialized society exiled men and women from themselves. They had developed a one-sided and over-rational approach to life. To counteract this, they must cultivate *chavayah,* an immediate, mystical experience of the sacred, by immersing themselves as fully as possible in the life of the natural landscape, because that was where the Infinite revealed itself to humanity. For Jews, that landscape must be in Palestine. "The soul of the Jew," Gordon insisted, "is the offspring of the natural environment of the Land of Israel." Only there could a Jew experience what Kabbalists had called "clarity, the depth of an infinitely clear sky, a clear perspective, mists of purity."[55] By means of labor *(avodah)* a pioneer would experience "the divine unknown," and would re-create himself, as the mystics had done in the course of their spiritual exercises. By working on the land, "the unnatural, defective, splintered person" that he had become in the Diaspora would be "changed into a natural, wholesome human being who is true to himself."[56] For Gordon it was no accident that *avodah,* the word for "labor" or "service," had once applied to the liturgy in the Temple. For the Zionist, holiness and wholeness were no longer to be found in conventional religious practices, but in their hard labor in the hills and farms of Galilee.

One of the most innovative and daring Jewish attempts to spiritualize the secular was developed by Rabbi Abraham Yitzak Kook (1865–1935), who also migrated to Palestine in 1904 to become the rabbi of the new settler communities. It was an odd appointment. Unlike most of the Orthodox, Kook had been deeply stirred by the Zionist movement, but he had been horrified to hear that the delegates to the Second Zionist Congress in Basel in 1898 had issued the statement: "Zionism has nothing to do with religion."[57] He condemned this remark in the strongest terms. It "spreads the terrible, black wings of death over our tender, lovely young national movement, by cutting it off from the source of its very life and the light of its splendor." It was an "abomination and perverse;" a "poison" that was corrupting Zionism, causing it to "putrify and be covered in worms." It could only turn Zionism "into an empty vessel . . . filled with a spirit of destructiveness and strife."[58] Kook often spoke like one of the ancient prophets, but many elements in his thought were modern. He was one of the first religious people who perceived, long before the First World War, that nationalism could become lethal and that, without a sense of the sacred, politics could become demonic. He pointed to the example of the French Revolution, which had begun with such high ideals but had degenerated into an orgy of bloodshed and cruelty. A purely secularist ideology could trample on the divine image in men and women; if it made the state its supreme value, there was nothing to stop a ruler from exterminating subjects who, in his view, obstructed the good of the nation. "When nationalism alone takes root among the people," he warned, "it is as likely to debase and dehumanize their spirit as elevate it."[59]

There have, of course, been secularist ideologies that have helped people to cultivate a deep sense of the sacred inviolability of each human being without recourse to the supernatural. And religions have been just as murderous as any secular ideal. But Kook uttered a timely warning, since the twentieth century, from start to finish, has been characterized by one act of genocide after another, committed by nationalist, secularist rulers. Kook was anxious lest Zionism become equally oppressive and the Jewish state a dangerous idolatry. But he was also convinced that any attempt to separate a Jewish state from God was doomed, because Jews were existentially connected to the divine, whether they knew it or not. When he arrived in Palestine, one of Kook's first duties was to deliver a eulogy in honor of Theodor Herzl, who had died tragically young. To the fury of the Orthodox community in Palestine, who saw Zionism as inherently evil, Kook presented Herzl as the Messiah of the House of Joseph, a doomed Redeemer in popular Jewish eschatology who was expected to arrive at the start of the messianic era to fight the enemies of the Jews and would die at the gates of Jerusalem. His campaign would, however, have paved the way for the final Messiah of the House of David, who would bring Redemption. This was how Kook saw Herzl. Many of his achievements had been constructive, but insofar as he had tried to eliminate religion from his ideology, his work had been damaging. It was, like the efforts of the Josephic Messiah, destined to fail. But Kook also argued that the Orthodox who opposed Zionism were equally destructive; by making themselves "an enemy of material change," they had made the Jewish people weak.[60] Religious and secularist Jews needed one another; neither could exist without the other.

This recast the old conservative vision. In the premodern world, religion and reason had occupied separate but complementary spheres. Both had been necessary and each would be the poorer without the other. Kook was a Kabbalist, inspired by the mythology and mysticism of the conservative period. But, like some of the other reformers we have considered, he was modern in his conviction that change was now the law of life and that it was essential to throw off the constraints of agrarian culture, however painful this might be. He believed that the young Zionist settlers would make Jews move forward and—ultimately—bring Redemption. Their ruthlessly pragmatic ideology was the *logos* that human beings needed in order to survive and function effectively in this world. But unless this was linked creatively to the *mythos* of Judaism, it would lose its meaning and, cut off from the source of life, would wither away.

When Kook arrived in Palestine, he met these young secularists for the first time. A few years earlier, their rejection of religion had appalled him, but when he saw them going about their work in the Holy Land he was forced to revise his ideas. He discovered that they had their own spirituality. Yes, they were brazen and insolent, but they also had the great qualities of "kindness, honesty, fairness, and mercy, . . . and the spirit of knowledge and idealism is ascendent [among them]." More important, their rebelliousness, which so offended the "weak who inhabit the world of order, the moderate, and well-mannered," would push the Jewish people forward; their dynamism was essential if Jews were to progress and fulfill their destiny.[61] When he praised the Zionist pioneers, he picked out those qualities which would have been utterly abhorrent to a sage of the premodern period, where people had to accept the rhythms and restrictions of the existing order and where individuals who stepped out of line could gravely damage society:[62]

> These fiery spirits assert themselves, refusing to be bound by any limitation. . . . The strong know that this show of force comes to rectify the world, to invigorate the nation, humanity and the world. It is only in the beginning that it appears in the form of chaos.[63]

Had not the rabbis of the Talmudic period predicted that there would be an "age of insolence and audacity,"[64] in which young men would rise up against their elders? This distressing rebellion was simply "the footsteps of the Messiah, . . . gloomy steps, leading to a rarefied, joyous existence."[65]

Kook was one of the first deeply religious thinkers able to embrace the new secularism, though he believed that ultimately the Zionist enterprise would lead to a religious renewal in Palestine. Instead of seeing the religious and secularists—representing *mythos* and *logos,* respectively—as coexisting peacefully, he developed a Hegelian vision of a dialectical clash of opposites leading to the synthesis of Redemption. The secularists clashed with the religious, but in this rebellion the Zionists were pushing history forward to new fulfillment. The whole of creation was being propelled, often painfully, toward a final reunion with the divine. One could see this in the evolutionary processes described by modern science, Kook believed, or in the scientific revolutions of Copernicus, Darwin, or Einstein, which seemed to destroy traditional ideas but which led to new understanding. Even the agony of the First World War could be seen, in Lurianic terms, as a "breaking of the vessels," part of the creative process, which would eventually reinstate the sacred in our world.[66] This was how religious Jews should see the Zionist rebellion. "There are times when the laws of the Torah must be overridden," Kook argued audaciously. When people were searching for a different path, everything was new and unprecedented, so "there is no one to show the legitimate way and so the aim is accomplished by a bursting of bounds." It was "outwardly lamentable but inwardly a source of joy!"[67]

Kook did not gloss over the difficulties. Between religious and secular Jews "there is a great war." Each camp had right on its side: the Zionists were correct to struggle against unnecessary restrictions, while the Orthodox were understandably anxious to avoid the chaos of a premature abandonment of tradition. But each side had only a partial truth.[68] The conflict between them would lead to a wonderful synthesis that would benefit not just the Jewish people but the whole world. "All the civilizations of the world will be renewed by the renaissance of our spirit," he prophesied; "all religions will don new and precious raiment, casting away all that is soiled, abominable, and unclean."[69] It was a messianic dream. Kook really believed that he was living in the last age and would shortly witness the final fulfillment of human history.

Kook was evolving a new myth, relating the extraordinary developments of his time to the timeless symbols of the Kabbalah. But as a man of the modern period, he directed his myth to the future; it depicts a painful and turbulent dynamic that is driving history onward. Instead of persuading his Jewish readers to accept the way things are and have to be, Kook argued that it was necessary to smash the sacred laws of the past and start afresh. But despite this modern thrust, Kook's myth still belongs in one important respect to the premodern world. His vision of the two camps, the religious and the secular Zionist, so similar to the old perception of *mythos* and *logos,* presented an equal division of labor. It was the rational pragmatists who were driving history forward, as *logos* had always done, while the religious, who represented the world of *mythos* and the cult, gave meaning to this activity. "We lay *tefillin* [phylacteries]," Kook was fond of telling the Orthodox, "and the pioneers lay bricks."[70] Without the myth, the Zionists' activities were not only meaningless but potentially demonic. The Zionists might not realize it, Kook believed, but they were the instruments of God, helping to bring about his divinely orchestrated plan. It was this alone that made their religious rebellion acceptable, and very soon—Kook indicated that this could happen in his own lifetime—there would be a spiritual revolution in the Holy Land and history would be redeemed.

True to the disciplines of the conservative age, Kook did not intend his myth to become an ideology, to be a blueprint for action. In any case, he had very few followers, and in his own lifetime was regarded as something of a crank. Kook put forward no political solution to the pressing problems of Zionist activity in Palestine. God had everything in hand. Kook's *mythos* simply enabled his followers to see what was really going on. Kook seemed utterly indifferent to the political form the future Jewish state should take. "As for me, my main concern is the spiritual content, grounded in holiness," he wrote to his son, Zvi Yehuda (1891–1981). "It is clear to me that, no matter how matters develop on the governmental level, if the spirit is strong it can lead to the desired goals, for with the sublime manifestation of free, shining holiness, we shall be able to illuminate all the paths of government."[71] In the present, unredeemed age, politics were corrupt and cruel. Kook was "disgusted with the terrible iniquities of ruling during the evil age." Fortunately, Jews had not been able to take an active political role since they had lost the Holy Land in 70 CE and gone into exile; until the world had been morally and spiritually transformed, Jews should stay out of politics. "It is not for Jacob to engage in government, as long as it entails bloodshed, as long as it requires a knack for wickedness." But very soon, "the world will be refined,"[72] and when that happened, Jews could put their minds to the type of polity and practical policies they wished to implement. "Once the Lord's people are established on their land in some definite way, they will turn their attention to the [geo]political realm, to purifying it of its dross, to cleansing the blood from its mouth and the abominations from between its teeth."[73] In the premodern world, myth was not supposed to be translated into practical action; that was the job of *logos* and—in Kook's scheme—of the pioneers.

Kook still felt that, in the present dispensation, religion and politics were incompatible, a conviction that had acquired the force of a taboo in the Orthodox world. The Zionists, who had cast off religion, were doing all the practical work.

Kook died in 1935, thirteen years before the establishment of the State of Israel. He did not live to see the terrible expedients to which Jews would feel driven in order to create a state for themselves in Arab Palestine. He never witnessed the expulsion of 750,000 Palestinians from their homes in 1948, nor the Arab and Jewish blood spilled in the course of the Arab-Israeli wars. Nor did he have to face the fact that, fifty years after the creation of the State of Israel, most of the Jews in the Holy Land would still be secularists. His son, Zvi Yehuda, would see these things, and, in his old age, would make his father's *mythos* a program for practical, political action and create a fundamentalist movement.

But in these terrible times, was it possible for Jews to keep out of political life? Not only was modern society becoming increasingly anti-Semitic, but secularism was making great inroads into Jewish communities and undermining the traditional way of life. In eastern Europe, modernization was only just beginning. Some of the rabbis of Russia and Poland continued to turn their backs on the new world and held aloof from politics. How could any Jew worthy of the name soil his integrity by taking part in the bargaining and compromise that were an essential part of modern political life in a democratic state? How could they square this with the absolute demands of the Torah? By making deals with gentiles and getting involved in their political institutions, Jews would bring the profane world into the community, and this would inevitably corrupt it. But the principals of the great Misnagdic *yeshivot* and the Hasidim of the Polish town of Ger disagreed. They could see that the various Zionist parties and the Jewish socialist parties were enticing Jews into a godless way of life. They wanted to stop the drift toward secularism and assimilation, and believed that these essentially modern dangers must be met on their own terms in modern ways. Religious Jews must fight the secularists with their own weapons. That meant the creation of a modern political party to protect Orthodox interests. This was not a wholly new idea, they contended. For a long time, the Jews of Russia and Poland had engaged in *shtadlanut* (political dialogue or negotiations) with the government to safeguard the welfare of the Jewish communities. The new Orthodox party would continue this work, but in a more efficient and organized manner.

In 1912, the Misnagdic *roshey yeshivot* and the Ger Hasidim founded a new party, Agudat Israel ("The Union of Israel"). They were joined by members of Mizrachi, an association of "religious Zionists" formed by Rabbi Isaac Jacob Reines (1839–1915) in 1901. Mizrachi was quite different from and less radical than Rabbi Kook, who saw the secular Zionist enterprise in Palestine as a profoundly religious development. More strictly Orthodox, Reines did not agree: the political activities of the Zionists had no religious significance whatsoever, but the creation of a Jewish homeland was a practical solution for a persecuted people, and therefore deserved the support of the Orthodox. If a homeland was established in Palestine one day, this might well, in the view of Mizrachi, lead to a spiritual renewal and to devout Torah observance there. In 1911, however, the Mizrachi delegates had walked out of the Tenth Zionist Congress at Basel, when the Congress failed to grant them equal funding for their religious schools in Palestine. Since they could no longer cooperate with mainstream Zionism, which seemed committed to radical secularism, they were prepared to throw in their lot with Agudat Israel, which soon had branches in both eastern and western Europe.

But the members of Agudat in the West saw the movement in a very different light from the Russian and Polish Jews, who still felt very cautious about direct activism.[74] The Jews of Russia and Poland saw Agudat as a

defensive organization only; its task was simply to safeguard Jewish interests at this crucial time when the governments of eastern Europe were trying
to modernize. They kept their activism to a minimum, worked to improve
the lot of Jews within a modern political framework, abjured Zionism, and
professed loyalty to the Polish state. But in the West, where modernization
was far advanced, Jews were ready for something different. Most Agudat
members in the West were Neo-Orthodox, which was itself a modernized
form of Judaism. They were now accustomed to the modern world, and
no longer sought simply to contain the shock of the new but wanted to
change it. Instead of seeing their party as a defensive organization, some
wanted Agudat to go on the offensive and were developing an incipient
fundamentalism.

For Jacob Rosenheim (1870–1965), the founding of Agudat was not
simply a slightly regrettable necessity, as it was for the eastern Jews, but a
cosmic event. For the first time since 70 CE, Jews had "a unified and will-
determining centre."[75] Agudat symbolized God's rule over Israel and
should become the central organization of the Jewish world. Nevertheless,
Rosenheim still felt slightly queasy about politics, and wanted Agudat to
confine its activities to maintaining Jewish schools and protecting Jews' economic rights. Younger members were more radical, and were closer in spirit
to Protestant fundamentalists. Isaac Breuer (1883–1946) wanted Agudat to
take the initiative and start a campaign for the reform and sacralization of
Jewish society. Like the premillennialists, he could see "signs" of God's
activity in the world. The Great War and the Balfour Declaration were the
"footsteps of the Messiah." Jews must reject the corrupt values of bourgeois
society, cease to cooperate with the governments of Europe, and create their
own sacred enclave in the Holy Land, where they would build a theocratic,
Torah-based state. Jewish history had gone awry; Jews had defected from
sacred tradition; it was now time to put Jewish history back on track and, if
Jews took the first step, made the exodus from the corrupt Diaspora, and
returned to their original values, living according to the Torah in their Land,
God would send the Messiah.[76]

The Jewish scholar Alan L. Mittelman notes that the early experience
of Agudat shows the way fundamentalism works. It is not an immediate,
knee-jerk response to modern secular society but only develops when the
modernization process is fairly advanced. At first, traditionalists—like the
eastern European members of Agudat—try simply to find ways of adapting
their faith to the new challenge. They adopt some modern ideas and institutions, and attempt to prove that these are not alien to tradition, that the faith
is strong enough to absorb these changes. But once society has become more
completely secular and rational, some find its innovations unacceptable.

They begin to realize that the whole thrust of secular modernity is diametrically opposed to the rhythms of conservative premodern religion, and that it threatens essential values. They begin to formulate a "fundamentalist" solution that returns to first principles and plans a counteroffensive.[77]

THE MUSLIMS we are considering had not yet reached this stage. Modernization was far from complete in Egypt, and had not really begun in Iran. Muslims were still either trying to absorb the new ideas in an Islamic context or adopting a secularist ideology. Fundamentalism would not appear in the Islamic world until these early stratagems had, in the eyes of some Muslims, proved to be inadequate. They would see secularism as an attempt to destroy Islam, and, indeed, in the Middle East, where Western modernity was being implemented in a foreign context, it often appeared very aggressive indeed.

This was obvious in the new secular state of Turkey. After the First World War, the Ottoman empire, which had fought on the side of Germany, was defeated by the European allies, who dismembered the empire and set up mandates and protectorates in the old Ottoman provinces. The Greeks invaded Anatolia and the old Ottoman heartland. From 1919 to 1922, Mustafa Kemal Atatürk (1881–1938) had led Turkish nationalist forces in a war of independence, and had succeeded in keeping the Europeans out of Turkey and in setting up a sovereign state, run on modern European lines. This was an unprecedented step in the Islamic world. By 1947, Turkey had acquired an efficient bureaucracy and a capitalist economy, and had become the first multiparty secular democracy in the Middle East. But this achievement began with an act of ethnic cleansing. Between 1894 and 1927, successive Ottoman and Turkish governments had systematically expelled, deported, or massacred the Greek and Armenian inhabitants of Anatolia to get rid of these foreign elements, who comprised about 90 percent of the bourgeoisie. Not only did this purge give the new state a distinctively Turkish national identity, but it gave Atatürk the chance to create a wholly Turkish commercial class which would cooperate with his government in creating a modern industrialized economy.[78] The massacre of at least one million Armenians was the first act of genocide in the twentieth century, and showed that, as Rabbi Kook had feared, secular nationalism could be lethal and certainly as dangerous as the crusades and purges conducted in the name of religion.

Atatürk's secularization of Turkey was also aggressive. He was determined to "Westernize" Islam and reduce it to a private creed, without legal, political, or economic influence. Religion must be made subordinate to the state. Sufi orders were abolished; all the *madrasahs* and Koran schools were closed; Western dress was imposed by law; women were forbidden to wear the veil, and men the fez. Islam made a last-ditch stand, when Shaykh Said Sursi, head of the Naqshbandi Sufi order, led a rebellion, which Atatürk crushed swiftly and efficiently in two months. In the West, secularization had been experienced as liberating; it had even, in its early stages, been regarded as a new and better way of being religious. Secularism had been a positive development that had led, for the most part, to greater tolerance. But in the Middle East, secularization was experienced as a violent and coercive assault. When later Muslim fundamentalists claimed that secularization meant the destruction of Islam, they would often point to the example of Atatürk.

Egypt did not achieve either independence or democracy as quickly as Turkey. After the First World War, Egyptian nationalists had demanded independence; there were riots, Englishmen were attacked, railway lines torn up, and telegraph lines cut. In 1922, Britain allowed Egypt a measure of independence. Khedive Fuad became the new king; Egypt was given a liberal constitution, and a representative, parliamentary body. But this was no true democracy. Britain retained control of defense and foreign policy, so there was no real independence. Between 1923 and 1930, the popular Wafd Party, which demanded the withdrawal of the British, won three large electoral victories under the liberal constitution, but each time it was forced to resign under pressure from either the British or the king.[79] The new democratic structures were only cosmetic, and this dependence would not help Egyptians to develop the autonomy that was essential to the modern spirit. Moreover, the more the British were seen to tamper with the electoral process, the more tainted the democratic ideal appeared.

Nevertheless, during the first three decades of the twentieth century, leading Egyptian thinkers seemed to lean toward a secularist ideal. Islam played very little part in the work of Lufti al-Sayyid (1872–1963), who was one of Abdu's disciples. He was convinced that the secret of Western success was the ideal of nationalism, and felt it essential to graft modern institutions onto an Islamic base. Lufti's view of Islam was entirely instrumental. Certainly religion played an important role in the creation of modern national consciousness, but it was one element among many. Islam had nothing special or distinctive to offer. It would have to be the state religion of Egypt, because most Egyptians were Muslims; it would help them to cultivate the civic virtues, but in another society, another faith would do the job just as well.[80] Even more radical was the book *al-Islam wa usul al-hukm* ("Islam and the Bases of Power," 1925) by Ali Abd al-Raziq (1888–1966), which argued that modern Egypt should sever its connection with Islam altogether. He pointed out that the institution of the caliphate was not mentioned in the Koran and that the Prophet Muhammad had not been the head of a state or a government in the twentieth-century sense, so there was nothing to stop Egyptians from setting up a wholly secularist, European-style polity.[81]

There was a great outcry against al-Raziq's book. In particular, the journalist Rashid Rida (1865–1935) declared that this kind of thinking could only weaken the unity of the Muslim peoples and cause them to fall prey more easily to Western imperialism. Instead of taking the secular option, Rida became the first Muslim to propose the establishment of a fully modernized Islamic state based on the Shariah. In his monumental work *al-Khalifa* (1922–23), he argued for the restoration of the caliphate. Rida was the biographer and fervent admirer of Abdu, but even though he was well versed in Western thought, he never felt as much at home with Europeans as Abdu had done. The caliphate was necessary because it would enable Muslims to unite effectively against the West, but this was a long-term solution. Before a truly modern caliphate could be established, there would have to be a lengthy period of preparation. Rida saw the future caliph as a great *mujtahid* who was so expert in Islamic law that he would be able to modernize the Shariah without diluting it. He would thus create laws that modern Muslims could truly obey because they would be based on their own traditions, instead of being imported from abroad.[82]

Rida was a typical Muslim reformer in the tradition of Ibn Taymiyyah and Abd al-Wahhab. He wanted to counter a foreign threat by returning *ad fontes*.[83] Modern Muslims could create a new and vibrant Islam only by returning to the ideals of the *salaf*, the first generation of Muslims. But Rida's *salafiyyah* movement was not a slavish return to the past. Like other reformers at an early stage of the modernization process, he was trying to absorb the learning and values of the modern West by placing them within an Islamic context. He wanted to establish a seminary where students could be introduced to the principles of international law, sociology, world history, the organization of religious institutions, and Western science, at the same time as they studied Islamic jurisprudence. In this way, a new class of *ulema* would emerge, who, unlike the scholars at the Azhar (whom Rida considered to be hopelessly behind the times), would truly be men of their time, able to exercise an innovative *ijtihad* that was faithful to tradition. One day, one of these new *ulema* might become the modern caliph.[84] Rida was no fundamentalist; he was still trying to effect a marriage between Islam and modern Western culture instead of creating a counterdiscourse, but his work would influence the fundamentalists of the future. Increasingly, toward the end of his life, Rida drew away from the Egyptian nationalists. He did not think that secularism was the answer. He was appalled by Atatürk's atrocities. Was this what happened when the state became the supreme value and there was nothing to restrain a ruler from pragmatic but cruel policies to further the interests of the nation? Rida believed that in the Middle East—if not in the Christian West—persecution and intolerance were due to the decline of religion.[85] At a time when many of the leading thinkers of Egypt were turning away from Islam, Rida came to believe that the modern Muslim states needed the restraints of religion as much as, if not more than, they had ever done before.

If in Egypt, people had come to believe that the "secret" of Europe's success was nationalism, Iranians in the early years of the twentieth century believed that this "secret" was constitutional government. At this point, like many Egyptians, Iranians wanted to be like the West. In 1904, Japan, which had recently adopted constitutional rule, inflicted a stunning defeat upon Russia. It was not long since Japan had been as ignorant and backward as Iran, the reformers argued, but now, thanks to its constitution, it was on the same level as the Europeans and could beat them at their own game. Even some of the *ulema* had become convinced of the need for representational government to curb the despotic rule of the shahs. As Sayyed Muhammad Tabatabai, a liberal *mujtahid*, explained:

> we ourselves had not seen a constitutional regime. But we had heard about it, and those who had seen the constitutional countries had told us that a constitutional regime will bring security and prosperity to the country. This created an urge and an enthusiasm in us.[86]

Unlike the Egyptian *ulema*, who had retreated defensively into the world of the *madrasahs*, the Iranian *ulema* were often in the vanguard of change and would continue to have a decisive role in forthcoming events.

In December 1905, the governor of Tehran gave orders that the feet of several sugar merchants be beaten for refusing to lower their prices as ordered by the government. They claimed that the high import duties made their high prices necessary. A large group of *ulema* and *bazaaris* took sanctuary in the royal mosque of Tehran, until ejected by the agents of Prime Minister Ain al-Dauleh. At once, a significant number of mullahs followed Tabatabai into one of the major shrines, whence they demanded that the shah establish a representative "house of justice." The shah agreed and the *ulema* returned to Tehran, but when the prime minister showed no signs of fulfilling this promise, rioting broke out there and in the provinces, and popular preachers denounced the government from the pulpits, stirring up the common people. Finally, in July 1906, the mullahs of Tehran staged a mass exodus to Qum, while some 14,000 merchants took refuge in the British legation. Business came to a halt, while the protesters demanded the dismissal of Ain al-Dauleh and the establishment of a *majlis* ("representative assembly"), and the more knowledgeable reformers began to discuss a *mashruteh* ("constitution").[87]

The Constitutional Revolution was initially successful. The prime minister was dismissed at the end of July, and the first Majlis, which included a significant number of elected *ulema*, opened in Tehran in October. A year later, the new shah, Muhammad Ali, signed the Fundamental Law, which was modeled on the Belgian constitution. This required the monarch to ask the approval of the Majlis in all important matters; all citizens (including those who belonged to a different faith) enjoyed equality before the law, and the constitution guaranteed personal rights and freedoms. There was a flurry of liberal activity throughout Iran. The First Majlis gave new freedoms to the press, and immediately satirical and critical articles began to be published. New societies were formed, there were plans for a national bank, and new municipal councils were elected. The brilliant young deputy for Tabriz, Sayyed Hasan Taqizadeh, led a left-wing, democratic party in the Majlis, while the *mujtahids*, Ayatollah Tabatabai and Seyyed Abdallah Behbehani, led the Conservative party, which managed to include some clauses in the constitution to safeguard the status of the Shariah.

But despite this show of cooperation between the liberal clergy and the reformers, the First Majlis revealed deep divisions. Many of the lay deputies belonged to the dissident circles, associated with Mulkum Khan and Kirmani, who felt only contempt for the *ulema*. They were often members of the *anjumans* ("secret societies") formed to disseminate revolutionary ideas, and even though some of the more radical clergy had links with these groups, the reformers were usually anticlerical and regarded the *ulema* as an obstacle to progress. If the *ulema* who had joined forces with the reformers had expected the constitution to make the Shariah the law of the land, they were disappointed. The First Majlis immediately took steps to curb clerical power in such matters as education, and, ironically, the Constitutional Revolution, which so many of the mullahs had supported, marked the beginning of the end of their enormous power in the country.[88]

The Shii *ulema* had never taken such an active role in politics before. Some scholars believe that they were motivated chiefly by the desire to protect their own prerogatives and interests, and to ward off the encroachment of the infidel West;[89] others point out that in promoting a constitution that would limit the despotic power of the shahs, the more liberal *ulema* were fulfilling the ancient Shii duty of opposing tyranny.[90] The lay reformers, mindful of the great power of the *ulema*, had been careful not to offend Muslim sensibilities during the revolution, but they had long been hostile to the clergy and, once in power, were determined to secularize the legal system and education. One of the first to spot the dangers of this secularization was Shaykh Fadlullah Nuri (1843–1909), one of the three leading clerics of Tehran, who began to agitate against the constitution in 1907: he argued that since all government was illegitimate during the absence of the Hidden Imam, the new parliament was un-Islamic. The *mujtahids*, not the Majlis, were the Imam's deputies and it was they who should make the laws and safeguard the rights of the people. Under this new system, however, the clergy would simply become one institution among others; they would no longer be the chief spiritual guides of the people and religion would be jeopardized. Nuri demanded that the Majlis should, at the very least, base its decisions on the Shariah. Because of his objections, the constitution was amended: a panel of five *ulema*, selected by the Majlis, was established with the power to veto legislation that contradicted the sacred law of Islam.[91]

Yet Nuri expressed a minority view. Most of the *mujtahids* at Najaf supported the constitution, and would continue to do so. They rejected Nuri's plea for a Shariah state on the grounds that it was not possible to implement law correctly without the direct guidance of the Hidden Imam. Yet again, the spiritual insights of the Shiah promoted a secularization of the polity, and still regarded state power as incompatible with religion. Many clergy had been disgusted by the growing corruption of the court and by the economic insecurity of the government which had led the Qajars to grant unacceptable financial concessions to foreigners and to take out expensive loans. They had seen that this shortsighted behavior had led in Egypt to military occupation. It seemed clearly preferable to limit the oppressive policies of the Qajar state by means of the constitution.[92] This point of view was expressed forcibly by Shaykh Muhammad Husain Naini (1850–1936), in his *Admonition to the Nation and Exposition to the People*, which was published in Najaf in 1909. Naini argued that representative government was the next best thing to the Hidden Imam; to set up an assembly capable of restraining a despotic ruler was clearly an act worthy of the Shiah. A tyrannical ruler was guilty of idolatry *(shirk)*, the cardinal sin of Islam, because he arrogated to himself divine power and behaved as though he were God himself, lording it over his subjects. The prophet Moses had been sent to destroy the power of Pharaoh, who had oppressed and enslaved his people, and force him to obey the commands of Allah. In the same way, the new Majlis with its panel of religious experts must ensure that the shahs obey God's laws.[93]

The most lethal opposition to the new constitution, however, came not from the *ulema* but from the new shah, who, with the help of a Russian Cossack brigade, led a successful coup in June 1908 and closed the Majlis; the most radical Iranian reformers and *ulema* were executed. But the popular guard in Tabriz held out against the shah's forces and, with the help of the Bakhtiari tribe, staged a countercoup the following month, unseated the shah, and put his minor son, Ahmad, on the throne with a liberal regent. A Second Majlis was elected, but, as in Egypt, this fledgling parliamentary democracy was cut down to size by the European powers. When the Majlis tried to break the stranglehold that Britain and Russia had long had on Iranian affairs by appointing a young American financier, Morgan Shuster, to help them reform Iran's ailing economy, Russian troops advanced on Tehran and closed the Majlis in December 1911. It was three years before the Majlis was permitted to reconvene, and by that time, many had become embittered and disillusioned. The constitution had not been the panacea they had hoped for, but had simply thrown the fundamental impotence of Iran into cruel and clear relief.

The First World War was very disruptive for Iran and left many Iranians longing for strong government. In 1917, British and Russian troops overran the country. After the Bolshevik Revolution, the Russians withdrew, but the British moved into the areas they had vacated in the north of the country, while holding on to their own bases in the south. Britain was now eager to make Iran a protectorate. Oil had been discovered in the country in 1908, and the concession had been granted to a British subject, William Knox D'Arcy; in 1909, the Anglo-Persian Oil Company was formed, and Iranian oil fueled the British navy. Iran was now a rich prize. But the Majlis held out against British control. There were anti-British demonstrations throughout the country in 1920, the Majlis appealed for help from Soviet Russia and the United States, and Britain was forced to abandon this plan. But Iranians were miserably aware that they had managed to retain their independence only by appealing to other great powers, who had their own designs on Iranian oil. Iran now had a constitution and representative government, but this was useless, since the Majlis had no real power. Even the Americans noted that the British constantly rigged the elections and that Iranians were "prevented from public expression of opinion or giving vent to feelings in any manner by the existing martial law and controlled press."[94]

The prevailing mood of dissatisfaction made it relatively easy for a small group, under the leadership of Seyyid Zia ad-Din Tabatabai, a civilian, and Reza Khan (1877–1944), the commander of the shah's Cossack brigade, to overthrow the government. In February 1921, Zia ad-Din became prime minister, with Reza Khan as his minister of war. The British acquiesced because Zia ad-Din was known to be pro-British, and they hoped that his election would further their plans for a protectorate, which they had not abandoned entirely. But Reza Khan was the stronger of the two leaders, and he was soon able to force Zia ad-Din into exile, form a new cabinet, and become sole ruler. Reza at once began to modernize the country, and, because the people were so frustrated and ready for any change, he was able to succeed where his predecessors had failed. Reza had no interest in social reform and no concern for the poor. His objective was simply to centralize the country, strengthen the army and the bureaucracy, and make Iran function more effectively. Any opposition was ruthlessly cut down. From the very beginning, Reza courted Soviet Russia and the United States in order to rid the country of the British, granting an oil concession to the Standard Oil Company of New Jersey in return for American technical advice and investment. In 1925, Reza was in a strong enough position to force the last Qajar shah to abdicate. His original intention was to establish a republic, but the *ulema* objected. In the Majlis, Ayatollah Muddaris declared that a republic was un-Islamic. It was tainted by its association with Atatürk, and the clergy had no wish to see Iran go the same way as Turkey. Reza had no objection to becoming shah, and was still anxious to court the clergy. He promised them that his government would honor Islam and that its legislation would not conflict with the Shariah. That done, a packed Majlis endorsed the foundation of the Pahlavi dynasty. But it would not be long before Shah Reza Pahlavi would feel able to break his promise to the *ulema* and not only equal but even surpass Atatürk's ruthless secularization.

By the end of the third decade of the twentieth century, secularism seemed to be winning the day. There was plenty of religious activity, though the more radical movements had been cut down to size and posed no threat to the secularist leadership. But the seeds that had been sown during these years would take root when some of the limitations of this modern secularist experiment became apparent.

7. Counterculture

(1925–60)

EVER SINCE Nietzsche had proclaimed the death of God, modern people had, in various ways, become aware of a void at the heart of their culture. The French existentialist Jean-Paul Sartre (1905–80) called it the God-shaped hole in human consciousness, where the divine had always been but had disappeared, leaving an emptiness behind. The astonishing achievements of scientific rationalism had made the very idea of God incredible and impossible for many Westernized people, since it had gone hand-in-hand with a suppression of the old mythical consciousness. Without a cult to evoke a sense of sacredness, the symbol of God had become attenuated and meaningless. But most modern people did not repine. The world was in many ways a much better place, and they were evolving new secularist spiritualities, seeking in literature, art, sexuality, psychoanalysis, drugs, or even in sport, a sense of transcendent meaning that gave their lives value and put them in touch with the deeper currents of existence hitherto revealed by the confessional religions. By the middle of the twentieth century, most Western people assumed that religion would never again play a major part in world events. It had been relegated firmly to the private sphere and, again, for many of the secularists who occupied positions of power or who controlled the media and the public discourse, this seemed right. In Western Christendom, religion had often been cruel and coercive; the needs of the modern state demanded that society be tolerant. There could be no going back to the age of crusade or inquisition. Secularism was there to stay. But at the same time, by the mid-twentieth century, the world also had to come to terms with the fact that the "void" was no longer merely a psychic vacuum, but had been given graphic and terrifying embodiment.

Between 1914 and 1945, seventy million people in Europe and the Soviet Union had died violent deaths.[1] Some of the worst atrocities had been perpetrated by Germans, who lived in one of the most cultivated societies in Europe. It was no longer possible to assume that a rational education would eliminate barbarism, since the Nazi Holocaust revealed that a concentration camp could exist in the same vicinity as a great university. The sheer scale of the Nazi genocide or the Soviet Gulag reveals their modern origins. No previous society could have dreamed of implementing such grandiose schemes of extermination. The horrors of the Second World War (1939–45) only ended with the explosion of the first atomic bombs over the Japanese cities of Hiroshima and Nagasaki. This, again, was a horrifying vision of the power of modern science and the germ of nihilism in modern culture. For decades, men and women had dreamed of a final apocalypse wrought by God; now, it appeared, human beings no longer needed a supernatural deity to end the world. They had used their prodigious skill and learning to find the means of doing this very efficiently for themselves. As they contemplated these new facts of life, people became aware as never before of the limitations of the rationalistic ethos. Faced with catastrophe on such a scale, reason is silent; there is—literally—nothing that it can say.

The Holocaust would become an icon of evil for modern times. It was a by-product of modernity, which, from the very beginning, had often involved acts of ethnic cleansing. The Nazis used many of the tools and achievements of the industrial age to deadly effect. The death camps were a fearful parody of the factory, right down to the industrial chimney itself. They made full use of the railways, the advanced chemical industry, and efficient bureaucracy and management. The Holocaust was an example of scientific and rational planning, in which everything is subordinated to a single, limited, and clearly defined objective.[2] Born of modern scientific racism, the Holocaust was the ultimate in social engineering in what has been called the "garden" culture of the twentieth century. Science itself was also deeply implicated in the death camps and the eugenic experiments carried out there. At the very least, the Holocaust showed that a secularist ideology could be just as lethal as any religious crusade.

The Holocaust was also a reminder of the dangers that can accrue from the death of God in human consciousness. In Christian theology, hell had been defined as the absence of God. The camps seemed an uncannily accurate reproduction of the imagery of the inferno, which had haunted Europeans for centuries. The flaying, racking, whipping, screaming, and mocking, the deformed, distorted bodies, the flames, and the stinking air all recalled the Christian hell depicted by the poets, painters, sculptors, and dramatists of Europe.[3] Auschwitz was a dark epiphany, giving human beings a glimpse of what life could be like once all sense of sacredness has been lost. At its best (and only at its best), religion had helped people to cultivate an appreciation of the holiness of humanity in its myths, rituals, and cultic and ethical practices. By the mid-twentieth century, it seemed that an unfettered rationalism could feel impelled to create a hell upon earth, an objective correlative of God's absence. There was a nihilistic impulse that could draw human beings who had more power than they had ever had before to expend enormous creativity in mass destruction. The symbol of God had marked the limit of human potential and, in the conservative period, had imposed a constraint upon what men and women could do. The commandments of the Law had reminded them that the world was not theirs to do with as they chose. Modern human beings now prized autonomy and freedom so greatly that the idea of an omnipotent divine legislator was abhorrent to them, and this development marked a great advance in human dignity. But the Holocaust and the Gulag show what can happen when people cast off all such restraint or make the nation or polity the supreme value. New ways of teaching human beings to respect the sacredness of life and the world would have to be found that would not compromise modern integrity with inadequate symbols of the "supernatural."

The death camp and the mushroom cloud are icons that we must contemplate and take to heart so that we do not become chauvinistic about the modern scientific culture that so many of us in the developed world enjoy. But these icons can also give us an insight into the way that some religious people regard modern secular society, in which they also experience the absence of God. Some fundamentalists see modernity as equally hubristic, evil, and demonic; their vision of the modern city or the secular ideology fills them with something of the same dread and helpless rage as overtakes the liberal secularist who gazes into the darkness of Auschwitz. During the middle of the twentieth century, fundamentalists in all three of the monotheistic faiths were beginning to retreat from the mainstream society to create countercultures that reflected the way they thought things ought to be. They were not simply withdrawing out of pique, but were often impelled to do so by horror and fear. It is important that we understand the dread and anxiety that lie at the heart of the fundamentalist vision, because only then will we begin to comprehend its passionate rage, its frantic desire to fill the void with certainty, and its conviction of ever-encroaching evil.

Some Jews had begun to see the modern world as demonic long before the Holocaust. Indeed, the Nazi atrocity only confirmed them in their conviction that not only was the gentile world irredeemably evil, but most modern Jews were horribly culpable too. Until the 1930s, most Orthodox Jews who wanted nothing to do with modern culture could immerse themselves in the life of the *yeshiva* or the Hasidic court. They had neither the desire nor the need to migrate to the United States or Palestine. But the convulsions of the 1930s and 1940s meant that survivors had no choice but to flee from Europe and the Soviet Union. Some of the Haredim went to Palestine and came face-to-face with the Zionists, who were now engaged in a desperate struggle to create a state that would save Jews from the coming catastrophe.

The Edah Haredis, the ultra-Orthodox community in Jerusalem, had been vehemently opposed to Zionism long before the Balfour Declaration. It was a small group, which had attracted only 9000 out of the 175,000 Jewish residents of Palestine by the 1920s.[4] Immersed in their sacred texts, the community had no idea how to organize themselves politically, but they would soon be joined by members of Agudat Israel, who had learned to play the modern political game. Agudat was still ideologically opposed to Zionism, but members had tried to balance the influence of the secularists by founding their own religious settlements in the Holy Land, where young people studied modern subjects along with Torah and Talmud. This concession appalled the more rigorous of the ultra-Orthodox, who believed that Agudat had gone over to the "Other Side." From this intra-Orthodox conflict, a fundamentalist movement was born, inspired in the first instance, as so often, by a quarrel between coreligionists.

The chief spokesman of this rejectionist Orthodoxy was Rabbi Hayyim Eleazer Shapira of Munkacs (1872–1937), one of the most eminent Hasidic leaders of Hungarian Jewry, who began a vehement campaign against Agudat in 1922. In his view, Agudat members were collaborating with the Zionists and infecting the minds of innocent schoolchildren with the "poisonweed and wormwood" of the *goyische* Enlightenment, as well as "songs that speak of the settlement of the Land, and the fields and the vineyards of Eretz Israel—just like the Zionist poets."[5] They were defiling the Holy Land, which was intended only for prayer and sacred study, by tilling its sacred soil. At a meeting in Slovakia, the most radical of the Haredim agreed with the Munkaczer rebbe, and signed a ban on any association with Agudat. Their view of Agudat, which had come into existence precisely to oppose Zionism, was inaccurate; the group was also aware that they were at odds with the vast majority of the Orthodox in eastern and western Europe, who disapproved of Zionism but regarded Shapira's ban on Agudat as too extreme. Nevertheless, they felt justified in this separatist policy by their instinctive horror of Zionism. One of the first of the Haredim to sign the ban was the young Rabbi Joel Moshe Teitelbaum (1888–1979), who would later become the leader of the Hasidim of Satmar, Hungary, and the most vigorous of all the Haredi opponents of Zionism and the State of Israel.

When Shapira and Teitelbaum contemplated the Zionist *kibbutzim* in Palestine, they felt the same outrage and dread as, later, people felt when they heard about the Nazi death camps. This is not an exaggeration. Teitelbaum, who narrowly escaped extermination by migrating with his people to America, put the entire blame for the Holocaust on the great sin of the Zionists, who had "lured the majority of the Jewish people into awful heresy, the like of which has not been seen since the world was created. . . . And so it is no wonder that the Lord lashed out in anger."[6] These rejectionists could see nothing positive in the agricultural achievements of the Zionists, who were making the desert bloom, or the political acumen of their leaders, who were striving to save Jewish lives. This was an "outrage," a "defilement," and the final eruption of the forces of evil.[7] The Zionists were atheists and unbelievers; even if they had been the most strictly observant of Jews, their enterprise would still be evil because it was a rebellion against God, who had decreed that Jews must endure the punishment of the Exile and must take no initiative to save themselves.

For Shapira, the Land was too holy to be settled by any ordinary Jew, let alone by self-confessed Zionist rebels. Only the religious zealot who devoted his entire life to study and prayer could live there safely. Wherever there is a holy object, like Eretz Israel (the Land of Israel), evil forces gather to attack it. The Zionists, Shapira explained, were simply the external manifestation of these demonic influences. The Holy Land itself, therefore, was teeming with wicked forces "which excite God's anger and fury." Instead of God, it was Satan that now dwelt in Jerusalem. The Zionists who "pretend to 'ascend' to the Land, are in fact, descending to the depths of hell."[8] The Holy Land was empty of God and had become an inferno. Eretz Israel was not a homeland, as the Zionists maintained, but a battlefield. The only people who could safely dwell there in these terrible times were not householders and farmers, but holy warriors, "zealous fearers of God," "valiant men of war" who set out "to fight the just war for the residue of God's heritage in the holy mountain of Jerusalem." The whole Zionist enterprise imbued Shapira with existential terror. Teitelbaum saw the Zionists as the latest manifestation of the evil hubris that had consistently brought disasters upon the Jewish people: the Tower of Babel, the idolatry of the Golden Calf, the Bar Kochba rebellion in the second century CE which had cost thousands of Jewish lives, and the Shabbetai Zevi fiasco. But Zionism was the heresy par excellence; this was brazen arrogance which shook the very foundations of the world. It was no wonder that God had sent the Holocaust![9]

Hence the faithful must separate themselves absolutely from this evil. Rabbi Yeshayahu Margolis, one of the most zealous of the Hasidim in Jerusalem, who wrote during the 1920s and 1930s, was a great admirer of both Shapira and Teitelbaum, and wanted Teitelbaum to become the leader of Edah Haredis. Margolis created a counterhistory of Israel which stressed the existence of an embattled minority that had consistently over the centuries felt obliged to rise up and fight other Jews in the name of God. The Levites had killed three thousand of the Israelites who had worshipped the Golden Calf while Moses was receiving the Torah on Mount Sinai; that was the reason that God had honored them above the other tribes, not because of their service in the Temple. Moses had been a great zealot who had fought other Jews all his life. Phinehas, the grandson of Aaron, had risen up against Zimri, even though he was a prince of Israel, because he had committed fornication. Elijah had stood up to Ahab and slaughtered the 450 prophets of Baal. These zealots, whose passion for God was often expressed in uncontrollable rage, were the true Jews, the faithful remnant.[10] Sometimes they had to fight gentiles, sometimes their fellow Jews, but the battle was always the same. Faithful Jews must cut themselves off, root and branch, from such Jews as the members of Agudat who had left God and gone over to the Evil One. By collaborating with the Zionists, Agudat had done Jews "more harm than all the wicked of the earth." To consort with them was sinful and to make a pact with Satan.[11]

Hence the duty of segregation. Just as the Torah separates sacred from profane, light from darkness, milk from meat, and Sabbath from the rest of the week, so the righteous must keep themselves apart. The renegades would never return to the fold; by living and praying separately from these wicked Jews, the true Haredim were simply expressing physically the onto-logical gulf that existed between them at a metaphysical level. But this fear-ful vision meant that, living as they were in the midst of satanic evil, every detail of the lives of the faithful had cosmic importance. Matters of dress, methods of study, even the cut of the beard, must be absolutely correct. Jew-ish life was gravely imperiled, and any innovation was utterly forbidden: "Care should be taken that the right lapel overlaps the left, so that the right hand of the Most High, 'the right hand of the Lord uplifted,' in its exalted Love (*hesed*), predominates over the left side, which represents Power (*din*), the strength of the Evil Impulse."[12] Where Protestant fundamentalists had sought to fill the void by seeking absolute certainty in stringent doctrinal correctness, these anti-Zionist ultra-Orthodox sought certainty in a minute observance of divine law and customary observance. It is a spirituality that reveals almost ungovernable fear which can only be assuaged by the meticu-lous preservation of old boundaries, the erection of new barriers, a rigid segregation, and a passionate adherence to the values of tradition.

This rejectionist vision is utterly incomprehensible to Jews who regard the Zionist achievement as wondrous and salvific. This is the dilemma that Jews, Christians, and Muslims have all had to face in the twentieth century: between the fundamentalists and those who adopt a more positive attitude to the modern secular world there is an impassable gulf. The different groups simply cannot see things from the same point of view. Rational arguments are of no avail, because the divergence springs from a deeper and more instinctual level of the mind. When Shapira, Teitelbaum, and Margolis contemplated the purposeful, pragmatic, and rationally inspired activities of the secular Zionists, they could only see them as godless and, hence, as demonic. When later they and their followers heard about the rationalized, practical, and ruthlessly directed activities of the Nazis in the death camps, they experienced them as similar to the Zionist enterprise. Both revealed the absence of God, and were, therefore, satanic and nihilistic, destructively trampling upon every sacred value that these Haredim held dear. To this day, the placards and graffiti on the walls of an anti-Zionist district in Jerusalem equate the political leaders of the State of Israel with Hitler. To an outsider, such an equation is shocking, false, and perverse, but it gives us some idea of the profound horror that secularism can inspire in the heart of a fundamentalist.

The very idea of Jewish apostates setting up a secular state in Eretz Israel violated a taboo. Over the centuries, the lost land had acquired a symbolic and mystical value that linked it with God and the Torah in a sort of holy trinity. To watch its profanation by men who made no secret of the fact that they had cast religion aside inspired the same kind of mingled fury and dread as the violation of a sacred shrine, which, especially in the Jewish world, has often been experienced as a rape.[13] The closer the Zionists came to achieving their objective, the more desperate some of the more radical Haredim became, until in 1938, Amram Blau and Aharon Katzenellenbogen, who had both defected from Agudat because of its alleged "collaboration" with the Zionists, seceded from the Edah Haredis. The Jewish community had recently levied a special tax to cover the cost of an organized defense against Arab attacks, and these rejectionists refused to pay it. To justify their refusal, Blau and Katzenellenbogen quoted a Talmudic story. In the third century, when armed guards were organizing the defense of one of the Jewish urban communities in Roman Palestine, two Jewish sages told them: "You are not the city's guardians but its destroyers. The scholars who study the Torah are the true guardians of the city."[14] The new group formed by Blau and Katzenellenbogen gave itself the Aramaic title Neturei Karta ("The Guardians of the City"): Jews would not be protected by the militant activities of the Zionists but by the devout and punctilious religious observance of the Orthodox. They challenged the perspective of the Zionists. In their view, when Jews had been given the Torah, they had entered a different realm from other nations. They were not supposed to get involved in politics or armed struggle, but to devote themselves to the affairs of the spirit. By summoning Jews back to the world of history, Zionists had in fact abandoned the Kingdom of God and entered a state which, for Jews, could make no existential sense. They had denied their very nature and set the Jewish people on a doomed course.[15]

The more successful the Zionists became, the more the Neturei Karta were baffled. Why had the wicked prospered? When the State of Israel was established in 1948, so soon after the Holocaust, Teitelbaum and Blau could only conclude that Satan had intervened directly in history to lead Jews into a realm of meaningless evil and sacrilege.[16] Most of the Orthodox and ultra-Orthodox were able to accommodate the new state. They declared that it had no religious value and that Jews who lived in Israel were still in exile, just as they had been in the Diaspora. Nothing had changed. Agudat Israel was prepared to engage in *shtadlanut*—dialogue and negotiations—with the Israeli government to safeguard the religious interests of Jews, just as they had with the gentile governments in Europe. But Neturei Karta would have none of this. Immediately after the proclamation of statehood on May 14, 1948, they imposed a ban on any participation in the elections, refused to accept government funding for their *yeshivot,* and vowed never to set foot in government institutions. They also redoubled their attacks on Agudat, whose pragmatic acceptance of the state they regarded as the thin end of the wedge. "If [we] let up even to the slightest degree, God forbid, from our hatred of evil, of seducers and corrupters," Blau insisted, "[if we breach] the separateness to which our holy Torah obliges us . . . then the way is open to every forbidden thing, for we will have left the straight and narrow path for a crooked one."[17] The Zionist venture, which had enticed almost the entire Jewish people away from God, was plunging into a nihilistic denial of all decent and sacred values.

The more rooted Zionism became in the Jewish world and the more successful the new state, the deeper and more principled was Neturei Karta's repudiation of both. There could be no possibility of reconciliation, because the State of Israel was the creation of Satan. As Teitelbaum explained, it was not possible for a Jew "to adhere to both faith in the state and faith in our holy Torah, for they are complete opposites." Even if the politicians and cabinet ministers were Talmudic sages and devout observers of the commandments, the state would still be a demonic profanity because it had rebelled against God and tried to snatch salvation and to advance the End of Days.[18] Neturei Karta had no time for Agudat's efforts to get religious legislation passed in the Knesset, the Israeli parliament. It was not a pious act to try to limit public transport on the Sabbath by law or to ensure that *yeshiva* students were exempt from the draft. This was simply converting a divine law into human law; it amounted to an annulment of the Torah and to a desecration of the Halakhah. As Rabbi Shimon Israel Posen, a leading scholar of the community of Satmar Hasidim in New York, said of the Agudat members of the Knesset:

> Woe unto them for the shame of it, that people who put on phylacteries every day sit in that assembly of the wicked called the "Knesset" and, signing their names to falsehoods, forge the signature of the Holy One, blessed be He, heaven forfend. For they think that they can decide by majority vote whether the Torah of truth will be trampled upon even further or whether God's Torah will be granted authority.[19]

Yet even the Neturei Karta felt the attraction of Zionism. Blau's description of the Zionists as "seducers" is significant. A Jewish state in a Jewish land is a temptation that tugs hard at the Jewish soul. This is part of the fundamentalists' dilemma. They often feel fascinated and drawn toward the very modern achievements from which they recoil in horror.[20] The Protestant fundamentalists' portrayal of Antichrist, the charming, plausible deceiver, shows something of the same conflict. There is a tension in the fundamentalist vision of modernity that can be explosive. As Blau indicated, the piety of the anti-Zionists is one of principled "hatred" and hatred often goes hand-in-hand with unacknowledged love. Haredim feel rage when they contemplate the State of Israel. They do not kill, but to this day they throw stones at cars in Israel whose drivers break the law by traveling on the Sabbath. Sometimes they will attack the house of a fellow Haredi who has failed to live up to the expected standard by, say, owning a television set or permitting his wife to dress immodestly. Such acts of violence are seen as *kiddush hashem,* "sanctification of God's Name," and a blow against the forces of evil that surround the Haredim on all sides and threaten to devour them.[21] But it is not impossible that these violent assaults are an attempt to kill a buried yearning and attraction in their own hearts.

These anti-Zionist Haredim constitute a small minority: there are only about ten thousand of them in Israel, and several tens of thousands in the United States. But their influence is considerable.[22] Even though most of the ultra-Orthodox are a-Zionist rather than anti-Zionist, the Neturei Karta and other radicals, such as the Satmar Hasidim, confront them with the dangers of cooperating too closely with the state. Their determined withdrawal from the State of Israel reminds the less zealous Haredim, who often feel a lack of integrity and authenticity in their cooperation with the Jewish state, that no matter how powerful and successful Israel has become in worldly terms, Jews are still in a state of existential exile and can take no legitimate part in the political and cultural life of the modern world.

This Haredi refusal to accept Israel as anything but a satanic creation amounts to an act of constant rebellion against the state in which many of them live. When they stone cars on the Sabbath or tear down posters displaying scantily clad women advertising swimwear, they are rebelling against the secularist ethos of the Jewish state in which the only criterion for a course of action is its rational, practical utility. Fundamentalists in all three of the monotheistic faiths are in revolt against the pragmatic *logos* that dominates modern society to the exclusion of the spiritual, and which refuses the restraints imposed by the sacred. But because the secular establishment is so powerful, most have to confine their revolt to small symbolic acts. Their sense of weakness and tacit acknowledgment of their dependence upon the state in times of war, for example, can only increase the fundamentalists' rage. The vast majority of Haredim confine their protest to a determined retreat from the secular state and to the establishment of a counterculture which challenges its values at every turn.

The alternative society of the Haredim is motivated by a desire to fill the void created by the modern ethos. For Jews after the Holocaust this void is horribly graphic. Those who survived feel impelled to rebuild the Hasidic courts and Misnagdic *yeshivot* in Israel and the United States. It is an act of piety to the millions of Haredim who died in Hitler's camps, and an act of rebellion against the forces of evil. They believe that by giving their Haredi institutions a new lease on life and making that dead world not only live again but become more powerful than ever, they are striking a blow for the sacred.[23] After the Second World War, new *yeshivot* were built in Israel and the United States. In 1943, Rabbi Aaron Kotler (1891–1962) founded the first Lithuanian *yeshiva* in America, when he established Bais Midrash Gedolah in New Jersey, modeled on the *yeshivot* of Volozhin, Mir, and Slobodka. After 1948, Bnei Brak near Tel Aviv became a "city of Torah"; its newly established *yeshivot* drew students from all over Israel and the Diaspora. Here the guiding spirit was Rabbi Abraham Yeshayahu Karlitz (1878–1943), who was known as the Hazon Ish (the title of one of his books). These new institutions made the *yeshiva* more central to Haredi life than ever before. Torah study became a lifelong, full-time pursuit; men would continue their studies after they were married, and would be supported financially by their wives. In the dangerous new world of modernity, which had nearly obliterated the whole of European Jewry, a cadre of scholars who lived in the *yeshiva*, had minimal contact with the outside world, and immersed themselves wholly in the study of sacred texts would become the new guardians of Judaism.[24]

Kotler believed that his students kept the whole world in existence. God had created the heavens and the earth simply in order that men could study the Torah. Only if the Jewish people studied the Holy Law day and night would it fulfill its vocation. If they stopped, "the universe would be immediately destroyed."[25] It was a piety that sprang from too close a brush with total annihilation. Any secular study not only was a waste of time, but was tantamount to assimilation with the murderous gentile culture. Any form of Judaism which tried to absorb aspects of modern culture—religious Zionism, Reform, Conservative, or Neo-Orthodox—was illegitimate.[26] In a world that had recently dedicated itself to the destruction of Judaism, there could be no such compromise. The true Jew must separate himself from this world and devote himself wholly to the texts. The new postwar *yeshivot* reflected the desperation of fundamentalist spirituality. The holy texts were all that remained from the Jews' crushing confrontation with modernity during the twentieth century. Six million of the Jewish people had been killed; the *yeshivot* and Hasidic courts had all been destroyed, together with countless classics of Jewish learning; the lifestyle of the ghetto had gone forever, and with it an intimate knowledge of centuries of traditional observance; the Holy Land was being polluted by the Zionists. All that a zealous Jew could do to fill the void was to cling to the texts which preserved his last link with the divine.

The destruction of the Holocaust had changed the nature of Torah study. In the ghetto world, many of the traditional rites and practices had been accepted as a "given"; there had been no alternative way of living or observing the Torah. The first generation of refugees still had that knowledge of exactly how these rites should be performed in their bones, but their children and grandchildren, who were so anxious to re-create the lost world of their murdered ancestors, were no longer so instinctively aware of this customal observance, which had never needed to be written down formally. The only way they could recover this vanishing Torah world was to comb the texts for scraps of information. From the 1950s, the *yeshiva* world was flooded by learned monographs describing in minute and complicated detail procedures which in pre-Holocaust Europe had seemed natural and a matter of course. Each succeeding generation would depend on such scholarship more than its predecessors.[27] As a result of the destruction, Jewish life was more text-bound and reliant on the written word than ever before.

There was a new stringency in fundamentalist Judaism. By the 1960s, Rabbi Simla Elberg, then visiting Bnei Brak, noted that an "extensive revolution in the entire alignment of the religious life" was taking place there. The Jews in the "city of Torah" were observing the commandments far more rigorously than ever before.[28] This effort to obey the law more fully than had been possible in previous ages was heroic: it was a way of incarnating the divine in a world that had been brutally emptied of God. The

Haredim of Bnei Brak were finding new ways of being punctilious and exact about such questions as diet and purification, even if this made their lives more difficult.

The Hazon Ish had set the tone in the 1930s, when he first arrived in Palestine. A group of religious Zionists had approached him with a query. They wanted to observe Jewish agricultural law in their settlement, and to farm the Holy Land according to the Torah. Did that mean that every seven years they should let their fields lie fallow, as the law enjoined?[29] To observe this "sabbatical year" would obviously cause great hardship and was a practice utterly opposed to the techniques of modern agriculture, which were designed for maximum efficiency. Rabbi Kook had found a legal loophole for the settlers, but the Hazon Ish was adamantly opposed to such leniency (kula). The challenge, he said, lay precisely in the difficulty. The law demanded that the farmer sacrifice his prosperity for a higher good. The sabbatical year was designed to celebrate the holiness of the Land, to make Jews aware of its inviolability and that, like all sacred objects, it was essentially separate from the needs and desires of individuals. The Land was not to be exploited by Jews for their own benefit, milked for increased productivity, or subjected to cost-effective projects. The truly religious farmer should challenge the rational materialism of the secular pioneers, which might be "Zionist" but was not at all "Jewish."[30]

At Bnei Brak, the Hazon Ish presided over what Rabbi Elburg called "the world of humrot ('stringencies')," and taught his disciples to find the "most restrictive, stringent, and punctilious" way to observe the commandments,[31] a discipline which would set them radically apart from the pragmatic ethos of modernity. This type of rigor had been frowned upon by the rabbinic establishment in the traditional Jewish communities in Europe. Rabbis had respected the scruples of people who were concerned about the finer points of the Law, but would not allow them to impose this stringency (humra) on the community as a whole, because it could become divisive. Jews who came from communities which had more rigorous standards about the slaughtering of animals would not be able to eat with a Jew who interpreted the rules more leniently. Too great a stringency could also be insulting to the great sages of the past, who had not been quite so punctilious in such matters. Rabbis had tended toward leniency in their interpretation of the Torah: a spiritual elite could not be allowed to make observance impossible for the more run-of-the-mill Jews.[32]

The revolutionary stringency of Bnei Brak was part of a new counter-culture that the Haredim were trying to create. It set a religious standard that was diametrically opposed to the rationalized spirit of modernity, which made efficiency and pragmatism the main criteria. At a time when Reform,

Conservative, and Neo-Orthodox Jews were discarding parts of the law or trying to find a more relaxed and rational religious life, the more rigorous observance of the Haredim refused to compromise with the norms of mainstream society. On his visit to Bnei Brak, Rabbi Elburg noted that it had become "a world in itself ";[33] Haredi Jews were not only withdrawing from modern society, but from other, less punctilious Jews. They needed different slaughterers, shops that were stricter about kosher food, and their own ritual baths. They were cultivating a distinct identity in opposition to the temper of the times.

Similarly, in the *yeshivot,* Jews did not study, like students in secular colleges, to acquire information that could later be put to practical use. Many of the laws of the Torah, such as those concerned with the rituals of the Temple and animal sacrifice, could no longer be implemented; the laws of torts and damages could be restored only by the Messiah when he established the Kingdom. Yet students spent hours, days, and even years immersed in intense discussion of this apparently obsolete legislation with their teachers, because these were God's laws. The repetition of the Hebrew words that God had—in some sense—spoken when he had given the law to Moses on Mount Sinai was a form of communion with the divine. Exploring every detail of the laws enabled a student to enter symbolically into the mind of God. In an age which had so horrifically cast the divine law aside, Jews would observe it more accurately than ever before. Familiarizing himself with the legal opinions of the great rabbis of the past was a way for the student to take the tradition into his own mind and heart, and commune with the sages. In the *yeshivot,* the methods of study were just as crucial as the material itself, and the object of *yeshiva* education was not greater facility in this world but a quest for the divine in a society which had tried to exclude God. Everything about the *yeshiva* world was different from the secularist world outside. In mainstream society, men (still considered the superior sex in the 1950s) went out to engage in business, while women stayed in the seclusion of the home. Among the Haredim, it was the inferior sex who went out into what the *goyim* considered the "real" world of affairs (tacitly proclaiming its secondary status), while the men led an enclosed, protected life with the true Reality in the *yeshiva*. In secular Israel, the army was becoming almost a sacred institution; national service was obligatory for both sexes, and a man would remain in his army unit for reserve duty for the whole of his active life. A *yeshiva* student, however, was excused military service, turned his back on the Israel Defense Forces (IDF), proclaimed that he was the true "guardian" of the Jewish people, and was on the front line of a holy war against the evil forces that pressed aggressively upon the *yeshiva* on all sides.[34]

For the Haredim, modernity—even in the State of Israel—was simply the latest manifestation of Galut, the state of exile, alienation, and distance from God. The Holocaust had revealed its essential malignity. A Jew was not supposed to feel at home in such a world, even though, paradoxically, in both Israel and America, Torah education was generously funded and flourished as never before. Students were, however, taught to keep apart from the secular world. As a Haredi educationalist explained, the *yeshiva* not only taught a young man "total dedication to Torah," but also how "to distance himself from the experiences of this world."[35] The *yeshiva* walls were a constant reminder that the Torah can never be at home in the Galut. The counterculture was designed to enhance the students' separation from the mainstream. As Avraham Woolf observed in *Education in the Face of the Generation* (1954), the *yeshiva* Jew was dedicated to the task of reviving the world of his father and grandfather, despite the indifference of the secularists. "We stand all alone in this. We are different from all around us. Reform historians . . . poets [are seen as great men by all the others]." Even in the Jewish state the Haredim were isolated. "Streets are named for historical figures whom we see in an utterly negative light. We stand all alone."[36]

The Haredi rebellion against rational modernity consists largely of retreat. But in this period, the Lubavitch Hasidim, who had long nurtured a militancy in the Habad *yeshiva* in Russia, went on the offensive. The Bolsheviks had virtually annihilated the Habad in Russia. Jewish schools and *yeshivot* were closed, Torah study was condemned as counterrevolutionary, and defiance meant starvation, imprisonment, or death. The Sixth Rebbe (Joseph Isaac Schneerson, 1880–1950) could only see these measures as the "birth pangs of the Messiah." It was not enough for the religious to retreat from the world; Hasidim must try to conquer the modern world for God. In Russia, the Rebbe organized a Jewish underground, where the graduates of the Habad *yeshiva* gave Torah and Talmud classes, and taught young Jews to observe the commandments. He was exiled, but continued his work from Poland, reorganizing and centralizing his court on modern lines, and using the new communications technology to keep in touch with the Lubavitch all over the world. When the Rebbe was forced to flee Hitler and arrived in the United States, he continued his mission and began a propaganda campaign to reclaim Jews who had assimilated or felt deracinated in the New World. Instead of withdrawal, there was outreach. In 1949, the Rebbe took the remarkable step of founding Kfar Habad, the first Hasidic settlement in Israel. He had not abated his hostility to Zionism one whit, but believed that in these Last Days, his mission must also reach the Jews in the defiled land of Israel.[37]

In 1950, the Rebbe died and was succeeded by his son-in-law, Rabbi

Menachem Mendel Schneerson (1904–94). This was an astonishing development, which must reflect the Habad's willingness to embrace the secular
world in an attempt to convert it. The Seventh Rebbe had not been educated
in a *yeshiva*, but had received a modern education. He had studied Jewish
philosophy in Berlin and marine engineering at the Sorbonne. When he
arrived in the United States in 1941, he had worked for the Navy, but had
also assisted in his father-in-law's mission. Here was a Rebbe who was a
product of the modern world, and able to mobilize his Hasidim in a vastly
efficient media campaign to redeem Jews all over the world. Now it was not
only the *yeshiva* students who were to be soldiers in the Rebbe's army but
every single Habad Jew. The Rebbe carefully prepared his campaign, and in
the 1970s launched an immense counteroffensive against secularization and
assimilation. Thousands of young Lubavitch, male and female, would be
dispatched to found Habad houses in distant cities, where Jews were either
wholly secularized or in a minority. The house would be a "drop-in" center
which provided information about Judaism, hosted Sabbath and festival
ceremonies, and held lectures and classes. Other young Hasidim would be
sent out onto the campuses and streets of America, where they would accost
passing Jews and persuade them to perform one of the commandments in
public, such as putting on *tefillin* and reciting a prayer. The idea was that the
rite would touch the divine "spark" lodged in the soul of every Jew and
awaken his or her essential holiness.[38]

The Rebbe was at home in the world. His scientific knowledge coexisted
with the old *mythos* of Habad Hasidism. His studies in marine biology had
not robbed him of his vision of the divine sparks; he would develop a strong
messianism, and won the election to the leadership of Habad by claiming to
be in mystic communion with the deceased Sixth Rebbe. In his spirituality,
logos and *mythos* were complementary sources of insight. He interpreted the
Bible as literally as any Protestant fundamentalist, convinced that the world
had been created by God in six days just under six thousand years ago. But
he also believed that the discoveries of modern science about the connection
between body and soul, or matter and energy, were leading human beings to
a new appreciation of the organic unity of reality, which, in turn, would pre-
dispose them to monotheism.[39] His immense campaign was organized upon
modern lines, and he understood how to exploit his resources and speak to
secularized men and women. It seems, however, to have been the mythology
and mysticism of Habad that gave the Lubavitch the confidence to sally
forth into the world instead of retreating defensively from it. Recent rebbes
had turned against the spirit of the Enlightenment, but Rabbi Schneur Zalman, the First Rebbe and founder of Habad, had helped his Hasidim to cultivate a positive view of the world of their day. The Seventh Rebbe seemed

to have returned to this original spirit, using his rational powers within a mythical context, as Zalman himself had done. Habad had refused to accept the modern separation of sacred and profane. Everything, however base and mundane, held a spark of the divine. There was no such person as a "secular Jew," and even the *goyim* had a potential for holiness. Toward the end of his life, convinced of the imminence of the Last Days, the Rebbe began a mission to the gentiles of America, which, he acknowledged, had been good to Jews. The Lubavitch had suffered greatly in the modern period and had even faced extinction, but the Rebbe trained them not to see the Galut in a wholly demonic light, not to nurture fantasies of hatred and revenge, but to see the world as a place to which they could reintroduce the divine.[40]

PROTESTANT FUNDAMENTALISTS in the United States would eventually launch a counteroffensive against the modernity that had defeated them, but during the period currently under discussion, they concentrated, like Haredi Jews, on creating their own defensive counterculture. After the Scopes trial, Protestant fundamentalists retreated from the public arena and withdrew to their own churches and colleges. The liberal Christians assumed that the fundamentalist crisis was over. By the end of the Second World War, the fundamentalist groups seemed marginal and insignificant, and the mainstream denominations drew most of the believers. But instead of disappearing, the fundamentalists were putting down strong roots at the local level. There was still a considerable number of conservatives within the mainstream denominations; they had lost all hope of expelling the liberals, but they had not relinquished their belief in the "fundamentals" and held aloof from the majority. The more radical formed their own churches, especially the premillennarians, who believed it to be a sacred duty, while waiting for Rapture, to separate themselves from the ungodly liberals. They began to found new organizations and networks masterminded by a new generation of evangelists. By 1930, there were at least fifty fundamentalist Bible colleges in the United States. During the Depression years, another twenty-six were founded, and the fundamentalist Wheaton College, in Illinois, was the fastest-growing liberal arts college in the United States. Fundamentalists also formed their own publishing and broadcasting empires. When television arrived during the 1950s, the young Billy Graham, Rex Humbard, and Oral Roberts began their ministries as "televangelists," replacing the old traveling revivalist preachers.[41] A huge, apparently invisible broadcasting network linked fundamentalists together all over the nation. They felt themselves to be outsiders, pushed to the periphery of society, but their new colleges and radio and television stations gave them a home in a hostile world.

In the counterculture that Protestant fundamentalists were creating, their colleges were safe, sacred enclaves amid the surrounding profaneness. They were attempting to create holiness by means of segregation. Bob Jones University, founded in 1927 in Florida, and moving to Tennessee before finding its final home in Greenville, South Carolina, epitomized the ethos of the new fundamentalist institution. The founder, an early-twentieth-century evangelist, was no intellectual, but wanted to found what he called a "safe" school, which would help young people preserve their faith while they prepared to fight the atheism which, he believed, now pervaded the secular universities.[42] Students were taught "common sense Christianity" alongside the liberal arts. Everybody was obliged to take at least one Bible course each semester, to attend chapel, and to adhere to a "Christian" lifestyle, with strong rules governing dress, social interaction, and dating. Disobedience and disloyalty were, Bob Jones insisted, "unpardonable sins" and were not tolerated.[43] Staff and students alike had to conform. Bob Jones University was a world unto itself: it made the difficult decision not to seek academic accreditation, believing any such compromise with the secular establishment to be sinful.[44] This sacrifice enabled the university to exert tighter control over admissions, curriculum, and library resources.

This discipline was essential, for BJU students knew that they were at war. As a recent undergraduate catalog explains, the school is against "all atheistic, agnostic and humanistic attacks upon the Scripture"; all "so-called Modernist," "Liberal," and "Neo-Orthodox" positions, and the "unscriptural compromise of the 'New Evangelicals' and the unscriptural practices of the 'Charismatics.' "[45] Students and staff retreated from the world to protect their faith from the assaults of these enemies. This "separation," according to Bob Jones's son (Bob Jones II), was "the very foundation and basis of a fundamental witness and testimony."[46] From this bastion of faith, students would militantly defend "biblical authority and infallibility" by attacking "the enemies of the faith."[47] BJU had little influence on American academia, but great influence on the Christian nation. Bob Jones University has become the largest supplier of fundamentalist teachers in the country; graduates are known for their self-discipline and self-motivation, if not for their broad education.

The Bible colleges and the fundamentalist universities created during these years were, like the Haredi *yeshivot*, separatist citadels. Fundamentalists felt that their faith was imperiled; they had been displaced from the center of American life, and were taught to regard themselves as "outside the gate."[48] The militancy expressed deep anger. This surfaced in the utterances of the more extremist Christians in these years, who voiced many of the fears, hatreds, and prejudices of the most marginalized sectors of the population. Gerald Winrod, a Baptist who organized the Defenders of the Christian Faith to combat the teaching of evolution during the 1920s, traveled in Nazi Germany during the 1930s and returned determined to expose the "Jewish menace" to the American people. At the same time, he denounced Roosevelt's "Jewish New Deal" as satanic. With Carl McIntyre and Billy James Hargis, Winrod condemned every "liberal" trend in the United States. Fundamentalists blamed liberals of any hue, secularist or Christian, for the marginal status of the "true" Christians. They were beginning their swing to the political Right. In the nineteenth century, evangelicals had seen patriotism as idolatrous. Now it became a sacred duty to defend the American way of life. Hargis, the founder of the Christian Crusade, an anti-communist ministry, saw the Soviet Union as demonic, and battled tirelessly against what he regarded as communist infiltration: the liberal press, leftist teachers, and the Supreme Court were all, in his view, part of a conspiracy to turn America "red." Carl McIntyre, who seceded from the Presbyterian Church to found the Bible Presbyterian Church and the Faith Theological Seminary, saw hidden enemies everywhere. The mainline denominations themselves were part of a satanic plot to destroy Christianity in America. In the 1950s, McIntyre joined Joseph McCarthy's anticommunist crusade. These extremists were not typical, but they were influential. By 1934, some 600,000 people subscribed to Winrod's *Defender Magazine;* 120,000 took McIntyre's *Christian Beacon.* McIntyre reached thousands more in his *Twentieth Century Christian Hour,* a radio program which condemned all Christians who did not subscribe to his theology of hatred, and all liberal clergy, who might seem loving and Christian to the uninformed, but who were really "atheistic, communistic, Bible-ridiculing, blood-despising, name-calling, sex-manacled sons of green-eyed monsters."[49]

Fundamentalism was becoming a religion of rage, but, as in Haredi Judaism, this rage was rooted in deep fear. This was evident in the pre-millennialism that became a hallmark of the movement during this period. By the Second World War, only premillennialists still called themselves "fundamentalists"; other conservative Christians, such as Billy Graham, preferred to call themselves "evangelicals": the duty of saving souls in this rotten civilization demanded some degree of cooperation with other Christians, whatever their theological beliefs. Fundamentalists proper, however, insisted on separatism and segregation.[50] The war years seemed to prove that the postmillennial optimism of the liberals had been deluded; fundamentalists regarded the new United Nations in as negative a light as they had the old League of Nations. It would prepare the world for the dictatorship of

Antichrist and the ensuing Tribulation. There could be no world peace. "The Bible contradicts such a utopian dream," wrote Herbert Lockyear in 1942. "This is not to be the last war. Present horrors are but the spawn to produce still more terrible anguish."[51] This was a vision diametrically opposed to the view of the liberal establishment. There were "two nations" in America, unable to share each other's vision of the modern world. The premillennial vision endorsed the fundamentalists' feeling of utter helplessness. The atomic bomb, they believed, had been foretold by St. Peter, who had predicted that on the last day, "with a roar the sky will vanish, the elements will catch fire and fall apart, the earth and all that it contains will be burnt up."[52] There was no hope of averting the final holocaust, David Grey Barnhouse reflected in *Eternity* magazine in 1945: "the divine plan moves forward to its inevitable fulfillment." In his best-seller *The Atomic Age and the Word of God* (1948), the fundamentalist author Wilbur Smith argued that the bomb proved that the literalists had been right all along.[53] The exact predictions of the atomic explosion in Scripture showed that the Bible was indeed inerrant and must be read according to its plain sense.

Yet this fatalistic scenario also gave the fundamentalists, who felt despised and ostracized by the mainstream culture, a sense of confidence and superiority. They had privileged information, denied to the secularist or liberal Christian, and knew what was really going on. The catastrophic events of the twentieth century were really heading toward Christ's final victory. Moreover, the atomic holocaust would not affect the true believers, since, as we have seen, they were convinced that they would be raptured up to heaven before the End. It was only the apostates and unbelievers who would suffer those final tortures. Premillennialism was, therefore, fueling the resentment experienced by fundamentalists by allowing them to cultivate fantasies of revenge that were quite out of keeping with the spirit of the Gospels. There was contradiction too in their apparently positive vision of the new State of Israel.

The Jewish people had been central to the vision of John Darby, the founder of premillennialism. Fundamentalists had been thrilled by the Balfour Declaration of 1917, and the actual creation of the State of Israel in 1948 was seen by fundamentalist preacher Jerry Falwell as "the greatest . . . single sign indicating the imminent return of Jesus Christ"; he saw May 14, 1948, when Ben-Gurion proclaimed the birth of the State of Israel, as the most important day in history since the ascension of Jesus into heaven.[54] Support for Israel became mandatory; Israel's history was beyond human influence and control, determined by God from all eternity. Christ could not return, the Last Days could not begin, unless the Jews were living in the Holy Land.[55]

Protestant fundamentalists were enthusiastic Zionists, but their vision had a darker side. John Darby had taught that Antichrist would slaughter two-thirds of the Jews living in Palestine in the End-time: Zachariah had predicted this, and, like all such prophecies, his words must be interpreted literally.[56] Some fundamentalists had seen the Holocaust as God's last effort to convert the Jews, and a foretaste of worse to come. In *Israel and Prophecy,* the prolific fundamentalist writer John Walvoord gave a detailed timetable of this final persecution of the Jews, based on a patchwork of prophecies. Antichrist would help the Jews to rebuild their Temple and convince many of them that he was the Messiah; but then he would set up his own image in the new Temple as an object of worship. After this apostasy, 144,000 Jews would reject Antichrist, be converted to Christianity, and die as martyrs. Then Antichrist would unleash a hideous persecution and Jews would die in ghastly numbers. Only a few would escape and be present to greet Jesus at his Second Coming.[57] At the same time as Protestant fundamentalists cele-brated the birth of the new Israel, they were cultivating fantasies of a final genocide at the end of time. The Jewish state had come into existence purely to further a Christian fulfillment. The Jews' fate in the Last Days is uniquely grim, since they are doomed to suffer whether or not they accept Christ. American Protestants had not suffered like the Jews, but their vision of modernity was also dark and doomed. They had evolved their literal and "scientific" reading of scripture in response to the rationalistic spirit of the modern world, yet if the true test of a religious vision is that it helps believ-ers to cultivate the cardinal virtue of compassion (a teaching that informs the Gospels and the letters of St. Paul, if not the Book of Revelation), Protestant fundamentalism seemed to be failing as a religious movement, just as at the Scopes trial its science had proved to be defective. Indeed, their literal reading of highly selected passages of the Bible had encouraged them to absorb the Godless genocidal tendencies of modernity.

MUSLIMS HAD AS YET produced no fundamentalist movement, because their modernization process was not yet sufficiently advanced. They were still at the stage of reshaping their religious traditions to meet the new challenge of modernity and using Islam to help the people understand the spirit of the new world. In Egypt, a young teacher brought the ideas of Afghani, Abdu, and Rida, whose reforms had always been confined to a small circle of intellectuals, to the more ordinary people. This in itself was a modern-izing move. The older reformers had still been shaped by the conserva-tive ethos, and, like most premodern philosophers, they had been elitists and did not consider the masses capable of abstruse thought. Hasan al-Banna

(1906–49) found a way to turn their reforming ideas into a mass movement. He had had a modern as well as a traditionally religious education. He had studied at the Dar al-Ulum in Cairo, the first teachers' training college to provide a higher education in the sciences, but Banna was also a Sufi and throughout his life the spiritual exercises and rites of Sufism remained important to him.[58] For Banna, faith was not a notional assent to a creed; it was something that could be understood only if it was lived and its rituals were carefully practiced. He knew that Egyptians needed Western science and technology; he also realized that their society must be modernized, politically, socially, and economically. But these were practical and rational matters that must go hand-in-hand with a spiritual and psychological reformation.[59]

As students in Cairo, Banna and his friends were moved almost to tears by the political and social confusion in the city.[60] There was a political stalemate: the parties engaged in fruitless and vociferous debate and were still manipulated by the British, who despite Egyptian "independence" remained very much in command of the country. When Banna took up his first teaching post in Ismailiyyah in the Suez Canal Zone, where the British were ensconced, the humiliation of his people affected his very soul. The British and other expatriates had no interest in the local population, but kept a firm hand on the economy and public utilities. He was shamed by the contrast between the luxurious homes of the British and the miserable hovels of the Egyptian workers.[61] For Banna, a devout Muslim, this was not merely a matter of politics. The condition of the *ummah*, the Muslim community, is as crucial a religious value in Islam as a particular doctrinal formulation in Christianity. Banna was as spiritually distressed by the plight of his people as a Protestant fundamentalist when he felt that the inerrancy of the Bible had been impugned, or a member of Neturei Karta when he saw what he regarded as the desecration of the Holy Land by the Zionists. Banna was especially concerned to see the people drifting away from the mosques. The vast majority of Egyptians had not been included in the modernization process, and they were bewildered by the Western ideas they encountered in the numerous newspapers, journals, and magazines that were published in Cairo, which seemed either to have nothing in common with or to be positively hostile toward Islam. The *ulema* had turned their backs on the modern scene, and could offer the people no effective guidance, and the politicians made no sustained attempt to deal with the social, economic, or educational problems of the masses.[62] Banna decided that something had to be done. It was no good having high-flown discussions about nationalism and Egypt's future relationship with Europe when the vast bulk of the population felt confused and demoralized. As he saw it, the only way the people could find spiritual healing was by returning to the first principles of the Koran and the Sunnah.

Banna organized a few of his friends to hold impromptu "sermons" in the mosques and coffeehouses.[63] He told his audience that the impact of the West and the recent political changes had knocked them off balance, and that they no longer understood their religion. Islam was not a Western-style ideology, or a set of creeds. It was a total way of life and, if lived whole-heartedly, would bring back that dynamism and energy that Muslims had had long ago, before they had been colonized by foreigners. To make the *ummah* strong again, they must rediscover their Muslim souls.[64] Even though he was only in his early twenties, Banna made an impression. He was strong-minded, charismatic, and could make people follow him. One evening, in March 1928, six of the local workers in Ismailiyyah came and asked him to take action:

> We know not the practical way to reach the glory of Islam and to serve the welfare of the Muslims. We are weary of this life of humiliation and restriction. So we see that the Arabs and the Muslims have no status and no dignity. They are not more than mere hirelings belonging to foreigners. We possess nothing but this blood . . . and these souls . . . and these few coins. We are unable to perceive the road to action as you perceive it, or to know the path to the service of the fatherland, the religion and the *ummah* as you know it.[65]

Banna was moved by this appeal. Together, he and his visitors made an oath to be "troops [*jund*] for the message of Islam." That night the Society of Muslim Brothers was born. From this tiny beginning, it spread. By the time of Banna's death in 1949, there were 2000 branches of the Society through-out Egypt, each branch representing between 300,000 and 600,000 Brothers and Sisters. It was the only organization in Egypt to represent every group in society, including civil servants, students, and the potentially power-ful urban workers and peasants.[66] By the Second World War, the Society had become one of the most powerful contestants on the Egyptian political scene.

Despite the militant imagery that characterized the Society from the first night of its existence, Banna always insisted that he had no intention of staging a coup or seizing power. The Society's chief aim was education. He believed that when the people had absorbed the message of Islam and allowed it to transform them, the nation would become Muslim without a violent takeover. At the very beginning, Banna formulated a six-point program, which revealed his debt to Afghani, Abdu, and Rida's *salafiyyah* reform movements: (1) the interpretation of the Koran in the spirit of the age, (2) the unity of Islamic nations, (3) raising the standard of living and achievement of social justice and order, (4) a struggle against illiteracy and poverty, (5) the emancipation of Muslim lands from foreign dominance, and (6) the promotion of Islamic peace and fraternity throughout the world.[67] Banna did not intend his Society to be violent or radical, but was principally concerned with the fundamental reform of Muslim society, which had been undermined by the colonial experience and cut off from its roots.[68] Egyptians had become accustomed to thinking themselves inferior to Europeans, but there was no need for this. They had fine cultural traditions too that would serve them better than any imported ideologies.[69] They should not have to copy the French or Russian revolutions, because the Prophet Muhammad had already proclaimed the need for liberty, equality, fraternity, and social justice 1300 years before.[69] The Shariah suited the Middle Eastern environment in a way no foreign law code could. As long as Muslims imitated other people, they would remain "cultural mongrels."[70]

But first the Brothers and Sisters had to reacquaint themselves with Islam. There was no shortcut to freedom and dignity; Muslims would have to rebuild themselves and their society from the ground up. Over the years, Banna evolved an efficient, modern system, constantly subject to review and self-appraisal, to achieve this. In 1938, members were divided into "battalions," each consisting of three groups—one for workers, one for students, and one for businessmen and civil servants. The groups met once a week to spend the night together in prayer and spiritual instruction. By 1943, when this system had not brought in the harvest of recruits that had been hoped for, the "battalions" were replaced by "families," each of which had ten members and was a unit, responsible for its actions. The family members would meet once a week, and keep each other up to the mark, ensuring that everybody observed the "pillars," and kept clear of gambling, alcohol, usury, and adultery. The family system stressed the bonding of Muslims at a time when Egyptian society was fragmenting under the pressures of modernization. Each family belonged to a larger "battalion," which kept it in touch with headquarters.[71]

A Christian reform movement at this time tended to pinpoint doctrine; this was partly due to the rationalism of modern Western culture, which had come to see faith as adherence to a set of beliefs. The Society, however, was run according to the conservative piety of the Shariah, which helped Muslims to build the Muhammadan archetype within themselves by living in a certain way. But this old-style piety was promoted in a modern guise. The rites, prayers, and ethical disciplines were designed to create an interior orientation to God, similar to the Prophet's own. Only in this spiritual context, Banna believed, could modern institutions and reforms make sense to a Muslim people. In 1945, at a packed meeting, Banna decided that it was time to establish a social and welfare program that was desperately needed, but which no government had addressed effectively. The Brothers had always built schools for boys and girls beside the mosque, as soon as they established a new branch.[72] They had also founded the Rovers, a modern scout movement, which trained young Brothers physically and practically; the Rovers had become the largest and most powerful youth group in the country by the Second World War.[73] Now these services were to become more streamlined and efficient. The Brothers ran night schools for workers, and tutorial colleges for the civil-service examinations[74]; they founded clinics and hospitals in the rural areas, and the Rovers were also actively involved in improving sanitation and health education in the poorer, country districts. The Society also founded modern trade unions, and instructed the workers on their rights. They made public some of the worst labor abuses, and were active in job creation, by establishing their own factories and light industries in printing, weaving, construction, and engineering.[75]

The Society's enemies always accused Banna of having created a "state within a state." He had indeed built a massively successful counterculture which highlighted the deficiencies of the government in a way that was clearly threatening.[76] It called attention to the government's neglect of education and labor conditions; the fact that the Society alone was able to appeal to the *fellahin* was also disturbing. But, more important, all the Society's institutions had a distinctly Muslim identity. Its factories all had mosques and gave the workers time to make the required prayers; in accordance with the social message of the Koran, working conditions and pay were good; workers had health insurance and decent holidays; disputes were arbitrated fairly. The extraordinary success of the Society was a dramatic demonstration of the fact that, whatever the intellectuals and pundits claimed, most of the Egyptian people wanted to be religious. It also showed that Islam could be progressive. There was no slavish return to the practices of the seventh century. The Brothers were extremely critical of the new Wahhabi Kingdom of Saudi Arabia, and condemned its literalistic interpretations of Islamic law, such as cutting off the hands of thieves or stoning adulterers.[77] The Brothers had no definite notions about the kind of polity the future Islamic state should have, but they insisted that to be faithful to the spirit of the Koran and Sunnah, there must be a fairer distribution of wealth than there was in the Saudi Kingdom. Their general ideas were certainly in tune with the times: rulers should be elected (as in the early Muslim period), and, as the *rashidun* ("righteous") caliphs had urged, a ruler must be accountable to the people and must not rule dictatorially. But Banna always felt that precise discussions about a possible Islamic state were premature, because there was still much basic preparation to be done.[78] Banna simply asked that Egypt be allowed to make its state Islamic; the Soviets had chosen communism, and the West democracy; countries where the population was predominantly Muslim should have the right to construct their polity on an Islamic basis, if and when they so wished.[79]

The Society was not perfect. Because of its appeal to the masses, it tended to be anti-intellectual. Its pronouncements were often defensive and self-righteous. The Brothers' image of the West, which stressed its greed, tyranny, and spiritual bankruptcy, had been distorted by the colonial experience. The object of Western imperialism had not simply been, as one of the Society's spokesmen maintained, "to humiliate us, to occupy our lands and begin destroying Islam."[80] The Society's leaders were intolerant of dissension in the ranks. Banna insisted on absolute obedience and did not delegate responsibility sufficiently. As a result, after his death, nobody could take his place, and the Society was virtually destroyed from within by fruitless infighting. But by far its most serious and damaging failing was the emergence in 1943 of a terrorist unit known as "The Secret Apparatus" *(al jihaz al-sirri)*.[81] It remained marginal to the Society as a whole. Because it was so clandestine, we have very little information about it, but in his definitive study of the Society, Richard P. Mitchell states his belief that by 1948, the unit only had about a thousand members, and that most of the Brothers had never heard of its existence until this date.[82] For the vast majority of members, social and spiritual reform was the raison d'être of the Society, and they abhorred the terrorism of the Apparatus. Nevertheless, once a movement has started killing in the name of God, it has embarked on a nihilistic course that denies the most fundamental religious values.

The 1940s were very turbulent years in Egypt. It had become obvious that liberal democracy had failed, and most Egyptians were thoroughly pessimistic about the parliamentary system. Neither the British nor the Egyptian nationalists had understood that it was not possible to impose a modern system of government on a country that, as a result of superficial and too rapid modernization, was still basically feudal and agrarian. Between 1923 and 1950, all seventeen general elections were won by the nationalist Wafd party, but they were only allowed to rule five times. Wafdists were usually forced to resign by either the British or the palace.[83] In 1942, even the Wafd lost the respect of the people when the British forced the pro-German prime minister to step down and replaced him with a Wafdist government, as the lesser of two evils. There was an atmosphere of violence in Cairo during the Second World War and a desperation, subsequently compounded by the ignominious defeat of the five Arab armies, including that of Egypt, which invaded Palestine after the creation of the State of Israel in 1948. The loss of Palestine and the world's apparent indifference to the plight of the 750,000 Palestinian refugees who were forced to leave their homes in 1948 demonstrated Arab impotence in the modern world. Arabs still call the events of 1948 *al-Nakhbah:* a "disaster" of cosmic proportions. In this grim atmosphere, some believed that terror was the "only path."[84] That was certainly the opinion of Anwar al-Sadat, later to become president of Egypt, who founded a "murder society" in the late 1940s to attack the British in the Canal Zone and Egyptian politicians who were seen to "collaborate" with the British. There were other paramilitary groups that also saw violence as the only way: the Green Shirts, who were attached to the palace, and the Blue Shirts, who were associated with the Wafd.[85]

It was, perhaps, inevitable that the Society of Muslim Brothers, which was now such a major player on the Egyptian political scene, should have its terrorist wing too, but it was a tragic development. It is not clear how far Banna himself was implicated in the activities of the Secret Apparatus. He always denounced them, but he was also virulent in his denunciation of the government during these years.[86] Banna could not control the terrorist unit, whose activities initiated a series of events that led to his death, tainted the moral credibility of the Society, and eventually resulted in its destruction. In March 1948, members of the Secret Apparatus started a campaign of terror, which began with the murder of Ahmed al-Khazinder, a respected judge, continued throughout the summer in violent raids and bombing of the Jewish district in Cairo, in which property was damaged and scores of people were injured or lost their lives, and culminated on December 28, 1948, in the assassination of Prime Minister Muhammad al-Nuqrashi.

The Society repudiated these killings, and Banna professed horror at the murder of Nuqrashi.[87] Nevertheless, the new prime minister, Ibrahim al-Hadi, who was loathed by all the articulate sectors of society, seized the opportunity of eliminating the Brotherhood, which had become far too powerful. The Society was suppressed, members were rounded up, arrested, and tortured, and by the end of July 1949, when Abd al-Hadi finally resigned, there were over four thousand Brothers in prison.[88] But on February 12, 1949, Banna had been shot in the street outside the headquarters of the Young Men's Muslim Association, almost certainly at the behest of the prime minister.

The Society began to regroup secretly in 1950 and elected a new leader, Hasan Ismail al-Hudaybi, a judge who was known for his moderation and aversion to violence. It was hoped that he would give the Society much-needed respectability. But Hudaybi was unequal to the task. Without

Banna's strong leadership, factional strife broke out among the leaders, and Hudaybi proved to be incapable of controlling the Secret Apparatus, which brought the Society down once again in 1954.

By that time, Egypt was ruled by the formidable young army officer Jamal Abd al-Nasser (1918–70), who had overthrown the old, discredited regime in a military coup on July 22, 1952, with his association of Free Officers, and set about creating a revolutionary republic in Egypt. Nasser espoused a militant nationalism that was quite different from the old liberal ideal. Unlike the Egyptian intellectuals of the 1920s and 1930s, the new Arab nationalists were not enamored of the West, and had no time for the parliamentary "liberalism" that had so signally failed in the Middle East. Nasser's regime was defiantly socialist, and he courted the Soviets. He was determined to get the British out of Egypt once and for all; his attitude toward both Israel and the West was cathartically defiant for his people. His foreign policy was pan-Arab and emphasized Egypt's solidarity with other Asian and African countries who were struggling to free themselves from European control. Nasser was also a determined secularist; nothing, including religion, must be allowed to interfere with the national interest; everything, including religion, must be subordinated to the state. Eventually Nasser would become the most popular ruler in the Middle East, and "Nasserism" the dominant ideology. But in these first years, Nasser was struggling: he was not very popular and could not permit any major rival to survive.

At first, however, Nasser wooed the Brotherhood. He needed them, and, because he was happy to use Islamic rhetoric, the Society supported him and the Rovers played an important part in restoring order after the July Revolution. But there was an incipient tension, especially when it became clear that, despite his populist Muslim rhetoric, Nasser had no intention of creating an Islamic state. When Hudaybi's demands for a full application of Islamic principles became importunate, Nasser's cabinet dissolved the Society once again, on January 15, 1954, on the grounds that it was planning a counter-revolution.[89] A nucleus of the Brotherhood went underground, and the government began a smear campaign which accused the Brothers of possessing illegal arms, and of plotting with the British. The regime began to stress its own Islamic credentials, and Anwar Sadat, now secretary-general of the new Islamic Congress, founded by Nasser, wrote a series of articles on the "true" and "liberal" Islam espoused by the government in the semi-official paper *al-Jamhariyyah*. Finally, however, the Brotherhood itself played into Nasser's hands on October 26, 1954, when Abd al-Latif, a member of the Society, shot Nasser during a rally.

Nasser survived the attack, and his courage and insouciance under fire did wonders for his popularity. He was now free to destroy the Society completely. By the end of November 1954, over one thousand Brothers had been arrested and brought to trial. Innumerable others, however, many of whom had been guilty of nothing more inflammatory than distributing leaflets, never appeared in court, were subjected to mental and physical torture, and languished in Nasser's prisons and concentration camps for the next fifteen years. Hudaybi was sentenced to life imprisonment, but six other leaders of the Society were executed.[90] Nasser seemed to have broken the Brotherhood, and to have stopped the only progressive Islamic movement in Egypt in its tracks. Secularism appeared to be victorious, especially after Nasser became the hero of the Arab world two years later after the Suez Crisis, in which he not only successfully defied the West but inflicted a crushing humiliation on the British. But his triumph over the Brotherhood proved in the end to be a Pyrrhic victory. The Brothers who spent the rest of Nasser's life in the camps had experienced the onslaught of secularism at its most aggressive. We shall see that it was in the camps that some of the Brothers abandoned Banna's reformist vision and created a new and potentially violent Sunni fundamentalism.

Iranians were also experiencing a vicious secularist assault. Reza Shah's modernization program was even more accelerated than that undergone by either Egypt or Turkey, because when he came to power, Iran had scarcely begun to modernize.[91] Reza was ruthless. Opponents were simply eliminated; one of the first to go was Ayatollah Mudarris, who had opposed the shah in the Majlis; he was imprisoned in 1927, and murdered in 1937.[92] Reza managed to centralize the country for the first time, but only by the most brutal means, quashing uprisings and impoverishing the nomadic tribes, who had hitherto been virtually autonomous.[93] Reza reformed the judiciary; three new secular law codes—civil, commercial, and criminal—replaced the Shariah.[94] He also tried to industrialize the country and bring it modern amenities. By the late 1930s, most cities had electricity and power plants. But government controls stifled the development of a truly aggressive capitalist economy, wages were low, and exploitation rife. These draconian methods proved to be fruitless; Iran was unable to achieve economic independence. Britain still owned the booming oil industry, which contributed almost nothing to the economy, and Iran was forced to rely on foreign loans and investment.

Reza's program was inevitably superficial. It simply imposed modern institutions on old agrarian structures, an approach that had failed in Egypt and would fail here. Ninety percent of the population who were involved in agriculture were ignored; traditional farming methods continued and remained unproductive. There was no fundamental reform of society. Reza was not in the least interested in the plight of the poor, and, while the army got fifty percent of the budget, only four percent was spent on education, which remained a privilege for the rich.⁹⁵ As in Egypt, two nations were developing in Iran, who were, increasingly, unable to understand each other. One "nation" comprised the small Westernized elite of the upper and middle classes, who had benefited from Reza's modernization program; the other "nation" consisted of the vast mass of the poor, who were bewildered by the new secular nationalism of the regime, and relied more than ever upon the *ulema* for guidance.

But the *ulema* themselves were reeling under the impact of Reza's secularization policy. He hated the clergy and was determined to curb their considerable power in Iran. His Iranian nationalism tried to cut out Islam altogether, and was based on the ancient Persian culture of the region. Reza tried to suppress the Ashura celebrations in honor of Imam Husain (recognizing their revolutionary potential), and Iranians were forbidden to go on the *hajj* to Mecca. In 1931, the scope of the Shariah courts was drastically reduced. The clergy were permitted to deal only with questions of personal status; all other cases were referred to the new civil courts. For over a century, the *ulema* had enjoyed almost unrivaled power in Iran. Now they watched their power systematically cut down to size, but, after the assassination of Mudarris, most of the clergy were too afraid to protest.⁹⁶

Reza's Laws on the Uniformity of Dress (1928) show both the superficiality and the violence of this modernization process. Western dress was made obligatory for all men (except the *ulema*, who were allowed to wear their cloaks and turbans, on condition that they pass a state examination admitting them to clerical status) and, later, women were forbidden to wear the veil. His soldiers used to tear off women's veils with their bayonets, and rip them to pieces in the streets.⁹⁷ Reza wanted Iran to *look* modern, despite the underlying conservatism, and was prepared to go to any lengths to achieve this. During Ashura, in 1929, the police surrounded the Fayziyah Madrasah in Qum, and when the students spilled out into the street, they stripped them of their traditional clothes and forced them into Western garb. Men particularly disliked wearing the wide-brimmed Western hats, because they prevented their making the ritual prostrations during prayer. In 1935, there was an ugly incident at the shrine of the Eighth Imam in Mashhad, when the police fired on a crowd who had staged a demonstration against the Dress Laws. Hundreds of unarmed demonstrators were either killed or wounded in the sanctuary. It was not surprising that many Iranians came to fear secularization as a lethal policy, designed not to free religion from the coercive state (as in the West) but to destroy Islam.⁹⁸

This was exactly the kind of atmosphere in which a fundamentalist movement was likely to thrive. It did not happen during this period, but four things did occur which foreshadowed later developments. The first was the creation of a counterculture. In 1920, Shaykh Abd al-Karim Hairi Yazdi (1860–1936), an eminent *mujtahid,* was invited to settle in Qum by the mullahs there. He was determined to put Qum back on the Shii map, because he feared for the future of the shrine cities of Kerbala and Najaf in Iraq, which had become the intellectual center of Iranian Shiism during the eighteenth century. Shortly after Shaykh Hairi's arrival in Qum, the British did indeed exile some of the leading *ulema* from Iraq and two of the most learned, one of them the "constitutionalist" *mujtahid* Naini, came to settle in Qum. The city began to revive. The *madrasahs* were refurbished, and distinguished scholars started to teach there, enabling them to attract better students. One of the newcomers was the scholarly and unworldly Ayatollah Sayyid Aqa Husain Borujerdi (1875–1961), who became the Marja-e Taqlid, the Supreme Model of the Shiah, and attracted still more scholars to Qum.⁹⁹ Gradually Qum began to replace Najaf and, in the 1960s and 1970s, it would become the religious "capital" of Iran, and the center of the opposition to the royal capital in Tehran. But in these early years, the mullahs of Qum adhered to the Shii tradition of holding aloof from politics; any political activism would have incurred the wrath of the shah, and the revival in Qum would have been crushed in its infancy.

The second fateful incident was the arrival in Qum in 1920 of the man who would become Iran's most famous mullah. Shaykh Hairi Yazdi had brought some of his pupils with him when he moved to Qum from western Iran, and one was the young Ruhollah Musavi Khomeini (1902–89). At first, however, Khomeini seemed a rather marginal figure. He taught *fiqh* at the Fayziyah Madrasah, but later he would specialize in ethics and mysticism *(irfan),* which were, compared with *fiqh,* definitely "fringe" subjects. Moreover, Khomeini practiced the mysticism of Mulla Sadra, upon which the establishment had long tended to look askance. He seemed interested in political questions, and this again was not calculated to advance his clerical career, especially after Ayatollah Borujerdi, who adhered strictly to the old Shii quietism and forbade the *ulema* to take part in politics, became the Marja. These were turbulent years in Iran, but despite his obvious political concern, Khomeini did not become an activist. Yet in 1944, he published *Kashf al-Asrar* ("The Discovery of Secrets"), which received very little attention at the time, but was the first serious attempt to challenge Pahlavi policy from a Shii perspective. At this point, Khomeini was still a reformer and not in any sense fundamentalist. His position was similar to that of the First Majlis in 1906, which had accepted the idea of a panel of *mujtahids* with the power to veto any parliamentary legislation that contravened the Shariah. Khomeini was still a supporter of the old constitution, and was trying to place this modern institution in an Islamic context. Only God had power to make laws, he argued; and it was not reasonable for Shiis to obey a ruler such as Atatürk or Reza Shah, who had done everything they could to destroy Islam. But Khomeini was still too much of a traditionalist to suggest at this early date that a cleric should rule the country directly: that would contravene centuries of Shii practice. The *mujtahids*, who were learned in God's law, were, in his theory, simply permitted to elect a lay sultan who they knew would not disobey the divine law or oppress the people.[100]

By the time Khomeini's book was published, the British had forced Reza Shah to abdicate because of his pro-German sympathies, showing that for all Reza's noisy assertions of independence, he was as much in thrall to the European powers as the Qajars. When Reza died in 1944, he was succeeded by his son, Muhammad Reza (1919–80), a much quieter and, at this point, weaker character. He came to the throne at a difficult time. The Second World War had been very disruptive in Iran; industry had come to a standstill, machinery had deteriorated, and there was widespread famine. The new middle classes were beginning to chafe at their lack of opportunity, nationalists wanted to shake off foreign control, and there was increasing discontent, at this time of economic hardship, about the British control of Iranian oil. The *ulema* were happier, however. The new shah was not yet strong enough to oppose their demands: the Ashura passion plays and recitations were allowed to resume, Iranians were permitted to go on the *hajj*, and women could wear the veil. Several new political parties emerged at this time: the pro-Soviet Tudeh, the National Front, led by Muhammad Musaddiq (1881–1967), which demanded that Iranian oil be nationalized, and a new paramilitary group, the Fedayin-e Islam ("Fighters of Islam"), which terrorized people who promoted a secularist agenda.

In 1945, Ayatollah Sayyid Mustafa Kashani (c. 1882–1962),[101] who had been imprisoned by the British during the war, was permitted to return to Iran. Huge crowds turned out to greet him, rolling out carpets under his car. Busloads of some of the most brilliant *ulema* traveled long distances to welcome Kashani home, and ecstatic *madrasah* students turned out en masse.[102] Kashani was the third portent of future events during this period. His extraordinary popularity might have shown a perceptive observer that Iranians might well follow a cleric in political matters far more enthusiastically than they would any layman. Kashani and Khomeini knew each other well, but in fact the two men were very different. Where Khomeini would be utterly disciplined and single-minded in pursuit of an objective, Kashani was much more erratic, willing to jump on any bandwagon, and some of his schemes were morally indefensible. He had been imprisoned by the British for pro-German activities in 1943: the iniquities of the Nazis were less important, in

Kashani's eyes, than the fact that they might help the Iranians to get rid of the British.[103] Kashani also had links with the Fedayin-e Islam, and when one of them tried to assassinate the shah in 1949, Kashani was sent into exile. From Beirut, he threw in his lot with the National Front party, issuing a *fatwa* in July 1949 in favor of the nationalization of oil. In 1950, Kashani was permitted to return to Iran and received another hero's welcome. The crowds started to assemble at Mehrabad Airport the evening before his arrival. Musaddiq, whose National Front had just made large gains in the elections because of the oil issue, joined the welcoming party of senior *ulema;* when Kashani alighted from his plane, the din was so tumultuous that the official speech in his honor had to be abandoned, and when he began his journey to his Tehran home, the crowds became delirious, sometimes even lifting his car off the road.[104]

The fourth crucial event of these years was the oil crisis,[105] which flared in 1953, when the prime minister, Ali Razmara, a supporter of the Anglo-Persian Oil Company, was assassinated by the Fedayin. Two days later the Majlis recommended that the government nationalize the oil industry, and Musaddiq became premier, replacing the shah's candidate. Iranian oil was nationalized, and, even though the International Court at The Hague ruled in favor of Iran's right to nationalize its own resources, British and American oil companies joined in an unofficial boycott of Iranian oil. In Britain and the United States, the media portrayed Musaddiq as a dangerous fanatic, a thief (even though he had always promised compensation), and a communist, who would hand Iran over to the USSR (even though Musaddiq was a nationalist who wanted to free Iran from all foreign control). In Iran, however, Musaddiq was a hero, rather as Nasser would be after he nationalized the Suez Canal. He began to arrogate more power to himself at the shah's expense. When he demanded control of the armed forces in July 1952, the shah dismissed him, but there were massive popular riots in Musaddiq's favor, which alarmed the royalists, since it suggested that Iranians were on the verge of demanding republican rule. The riots also disturbed London and Washington, who wanted Musaddiq out. Ayatollah Kashani played a leading role in these demonstrations, rushing through the streets in a shroud to declare his willingness to die in the holy war against tyranny. After only two days, the shah was forced to reinstate Musaddiq.

It was at this moment that the United States, which had hitherto been seen as a benevolent power, lost its political innocence in Iran. By 1953, Musaddiq's support was on the wane. He had never commanded the full allegiance of the army, but now the oil embargo was causing a grave economic crisis, and the *bazaaris* deserted him. So did the *ulema,* including Kashani: Musaddiq was an avowed secularist, and was determined to relegate religion to the private sector. He had also felt strong enough to dismiss the Majlis, which made the Shii clergy nervous of tyranny. But just as these old allies abandoned Musaddiq, Tudeh, the socialist party, swung to his support. This alarmed the U.S. government under President Dwight Eisenhower, who feared a pro-communist coup. He therefore approved United States participation in Operation Ajax, a coup engineered by British intelligence and the CIA to depose Musaddiq. In August 1953, however, Musaddiq got wind of the plot and, as agreed in case of discovery, the shah and the queen left the country, only to return under the aegis of CIA agents, who, three days later, orchestrated the dissaffected Iranians and key men in the military in an uprising which unseated Musaddiq. He was later tried by a military court, defended himself brilliantly, and escaped the death penalty, though he spent the rest of his life under house arrest.

The 1953 coup could not have succeeded had there not been considerable disaffection in the country, but it is also true that it would not have taken place without foreign intervention. Iranians felt betrayed and humiliated by the United States, which they had previously considered a friend. America was now following in the footsteps of the Russians and the British, who had cynically manipulated events in Iran for their own gain. This seemed clear in 1954, when a new oil treaty was made which returned the control of oil production, its marketing, and fifty percent of the profits to the world cartel companies.[106] This sickened the more thoughtful Iranians. They had tried to take control of their own wealth, with the backing of the international court, but this had not been respected. Ayatollah Kashani was appalled. American aid to Iran benefited only a few people, he protested, and did not reach a hundredth of what the United States took from Iran in petrodollars. "For the hundreds of millions of dollars that the American colonialist imperialists will gain in oil," he predicted, "the oppressed nation will lose all hope of liberty and will have a negative opinion about all the Western world."[107]

In this, at least, Kashani was a true prophet. When Iranians looked back on Operation Ajax, they would forget the defection of their own people from Musaddiq, and believe implicitly that the United States had single-handedly imposed the shah's dictatorship upon them, for its own interests. Bitterness increased in the early 1960s, when the shah's rule became more autocratic and cruel. There seemed to be a double standard. America proudly proclaimed its belief in freedom and democracy, but warmly supported a shah who permitted no opposition to his rule, and denied Iranians fundamental human rights. After 1953, Iran became a privileged American ally. As a major oil-producing country, Iran was a prime market for the sale of American services and technology. Americans looked upon Iran as an economic goldmine, and, over the years, the United States repeated the old political patterns used by the British: strong-arm tactics in the oil market, undue influence over the monarch, demands for diplomatic immunity, business and trade concessions, and a condescending attitude toward the Iranians themselves. American businessmen and consultants poured into the country and made a great deal of money. There was a glaring discrepancy between their lifestyle and that of most Iranians; they lived isolated from the people, and since most worked under contracts associated with the throne, they became fatally associated with the regime. It was a shortsighted, self-interested policy that would eventually cast the United States in a demonic light.

Iran was becoming a polarized country: a few benefited from the American boom, but the vast majority were being left behind. And Iran was not unique. By the middle of the twentieth century, the societies of all the countries we are considering were being divided into two camps. Some saw the modern age as liberating and empowering; others experienced it as an evil assault. There was fear, hatred, and a barely suppressed rage. It would not be long before fundamentalists, who felt this anger acutely, would decide that it was no longer sufficient to hold aloof from society and build a counter-culture. They must mobilize and fight back.

8. Mobilization
(1960–74)

BY THE 1960S, revolution was in the air throughout the West and the Middle East. In Europe and America the young people took to the streets and rebelled against the modern ethos of their parents. They called for a more just and equal system, protested against the materialism, imperialism, and chauvinism of their governments, refused to fight in their nation's wars or to study in its universities. Sixties youth began doing what the fundamentalists had been doing for decades: they started to create a "counterculture," an "alternative society" in revolt against the values of the mainstream. In many ways, they were demanding a more religious way of life. Most had little time for institutional faith or for the authoritarian structures of the monotheisms. Instead, they went to Katmandu or sought solace in the meditative or mystical techniques of the Orient. Others found transcendence in drug-induced trips, transcendental meditation, or personal transformation in such techniques as the Erhard Seminars Training (est). There was a hunger for *mythos* and a rejection of the scientific rationalism that had become the new Western orthodoxy. This was not a rejection of rationality *per se,* but of its more extreme forms. Twentieth-century science itself was cautious, sober, and highly conscious in a disciplined, principled way of its limitations and areas of competence. But the prevailing mood of modernity had made science ideological and had refused to countenance any other method of arriving at truth. During the sixties, the youth revolution was in part a protest against the illegitimate domination of rational language and the suppression of *mythos* by *logos.*

But because the understanding of such disciplined ways of arriving at a more intuitive knowledge had been neglected in the West since the advent of modernity, the sixties quest for spirituality was often wild, self-indulgent, and unbalanced. There were flaws too in the visions and policies of the religious radicals, who were beginning to organize their own offensive against the secularization and rationalism of modern society. The fundamentalists were beginning to mobilize. They had often experienced modernity as an aggressive onslaught. The modern spirit had demanded freedom from the outmoded thought patterns of the past; the modern ideal of progress had entailed the elimination of those beliefs, practices, and institutions that were deemed to be irrational and, therefore, retarding. Religious establishments and doctrines had often been key targets. Sometimes, as in the case of the liberals at the time of the Scopes trial, the weapon had been ridicule. In the Middle East, where modernization was more problematic, the methods had been more brutal, involving massacre, despoliation, and the concentration camp. By the 1960s and 1970s, many religious people were angry and were determined to fight the liberals and secularists who had, they believed, oppressed and marginalized them. But these religious radicals were men of their time. They would have to fight with modern weapons and devise a modern ideology.

Ever since the American and French revolutions, Western politics had been ideological; people had engaged in mighty battles for the Enlightenment ideals of the Age of Reason: liberty, equality, fraternity, human happiness, and social justice. The Western liberal consensus believed that with education, society and politics would become more rational and united. The secular ideology, a way of mobilizing people for the battle, was a modern belief system which justified the political and social struggle and gave it a rationale.[1] In order to appeal to as many people as possible, an ideology was expressed in simple images that could often be reduced to such slogans as "Power to the People!" or "Traitors within!" These highly simplified truths were thought to explain everything. Ideologists believe that the world is in a parlous state, find reasons for the current crisis, and promise to find a way out. They direct the attention of the people to a group that is to blame for the world's ruin, and to another group that will put things right. Since in the modern world, politics can no longer be an entirely elitist pursuit, the ideology must be simple enough to be grasped by the meanest intelligence, in order to gain the support of the people as a whole.

Crucial is the conviction that some groups will never be able to understand the ideology, because they have been infected by a "false consciousness." The ideology is often a closed system that cannot afford to take alternative views seriously. Marxists, who see capitalists as the source of the world's ills, cannot understand the values of capitalism, and vice versa. Colonialists are impervious to the truths of emerging nationalisms. Zionists and Arabs are unable to appreciate one another's point of view. All ideologies imagine an unrealistic and, some would say, unrealizable utopia. They are by their very nature highly selective, but ideas, passions, and enthusiasms that are in the air at any given time, such as nationalism, personal autonomy, or equality, are likely to be picked up by a number of competing ideologies, which will often, therefore, appeal to the same ideals, since all derive from the same zeitgeist.

The historian Edmund Burke (1729–97) was one of the first people to realize that if a group of people wished to challenge the ideology of the establishment (which may itself once have been revolutionary), they will have to develop a counterrevolutionary ideology of their own. This was the position of some of the most discontented Jews, Christians, and Muslims by the 1960s and 1970s. In order to counter what they regarded as the rational fantasies of the modern establishment, they would have to challenge ideas which had once been radical and revolutionary but had now become so authoritative and pervasive that they seemed self-evident. They were all in a weak position and all convinced, sometimes with reason, that the secularists and liberals wanted to annihilate them. In order to create a religious ideology, they would have to reshape the myths and symbols of their tradition in such a way that they became a persuasive blueprint for action that would compel the people to rise up and save their faith from extinction. Some of these religious ideologues were deeply imbued with the spirituality of the conservative age. They were mystics and had a deep appreciation of myth and ritual, which made them acutely aware of the reality of the unseen. But there was a difficulty. In the premodern period, myth had never been intended to have a practical application. It was not meant to provide a concrete plan of action; on occasions when people had used myth as a springboard for political activity, the results had been disastrous. Now, as they planned their counterattack on the secular world, these religious radicals would have to turn their myths into ideology.

In Egypt, Islam had come under sustained ideological attack during the 1960s. Nasser was at the height of his popularity, and had called for a "cultural revolution" and the implementation of what he called "scientific socialism." In the National Charter of May 1962, he reinterpreted history from a socialist perspective; it was an ideology that "proved" that capitalism and monarchy had both failed, and that socialism alone would lead to "progress," defined as self-government, productivity, and industrialization. Religion was regarded by the regime as irredeemably passé. After the destruction of the Muslim Brotherhood, Nasser no longer bothered to use the old Islamic rhetoric. In 1961, the government castigated the *ulema* for their timorous adherence to their old medieval studies, and for the "defensive, reserved and rigid attitude" of the Azhar, which made it impossible to "adapt itself to contemporary times." Nasser had a point. The Egyptian *ulema* had indeed closed ranks against the modern world and would continue to resist reform.[2] They were making themselves an anachronism and losing all influence over the modernizing sectors of Egyptian society. Similarly, the immoral, injudicious terrorism of a fringe group of the Muslim Brotherhood had been largely responsible for the destruction of the Society. The Muslim establishment seemed to be putting itself out of business and demonstrating its incompatibility with the modern world.

In both Egypt and Syria during the 1960s, "Nasserist" historians reinforced the new secularist ideology. Islam had become the cause of the nations' ills; it was made to fill the role of the "out group" which must be eliminated if the Arab countries were to progress. The Syrian scholar Zaki al-Arsuzi believed that instead of dwelling on the fact that the Arabs had given Islam to the world, historians should stress their contribution to material culture (their transformation of the alphabet from hieroglyphics to letters, for example). It was their concentration upon religion that had put Arabs behind the Europeans, who had focused on the physical world instead of the spiritual, and created modern science, industry, and technology. Shibli al-Aysami argued that it was deplorable that the pre-Islamic Arabian civilization should be dismissed by Muslim historians as *jahiliyyah* ("the Age of Ignorance"), since its cultural achievements in the ancient Yemen had been considerable. Yasin al-Hafiz cast doubt on the reliability of the Islamic historical sources which had simply reflected the views of the ruling classes. It was pointless and impossible to build a modern ideology on inaccurate memories of a dead and distant past. Historians must construct a more scientific and dialectical historiography, "one of the battle fronts one ought to join in order to destroy all the superstructures of the old society."[3] Religion was responsible for the "false consciousness" that held the Arabs back. It must, therefore, be eliminated like all other impediments to rational and scientific progress. As with any ideology, the arguments were selective; the portrayal of religion simplistic and inaccurate. It was also unrealistic. Whatever the place religion would have in the modern world (and that was still to be decided), it is always impossible to obliterate the past, which continues to live on in the minds of the people who make up a nation, even if old institutions and their personnel have been removed.

In response, the new religious ideologues were just as simplistic and aggressive. They believed that they were fighting for their lives. In 1951, the work of the Pakistani journalist and politician Abul Ala Mawdudi (1903–79) began to be published in Egypt.[4] Mawdudi feared that Islam was about to be destroyed. He saw the mighty power of the West gathering its forces together to crush Islam and grind it into oblivion. This was a moment of grave crisis, and Mawdudi believed that devout Muslims could not retire from the world and leave politics to others. They must combine together and form a tight-knit group to fight this encroaching and *la dini* ("religionless") secularism. To mobilize the people, Mawdudi tried to present Islam in a reasoned, systematic way, so that it could be taken as seriously as the other leading ideologies of the day.[5] He was, therefore, attempting to turn the whole complex *mythos* and spirituality of Islam into *logos,* a rationalized discourse designed to persuade and to lead to pragmatic activism. Any such attempt would have been condemned as utterly wrongheaded in the old conservative world, but Muslims were not living in the premodern period any longer. If they wanted to survive in the dangerous, violent twentieth century, maybe they had to revise their old conceptions and make their religion modern?

The basis of Mawdudi's ideology, like that of the other modern Muslim thinkers whose work we shall consider, was the doctrine of God's sovereignty. This immediately threw down the gauntlet to the modern world, because it contradicted every one of its sacred truths. Because God alone ruled human affairs and was the supreme legislator, human beings had no right to make up their own laws or take control of their destiny. By attacking the whole notion of human freedom and human sovereignty, Mawdudi was defying the whole secularist ethos:

> It is neither for us to decide the aim and purpose of our existence nor to prescribe the limits of our worldly authority, nor is anyone else entitled to make these decisions for us. . . . Nothing can claim sovereignty, be it a human being, a family, a class, or a group of people, or even the human race in the world as a whole. God alone is the Sovereign, and His commandments the Law of Islam.[6]

Locke, Kant, and the Founding Fathers of America would be turning in their graves. But in fact Mawdudi was as enamored of liberty as any modern, and was proposing an Islamic liberation theology. Because God alone was sovereign, nobody was obliged to take orders from any other human being. No ruler who refused to govern according to God's will (as revealed in the Koran and the Sunnah) could command the obedience of his subjects. In such a case, revolution was not simply a right but a duty.

The Islamic system, therefore, ensured that the state was not subject to the whims and ambitions of the ruler. It freed Muslims from the caprice and possible evil of human control. By the principle of *shurah* ("consultation") in Islamic law, the caliph was bound to deliberate with his subjects, but that did not mean that government derived its legitimacy from the people, as in the democratic ideal. Neither the caliph nor the people could create their own legislation. They could simply administer the Shariah. Muslims, therefore, must resist the Westernized forms of government imposed upon them by the colonial powers, since such governments constitute a rebellion against God and usurp his authority.[7] Once human beings hubristically seized control, there was danger of evil, oppression, and tyranny. It is a liberation theology that sounds bizarre to a confirmed secularist, but it is in the nature of an ideology that its insights cannot be appreciated by opponents. Mawdudi had imbibed and shared the values of the current zeitgeist; he believed in liberty and the rule of law, which he also saw as a device to prevent corruption and dictatorship. He just defined these ideals differently and gave them an Islamic orientation, but this would be impossible for somebody with the "false consciousness" of secularism to understand.

Mawdudi also believed in the value of an ideology. Islam, he declared, was a revolutionary ideology that was similar to Fascism and Marxism, but there was an important difference.[8] The Nazis and Marxists had enslaved other human beings, whereas Islam sought to free them from subjection to anything other than God. A true ideologist, Mawdudi saw all other systems as irredeemably flawed.[9] Democracy led to chaos, greed, and mob rule; capitalism fostered class warfare and subjected the whole world to a clique of bankers; communism stifled human initiative and individuality. These were the usual ideological oversimplifications. Mawdudi skirted over details and difficulties. How would Islamic *shurah* differ in practice from Western-style democracy? How would the Shariah, an agrarian law code, cope with the political and economic difficulties of the modern industrialized world? An Islamic state, Mawdudi argued, would be totalitarian, because it subjected everything to the rule of God; but how would that differ in practice from dictatorship, which, Mawdudi rightly insisted, was condemned by the Koran?

Like any ideologist, Mawdudi was not developing an abstruse scholarly theory, but issuing a call to arms. He demanded a universal *jihad,* which he declared to be the central tenet of Islam. No major Muslim thinker had ever made this claim before. It was an innovation required, in Mawdudi's eyes, by the current emergency. *Jihad* ("struggle") was not a holy war to convert the infidel, as Westerners believed, nor was it purely a means of self-defense, as Abdu had argued. Mawdudi defined *jihad* as a revolutionary struggle to seize power for the good of all humanity. Here again, Mawdudi, who developed this idea in 1939, shared the same perspective as such militant ideologies as Marxism. Just as the Prophet had fought the *jahiliyyah,* the ignorance and barbarism of the pre-Islamic period, so all Muslims must use all means at their disposal to resist the modern *jahiliyyah* of the West. The *jihad* could take many forms. Some people would write articles, others make speeches, but in the last resort, they must be prepared for armed struggle.[10]

Never before had *jihad* figured so centrally in official Islamic discourse. The militancy of Mawdudi's vision was almost without precedent, but the situation had become more desperate since Abdu and Banna had tried to reform Islam and help it to absorb the modern Western ethos peacefully. Some Muslims were now prepared for war. One of the people most profoundly affected by Mawdudi's work was Sayyid Qutb (1906–66), who had joined the Muslim Brotherhood in 1953, was imprisoned by Nasser in 1954 and sentenced to fifteen years hard labor, and witnessed the brutality of the regime toward Islamists.[11] His experiences in Nasser's camps scarred him and his ideas became far more radical than Mawdudi's. Qutb can be called the founder of Sunni fundamentalism. Almost all radical Islamists have relied upon the ideology that he developed in prison,[12] but he had not always been hostile to Western culture or an extremist. Qutb had studied at the Dar al-Ulum college in Cairo, where he fell in love with English literature and became a man of letters. He was also a nationalist and a member of the Wafd party. He did not look like a firebrand, being small, soft-spoken, and not physically strong. But Qutb was a devoutly religious man. By the age of ten he had memorized the whole of the Koran, and it remained the lodestar of his life, but as a young man his faith sat easily with his enthusiasm for Western culture and secular politics. By the 1940s, his admiration of the West had worn thin, however. The colonial activities of Britain and France in North Africa and the Middle East had begun to sicken him, as did Western support for Zionism.[13] A period of study in the United States was also a disillusioning experience.[14] He found the rational pragmatism of American culture disturbing: "Any objectives other than the immediate utilitarian ones are by-passed, and any human element other than ego is not recognized," he wrote later. "While the whole of life is dominated by such materialism, there is no scope for laws beyond provisions for labor and production."[15] But still, he remained a moderate and a reformer, trying to give modern Western institutions, such as democracy and parliamentarianism, an Islamic dimension in the hope of avoiding the excesses of a wholly secularist ideology.

But Qutb's experience in prison convinced him that religious people and secularists could not live at peace in the same society. When he looked around his prison, recalled the torture and execution of the Brothers, and reflected upon Nasser's avowed determination to cast religion to one side, he could see all the hallmarks of *jahiliyyah*, which, like Mawdudi, he defined as the ignorant barbarism that was forever and for all time the enemy of faith, and which Muslims, following the example of the Prophet Muhammad, who had fought the *jahili* (ignorant) society of Mecca, were bound to fight to the death. Yet Qutb went much further than Mawdudi, who had only seen the non-Muslim world as *jahili*. By the 1960s, Qutb was convinced that the so-called Muslim world was also riddled with the evil values and cruelty of *jahiliyyah*. Even though a ruler such as Nasser outwardly professed Islam, his words and actions proved that he had in fact apostatized. Muslims were duty-bound to overthrow such a government. He now looked back to the life and career of the Prophet to create an ideology that would mobilize a dedicated vanguard in a *jihad* to turn back the tide of secularism and force its society to return to the values of Islam.

Qutb was a man of the modern world, and he would create a compelling *logos,* but he was also profoundly aware of the world of myth. He respected reason and science but did not see them as the sole guides of truth. During his long years in prison, at the same time as he evolved his new fundamentalist ideology, he worked on a monumental commentary on the Koran, which showed his spiritual awareness of the ineffable and the unseen. No matter how rational the human intellect became, he wrote, it was constantly swimming in "the sea of the unknown." All philosophical and scientific developments certainly constituted progress of a sort, but they were simply glimpses of permanent cosmic laws, as superficial as the waves "in a vast ocean; they do not change the currents, being regulated by constant natural factors."[16] Where modern rationalism concentrated on the mundane, Qutb still cultivated the traditional discipline of looking through the earthly reality to what was beyond time and change. This mythical, essentialist mentality, which saw worldly events as reflecting more or less perfectly eternal, archetypal realities, was crucial to his thought. Its apparent absence in the United States had disturbed him. When Qutb gazed at modern secular culture, like other fundamentalists he saw a hell, a place utterly drained of sacred and moral significance, which filled him with horror.

> Humanity today is living in a large brothel! One has only to glance at its press, films, fashion shows, beauty contests, ballrooms, wine bars, and broadcasting stations! Or observe its mad lust for naked flesh, provocative postures, and sick, suggestive statements in literature, the arts and the mass media! And add to all this, the system of usury which fuels man's voracity for money and engenders vile methods for its accumulation and investment, in addition to fraud, trickery, and blackmail dressed up in the garb of law.[17]

He wanted Muslims to revolt against this secular city, and to restore a sense of the spiritual to modern society.

Qutb saw history mythically. He did not approach the Prophet's life like a modern, scientific historian, seeing these events as unique and located in a distant period. He had been a novelist and a literary critic, and knew that there were other ways of arriving at the truth of what had really happened. For Qutb, Muhammad's career was still an archetype, a moment when the sacred and the human had come together and acted in concert. It was in the deepest sense a "symbol," which linked the mundane with the divine. Muhammad's life thus represented an ideal beyond history, time, and place and, like a Christian sacrament, it provided humanity with a "constant encounter" with the ultimate Reality.[18] It was, therefore, an epiphany, and the different stages of the Prophet's career represented "milestones" that guided men and women to their God. In the same way, the term *jahiliyyah* could not simply refer to the pre-Islamic period in Arabia, as in conventional Muslim historiography. "*Jahiliyyah* is not a period in time," he explained in *Milestones*, his most controversial book. "It is a condition that is repeated every time society veers from the Islamic way, whether in the past, the present, or the future."[19] Any attempt to deny the reality and sovereignty of God is *jahili*. Nationalism (which makes the state a supreme value), communism (which is atheistic), and democracy (in which the people usurp God's rule) are all manifestations of *jahiliyyah*, which worships humanity instead of the divine. It is a state of Godlessness and apostasy. For Qutb, the modern *jahiliyyah* in both Egypt and the West was even worse than the *jahiliyyah* of the Prophet's time, because it was not based on "ignorance" but was a principled rebellion against God.

But in premodern spirituality, the Muhammadan archetype had been created in the ground of each Muslim's being by means of the rituals and ethical practices of Islam. It was certainly a *mythos* in this way for Qutb still, but he now recast it so that the myth became an ideology, a blueprint for action. The first *ummah* created by the Prophet in Medina was a "bright beacon," designed by God "so that this unique image might be materialised in the situations of real life and recourse might be had to it, in order to repeat it within the limit of human capacity."[20] The archetypal society of Medina had indeed been achieved by "an exceptional generation of men" but it was not an "unrepeatable miracle"; it was "the fruit of human exertion," and could be achieved wherever that exertion was made.[21] In the life of Muhammad, Qutb argued, God had revealed a divine program *(manhaj)*, and it was, therefore, superior to all man-made ideologies. In contemplating the "milestones" of the Prophet's life, God had shown human beings the only way to build a properly oriented society.[22]

Unlike Christians, Muslims had always experienced the divine not so much in a doctrine as in an imperative; Muslim fundamentalism would always be activist and centered on the *ummah*. But when Qutb converted the *mythos* of the Prophet's life into an ideology, he inevitably simplified it, limited its spiritual potential, and cut it down to size. He removed the complexities, ambiguities, and contradictions of the Prophet's personal, multifaceted struggle, to create the kind of streamlined program that a modern ideology requires, but in the process, the ruthless selection that this involved inevitably distorted the Islamic vision.

Qutb saw the Prophet's career proceeding in four stages; to re-create a rightly guided community in the twentieth century, Muslims must also go through this four-fold process.[23] First God had revealed his plan to one man, Muhammad, who then went on to form a *jamaah*, a party of committed individuals who vowed to fulfill God's command and replace the *jahiliyyah* of Mecca with a just, egalitarian society that recognized only the sovereignty of God. During this first phase, Muhammad trained this vanguard to separate themselves from the pagan *jahili* establishment, which operated on quite a different set of values. Like other fundamentalists, Qutb saw the policy of dissociation *(mafasalah)* as crucial. The Prophet's program showed that society was divided into two utterly opposed camps. Muslims today, Qutb urged, must also reject the *jahiliyyah* of their own age and withdraw from it to create a pure Muslim enclave. They could, and indeed should, be courteous to unbelievers and apostates in their society, but should keep contacts to a minimum and in general pursue a policy of noncooperation in such crucial matters as education.[24]

This segregation of the faithful from the *jahili* mainstream intensified in the Prophet's life when the pagan establishment of Mecca began to persecute the small Muslim community and eventually forced them in 622 to undertake the migration *(hijrah)* to the settlement of Medina, some 250 miles north of Mecca. Eventually there must be a complete rupture between the true believers and the rest of their Godless society. In Medina, during the third stage of his program, the Prophet established an Islamic state. It was a period of consolidation, brotherly affirmation, and integration, when the *jamaah* prepared itself for the coming struggle. In the fourth and final stage of the program, Muhammad initiated a period of armed struggle against Mecca, at first in small-scale raids against the Meccan trading caravans, and then by sustaining the attacks of the Meccan army. Given the polarization of this society, the violence was inevitable, as it was for Muslims today. But eventually in 630, Mecca voluntarily opened its gates to Muhammad and accepted the rule of Islam and the sovereignty of God.

Qutb always insisted that the armed struggle for God would not be an oppressive, coercive campaign to impose Islam by force. Like Mawdudi, he saw his proclamation of the sovereignty of God as a declaration of independence. It was

> a universal declaration of human liberation on earth from bondage to other men or to human desires. . . . To declare God's sovereignty means: the comprehensive revolution against human governance in all its perceptions, forms, systems, and conditions, and the total defiance against every condition in which human beings are sovereign.[25]

Qutb's ideology was essentially modern; apart from the centrality of God in his thought, he was in many ways a man of the sixties in his rejection of the modern system. His depiction of the Prophet's program had everything that an ideology required. It was simple; it identified the enemy, and pointed to the *jamaah* who would regenerate society. For many Muslims who were disturbed by the fragmentation and reorientation of their society, Qutb's ideology translated the crucial aspects of the modern ethos into an Islamic idiom to which they could relate. They had certainly not found the "independence" granted by the British either liberating or empowering. Nasser's catastrophic defeat by Israel in the Six Day War of June 1967 had discredited the secular ideologies of Nasserism, socialism, and nationalism for many people. There was a religious revival throughout the Middle East, and a significant number of Muslims would find Qutb's ideology an inspiration.

But by making *jihad* central to the Muslim vision, Qutb had in fact distorted the Prophet's life. The traditional biographies make it clear that even though the first *ummah* had to fight in order to survive, Muhammad did not achieve victory by the sword but by a creative and ingenious policy of nonviolence. The Koran condemns all warfare as abhorrent, and permits only a war of self-defense. The Koran is adamantly opposed to the use of force in religious matters. Its vision is inclusive; it recognizes the validity of all rightly guided religion, and praises all the great prophets of the past.[26] The last time Muhammad preached to the community before his death, he urged Muslims to use their religion to reach out to others in understanding, since all human beings were brothers: "O men! behold we have created you all out of a male and a female, and have made you into nations and tribes so that you may know one another."[27] Qutb's vision of exclusion and separation goes against this accepting tolerance. The Koran categorically and with great emphasis insisted that "There shall be no coercion in matters of faith."[28] Qutb qualified this: there could only be toleration *after* the political victory of Islam and the establishment of a true Muslim state.[29]

The new intransigence springs from the profound fear that is basic to fundamentalist religion. Qutb had personally experienced the murderous and destructive power of the modern *jahiliyyah*. Nasser did seem bent on wiping out Islam, and he was not alone. When Qutb looked back into history, he saw what looked like one *jahili* enemy after another intent on the destruction of Islam: pagans, Jews, Christians, Crusaders, Mongols, Communists, capitalists, colonialists, and Zionists.[30] Today, these were linked in a vast conspiracy yet again. With the paranoid vision of the true fundamentalist who has been pushed too far, Qutb saw connections everywhere. Jewish and Christian imperialists had conspired together to dispossess the Arabs of Palestine; Jews had created both capitalism and communism; Jews and Western imperialists had put Atatürk in power to get rid of Islam, and when other Muslim states had not followed Turkey's example, they had supported Nasser.[31] Like most neuroses, this conspiracy fear flew in the face of the facts, but once human beings feel that they are fighting against great odds simply to survive, their views are not likely to be reasonable.

Qutb did not survive. In 1964, possibly at the request of the prime minister of Iraq, he was released from prison. During his incarceration, his sisters had smuggled his work out and distributed it secretly, but after his release, Qutb published *Milestones*. The following year, the government uncovered a network of terrorist cells which it alleged to be plotting to assassinate Nasser. Hundreds of Brothers, including Qutb, were arrested, and in 1966, as a result of Nasser's insistence, Qutb was executed. To the end, however, Qutb himself remained an ideologue rather than an agitator. He always argued that the stockpiling of weapons by the Brothers was a defensive measure only, to prevent a repetition of the events of 1954. He probably thought that the time was not yet ripe to commence a *jihad*. The vanguard had to go through the first three stages of the Muhammadan program before they were spiritually and strategically ready to commence the assault on the *jahiliyyah*. Not all the Brothers would follow him. Most remained true to the more moderate, reformist vision of Hudaybi, but in the prisons and camps a number of Muslims studied Qutb's work, discussed it, and, in the more religious climate after the Six Day War, began to create a cadre.

The Shii Muslims of Iran also experienced a new wave of secularist aggression when Shah Muhammad Reza Pahlavi announced his White Revolution in 1962. This consisted of the establishment of state capitalism, the institution of increased profit-sharing for the workforces and reforms to undermine the semifeudal forms of land ownership, and the creation of a literacy corps.[32] Some of the shah's projects were successful. The industrial, agricultural, and social projects looked impressive, and the 1960s saw a large increase in the Gross National Product. Even though the shah personally thought women an inferior sex, he introduced reforms that improved their status and education, though this only benefited women of the upper classes. In the West, the shah's achievements were hailed with enthusiasm: Iran seemed a beacon of progress and sanity in the Middle East. After the Musad-diq crisis, the shah courted America, supported the State of Israel, and was rewarded with foreign investment that kept the economy afloat. But even at the time, astute observers noted that these reforms did not go far enough. They favored the rich, concentrated on city dwellers, and ignored the peas-antry. The profits derived from oil and natural gas were not used efficiently but were spent on showy projects and the latest in military technology.[33] As a result, the basic structures of society remained untouched and an even greater gulf yawned between the Westernized rich and the traditional poor, who had been left behind in the old agrarian ethos.

Because of the decline in agriculture, there was a massive exodus from the country to the cities: between 1968 and 1978, the urban population rose from 38 percent to 47 percent. The population of Tehran almost doubled during these years, increasing from 2.719 million to 4.496 million.[34] The rural migrants did not integrate successfully, but lived in shantytowns on the outskirts of the cities, eking out a precarious living as porters, taxi drivers, and street vendors. Tehran split into modernized and traditional sectors: the Westernized upper and middle classes moved away from the old city to the new residential neighborhoods and the business area in the north of the city, where there were bars and casinos, and where women dressed like Euro-peans and mixed freely with men in public. It seemed like a foreign country to the *bazaaris* and the poor, who remained in the old city and the adjacent southern areas.

The vast majority of Iranians were thus experiencing one of the most unsettling of human emotions. The familiar world had grown unfamiliar; it was itself and yet not itself, like a close friend whose appearance and personality have been disfigured by illness. When the world we know changes as rapidly as Iran did during the 1960s, men and women begin to feel like strangers in their own country. Increasingly, a worrying number of Irani-ans found that they did not feel at home anywhere. The debacle of 1953 had left many with a corrosive sense of defeat and humiliation at the hands of the international community. Those few who had had a Western education felt estranged from their parents and families, caught between two worlds and at ease in neither. Life seemed drained of meaning. In the prolific literature of the 1960s, the most recurrent symbols expressed the growing alienation: walls, solitude, nothingness, loneliness, and hypocrisy. The contemporary Iranian critic Fazaneh Milani noted the persistence during the 1960s and 1970s of imagery depicting "ingenious forms of protection and secrecy."

Walls surround houses. Veils cover women. Religious *taqiyyah* protects faith. *Taarof* [ritualistic modes of discourse] disguise real thoughts and emotions. Houses become compartmentalized with their *darni* [inner] and *biruni* [external] and *batini* [hidden] spheres.[35]

Iranians were hiding from themselves and from one another. They no longer felt safe in the Pahlavi state, which was becoming a very frightening place.

The shah had begun his White Revolution by closing the Majlis, believing that he could only push his reforms forward by dictatorial rule and by silencing all opposition. He was supported by the SAVAK, his secret police, formed in 1957 with the help of the American CIA and the Israeli Mossad. SAVAK's brutal methods, its regime of torture and intimidation, made people feel that they were held prisoner in their own country, with the connivance of Israel and the United States.[36] During the 1960s and 1970s, two paramilitary organizations were formed, similar to other guerrilla groups that were emerging in the developing world at this time: the Fedayin-e Khalq, a Marxist group founded by members of the now suppressed Tudeh and National Front parties, and an Islamic corps, the Mujahedin-e Khalq. Force seemed the only way to fight a regime which blocked all normal opposition and which was based on coercion rather than consent.

Intellectuals tried to fight the regime with ideas. They were disturbed by the malaise in the country, and could see that modernization had been too rapid and had resulted in widespread alienation. The brilliant philosopher Ahmed Fardid (1912–94), who became a professor at the University of Tehran in the late 1960s, coined the term *gharbzadegi* ("West-toxication") to describe the Iranian dilemma: the people had been poisoned and polluted by the West; they must create a new identity for themselves.[37] This theme was amplified by the secularist and onetime socialist Jalal Al-e Ahmad (1923–69), whose *Gharbzadegi* (1962) became a cult book for Iranians during the 1960s. This "rootlessness" and "Occidentosis" was "a disease from without, spreading in an environment susceptible to it." It was the plight of a people "having no supporting tradition, no historical continuity, no gradient of transformation."[38] This plague could devastate Iran's integrity, eradicate her political sovereignty, and destroy the economy. But Al-e Ahmad was himself torn both ways: he was influenced by such Western writers as Sartre and Heidegger, and attracted by the Western ideals of democracy and liberty; but he did not see how they could be successfully transplanted in the alien soil of Iran. He expressed what has been described as the "agonized schizophrenia" of the Western-educated Iranians, who felt pulled in two directions,[39] and though he could articulate the problem memorably, he had no solution to propose—though it appears that, toward the end of his life, he was beginning to see Shiism as an authentically Iranian institution that could provide a basis for a genuine national identity and become a healing alternative to the Westernizing disease.[40]

The Iranian *ulema* were quite unlike the Egyptian clergy. Many were aware that they would have to modernize themselves and their institutions if they were to support the people. They were increasingly distressed by the shah's autocratic rule, which offended fundamental Shii principles, and his obvious indifference to religion. In 1960, even Ayatollah Borujerdi, the supreme Marja, who had forbidden the clergy to take any part in politics, was moved to condemn the shah's Land Reform Bill. It was a pity that he chose this issue, because it made the *ulema,* many of whom were landowners, seem selfish and reactionary. In fact, Borujerdi's intervention probably sprang from an instinctive feeling that this could be the thin end of the wedge.[41] The Land Reform contravened Shariah laws of ownership, and Borujerdi may have feared that to deprive the people of rights guaranteed by Islamic Law in one sphere could lead to worse abuses in other areas. When Borujerdi died in March the following year, the post of Marja was not filled. A group of *ulema* argued that Shiism should become more democratic, and that it was not realistic to expect one man to be the Supreme Guide in this complex new world. Perhaps the new leadership should consist of several *maraji,* each with his own specialty. This was clearly a modernizing move, and this group of reformist *ulema* included several clerics who would later play a key role in the Islamic Revolution: Ayatollah Seyyed Muhammad Bihishti; the learned theologian Morteza Motahhari; Allameh Muhammad-Husain Tabatabai; and the most politically radical Iranian cleric, Ayatollah Mahmoud Taleqani. In the autumn of 1960, they held a series of lectures, and the following year published a volume of essays that discussed ways of bringing the Shiah up to date.

The reformers were convinced that, because Islam is a total way of life, the *ulema* should not be so wary of intervening in politics. They did not envisage clerical rule, but believed that when they felt that the state was becoming tyrannical or indifferent to the needs of the people, the *ulema* should stand up to the shahs, as they had done at the time of the Tobacco Crisis and the Constitutional Revolution. They argued that the curriculum of the *madrasahs* should be revised, to dilute the heavy concentration on *fiqh*. The clergy should also rationalize their finances: at present, they relied too much on voluntary contributions, and, as the people tended to be conservative, this inhibited them from making fundamental changes. The importance of *ijtihad* was stressed. Shiis must come to terms with such modern realities as trade, diplomacy, and war if they were to be of real service to the people. Above all, they should listen to their students. Young people in the 1960s were better educated, and would not swallow the old propaganda. They were drifting away from religion because the vision of Shiism they had been given was lifeless and old-fashioned. Before the youth culture had fully developed in the West, the Iranian clergy were already aware of the need to revise their view of the young. Their reform movement involved only a handful of *ulema;* it did not reach the masses, and made no attempt to criticize the regime. It was concerned solely with the internal affairs of the Shiah. But it did lead to a great deal of discussion in religious circles and predisposed more of the clergy toward change.[42] Suddenly, however, the *ulema* were taken by surprise when a hitherto unnoticed cleric hit the headlines, and took a far more radical stance.

By the early 1960s, more and more students were drawn to the course in Islamic ethics taught by Ayatollah Khomeini at the Fayziyah Madrasah in Qum. He used to leave his pulpit during class, coming, as it were, "off the record," and would sit on the floor beside his students, openly criticizing the government. But in 1963, Khomeini suddenly broke his cover, and speaking from his pulpit, in his official capacity, began a sustained and outright attack upon the shah, whom he portrayed as the enemy of Islam. At a time when nobody else dared to speak out against the regime, Khomeini protested against the cruelty and injustice of the shah's rule, his unconstitutional dismissal of the Majlis, the torture, the wicked suppression of all opposition, the shah's craven subservience to the United States, and his support of Israel, which had deprived Palestinians of their homes. He was particularly concerned about the plight of the poor: the shah should leave his splendid palace and go and look at the shantytowns in South Tehran. On one occasion, he is said to have held a copy of the Koran in one hand, and a copy of the 1906 constitution in the other, and accused the shah of violating his oath to defend them. Reprisals were swift and inevitable. On March 22, 1963, the anniversary of the martyrdom of the Sixth Imam (who had been poisoned by Caliph al-Mansur in 765), SAVAK forces surrounded the *madrasah*, and attacked it, killing a number of students. Khomeini was arrested and taken into custody.[43] It was inept and self-destructive of the regime to choose that date to make its move. Constantly, in the course of the long struggle with Khomeini, the shah seemed to go out of his way to cast himself as a tyrannical ruler and the enemy of the Imams.

Why did Khomeini choose this moment to speak out? Throughout his life, he had practiced the mystical disciplines of *irfan,* as taught by Mulla Sadra. For Khomeini, as for Sadra, mysticism and politics were inseparable. There could be no social reformation of society unless it was accompanied by a spiritual reformation. In the very last testimony he made to the people of Iran before his death, Khomeini begged them to continue to study and practice *irfan*, a discipline which the *ulema* had tended to neglect. For Khomeini, the mystical quest associated with *mythos* must always accompany the practical activities of *logos*. People who met Khomeini were always struck by his obvious absorption in the spiritual. His withdrawn demeanor, inward-looking gaze, and the studied monotone of his delivery (which Westerners found repellent) were easily recognizable by Shiis as the mark of a "sober" mystic. Where some Sufis and mystical practitioners were known as "drunken" mystics because they surrendered to the emotional extremes that are often unleashed in the course of this interior journey, the "sober" mystic cultivated an iron self-control as a means of keeping extremity at bay. Mulla Sadra had described the spiritual progress of a leader *(imam)* of the *ummah*. Before he could begin his political mission, he must first journey from man to God, expose himself to the transforming vision of the divine, and strip himself of the egotism that impedes his self-realization. Only at the end of this long and disciplined process, could he, as it were, return to the world of affairs, preach the word of God, and implement the divine law in society. The American scholar Hamid Algar suggests that when he began to speak against the shah in 1963, Khomeini had completed the preliminary and essential "journey to God," and felt ready to take an active role in politics.[44]

Khomeini was released after spending a few days in custody, but he returned at once to the offensive. Forty days after SAVAK's attack on the Fayziyah Madrasah, the students held the traditional mourning ceremonies for those who had been killed. Khomeini delivered a speech in which he compared the assault to Reza Shah's violation of the shrine of Mashhad in 1935, when hundreds of protesters had died. Throughout the summer, he continued to denounce the regime, until finally, on the feast of Ashura, the anniversary of the martyrdom of Imam Husain at Kerbala (June 3, 1963), Khomeini delivered a mourning eulogy, while the people sobbed and wept, as was customary during a *rawdah*. The shah, Khomeini claimed, was like Yazid, the villain of Kerbala. When they had attacked the Fayziyah Madrasah last March, why had the police bothered to tear the Koran apart? If they just wanted to arrest one of the *ulema*, why did they kill an eighteen-year-old student, who had never done anything against the regime? The answer was that the shah wanted to destroy religion itself. He begged him to reform:

> Our country, our Islam are in danger. What is happening, and what is about to happen worries and saddens us. We are worried and saddened by the situation of this ruined country. We hope to God it can be reformed.[45]

The following morning, Khomeini was arrested again, and this time the lid blew off. When they heard the news, thousands of Iranians went out onto the streets in protest in Tehran, Mashhad, Shiraz, Kashan, and Varamin. SAVAK forces were given orders to shoot to kill; tanks surrounded the mosques in Tehran to stop people from attending Friday prayers. In Tehran, Qum, and Shiraz, prominent *ulema* led the demonstrations, while others called for a *jihad* against the regime. Some put on white shrouds to show that, like Imam Husain, they were willing to die in the war against tyranny. University and *madrasah* students fought side by side, laymen alongside mullahs. It took SAVAK days to suppress the uprising, which revealed the immense tension and resentment that had been smoldering under the surface. When order was finally restored on June 11, hundreds of Iranians had died.[46]

Khomeini himself narrowly escaped execution. Ayatollah Muhammad-Kazim Shariatmadari (1904–85), one of the most senior *mujtahids,* saved his life by promoting Khomeini to the rank of Grand Ayatollah, which made it too risky for the regime to kill him.[47] After his release, Khomeini became a hero to the people. His photograph appeared everywhere as a symbol of opposition. He had put himself on the line and given voice to the aversion that many more inarticulate Iranians had come to feel for the shah. Khomeini's vision was flawed by the usual fundamentalist paranoia. Constantly in his speeches, he referred to a conspiracy of Jews, Christians, and imperialists, a fantasy that for many Iranians seemed credible because of the association of the CIA and Mossad with the hated SAVAK. It was a theology of rage.[48] But Khomeini enabled Iranians to express legitimate grievances in terms that they could understand. Where a Marxist or liberally inspired critique of the shah would have left the vast majority of unmodernized Iranians unmoved, everybody could understand the symbolism of Kerbala. Unlike the other ayatollahs, Khomeini did not speak in remote, academic language; his speech was direct and down-to-earth, addressed to ordinary people. Western people tended to see Khomeini as a throwback to the Middle Ages, but in fact much of his message and developing ideology was modern. His opposition to Western imperialism and his support of the Palestinians were similar to other Third World movements at this time; so was his direct appeal to the people.

Eventually, Khomeini went too far. On October 27, 1964, he delivered a strong attack against the recent granting of diplomatic immunity to American military personnel and other advisers, and to the shah's acceptance of 200 million dollars for arms. Iran, he claimed, was virtually an American colony. What other nation would submit to such indignity? An American maidservant would go virtually unpunished for a serious crime committed in Iran, whereas the case of an Iranian citizen who inadvertently ran over an American's dog would have to come to trial. For decades foreigners had been plundering Iran's oil, so that it was of no benefit to the Iranian people, and meanwhile the poor were suffering. He concluded:

> There is no redress for the Iranian people. I am deeply concerned about the condition of the poor next winter, as I expect many to die, God forbid, from cold and starvation. The people should think of the poor and take action now to prevent the atrocities of last winter. The *ulema* should appeal for contributions for this purpose.[49]

After this speech, Khomeini was deported, and eventually took up residence in the holy Shii city of Najaf.

The regime was now determined to muzzle the clerics. After Khomeini's departure, the government began to appropriate the religiously endowed properties *(awqaf)* and brought the *madrasahs* under stricter bureaucratic control. As a result, by the late 1960s, the number of theological students had markedly declined.[50] In 1970, Ayatollah Riza Saidi was tortured to death for objecting to a conference to promote American investment in Iran, and for denouncing the regime as a "tyrannical agent of imperialism." Thousands of demonstrators poured onto the streets in Qum, and in Tehran, outside Ayatollah Saidi's mosque, a huge crowd gathered to listen to an address by Ayatollah Taleqani.[51] At the same time, the government attempted to create a form of "civil Islam," obedient to the state: a Religious Corps was established, composed of lay graduates from the theological faculties of the secular universities, to work closely with the new Department of Religious Propaganda for Rural Areas. These "mullahs of modernization" would explain the White Revolution to the peasants, promote literacy, build bridges and reservoirs, and vaccinate livestock. It was a transparent attempt to undermine the traditional *ulema*.[52] But the shah was also anxious to sever the connection between Iran and the Shiah. In 1970, he abolished the Islamic calendar, and the following year there were lavish celebrations in Persepolis to commemorate the 2500th anniversary of the ancient Persian monarchy. Not only was this a tasteless demonstration of the immense gap that now existed between rich and poor in Iran, but it was a very public assertion of the regime's desire to found its identity on Islam's pre-Islamic heritage.

If Iranians lost Islam, they would lose themselves. That was the message of the charismatic young philosopher Dr. Ali Shariati (1933–77), to whose lecture halls the young Western-educated Iranians flocked in ever-increasing numbers during the late 1960s.[53] Shariati had not had a conventional *madrasah* education, but had studied at the University of Mashhad and at the Sorbonne, where he had written a dissertation on Persian philosophy and studied the work of the French orientalist Louis Massignon, the existential philosopher Jean-Paul Sartre, and the Third World ideologist Frantz Fanon. He had become convinced that it was possible to create a distinctively Shii ideology which would meet the spiritual needs of modern Iranians without cutting them off from their roots. After returning to Iran, Shariati eventually taught at the *husainiyyah* in north Tehran, which had been founded in 1965 by the philanthropist Muhammad Humayun. Humayun had been much moved by the lectures of the reforming *ulema* in the early sixties, and had established the *husainiyyah* to try to reach Iranian youth. In Iran, a *husainiyyah* was a center of devotion to Imam Husain, and was usually built beside the mosque. The hope was that the Kerbala story would inspire the young who attended classes at the *husainiyyah* to work for a better society. Iran was also experiencing the swing toward religion that had taken place in the Middle East after the 1967 war, and by 1968, Ayatollah Motahhari, one of the reformers who had helped to set it up, could write that, thanks to the *husainiyyah*, "our educated youth, after passing through a period of being astonished, even repulsed [by religion] are paying an attention and a concern for it that defies description."[54] None of the lecturers made as great an impact as Shariati. Students rushed to hear him during their lunch hour or after work, inspired by the passion and vehemence of his delivery. They could relate to him. Shariati dressed as they did, shared their dilemma of torn cultural allegiance, and some felt that he was like an older brother.[55]

Shariati was a creative intellectual, but he was also a spiritual man. The Prophet and the Imams were real presences in his life, and his devotion to them was obvious. His was a truly mythical piety. The events of Shii history were not merely historical incidents of the seventh century, but timeless realities that could inspire and guide people in the present. The Hidden Imam, he used to explain, had not disappeared like Jesus. He was still in the world, but concealed; Shiis could encounter him in that merchant or this beggar. He was waiting to make his appearance, and Shiis must live in constant expectation of hearing the sound of his trumpet, ready at all times to respond to the Imam's summons to the *jihad* against tyranny. Shiis must look through the concrete, perplexing realities that surrounded them in their everyday lives to catch a glimpse of their secret essence *(zat)*.[56] Because the spiritual was not in a realm apart, it was, therefore, impossible to separate religion from politics in the way that the regime was attempting. Human beings were two-dimensional creatures; they had a spiritual as well as a corporeal existence, needed *mythos* as well as *logos*, and every polity must have a transcendent dimension. That was the real meaning of the doctrine of the Imamate: it was a symbolic reminder that a society could not exist without an Imam, a divine guide, to help the people achieve their spiritual as well as their earthly objectives. To split religion and politics was to betray the principle of *tawhid* ("unification"), the cardinal tenet of Islam, which should help Muslims to achieve an integrity that reflected the divine unity.[57]

Tawhid would also heal the alienation of the West-toxicated Iranians. Shariati insisted on *bazgasht beh khishtan*, a "return to the self." Where the Greek spirit was characterized by philosophy, and the Roman spirit by art and militarism, Iran's archetypal self was religious and Islamic. Where the rational empiricism of the West concentrates on what *is*, the Orient seeks the truth that shall be. If Iranians tried to conform too closely to the Western ideal, they would lose their identity and assist in their own ethnicide.[58] Instead of glorying in the ancient Persian culture like the shah, they should celebrate their Shii heritage. But this could not be a superficial or a purely notional process. Muslims needed the rituals of their faith to transform them at a deeper level than the rational. In his beautiful monograph *Hajj*, Shariati reinterpreted the ancient cult connected with the Kabah and the pilgrimage to Mecca, which perfectly epitomized the conservative spirit, so that they could speak to Muslims in the rapidly changing world of modernity. In Shariati's book, the pilgrimage became a journey to God, not unlike the fourfold interior journey described by Mulla Sadra. Not everybody is capable of mysticism, which requires a special talent and temperament, but the rites of the *hajj* are accessible to all Muslim men and women. The decision to embark on the pilgrimage—a once-in-a-lifetime experience for most Muslims—represents a new orientation. Pilgrims must leave their confused and alienated selves behind. While making the seven circumambulations around the Kabah, the immense crush of the thronging crowds, Shariati explained, caused the pilgrim to "feel like a small stream merging with a big river":

> the pressure of the crowd squeezes you so hard that you are given a new life. You are now part of the People; you are now a Man, alive and eternal. . . . Circumambulating around Allah, you will soon forget yourself.[59]

Egotism was transcended in this union with the *ummah* and a new "center" had been attained. During the night vigil on the plain of Arafat, the pilgrims exposed themselves to the light of the divine knowledge, and must now prepare to reenter the world and struggle against the enemies of God (a *jihad* represented by the ritual stoning of three pillars at Mina). Then the *hajji* was

ready to return to the world with the spiritual consciousness that was indispensable to the social struggle to create a just society, which is incumbent
upon every Muslim. The rational effort involved in this depends upon, and
is given meaning by, the spirituality evoked in the cult and the myth.

For Shariati, Islam must be expressed in action. The timeless realities that
the Shiis learned to see at the core of existence must be activated in the present. The example of Imam Husain at Kerbala should, Shariati believed, be
an inspiration to all the oppressed and alienated people in the world. Shariati
was disgusted by the quietist *ulema,* who had locked themselves away in
their *madrasahs* and had, in his view, distorted Islam by making it a purely
private creed. The period of the Occultation should not be a period of pas-
sivity. If the Shiah followed Husain's example and led all the people of the
Third World in a campaign against tyranny, they would compel the Hidden
Imam to appear.[60] But the *ulema* had ruined the religious experience for
young Iranians, bored them to distraction, and driven them into the arms of
the West. They saw Islam in purely literal terms, as a set of clear directives
to be followed to the letter, whereas the genius of Shiism was its symbolism.
This taught Muslims to see all earthly reality as "signs" of the Unseen.[61] The
Shiah needed a Reformation. The original Shiism of Ali and Husain
had been obliterated in Iran by what Shariati called "Safavid Shiism." An
active, dynamic faith had been converted into a privatized, passive affair,
whereas the disappearance of the Hidden Imam meant that the mission of
the Prophet and the Imams had in fact passed to the people. The period of
the Occultation was thus the age of democracy. The ordinary people should
no longer be in thrall to the *mujtahids* and forced to imitate *(taqlid)* their religious behavior, as Safavid Shiism required. Each Muslim must submit to
God alone and take responsibility for his own life. Anything else was idolatrous and a perversion of Islam, turning it into a lifeless observance of set
rules. The people must elect their own leaders; they must be consulted, as
the principle of *shurah* demanded. By their consensus *(ijmah),* they would
give legitimacy to the decisions of their leaders. There should be an end
of clerical control. Instead of the *ulema,* the "enlightened intellectuals"
(raushanfekran) should be the new leaders of the *ummah.*[62]

Shariati was not entirely fair to the Usuli doctrines of "Safavid Shiism."
They had arisen in response to a particular need, and, though they had
always been controversial, they had expressed the spirituality of the premodern age, which could not permit the individual too much freedom.[63] But
the world had changed. Iranians who had been affected by the Western
ideals of autonomy and intellectual liberty could no longer submit to the rulings of a *mujtahid* as their grandparents had done. Conservative spirituality
had been designed to help people accept the limitations of their society and

submit to the status quo. The myth of Husain had kept the passion for social justice alive in the Shiah, but his story and the story of the Imams also showed how impossible it was to implement this divine ideal in a world that could not accommodate radical change.[64] But this no longer applied in the modern world. Iranians were experiencing change to an alarming degree; they could not respond to the old rites and symbols in the same way. Shariati was attempting to reformulate Shiism so that it could speak to Muslims in this deeply altered world.

Shariati insisted that Islam was more dynamic than any other faith. Its very terminology showed its progressive thrust. In the West, the word "politics" derived from the Greek *polis* ("city"), a static administrative unit, but the Islamic equivalent was *siyasat,* which literally meant "taming a wild horse," a process implying a forceful struggle to bring out an inherent perfection.[65] The Arabic terms *ummah* and *imam* both derived from the root *amm* ("decision to go"): the Imam, therefore, was a model who would take the people in a new direction. The community *(ummah)* was not simply a collection of individuals but was goal-oriented, ready for perpetual revolution.[66] The notion of *ijtihad* ("independent judgment") implied a constant intellectual effort to renew and rebuild; it was not, Shariati insisted, the privilege of a few *ulema,* but the duty of every Muslim.[67] The centrality of *hijrah* ("migration") to the Muslim experience implied a readiness for change, and an uprooting that kept Muslims in touch with the newness of existence.[68] Even *intizar* ("waiting for the return of the Hidden Imam") suggested a constant alertness to the possibility of transformation and implied a refusal to accept the status quo: "It makes [man's] responsibility for his own course, the course of truth, the course of mankind, heavy, immediate, logical, and vital." The Shiism of Ali was a faith that compelled Muslims to stand up and say "No!"[69]

The regime could not permit this kind of talk, and in 1973 the *husainiyyah* was closed down. Shariati was arrested, tortured, and imprisoned. He then endured a period of internal exile in Iran, before being permitted to leave the country. His father recalled that one night during this period, he heard Shariati weeping as he bade farewell to the Prophet and Imam Ali before his death.[70] In 1977, Shariati died in London, almost certainly at the hands of SAVAK agents. Shariati prepared the educated, Westernized Iranians for an Islamic revolution. He was as pivotal a figure for intellectuals during the 1970s as Al-e Ahmad had been in the sixties. In the days leading up to the Revolution in 1978, his picture was often carried in procession alongside Khomeini's.

The majority of Iranians, however, continued to look to Khomeini for guidance. Paradoxically, he was freer to express his opposition in exile in

Iraq than he had been in Qum. His books and tapes were smuggled into the country, and his *fatwas*, such as the one that declared the regime to be incompatible with Islam after the shah had changed the calendar, were taken very seriously. In 1971, Khomeini published a landmark book, *Hokomat-e eslami* ("Islamic Government"), which developed a Shii ideology of clerical rule. His thesis was shocking and revolutionary. For centuries, Shiis had declared all government to be illegitimate during the absence of the Hidden Imam, and had never thought it correct for the *ulema* to rule the state. But in *Islamic Government*, Khomeini argued that the *ulema* must take over the government in order to safeguard the sovereignty of God. If a *faqih*, an expert in Islamic jurisprudence, took control of the administrative and political institutions, he could ensure that the Shariah was implemented correctly. Even though the *faqih* was not on the same level as the Prophet and the Imams, his knowledge of the divine Law meant that he could command the same authority as they did. Since God was the only true Lawgiver, instead of a parliament creating its own man-made legislation, there should be an assembly to apply the Shariah to every aspect of day-to-day life.

Khomeini knew that his argument was highly controversial and challenged a fundamental Shii conviction. But, like Qutb, he believed that this innovation was justified by the present emergency. Like Shariati, he did not believe that religion could be privatized any longer. The Prophet, Imam Ali, and Imam Husain had all been political as well as spiritual leaders, and had struggled actively against the oppression and idolatry of their day. Faith was not a matter of personal belief but an attitude "that compels men to action":

> Islam is the religion of militant individuals who are committed to faith and justice. It is the religion of those who desire freedom and independence. It is the school of those who struggle against imperialism.[71]

It was a very modern message. Like Shariati, Khomeini was trying to prove that Islam was not a medieval faith but had always championed values that the West thought it had invented. But Islam had been infected and weakened by the imperialists. People wanted to separate religion and politics on the Western model, and this had perverted the faith: "Islam lives among the people as if it were a stranger," Khomeini lamented. "If somebody were to present Islam as it truly is, he would find it difficult to make people believe him."[72] The Iranians were in the grip of spiritual malaise. "We have completely forgotten our identity, and have replaced it with a Western identity," Khomeini used to say. Iranians had "sold themselves and do not know themselves, becoming enslaved to alien ideals."[73] He believed that the way to heal this alienation was to create a society based entirely on the laws of Islam, which were not only more natural for Iranians than the imported law codes of the West, but were of sacred origin. If they lived in a divinely ordered milieu, impelled by the law of the land to live exactly as God intended, they themselves and the meaning of their lives would be transformed. The disciplines, practices, and rituals of Islam would create within them the Muhammadan spirit that was the ideal for humanity. For Khomeini, faith was not a notional acceptance of a creed, but an attitude and lifestyle that embodied a revolutionary struggle for the happiness and integrity that God intended for humanity. "Once faith comes, everything follows."[74]

Such faith was revolutionary because it constituted a revolt against the hegemony of the Western spirit. A Westerner was likely to find Khomeini's theory of Velayat-e Faqih ("the Government of the Jurist") sinister and coercive, but the "modern" government that Iranians had experienced had not brought them the freedoms that people took for granted in Europe and America. Khomeini was coming to embody in his own person an alternative Shii ideal to the Pahlavi monarchy. He was known to be a mystic and to embody divine knowledge in a way that was similar, if not identical, to that of the Imams. Like Husain, he had challenged the corrupt rule of a tyrant; like the Imams, he had been imprisoned and almost put to death by an unjust ruler; like some of the Imams, he had been forced into exile and deprived of what was rightfully his. Now in Najaf, living beside the shrine of Imam Ali, Khomeini seemed rather like the Hidden Imam: physically inaccessible to his people, he still guided them from afar and would one day return. There was a rumor that Khomeini had dreamed that, despite his present exile, he would die in Qum. Western people found it difficult to understand how Khomeini, who had none of the charm or charisma that they expected in a political leader, had managed to inspire such devotion in the Iranian people. Had they known more about Shiism, they might have found this less of a mystery.

When Khomeini wrote *Islamic Government*, he probably had no idea that revolution was imminent. He believed that it would be two hundred years before Iran would be ready to implement Velayat-e Faqih.[75] Khomeini was at this date more concerned with the religious ideal than with the practical underpinning of his theory. In 1972, the year after the publication of *Islamic Government*, Khomeini wrote an article which he called "The Greater Jihad," which found a mystical justification for the controversial Velayat-e Faqih. The title refers to one of his favorite *hadith*, which has the Prophet say after returning home from a battle: "We are returning from the lesser *jihad* to the greater *jihad*." This perfectly expressed Khomeini's conviction that the battles and campaigns of politics were the "lesser" struggle, of far less import than the effort to effect the spiritual transformation of society and to integrate one's own heart and desires. He was convinced, like Shariati, that a political solution could not succeed without a deeply religious renewal in Iran.

In his 1972 article, Khomeini suggested that a *faqih* who engaged in the mystical quest described by Mulla Sadra could acquire the same "infallibility" *(ismah)* as the Imams. This did not mean, of course, that the jurist was on the same level as the Imams, but as the mystic approached God, he had to rid himself of the egotism that held him back from the divine. He had to divest himself of the "veils of darkness," "attachment to the world," and the lure of sensuality. At the peak of his journey to God, he was thus purged of the inclination to sin: "If a man believes in God Almighty and with the eye of his heart sees Him as clearly as he sees the sun, it is impossible for him to commit any act of sin." The Imams had had special divine knowledge, which was a unique gift, but they had also acquired this lesser infallibility by the ordinary processes of spirituality, Khomeini believed. Thus, it would not be impossible for a *faqih* who was expert in Islamic Law and mystically reborn in this way to lead the people to God.[76] There was a potential idolatry here, but, again, it must be emphasized that in 1972 nobody, not even Khomeini, believed that it would be feasible to topple the shah in an Islamically inspired revolution. Khomeini was now seventy years old. He must have thought it very unlikely that he would become the ruling *faqih*. In both *Islamic Government* and "The Greater Jihad," Khomeini was trying to see how the mythology and mysticism of the Shiah could be adapted to break centuries of sacred tradition and allow a cleric to rule Iran. He had yet to see how this *mythos* would work out in practice.

IN ISRAEL, a new form of Jewish fundamentalism had already started to translate myth into hard political fact. It had its roots in the religious Zionism which had grown up in the shadow of secular Zionism in the pre-state days in Palestine. These religious Zionists were modern Orthodox, and from an early date, they had started to found their own observant settlements alongside the socialist kibbutzim. Unlike the Haredim, this small group of religious Jews did not see Zionism as incompatible with Orthodoxy. They interpreted the Bible literally: in the Torah, God promised the Land to the descendants of Abraham, and thus gave Jews a legal title to Palestine. Moreover, in Eretz Israel, Jews would be able to observe the Law more fully than had been possible in the Diaspora. In the ghetto, it was obviously not feasible to observe many commandments relating to the farming and settlement of the Land, or the laws regarding politics and government.

As a result, Diaspora Judaism had perforce been fragmented and compartmentalized. Now at last in their own land, Jews would be able to observe the whole of the Torah once again. As Pinchas Rosenbluth, one of the pioneers of Zionist Orthodoxy, explained:

> We accept upon ourselves the entire Torah, its commandments and ideas. The [old] Orthodoxy made do in fact with a small part of the Torah . . . observed in synagogue or the family . . . or certain areas of life. We want to carry out the Torah all the time and in every area, to grant [Torah] and its laws sovereignty in the life of the individual and the public.[77]

Far from being incompatible with modernity, the Law would complete it. The world would see that Jews could create a new social order that was truly progressive because it had been planned by God.[78]

There was a desire for wholeness that would always characterize religious Zionism; it was a way of finding healing and a more holistic vision after the trauma and constrictions of exile. But it was also a rebellion against the rationalist vision of the secular Zionists, who did not take these religious settlers seriously and who saw their ambition to create a Torah state in Eretz Israel as not only anachronistic but repellent. The religious Zionists were very conscious of being rebels. When they established their own youth movement, Bnei Akiva ("Sons of Akiva"), in 1929, these youngsters took as their role model Rabbi Akiva, the great mystic and scholar of the second century CE, who had supported a Jewish revolt against Rome. The secular Zionists had also been rebels, but against religious Judaism. Now the Bnei Akiva felt that they "must call for a rebellion against the rebellion, against the views of the [secular] youth which is opposed to Judaism and to Jewish tradition."[79] They were fighting a battle for God. Instead of wanting to marginalize and exclude the divine from political and cultural life, they wanted religion to suffuse their existence "all the time and in every area." They refused to allow the secularists to "own" Zionism completely. Tiny minority though they were, they were staging a mini-revolution against what they regarded as the illegitimate domination of the secularists' wholly rational ideology.

They needed their own schools and institutions. During the 1940s, Rav Moshe Zvi Neria founded a series of elite boarding schools for religious Zionist boys and girls. In these *yeshiva* high schools, academic standards were high; students studied secular subjects alongside Torah. Unlike the Haredim, these neo-Orthodox religious Zionists did not feel that they should cut themselves off from major currents of modern life. This would betray their holistic vision; they believed that Judaism was quite large enough to accommodate these gentile sciences, but they also took Torah study very seriously indeed, and employed graduates from the Haredi *yeshivot* to teach them Torah and Talmud. In the *yeshiva* high schools, *mythos* and *logos* were still seen as complementary. Torah provided a mystical encounter with the divine and gave meaning to the whole, even though it had no practical utility. As Rabbi Yehoshua Yogel, the principal of Midrashiat Noam, explained, students did not study Torah to make a living or "as a means for economic, military, and political existence." Rather, Torah must be studied "for its own sake"; unlike the *logoi* of the secular subjects, it had no practical use, but was simply the whole "purpose of man."[80] Study, however, was not enough for the young religious Zionists after the foundation of the State of Israel. In the 1950s, *yeshivot* were established for older students which had a special "arrangement" *(hesder)* with the new Israeli government, giving religious youth a way of combining their national service in the IDF with Torah study.

Religious Zionists had thus carved out for themselves a distinctive way of life, but during the early years of the state, some suffered a crisis of identity. They seemed to fall between two worlds: they were not Zionist enough for the secularists, and their achievements could not compete with the triumph of the secular pioneers, who had brought the state into being. In the same way, they were not Orthodox enough for the Haredim, and knew that they could not match their expertise in Torah. This crisis led, during the early 1950s, to yet another youth rebellion. A small circle of about a dozen fourteen-year-old boys, who were pupils at Kfar Haro'eh, one of the *yeshiva* high schools, began to live more stringently religious lives, in much the same way as the Haredim. They insisted upon modest dress and the segregation of the sexes, banned frivolous conversations and trivial recreations, and supervised one another's lives in a system involving public confession and trials for miscreants. They called themselves Gahelet ("glowing embers"), linking their Haredi rigor with an intense nationalism. They dreamed of building a kibbutz with a *yeshiva* in the center, where the men would study Talmud day and night, like Haredim, while the women, relegated, ultra-Orthodox style, to the inferior but complementary sphere of *logos,* supported them and farmed the land. The Gahelet became an elite group in religious Zionist circles, but they felt that their Orthodoxy would not be complete until, like the Hasidim and Misnagdim, they found a rabbi to bless and guide them. In the late 1950s they fell under the spell of the ageing Rabbi Zvi Yehuda Kook, the son of Rabbi Abraham Yitzhak Kook, whose work we considered in Chapter Six.[81]

By the time the Gahelet discovered Rabbi Zvi Yehuda, he was almost seventy years old, and was generally considered to be not half the man his father had been. He was the principal of the Merkaz Harav Yeshiva in north Jerusalem, which had been founded by his father but was now dwindling, with only twenty students. But Kook the Younger's ideas appealed immediately to the Gahelet, because he went much further than Abraham Yitzhak and yet, at the same time, had so simplified the elder Kook's complex dialectical vision that it had the streamlined form of a modern ideology. Where Kook the Elder had seen a divine purpose in secular Zionism, Rabbi Zvi Yehuda believed that the secular State of Israel was the Kingdom of God *tout court;* every clod of its earth was holy:

> Every Jew who comes to Eretz Yisrael, every tree that is planted
> in the soil of Israel, every soldier added to the army of Israel,
> constitutes another spiritual stage, literally; another stage in the
> process of redemption.[82]

Where the Haredim forbade their students to watch the army parade on Independence Day, Kook the Younger insisted that, because the army was sacred, it was a religious duty to watch it. The soldiers were as righteous as Torah scholars, and their weapons as holy as a prayer shawl or phylacteries. "Zionism is a heavenly matter," Rabbi Zvi Yehuda insisted. "The State of Israel is a divine entity, our holy and exalted state."[83]

Where Kook the Elder had believed that Jews should take no part in politics, because in the unredeemed world, all politics was tainted, Kook the Younger believed that the messianic age had begun and that political involvement was, like the mystical journey of the Kabbalist, an ascent to the pinnacles of holiness.[84] His vision was literalistically holistic. The Land, the People, and the Torah formed an indivisible triad. To abandon one was to abandon all three. Unless Jews settled in the whole Land of Israel, as this was defined in the Bible, there could be no Redemption: the annexation of the whole land, including territory at this time belonging to the Arabs, had become a supreme religious duty.[85] But when the Gahelet met Kook in the late 1950s, there seemed little hope of achieving this. The borders of the State of Israel, established in 1948, included only Galilee, the Negev, and the coastal plain. The biblical land on the West Bank of the Jordan currently belonged to the Hashemite Kingdom of Jordan. But Kook was confident. Everything was proceeding in accordance with a preordained pattern. Even the Holocaust had pushed Redemption forward, since it had forced Jews to leave the Diaspora and return to the Land. Jews had "clung so determinedly to the impurity of foreign lands, that, when the End Time arrived, they had to be cut away with a great shedding of blood," Kook explained in a Holocaust Day sermon in 1973. These historical facts revealed God's divine hand, and had brought about "the rebirth of the Torah and all that was holy." History thus provided an encounter, "an encounter with the Master of the Universe."[86]

The transposition of myth into fact had finally occurred. In the premodern world, mythology and politics had been distinct. State-building, military campaigns, agriculture, and the economy had all been the preserves of the rational disciplines of *logos*. The myth contained these pragmatic activities and gave them meaning; myth could also serve as a corrective, and remind men and women of values, such as compassion, that transcended the pragmatic considerations of reason. An earthly reality could become a symbol of the divine, but was never itself holy; it pointed beyond itself to where reason could not go. But Kook had overridden these distinctions and created what some might call idolatry. Can an army be "holy" when it is often obliged to do terrible things, such as killing the innocent with the guilty? Traditionally, messianism had inspired people to criticize the status quo, but Kook would use it to give absolute sanction to Israeli policy. Such a vision could lead to a nihilism that denies crucial values. In making the State of Israel holy and its territorial integrity supreme, Kook had succumbed to the very temptation responsible for some of the worst nationalist atrocities of the twentieth century. Rabbi Kook the Elder's inclusive vision, which had reached out to other faiths and to the secular world, had been lost. Kook the Younger was filled with burning hatred of Christians, of the *goyim* who interfered with Israeli ambitions, and of the Arabs.[87] There had been wisdom in the older vision, which had seen reason and myth as complementary though separate. There was great danger in Kook the Younger's yoking of the two together.

The Gahelet did not take this view, however. Rabbi Kook's holistic ideology made Zionism a religion, and was just what they had been looking for. They became full-time students at Merkaz Harav, and put this obscure *yeshiva* on the map of Israel. They also made Kook a sort of Jewish pope, whose decrees were binding and infallible. These young men became Kook's cadre and would become the leaders of the new fundamentalist Zionism: Moshe Levinger, Yaakov Ariel, Shlomo Aviner, Haim Drukman, Dov Lior, Zalman Melamed, Avraham Shapira, and Eliezar Waldman. In Merkaz Harav during the 1960s, they planned an offensive designed to win the nation back to God and to make the secular state realize its religious potential. Instead of the dialectical synthesis of secular and religious envisaged by Kook the Elder, Rabbi Zvi Yehuda expected an imminent takeover of the secular by the divine.

For all their enthusiasm, however, the Gahelet could do no more than plan. There was nothing they could effectively do to settle the whole land or to change the heart of the nation. But in 1967, history took a hand.

On Independence Day 1967, some three weeks before the outbreak of the Six Day War, Rabbi Kook was delivering his usual sermon at the Merkaz Harav *yeshiva*. Suddenly he emitted a sobbing scream, and uttered words that completely broke the flow of his speech: "Where is our Hebron, Shechem, Jericho and Anatoth, torn from the state in 1948 as we lay maimed and bleeding?"[88] Three weeks later, the Israeli army had occupied these biblical cities which had previously been in Arab hands, and Rabbi Kook's disciples were convinced that he had been inspired by God to make a true prophecy. By the end of this short war, Israel had conquered the Gaza Strip from Egypt, the West Bank from Jordan, and the Golan Heights from Syria. The holy city of Jerusalem, which had been divided between Israel and Jordan since 1948, was now annexed by Israel and declared to be the eternal capital of the Jewish state. Once again, Jews were able to pray at the Western Wall. A mood of exultation and near-mystical euphoria gripped the entire country. Before the war, Israelis had listened on their radios to Nasser vowing to throw them all into the sea; now they were unexpectedly in possession of sites sacred to Jewish memory. Many of the most diehard secularists experienced the war as a religious event, reminiscent of the crossing of the Red Sea.[89]

But for Kookists the war was even more crucial. It seemed conclusive proof that Redemption was indeed under way and that God was pushing history forward to its final consummation. The fact that no Messiah had actually appeared did not worry the Gahelet; they were moderns, and perfectly prepared to see the "Messiah" as a process rather than a person.[90] Nor were they disturbed that the "miracle" of the war had a perfectly natural explanation: the Israeli victory was entirely due to the efficiency of the IDF and the ineptitude of the Arab armies. The twelfth-century philosopher Maimonides had predicted that there would be nothing supernatural about the Redemption: the prophetic passages that spoke of cosmic wonders and universal peace referred not to the Messianic Kingdom in this world but to the World-to-Come.[91] The victory convinced Kookists that it was now time to mobilize in earnest.

A few months after the victory, rabbis and students held an impromptu conference at Merkaz Harav to find ways of foiling the plan of the Labor government to relinquish some of these newly occupied territories in exchange for peace with their Arab neighbors. For Kookists, the return of even one inch of the sacred land would be a victory for the forces of evil. And they found, to their surprise, that they had secular allies. Shortly after the war, a group of distinguished Israeli poets, professors, retired politicians, and army officers had formed the Land of Israel Movement to prevent the government from making any territorial concessions. Over the years, the Movement helped the Kookists to formulate their ideology in a way that would appeal to the public, and gave them financial and moral support. Gradually, the Kookists were being drawn into the mainstream.

In April 1968, Moshe Levinger led a small group of Kookists and their families to celebrate Passover in Hebron, the city where Abraham, Isaac, and Jacob are thought to be buried. Since Muslims also venerate these Jewish patriarchs as great prophets, Hebron was a holy city for them too. For centuries, Palestinians had called Hebron al-Khalil, because of its sacred associations with Abraham, the "friend" of God. But Hebron also evoked darker memories. On August 24, 1929, during a period of great tension between Arabs and Zionists in Palestine, fifty-nine Jewish men, women, and children had been massacred in Hebron. Levinger and his party checked into the Park Hotel, pretending to be Swiss tourists, but when Passover was over they refused to leave and stayed on as squatters. This was embarrassing for the Israeli government, since the Geneva conventions forbade any settlement in territory occupied during hostilities, and the United Nations was demanding that Israel withdraw from the land they had conquered. But the *chutzpa* of the Kookists reminded Laborites of their own pioneers in their Golden Age, and the government was, therefore, reluctant to evict them.[92]

Levinger's group immediately went on the offensive in the Cave of the Patriarchs. After the Six Day War, the Israeli military government had opened the shrine, which had been closed during the hostilities, for worship once again, making special arrangements for Jews to pray there without disturbing the Arabs. This was not good enough for the Jewish settlers, who began to press for more space and time in the Cave. They would refuse to leave on Fridays in time to let the Muslims in for their weekly communal prayer; sometimes they would leave the halls, but block the main entrance, so that the Muslim worshippers could not get in; they would hold a *kiddush* in the Cave, drinking wine, which they knew the Muslims would find offensive, and, on Independence Day 1968, they flew the Israeli flag at the shrine, in defiance of government regulations. Tension escalated and—inevitably, perhaps—a hand grenade was thrown at some Jewish visitors by a Palestinian outside the mosque.[93] Reluctantly, the Israeli government established an enclave for the settlers outside Hebron; the new settlement was protected by the IDF. Levinger called it Kiryat Arba (the biblical name for Hebron) and it has remained a bastion for the most extreme, violent, and provocative Zionist fundamentalists. By 1972, Kiryat Arba had grown to a small town with a population of about five thousand settlers. For the Kookists, it represented a victory in a holy war that pushed against the frontiers of the "Other Side" and liberated an important area of the Holy Land for God.

Otherwise, however, Kookists made little progress. To their exasperation, redemption seemed to have stalled. The Labor government did not annex the occupied territories, and, though they built military settlements there, there was still talk of exchanging land for peace. The victory of 1967 had led to an Israeli complacency, which was shattered when, in October 1973 on Yom Kippur (the Day of Atonement), the most solemn day in the Jewish year, Egypt and Syria invaded Sinai and the Golan Heights, taking the Israelis completely by surprise. This time the Arab armies made a much better showing and were only pushed back by the IDF with great difficulty. Israelis were shocked, and a mood of depression and doubt settled on the country. Israel had been caught off-guard, and this near-defeat seemed the result of ideological decline. Kookists agreed. In 1967, God had made his will clear, but instead of capitalizing on this victory and taking over the territories, the Israeli government had temporized and worried about antagonizing the *goyim*, especially in the United States. The Yom Kippur War was God's punishment and a reminder. Now religious Jews must come to the nation's rescue. One Kookist rabbi compared secular Israel to a soldier falling in the desert after fighting an heroic war. Faithful Jews, who had never abandoned religion, would take over and carry on his mission.[94]

The Six Day War had confirmed the Kookists in their vision and led to a couple of settlement ventures, but their movement did not really take wing until after the shock of the war of Yom Kippur. An article by the Kookist rabbi Yehuda Amital expressed the new militancy. In "The Meaning of the Yom Kippur War," Amital demonstrated that deep fear of annihilation that lies at the heart of so many fundamentalist movements. The October assault had reminded all Israelis of their isolation in the Middle East and shown that they were encircled by enemies who seemed dedicated to the destruction of their state. This raised the specter of the Holocaust. Now Amital declared that the old Zionist policy had been discredited. The secular state had not solved the Jewish problem; anti-Semitism was worse than ever. "The State of Israel is the only state in the world which faces destruction," he argued. There was no way that Jews could be "normalized," becoming like all the other nations, as the secular Zionists had hoped. But there was another Zionism, that preached by Rabbi Zvi Yehuda Kook, which declared that the redemptive process was now far advanced. Instead of seeing the war as yet another Jewish catastrophe, it should be regarded as an act of purification. The secular Jews, whose Zionism had been so lamentably inadequate that it had brought the nation to the brink of catastrophe, had tried to fuse Judaism with the empirical rationalism and democratic culture of the modern West. This foreign influence must be eliminated.[95]

Amital was articulating a theory which had much in common with the fundamentalism that was then emerging in Egypt and Iran. God had permitted the Yom Kippur War to warn the Jews to return to themselves. It had been a reminder of true values to "West-toxicated" Israel. As such, it was part of the messianic process, a holy war against Western civilization. But the tide had turned. The war also revealed that it was not just the Jews who were struggling to survive. In this life-or-death conflict, Amital believed, the gentiles were also fighting their final battle. The revival and expansion of the Jewish state had shown them that God was in control, that there was no room for Satan, and that Israel had succeeded in turning back the forces of iniquity. Israel had conquered the Land; all that remained to be done before the Redemption was to purge the last relics of the Western secular spirit from the souls of Jews, who must return to their religion. The war had sounded the death knell of secularism. The Kookists were now ready to mobilize and become more politically active in the struggle—a struggle against the West which sought to restrain Israeli expansionism, against the Arabs, and against the secularism which the West had spawned in Israel.

THERE WAS a similar readiness among Protestant fundamentalists in the United States. The chaos of the 1960s, with its permissive youth culture, sexual revolution, and the promotion of equal rights for homosexuals, blacks, and women, seemed to shake the very foundations of society. Many were convinced that this cataclysm, plus the tumult in the Middle East, could only mean that Rapture was nigh. Ever since the Revolution, American Protestantism had been divided into two warring camps, and for some forty years, the fundamentalists had been creating their own separate world, which rejected the modern ethos of secularists and liberal Christians alike. They saw themselves as outsiders, but in fact they represented a large constituency of Americans who resented the cultural hegemony of the eastern, secularist establishment, and who felt more at home with the conservative religion of the fundamentalists. They had not yet mobilized to form a political movement to redeem American society, but by the end of the 1970s, the potential was there, and fundamentalists were becoming conscious of their power. In 1979, the year that fundamentalists staged their comeback, George Gallup's national poll showed that one out of every three of the American adults questioned had experienced a religious ("born-again") conversion; nearly 50 percent believed that the Bible was inerrant, and over 80 percent saw Jesus as a divine figure. The poll also revealed that there were about 1300 evangelical Christian radio and television stations, which had an audience of about 130 million and made profits estimated from $500 million to "billions" of dollars. As a leading fundamentalist, Pat Robertson, proclaimed during the 1980 election: "We have enough votes to run this country!"[96]

There were three factors that contributed to this new growth and confidence during the 1960s and 1970s. First was the development of the South. Hitherto, fundamentalism had been a product of the big northern cities. The South was still predominantly agrarian. Liberal Christianity had made little progress in the churches, and there had, therefore, been no need for "fundamentalists" to fight against the new ideas and the Social Gospel. But during the 1960s, the South began to modernize. There was an influx of people from the North. They were looking for employment in the oil industry and the new technical and aerospace projects located there. The South had begun to experience the same kind of rapid industrialization and urbanization as the North had a century earlier. During the 1930s, two-thirds of southerners had lived in the country. By 1960, less than half lived there. The South was beginning to acquire a higher national profile. In 1976, Jimmy Carter became the first southerner since the Civil War to be elected to the presidency; he was succeeded in 1980 by Ronald Reagan, the governor of California. But though southerners welcomed their new preeminence, they found their world completely changed. The immigrants from the North brought modern and liberal ideas with them. Not all were Protestants or even Christians. Values and beliefs that had hitherto been taken for granted now had to be defended. In the Baptist and Presbyterian denominations especially, conservative Protestants were as ripe for a fundamentalist movement as their northern co-religionists had been at the turn of the century, and for all the same reasons.[97]

The people of the new South, who felt uprooted and alienated from the society in which they lived, were often newcomers from the rural districts to the rapidly expanding cities. Many country people started to send their children to college and on the campus they had to encounter the new sixties liberalism. They also witnessed the loss of faith suffered by many of their fellow students.[98] Parents felt alienated and alarmed by children who were adopting apparently Godless ideas. In the churches, they encountered even more shocking notions, brought from the North by the new arrivals. Increasingly, people turned to the fundamentalist churches, and especially to the "electric" churches of the airwaves. Powerful new televangelists built empires during this period. The potential converts to fundamentalism lived along the southern rim, starting in Virginia Beach, where Pat Robertson had established his Christian Broadcasting Network and the immensely popular

"700 Club." Next came Lynchburg, Virginia, where Jerry Falwell had begun his television ministry in 1956; in Charlotte, North Carolina, was the ministry of the exuberant Jim and Tammy Faye Bakker, and the "Bible-Belt" ended in southern California, an area with a long tradition of political and religious conservatism.[99]

The second factor that led many traditionalists to become fundamentalists was the rapid expansion of state power in the United States after the Second World War. Americans had been mistrustful of centralized government since the Revolution, and had often used religion to voice their distaste for the secularist establishment. Fundamentalists were particularly outraged by the Supreme Court decisions banning obligatory worship in public schools on the grounds that this violated the "wall of separation" that Jefferson had decreed should divide religion and politics. Secularist judges had come to the conclusion that it was unconstitutional for the state to sponsor a program of prayer in its schools, even if this did not involve funds derived from taxes, and even if the worship was voluntary and nondenominational. Rulings to this effect were passed in 1948, 1952, and 1962. In 1963, the Supreme Court also banned Bible readings in public schools, quoting the religion clause of the First Amendment. During the 1970s, the Court passed a series of judgments declaring that any law would be struck down (1) if it intended to promote the cause of religion, (2) if its consequence, regardless of its intention, was the advancement of religion, and finally (3) if it entangled government in religious affairs.[100] The Court was responding to the increasing pluralism of American culture; it declared that it had nothing against religion, but insisted that it be confined to the private domain.

These rulings were secularizing but could not be compared to the aggressive attempts of either Nasser or the shah to marginalize religious faith. Nevertheless, fundamentalists and evangelical Christians alike were outraged by what they regarded as a Godless crusade. They did not believe that religion could be legitimately cordoned off and limited in this way, because Christianity's demands were total and should be sovereign. They were offended that the Court was willing to extend the principle of the "free exercise" of faith (demanded by the First Amendment) to religions that were not even Christian, and incensed by the judges' principled determination to put all faiths on the same level. This seemed tantamount to saying that their religion was false. The ruling that religion be confined to private life seemed even more outrageous to fundamentalists, when it was combined with what seemed an excessive and unprecedented intrusion of the Court into the private sphere. When the Internal Revenue Service threatened to withdraw charitable tax-exempt status from certain fundamentalist colleges on the grounds that their rules contravened public policy, it seemed an act of war on the part of liberal society. Only fundamentalists, it appeared, were not allowed "free exercise" of the principles of their faith. In the mid-1970s, the Supreme Court endorsed IRS rulings against Goldsborough Christian Schools in North Carolina, which did not admit Afro-Americans, and Bob Jones University, which was not segregationist but which banned interracial dating on campus, claiming that it was forbidden by the Bible.

It was another clash between two value systems, similar to the Scopes trial of 1925. Both sides believed that they were absolutely in the right. A deep rift ran through the nation. Increasingly, during the late 1960s and 1970s, as the state expanded its notion of what constituted the public arena, very conservative Christians on the margins of modern society experienced these interventions as a secularist offensive. They felt "colonized" by the world of Manhattan, Washington, and Harvard. Their experience was not entirely dissimilar to that of the Middle Eastern countries who had so bitterly resented being taken over by an alien power. The government seemed to have invaded the inner sanctum of the family: a Constitutional amendment giving women equal rights of employment seemed to fly in the face of biblical injunctions that a woman's place was in the home. Legislation limited the physical chastisement of children, even though the Bible made it clear that a father had a duty to discipline his children in this way. Civil rights and freedom of expression were granted to homosexuals, and abortion was legalized. Reforms that seemed just and moral to liberals in San Francisco, Boston, or Yale seemed sinful to religious conservatives in Arkansas and Alabama, who believed that the inspired word of God must be interpreted and obeyed to the letter. They did not feel liberated by the permissive society. When they reflected that in the 1920s, two-thirds of the states had voted for the prohibition of liquor, but that now throughout North America people were openly campaigning for the legalization of marijuana, they could only conclude that America was falling under the influence of Satan.[101]

There was a new urgency. People felt that true religion was being destroyed. If Christians did not fight back, there might not be another generation of believers. During the 1970s, more parents than ever before removed their children from the public schools to Christian establishments, where they could be instructed in Christian values and were given Christian role models, and where all learning was conducted within a biblical context. Between 1965 and 1983, enrollment in these evangelical schools increased six-fold, and about 100,000 fundamentalist children were taught at home.[102] The Independent Christian School movement began to mobilize. Hitherto, fundamentalist schools had been scattered and isolated, but during the 1970s they began to form associations to monitor legislation

on educational matters, create insurance packages, organize teacher place-
ment, and act as lobbying groups at the state and federal levels. These
have continued to grow. By the 1990s, the American Association of Christian Schools had 1360 member schools, while the Association of Christian
Schools International had 1930.[103] Like many of the other schools, colleges,
and educational establishments we have considered, there was a desire
for a "holistic" education, where everything—patriotism, history, morality,
politics, and economics—could be seen from a Christian perspective. Spiritual and moral training were considered to be as important as academic
achievement (though this, in general, compared well to education in the
public sector). It was a "hothouse" atmosphere to form committed and,
if need be, militant Christians prepared to fight the secularization of life
in the United States. They studied the Christian history of America, for
example, and examined the religious credentials of such figures as George
Washington and Abraham Lincoln, read only that literature and philosophy that "pretty much" agreed with the Bible, and stressed biblical "family
values."[104]

As we have seen, in order to mobilize effectively, a group needs an ideology with a clearly defined enemy. During the 1960s and 1970s, Protestant fundamentalist ideologues defined the enemy as "secular humanism."
Unlike the Islamists and the Kookists, who could decry the secular culture of
"the West," the American Protestants, who were fiercely patriotic, had no
such easy target. They had to fight "the enemy within." Over the years,
"secular humanism" became a portmanteau term into which fundamentalists
threw any value or belief that they did not like. Here, for example, is the
definition of secular humanism given by the fundamentalist "Pro-Family
Forum" (n.d.). It:

> Denies the deity of God, the inspiration of the Bible and the
>   divinity of Jesus Christ.
> Denies the existence of the soul, life after death, salvation and
>   heaven, damnation and hell.
> Denies the Biblical account of Creation.
> Believes that there are no absolutes, no right, no wrong—that
>   moral values are self-determined and situational. Do your
>   own thing, "as long as it does not harm anyone else."
> Believes in the removal of distinctive roles of male and female.
> Believes in sexual freedom between consenting individuals,
>   regardless of age, including premarital sex, homosexuality,
>   lesbianism, and incest.
> Believes in the right to abortion, euthanasia, and suicide.

Believes in the equal distribution of America's wealth to reduce
poverty and bring about equality.
Believes in control of the environment, control of energy, and
its limitation.
Believes in the removal of American patriotism, and the free-
enterprise system, disarmament, and the creation of a one-
world socialistic government.[105]

This list, which seems to have been compiled from the first and second Man-
ifestos of the American Humanist Society (1933 and 1973), an organization
of little influence, could, nevertheless, be described as a reasonably accurate
description of the liberal mind-set that evolved during the sixties.

But in the way of most ideologies, it was, of course, also a caricature and
an oversimplification of liberalism. Not all liberals who desire sexual equality or the equal distribution of wealth are atheists. Liberals who believe in
gay rights would never sanction incest. No liberal would agree that there
is "no right, no wrong"; instead they believe that there needs to be some
revision of the moral strictures of the past. A desire to achieve a coming-
together of previously hostile nation-states, in such organizations as the
European Union or the United Nations, by no means implies a desire for
"one-world socialistic government." But the list is useful in showing how
values which many liberal Christians and secularists alike would regard as
self-evidently good (such as concern for the poor or for the environment)
were regarded by fundamentalists as manifestly evil. It would appear that
there were "two nations" in the United States at this time in rather the same
way as in Iran or Israel. Modern society seemed to have become polarized in
such a way that it was increasingly difficult for people in the different camps
to understand one another. Because the subcultures were so isolated and
separatist, many may not even have realized that there *was* a problem.

But Protestant fundamentalists did not regard this definition of secular
humanism as a caricature. They saw secular humanism as a rival religion,
which had its own creed, its own objectives, and a distinctive organization.
They drew support for this belief from a footnote to the Supreme Court
judgment *Torcaso v. Watkins* (1961), which explicitly listed "secular humanism" among those world religions "which do not teach what would generally be considered a belief in the existence of God," such as Buddhism,
Taoism, and Ethical Culture.[106] Fundamentalists would use this later to
argue that the beliefs and values of the "secular humanism" practiced by the
government and the legislators should be outlawed from public life as firmly
as conservative Protestantism.

It would, however, be a mistake to regard this fundamentalist preoccupation with secular humanism as a ploy, or as an ingeniously concocted distortion designed to discredit the liberal attitude. The term "secular humanism" and all that it stands for filled fundamentalists with visceral dread. They saw it as a conspiracy of evil forces that, in the words of Tim LaHaye, one of the chief and most prolific fundamentalist ideologues, was "anti-God, anti-moral, anti-self-restraint, and anti-American." Secular humanism was run by a small cadre which controlled the government, the public schools, and the television networks, in order to "destroy Christianity and the American family."[107] There were 600 humanist senators, congressmen, and cabinet ministers, some 275,000 in the American Civil Liberties Union. The National Organization for Women, trade unions, the Carnegie, Ford, and Rockefeller foundations, and all colleges and universities were also "humanist." Fifty percent of the legislators were committed to the religion of secular humanism.[108] America, which had been founded as a Bible-based republic, had now become a secular state, a catastrophe, John Whitehead (president of the conservative Rutherford Institute) attributed to a gross misreading of the First Amendment. Jefferson's "wall of separation" was designed, Whitehead believed, to protect religion from the state, not vice versa.[109] But now the humanist judges had made the state an object of worship: "The state is seen as secular," he argued, but "the state is religious, because its 'ultimate concern' is the perpetuation of the state itself." Secular humanism, therefore, amounted to a rebellion against God's sovereignty, and its worship of the state was idolatrous.[110]

Not only had the conspiracy completely infiltrated American society, but it had also conquered the world. For the fundamentalist writer Pat Brooks, the secular humanists formed "a huge conspiratorial network" which was "fast approaching its goal of bringing in a 'new world order,' a vast world government that would reduce the world to slavery."[111] Like other fundamentalists, Brooks saw the enemy as omnipresent, and pursuing its objective relentlessly over a long period. He saw it at work in the Soviet Union, on Wall Street, in Zionism, in the International Monetary Fund, the World Bank, and the Federal Reserve System. The cabal that was masterminding this international conspiracy included the Rothschilds, the Rockefellers, Kissinger, Brzezinski, the shah, and Omar Torrijos, the former Panamanian dictator.[112] This terror of secular humanism was as irrational and as ungovernable as any of the other paranoid fantasies we have considered, and sprang from the same fear of annihilation. The Protestant fundamentalists' view of modern society in general and of America in particular was as demonic as that of any Islamist. For Franky Schaeffer, for example, the West was about to enter an electronic dark age, in which the new pagan hordes, with all the power of technology at their command, are on the verge of obliterating the last strongholds of civilized humanity. A vision of darkness lies before us. As we leave the shores of Christian western man behind, only a dark and turbulent sea of despair stretches endlessly ahead . . . unless we *fight*.[113]

Like Jewish and Muslim fundamentalists, American Protestants also felt that their backs were to the wall and that they would have to fight in order to survive.

Just as Sayyid Qutb's description of a modern *jahili* city was difficult for liberal Muslims to recognize, the vision of America that Protestant fundamentalists were evolving was radically different from that of the liberal mainstream. Fundamentalists were convinced that the United States was God's own country, but did not seem to share the values that were so prized and lauded by other Americans. When they wrote about American history, nearly all looked back nostalgically to the Puritan Pilgrim Fathers, but praised those traits in them that were least attractive to liberals. What kind of society had the Puritans tried to establish in New England? asked Rus Walton, founder of the Plymouth Rock Foundation. "*A democracy? Not on your life!* The early Americans brought no such idea to this new world," he noted approvingly.[114] Nor had the Puritans had any time for liberty; they were more interested in "right government in church and state" which would "compel other men to walk in the right way."[115] Similarly, the Revolution was not regarded as "democratic." American Protestant fundamentalists could regard democracy with as much suspicion as their Jewish and Muslim counterparts, and for the same reason. The Founding Fathers of the American Republic, according to Pat Robertson, were inspired by Calvinist, biblical ideals. This saved the American Revolution from going the same way as the French and Russian revolutions. The American revolutionaries had wanted nothing to do with mass rule; they wanted to establish a republic in which the will of the majority and all egalitarian tendencies would be controlled by biblical law.[116] The Founding Fathers certainly did not want a "pure, direct democracy in which the majority can do as it pleases."[117] They were as appalled as any Muslim fundamentalist by the idea of a government implementing its own laws: the Constitution was "not endowed with ability to create laws apart from the higher law [of God] but only to administer fundamental law as man is able to grasp and approximate it."[118]

This version of the American past is very different from that of the liberal establishment. Fundamentalist history was the creation of a counterculture determined to put the United States back onto the right path. All saw a falling-off and a decline from America's godly beginnings: the Supreme Court rulings, the social innovations, and legalization of abortion had promoted secularization in the name of "freedom." But by the end of the 1970s, fundamentalists were beginning to realize that they themselves must accept some of the blame.[119] They had retreated and isolated themselves after the Scopes trial and allowed the secular humanists to have it all their own way. Now they began to move toward a commitment to political activism. At the beginning of the 1970s, Tim LaHaye had never suggested that fundamentalists should become politically involved, but by the end of the decade, he had come to believe that the humanists would "destroy America" within a few years, "unless Christians are willing to become much more assertive in defense of morality and decency than they have been in the last three decades."[120]

One of the factors that had made fundamentalists hold aloof from politics had been their premillennialism: since the world was doomed, there was no point attempting to reform it. But even here there was a change. In 1970, Hal Lindsey published his extremely successful book *The Late Great Planet Earth,* which had sold 28 million copies by 1990. It rehashed the old premillennial ideas in racy, trendy prose. Lindsey saw no special role for America in the Last Days, and implied that Christians should content themselves with spotting "signs" of the approaching End in current events. But by the end of the 1970s, he, like Tim LaHaye, had changed his mind. In *The 1980s, Countdown to Armageddon,* he argued that, if America came to its senses, it could remain a world power right through the millennium. But

> that means that we must actively take on the responsibility of being a citizen and a member of God's family. We need to get active, electing officials who will not only reflect the Bible's morality in government, but will shape domestic and foreign policies to protect our country and our way of life.[121]

Fundamentalists were ready. They had an enemy to fight, a vision of what America should be that was very different from that of the liberal mainstream, and they now believed, despite all their fears, that they were powerful enough to succeed in their crusade.

By the late 1970s, Protestant fundamentalists in the United States had achieved a much higher profile and a greater self-confidence. This was the third reason for their mobilization in the early 1980s. They were no longer the impoverished backwoodsmen who had scuttled away from the Scopes trial. The affluence that had made the permissive society a possibility had affected them too. The new prominence of the South and the rise of fundamentalism there made many feel that it was now possible for them to challenge the establishment. They knew that membership in the liberal mainstream denominations had dropped during the 1960s, whereas the evangelical churches had increased at an average five-year rate of 8 percent.[122] Televangelism had also become more adept at packaging and marketing Christianity. It seemed to make the God who was being banished from so much of the public sphere a dramatic and tangible presence. When they watched the Pentecostalist preacher Oral Roberts apparently healing sick and disabled people on the air, they could see the divine power at work. When they heard the hugely powerful televangelist Jimmy Swaggart, who claimed to save 100,000 souls a week, hurling vitriolic abuse at Roman Catholics, homosexuals, and the Supreme Court, they felt that somebody was giving public voice to their own views. When they heard of the vast sums of money that Pat Robertson or the Bakkers could raise in their programs each week in donations, fundamentalists became convinced that God was the answer to the problems of the economy. Christians, they insisted, must give in order to get. In the Kingdom of God, according to Robertson, "there is no economic recession, no shortage."[123] It was a truth that seemed borne out by the immense success of the top ten Christian television empires, which took in over a billion dollars each year, employed over a thousand people, and turned out a highly professional product.[124]

The man of the hour, however, was Jerry Falwell. It has been estimated that during the 1960s and 1970s four out of every ten households in the United States tuned in to his station in Lynchburg, Virginia. He had begun his ministry there in 1956 with only a handful of members in a disused soda plant. Three years later, the congregation had grown to three times its original size, and by 1988 the Thomas Road Baptist Church had 18,000 members and sixty associate pastors. The total income of the church was over sixty million dollars per annum, and services were broadcast on 392 television channels and 600 radio stations.[125] A typical fundamentalist, Falwell wanted to build a separate, self-sufficient world. At Lynchburg, he created a school run on biblical lines; by 1976, Liberty Baptist College had 1500 students. Falwell also established philanthropical ventures: a home for alcoholics, a nursing home, and an adoption agency to offer an alternative to abortion. By 1976, Falwell regarded himself as the leading born-again broadcaster.

Falwell was creating an alternative society to undercut secular humanism. From the start, he wanted Liberty College to become a world-class university; it was to be what Notre Dame was to the Roman Catholics, or Brigham Young to the Mormons. Fundamentalism had changed since Bob Jones had founded his university in the 1920s. Separation from society was no longer enough. Like other fundamentalist educators, Falwell was creating a cadre for the future, "a spiritual army of young people who are pro-life, pro-moral, and pro-America."[126] Where Bob Jones had turned away from the secular world to prepare teachers for Christian schools, Falwell wanted to take on the secularist establishment. Liberty would train students for all walks of life and the major professions. They would "save" society. But that meant that they had to submit to the fundamentalist ethos: the faculty must subscribe to the articles of faith; all students had to complete a "Christian service assignment" in the parish each semester; there was to be no drinking or smoking; students must wear Sunday-best clothes at all times, and attend services at Thomas Road thrice weekly. Unlike Bob Jones, Falwell sought academic accreditation and was thus able to attract nonfundamentalist students, whose parents approved of the sobriety of the campus and its good academic standards. Falwell had charted a middle course. Liberty provided an alternative to the permissive liberal arts colleges of the sixties and seventies, on the one hand, and to the mediocre standard of some of the old Bible colleges on the other. Despite its doctrinal emphasis, the campus was open to serious debate of intellectual and social issues; this would enable students to engage with the secular world on its own terms, and initiate its *reconquista*.[127]

Falwell was planning an offensive, and was doing so in modern terms. His industrious regime in the college, church, and radio station was an attempt to reach out to a lost and dying world. There were no gimmicks and no wild antics on his station; the *Old Time Gospel Hour* eschewed the extravagances of Roberts, Swaggart, and the Bakkers. A literalist as a broadcaster as in theology, he had his services screened and recorded exactly as performed, with no concessions to the camera and its love of spectacle. Lynchburg stood for restraint, capitalism, and the Calvinist work ethic. Falwell modeled his empire on the new shopping malls, which offered a combination of services. As Elmer Towns, his chief theological adviser, explained, Falwell believed that he could win souls with similar entrepreneurial expertise. Business, Falwell judged, was at the cutting edge of innovation, and "the Thomas Road Baptist Church believed that the combined ministeries of several agencies in one church can not only attract the masses to the Gospel, but can better minister to each individual who comes."[128] During the 1960s and 1970s, Thomas Road seemed to prove the Godly viability of capitalism, adding one ministry after another, with continued growth and expansion. When secular power brokers were looking around for somebody to lead a right-wing resurgence in the 1980s, Falwell was their man. He clearly understood the dynamic of modern capitalist society and would be able to engage with it as an equal.

Yet for all Falwell's apparently hardheaded approach, the fundamentalists who responded to him were filled with fear. It was no use arguing with Fal-well, LaHaye, or Robertson in the hope of convincing them that there was no secular humanist conspiracy. This paranoid fear of annihilation and destruction, which they shared with Jewish and Muslim fundamentalists, would add urgency and conviction to their campaign. Modern society had achieved a great deal, materially and morally. It had reason to believe in its righteousness. In Europe and the United States, at least, democracy, free-dom, and toleration were liberating. But fundamentalists could not see this, not because they were perverse, but because they had experienced moder-nity as an assault that threatened their most sacred values and seemed to put their very existence in jeopardy. By the end of the 1970s, Jewish, Christian, and Muslim traditionalists were poised to fight back.

9. The Offensive
(1974–79)

THE FUNDAMENTALIST ASSAULT took many secularists by surprise. They had assumed that religion would never again be a major player in politics, but during the late 1970s there was a militant explosion of faith. In 1978–79, the world watched in astonishment as an obscure Iranian ayatollah brought down the regime of Shah Muhammad Reza Pahlavi, which had seemed to be one of the most progressive and stable states in the Middle East. At the same time as governments applauded the peace initiative of President Anwar Sadat of Egypt, his recognition of the State of Israel, and his overtures to the West, observers noted that the young Egyptians appeared to be turning to religion. They were donning Islamic dress, casting aside the freedoms of modernity, and many were engaged in an aggressive takeover of the university campuses. In the United States, Jerry Falwell founded the Moral Majority in 1979, urging Protestant fundamentalists to get involved in politics and to challenge state and federal legislation that pushed a "secular humanist" agenda.

This sudden eruption of religion seemed shocking and perverse to the secularist establishment. Instead of embracing one of the modern ideologies, which had proved so effective, these radical traditionalists quoted scripture and cited archaic laws and principles that were quite alien to twentieth-century political discourse. Their initial success seemed inexplicable; it was (surely?) impossible to run a modern state along these lines. The fundamentalists seemed engaged in an atavistic return to the past. Further, the enthusiasm and the support that these policies inspired were an affront. Those Americans and Europeans who had imagined that religion had had its day were now forced to see that not only could the old faiths still inspire a passionate allegiance, but that millions of committed Jews, Christians, and Muslims loathed the secular, liberal culture of which they were so proud.

In fact, as we have seen, the fundamentalist resurgence was neither sudden nor surprising. For decades, the more conservative religious people who felt, for different reasons, slighted, oppressed, and even persecuted by their secular governments, had been seething with resentment. Many had withdrawn from modern society to create a sacred reservation of pure faith. Convinced that they were in danger of being wiped out by regimes committed to their destruction, they felt embattled and defensive. They had evolved ideologies to mobilize the faithful in a struggle for survival. Surrounded by social forces that were either indifferent to religion or hostile to it, they had developed a siege mentality that could easily tip over into aggression. By the mid-1970s, the time was ripe. All had become aware of their strength, and were convinced that a crisis was at hand and that they were facing a unique moment in their history. All were determined to change the world before it changed them. In their view, history had taken a fatal turn; everything was awry. They now lived in societies which had either marginalized or excluded God, and they were ready to re-sacralize the world. Secularists must abandon their proud self-reliance, which made man the measure of all things, and acknowledge the sovereignty of the divine.

Secularist observers had, for the most part, been unaware of this religious reaction. The various societies had become so polarized that liberals in the United States or Westernized secularists in a country such as Iran tended to underestimate the religious counterculture that had been developing over the years. They were wrong to imagine that this aggressive piety belonged to the old world; these were modern forms of faith that were often highly innovative, ready to jettison centuries of tradition. At the same time as the fundamentalists, in all three religions, had rejected modernity, they had also been influenced by modern ideas and enthusiasms. But they had a lot to learn. These early offensives represented the glory days of the fundamentalist era, but, as we shall see in the following chapter, it is very difficult for a religiously inspired movement to retain its integrity once it has entered the plural, rational, and pragmatic world of modern politics. A revolution against tyranny could become tyrannical in its turn; a campaign to abolish the separations of modernity in order to achieve an integrated, holistic state could become totalitarian; the translation of the mythical, messianic, or mystical visions of the fundamentalists into political *logoi* was dangerous. But at first, fundamentalists felt that after decades of humiliation and oppression they carried all before them and that they would indeed reconquer the world for God.

The Iranian Revolution was the event that first drew the attention of the world to the fundamentalist potential, but it was not the first movement to make a successful venture into the world of politics. We have seen that after

the Yom Kippur War of 1973, the Kookists in Israel had been convinced that
the Jewish people were engaged in a war against the forces of evil. The war
had been a warning; redemption was under way, but if the government was
determined to promote policies that would impede the messianic process,
they themselves must take the initiative. Somewhat to their surprise, they
had found secularist allies, who did not share the vision of Rabbi Kook, but
who were equally determined to hold on to every inch of occupied territory.
People who were neither Kookists nor observant Jews, such as the army
chief of staff, Rafael Eitan, or the nuclear physicist and ultranationalist
Yuval Ne'eman, were willing to work with the religious Zionists to secure
the occupied territories for Israel. In February 1974, a group of rabbis,
hawkish young secularists, Kookists and other religious Zionists who had
served in the IDF and fought in Israel's wars formed a group which they
called Gush Emunim, the "Bloc of the Faithful."

Shortly afterward, they put together a position paper outlining their
objectives. The Gush would not be a political party, competing for seats in
the Knesset, but a pressure group, working to bring about "a great awakening of the Jewish people towards full implementation of the Zionist vision,
realizing that this vision originates in Israel's Jewish heritage, and that its
objective is the full redemption of Israel and the entire world."[1] Where the
early Zionists had cast religion aside, the Gush insisted on rooting their
movement in Judaism. Where secular members of the Gush could interpret
the word "redemption" in a looser, more political sense, the religious
activists who had adopted Rabbi Kook's holistic vision were convinced that
messianic redemption had already begun, and that unless the Jewish people
were settled in the whole of Eretz Israel there would be no peace for the rest
of the world.

From the start, Gush Emunim posed a challenge to secular Israel. The
position paper emphasized the failure of the old Zionism. Even though Jews
were engaged in a fierce struggle for survival in their land,

> we are witnessing a process of decline and retreat from the
> realization of the Zionist ideal, in word and deed. Four related
> factors are responsible for this crisis: mental weariness and
> frustration induced by the extended conflict; the lack of chal-
> lenge; preference for selfish goals; the attenuation of Jewish
> faith.[2]

It was the last cause—the weakening of religion—which, in the view of the
religious members of the Gush, was crucial. Divorced from Judaism, Zionism, they believed, could make no sense. At the same time as the Kookists

sought to conquer the occupied territories from the Arabs, they were also engaged in a war against secular Israel. They were determined to replace the old socialist and nationalist discourse with the language of the Bible. Where Labor Zionists had sought to normalize Jewish life and make Jews "like all the other nations," the Gush Emunim emphasized the "uniqueness" of the people of Israel;[3] because Jews had been chosen by God, they were essentially different from all other nations and were not bound by the same rules. The Bible made it clear that as a "holy" people, Israel was set apart, in a category of its own.[4] Where Labor Zionism had tried to incorporate the liberal humanism of the modern West, Gush Emunim believed that Judaism and Western culture were antithetical. There was, therefore, for Kookists, no way that secular Zionism could ever have worked.[5] Their task was to reclaim Zionism for religion, correct the mistakes of the past, and make history right again.

The near-disaster of the Yom Kippur War had shown that it was essential to act immediately in order to hasten the redemptive process, which the policies of the "false" secular Zionism had retarded. It would take over a year for the Gush Emunim to develop fully, but eventually it provided its members with a total way of life. There would be a Gush style of dress, music, decor, books, and choice of children's names, and even a particular style of speech.[6] Over the years, the Gush created a counterculture that enabled members to withdraw, in time-honored fundamentalist style, from secular Israel. There was a certain aggression, however, in the way religious members of the Gush flaunted their piety and Torah observance. In the early years of the state, secular Israelis had ridiculed Jews who wore traditional skullcaps; now these pious activists sported the knitted *kipa*, which became an item of radical religious chic.[7] The cadres of the Gush saw themselves as more authentically Jewish and Zionist than the Laborites, linking themselves not only with such holy warriors of ancient times as Joshua, David, and the Maccabees, but also with such Zionist heroes as Theodor Herzl, Ben-Gurion, and the early pioneers, who were also possessed by a mystical vision of sorts, and had sometimes been regarded as madmen in their own day.

While the secular and religious members of the Gush had been occupied in the establishment of their organization, a group of Kookists, with the help of the veteran settler Moshe Levinger, attempted to create a *garin* (a "seed," or nucleus, for a small settlement) in a railway depot near the Arab town of Nablus on the West Bank. This was a sacred area for Jews: Nablus occupied the site of the biblical city of Shechem, associated with Jacob and Joshua. The settlers were attempting to re-sacralize land which, in their view, was profaned by the Palestinians. They called their settlement Elon Moreh, one of the city's other biblical names, and tried to turn their railway depot into a *yeshiva* for the study of sacred texts. They also agreed to join Gush Emunim. The government tried to dislodge the settlers, since the *garin* was illegal, but the Gush felt no need to comply with the declarations of the United Nations that demanded Israel's withdrawal from the occupied territories, since Jews were not bound by the laws of other peoples. The settlers won considerable support in Israel, while the government seemed feeble and hesitant. In April 1975, Moshe Levinger led a march of twenty thousand Jews into the West Bank. From his tent in Elon Moreh, which he called his "war situation room," he negotiated with Israeli defense minister Shimon Peres. There was a battle with soldiers of the IDF: no shots were fired, but rocks were hurled and rifle butts used. Eventually, Peres was flown in by helicopter, confronted Levinger in his tent, and after the meeting, the rabbi stormed out, tearing his white shirt in the traditional sign of mourning. As elections were looming and Peres feared to lose the religious vote, he finally caved in and in December 1975, he agreed to accommodate thirty of the Elon Moreh settlers in a nearby army camp. Levinger was carried in a triumphal procession on the shoulders of cheering youths.[8] A thin, balding man, with a straggling beard, thick glasses, and a gun perpetually slung over his shoulder, Levinger had become a new kind of Jewish hero. For some, the Settler was beginning to rank alongside the Zaddik, the Torah scholar, and the Hasid. He also won the support of secularists. "Levinger symbolizes the return of Zionism," maintained the veteran and self-confessed terrorist Geula Cohen. "He is standing like a candle in Judea and Samaria [the Biblical names for the West Bank]. He is the leader of the Zionist revolution."[9]

Elon Moreh, now renamed Kedamim, was finally established during the season of Hanukkah, the festival that celebrates the liberation of Jerusalem by the Maccabees from the Seleucids in 164 BCE and the rededication of the Temple. In the mythology of Gush Emunim, the *garin* became a new Hanukkah, a divine breakthrough, and a victory for God. It was a formative moment: the tide seemed to have turned; secular Zionism had been forced to submit to the divine will. Levinger had put history back on track.

The years 1974–77 marked the golden age of the Gush. Members toured the country, giving lectures and recruiting young men and women, secularists as well as religious, who were prepared to settle in the territories. Gush branches opened all over the country. The cadre formed a master plan for the settlement of the whole of the West Bank: the aim was to import hundreds of thousands of Jews into the area and to colonize all the strategic mountain strongholds. Experts on the geography of the region, on demography, and on settlement were consulted. Administrative bodies were established for planning and propaganda. One of these was Mate Mirtzai, which organized settlement operations.[10] Squatters, often led by Levinger, would drive their old, battered trailers to a desolate West Bank hilltop in the dead of night. When the army arrived to expel them, the right-wing parties in the Knesset accused the Labor government of behaving exactly the same way as the British in pre-state days. It was a clever stratagem. The Israeli government was now cast in the role of oppressor, and it was the Gush settlers who seemed to embody Israel's heroic past.

The Gush managed to establish only three settlements during these years, however. Prime Minister Yitzhak Rabin was anxious to conciliate Egypt and Syria during this postwar period, and was ready to make small territorial concessions. He continued to resist the combined pressure of the Gush and the Right. But the Gush continued its propaganda efforts, organizing huge rallies and hikes across the West Bank. In 1975, crowds carried Torah scrolls through the occupied territories, singing, dancing, and clapping, secularists joining the religious Zionists. On Independence Day 1976, nearly twenty thousand armed Jews attended a West Bank "picnic," marching from one part of Samaria to another.[11] These militant hikes and demonstrations were often timed to coincide with the establishment of a new settlement or with another illegal squat. All these actions encouraged some Israelis to see the territories as essentially Jewish, and helped to break down the taboo against settling in occupied land.

Gush was pragmatic, clever, and resourceful. It appealed to atheists and secularists, but for its Orthodox members it was an essentially religious movement. From the Rabbis Kook, they had inherited a kabbalistic piety. Establishing a settlement in what the Gush believed to be Jewish land was to extend the realm of the sacred and to push back the frontiers of the "Other Side." A settlement was what Christians would call a sacrament, an outward symbol of hidden grace that made the divine present in the profane world in a new and more effective way. It was what Isaac Luria had called *tikkun,* an act of restoration that would one day transform the world and the cosmos. The hikes, marches, battles with the army, and illegal squats were a form of ritual that brought a sense of ecstasy and release. After years of feeling inferior to both the secular pioneers and the scholarly Haredim, Kookists suddenly felt that they were at the center of things and on the front line of a cosmic war. By hastening the advent of Redemption, they felt at one with the fundamental rhythms of the universe. Observers noted that when they prayed, they swayed backward and forward, with their eyes tightly shut, their faces contorted and pained, and wailed aloud. These were all signs of what the Kabbalists called *kawwanah,* an effort of intensive concentration during the performance of one of the commandments that enables the Jew to see through its symbolic form to the essential significance of the rite.[12] An act performed with *kawwanah* not only brings the worshipper closer to God but helps to rectify the imbalance that separates the mundane world from the divine. Gush activists not only experienced this ecstasy when they prayed; they saw their political activities in the same light. The spectacle of Rabbi Kook preaching and weeping before a huge crowd at the inauguration of a new settlement was a "revelation." So was the occasion when squatters wrapped themselves, screaming, in their prayer shawls, clinging with bleeding fingers to the sacred land, while the army pried them away from a hill near Ramallah.[13] These were not simply political moments. Activists believed that they had looked through the earthly shell of these events to the divine drama at the core of reality.

Politics had thus become an act of worship *(avodah)*. Before a Jew attends a synagogue service, he bathes in the *mikveh,* a ritual bath. In the same way, Gush rabbis have declared: "Before we sink into the gutter of politics, we should purify ourselves in the *mikveh,* as it is like delving into the secrets of the Torah."[14] This is a revealing remark, because it shows the dualism at the heart of Gush piety. Politics is as holy as the Torah, but—as Kook the Elder had pointed out so long ago—it is also a gutter. Since 1967, Kookists had often experienced the shock of historical events as a "burst of light," a favorite image of Kook the Elder, but they were also acutely aware of the darkness of political failure, setbacks, and obstacles. Israeli victories were hailed as great miracles, but they were also recognized to have been brought about by modern technology and military expertise.

Kookists, therefore, were actually strongly aware of the profane as well as the sacred. Their yearning for the divine was balanced by an experience of the opacity and intransigence of recalcitrant mundane reality. Hence the extremity and anguish of their prayer and activism. Their mission was to bring the whole of life—even those aspects that are most impure, banal, and perverse—under the canopy of the sacred. But where the Hasidim found joy and a new lightness in this task, the ecstasy of the Gush was often imbued with rage and resentment. They are men and women of the modern era. The divine is more distant, and it is more of a strain to transcend the pressing and insistent reality of the profane, which, as many now think, is all there is. Gush activists overcame their personal alienation in the secular State of Israel by attempting to wrest the land from the alien Arabs. They settled their own minds by uprooting themselves, going beyond the borders of Israel, and colonizing the long-lost land. The "return" to Eretz Israel was an attempt to retrieve a value and a state of mind that is more fundamental than the confusing present.

There are obvious difficulties in this spirituality of rage and *reconquista.* In 1977, for the first time in Israeli history, Labor was defeated in a general election and the new right-wing Likud party, headed by Menachem Begin, came to power. Begin had always advocated a Jewish state on both sides of the River Jordan, so his election seemed at first to be another act of God. This seemed clear shortly after the election, when Begin visited the aged Rabbi Kook at Merkaz Harav, knelt at his feet, and bowed before him. "I felt that my heart was bursting within me," Daniel Ben Simon, who was present at this "surrealistic scene," recalled later. "What greater empirical proof could there be that [Kook's] fantasies and imaginings were indeed reality."[15] Begin was an outspoken admirer of Levinger, he liked to call Gush Emunim his "very dear children," and often used biblical imagery when expounding his hawkish policies.

After the election, the Likud government began a massive settlement initiative in the occupied territories. Ariel Sharon, the new head of the Israel Lands Commission, declared his intention of settling one million Jews on the West Bank within twenty years. By the middle of 1981, Likud had spent $400 million in the territories and built twenty settlements, manned by some 18,500 settlers. By August 1984, there were about 113 official government settlements, including six sizable towns, all over the West Bank. Surrounded by 46,000 militant Jewish settlers, the Arabs became frightened and some resorted to violence.[16] This should have been the perfect political environment for the Gush Emunim, who received much government support. In 1978, Raphael Eitan made each West Bank settlement responsible for the security of its own area, and hundreds of settlers were released from their regular army units to protect their community and police the roads and fields. They were given a great deal of sophisticated arms and military equipment. In March 1979, the government established five regional councils on the West Bank with the power to levy taxes, supply services, and employ workers. Gush members usually had key roles, even though they now supplied only 20 percent of the West Bank settlers.[17] They had become in effect state officials, but their years of confrontation had made the Gush skeptical of government, however friendly, and after the Likud victory, members established Armana ("Covenant") to organize and unify their own settlement activities, and Moetzet Yesha, a council of Gush settlements, to give them some independence.

The Gush were right to be skeptical, for the honeymoon with Likud was short. On November 20, 1977, President Anwar Sadat of Egypt made his historic journey to Jerusalem to initiate a peace process and, the following year, Begin and Sadat signed the Camp David Accords. Israel would return the Sinai peninsula, conquered in 1967, to Egypt and, in return, Egypt recognized the State of Israel and guaranteed security along their common borders. The Accords looked forward to a "Framework for Peace," possible future negotiations between Israel, Egypt, Jordan, and the "representatives of the Palestinian people" about the future of the West Bank and the Gaza Strip. On both sides, Camp David was a pragmatic agreement. Egypt got important territory back, and Israel gained a measure of peace. The Sinai was not sacred land; it was not included within the borders of the Promised Land described in the Bible. Begin had always been adamant that there was no question of returning the West Bank to the Arabs; he was also confident that the Framework for Peace discussions would never happen, since no other Arab state would countenance them. On the day the Camp David treaty was signed, Begin announced that the government would establish twenty new settlements on the West Bank.

This did not appease the religious Zionists, the Gush Emunim, or the Israeli right in general. On October 8, 1979, the new Tehiya ("Renaissance") party was officially launched, with the blessing of Rabbi Kook, to fight Camp David and prevent further territorial concessions. Religious and secular radicals now worked together in the same political party. In 1981, the Kookist and former Gahelet member Haim Drukman founded his own Morasha ("Heritage") party to press for more West Bank settlement. For the Gush, Camp David was no peace. They pointed out the etymological connection between the words *shalom* ("peace") and *shlemut* ("wholeness"): true peace meant territorial integrity and the preservation of the complete land of Israel. There could be no compromise. As Gush rabbi Eleazar Waldman explained, Israel was engaged in a battle against evil, on which hung the fate of the entire world:

> The Redemption is not only the Redemption of Israel, but the Redemption of the whole world. But the Redemption of the world *depends* upon the Redemption of Israel. From this derives our moral, spiritual, and cultural influence over the entire world. The blessing will come to all of humanity from the people of Israel living in the whole of its land.[18]

But it appeared to be impossible to implement this mythical imperative in a world run along pragmatic, secular lines. However hawkish or biblical Begin's rhetoric, he had no intention of letting *mythos* interfere with the practical *logos* of politics. From the very beginning, efficiency and effectiveness had been the watchwords of the modern spirit. Absolute principles had to be accommodated to practical political considerations and policies. Begin had to remain in good odor with the United States, which wanted the peace process.

This would always be one of the main problems for fundamentalists who tried to battle for God in the modern political world. Gush Emunim did make some gains during these years. In 1978, a French graduate of the Sorbonne and Merkaz Harav, Shlomo Aviner, set up the Ateret Cohanim ("Crown of Priests") *yeshiva* in the Muslim quarter of East Jerusalem. The *yeshiva* overlooked the Temple Mount, now occupied by the Dome of the Rock, the third-holiest place in the Islamic world, and the *yeshiva*'s purpose was the study of texts relating to the priestly cult and sacrifices in the biblical Temple, in preparation for the coming of the Messiah and the rebuilding of the Temple on its ancient site. Since a new Jewish Temple would mean the destruction of the Muslim shrine, the founding of the *yeshiva* was itself provocative, but Ateret Cohanim also initiated a settlement project in the Old City of Jerusalem, which Israel had annexed, in defiance of the international community, in 1967. The *yeshiva* began secretly to purchase Arab property in the Muslim quarter and to reconstruct old synagogues there in order to establish a strong Jewish presence in Arab Jerusalem.[19] The second gain made during these years occurred in 1979, when Gush Emunim challenged a ruling of the Israeli Supreme Court that ordered their new settlement of Elon Moreh, southeast of Nablus, to be dismantled. Gush Emunim threatened civil war and a hunger strike, and eventually, at the end of January 1980, the cabinet set up a special committee to find means of safeguarding existing settlements and to create new opportunities within the constraints imposed by the Supreme Court. On May 15, the government announced a five-year plan to establish fifty-nine new settlements in the West Bank.[20]

But despite these isolated successes, Gush Emunim's glory days were over. The new peace was popular with the Israeli public and in 1982, the Gush suffered a serious defeat. To comply with the Camp David Accords, Israel had evacuated the settlement of Yamit, a thriving secular town built by the Labor government on the shores of the Sinai. Moshe Levinger declared that Zionism had been infected by the "virus of peace."[21] He led thousands of West Bank settlers back to Yamit, where they camped in the abandoned houses, daring the IDF to force them out. It was a desperate step. Levinger reminded the settlers of the Jewish wars against Rome (66–72 CE), during which 960 men, women, and children had committed suicide in the fortress of Masada rather than submit to the Roman army. The Gush rabbis consulted Israel's two chief rabbis, who ruled against martyrdom, however, and once again Rabbi Levinger tore his garments in mourning.[22] When the IDF arrived to remove the settlers, no Jewish blood was spilled but the Gush had been ready for a showdown and, for a moment, religious and secular Israel had seemed to stand on opposite sides of a battlefield.

The last stand at Yamit may have been an unconscious stratagem to deny a terrible truth. The Great Awakening that the Kookists had so confidently expected had not taken place; maybe Redemption was not, after all, imminent? How could a state which made such craven territorial concessions be holy? The religious members of the Gush were experiencing "the great disappointment" of a messianic hope, which could lead to more desperate measures. Despite their best endeavors, the Gush could not make God's politics *work* in the real world. Shortly before the withdrawal from Sinai, Rabbi Kook died, which increased this sense of abandonment. No single figure emerged as Kook's undisputed successor, and the movement split. Some advocated patience, prayer, and a new focus on education to revive the true spirit of Israel. Others were ready for violence.

BEGIN WAS NOT ALONE in encountering religious opposition to Camp David. Anwar Sadat, his Egyptian opposite number, had met with the Muslim opposition in that country. Sadat's peace initiative made him beloved and admired in the West, but, even though the peace was popular with many sectors of society, Egyptians felt more ambivalent about their president. Despite the catastrophe of the Six Day War, Nasser had been greatly loved by most of the people. Sadat never inspired the same affection. He had always been regarded as a lightweight politically, and on first coming to power in 1971, he had had to defeat an attempted palace coup against him. The comparative success of the Yom Kippur War of 1973 did much to establish Sadat's legitimacy, however.[23] Having proved himself on the battlefield and restored Arab confidence, he was able to take his people into the peace process, which, he believed, would help Egypt and repair relations with the West.

After the 1967 defeat, Nasser had retreated somewhat from socialism and had initiated a rapprochement with the United States. He had also acknowledged the new religious mood in the Middle East, and, though the Muslim Brothers remained in prison, Nasser began to lard his speeches with Islamic references once again. These two tendencies became more marked under Sadat. In 1972, he dismissed the 1500 Soviet advisers installed by Nasser, and, after the Yom Kippur War, announced a new policy designed to bring Egypt into the capitalist world market. He called this new economic initiative *infitah* ("Open Door").[24] Sadat, however, was no economist and Egypt's financial problems, always an Achilles' heel, were exacerbated by *infitah*. It certainly opened Egypt up: foreign currency and foreign imports poured into the country. Western investors were wooed by advantageous tax deals, and Egypt did become closer to the United States. Open Door also benefited a small percentage of the rising bourgeoisie, and a few Egyptians made a great deal of money. But the vast majority suffered. Inevitably, Egyptian businesses could not cope with this foreign competition; there was corruption, and the ostentatious consumerism of the elite aroused intense disgust and discontent. The young especially felt alienated. Only about 4 percent of them could expect a decent job; the rest had to survive on very meager public-sector salaries, which they were forced to supplement by moonlighting in their spare time, working—often ineptly—as taxi drivers, plumbers, and electricians. Decent accommodation was prohibitively expensive, and this meant that a young couple often had to wait for years before they could marry and set up house together. Their only hope was emigration. Hundreds of thousands of Egyptians were forced to leave home for long periods to find work in the wealthy oil states, where they could earn a good salary, send money to their families, and save for the future. Peasants also joined this exodus to the Gulf, returning only when they had enough money to build a house or buy a tractor.[25] *Infitah* endeared Sadat to the West, but it meant that most Egyptians simply could not afford to live in their own country, and were forced into exile.

As American business and culture took root, Egypt began to seem alien and Westernized to many Egyptians. Sadat was also becoming estranged from many of his people. He and his wife, Jihan, had a glitzy Western lifestyle, were frequently seen entertaining foreign celebrities and film stars, were known to drink alcohol, and lived in luxury in their numerous magnificent rest-houses, refurbished at the cost of millions of dollars, isolated from the hardship endured by most of the population. This accorded ill with Sadat's carefully cultivated religious image. In the Sunni tradition, a good Muslim ruler is commanded not to separate himself from the people, but to live simply and frugally, and to ensure that the wealth of society is distributed as fairly as possible.[26] By calling himself "the Pious President" in an attempt to align himself with the new religious mood in the country, and by encouraging the press to photograph him in the mosques, with a prominent "ash mark" on his forehead to show that he prostrated himself five times daily in prayer, Sadat inevitably invited Muslims to make unflattering comparisons between his own actual behavior and the ideal.

Yet, on the surface, Sadat was good to religion. He needed to create an identity for his regime that was different from Nasser's. Since the time of Muhammad Ali, Egyptians had repeatedly tried to enter the modern world and find their own niche there. They had imitated the West, adopted Western policies and ideologies, fought for independence, and tried to reform their culture along modern European lines. None of these attempts had been successful. Like the Iranians, many Egyptians felt that it was time to "return to themselves" and create a modern but distinctively Islamic identity. Sadat was happy to capitalize upon this. He was attempting to make Islam a civil religion on the Western model, firmly subservient to the state. Where Nasser had persecuted Islamist groups, Sadat appeared to be their liberator. Between 1971 and 1975, he gradually released the Muslim Brothers who had been languishing in the prisons and camps. He relaxed Nasser's strict laws controlling religious groups, and allowed them to meet, preach, and publish. The Muslim Brotherhood was not allowed to reestablish itself as a fully functioning political society, but the Brothers could preach and establish their own journal, *al-Dawah* ("The Call"). There was much mosque-building and more air time was given over to Islam. Sadat also courted Islamic student groups, encouraging them to wrest control of the campuses from the socialists and Nasserites. Nasser had tried to suppress religion and found that this coercive policy was counterproductive. It had led to the rise of the more extreme religiosity promoted by Sayyid Qutb. Now Sadat was attempting to co-opt religion and use it for his own ends. This would also prove to be a tragic miscalculation.

At first, however, Sadat's policy seemed a success. The Muslim Brotherhood, for example, appeared to have learned its lesson. The older generation of leaders released from the jails seemed determined to disown Sayyid Qutb and the Secret Apparatus, and wished to return to the nonviolent, reforming policies of Hasan al-Banna. The Brothers wanted a state ruled by Muslim law, but saw this as a long-term goal which could only be achieved by peaceful and legal methods.[27] Yet even though the Brotherhood claimed to be returning to the pristine spirit of the Society, it was now in fact a very different organization. Where Banna had appealed especially to the working and middle classes, in the 1970s what scholars sometimes call the "Neo-Brotherhood" attracted those members of the bourgeoisie who had profited from Sadat's Open Door. They were prosperous, comfortable, and ready to cooperate with the regime. This new Brotherhood would not appeal to the majority, who felt increasingly alienated from Sadat's Egypt and endured a wearisome deprivation. In the absence of any other permitted form of opposition to the regime, many of the most discontented would seek a more extreme Islamic alternative.[28]

But soon Sadat's policies even antagonized the Neo-Brotherhood. Each month, its journal, *al-Dawah*, which had a circulation of about 78,000, published news about the four "enemies" of Islam: Western Christianity (habitually called *al-Salibiyyah*, the Crusade, to highlight its perceived imperialism), communism, secularism (typified by Atatürk), and Zionism. "Jewry" in particular was regarded as the ultimate abomination, linked inextricably with the other three enemies. Articles in *al-Dawah* quoted passages in the Koran that speak of those Jews who rebelled against the Prophet in

Medina, and ignored those other verses that speak positively of the Jewish faith.[29] The anti-Semitism of *al-Dawah* claimed to go back to the Prophet, but was in fact a recent Islamic innovation, which relied heavily on *The Protocols of the Elders of Zion* rather than on Islamic sources. It was, therefore, impossible for the Neo-Brotherhood to remain loyal to Sadat after Camp David. Throughout 1978, *al-Dawah* called the Islamic legitimacy of the regime into question. The cover of the issue for May 1981 depicted the Dome of the Rock ringed with a chain, and locked with a padlock displaying the Star of David.[30]

But at the time of Sadat's historic visit to Jerusalem a more extreme Muslim sect had come to light. Its leaders were standing trial for the murder of Muhammad al-Dhahabi, a distinguished religious scholar and former government minister. Egyptians were shocked to hear these young Muslims declare that Islam had been in decline since the era of the first four "rightly guided" *(rashidun)* caliphs, that all Islamic developments since that time were nothing but idolatry, and that the whole of Egypt, including the president and the religious establishment, belonged to the *jahiliyyah*. The sect declared that this *jahili* society must be destroyed and a truly Muslim society based on the Koran and the Sunnah built on its ruins. God had chosen Shukri Mustafa, the founder of the sect, to create a new law and to put Muslim history back on the straight path.[31]

Shukri had been arrested and imprisoned by Nasser's regime in 1965, when he was twenty-three years old, for distributing the leaflets of the Society of Muslim Brothers.[32] For this paltry offense, he had spent six years in Nasser's camps, reading Mawdudi and Qutb, and, like many of the younger Brothers, he was drawn to their ideas. In the prisons, these more extreme Muslims practiced the strict segregation demanded by Qutb. They withdrew from the other inmates and the older, more moderate Brothers, declaring that they were *jahili*. Some, however, decided to keep their views secret. Qutb had believed that it would be a long time before his vanguard were ready to begin a *jihad* against *jahili* society. First they must go through the first three stages of the Muhammadan program, and prepare themselves spiritually. Some of the young extremists in the prisons, therefore, agreed that they were currently in a state of "weakness" and in no position to challenge the evil regime. For the time being they would continue to live a normal life in the *jahiliyyah* until the time was ripe. Shukri, however, belonged to the more ardent group which advocated "total separation" *(mufsalah kamilah)*: anybody who did not join their sect was an infidel and true believers could have nothing to do with him. They would refuse to speak to their fellow prisoners, and there were frequent fistfights.[33]

When Shukri was released from the Abu Zabal camp on October 16, 1971, he founded a new group which he called the Society of Muslims. Members were convinced that they were Qutb's vanguard and dedicated themselves to fulfilling his program. Accordingly, they withdrew from mainstream society to prepare for the *jihad*. Since the whole of Egyptian society was corrupt, they refused to worship in the mosques and pronounced the edict of excommunication *(takfir)* upon the religious and secularist establishment alike. Some migrated to the deserts and mountain caves around Asyut, Shukri's hometown. Most lived in furnished rooms in the poorest and most deprived neighborhoods on the outskirts of the large cities, where they tried to live a truly Islamic life. By 1976, the Society of Muslims had about two thousand members, men and women, who were convinced that God had chosen them to build a pure *ummah* on the ruins of the present *jahiliyyah*. They were in God's hands. Now that they had taken the initiative, God would do the rest. The police kept a watchful eye on the Society, but dismissed them as harmless cranks and dropouts.[34] But if Sadat and his advisers had bothered to look at the lives of these young, desperate fundamentalists, they might have seen that these Muslim communes were a reverse image of the Open Door policy and reflected the shadow side of modern Egypt.

Shukri's excommunication of the whole of Egyptian society may have been extreme, but it was not wholly without foundation. However many mosques were built in Sadat's Egypt, there was nothing Islamic about a nation in which wealth was commandeered by a small elite while the majority languished in hopeless poverty. The *hijrah* or "migration" which members of the Society made to the most desperate neighborhoods of the cities also demonstrated the plight of so many young Egyptians, who felt that there was no place for them in Egypt, that they had been pushed out of their own country. The Society's communes were maintained by young men whom Shukri sent to the Gulf states, like so many other Egyptian youths. Many members of the Society had received a university education, but Shukri declared that all secular learning was a waste of time; all a Muslim needed was the Koran. This was another extreme position, but there was a grain of truth in it. The education that many Egyptians were receiving during the 1970s was entirely useless to them. Not only were the teaching and methods of study grossly inadequate, but a university degree did not even ensure that a graduate would get a decent job: a lady's maid in a foreign household was likely to earn more than an assistant university professor.[35]

As long as the Society kept a low profile, the regime left them alone. But in 1977 Shukri broke his cover. In November 1976, rival Islamic groups had enticed some members of the Society away and, in Shukri's eyes, these defectors had become apostates worthy of death. His disciples launched a series of raids against them and, as a result, fourteen members of the Society were arrested for attempted homicide. Shukri immediately went on the offensive. For the first six months of 1977, he campaigned for the release of his colleagues, sending articles to the newspapers and trying to broadcast on radio and television. When these peaceful methods failed, Shukri resorted to violence. On July 7, he kidnapped Muhammad al-Dhahabi, who had written a pamphlet denouncing the Society as heretical. The day after the kidnapping, Shukri published a communiqué in three Egyptian newspapers, as well as in several other Muslim countries, New York, Paris, and London. He demanded the immediate release of his disciples, insisted on a public apology for the negative press the Society had received in the media, and requested the setting up of a committee to investigate the legal system and intelligence services of the regime. There was no chance that Sadat would permit any discussion of the methods of his secret police: Shukri clearly did not understand the nature of the state that he had defied. When Dhahabi's body was discovered a few days later, Shukri and hundreds of his disciples were arrested. After a swift trial, Shukri himself and five of the leading members of the Society were executed. The press called the sect Takfir wal Hijrah ("Excommunication and Migration"), because of its rejectionist and condemnatory ideology.[36] Like so much fundamentalist theology, it sprang from the experience of rage and marginalization, but Shukri's story reminds us that it is not always accurate to condemn such a movement as merely lunatic. Unbalanced and tragically mistaken as he was, Shukri had created a counterculture that mirrored the darker side of Sadat's new Egypt, which was being hailed with such enthusiasm in the West. It revealed in a distorted, exaggerated form what was really going on, and expressed the alienation experienced by so many young Egyptians in a country which they no longer felt to be their own.

Just as revealing, but more successful and enduring, were the *jamaat al-islamiyyah,* the Islamist student associations which dominated the university campuses during the presidency of Sadat. Like Shukri's Society, the *jamaat* saw themselves as Qutb's vanguard; however, they did not practice a radical withdrawal from the mainstream, but tried to create an Islamic space for themselves in a society that seemed oblivious to their needs. Egyptian universities were not like Oxford, Harvard, or the Sorbonne. They were huge, heartless, mass institutions with lamentably poor facilities. Between 1970 and 1977, the number of students rose from about 200,000 to half a million. As a result, there was appalling overcrowding. Two or three students would have to share a seat, and the lecture halls and laboratories were so packed that it was virtually impossible to hear the teacher's voice, especially since the microphones were often broken. The overcrowding was especially difficult for women students, many of whom had come from a traditional background and found it intolerable to be crammed up against young men on the benches or in the buses that conveyed the students back to their equally crowded halls of residence. Learning was by rote and success in the examinations required the mechanical regurgitation of the lecture notes and manuals issued by the professors. The humanities, law, and the social sciences were known as "garbage faculties," and virtually written off. Whatever their personal inclinations, able students would be forced to study medicine, pharmacology, odontology, engineering, or economics, or else resign themselves to being taught by the worst professors and to having even less chance of a reasonable job after graduation. In this setting, the students were not trained to think creatively about the problems of humanity or of society. Instead, they were required to absorb information passively and soullessly. Their introduction to modern culture was chronically superficial, therefore, and left their religious beliefs and practices entirely untouched.[37]

The *jamaat* produced few books or pamphlets, but an article written for *al-Dawah* in 1980 by Isam al-Din al-Aryan sums up their main ideas. Sayyid Qutb was clearly an inspiration; the *jamaat* believed that it was time for Egyptians to shake off the Western and Soviet ideologies that had dominated the country for so long, and return to Islam. Egypt was still in effect controlled by infidels, and there could be no true independence unless there was a great religious awakening.[38] The *jamaat* did not confine themselves to the discussion of ideas, but applied the Islamic ideology creatively and practically to their own circumstances. In 1973, the students began to set up summer camps in the major universities.[39] They studied the Koran, prayed together at night, and listened to sermons about the Golden Age of Islam, the career of the Prophet, and the four *rashidun*. By day, there were sporting activities and classes in self-defense. For a few weeks, the students lived, thought, and played in a wholly Islamic setting. It was, in a sense, a temporary *hijrah*, a migration from mainstream society to a world where they could live out the Koran and experience for themselves its impact on their lives. They learned what it was like to live in an environment which really did endorse the teachings of scripture. The camps gave them a taste of an Islamic utopia, in marked contrast to the inauthentically Muslim life of the regime. Preachers and speakers discussed the bitter disappointment of the modern experiment, which may have worked beautifully in Europe or America, but which only worked to the advantage of the rich in Egypt.

When they returned to university life, students tried to reproduce some of this experience on campus. They set up a minibus service for women students, to spare them the harassment they frequently suffered on public transport. They insisted on the segregation of the sexes in separate rows in the lecture halls for the same reason, and also advocated the wearing of Islamic dress for both men and women. The long, concealing robes were more practical in a traditional society, which did not look kindly upon Western-style dating, and where (since marriage, for economic reasons, was not an option) sexual frustration was a major problem for Egyptian youth. The *jamaat* also organized revision sessions in the mosques, where students could study quietly in a way that was impossible in the noisy, overcrowded halls of residence. These policies were effective. A student might wear traditional dress or join a segregated row in a lecture hall simply to avoid embarrassment, in the first instance, but at the same time she would become aware that the regime was less concerned for her well-being than the cadre of *jamaat*. By leaving his turbulent dormitory to study in a mosque, a student had made a small, symbolic *hijrah,* and learned that an Islamic setting worked far better for him.[40] Many of the students had come from rural backgrounds and a traditional, premodern society. Not only did they experience modernity in the university as alien, impersonal, and bewildering, but they were given no other intellectual tools to enable them to criticize the regime in the course of their mediocre education. Many would find that in this world, only Islam made sense.

Western observers were particularly dismayed by the spectacle of women returning to the veil, which they had seen as a symbol of Islamic backwardness and patriarchy since the days of Lord Cromer. But it was not experienced in this way by those Muslim women who voluntarily assumed Islamic dress for practical reasons and also as a way of casting off an alien Western identity. Donning a veil, a scarf, and a long dress could be a symbol of that "return to the self" which Islamists were attempting with such difficulty in the postcolonial period. There is, after all, nothing sacred about Western dress *per se.* The desire to see all women wearing it has been construed by Islamists as a sign of that tendency to regard "the West" as the norm to which "the rest" are obliged to conform. The veiled woman has, over the years, become a symbol of Islamic self-assertion and a rejection of Western cultural hegemony. Opting for concealment, she defies the sexual mores of the West, with its strange compulsion to "reveal all." Where Western men and women attempt to bring the body under the control of the human will in their gyms and workouts, and cling to this life by making their bodies impervious to the process of time and ageing, the veiled Islamic body tacitly declares that it is under divine orders and oriented not toward this world but to transcendence. In the West, men and women often display and even flaunt their expensively acquired tans and finely honed bodies as a mark of privilege; Muslim bodies, concealed under layers of very similar clothing, emphasize the equality of the Islamic vision. By the same token, they assert the Koranic ideal of community over the individualism of Western modernity. In rather the same way as Shukri Mustafa's communes, the veiled Islamic woman is a tacit critique of the darker side of the modern spirit.[41]

A woman who decided to wear Islamic dress had not necessarily reverted to the old female submission of premodernity. A survey conducted in Egypt in 1982 showed that while veiled women were generally more conservative than those who preferred Western clothes, a remarkably high proportion of the Islamists held progressive views on gender issues. Eighty-eight percent of veiled women believed that women's education was important (as opposed to 93 percent of the unveiled); 88 percent of the veiled women thought it acceptable for women to work outside the home, and 77 percent of them intended to work after graduation (compared with 95 and 85 percent respectively of the unveiled). The gap was larger in other areas, but a majority of veiled women (53 percent) still believed that men and women should have the same political rights and duties, and that women should be able to occupy the highest positions in the state (63 percent). Only 38 percent of the veiled women thought that men and women should be equal in marriage, but only 66 percent of the unveiled women believed in marital equality. It is also interesting that a majority of both veiled (67 percent) and unveiled (52.7 percent) believed that the Shariah should be the law of the land.[42]

It is true that, like all premodern law, the Shariah reduces women to a secondary, inferior position. But, as Leila Ahmed points out in *Women and Gender in Islam,* these women were attempting to return, like so many Muslim reformers of the past, to the "true Islam" of the Koran and the Sunnah, rather than to the medieval *fiqh* of al-Azhar. They believed that "true Islam" preached equality and justice to all, women included. But Ahmed agrees that they could be vulnerable to cooption by the patriarchal establishment, and notes that when an Islamic regime comes to power, this has generally led to a deterioration in the status of women.[43] When things are not going well, it is easy to quell incipient discontent by giving males more control over their women. Nevertheless, it remains true that Islamic dress does not always indicate a submissive female heart. The Turkish scholar Nilufar Göle argues that veiled women are often militant, outspoken, and well-educated.[44] Many veiled women took an active and sometimes a heroic role in the new fundamentalist offensive.

Ahmed also points out that in Egypt, Islamic dress is not a return to the past. There was nothing traditional about the clothes that many women preferred in the 1970s and 1980s. It was a new fashion, resembling Western styles (apart from the long sleeves and skirts) rather than the garb worn by their grandmothers. Indeed, it could be seen as a "halfway house" and as the uniform of transition to modern society. More and more women than ever before had started to receive a higher education during these years. A

large number of the women who opted for Islamic dress in the universi-
ies were among the first members of their family to have advanced beyond
basic literacy; they often came from a rural background. Their dress was,
therefore, a "modern" version of the clothes worn by the women in their
family. When they encountered the alarming modernity of the big city—
its cosmopolitanism, aggressive consumerism, inequalities, violence, and
overcrowding—they could easily have been overcome. Their dress proclaimed their upward mobility, but it also provided some continuity with
what they had worn before. An Islamic identity and the community that
went with it enabled them to make what could have been a traumatic rite of
passage more easily and peacefully. We have seen that in the past, religion
has helped people to cross over from a conventional to a more modern
lifestyle and ideology. Islamic dress, for both men and women, could be
another of these stratagems.[45]

All transitions are painful, however. The Islamic *jamaat* on the campuses
during the late 1970s was a youth movement which helped young men and
women to articulate their frustration and confusion. It often spilled over into
violence. The *jamaat* were the least aggressive of the Egyptian Islamic
movements during the 1970s, but some of the more militant leaders would
resort to strong-arm tactics on occasion to get control of the campus.
The American Arabist Patrick Gaffney made a study of the Jamaah al-
Islamiyyah at the new University of Minya in Upper Egypt, where the student body was still undeveloped and the small Islamic cadre had few rivals.
They began by establishing special places as Islamic zones: a bulletin board,
a section of the cafeteria, or the shady spots on lawns. By 1977, by dint of
bullying to deter rivals, the Islamists had gained control of the student
union. They made a mosque in the shared grounds of the Colleges of Art
and Education, where students had to congregate between classes. The
Islamists took the place over, spreading prayer mats, amplifying the prayers
over a loudspeaker, and bearded youths occupied the area at all times, studying the Koran.[46]

This aggressive encroachment into secular space can be seen as a crude
attempt to reconstruct Islam and implant it in a Westernized world. The
Islamists of Minya refused to accept the universal expansion of Western
civilization and were trying to change the map. Like the adoption of Islamic
dress, the conversion of a profane space into a mosque constituted a rebellion against a wholly secularized way of life. For almost a century, Egyptians, like other people in the developing world, had been deemed incapable
of creating history and establishing a modern society on their own terms.
Now the Islamists were making something happen, on however small a
scale. They were protesting against the centrality of the Western viewpoint,

and pushing their own out of the margins and into the limelight once more. Like the civil rights or ethnic movements, like feminism or environmentalism, the student Muslim organizations were struggling to reassert an identity, values and issues which they felt had been repressed by industrial modernity, and to emphasize the vitality of the local and particular over against the uniformity of the global society imposed by the West. Like other postmodern movements, it was an act of symbolic decolonization, an attempt to de-center the West, and demonstrate the fact that there were other possibilities for humanity. As Sadat moved ever closer to the West and made peace with Israel (which was regarded by Islamists as the alter ego of America in the Middle East), a rupture with the regime became almost inevitable. At Minya the students became more violent. They vandalized churches, attacked students who refused to wear Islamic dress, and, in February 1979, occupied the municipal government building for a week. When the police closed down one of their mosques, the students held the Friday community prayer in the middle of the street on an important bridge, holding up traffic. Next they took over University City, the student resident block, and held thirty Christian students as hostages. Two days later, a thousand troops arrived to quell the uprising.[47]

Until 1977, Sadat had supported the *jamaat al-islamiyyah*, but the events at Minya changed his mind. On April 14, 1979, he visited Upper Egypt and addressed the faculties of the Universities of Minya and Asyut: the government would no longer tolerate this abuse of religion. In June, the General Union of Egyptian Students was banned, and its assets were frozen. But the *jamaat* were too strongly entrenched to disappear. At the end of the Ramadan fast, they held huge rallies in the major cities of Egypt. In Cairo, fifty thousand Muslims gathered in prayer outside the presidential Abidin Palace, tacitly reminding Sadat that he must rule according to God's law. The distinguished Muslim Brother Yusuf al-Qaradawi was flown in from the Gulf to address the crowds. He reminded Sadat, who was currently devoting much attention to the preservation of the mummy of Ramses II:

> Egypt is Muslim, not pharaonic . . . the youth of the *jamaat islamiyyah* are the true representatives of Egypt, and not the Avenue of the Pyramids, the theatre performances, and the films. . . . Egypt is not naked women, but veiled women who adhere to the prescriptions of divine law. Egypt is young men who let their beards grow. . . . It is the land of al-Azhar![48]

Repression and coercion had their usual effect. The Islamist students now redoubled their efforts to turn the campuses into Islamic bastions; there were more attacks on cinemas, theaters, Christians, and unveiled women. They also began to spread the word outside the universities. There was now a state of open warfare against the regime and its secularized ethos. The *jamaat* were not allowed to regroup, and many of their members joined the new secret cells dedicated to a more violent *jihad*.

These events all took place against the backdrop of the Iranian Revolution. While Sadat, in his attempt to draw closer to the West, spoke proudly of the shah as his friend, Islamic militants in Egypt gloried in the reports of the Iranian revolutionaries who were bringing the shah down. The Iranian Revolution of 1978–79 was a watershed. It was an inspiration to thousands of Muslims all over the world, who had long felt that their religion was under attack. Khomeini's victory showed that Islam was not destined for destruction; it could take on powerful secularist forces and win. But the Revolution filled many in the West with horror and dismay. Barbarism seemed to have triumphed over Enlightenment. For many committed secularists, Khomeini and Iran would come to typify all that was wrong—and even evil—in religion, not least because the Revolution revealed the hatred that so many Iranians felt for the West in general and America in particular.

In the early 1970s, Iran seemed to be booming. American investors and the Iranian elite alike both made a great deal of money out of the new businesses and industries created by the White Revolution. The American embassy in Tehran, far from being a center of espionage (as the revolutionaries would claim) was more like a brokerage center to put rich Americans in touch with rich Iranians.[49] But—again—it was only the elite that benefited. The state had grown rich, but the people had grown poorer. There was rampant consumerism in the upper echelons of society, and corruption and deprivation among the petty bourgeoisie and the urban poor. After the oil price increase in 1973–74, there was tremendous inflation, owing to lack of investment opportunity for all but the very wealthy. A million people were unemployed, many of the smaller merchants had been ruined by the influx of foreign goods, and by 1977 inflation had even begun to affect the rich. In this climate of discontent and desperation, the two major guerrilla organizations became active, assassinating American military personnel and advisers. There was much resentment of the American expatriates in Iran, who seemed to be profiting from the disastrous mess. During these years too, the shah's regime became more tyrannical and autocratic than ever.[50]

Many disaffected Iranians looked to the *ulema*, who responded to the crisis in different ways. In Qum, Ayatollah Shariatmadari, the most senior *mujtahid*, opposed any political confrontation with the regime, though he was anxious to see the 1906 constitution restored. Ayatollah Taleqani, who had been jailed many times for demanding a strict application of the constitution and protesting against the excesses of the regime, worked alongside such lay reformers as Mehdi Bazargan and Abolhassan Bani Sadr, who wanted to see an Islamic republic in Iran but not clerical rule. Taleqani did not believe that the clergy should have any privileged role in government; he certainly did not agree with Khomeini's vision of Velayat-e Faqih, government by a charismatic jurist.[51] But Khomeini was still a symbol of steadfast and unbowed resistance to the regime. In June 1975, the students of the Fay-ziyyah Madrasah staged a demonstration to mark the anniversary of Khomeini's arrest there in 1963. The police invaded the building, using tear gas, and killed one of the students by throwing him off the roof. The government closed the *madrasah*, and its silent, empty courtyards remained a potent symbol of the shah's fundamental hostility to any murmur of protest and his opposition to religion.[52] Increasingly, in the popular imagination, he was identified with Yazid, the enemy of the faith, the murderer of the martyr Husain, and the enemy of Khomeini, whom the people now called their Imam.

At the beginning of 1977, however, the regime relaxed somewhat and appeared to bow to public pressure. Jimmy Carter had been elected to the presidency of the United States the previous year, and his human rights campaign, plus a damning report from Amnesty International about the state of Iran's courts and prisons, may have inclined the shah to make some concession to the prevailing discontent. There was little real change, but the censorship laws were eased and a flood of literature hit the market revealing frustration in nearly every sector of society. The students were angry about government interference in the universities; farmers protested about the agricultural imports, which had increased the poverty in the countryside; businessmen were worried about inflation and corruption; lawyers protested against the decision to downgrade the Supreme Court.[53] But there was still no call for revolution. Most of the *ulema* in Iran followed the lead of Shariat-madari and maintained the traditional quietist line. It was not the clergy but the writers of Iran who made the most eloquent protest against the government in 1977. From October 10 to 19, in the Goethe Institute in Tehran, about sixty leading Iranian poets and writers read their work to thousands of adults and students. SAVAK did not interrupt these poetry recitals, despite their outright hostility to the regime.[54] It seemed as though the government was learning to accommodate peaceful protest.

But the new era did not last long. Not long after the poetry meetings, the shah clearly felt that matters were getting out of hand. A number of known dissidents were arrested and on November 3, 1977, Khomeini's son Mustafa died mysteriously in Iraq, almost certainly at the hands of SAVAK agents.[55] Yet again, the shah had cast himself in the role of Yazid. Khomeini was already surrounded by a Shii aura and had begun to seem a little like the Hidden Imam in his exile; now, like Imam Husain, his son had been killed by a tyrannical ruler. All over Iran, the people gathered to mourn Mustafa Khomeini, weeping and beating their breasts in the traditional manner. In Tehran, the police attacked the mourners, and there were more arrests and beatings during poetry readings held in Tehran on November 15, 16, and 25. But still there was no sign of a general uprising. In Najaf, Khomeini, who used to call Mustafa the "light of his eyes," was silent.

Meanwhile, on November 13, 1977, the shah had flown to the United States for talks with President Carter. Each day, crowds of Iranian students who were attending American universities poured into Washington to shout anti-shah slogans outside the White House. At a ceremonial dinner, Carter delivered a moving address about the importance of the special relationship between Iran and the United States, calling Iran an "island of stability in a turbulent corner of the world."[56] On December 31, Carter interrupted a journey to India by making a flying visit to Tehran, where, again, he expressed his warm support for the regime. Right up to the very end, Carter continued to express his confidence in the shah. His visit to Tehran coincided with the sacred month of Muharram, when the Kerbala tragedy was uppermost in everybody's minds; this year, everybody was also thinking about Khomeini: the shah had just forbidden the traditional mourning ceremonies, which are usually held forty days after a death, for Mustafa Khomeini. When, at this crucial juncture, Carter made a special trip to endorse the shah's rule, he stepped neatly into the role of the Great Satan.

Americans were shocked to hear their nation described as satanic during and after the Revolution. Even those who were aware of the resentment that so many of the Iranian people had felt for the United States since the 1953 CIA coup, were repelled by this demonic imagery. However mistaken American policy may have been, it did not deserve to be condemned in this way. It confirmed the prevailing belief that the Iranian revolutionaries were all fanatical, hysterical, and unbalanced. But most Western people misunderstood the image of the Great Satan. In Christianity, Satan is a figure of overpowering evil, but in Islam he is a much more manageable figure. The Koran even hints that Satan will be forgiven on the Last Day,[57] such is its confidence in the all-conquering goodness of God. Those Iranians who called America "the Great Satan" were not saying that the United States was diabolically wicked but something more precise. In popular Shiism, the Shaitan, the Tempter, is a rather ludicrous creature, chronically incapable of appreciating the spiritual values of the unseen world. In one story, he is said to have complained to God about the privileges given to humans, but was easily fobbed off with inferior gifts. Instead of prophets, the Shaitan was quite happy with fortune-tellers, his mosque was the bazaar, he was most at home in the public baths, and instead of seeking God, his quest was for wine and women.[58] He was, in fact, incurably trivial, trapped forever in the realm of the exterior (ʒahir) world and unable to see that there was a deeper and more important dimension of existence. For many Iranians, America, the Great Shaitan, was "the Great Trivializer." The bars, casinos, and secularist ethos of West-toxicated North Tehran typified the American ethos, which seemed deliberately to ignore the hidden (batin) realities that alone gave life meaning. Furthermore, America, the Shaitan, had tempted the shah away from the true values of Islam to a life of superficial secularism.[59]

Iranian Shiism had always been motivated by two passions: for social justice and the Unseen (al-ghayb). Where Western people had, over the centuries, carefully cultivated a rational ethos which concentrated entirely on the physical world perceived by the senses, Iranian Shiis, like other premodern peoples, had nurtured a sense of the hidden (batin) world evoked by cult and myth. During the White Revolution, Iranians had acquired electricity, television, and modern transport, but the religious revival in the country showed that for many people these external (ʒaheri) achievements were simply not enough. Modernization had been too rapid and was inevitably skin-deep. Many Iranians still hungered for the batin and felt that without it their lives had neither value nor significance. As the American anthropologist William Beeman explained, an Iranian who believed himself to be trapped on the material surface of life felt that he had lost his soul. The drive for a pure inner life was still a supreme value in Iranian society, so much so that one of the greatest compliments one person could pay another was to say that "his/her inside (batin) and outside (ʒahir) are the same."[60] Without a strong sense of the spiritual, many Iranians felt utterly lost. During the White Revolution, some had become convinced that their West-toxicated society had been poisoned by the materialism, consumer goods, alien modes of entertainment, and the imposition of foreign values. Further, the shah, with the enthusiastic support of the United States, seemed determined to destroy Islam, the source of the nation's spirituality. He had exiled Khomeini, closed the Fayziyyah Madrasah, insulted the clergy, cut their revenues, and killed theology students.

The Iranian Revolution was not merely political. Certainly, the cruel and autocratic regime of the shah and the economic crisis were crucial: there would have been no uprising without them. Many secularist Iranians who did not experience this spiritual malaise would eventually join the ulema simply to get rid of the shah, and without their support, the Revolution would not have succeeded. But it was also a rebellion against the secularist ethos which excluded religion and which many ordinary Iranians felt was being imposed upon them against their will. This was most graphically expressed in the depiction of the United States as the Great Satan. Rightly or wrongly, many believed that if he had not been so warmly supported by the United States, the shah would not have behaved as he did. They knew that Americans were proud of their secular polity, which deliberately separated religion from the state; they had learned that many Westerners thought it praiseworthy and necessary to focus exclusively on the *zahir*. The result, as far as they could see, was the empty, hedonistic nightlife of North Tehran. Iranians were aware that many Americans were religious, but their faith seemed to make no sense. The "inside" and "outside" of Jimmy Carter were *not* "the same." They could not understand how the President could continue to support a ruler who by 1978 had started to murder his own people. "We didn't expect Carter to defend the shah, for he is a religious man who has raised the slogan of defending human rights," Ayatollah Husain Montazeri told an interviewer after the Revolution. "How can Carter, the devout Christian, defend the shah?"[61]

When Carter visited the shah on New Year's Eve, during the sacred month of Muharram, to boost his regime, he could not, if he had tried, have cast himself more perfectly as the villain. During the next turbulent year, the United States came to seem the ultimate cause of Iran's spiritual, economic, and political problems. Street graffiti identified Carter with Yazid, and the shah with Shimr, the general dispatched by Yazid to massacre Husain and his little army. In one series of street drawings, Khomeini was depicted as Moses, the shah as Pharaoh, while Carter was the idol adored by the Pharaoh/shah.[62] America, it was thought, had corrupted the shah and Khomeini, now increasingly bathed in a Shii light, came to stand as an Islamic alternative to the present unholy dictatorship.

At the end of Muharram 1978, the shah yet again cast himself as the enemy of the Shiah. On January 8, the semiofficial newspaper *Ettelaat* published a slanderous article about Khomeini, calling him "an adventurer, without faith, and tied to the centers of colonialism." He had led a dissolute life, the article averred, had been a British spy, and was even now in the pay of the British, who wanted to undermine the White Revolution.[63] This scurrilous and preposterous attack was a fatal mistake on the part of the shah. The next day four thousand students turned out onto the streets of Qum: they demanded a return to the 1906 constitution, freedom of speech, the release of political prisoners, the reopening of the Fayziyyah Madrasah, and that Khomeini be permitted to return to Iran. What they got was a massacre. The police opened fire on the unarmed demonstrators, and, according to the *ulema*, seventy students were killed (though the regime claimed that only ten had died).[64] It was the bloodiest day in Iran since the 1963 riots, and for the shah it was the beginning of the end. William Beeman points out that Iranians will put up with a great deal, but that a single act of bad faith can cause an irrevocable breach in personal, business, and political relationships. Once this line has been crossed, there can be no going back.[65] For millions of ordinary religious Iranians, the shah crossed that line when he ordered SAVAK to shoot the demonstrators in Qum. They responded to the massacre with raw outrage, and the Revolution began.

In recent months, the intellectuals, writers, lawyers, and businessmen had led the opposition to the shah's regime. In January, however, after this blatant attack on the Shiah, the leadership passed to the *ulema*. The massacre had been so shocking that it even moved Ayatollah Shariatmadari to abandon his usual quietism and he condemned the shooting in the strongest terms. This passed a signal to the *ulema* throughout the country. Nothing was planned or prearranged. Khomeini issued no strategic orders from Najaf, but from the moment the *Ettelaat* article appeared, he was the unseen instigator and inspiration of the uprising. The struggle centered on the traditional mourning ceremonies held on the fortieth day after a death. These turned into demonstrations against the government, during which there were more killings; and, forty days later, a new series of rallies were held to commemorate the latest martyrs. The Revolution acquired an unstoppable momentum. The forty-day period between each demonstration gave the leaders time to spread the word, and, at the appointed time, the crowd would know exactly when to assemble, without any need for elaborate planning or advertising.

Thus on February 18, forty days after the Qum massacre, crowds of mourners, led by the *ulema* and *bazaaris,* swarmed onto the streets of major Iranian cities to weep for the dead. Women students, many of whom wore the veil to dissociate themselves from the regime, and chadored women from the bazaar often led the processions, as if to challenge the police to fire directly at them. The police did shoot and there were more martyrs. The confrontation was especially violent in Tabriz, where as many as one hundred mourners may have died, and six hundred people were arrested. Young men broke away from the procession to attack the cinemas, banks, and liquor stores (symbols of the Great Satan), but no people were assaulted.[66] Forty days later, on March 30, the mourners turned out onto the streets once again, this time to weep for the martyrs of Tabriz. On this occasion, about a hundred demonstrators were shot in Yazd, as they left the mosques. On May 8, there were new processions to honor the martyrs of Yazd.[67] The jails were crammed with political prisoners, and the number of dead revealed the naked aggression of a regime that had turned against its own people.

This was the ultimate passion play. Demonstrators carried placards read-

ing "Everywhere is Kerbala, and every day is Ashura."[68] The word for martyr, *shaheed,* meant "witness," as in Christianity. The demonstrators who
died were bearing witness to the duty to fight tyranny, as Imam Husain had
done, and to defend the values of the Unseen spiritual world, which the
regime seemed determined to violate. People spoke of the Revolution as a
transforming and purifying experience; they felt that they were purging
themselves and their society of a poison that had debilitated them and that,
in the struggle, they were returning to themselves. This was not a revolution
that was simply using religion for political ends. It was the Shii mythology
that gave it meaning and direction, especially among the poor and uneducated, who would have been quite unmoved by a more strictly secularist
ideology.[69]

In June and July, the shah made some concessions, promising free elections and the restoration of the multiparty system. During these months, the
demonstrations were quieter. There seemed to be a lull, and the Western-
educated secularists and intellectuals, who had hitherto taken no part in the
mourning processions but had supported the demonstrators by making
purely verbal protests against the regime, assumed that the battle had been
won. But on August 19, the twenty-fifth anniversary of the restoration of
the Pahlavi monarchy in 1953, an arson attack on the Rex Cinema in Abadan
killed four hundred people. This was immediately attributed to SAVAK, and
ten thousand mourners attended the funeral, chanting "Death to the shah!
Burn him!"[70] Iranian students organized big demonstrations against the
regime in Washington, Los Angeles, and The Hague. The shah made more
concessions: the Majlis debates became freer, orderly demonstrations were
permitted, some of the casinos were closed, and the Islamic calendar was
restored.[71]

But it was too late. During the last week of Ramadan, when Muslims usually keep vigil in the mosques, there were demonstrations in fourteen Iranian
cities, in which between fifty and one hundred people died. On September 4,
the last day of Ramadan, there was a massive peaceful demonstration in
Tehran. The crowds prostrated themselves in prayer in the streets, and
handed out flowers to the soldiers. For the first time, the army and the police
did not open fire, and on this occasion—a highly significant development—
the middle classes began to join in. A small group of marchers processed
through the streets of some of the residential districts, shouting: "Independence! Freedom! and Islamic Government!" On September 7, a huge parade
marched from North Tehran down to the Parliament building, carry-
ing large pictures of Khomeini and Shariati, and calling for an end to Pahlavi rule and for an Islamic government.[72] Lay thinkers such as Shariati,
Bazargan, and Bani Sadr had prepared the Western-educated elite for the

possibility of modern Islamic rule. Even though their views were different
from those of Khomeini, the middle-class liberals could see that he had
grassroots support that they could never command, and were willing to join
forces with him to get rid of the shah. Secularist rule had been a disaster in
Iran, and they were ready to try something different.

Once he had been deserted by the middle classes, it was all up for the
shah, and he must have realized the danger. At 6:00 a.m. on Friday, September 8, martial law was declared and all large gatherings were banned. But the
twenty thousand demonstrators who had already started to gather in Jaleh
Square that morning for another peaceful rally did not know about this.
When they refused to disperse, the soldiers opened fire and as many as nine
hundred people may have died. After this massacre, the crowds raged
through the streets, erecting barricades and burning buildings, while soldiers fired at them from their tanks.[73] At 8:00 a.m. on Sunday, September 10,
President Carter called the shah from Camp David to assure him of his support, and a few hours later, the White House confirmed that this telephone
conversation had taken place, reaffirmed the special relationship between the
United States and Iran, and reported that though the President regretted the
loss of life in Jaleh Square, he hoped that the political liberalization which
the shah had just begun would continue.[74]

But after the Jaleh Square massacre, not even the support of the Great
Satan could save the shah. The oil workers now came out on strike, and by
late October, production had dropped to 28 percent of its former level. The
guerrilla groups, who had been quieter in recent years, began once again to
attack military leaders and government ministers. On November 4, students
pulled down the statue of the shah at the gates of Tehran University: on
November 5, the bazaar closed, and students attacked the British embassy,
the offices of various United States airlines, cinemas, and liquor stores.[75]
This time, the army did not intervene.

By this date, the Iraqi government, responding to pressure from Tehran, had expelled Khomeini from Najaf and he had taken up residence
in Paris. Here he was visited by a delegation from the recently revived
National Front, who issued a statement that both they and Khomeini were
committed to restoring the 1906 constitution. On December 2, as Muharram
approached, Khomeini gave orders that instead of holding the usual passion
plays, *rawdahs,* and processions in honor of the martyrdom of Husain, the
people should demonstrate against the regime. The radical potential of these
pious ceremonies had reached its apotheosis. On the first three nights of
Muharram, men put on white shrouds to symbolize their readiness for martyrdom, and ran through the streets, defying the government curfew. Others
shouted anti-shah slogans through loudspeakers from the rooftops. The

BBC claimed that seven hundred people were killed by the police and army in these few days alone.[76] On December 8, six thousand people gathered at the Behest-e Zahra cemetery in south Tehran, where many of the revolutionary martyrs were buried, crying "Death to the shah!" In Isfahan, twenty thousand people marched through the streets, and then attacked banks, cinemas, and a block of flats inhabited by American technicians. On December 9, on the eve of Ashura, Ayatollah Taleqani, who had just been released from prison, led a magnificent peaceful march, which wound through the streets of Tehran for six hours; between 300,000 and a million and a half people took part, walking quietly, four abreast. There were other peaceful demonstrations in Tabriz, Qum, Isfahan, and Mashhad.[77]

On Ashura itself, there was an even bigger march in Tehran, lasting eight hours, in which almost two million people participated. The demonstrators carried green, red, and black flags (symbolizing, respectively, Islam, martyrdom, and the Shiah) interspersed with banners reading "We will kill Iran's dictator!" and "We will destroy Yankee power in Iran!" There was growing confidence that, united as never before, the people of Iran would really manage to get rid of the Pahlavi state.[78] Many felt as though Imam Husain himself was leading them into battle that Ashura, and that Khomeini was directing them from afar, like the Hidden Imam.[79] At the end of the demonstration, a resolution was passed: Khomeini was invited to become the new leader of Iran, and Iranians were urged to band together until the shah was overthrown.[80]

Three days later, the army tried to organize pro-shah demonstrations, and clashes between the revolutionaries and the military became more violent. The shah made a last effort at appeasement, appointing Shahpour Bakhtiar, a known liberal, to form a constitutional government; the shah promised that he would dismantle SAVAK, release political prisoners, and make fundamental changes in his economic and foreign policy. But this came a year too late; the people had heard too many promises made under duress to give these latest offers credence. Khomeini declared December 30 (which, according to the Islamic calendar, was the first anniversary of the Qum massacre) to be a day of mourning. There were more deaths in Mashhad, Tehran, and Qazrin; pictures of these latest martyrs were displayed alongside portraits of Khomeini. On December 23, when soldiers tore up pictures of Khomeini in Mashhad, there was a skirmish, and twelve civilians were killed. Immediately, crowds gathered at the spot and walked toward the soldiers, led by young men who were willing to sacrifice their lives. The army began to retreat, the soldiers firing at the ground to keep the people at bay. The next day, tens of thousands went back onto the streets to protest against these killings.[81]

By mid-January, it was all over. Prime Minister Bakhtiar negotiated the shah's departure, which, to save face, was declared to be only temporary. The royal family flew to Egypt, where Sadat took them in. Bakhtiar tried to stall the Revolution by ordering the release of political prisoners, dismantling SAVAK, refusing oil to Israel and South Africa, and promising to review all foreign contracts and to make major cuts in military expenditure. Again, it was too late. The crowds were clamoring for the return of the man they called their Imam, and on February 1, 1979, Bakhtiar was forced to allow Khomeini to return.

Khomeini's arrival in Tehran was one of those symbolic events, like the storming of the Bastille, which seem to change the world forever. For committed liberal secularists, inside and outside Iran, it was a dark moment, a triumph of superstition over rationality. But for many Muslims, Sunni as well as Shii, who had long feared that Islam was about to be annihilated, it seemed a luminous reversal. For some Iranian Shiis, Khomeini's return seemed a miracle, and inevitably, it resembled the mythical return of the Hidden Imam. As he drove through the streets of Tehran, the crowds shouted for "Imam Khomeini," confident that a new age of justice had dawned. Senior *mujtahids*, such as Ayatollah Shariatmadari, were incensed by this use of the title of Imam, and it was firmly and officially stated that Khomeini was *not* the Hidden Imam. But whatever the official line, for millions of the Iranian masses, Khomeini was an Imam until the day he died. His life and career seemed clear evidence that the divine was present and active in history after all. Like the Revolution itself, Khomeini seemed to make an ancient myth an actual reality.

Immediately before Khomeini's return, Taha Hejazi published a poem that expressed the eager anticipation of many Iranians: "On the Day the Imam Returns" looks forward to universal brotherhood. No one would tell lies any more, there would be no need to lock the door against thieves, everybody would share their food with each other:

> The Imam must return . . .
> so that right can sit on his throne,
> so that evil, treachery, and hatred
> are eliminated from the face of time.
> When the Imam returns,
> Iran—this broken, wounded mother—
> will be forever liberated
> from the shackles of tyranny and ignorance
> and the chains of plunder, torture and prison.[82]

Khomeini liked to quote the *hadith* in which the Prophet Muhammad, on returning from battle, announces that he is returning from the lesser to the greater *jihad;* the more difficult, crucial, and exacting struggle was not the physical, political battle, but the conquest of self and the implementation of justice and truly Islamic values in society. When he returned to Tehran, Khomeini must have reflected that the lesser *jihad* was now over and that the infinitely more arduous greater *jihad* was about to begin.

THE FUNDAMENTALIST REVIVAL in the United States during the late 1970s was far less dramatic. American Protestants did not need to take such extreme action. They were not, as were the Jews, still haunted by memories of Holocaust and genocide, nor were they, like the Muslims, victims of political and economic oppression. They felt alienated from modern secular culture, but their leaders, at least, enjoyed prosperity and success. This would later prove to be one of their problems. Despite their conviction that they were outsiders, Protestant fundamentalists were very much at home in America. Democracy was firmly established in the United States, and they were able to voice their views freely without fear of reprisal and use democratic institutions to further their cause. Nevertheless, by the late 1970s, as we have seen, fundamentalists were beginning to feel that instead of withdrawing from society as had been their policy for some fifty years, they should become politically active. They believed that they had a chance to make an impact and put America back on the right path. It had become clear that a substantial evangelical constituency could be mobilized on such issues as family values, abortion, and religious education. The old fears remained, but there was new confidence too.

The symbol of this revived fundamentalism was the Moral Majority, created in 1979 under the leadership of Jerry Falwell. The original inspiration for the group, however, came not from the fundamentalists themselves but from three professional right-wing organizers, who had already created a number of political action committees. Richard Vignerie, Howard Phillips, and Paul Weyrich had become frustrated with the Republican party and alienated even from Ronald Reagan, who had chosen the liberal Richard Schweiker as his running mate in his campaign for the presidency. Conservative on such issues as defense and the reduction of government interference in the economy, they wanted to build a new conservative majority to oppose the moral and social liberalism that had entered American public and private life during the 1960s. They noted the strength of the evangelical and fundamentalist Protestants, and saw Jerry Falwell as perfect for their needs. He already had a huge ready-made constituency, based on his congregation, Liberty College, and his television audience.[83] Other fundamentalists who came to be prominent in Moral Majority, such as Tim LaHaye and Greg Dixon, had also founded superchurches, enjoyed considerable autonomy, and would fear no censure from a denomination. They already had close links with one another: they were nearly all Baptists and members of the Baptist Bible Fellowship.

The Moral Majority did not confine itself to fundamentalists. The leaders wanted to cooperate with other people who shared their views on ethical and political issues, and create a forum for all the conservatives of America. If the new group was to make a significant impact, it needed the support of like-minded Roman Catholics, Pentecostalists, Mormons, Jews, and secularists, since only 15 to 20 percent of the population of the United States were evangelical Protestants.[84] For the first time, driven by pragmatic considerations, fundamentalists felt compelled to lay aside their separatism, leave their enclaves, and embrace the pluralism of modern life. This was reflected in the leadership. Falwell, LaHaye, Dixon, and Bob Billington were fundamentalists, but Paul Weyrich was Jewish, and Howard Phillips and Richard Vignerie were Catholics. This pluralism cost them some Christian fundamentalist support: Bob Jones II, for example, called Falwell "the most dangerous man in America."[85] But, in fact, popular support for Moral Majority remained predominantly Protestant. Grassroots sympathy was centered in the South, and the movement had little appeal outside WASP circles. Conservative Catholics could endorse Moral Majority's position on abortion and homosexual rights, and tax relief for independent schools, but many could not forget the fundamentalists' traditional hatred of Roman Catholicism. By the same token, Jews, black Baptists, and Pentecostalists would be repelled by the racism of some of the most prominent leaders and patrons of the movement. Senator Jesse Helms, for example, was a committed opponent of the civil rights movement.[86]

The message of Moral Majority was not new. It was declaring war on the liberal establishment and fighting a battle for the future of America. Members were convinced that the civilization of the United States must be religious, and its policy dictated by the Bible. At present, America was degenerate. After the Second World War, a secularist elite, centered on the East Coast, had dominated political and cultural life. These liberals had become what Jerry Falwell called "an immoral minority." Conservatives should not see themselves as a reactionary, marginal group. In fact, they represented the majority, and they must fight to preserve traditional values. "There are millions of us—and only a handful of them," claimed Tim LaHaye.[87] "We have together with the Protestants and Catholics enough votes to run this country," Pat Robertson told an audience. "And when the people say, 'We've had enough,' we are going to take over."[88]

During the late 1970s and early 1980s, some fundamentalists were beginning to modify the old premillennial pessimism. The world as a whole was doomed, but Christians had an obligation to evangelize the world, spread the Gospel, and try to ensure that it reached as many people as possible. If Christians took action, America could be reprieved before the Rapture. "Is there hope for our country?" Falwell asked on *Old Time Gospel Hour* in 1980:

> I think so. I believe as we trust in God and pray, as we Christians lead the battle to outlaw abortion, which is murder on demand, as we take our stand against pornography, against the drug traffic, as we take our stand against the breakdown of the traditional family in America, the promotion of homosexual marriages, as we stand up for strong national defense so that this country can survive and our children will know the America we've known. . . . I think there is hope that God may one more time bless America.[89]

Fundamentalists in what soon became known as the New Christian Right had gone on the offensive, after fifty years of quietism, but they were *against* more than they were *for*. Not all were involved in, or even approved of, the Moral Majority, but these newly militant Christians were anti-abortion, anti–gay rights, anti-drugs. They were adamantly opposed to any détente with the Soviet Union, which they had always regarded as a Satanic empire. For the televangelist James Robison, "Any teaching of peace prior to [Christ's] return is heresy. . . . It's against the word of God; it's Antichrist."[90] The agenda of the Moral Majority and the New Christian Right was rejectionist, a crusade against an impending evil that threatened to overwhelm America.

In the light of what came later, the emphasis placed on sexuality was significant. The New Christian Right was just as concerned about the position of women as the Islamists, but theirs was a far more frightened vision. The women's liberation movement filled fundamentalist men and women alike with terror. For Phyllis Schlafly, one of the Roman Catholic leaders of Moral Majority, feminism was a "disease," the cause of all the world's ills. Ever since Eve disobeyed God and sought her own liberation, feminism had brought sin into the world and with it "fear, sickness, pain, anger, hatred, danger, violence and all varieties of ugliness."[91] The proposed Equal Rights Amendment was a government plot to create higher taxes, Soviet-style nurseries, "and the federalization of all remaining aspects of our life."[92] For Beverley LaHaye, feminism was "more than an illness"; based on Marxist and humanist teachings, "it is a philosophy of death. . . . Radical feminists are self-destructive and are trying to bring about the death of an entire civilization as well." It was up to Christian women to take active steps to move their husbands back to center stage and reeducate themselves in the ethos of feminine self-sacrifice. It was their duty "to save our society," bringing "civilization and humanity to the twenty-first century."[93] The conflation of feminism with the other evils that had long haunted the fundamentalist imagination is evidence of conspiracy fear. They associated the integrity and even the survival of their society with the traditional position of women.

Protestant fundamentalists and Christian conservatives in most of the denominations seem to have felt unmanned by the evil forces of secular humanism. They appeared deeply concerned about male impotence. Modern men were much "less certain of their manhood than formerly," lamented Tim and Beverley LaHaye in *The Act of Marriage: The Beauty of Sexual Love* (1976), their best-selling sex manual. Men were impotent, sexually troubled, worried about satisfying their wives, or about how their performance compared with that of other men.[94] The reason for this was the new self-assertion of women; even fundamentalist women were infected by this cultural virus and, as a result, men were becoming "feminized" or even "castrated."[95] This fear also underlay the fundamentalist hatred of homosexuality, which, like feminism, they regarded as an epidemic, the cause of America's decline.[96] "It is a perversion of the highest order," thundered James Robison, who became famous for the virulence of his attacks on homosexuality in his television program. "It is against God, against God's word, against society, against nature. It is almost too repulsive to imagine or describe."[97] Fundamentalists were almost unanimous in seeing homosexuality as identical with pederasty. They were also convinced that it was the result of failed homes which had fallen prey to "secular humanism."[98] Fundamentalist writers on family values were united in their conviction that America needed real men. But, interestingly, some fundamentalists seemed to have buried worries about what they considered to be an emasculating tendency in Christianity itself, which had become a religion of womanly values: forgiveness, mercy, and tenderness. But Jesus was no sissy, expostulated Edwin Louis Cole: he was "a fearless leader, defeating Satan, casting out demons, commanding nature, rebuking hypocrites."[99] He could be ruthless: Christians must also be aggressive, Tim LaHaye insisted in *Battle for the Family*. They must become politically active.[100] This desire for a militant, virile Christianity also explains Moral Majority's hostility to gun-control legislation. This too was part of their campaign to revive upright, potent, and combative manhood.

The activism of the New Christian Right sprang in part from fundamental fear. Fundamentalists felt obscurely castrated and profoundly undermined. Their ideology had not changed, but they were now determined to make their flocks, whom for years they had commanded to hold aloof from mainstream society, politically active in public life. The Moral Majority network began to work in the same way as other political campaigning movements. Their main job was to make sure that their members registered for the vote, were taught how to use their vote correctly, and were able to get to the polls. They held rallies to explain the need for activism, and to educate the people in lobbying and the preparation of newsletters; they also taught them how to influence the media. Christians were exhorted to stand for public office, at however lowly and local a level. Liberals and secularists gradually became aware of a vociferous born-again presence in public life. In the course of the next decade, militant Christians began to colonize mainstream institutions. In 1986, Pat Robertson even made a bid for the presidency. Christians began to be a thorn in the side of some politicians. For years, public action committees had targeted candidates for office who, in their view, promoted undesirable policies. They had issued "report cards," making their ideas public property. Now Christian activists began to target candidates who voted the "wrong" way on the gun laws, funding for abortion clinics, or the Equal Rights Amendment. To hold the wrong views on defense, school prayer, or gay rights was to be anti-family, anti-America, and anti-God.

At first, the fundamentalist activists tended to be inept, but gradually they learned to play the modern political game. They were preachers and television presenters and not natural politicians, but they did achieve some success. Their most notable achievement was probably the blocking of the Equal Rights Amendment. It was necessary that thirty-eight states vote for the amendment in order to procure the necessary two-thirds majority, and by 1973 thirty states had voted for it.[101] But the efforts of Phyllis Schlafly and the campaigning of local Christian Right activists halted the amendment's momentum: Nebraska, Tennessee, Kentucky, Indiana, and South Dakota would all reverse their previous endorsements. Otherwise, the Moral Majority did not manage to change either federal or state legislation, even on such issues as school prayer and abortion. In Arkansas and Louisiana, however, bills were passed to ensure that the literal teachings of Genesis were given equal time with Darwinian evolution in the school curriculum. This apparent lack of success did not worry Christian activists, however, who pointed out that their long-term objective was to build an ultraconservative majority in both chambers of Congress. Once that had been achieved, the reforms that they wanted would take place as a matter of course.

At this writing, twenty years after the Moral Majority initiated this type of political activism, it is not easy to assess its long-term effectiveness. There is evidence that more committed Christians vote than before, especially in the South, but this type of negative campaigning can sometimes backfire. When Christian Right supporter Linda Chavez called her liberal opponent in the Maryland mid-term elections in 1986 a communist and a child-murdering lesbian, for example, this may have contributed to her defeat.[102] The efforts of fundamentalists and other conservatives in 1998–99 to impeach President Bill Clinton because of his sexual relationship with Monica Lewinsky and subsequent alleged perjury also proved counterproductive. The spectacle of the President having to answer intimate questions about his sexual behavior and the inevitable trivialization of political discourse that this involved caused widespread revulsion, and possibly resulted in a liberal backlash in Clinton's favor.

Nevertheless, the fact that at the height of the scandal the President felt it necessary to address a breakfast meeting of the religious leaders of the United States and tearfully confess that he had sinned showed that politicians could no longer treat the conservative views of the faithful with secularist disdain. By the end of the twentieth century, religion was a force to be reckoned with in North America. The United States had come a long way since the Founding Fathers had promoted the secular humanism of the Enlightenment. Since the Revolution, the Protestants of America had used religion as a way of protesting against the policies and conduct of the liberal establishment; the fundamentalist campaigning of Jerry Falwell, Pat Robertson, and other members of the Christian Right was simply a late-twentieth-century manifestation of this tendency. As a result of all these Christian efforts, the sacred plays a far greater role in the political life of the United States than in such countries as Britain and France, where a politician would be damaged by the display of overt and emotional religiosity.

National politics aside, it is also true that some of the greatest victories of the Christian Right in the 1970s and 1980s were at the local level. In 1974, for example, Alice Moore, wife of a fundamentalist minister in Kanawa County, West Virginia, led a campaign against the "secular humanist slant" of school textbooks, which implied that the Bible was a myth, were critical of authority, and presented Christianity as hypocritical and atheism as intelligent and attractive. Christians withdrew their children from the schools, and picketed them. Moore displayed the long American Protestant tradition of distrust of the experts. Who should control the schools in Kanawa County: "the people who live here, or the educational specialists, the administrators, the people from other places who have been trying to tell us what is best for our children?"[103] In January 1982, the local Christians of St. David's, Arizona, managed to get books by William Golding, John Steinbeck, Joseph Conrad, and Mark Twain banned from their schools. In 1981, Mel and Norma Gabler began a similar campaign to "get God back into the schools" of Texas. They objected to the present "liberal slant," which could be seen in:

> open-ended questions that require students to draw their own conclusions; statements about religions other than Christianity; statements that they construe to reflect negatively on the free enterprise system; statements that they construe to reflect positive aspects of socialist or communist countries (e.g., that the Soviet Union is the largest producer in the world of certain grains); any aspect of sex education other than the promotion of abstinence; statements which emphasize contributions made by blacks, Native American Indians, Mexican-Americans, or feminists; statements which are sympathetic to American slaves or are unsympathetic to their masters; and statements in support of the theory of evolution, unless equal space is given to explain the theory of creation.[104]

The courts ruled against the Gablers, but the publishers were so alarmed by the prospect of damage to the big Texas market, where the state chooses textbooks for all the schools, that they amended the books themselves.

The campaigners had revealed all the worries that had long plagued fundamentalists about modern culture: the fear of colonization, of experts, of uncertainty, of foreign influence, of science and sex. They also showed the quintessentially WASP orientation of the New Christian Right. America was to be white and Protestant. Like the Jewish and Muslim activists, the Christians of Moral Majority were fighting to extend the domain of the sacred, to limit the advance of the secularist ethos, and to reinstate the divine. Their victories might seem small and insignificant, but the Christian Right had learned how to conduct themselves in the political arena; they had re-enfranchised themselves, and, to an extent, resacralized American politics in a way that never ceases to amaze the more secular countries of Europe.

The liberal organization People for the American Way, which took on the Gablers in the Texas case, pointed out that the conservatives have only won 34 out of 124 similar conflicts. The liberals began to create their own organizations and fight back. Progress was, therefore, slow, and this worried fundamentalists who believed that time was running out, that Rapture was nigh, and that an omnipotent God was active in history, upholding the righteous with his might. Some fundamentalists believed that their leaders were selling out. In 1982, for example, instead of campaigning for the total abolition of abortion, Falwell moved to the more pragmatic objective of limiting its availability. During his presidential campaign, Pat Robertson spoke guardedly but politely about the mainstream denominations, even though fundamentalist orthodoxy demands that the apostate churches be attacked at every available opportunity.

During these early years of the Protestant resurgence, Falwell and Robertson both learned that modern politics demands compromise. Absolute policies cannot succeed in a democratic context, where the contest for power entails bargaining, and giving some ground to opponents. This is difficult to square with a religious vision which sees certain principles as inviolable, and, therefore, nonnegotiable. In the world of secular politics, where fundamentalists are forced to contend, whether they like it or not, nothing is sacred in this way. To achieve any measure of success, Falwell and Robertson had to make concessions to enemies whom they regarded as satanic. There was a tension: by entering the modern political world, fundamentalists found that they not only had to sup with the devil but were tainted by some of the evil influences that they had entered the political lists to fight. This was just one of their difficulties. During the last two decades of the century, some of the solutions to which fundamentalists felt driven meant a defeat for religion itself.

10. Defeat?
(1979–99)

THE FUNDAMENTALIST *reconquista* had shown that religion was anything but a spent force. It was no longer possible to ask, as an exasperated United States government official had demanded after the Iranian Revolution: "Whoever took religion seriously?"[1] The fundamentalists had brought faith out of the shadows and demonstrated that it could appeal to a huge constituency in modern society. Their victories filled secularists with dismay; this was not the tamed, decorous, privatized faith of the Enlightenment era. It seemed to deny sacred values of modernity. The religious offensive of the late 1970s had shown that societies were polarized; by the end of the twentieth century, it was clear that religious and secularists were even more divided. They could not speak each other's language, nor share one another's vision. From a purely rational perspective, fundamentalism was a disaster, but, since it amounted to a rebellion against what fundamentalists regarded as the illegitimate hegemony of scientific rationalism, this was not surprising. How should we assess these fundamentalisms as religious movements? What can they tell us about the peculiar challenges that religion faces in the modern and postmodern world? Did the fundamentalist triumphs amount, in fact, to a defeat for religion, and has the fundamentalist threat subsided?

The Islamic Revolution in Iran was particularly troubling to those who still adhered to the principles of the Enlightenment. Revolutions were supposed to be strictly secularist. They were thought usually to occur at a time when the mundane realm had acquired new dignity, and was about to declare its independence of the mythical realm of religion. As Hannah Arendt explained in her celebrated study *On Revolution* (1963): "it may ultimately turn out that what we call revolution is precisely that transitory phase which brings about the birth of a new secular realm."[2] The idea of a popular uprising ushering in a theocratic state seemed an utterly fantastic notion, almost embarrassing in its apparently naive rejection of accepted Western wisdom. In the immediate aftermath of the Iranian Revolution, nobody expected Khomeini's regime to survive. The very idea of a religious revolution, like that of a modern Islamic government, seemed a contradiction in terms.

But Westerners had to face the fact that most Iranian people did want Islamic rule. The "moderates" whose emergence many American and European observers had confidently predicted did not arise to oust the "mad mullahs." Those nationalists who wanted a secular and democratic republic in Iran found themselves in a minority after the Revolution. There was no agreement about what form an Islamic government should take, however. Western-educated intellectuals, followers of Shariati, wanted a regime governed by laymen, with reduced clerical rule. Mehdi Bazargan, Khomeini's new prime minister, wanted a return to the 1906 constitution (without the monarchy), with a council of *mujtahids* with the power to veto un-Islamic parliamentary legislation. The *madrasahs* of Qum pressed for Khomeini's Velayat-e Faqih, but both Ayatollah Shariatmadari and Ayatollah Taleqani were vehemently opposed to this vision of a mystically inspired cleric ruling the nation, since it violated centuries of sacred Shii tradition. They saw great dangers in such a polity. By October 1979, there was serious conflict.[3] Bazargan and Shariatmadari attacked the draft constitution drawn up by Khomeini's followers, which gave supreme power to a *faqih* (Khomeini), who would control the armed forces and could summarily dismiss the prime minister. The constitution also made provision for an elected president and parliament, a cabinet, and a twelve-man Council of Guardians with the power to veto laws that contravened the Shariah.

Opposition to the draft constitution was strong. The left-wing guerrilla movements, the ethnic minorities within Iran, and the influential Muslim People's Republican party (founded by Ayatollah Shariatmadari) were all adamantly against it. The liberals and the Western-educated middle classes now became increasingly depressed by what they regarded as the religious extremism of the new regime: it seemed to them that they had fought bravely to free themselves from the tyranny of the former shah only to find themselves subject to Islamic despotism. They noted that in the draft constitution, freedom of the press and liberty of political expression (for which the liberals had fought the Pahlavi regime) were guaranteed only provided that they did not contravene Islamic law and practice. Prime Minister Bazargan was particularly outspoken. He was careful never to attack Khomeini himself, but was sharply critical of what he called the reactionary clergy in the Islamic Revolutionary Party who were responsible for the proposed constitutional clauses which, he claimed, violated the whole purpose of the Islamic Revolution.

Khomeini faced a crisis. On December 3, 1979, the people were due to vote on the draft constitution in a national referendum, and it seemed likely that the Velayat-e Faqih would be soundly defeated. Until this point, Khomeini had been a pragmatist, adroitly managing a coalition of left-wingers, Islamists, intellectuals, nationalists, and liberals to overthrow the Pahlavi regime, but by the end of 1979 it was clear that this uneasy alliance of groups with mutually contradictory objectives was about to split apart and the future of the Revolution—as he himself saw it—was imperiled. Then, unwittingly, the United States came to his aid.

Despite the denunciation of America as the Great Satan, relations between the United States government and the new Islamic regime in Tehran after the Revolution had been cautious but correct. On February 14, 1979, shortly after Khomeini's return to Iran, students had stormed the American Embassy in the capital and attempted to occupy it, but Khomeini and Bazargan had moved quickly to expel the intruders. Nonetheless, Khomeini remained mistrustful of the Great Satan and could not believe that America would forgo its interests in Iran without a struggle. With the paranoia that we have seen to haunt most fundamentalist leaders, Khomeini was convinced that the United States was simply biding its time and would eventually threaten the new Islamic Republic with a coup similar to that which had overthrown Musaddiq in 1953. When, on October 22, 1979, the former shah flew into New York City to receive medical treatment for the cancer which was killing him, Khomeini's suspicions seemed to be confirmed. The United States government had been warned by its own experts and by Tehran not to admit the former shah, but Carter believed that he could not deny his erstwhile loyal ally this humanitarian service.

Immediately Khomeini's rhetoric against the Great Satan became more scathing; he demanded that Muhammad Reza Pahlavi be returned to Iran for punishment, and called for a purge from the government of all those who remained loyal to the former regime. There were within Islamic Iran, he proclaimed, traitors who were still dependent upon the West and must be expelled from the nation. It took no genius to realize that Prime Minister Bazargan was the principal target of this attack, together with all opponents of the draft constitution. On November 1, Bazargan played into Khomeini's hands by flying to Algiers for the anniversary celebrations of Algerian independence, and was photographed there shaking hands with Zbigniew Brzezinski, Carter's National Security Adviser. Bazargan was gleefully denounced by his enemies in the Islamic Revolutionary Party as an American agent. It was in this heightened atmosphere that on November 4 some three thousand Iranian students stormed the American Embassy in Tehran and took ninety hostages. At first, it was assumed that Khomeini would secure their immediate release and command the students to withdraw, as he had before. To this day, it is not clear whether Khomeini knew of the students' decision to invade the embassy beforehand. In any case, for some three days he kept a low profile. But when Bazargan realized that he could not get Khomeini's support for the evacuation of the embassy, he recognized his political impotence and resigned on November 6, together with the foreign secretary, Ibrahim Yazdi. Rather to their own surprise, the students, who had expected their siege to last only a few days, found that they had spearheaded a major confrontation between Iran and the United States. Khomeini and the Islamic Revolutionary Republic threw their support behind the students. The huge publicity surrounding the hostage crisis worldwide gave Khomeini a new assertiveness. In the event, even though the women hostages and black Marine guards were released, the remaining fifty-two American diplomats were held for 444 days and became an icon of Iranian radicalism.

For Khomeini, the hostages were a godsend. By focusing attention on the Great Satan, an external enemy, their capture and the post-revolutionary hatred of America that ensued united Iranians behind Khomeini during a period of internal turbulence. The departure of Bazargan removed, at a stroke, the most vociferous opponent of the draft constitution, and weakened the strength of the opposition. Accordingly, the new constitution was passed in the December referendum with an impressive majority. Khomeini saw the hostage crisis simply in terms of his own domestic situation. As he explained to Bani Sadr, his new prime minister, at the outset:

> This action has many benefits. The Americans do not want to see the Islamic Republic taking root. We keep the hostages, finish our internal work, then release them. This has united our people. Our opponents do not dare act against us. We can put the constitution to the people's vote without difficulty, and carry out presidential and parliamentary elections. When we have finished all these jobs, we can let the hostages go.[4]

This was a policy dictated not by the *mythos* of Islam, despite Khomeini's fiery rhetoric, but a piece of pragmatic *logos*. Nevertheless, the crisis also changed Khomeini's own profile. Instead of remaining a practical politician, he became, in his own view, the leader of the *ummah* in its struggle against Western imperialism; the word "revolution" acquired an almost sacred value in his speech, on a par with conventional Islamic terminology: he alone was able to take a stand against the most powerful imperialist power in the world and reveal the limits of its might. At the same time, the hatred of Iran and Islam that the crisis not unnaturally unleashed throughout the world made Khomeini more aware than ever of the fragility of the Revolution, threatened as it was by enemies within and without. Between late May and mid-July 1980, four separate coups against the regime were discovered, and until the end of the year, there were constant street battles between secularist guerrillas and Khomeini's Revolutionary Guards. The confusion and terror of these days was increased by the proliferation all over Iran of so-called revolutionary councils, which the government was unable to control. These *komitehs* executed hundreds of people for such "un-Islamic behavior" as prostitution or having held office under the Pahlavis. The emergence of such local bodies after the collapse of a central power seems a universal characteristic of revolutions designed to reconstruct society. Khomeini condemned the excesses of these *komitehs*, which, he declared, contravened Islamic law and undermined the integrity of the Revolution. But he did not disband them and was, eventually, able to bring them under his aegis, control them, and make them a grassroots support for his regime.[5] Khomeini also had to face war with Iraq. On September 20, 1980, the forces of Saddam Hussein, president of Iraq, invaded southwest Iran, with the encouragement of the United States. This meant that the social reforms planned by Khomeini had to be put on hold. Throughout this period, the American hostages served a purpose. Only when they had outgrown their usefulness were the hostages released, on January 20, 1981 (the inauguration day of the new U.S. president, Ronald Reagan).

Inevitably, however, the plight of the hostages tarnished the image of the new Islamic republic. Despite the high-flown talk during the crisis of the iniquity of the Great Satan, there was nothing religious or Islamic about this hostage-taking. Quite the contrary. Even though the capture of the hostages was not popular with all Iranians, many could appreciate its symbolism. An embassy is regarded as the given country's territory on foreign soil, and the occupation of the students thus amounted to an invasion of American sovereignty. Yet to some it seemed appropriate that American citizens should be held captive in their own embassy in Iran, because for decades Iranians felt that they had been prisoners in their own country with the connivance of the United States, which had supported the Pahlavi dictatorship. But this was revenge politics, not religion. In the occupation's early days, some of the hostages had been bound hand and foot, forbidden to speak, and told that the United States had abandoned them. Later, the hostages were moved to more comfortable quarters,[6] but this type of cruelty and ill-treatment contravenes the cardinal insight of all the major confessional faiths, Islam included: no religious doctrine or practice can be authentic if it does not lead to practical compassion. Buddhists, Hindus, Taoists, and monotheists all agree that the sacred reality is not simply transcendent, "out there," but is enshrined in every single human being, who must, therefore, be treated with absolute honor and respect. Fundamentalist faith, be it Jewish, Christian, or Muslim, fails this crucial test if it becomes a theology of rage and hatred.

Indeed, this type of hostage-taking violates specific Islamic laws about the treatment of prisoners. The Koran demands that Muslims treat their opponents humanely. It insists that it is unlawful to take prisoners, except during the fighting of a regular war (which, in itself, rules out the taking and retention of the American hostages). Prisoners must not be ill-treated and should be released, either as a favor or for ransom, after hostilities have ended. If no ransom is forthcoming, the prisoner must be free to seek employment, so that he can pay it off himself; the Muslim to whose care he has been consigned must help the captive to raise the required sum out of his own resources.[7] A *hadith* attributes this directive about the treatment of prisoners to the Prophet himself. "You must feed them as you feed yourselves, and clothe them as you clothe yourselves, and if you should set them a hard task, you must help them in it yourselves."[8] For Shiis, who venerate Imams who were held hostage in a foreign land by a tyrannical government for its own pragmatic ends, hostage-taking should be especially repugnant. Holding hostages in this way may have made political sense, but it was neither authentically religious nor Islamic.

Fundamentalism is an embattled faith and sees itself fighting for survival in a hostile world. This affects and sometimes distorts vision. Khomeini, as we have seen, suffered from the paranoid fantasies that afflict so many fundamentalists. On November 20, 1979, shortly after the hostages were first taken, several hundred armed Sunni fundamentalists in Saudi Arabia occupied the Kabah in Mecca and proclaimed their leader as Mahdi. Khomeini denounced this sacrilege as the combined work of the United States and Israel.[9] This type of conspiracy thinking commonly emerges when people feel imperiled. The outlook was bleak in Iran. There was growing disillusion with the regime, despite Khomeini's personal popularity. No criticism of or opposition to the government was permitted. Khomeini's relationship with the other Grand Ayatollahs deteriorated during 1981, and there was virtually a state of war between the radical Islamists, who wanted a complete return to Shariah law on the one hand, and the secularists and laymen on the left. On July 22, 1981, Bani Sadr, who had been president for only a year, was deposed and fled to Paris. On June 28, Khomeini's chief clerical ally, Ayatollah Bihishti, and seventy-five members of the Islamic Revolutionary party were killed in a bomb attack on the party headquarters.[11] Until this point,

Khomeini had preferred to give laymen the top jobs, but in October, he permitted Hojjat ol-Islam Ali Khameini to become president. Clerics were now in a majority in the Majlis. By 1983, all political opposition to the regime had been suppressed. The Mujahedin-e Khalq went underground after the departure of Bani Sadr; the National Front, the National Democratic party (led by Musaddiq's grandson), and Shariatmadari's Muslim People's Republican party had all been disbanded. Increasingly, Khomeini called for "unity of expression."[12]

As often happens after a revolution, the new regime appeared to become as autocratic as its predecessor. Beset by enemies, Khomeini began to insist upon ideological conformity, like other, modern secularist revolutionary ideologues; but in Islamic terms, this represented a new departure. Like Judaism, Islam had demanded uniformity of practice, but never doctrinal orthodoxy. Shiis had been supposed to imitate *(taqlid)* the religious behavior of a *mujtahid*, but were not expected to conform to his beliefs. Now Khomeini insisted that Iranians accept his theory of Velayat-e Faqih, and quashed all opposition. "Unity of expression," he told the *hajj* pilgrims in 1979, was the "secret of victory."[13] The people would not achieve the spiritual perfection he desired for them unless they adopted the right ideas. There could be no democracy of opinion; the people must follow the Supreme Faqih, whose mystical journey had given him "perfect faith." They would then walk in the path of the Imams.[14] But this did not mean dictatorship. Muslims needed unity if they were to survive in an inimical world. "Today Islam is confronted with the enemy and with blasphemy," he told a delegation from Azerbaijan. "We need power. Power can be obtained by turning toward God, the exalted and blessed, and through unity of expression."[15] Muslims could not afford infighting, if they were to stand up to the superpowers. Desperate measures were necessary if Iran, long divided into "two nations" as a result of the modernization process, was to be reunited and brought back to the Islamic ideal.

Westerners were understandably horrified when they heard that Khomeini told parents to denounce children who were hostile to the regime, and that Iranians who made fun of religion were declared apostates and judged worthy of death. This violated the ideal of intellectual freedom, which had become a sacred value in Europe and America. But Western people were also forced to note that Khomeini never lost the love of the masses of Iranians, especially the *bazaaris*, the *madrasah* students, the less-eminent *ulema*, and the poor.[16] These people had not been included in the modernization program of the shah and could not understand the modern ethos. Where Western secularists had come to see defiance of tradition as Promethean and heroic, Khomeini's followers still saw the sovereignty of God as the highest value and did not yet see the rights of the individual as absolute. They could understand Khomeini but not the modern West. They still spoke and thought in a religious, premodern way that many Westerners could no longer comprehend. But Khomeini was not giving himself papal airs. He insisted that his "infallibility" did not mean that he did not make mistakes. He would become impatient with followers who took his every word as a divinely inspired pronouncement. "I may have said something yesterday, changed it today, and will again change it tomorrow," he told clerics on the Council of Guardians in December 1983. "This does not mean that simply because I made a statement yesterday, I should adhere to it."[17]

Nevertheless, "unity of expression" was a limitation and, some would say, a distortion of Islam. Jewish and Christian fundamentalists also insisted, in their different ways, on dogmatic conformity, asserting—sometimes stridently—that only their version of the faith was authentic. Khomeini's "unity of expression" reduced the essentials of Islam to an ideology; by giving so much prominence to Khomeini's own theories, it ran the risk of idolatry, the raising of a purely human expression of divine truth to absolute status. But it also sprang from Khomeini's sense of danger. For years he had been fighting an aggressively secularizing regime which had been destructive to religion; he was now fighting Saddam Hussein, and was acutely aware of extreme international hostility to the Islamic Republic. "Unity of expression" was a defensive device. In making Iran an Islamic country once again, Khomeini was building a new, giant sacred enclave in a Godless world that wanted to destroy it. The experience of suppression, the perceived danger, and the knowledge that he was fighting against the grain of an increasingly secular world made for an embattled spirituality and would produce a contorted version of Islam. The experience of suppression had been scarring, and had resulted in a repressive religious vision.

Khomeini was convinced that the Revolution had been a rebellion against the rational pragmatism of the modern world. The people had shown that they were willing to die in order to achieve a polity with transcendent goals. "Could anyone wish his child to be martyred in order to obtain a good home?" he asked an audience of craftsmen in December 1979. "This is not the issue. The issue is another world. Martyrdom is meant for another world. This is the martyrdom sought by all God's saints and prophets . . . the people want this meaning."[18] Scientific rationalism could not answer questions about the ultimate meaning of life; that had always been the preserve of myth. In the West, the abandonment of mythology had led, in some quarters, to the perceived void, which Sartre had described as a God-shaped hole. Many Iranians had been disoriented by the sudden lack of inwardness in their daily and political life. Khomeini was convinced that people were three-dimensional beings; they had spiritual as well as material needs, and in showing that they were willing to die for a state that made religion central to its identity, they had been trying to regain their full humanity.[19] Khomeini himself rarely forgot the transcendent aspect of politics, even during a crisis. When the Iran-Iraq war broke out, Bani Sadr suggested that it might be useful to release the former shah's military personnel from prison to direct operations. Khomeini refused. The Revolution, he said, had not been about economic prosperity or territorial integrity. He cited a story about Imam Ali during his struggle in Syria with Muawiyyah, the founder of the Umayyad dynasty, who was challenging his rule. Just before the army went into battle, Ali delivered a sermon to the soldiers about the divine unity *(tawhid)*. When his officers asked if this homily had been appropriate at such a time, Ali replied: "This is the reason we are fighting Muawiyyah, not for any worldly gain."[20] The battle was to preserve the unity of the *ummah,* which must reflect the unity of God. The Muslims were fighting for *tawhid,* not for the conquest of Syria.

This, of course, was admirable, but it posed a problem. Human beings need meaning and *mythos,* but they also need hard, rational *logos,* too. In premodern society, these two spheres had both been seen as indispensable. But just as myth could not be explained in rational or logical terms, it could not be expressed in practical politics. This had been difficult, and had sometimes resulted in a de facto separation of religion and politics. The theology of the Imamate had suggested that there was an incompatibility between the mystical vision and the hardheaded pragmatism that is required of a head of state. Khomeini sometimes blurred the crucial distinction between *mythos* and *logos.* As a result, some of his policies were disastrous. The economy suffered from the sudden sharp fall in oil revenue after the hostage crisis and from the lack of sound state investment. The ideological purges deprived state departments and industry of competent management. By antagonizing the West, Iran had forfeited essential equipment, spare parts, and technical advice. By 1982, inflation was high, there was a severe shortage of consumer goods, and unemployment had risen to 30 percent of the general population (50 percent in the cities).[21] The hardships suffered by the people were embarrassing to a regime that, for religious reasons, had put social welfare at the top of its original agenda on coming to power. Khomeini did his best for the poor. He set up the Foundation for the Downtrodden to relieve the distress of those who had suffered most under the Pahlavis. Islamic associations in the factories and workshops provided workers with interest-free loans. In the rural areas, Construction Jihad employed young people in building new houses for the peasants, and in agricultural, public health, and welfare projects, especially in the war zones. But these efforts were offset by the war with Iraq, which had not been of Khomeini's making.

Khomeini was aware of the tension between the mystical and the practical. He understood that a modern state needed popular participation and a fully representative government. As the West had discovered in the course of its own modernization, this was the only type of polity that worked in an industrialized, technicalized society. His theory of Velayat-e Faqih had been an attempt to provide modern political institutions with an Islamic context that would give them meaning to the people. The Supreme Faqih and the Council of Guardians would give the elected Majlis a mystical, religious significance that a Muslim people, who could not relate to the Western secularist ideal, needed: Velayat-e Faqih was thus an attempt to provide a mythical foundation for the practical activities of parliament, and contain the modern within a traditional vision. But Khomeini had evolved the theory of Velayat-e Faqih in a *madrasah* in Najaf. What sounded good on paper, as it were, proved to be problematic when put into practice in Iran. This became apparent as early as 1981, and the difficulty continued to exercise Khomeini for the rest of his life.[22]

In 1981, the Majlis proposed some important land reforms, which would ensure a fairer distribution of resources. Khomeini sympathized with this move, which would be beneficial to the people, even though it contradicted the letter of the Shariah. He could also see that unless Iran was able to achieve this type of basic reform, it would remain feudal and agrarian, and any modernization would be superficial. But the Land Reform Bill ran into difficulties. According to the constitution, all legislation had to be passed by the Council of Guardians, who had the right to reject laws which they deemed un-Islamic. Many of the *ulema* on the Council had large landholdings, and when they were presented with the bill, they exercised their right of veto, citing the Shariah laws to support their decision. Khomeini tried to reason with them. The clergy, he said, "should in no way interfere in matters for which they are not qualified." This "would be an unforgivable sin, because it will lead to the nation's mistrust of the clergy."[23] The clergy understood religion and *fiqh*, but not modern economics; the Islamic republic must be a modern state, which required specialists to work within the field of their expertise.

But the deadlock continued. The Council of Guardians refused to budge on the issue, so Khomeini tried a more spiritual approach. In March 1981, he told a group of clerics: "One should not expect, without having been reformed himself, to attempt to reform another." The clergy could not bring the people back to Islam if they were themselves crippled by selfishness and locked in futile power struggles. Every single one of the *ulema* must over-come this egotism that was impeding the Islamic development of the country. The solution was to "reach a stage where you . . . overlook yourself." "When there is no self to contend with," Khomeini concluded, "there is no dispute, no quarrel."²⁴ This sprang directly from Khomeini's practice of mystical *irfan;* as the seeker approaches God, he gradually divests himself of his selfish desires until he is able to behold the transforming vision of God. But the dynamic of modern politics is very different from spiritual con-templation. The *ulema* of the Council of Guardians remained deaf to Kho-meini's plea. Politics usually attracts men and women with a heightened sense of self. Modern governmental institutions work by means of a balance of competing interests, not by this kind of self-effacement. When he had evolved his theory of Velayat-e Faqih, Khomeini had believed that the *ulema* on the Council of Guardians would assert the mystical, hidden *(batin)* values of the Unseen; instead, they seemed mired, like most ordinary mor-tals, in the materialism of the *zahir.*

To break the deadlock with the Council of Guardians, the energetic Speaker of the Majlis, Hojjat ol-Islam Hashemi Rafsanjani, urged Khomeini to use his authority as Supreme Faqih to get the Land Bill passed. The con-stitution gave the Faqih final say on all Islamic matters, and he could over-rule the decision of the Council of Guardians. Khomeini could, Rafsanjani suggested, cite the Islamic principle of *maslahah* ("public necessity"), which allowed a jurist to legislate "secondary ordinances" about issues not directly provided for in the Koran and the Sunnah, if the welfare of the people demanded it. But Khomeini did not wish to do this. He was beginning to realize that the position of the Supreme Faqih could weaken the authority of the institutions that the Islamic republic needed if it was to survive in the modern world. He was an old man. If he kept intervening and overturning the decisions of government institutions on the basis of his personal charisma, the Majlis and Council would lose their credibility and integrity, and the Islamic constitution would not survive his death. The impasse between the Council and the Majlis continued.

Khomeini tried to shame the *ulema* by pointing to the example of the Iranian children who were dying every day as martyrs in the war with Iraq. These child martyrs show the moral dangers of translating a mystical insight into practical policy. From the moment war was declared, adolescents had crowded into the mosques begging to be sent to the front. Many of them came from the slums and shantytowns and had been radicalized during the Revolution. Afterward, they found their inevitably dull and grim lives an anticlimax. Some had joined the Foundation for the Downtrodden or worked for Construction Jihad, but this could not compare with the excitement of the battlefield. Iran was technically ill-equipped for the war; there had been a population explosion, and the youth formed the majority group in the country. The Foundation for the Downtrodden became the nucleus of an army of twenty million young people who were eager for action. The government passed an edict which allowed male children from the age of twelve to enlist at the front without their parents' permission. They would become the wards of the Imam, and could be assured of a place in paradise in the event of their death. Tens of thousands of adolescents, wearing crimson headbands (the insignia of a martyr), poured into the war zone. Some cleared minefields, running ahead of the troops and often getting blown to pieces. Others became suicide-bombers, attacking Iraqi tanks kamikaze-style. Special scribes were sent to the front to write their wills, many of which took the form of letters to Imam Khomeini, and spoke of the light he had brought into their lives and of the joy of fighting "alongside friends on the road to Paradise."[25]

These young people restored Khomeini's faith in the Revolution; they were following the example of Imam Husain, dying in order to "witness" to the primacy of the Unseen. It was the highest form of asceticism, through which a Muslim transcends self and achieves union with God. Unlike their elders, these children had ceased to be "slaves of nature," wedded to self-interest and the material world. They were helping Iran achieve "a situation which we cannot describe in any other way except to say that it is a divine country."[26] As long as men and women focused solely on the material and the mundane, they became less than human. "Dying does not mean nothingness," Khomeini declared, "it is life."[27] Martyrdom had become a crucial part of Iran's revolt against the rational pragmatism of the West and essential to the Greater Jihad for the nation's soul.[28] But despite Khomeini's insistence that martyrdom was not "nothingness," there was nihilism in this shocking dispatch of thousands of children to an early, violent death. It contravened fundamental human values, crucial to religious and secularists alike, about the sacred inviolability of life and our instinctive urge to protect our children at the cost of our own lives, if necessary. This cult of the child martyr was another fatal distortion of faith, to which fundamentalists in all three monotheistic traditions are prone. It sprang, perhaps, from the terror that comes from battling against powerful enemies who seek our destruction. But it also shows how perilous it can be to translate a mystical, mythical imperative into a pragmatic, military or political policy. When Mulla Sadra had spoken of the mystical death to self, he had not envisaged the physical, voluntary death of thousands of young people. Again, what works well in the spiritual domain can become destructive and even immoral if interpreted literally and practically in the mundane world.

It was clearly proving very difficult to create a truly Islamic polity. In December 1987, Khomeini, now frail and ailing, addressed himself once again to the constitutional issue. This time, the Council of Guardians was blocking the labor laws, which, they claimed, contravened the Shariah. Khomeini, who supported the populist Majlis against the more elitist and reactionary *ulema* on the Council, declared that the state had the power to replace fundamental Islamic systems if the welfare of the people demanded it. The Shariah was a preindustrial code, and needed to be radically adapted to the needs of the modern world, and Khomeini seemed to sense this. The state, he said, could substitute

> those fundamental Islamic systems, by any kind of social, eco-
> nomic, labor . . . urban affairs, agricultural, or other system, and
> can make the services . . . that are the monopoly of the state into
> an instrument for the implementation of general and comprehen-
> sive policies.[29]

Khomeini had made a declaration of independence. The state must have a "monopoly" in such practical matters, and must be emancipated from the constraining laws of traditional religion. Two weeks later, he went further. President Khameini had interpreted his remarks to mean that the Supreme Faqih had the right to *interpret* the law. Khomeini replied that this was not what he had meant. Government, he repeated, making no mention of his own rule as Faqih, did not merely have the power to interpret divine law, but was the vehicle of that law itself. Government was a crucial part of that divine rule which God had delegated to the Prophet, and had "priority over all peripheral divine orders." It even took precedence over such "pillars" of Islam as prayer, the Ramadan fast, and the Hajj:

> The government is empowered to unilaterally revoke any lawful
> agreement . . . if the agreement contravenes the interests of Islam
> and the country. It can prevent any matter, whether religious or
> secular, if it is against the interests of Islam.[30]

For centuries, Shiis had insisted on a separation of spheres: the absolute *mythos* of religion and spirituality gave meaning to but was quite distinct from the pragmatic *logos* of politics. Now Khomeini seemed to be insisting that government must not be impeded in its utilitarian pursuit of the interests of the people and the greater good of Islam.

Some assumed that Khomeini was referring to his *own* government and thought that he was promoting his doctrine of Velayat-e Faqih to a status that was superior to the "pillars" of Islam. Western observers accused Khomeini of megalomania. But Speaker Rafsanjani noted that Khomeini had not mentioned the Faqih. To the consternation of Khomeini's most radical supporters, he suggested that by "government" Khomeini had meant the Majlis. In an extraordinary sermon on January 12, 1988, Rafsanjani gave a new interpretation of Velayat-e Faqih. God had not revealed all the laws that were needed by the *ummah* to the Prophet in the Koran. He had delegated his authority to Muhammad, who had become his "vice-gerent" and allowed him to use his own initiative on these secondary matters. Now Imam Khomeini, the Supreme Faqih, had delegated his authority to the Majlis, which must also make up new laws, on its own initiative. Did this mean that Iran was embracing Western-style democracy? By no means. This right to legislate did not come from the people but from God, who had passed his authority to the Prophet, to the Imams, and now to Imam Khomeini, and it was they—not the people—who gave legitimacy to the rulings of the Majlis. "So you see," Rafsanjani argued, "democracy is present in a form better than the West," because it was rooted in God. It was a "healthy style of government of the people, by the people, with the permission of Velayat-e Faqih."[31] Yet again, as had happened in the West, the needs of the modern state had propelled Iran toward a democratic polity, but this time it came in an Islamic package to which the people could relate and link with their own Shii traditions.

Rafsanjani had probably gone beyond his brief, but Khomeini seemed pleased. In the spring elections of 1988, he merely asked the people to support the Majlis, making no mention of the clergy. The people, who were longing for economic reconstruction, did not miss this implied rebuke, and the *ulema* lost half their seats. In the new Majlis, only 63 out of the 270 members had received a traditional *madrasah* education.[32] Again, Khomeini seemed pleased with the results. He also gave the green light to the more pragmatic politicians who, in the winter of 1988, sought to amend the constitution. In October, he insisted that the *ulema* must not be permitted to impede the progress of the country. The reconstruction program should be led by "experts, in particular, cabinet ministers, the appropriate Majlis committees, . . . scientific and research centers, . . . inventors, discoverers and committed specialists."[33] Two months later, he allowed a committee to convene to revise the constitution. The more radical Islamists, who saw any dilution of Velayat-e Faqih as a betrayal of the revolution, were dismayed, but the pragmatists seemed to be winning the day, with the Imam's approval.

It was in this context of internal conflict that, on February 14, 1989, four months before his death, Khomeini issued his *fatwa* against the British Indian author Salman Rushdie. In his novel *The Satanic Verses*, Rushdie had created what many Muslims regarded as a blasphemous portrait of the Prophet Muhammad, which presented him as a lecher, a charlatan, and a tyrant, and—most dangerously—suggested that the Koran had been tainted by satanic influence. It was a novel that brilliantly expressed the giddy confusion of the postmodern world, where there are no boundaries, no certainties, and no clearly or easily defined identity. The passages that gave offense were the recorded dreams and fantasies of a deracinated Indian film star, who is suffering a breakdown and has interiorized the anti-Islamic prejudices of the West. The blasphemy was also an attempt to cancel the clinging relics of the past and to achieve an independent identity, free of old shibboleths. But many Muslims experienced this portrait of Muhammad as profoundly wounding. It seemed a violation of something sacred to their own Muslim *personae*. Dr. Zaki Badawi, one of Britain's most liberal Muslims, told *The Guardian* newspaper that Rushdie's words were "far worse to Muslims than if he had raped one's own daughter." So internalized was the Prophet by the practices of Islam in every Muslim's being, that the novel was "like a knife being dug into you or being raped yourself."[34] There were riots in Pakistan, and the novel was ceremonially burned in Bradford, England, where there was a large community of Muslims of Indian and Pakistani origin, who objected to the British blasphemy laws that punished only insults to Christianity, and were aware of widespread prejudice in England against Islam. On February 13, Khomeini saw the Pakistani police open fire on the demonstrators and concluded that the novel must be evil. His *fatwa* commanded Muslims all over the world "to put to death Salman Rushdie and his publishers, wherever they are found."

At the Islamic Conference the following month, the *fatwa* was condemned by forty-four out of the forty-five member countries as un-Islamic. It is not permissible in Islamic law to sentence an offender without trial, nor to apply Muslim law in a non-Muslim country. The *fatwa* was yet another distortion of Islam. Mulla Sadra, one of Khomeini's chief spiritual mentors, had been adamantly opposed to any such inquisitorial violence and coercion. He had insisted upon freedom of thought. Muslim outrage sprang, yet again, from a conviction that Islam had received a deadly blow; the years of suppression, denigration, and secularist attack had scarred Muslim sensibilities. The *fatwa* was an act of war, and was experienced as such by secularists and liberals in the West, who felt that *their* most sacred values had been violated. For them, humanity—not a supernatural God—was the measure of all things; men and women must have the freedom to fulfill their potential in their pursuit of artistic excellence. Muslims, for whom the sovereignty of God is the supreme value, could not accept this. The Rushdie affair was a clash of two irreconcilable orthodoxies; neither side could understand the viewpoint of the other. Different groups, living in the same country, were diametrically opposed to one another and in a state of potential war.

This polarization between religious and secularists became clear when Khomeini died in June 1989. In the West, Khomeini was regarded as the enemy, and people were bewildered to see the unfeigned grief of the Iranians at his funeral. The mob surged around his coffin with such passion that the corpse fell out; it was as though they wanted to keep the Imam with them forever. However, the Islamic Republic did not fall apart after his death. Indeed, it showed signs of greater flexibility. Even though the *fatwa* had, like the Hostage Crisis, incurred the enmity of the West, Iran seemed to be moving closer to the Western spirit. The new constitution, which was passed on July 9, 1989, showed a marked move toward a more secular, pragmatic style of government. Mystical powers were no longer attributed to the Supreme Faqih, nor was he to be instated, as Khomeini had been, by popular acclaim. He had to be reasonably well-versed in Islamic law, but need no longer be one of the senior *mujtahids*. If there were several possible candidates, "political perspicacity" was to be the decisive quality of the new leader. The Council of Guardians retained its right of veto, but its power was qualified by the new Expediency Discernment Council, which would adjudicate all disputes with the Majlis. As a result of these changes, the Majlis was able to enact all the reforms that had been blocked by the Guardians.[35]

On the day after Khomeini's funeral, Ayatollah Khameini was proclaimed Faqih, and on July 28, 1989, Rafsanjani became the new elected president. His cabinet excluded the radicals; a third of his ministers had been educated in the West, and they pushed for more Western investment and a more capitalist, diminished role for the government in economic matters. There would still be problems. The hard-liners continued to fight the pragmatists; the conservatives on the Council of Guardians would still manage to block reforms, and the institutional apparatus remains faulty. But the needs of the state seem to be pushing Iranians toward greater pluralism and to a secularization based on Shii rather than on Western tradition. The people are less hostile to modern values than before, because they are able to approach them in an Islamic milieu.

The shift in emphasis can be seen in the work of Abdolkarim Sorush, one of Iran's leading intellectuals. Sorush had studied the history of science at London University and held important posts in Khomeini's government after the Revolution. Today he is no longer part of the political establishment, but he strongly influences those in power. His Friday lectures are frequently broadcast, and he is one of the most prominent speakers in the mosques and universities. Sorush admires both Khomeini and Shariati, but goes beyond them. He has a more accurate view of the West, going so far as to say that by the end of the twentieth century, many Iranians had three identities: pre-Islamic, Islamic, and Western, which they must try to reconcile. Not everything Western was contaminating or toxic.[36] But Sorush will not accept the more radical secularist ethos of the West. Scientific rationalism cannot, in his view, provide a viable alternative to religion. Human beings will always need a spirituality that takes them beyond the material. Iranians should learn to appreciate the values of modern science, but hold on to their own Shii traditions too.[37] Islam must also change: *fiqh* must adapt to the modern industrial world, develop a philosophy of civil rights and an economic theory capable of holding its own in the twenty-first century.[38] Sorush is also opposed to *ulema* rule, because "the cause of religion is too great to be entrusted only to the clergy."[39] Sorush is often harassed by the more conservative clerics, but his popularity suggests that the Islamic republic is moving toward a postrevolutionary phase that will bring it closer to the West.

This seemed clear on May 23, 1997, when Hojjat ol-Islam Seyyed Khatami came to the presidency in a landslide victory, gaining 22 million out of a possible 30 million votes. He immediately made it clear that he wanted to achieve a more positive relationship with the Western world, and in September 1998, he dissociated his government from the *fatwa* against Salman Rushdie. This was later endorsed by the Faqih, Ayatollah Khameini. Khatami still finds his reforms impeded by the Council of Guardians, but his election signaled the deep desire of a large segment of the population for greater pluralism, a gentler interpretation of Islamic law, economic protection for the "downtrodden," and more progressive policies for women.* There is no retreat from Islam. Iranians still seem to want their polity to be contained within a Shii package, which seems to have made modern values more acceptable than when they were regarded as a foreign import. It could be that if a radical religious movement is allowed its head, works through its aggressions and resentment, it can learn to interact creatively with other traditions, eschew the violence of the more recent past, and make peace with former foes. Religion becomes most violent when suppressed.

This had become clear in Egypt in 1981, when the Western world was grieved to hear of the assassination of President Anwar Sadat by Sunni fundamentalists. Sadat had been officiating on October 6 at the parade celebrating the achievements of the 1973 war against Israel. Suddenly, one of the trucks in the parade pulled out of line just in front of the presidential stand,

---

*This became even more evident in the summer of 1999, when Iranian students came out onto the streets to demand more democracy and an Islamic government that is not impeded by reactionary *ulema.*

and when Sadat saw First Lieutenant Khaled Islambouli jump out and run toward him, he stood up, assuming that the officer wanted to salute him. But instead there was a volley of machine-gun fire. Islambouli shot round after round into the body of Sadat, even after he had himself been wounded in the stomach, shouting, "Give me that dog, that infidel!" The attack lasted only fifty seconds, but seven people besides Sadat were killed, and twenty-eight others injured.

Westerners were shocked by the ferocity of the assault. They had liked Sadat. Unlike Khomeini, Sadat was a Muslim ruler they could understand. He seemed devout without being a "fanatic"; Westerners admired his peace initiative with Israel and his Open Door policy. A bevy of American and European princes, politicians, and presidents attended Sadat's funeral. No Arab leaders came, however, and there were no crowds lining the streets. On the night of Sadat's death, the streets of Cairo were eerily quiet. The Egyptian people did not weep for Sadat, nor did they mass, grief-stricken, around his coffin as the Iranians would later mob the corpse of Khomeini. Once again, the modern West and the more traditional societies of the Middle East were poles apart and could not share each other's vision of events.

As we have seen, there were a significant number of Egyptians who thought that Sadat's rule had more in common with the *jahiliyyah* than with Islam. In 1980, on the Eid al-Adha, one of the holiest days in the Muslim year, the student members of the *jamaat al-islamiyyah*, who had been forbidden to hold their summer camp in Cairo, occupied the Saladin Mosque, denounced Camp David, and condemned Sadat as a "Tartar," one of the Mongol rulers of the thirteenth century who had supposedly converted to Islam but were Muslim only in name.[40] Other members of the suppressed *jamaat* had joined the network of secret cells, dedicated to violent *jihad* against the regime. Khaled Islambouli, who had studied at the University of Minya, was a member of this Jihad organization.

Sadat was aware of this dissent and was determined to avoid the fate of his friend the shah. In 1978, while revolution mounted in Iran, he had issued what he called the Law of Shame. Any deviation in thought, word, or deed from the established order was to be punished with loss of civil rights and confiscation of passports and property. Citizens were forbidden to join any organization, take part in any broadcast, or publish anything critical of the regime that was deemed to threaten "national unity or social peace." Even a casual private remark, made in the privacy of one's own family, was not to go unpunished.[41] In the last months of Sadat's life, the regime became even more oppressive. On September 3, 1981, Sadat rounded up 1536 of his known critics; they included cabinet ministers, politicians, intellectuals, journalists, preachers, and members of the Islamist groups. One of the Islamists thus imprisoned was Muhammad Islambouli, the brother of Sadat's assassin.[42]

We can gain some insight into the motivation of Sadat's killers in a treatise written by Abd al-Salam Faraj, the spiritual guide of Islambouli's Jihad organization. *Al-Faridah al-Ghaybah* ("The Neglected Duty") was published after the assassination in December 1981. It was not an apologia and was not originally intended for the general public. It seems to have been circulated privately among the members of the organization and affords a unique opportunity to learn what militant Muslims were talking to one another about, what their concerns, anxieties, and fears were. Muslims, Faraj argued, had an urgent task. God had commanded the Prophet Muhammad to establish a truly Islamic state. Faraj opened his treatise with a Koranic quotation that shows that only thirteen years after the first revelations to Muhammad, God was already growing impatient with Muslims who failed to obey his orders. "Is it not high time" for Muslims to act? God asks indignantly.[43] How much more impatient he must be after fourteen centuries! Muslims must, therefore, make "every conceivable effort" to do God's will. They must not be like the previous generations, who imagined that they could establish an Islamic state by peaceful, nonviolent means. The only way was by *jihad*, a holy war.[44]

The *jihad* was the "neglected duty" of the title. Even though Muslims no longer practiced this sacred violence, Faraj argued that it was the most important duty of all. This was flying in the face of centuries of Islamic tradition. To argue his case, Faraj, like Qutb, had to be ruthlessly selective, and, in the process, he inevitably distorted the Muslim vision. Again, it was a distortion that sprang from the experience of suppression. Faraj insisted that the sword was the only way to establish a just society. He cited a *hadith* in which the Prophet is reported to have said that anyone who was not willing to fight for his religion would die "as if he had never been a Muslim, or like someone who, filled with some form of hypocrisy, only outwardly pretended to be a Muslim."[45] In the Koran, God tells Muslims clearly that "fighting is ordained for you, even though it be hateful to you."[46] He commands Muslims to

> slay those who ascribe divinity to aught beside God wherever you may come upon them, and take them captive, and besiege them and lie in wait for them in every conceivable place.[47]

These Verses of the Sword, Faraj believed, were revealed to Muhammad later than those which urged Muslims to make peace with their enemies and address them courteously. They had, therefore, abrogated those teachings in which the Koran seems averse to violence.[48]

But Faraj had a difficulty. The Koran targets only idolaters ("who ascribe divinity to aught beside God"), whereas Sadat claimed that he was a Muslim who observed the five "pillars." How could Muslims fight him? Faraj found help in a *fatwa* of Ibn Taymiyyah, who had argued in the fourteenth century that the Mongol rulers, who had converted to Islam, were in fact apostates, because they ruled according to their own laws instead of the Shariah.[49] The current rulers of Egypt, Faraj declared, were worse than the Mongols. The Mongol codes had, at least, contained some Jewish and Christian legislation, but the legal system of Egypt today was based on the "laws of unbelief," created by infidels and imposed on the Muslim people by the colonialists.[50]

> The rulers of this age are in apostasy from Islam. They were raised at the tables of imperialism, be it Crusaderism, or Communism or Zionism. They carry nothing from Islam but their names, even though they pray and fast and claim to be Muslims.[51]

The students who had occupied the Saladin Mosque in 1980 had also compared Sadat to the Mongol rulers. Faraj's ideas do not seem to have been confined to a small group of extremists. By the 1980s, they were in the air and were widely discussed.

Faraj admitted that in Islamic law, *jihad* had been defined as a collective duty. It was not up to an individual to wage a holy war, but was a decision that could only be taken by the community as a whole. But, Faraj insisted, this law only applied when the *ummah* was under attack from external enemies. The situation today was far more serious, because the infidels had actually taken over in Egypt. *Jihad,* therefore, had become a duty for every single Muslim who was capable of fighting.[52] The whole complex tradition of Islam had thus narrowed to a single point: the only way to be a good Muslim in Sadat's Egypt was to take part in a violent holy war against the regime.

Faraj answered questions that were troubling his young disciples. Even though they were planning an assassination, Jihad members wanted to behave as morally as possible. Was it acceptable to tell lies in order to conceal their plans? What about the possibility of killing innocent bystanders as well as the guilty rulers? In Egypt, where family authority is very important, younger members wanted to know if it was all right to take part in the conspiracy without asking their parents' permission.[53] There was obviously concern about undertaking a *jihad* against Sadat before Jerusalem had been liberated from Israel: which should take priority? Faraj replied that the *jihad* for Jerusalem should be led only by a devout Muslim leader, not by an infidel. He also revealed a fatal confidence in God's direct intervention. Once a truly Islamic state had been established, Jerusalem would automatically revert to Muslim rule.[54] God had promised in the Koran that if Muslims fought the unbelievers, "God will chastise them by your hands, and will bring disgrace upon them, and will succour you against them."[55] From a literal reading of this text, Faraj concluded that if Muslims took the initiative, God "will then intervene [and change] the laws of nature." Could militants expect miraculous help? Faraj tragically answered "yes."[56]

Observers were puzzled that there was no follow-up to Sadat's assassination. The conspirators seem to have made no plans for a coup, nor did they try to orchestrate a general uprising. The reason for this was probably their confidence in divine intervention after Muslims had taken the first step, by killing the president. Faraj appeared to take this for granted. Even though the conspirators knew that they were up against enormous odds,[57] Faraj considered it "stupid" to fear failure. A Muslim's duty was to obey God's commands. "We are not responsible for the results." Once "the Rule of the Infidel has fallen, everything will be in the hands of the Muslims."[58]

Like so many other fundamentalists, Faraj was a literalist. He read the words of scripture as though they were factually true in every detail, and could be applied, simply and directly, to everyday life. This showed yet another danger of using the *mythos* of scripture as a blueprint for practical action. The old ideal had been to keep *mythos* and *logos* separate: political action was the preserve of reason. In their revolt against the hegemony of scientific rationalism, these Sunni fundamentalists were abandoning reason and had to learn the bitter truth that even though the assassins of Sadat had, as they thought, obeyed God to the letter, God did not intervene and establish an Islamic state. After Sadat's death, Hosni Mubarak became president with the minimum of fuss, and the secularist regime remains in place to this day.

It appears that the ideas outlined in *The Neglected Duty* were not confined to a tiny group of extremists, but were more widespread in Egyptian society than observers believed at the time.[59] Few Egyptians would have wanted actually to kill Sadat and most were shocked by the assassination, but their composure after his death was marked and chilling. The Shaykhs of al-Azhar, for example, condemned the assassination, but they did not seem to be heartbroken to have lost Sadat. In the first issue of the Azhari magazine immediately after the murder, there was no photograph of Sadat, and the killing was only obliquely mentioned on the second page. The one member of the religious establishment to come out strongly and unambiguously against *The Neglected Duty* was the Mufti, who gave a detailed answer to Faraj's treatise. He declared that it was forbidden to call another practicing Muslim an apostate. The practice of *takfir* (excommunication) had never been common in Islam, since nobody but God could read a person's heart. He discussed the Verses of the Sword in their historical context, showing them to have arisen in response to the particular circumstances of seventh-century Medina; they could not be applied verbatim to conditions in twentieth-century Egypt. Yet in an article in the *Journal of Islamic Mysticism*, the main Sufi periodical, in December 1981, the Mufti took it for granted that his readers would be familiar with the teachings of Faraj, even though *The Neglected Duty* had only just been published and they could not possibly all have read it yet. The ideas had probably percolated through devout circles and become common coin.[60] The vast majority of Egyptians regarded the assassination as a great sin, but many felt ambivalent about Sadat. Times had changed since Nasser's death; Egyptians now wanted to see genuine Islamic qualities in their leaders, and were turning away from the secularist ethos.

Mubarak had to acknowledge the religious mood of the country. He immediately released most of the people imprisoned during Sadat's crackdown in September 1981. He has continued to try to control the Islamic movements, but has targeted only specific groups, and has allowed the Muslim Brotherhood (which is still not officially recognized) to participate in party elections and permitted them to build a position for themselves in the government. The Islamic Alliance, the Society's new political organization, has carefully distanced itself from extremists, has tried to improve relations with the Coptic Christians of Egypt, and to work peacefully for the creation of an Islamic state. Egypt is now a very religious country. Today Islam is as dominant as Nasserism was in the 1960s. The Brothers' slogan, "Islam is the solution," seems to resonate with an increasing number of people.[61] Questions of personal piety now dominate the letter-pages of magazines and periodicals, and there are lively discussions of Islamic issues in the media. Religious dress is ubiquitous, men and women are now regularly segregated in classrooms, and designated areas for prayer are now taken for granted in public life.[62] There is still a widespread desire to return Egypt to full Islamic law and to make Islam the basis of the constitution. Religious candidates become stronger in every election. Egypt is a nominally multiparty, democratic country, but corruption is still widespread, the executive autocratic, and the state party refuses to become a mere ruling party. There is a suspicion that if the elections were fair, the people would vote for more religious leaders. As a result, Islam has become the chief challenge to Mubarak's regime.[63]

The religious revival of the 1970s has matured. Many of the mainstream, which includes Egyptians of all ages and classes, now adopt a moderate form of fundamentalism. Most are not interested in politics, but given the predisposition to religion, they would be easy to mobilize by Islamic leaders in a social or economic crisis. Many of the young, however, still feel that modern Egyptian society does not have their interests at heart. Students in the science, engineering, and mathematics faculties are still drawn to the more extreme groups. They find that a stringent Muslim lifestyle gives them a viable alternative to the secularist option, helps them to make the difficult transition from a rural to a modern urban culture, and gives them a sense of authenticity and belonging.[64] It also provides them with a community, something which is more difficult to achieve in modern society but which is a crucial human need. They are not seeking to turn the clock back but are looking for new ways to apply the Islamic paradigm, which served Muslims well for centuries, to current conditions.

The deep discontent which erupted so horribly in the assassination of Sadat still simmers beneath the surface, after two decades of Mubarak's limited liberalization and partial implementation of democracy. The difference now is that the Islamists are much more organized. Patrick Gaffney, the American Arabist, revisited Minya in 1991 and noted that the crowds performing the noon prayers every Friday in the main street outside the tiny fundamentalist mosque were much more disciplined than they had been in the 1970s. Gone was the old ragged and disorderly defiance. Many of the participants were in their thirties and forties; they wore a uniform white *jalabiyyah* and the correct Islamic head covering. They gave the impression of forming a distinct and focused subculture, with its own direction and identity. Gaffney also noted a huge new government building housing the offices of the Ministry of the Interior, which was meant to symbolize the massive power of the state. An emblem of control in a former trouble spot, it seemed to have nothing to do with the dedicated Islamists, who were oriented to Mecca rather than Cairo.[65] Two realms existed side by side in Egypt in a schizophrenic rift that shows no sign of healing.

Not surprisingly, therefore, there is war between the "two nations." Periodically, there are reports of arrests and shoot-outs between the police and the most extreme Muslim groups. Where the majority of Islamists are content with a fundamentalist separation from secular society, a small minority resort to terror. Since 1986, there have been politically motivated attacks on Americans, Israelis, and prominent Egyptians. In 1987, Islamists shot Hasan Abu Bawha, a former minister of the interior, and Nabawi Ahmed, the editor of the weekly journal *al-Mussawar*. In October 1990, they killed the Speaker of the Egyptian parliament, Rifaat Mahjub, and gunned down the determined secularist Faraj Foda in 1992. That year saw the first Islamist attacks on European and American tourists.[66] Since tourism is crucial to the economy, Mubarak responded with raids and indiscriminate, clumsy mass arrests, which put more fuel on the flames. By 1997, human rights groups claimed that 20,000 suspected guerrillas were being detained without trial in Egyptian prisons, many—yet again—arrested for simply possessing an inflammatory pamphlet or attending a meeting. On November 17, 1997, the terrorist group Jamaat al-Islamiyyah massacred fifty-eight foreign tourists and four Egyptians at Luxor, insisting that this attack would "not be the last, because the Mujahedin will continue their work as long as the government continues to torture and kill the sons of the Islamic movement."[67] The war continues. Desperation and helplessness have continued to inspire a minority of Sunni Muslims in Egypt to turn Islam into an ideology that, in its justification of murder, is a total distortion of religion.

LIKE EGYPT, Israel was also becoming a more religious country. This was nowhere more evident than in the political rise of the Haredim during the 1980s. A minority of the ultra-Orthodox Jews continued to regard the State of Israel as inherently evil, "a pollution that encompasses all other pollutions, a complete heresy that includes all other heresies."[68] "In its very essence, Zionism utterly denies the essentials of our faith," wrote Yeramiel Domb in the Neturei Karta newsletter in 1975. "It is an absolute denial that reaches down to the very depths, the very foundations, the very roots."[69] But most of the Haredim did not go so far; they simply saw the state as having no religious significance and regarded it with utter indifference. This neutrality enabled them to take part in the political process. The Hasidim could even see their political work in a religious light, as a redemption of the divine sparks trapped in the secular institutions of the state. By pressing for such religious legislation as the banning of pork, or promoting more stringent Sabbath observance, they could make Israeli society more open to the possibility of messianic transformation. The Lithuanian Misnagdim had a more pragmatic attitude. They had entrenched themselves more deeply than ever in the *yeshiva* world, and used the state to buttress their own institutions. They were entirely uninterested in questions of state, of defense, of domestic or foreign policy; their sole criterion for the support of one party rather than another was the amount of funding and political backing it was willing to devote to the *yeshivot*.[70]

Survival was still the major objective of the Haredim. Their attitude to the gentile world had hardened since the 1960s. The trial of Adolf Eichmann in Jerusalem in 1961 had led to a new consciousness of the Holocaust, which made the Haredim even more determined to keep their distance from *goyische* culture and those secular Jews who participated in it. They saw themselves at war with modern civilization and had nothing to say to the gentiles or to those Jews, secular or religious, who did not share their view of Judaism. Once again, the experience of suppression and persecution had led to a narrowing of religious horizons and to new emphasis on ideological conformity. Increasingly, Haredim had neither the language nor the concepts to relate in any meaningful way outside the *yeshivot* or the Hasidic courts.[71] They felt as estranged from their Israeli neighbors as their ancestors had felt from the gentiles in the Diaspora.

Yet their new awareness of the Holocaust had made them hyperconscious of the vulnerability of Judaism. In order to preserve the Torah, they were willing to enter the political process. Their attitude had been well expressed by a member of Edah Haredis in 1950:

> We are weak; the strong instruments are in the hands of our opponents; separated and divided, we stand against storms that threaten to annihilate us, God forbid. Laws that injure our inmost being will make our situation tragic and unbearable. We must therefore maintain our guard and repulse the attacks against us from within the government.[72]

But in the 1950s, conditions were not right. Agudat Israel had broken with the Labor government in 1952 on the issue of drafting women into the IDF, and had not been represented in the Knesset since. But after the Likud victory in 1977, Agudat became a member of the coalition government. The Moetzet G'dolay ha-Torah (Council of Torah Sages), the advisory body of Agudat, thus brought elderly rabbis, whom the Zionists had mentally consigned to the scrap heap of history, close to the centers of power. But the old hostility between Hasidim and Misnagdim, muted for decades, surfaced once again in the council; they began to see one another as rivals, in competition for the same funding. This led to the emergence of new Haredi parties and new political players.

Rabbi Eliezer Schach, for example, head of the Ponovez Yeshiva and leader of Lithuanian Jewry in Israel, became worried about the influence of the Sephardic Jews, who had immigrated to Israel from the Arab countries after 1948. Many of the Sephardics were coming under the influence of the Hasidic members of Agudat Israel, and Schach feared that this increased Hasidic constituency would draw funds away from the Misnagdic *yeshivot*. To counter the danger and to woo the Sephardics, he founded a new Sephardic party, Shas Torah Guardians, with the Sephardic Chief Rabbi, Ovadia Yosef. Sephardics did not have the same aversion to Zionism as the European Jews. Until the creation of the State of Israel in 1948, they had not

been persecuted in the Muslim world and had not developed a ghetto mentality. They were not squeamish about taking part in state affairs and took to
political life with gusto. In the 1984 elections, Shas won four seats in the
Knesset.

In 1988, however, the Seventh Lubavitcher Rebbe decided to counter the
influence of Rabbi Schach and the Misnagdim. He ordered all his followers
to vote for Agudat in the forthcoming elections.[73] He also wanted to force
Agudat to press for a more stringent government definition of Jewishness.
This move showed the indifference of the Haredim toward the political welfare of the State of Israel. Had the Israeli government complied with the
Rebbe's wishes and declared that an offspring of a mixed marriage or somebody who had been converted by a Reform rabbi was not Jewish, it would
have antagonized many of the American Jews who lobbied so successfully
for Israel in the United States. American support was absolutely crucial to
Israel's survival, but the Lubavitcher Rebbe did not care about that. He simply wanted to further his own mission to the Jewish world. Some of his
emissaries had difficulty with people who considered themselves Jewish but
did not meet halakhic criteria. If the State of Israel would formally declare
that such people were not Jewish, that would make life a great deal easier for
the Lubavitch. The Rebbe's intervention, however, greatly increased the
Hasidic membership of Agudat, so to oppose this, Rabbi Schach formed a
new Misnagdic party, Degel ha-Torah (Torah Banner).

To the astonishment of the Israeli public, the religious parties gained a
record number of eighteen seats in the 1988 elections, and as a result found
that they now held the balance of power between Labor and Likud. The secularist politicians, who had previously despised the Orthodox and regarded
them as hopeless anachronisms, now had to come to them cap in hand to
ask them to join their camp and enable them to form a government. The
Haredim were as deeply opposed to the State of Israel as ever; they still
believed that secular Jews were determined to destroy religion. They
regarded their political work as a necessary evil, an act of self-defense. It
could "be defined as stealing into the camp of the enemy," wrote Rabbi
Nathan Grossman in 1991 in the Lithuanian newspaper *Yated Neeman*.[74] Yet,
almost in spite of themselves, the Haredim had acquired unprecedented
power in the state with which they felt at war. Ever since the Holocaust, the
Haredim had striven to re-create the lost world of European Jewry. They
saw the old life in Eastern Europe as a Golden Age and looked for inspiration to the great rabbis of the past. But by the late 1980s, they had surpassed
them. Since the destruction of the Temple in 70 CE, no religious Jew had
been as powerful as Rabbi Schach, who by 1988 led two political parties and
was courted by major politicians for his decisive vote.[75]

This became dramatically evident on March 26, 1990. The Yad Eliahu basketball stadium in Tel Aviv is the symbolic temple of Israeli secular culture. In Israel, basketball is almost a national religion. The sport represents the Zionist dream of the new Jew, no longer bowed palely over a volume of Talmud in a musty *yeshiva*, no longer shrouded in the black robes of Orthodoxy, but stripped for action, tanned, fit, healthy, and able to compete internationally with the *goyim* and beat them at their own game. On that March evening in 1990, however, the stadium was crammed not with eager supporters of the Maccabees (the national basketball team) but with ten thousand bearded, caftaned Haredim. The ultra-Orthodox had invaded the heart of secular Israel and, for that evening at least, had taken over one of its chief citadels. Moreover, the event was televised and watched breathlessly by religious and secularist Israelis alike, throughout the country. The occasion? Rabbi Schach was about to address his followers and instruct them on how they should vote in the forthcoming election. The nation had awoken to the fact that the balance of power was held by an aged rabbi with a top hat and side curls, who spoke a strange mixture of Hebrew, Aramaic, and Yiddish that most of his secular listeners could not understand. That evening Rabbi Schach would determine the fate of Labor and Likud.

A peace process between Israel and the Palestinians was inching its way painfully forward, but it had split the National Coalition Government. Both Labor and Likud began to seek alliances with the smaller parties, of which the religious formed the largest single bloc. Labor had made informal agreements with Agudat and Shas, but Rabbi Yosef, one of the leaders of Shas, feared that a Labor alliance would split the party. The Sephardics tended to be ultranationalists, hated the Arabs, and were adamantly opposed to the territorial concessions envisaged by Labor. Rabbi Schach, cofounder of Shas, came to the rescue. He would address his disciples in Shas and Degel ha-Torah and advise them about the imminent coalition talks.

The rabbi's ten-minute speech was not only bewildering, but obscurely disturbing to the Israelis who watched him on their television sets. He did not mention the coalition talks directly and addressed none of the issues that obsessed the rest of the nation. He was clearly quite indifferent to such issues as Palestinian rights, national defense, or the feasibility of exchanging territory for peace. He had not a single good word to say about the State of Israel. Instead of seeing the Jewish state as a savior, he referred bleakly to the "terrible and awful" time in which the Haredim now lived. The wars that worried the rabbi were not the Arab-Israeli wars, but the long battle waged by the Zionists against religion. "The wars we are fighting [against those who oppose tradition] did not begin today; they began already at the time of the First World War, and only the Master of the Universe knows what else is expected," the rabbi said with great emotion. But the outcome was not in doubt: "The Jew cannot be destroyed. He may be killed, but his children will continue to cleave to the Torah."

Bad enough that they were cast as the enemy; but, to their dismay, Laborites had to hear their sacred institutions and themselves denounced as not merely un-Jewish but positively anti-Jewish. "Is Labor something holy?" asked the rabbi derisively. "Have they not separated themselves from the past, and seek a new Torah?" These *kibbutzniks* were no better than gentiles; they did not even know what Shabbat or Yom Kippur was. How could such people be trusted to decide "critical and essential matters facing the Jewish people?" There could be no deal with Labor politicians. "When they are in the Knesset, they are not interested in strengthening religiosity. To the contrary, they seek to pass laws that will destroy the Jewish religion."[76] The significance of that evening in Yad Eliahu Stadium did not lie simply in the fact that Rabbi Schach, alone and unaided, appeared effortlessly to have swung the balance in favor of Likud, but that it marked the extraordinary journey of the Haredim from a despised out-group to the heart of power. The occasion also showed that there were "two nations" in Israel, who scarcely understood one another's language and shared none of the same concerns. It also revealed the deep hatred that inspired the piety of so many of the Haredim, a rage directed not merely against gentiles, but also against their fellow Jews.

The extreme religious Zionists and members of Gush Emunim were also ready for a fight. They were rebels, mounting what they saw as a revolution against secular nationalism on the one hand, and Orthodoxy on the other. Life had changed drastically for Jews. They felt that there was no need for Jews to be constricted by the traditions belonging to the Diaspora, because the messianic age had begun. This was the first major outbreak of Jewish messianism since Shabbetai Zevi. At that time, too, Jews had felt in transition and believed that they were about to experience unprecedented change. But where Shabbateans had rebelled against the restrictions of the ghetto, Gush members felt territorially circumscribed. They were as obsessed with boundaries as the Shabbateans, and though they focused chiefly on the frontiers of Eretz Israel, they were also fighting a battle to define the limits and borders of Judaism. They wanted to break down the barriers between secular and religious Jews.[77] Kookists were convinced that, whatever the Haredim thought, it was possible to be at once fully Orthodox and Zionist; they also insisted, against the secularists, that without a religious dimension, Zionism was incomplete. But these were difficult years. Kookists felt betrayed by the Likud government, which had expelled them from Yamit, and, by making peace with the Arabs, had stalled the redemptive process.

This seemed clearer than ever when the Palestinian uprising known as the *intifadah* (an Arabic term meaning "a shaking off") broke out in 1987, and eventually impelled the Labor government to sign a peace treaty which, in Kookist eyes, was even more unacceptable than Camp David, because it promised to surrender parts of the holy land of the West Bank. Increasingly, Kookists felt that they were surrounded—rather as Jews had been in the Diaspora—by a hostile gentile world, but also by their fellow Jews, who were holding them back from the fulfillment they felt to be within their grasp.

As a result, the Gush's mystical joy in the Land became an ecstasy of rage, which could on occasion erupt in terrifying violence, in the first instance against the Arabs. In the early, more hopeful days of their movement, Gush settlers declared that they had come to "help" the Palestinians in the occupied territories, and to break down the "wall of hatred" between the two peoples, though the very terms in which this offer was couched revealed implacable hostility: "We have come to cleanse you of the air of murder to which you have become accustomed," Levinger had promised in the 1970s.[78] His behavior grew increasingly provocative. He used to walk aggressively, gun in hand, through Arab towns in the West Bank. If there had been a recent Palestinian attack on a settlement, he would lead activists in retaliatory, vigilante raids, smashing car windows or burning shops. After the outbreak of the *intifadah*, he said that whenever he approached Hebron, "there awakened within me raging spirits that did not give me peace."[79] In 1988, when his car was stoned by Palestinians in Hebron, Levinger jumped out and opened fire on his assailants, killing Khaled Salah, who was simply standing by his shoe store taking no part in the stoning. Afterward, Levinger ran amok, shooting indiscriminately, overturning vegetable carts, and cursing at the top of his voice. At his trial, he stated that though he had not murdered anybody, he wished he had had "the honour of killing an Arab."[80]

Gush members had different theories about what should be done about the Arabs in Eretz Israel. All agreed that the Palestinians had no rights to the land and that there was no place for them there. This theology of hatred and exclusion was, of course, a distortion of the Jewish faith. The Prophets of Israel, the Torah, and the rabbinical sages of the Talmud had all insisted on the paramount duties of justice and lovingkindness, even to "the stranger" who did not belong to their ethnic group but who lived with them in their Land.[81] Rabbi Hillel, an older contemporary of Jesus, had summed up the teachings of Judaism in the Golden Rule: "Do not do unto others as you would not have done unto you."[82] With fundamentalist selectivity, however, Kookists concentrated only on the more aggressive biblical passages, in which God commanded the Israelites to drive out the indigenous people of the Promised Land, to make no treaty with them, to destroy their sacred symbols, and even to exterminate them.[83] They interpreted the belief that the Jews were God's chosen people to mean that they were not bound by the laws obligatory for other nations, but were unique, holy, and set apart. God's command to conquer the land, argued Shlomo Aviner, was more important than "the human and moral considerations of the national rights of the gentiles to our land."[84]

Most Kookists believed that Arabs should be allowed to stay in Eretz Israel, but only as *gerim toshavim* ("resident aliens"). As long as they respected the State of Israel, they must be treated decently, but they could never become citizens or have political rights. Others would deny the Palestinians even this much consideration, and would press them to emigrate. A tiny minority have proposed extermination, using the biblical precedent of the Amalekites, a people so cruel that God commanded the Israelites to slay them without mercy.[85] In 1980, Rabbi Israel Hess published an article entitled "Genocide: A Commandment of the Torah" in the official magazine of Bar-Ilan University. He argued that the Palestinians were to Jews what darkness was to light, and that they deserved the same fate as the Amalekites.[86] In the same year, the Gush settler Haim Tzuria wrote that hatred was "natural and healthy":

> In each generation we have those who rise up to wipe us out, therefore each generation has its own Amalek. The Amalekism of our generation expresses itself in the extremely deep hatred of the Arabs to our national renaissance in the land of our forefathers.[87]

On May 3, 1980, six *yeshiva* students were murdered in Hebron. This inspired some of the most extreme Kookists to take revenge. Menachem Livni, a settler at Kiryat Arba, and Yehuda Etzion, a veteran Gush settler, planted bombs in the cars of five Arab mayors, intending not to kill but to mutilate them, so that they should be living reminders of the consequences of anti-Jewish terror. When he heard the news, Rabbi Haim Drukman exclaimed in rapture: "Thus may all Israel's enemies perish!"[88] Most Israelis, however, were horrified by this attack, which, in the event, only maimed two of the targeted mayors. They were even more disgusted when they learned that for Livni and Etzion this act of terror was just a sideline. In April 1984, the government revealed the existence of a Jewish underground in Israel which had plotted to blow up the Dome of the Rock, the third-holiest place in the Islamic world.

During the Six Day War in 1967, the IDF had conquered and taken East

Jerusalem and the Old City from Jordan, and, a few days after the war, Israel had annexed these districts and, in defiance of the international community, had declared Jerusalem to be the eternal capital of the Jewish state. It was a controversial decision, since in 1947 the United Nations had declared that Jerusalem should be an international zone, and after the Six Day War had demanded that Israel withdraw from all the territories occupied during the hostilities, including Jerusalem. Jerusalem had been a Muslim city since 638, apart from a brief period of Crusader rule (1099–1187); Jerusalem, which Muslims call al-Quds ("the Holy") is the third-holiest city in the Islamic world, after Mecca and Medina. The Dome of the Rock, which was completed in 691, was the first major Muslim monument ever built and was believed to mark the spot where Abraham offered his son to God in sacrifice; later tradition had it that the Prophet Muhammad had made a mystical ascent to heaven from this rock. This place is also deeply sacred in the Jewish world, since the Dome is on the Temple Mount, thought to be the site of the Temple built by King Solomon.

For centuries, however, there had been no tension between Jews and Muslims in Jerusalem; Jews had come to believe that their Temple, which had been destroyed by the Romans in 70 CE, could only be rebuilt by the Messiah, so they had no designs on the area, which Muslims call the Haram al-Sharif (the Most Noble Sanctuary). Since the sixteenth century, the single most sacred place in the Jewish world has been the Western Wall, just below the Dome of the Rock, the last relic of the Temple built by King Herod in the first century CE. The Ottoman sultan Suleiman the Magnificent (1494–1566) granted Jews permission to make this an official sanctuary and, it is said, his court architect, Sinan, designed the simple shrine there.

The Arab-Israeli conflict ended this period of harmony between Muslims and Jews in the Holy City, and this sacred district had seen much violence since the 1920s. During the period of Jordan's occupation of East Jerusalem and the Old City, between 1948 and 1967, Jews were not permitted to visit the Western Wall and ancient synagogues in the Jewish district of the Old City were destroyed. The Jews' return to the Western Wall in 1967 was one of the most emotional moments of the Six Day War and was experienced, even by secular Israelis, as a profoundly spiritual event.

When the Israelis annexed Jerusalem after the war, they promised that Christians and Muslims would have unrestricted access to their holy places. Muslims continued to control the Haram al-Sharif, even though this official government policy was deeply unpopular with both ultranationalist Israelis and the more extreme religious Zionists, who maintained that it should be returned to the Jewish people. However, the official Jewish position remained unchanged. The Temple could not be rebuilt until the Messiah had brought about the Redemption; it was a prohibition that over the centuries had acquired the force of a taboo.

By the early 1980s, however, this was beginning to change. Livni and Etzion were not the only Jewish extremists who dreamed of rebuilding the Temple as a prelude to the Redemption. How could the Messiah return when the sacred site was "polluted" by the Dome of the Rock? Like other fundamentalists, they believed that they should take the initiative, cast caution to the winds, and clear the Temple Mount of this Muslim shrine in order to prepare the way for the Messiah. If they took the first step, God would certainly intervene and reward this act of faith by intervening in history, sending the long-awaited Messiah and redeeming the people of Israel. Livni and Etzion and their fellow-conspirators believed that the Israeli government had committed a great sin in permitting the Arabs to remain in control of the Haram al-Sharif, the Temple Mount. The Dome of the Rock, in their eyes, was an "abomination," and the "root cause of all the spiritual errors of our generation."[89]

One of the chief ideologues of the Jewish underground was Yeshua ben Shoshan, a gentle, soft-spoken Kabbalist who believed that the Dome of the Rock was the abode of the evil forces of the "Other Side" that were impeding redemption. It was he who had approached Livni and Etzion with the idea of purging the "abomination" during the Camp David negotiations, which, in his view, had been inspired by these demonic influences. Their power would be neutralized by the destruction of the Dome, and the accursed peace process would come to an abrupt end. At the very least, the dramatic action would shock the Jewish people worldwide into a proper awareness of their religious responsibilities, and cause them to abandon this talk of reconciliation with the enemy.

It had been a perilous moment. Not only would the bombing of the Dome of the Rock have ended the peace process, it would almost certainly have resulted in a war in which, for the first time, the whole Muslim world would have joined forces against Israel. Strategists in Washington agreed that, in the context of the Cold War, when the Soviets supported the Arabs and the United States, Israel, the destruction of the Dome of the Rock could well have sparked World War III.[90] The specter of nuclear catastrophe did not trouble these extreme Kookists, however. They were convinced that by instigating an apocalypse here on Earth, they would activate powers in the divine world and "oblige" God to intervene on their behalf and send the Messiah to save Israel.[91]

This was kabbalistic thinking gone mad. It is a terrifying example of the fundamentalist tendency to use mythology as a blueprint for action. On the practical level, there was nothing irrational about the conspirators' plans.

Livni had been trained as an explosives expert in the IDF. He had studied the Haram al-Sharif meticulously for two years, and purloined a large quantity of explosives from military camps in the Golan Heights. He had manufactured twenty-eight precision bombs that would have destroyed the Dome but not its surroundings.[92] They were entirely ready for the attack. All that stopped them was that they could find no rabbi who was willing to sanction their plan.

The Dome of the Rock plot represented an abdication of reason, a reliance upon the miraculous, and a nihilism that could have entirely destroyed the Jewish state. This catastrophic messianism exhibited the death wish that has long been part of the modern experience. It was also self-destructive in that it badly damaged the credibility of Gush Emunim, which never recovered the admiration it had won in certain sectors of the Israeli public during its golden age.

A moral nihilism also characterized the movement founded by Rabbi Meir Kahane, who, to the distress of most Israelis, was elected to a seat in the 1984 Knesset with 1.2 percent of the vote.[93] His career had begun in New York City, where he had organized the Jewish Defense League to avenge attacks on Jews made by black youths. In 1974, he had arrived in Israel, and eventually settled in Kiryat Arba, where he changed the name of his organization to Kach ("Thus!"). His objective now was to harass the Arabs and force them to leave Eretz Israel. Kahane's fundamentalism was almost archetypal. His Judaism was so reductionist and ruthlessly selective that it become a deadly caricature of the faith. "There are not several messages in Judaism," he explained to an interviewer. "There is only one. And this message is to do what God wants." The message was simply this: "God wanted us to come to this country and create a Jewish state."[94] The Jewish doctrine of holiness (*kodesh:* "separateness" "a setting apart"), which had symbolically celebrated the distinction of things by means of ritual, now had, in Kahane's interpretation, a uniquely political meaning: "God wants us to live in a country on our own, isolated, so that we have the least possible contact with what is foreign."[95] That meant that the Arabs must go. The promise to Abraham was as valid today as in the patriarchal period, so the Arabs were usurpers.[96] The *mythos* of Genesis thus became the rationale for a political program of ethnic cleansing. This reductive vision led logically to a messianic vision of utter horror. After the victory of the Six Day War, Jews had stood "on the brink of redemption." Because of the single directive of Judaism, their mission was clear. They should have occupied the territories, expelled the Arabs, and expunged "the gentiles' abomination from the Temple Mount." If they had done all this, redemption would have come effortlessly and joyously. Because Israel failed, the Messiah would still come, but in a huge anti-Semitic catastrophe, far worse than the Holocaust, which would finally force all Jews to obey God's one commandment and settle in Israel.[97]

This dark vision of destruction and death is profoundly nihilistic. It is also suffused with hatred and a desire for revenge. Kahane's horribly distorted version of the faith shows the effects of long persecution and suppression, which can, if permitted to do so, enter deeply into the soul and warp it. Kahane's theology sees enemies everywhere, enemies that are ultimately one and the same, whether they are Christians, Nazis, blacks, Russians, or Arabs. Everything is seen from the perspective of Jewish suffering, and vengeance for that suffering. The State of Israel was not a blessing for Jews but God's revenge on the gentiles:

> God created this state not for the Jew and not as a reward for his justice and good deeds. It is because He, be blessed, decided that He could no longer take the desecration of His Name and the laughter, the disgrace, and the persecution of the people that were named after Him, so He ordered the State of Israel to be, which is a total contradiction of the Diaspora.[98]

God's name was desecrated every time a Jew was beaten or raped by a gentile: "When the Jew is humiliated, God is shamed! When the Jew is attacked—it is an assault upon the Name of God!" But the opposite was also true. Violent retaliation was *kiddush ha-Shem*, a sanctification of God's name: "A Jewish fist in the face of the astonished gentile world that has not seen it for two millenniums, this is *kiddush ha-Shem*."[99]

This ideology inspired a Kahanist, Baruch Goldstein, to shoot twenty-nine Palestinian worshippers in the Cave of the Patriarchs in Hebron on the festival of Purim, February 25, 1994. He acted to avenge the massacre of the fifty-nine Jews murdered by Palestinians on August 24, 1929. This act of revenge led to an escalation of Islamically inspired terror in the territories and in Israel itself.

The Palestinians had not been caught up in the religious renewal that had seized the Muslim world after 1967. Their response to the Arab defeat was political, secularist, and nationalist. Yasir Arafat reorganized the Palestine Liberation Organization and initiated a campaign of guerrilla action, terrorism, and diplomacy to find a solution to the Palestinian problem. This was a decisively secular movement. But after the PLO nationalists were suppressed in the Gaza Strip by Ariel Sharon in 1971, Sheikh Ahmed Yasin founded an Islamic movement which he called Mujamah ("Congress"), which initiated the type of welfare program that was associated with the

Muslim Brotherhood. By 1987, Mujamah had established a charitable empire in the Strip, consisting of clinics, drug-rehabilitation programs, youth clubs, sporting facilities, and Koran classes, supported by *zakat* (the Islamic tax), by the oil-rich Gulf states, and by Israel, which hoped to undermine the PLO by supporting Mujamah. For Yasin at this point was not interested in armed struggle against Israel. He was a reformer, who wanted to bring the fruits of modernity to the refugees of Gaza in an Islamic setting. He was also contending for the soul of Palestine against the nationalists: the cultural identity of the Palestinian people, he believed, should be Muslim rather than secular. The popularity of Mujamah showed that many Palestinians agreed. They were proud of Arafat, but his secularist ethos only made perfect sense to an elite who had the benefit of a modern Western education.[100]

Quite different was the ideology of Islamic Jihad, an underground network of cells similar to the Jihad organization in Egypt. Islamic Jihad applied the ideology of Sayyid Qutb to the Palestinian tragedy, which they interpreted in religious terms. At present, they believed, Palestinian secular society was *jahili*. Members of Islamic Jihad saw themselves as a vanguard, fighting a battle "against the forces of arrogance—against the colonial enemy all over the world," explained their ideologue, Sheikh Auda. They were fighting a battle for the future of the entire *ummah*. Unlike Mujamah, Islamic Jihad was interested in armed struggle against Israel, and its targets were religious. In October 1985, for example, activists threw hand grenades into a crowd of soldiers and civilians at an IDF induction ceremony at the Western Wall, killing the father of one of the new recruits. By this date the organization had spread from Gaza to the West Bank.[101]

On December 9, 1987, the popular Palestinian uprising known as the *intifadah* broke out in Gaza and spread to East Jerusalem and the West Bank. Since 1967, a whole generation of Palestinians had grown up in these territories under Israeli occupation; they were impatient with the old PLO leadership, which had not managed to achieve Palestinian independence, and frustrated by the daily humiliations and hardships of living under what they perceived as an oppressive, alien power. The Israelis had hoped that the Arabs in the occupied territories would become resigned to their rule in time, but resentment against Israel had reached boiling point by 1987, and the desire for a Palestinian state had become intense. The young leadership of this new revolt concentrated on undermining the occupation; they encouraged every single Palestinian to take part, so women and children threw stones at the Israeli soldiers, braving their guns and superior strength. The *intifadah* impressed both the rest of the Arab world and the international community; it also strengthened the hand of the Israeli peace movement, since it powerfully demonstrated the Palestinians' determination to achieve independence and liberation from Israeli hegemony at all costs. The *intifadah* also made an impression upon such relative hard-liners as Yitzhak Rabin, who as a soldier now appreciated the impossibility of using the IDF to batter women and children into submission. When he became prime minister in 1992, Rabin was prepared to enter into negotiations with the PLO, and, the following year, Israel and the PLO signed the Oslo Accords.

But in the early days of the *intifadah*, a new organization was formed which gave the Palestinian struggle a disturbingly nihilistic Islamic dimension. The leadership of the *intifadah* was secularist, but some members of Mujamah founded HAMAS (Haqamat al-Muqawamah al-Islamiyyah: Islamic Resistance Movement), which fought both the Israeli occupation and the Palestine nationalist movement. They were fighting the secularists for the Muslim soul of Palestine, and young men joined HAMAS in droves. Many came from the refugee camps, but others were middle-class and white-collar workers. It was a violent movement that, yet again, was born of oppression. HAMAS terrorism escalated after the killing of seventeen Palestinian worshippers on the Haram al-Sharif on October 8, 1990. Impelled by a fear of annihilation, HAMAS also attacked Palestinians whom they judged to be collaborators with Israel. "Our enemies are trying with all their might to obliterate our nation," a spokesman explained in 1993, so any cooperation with Israel was "a terrible crime."[102] Like Islamic Jihad, HAMAS saw the Arab-Israeli conflict in religious terms. The Palestinian tragedy had, members believed, come about because the people had neglected their religion; Palestinians would only shake off Israeli rule when they returned to Islam.[103] HAMAS believed that the success of Israel was due to Jewish faith, and that Israel was dedicated to the destruction of Islam.[104] They claimed, therefore, to be fighting a war of self-defense. After Baruch Goldstein massacred Palestinian worshippers at Hebron, HAMAS vowed to take a life for a life. Activists waited until after the forty-day mourning period and then a suicide bomber killed seven Israeli citizens not in the occupied territories but in Afula, in Israel proper. A week later, on April 13, 1994, another suicide bomber killed five Israelis on an Egged bus in Hadera. Violence had bred new violence.

These suicide bombings made many Israelis wary of the Oslo Accords signed the previous year, by which the PLO recognized Israel's existence within its 1948 borders, and promised to put an end to violence and terror. In return, Palestinians were offered limited autonomy in the West Bank and Gaza for a five-year period, after which final status negotiations would begin on such issues as the Israeli settlements in the territories, compensation for Palestinian refugees, and the future of Jerusalem. But the suicide bombings in Israel indicated that Arafat could not control the Islamic militants opposed to his secularist regime, and some Israelis, especially those on the right of the political spectrum, accused Rabin of having jeopardized Israeli security at Oslo.

The Kookist rabbis were especially incensed by the Oslo Accords: by signing away the sacred land, the government had committed a criminal act. So in July 1995, Rabbi Avraham Shapira and fourteen other Gush rabbis ordered soldiers to disobey the commands of their superior officers when the IDF began to evacuate the territories. This was tantamount to a declaration of civil war. Other Gush rabbis raised the question whether Rabin had become a *rodef* ("pursuer"), one who actively threatens the life of a Jew, and so is deemed worthy of death under Jewish law.[105] On November 4, 1995, Yigal Amir, a former student of a hesder *yeshiva*, an army veteran, and a student at Bar Ilan University, assassinated Rabin during a peace rally in Tel Aviv. His study of Jewish law, he said later, had persuaded him that Rabin was just such a *rodef*, an enemy of the Jewish people; he had a duty to kill him.[106]

Like the murder of Sadat, the assassination of Rabin showed that two wars are being fought in the Middle East. One is the Arab-Israeli conflict; the other is a war within such individual countries as Israel and Egypt, between secularists and religious. Religious Jews are not alone in feeling outraged and attacked at a profound level. Secularists in Israel likewise feel repelled and assaulted by religious Jews. Walking around a Haredi district in Jerusalem, the celebrated Israeli novelist Amos Oz recalled that the early Zionists detested Orthodox Judaism and "would have banished this reality from the world around them and from within their souls. In an eruption of hatred and loathing, they portrayed this world as a swamp, a heap of dead words and extinguished souls." To this secular hatred the Haredim have responded in kind. On the walls of the districts inhabited by members of Neturei Karta, Oz noted the black swastikas and graffiti: "Death to the Zionist Hitlerites." "To hell with [the Laborite mayor of Jerusalem] Teddy Kollek." Oz was also reminded of his teacher, Dov Sadan, who had argued that secular Zionism was just a passing episode in Jewish history, and that Orthodox Judaism would reemerge, "swallow Zionism and digest it." Now as he wandered around the streets of this ultra-Orthodox neighborhood, Oz felt claustrophobic and overwhelmed by the vitality of Haredi Judaism, "for as it grows and swells, it threatens your own spiritual existence and eats away at the roots of your own world, prepared to inherit it all when you and your kind are gone."[107] Secularist Israelis, it appears, also fear annihilation and feel irrational dread when confronted with their religious enemies.

Oz touched upon the core of the problem. Fundamentalists and secularists—of whatever faith—are at war because they have entirely different conceptions of the sacred. When speaking about Gush Emunim, Oz called it "a cruel and obdurate sect" which had emerged "from a dark corner of Judaism, and is threatening to destroy all that is dear and holy to us." For secularists and liberals—be they Jewish, Christian, or Muslim—such Enlightenment values as the autonomy of the individual and intellectual liberty, are inviolable and holy. They cannot compromise or make concessions on such issues. These principles are so central to the liberal or secular identity that if they are threatened, people feel that their very existence is in jeopardy. Just as fundamentalists fear annihilation at the hands of the secularist, a liberal like Oz saw the Gush as threatening "to bring down upon us a savage and insane bloodlust." The real aim of the Gush, he continued, was not the conquest of Nablus or Hebron, but

> the imposition of an ugly and distorted version of Judaism upon the State of Israel. The real aim of this cult is the expulsion of the Arabs so as to oppress the Jews afterwards, to force us all under the brutality of their false prophets.[108]

Each, the religious and the secularist, gazes at the other with horror. Neither can see the other clearly. Both recall the excesses, cruelties, and intolerance of the "other side" and, wounded to the core, they cannot make peace.

THERE WAS ALSO polarization and hostility in America. In the United States, religious fundamentalists seemed more restrained and law-abiding. Fundamentalists did not assassinate their presidents, lead revolutions, or take hostages. But a deep ravine ran through American religion nonetheless. Polls showed the religious population of the United States to be neatly divided into two almost equal and mutually antagonistic camps. A Gallup Poll carried out in June 1984 revealed that 43 percent of Americans called themselves "liberals" and 41 percent "conservatives"; and that the major denominations were split down the middle. Most of the respondents argued that the rift was "serious" and had a negative image of the "other side," which did not, as did other forms of prejudice, recede when there was greater contact.[109] Other polls showed that even though only 9 percent of Americans identified themselves as "fundamentalists," core tenets of Protestant fundamentalism were more widely held.

> 44 percent believed that salvation comes only through Jesus Christ.
> 30 percent describe themselves as "born-again."

28 percent believe that every word of the Bible must be read
  literally.
27 percent denied that the Bible could contain scientific and
  historical errors.[110]

The success of American fundamentalism was not entirely due to the adroit
marketing of Jerry Falwell and other televangelists. There were elements in
American culture and religious life that were favorable to this literalistic
form of faith, and which provided it with a fertile soil.[111]

During the 1980s, however, fundamentalism received a severe setback.
There was no murder of a president, no terrorist campaign. Instead the fundamentalist cause was damaged by a scandal that was just as destructive and
nihilistic in its own way, threatening to drown the televangelists in a sea of
triviality, money-grubbing, and sexual intrigue. Was there anything about
the nature of American fundamentalism that contributed to the Television
Scandals of 1987?

Because of the Christian concern with doctrine, Protestant fundamentalism had set out in a different direction from the other movements we have
considered. The Jewish and Muslim emphasis on practice had meant that
fundamentalists in these faiths had turned the myths of their traditions
into ideologies. Some of their worst excesses had come about because they
had tried to realize these mythologies literally in the practical world of
affairs. They had sought to meet the modern criterion of efficiency, in which
a "truth" had to work effectively in order to be taken seriously. Jewish
and Muslim fundamentalists had turned their *mythoi* into pragmatic *logoi*
designed to achieve a practical result. Protestant fundamentalists had perverted myth in a different way. They had turned the Christian myths into
scientific facts, and had created a hybrid that was neither good science nor
good religion. This had run counter to the whole tradition of spirituality and
had involved great strain, since religious truth is not rational in nature
and cannot be proved scientifically. Because Protestant fundamentalists
tended to overlook the intuitive and the mystical, they had also lost touch
with the unconscious, deeper impulses of the personality. As a result, American revivalism had sometimes been anarchic and neurotic. By the late 1980s,
some fundamentalists were ready to revolt against the constraints of this
rationalistic faith. Sex, as we have seen, was problematic for fundamentalists, many of whom appeared to be anxious about potency and gender
boundaries. It was not surprising, perhaps, that the rebellion, when it came,
took a sexual form.

Television and the public adulation that sometimes comes with it are also
traps for the spiritually unwary. Not only is the narcissism involved in a per-

sonality cult incompatible with the transcendence of ego that should characterize the spiritual quest, but the televangelist could also lose touch with reality. The vast sums of money that the more successful networks could command sat uneasily with the Gospel demand to abandon the pursuit of material wealth. Jim and Tammy Faye Bakker of PTL (Praise The Lord and People That Love) network in North Carolina had attracted adverse criticism for their extravagant lifestyle. The *Charlotte Observer* had for some years been pointing out that while they urged their viewers to make sacrifices and give their money to the needy, the Bakkers themselves had spent $375,000 on an ocean-front condominium and $22,000 on floor-to-ceiling mirrors.[112] All this was a far cry from Jerry Falwell's regime in Lynchburg, which was characterized by sobriety and self-restraint.

The Bakkers were chiefly known for their Christian theme park, Heritage USA, which portrayed the evangelical experience of North America Disney-style, and attracted huge numbers of visitors. In an intriguing article, the American anthropologist Susan Harding suggests that the Bakkers were quite consciously staging a revolt against Falwell's commonsense religiosity and pushing fundamentalism into a new, postmodern phase.[113] Since the late nineteenth century, American fundamentalists had responded to the challenge of modernity by trying to make their faith wholly rational. They had emphasized the virtues of reason and plain sense; they had embraced a sober literalism that eschewed imagination and fantasy; they had organized the world into watertight compartments in which right was utterly and obviously distinct from wrong, and true believers in an entirely different category from secularists and liberal Christians. Theirs had been an ethic of separation; fundamentalists had created a counterculture that was supposed to be everything that the Godless mainstream was not: it was a faith that offered cast-iron certainty and hierarchy to challenge the doubts, open questions, and shifting roles of the modern world. Heritage USA, however, like other forms of postmodern culture, was characterized by a mixing of genres, play, indulgence, and vivid spectacle.

By trying to make their faith scientific and rational, the fundamentalists had pushed religion into an unnatural mode. As fundamentalists had rebelled against the scientific rationalism of Darwin, based on hypothesis and free inquiry, by clinging to the Baconian ideal, so now the Bakkers revolted against the rationalism of the old-style fundamentalists like Falwell. As Harding points out, in its depiction of American Christian history, Heritage USA was an ensemble of categories in a wild mélange. Instead of insisting that truth was factual, the exhibits in Heritage USA drew attention to their artificial and unnatural assemblage in the park. The shopping mall was a hodgepodge of Victorian and colonial architecture, an eclectic mix of styles and periods that did not attempt verisimilitude. At the entrance, Billy Graham's "actual" home was displayed, but there were photographs on the walls showing its dismantling and rebuilding in the theme park, its displacement from the original site being part of the point. There was an "exact replica" of the Upper Room in Jerusalem (where Jesus was believed to have eaten the Last Supper and instituted the Eucharist), but it was deliberately made to look like a reproduction. Church services were held in a television studio, and, unlike Falwell, the Bakkers never televised a regular communion service or a sermon. The emphasis was always on performance, spectacle, and fantasy rather than on the literal fundamentalist Word.

Harding suggests that the Bakkers, who emphasized the endless love of God, were also evolving a folk theology of infinite forgiveness, which almost seemed to sanction sin, since it promised divine pardon beforehand.[114] We have seen that in the past, an antinomian rebellion has sometimes erupted during a time of transition. The old rules and lifestyle no longer suit the changing circumstances of some of the faithful, who feel restricted and reach out for something new. They find relief in the breaking of old taboos. Some have even gone so far as to evolve a theology of "holy sin." When the scandal which held the nation enthralled finally broke in March 1987, it appeared that something of the sort may have been going on in PTL circles. The *Charlotte Observer* alleged that in 1980, Jim Bakker had drugged and seduced Jessica Hahn, a church secretary from Long Island, and then paid her $250,000 to keep quiet.[115] On the heels of this revelation, it emerged that Tammy Faye had become so infatuated with country-and-western singer Gary Paxton that she had broken up his marriage. When the sordid truth was out, however, the Bakkers did not slink away in shame, but went public with their contrition, chattering to huge television audiences about God's love and forgiveness.

Falwell's regime in Lynchburg had been an attempt to hold on to the restraints of the conservative, premodern religion, which had helped people to accept necessary limitations. The Bakkers' story shows what happens when these restraints are entirely cast aside. Where other fundamentalist movements sprang from the experience of suppression, the Bakkers' postmodern Christianity expressed the late-twentieth-century conviction that "anything goes." With vast sums of money at their command, the Bakkers felt they could make anything happen. There were no limitations, and old categories of right and wrong could be dissolved as easily as truth and fiction in Heritage USA. That this was all a distortion of Christianity goes without saying.

Then new horrors came to light. Jim Bakker resigned from PTL and asked Jerry Falwell to rescue the network by acting as temporary caretaker.

Jim then turned on Jimmy Swaggart, who had brought the scandal to light, claiming that Swaggart had been plotting to take over PTL. Swaggart, for his part, had been making his own foray into antinomianism. At this time, Swaggart was probably the most successful of the televangelists. His shows were screened in 145 countries and, so he claimed, were available to half the homes on the planet. But he had taken to visiting a prostitute in Baton Rouge, Louisiana. The woman, who later sold her story, made it clear that Swaggart was less interested in sex than in ritual humiliation and abasement. He also seemed to be courting self-destruction, since he knew that people had seen and recognized him at the motel and yet continued to go there until all hell broke loose. His misconduct was revealed by another minister, Marvin Gorman, whom Swaggart had attacked on his show.[116]

Swaggart was a Pentecostalist. In its early days, Pentecostalism had been the polar opposite of fundamentalism, attempting to bypass reason and give voice to the ineffability of divine truth. As such, it had always courted the danger of an undisciplined entry into the unconscious world and the perils that always attend an abdication of reason. But early Pentecostalism at its best had been characterized by inclusion and a compassionate breaking down of racial and class barriers. Swaggart, however, preached a religion of hatred. He had become famous for his foulmouthed attacks on homosexuals, an obsession that almost certainly revealed buried anxieties about his own sexual proclivities. He had also turned viciously on other ministers and rival televangelists, and joined the judgmental crusade of Moral Majority. By casting off the restraints imposed by the discipline of charity as well as those of reason, Swaggart had embraced a religiosity that was, in its way, as self-destructive and nihilistic as some of the other movements we have considered.

American journalist Lawrence Wright found himself attracted to Swaggart's emotional preaching style. He sensed that Swaggart was rebelling against the strictures of rational modernity; it was "defiantly emotional," light-years away from the "arid intellectual refinements" of Wright's own childhood religion. He found that a part of himself craved Swaggart's "ecstatic abandonment of my own busy, judgmental, ironic mentality."[117] And so did Swaggart's audience, who responded ecstatically to his orgasmic preaching:

> He would sink deeper and deeper into his subconscious, he would journey past reason and conscious meaning into the slashing emotions and buried fears and unnamed desires that bubble below. His voice would rise and tremble, his grammar would fall away, but still he stumbled toward that cowering raw nerve of

longing. He knew where it was. One watched him with both dread and desire, because this is the nerve that is attached to faith. Longing to be loved and saved—it is when he finally touches this nerve that the tears flow and the audience stands with its hands upraised, laughing, wailing, praising the Lord, speaking in unknown languages and quivering with the pain and pleasure of this thrilling public exposure.[118]

The best premodern spirituality, such as that of John of the Cross, Isaac Luria, or Mulla Sadra, had eschewed such emotional excess, claiming that it had nothing to do with religion; they had insisted that the interior journey was calm, disciplined, and complemented by reason. No one was initiated into the Kabbalah until he was at least forty years old and married, and had achieved sexual equilibrium. The modern world, which had neglected the more intuitive paths to knowledge, had for the most part lost this mystical lore. Swaggart's success shows that people longed for ecstasy in an over-rationalized world, but also shows that such a quest can become unbalanced. Swaggart's frenzy seemed to have more to do with the sexual needs that drove him (to use Wright's words in a different context) to the "thrilling public exposure" in the Baton Rouge motel than with spirituality.

Yet the failure of fundamentalist faith is most plainly demonstrated in the rage and hatred that the televangelists displayed toward one another during the scandal. When Swaggart got wind of Bakker's sexual relationship with Jessica Hahn, he "took on Jim Bakker like a pit bulldog taking on a French poodle," one of Swaggart's former aides recalled. "Just ripped him to shreds, destroyed the man."[119] Next, Bakker turned on Jerry Falwell, who had come to the rescue of PTL, and accused him of exploiting the situation to get control of the network. Falwell retaliated by calling a press conference where he produced sworn affidavits by men who claimed to have had homosexual relations with Jim Bakker, together with a note from Tammy Faye listing what she wanted from PTL in return for going quietly: $300,000 a year for Jim, and $100,000 for herself; royalties on all PTL records and books; their $400,000 mansion, two cars, security staff, legal fees, plus the fees of the accountants who were trying to sort out the Bakkers' highly irregular finances. The grand fundamentalist enterprise seemed to have ended in a barren, unedifying cul-de-sac. The year before the scandals, Falwell had been full of confidence. He had renamed the Moral Majority "the Liberty Federation," and declared that many of its members would be running for office in the 1988 elections at the local, state, and federal levels. But after the PTL debacle, Falwell resigned on November 4, 1987, from the presidency of the Moral Majority and the Liberty Federation and announced that his political career was over. He would never again work for a candidate as he had for Ronald Reagan, and never again lobby for legislation. In the wake of the scandals, the income from his own *Old Time Gospel Hour* had declined, and Falwell felt compelled to return to his private Gospel ministry.[120] He would still surface from time to time to fulminate about the nation's ills, but he could no longer look forward to the imminent creation of a coalition of religious conservatives that would take America by storm. When Pat Robertson's bid for the presidency failed, the fundamentalist offensive, which had started in 1979 with such great hopes, seemed to have failed. The New Christian Right, discredited, appeared to have ignominiously fizzled out, and though Christians would individually continue to lobby and try to bring voters to the polls, it was generally assumed by secularists that the fundamentalist threat was over.

However, fundamentalism was not dead; it had, in fact, entered a new and more extreme phase in America. On November 28, 1987, Randall Terry, a born-again Christian from upstate New York, led three hundred "rescuers" to an abortion clinic in Cherry Hill, New Jersey. They held a service on what Terry described as "the doorstep of hell" for almost eleven hours, praying, singing psalms, and preventing women and staff from entering the clinic. By the end of the day, 211 of the "rescuers" had been arrested, but, Terry recorded triumphantly, "no babies died."[121] This was the first action of Operation Rescue, which declared war on mainstream culture by depicting it as inherently murderous. The imagery was militant. During the Democratic Convention in Atlanta in 1988, the movement began what Terry called the "siege of Atlanta," in which over thirteen hundred demonstrators were arrested for blockading the city's abortion clinics. They have since held Days of Rescue all over Canada and the United States, and held training days to lecture potential rescuers on the evils of feminism and liberal government and to give them instruction on lobbying techniques. They described their "operations" as acts of "biblical disobedience." Unlike Falwell and Robertson, Terry was prepared to work outside the law. His aim was fundamentalist: to create "a nation where once again the Judeo-Christian ethic is the foundation for our politics, our judicial system, and our public morality; a nation not floating in the uncertain sea of humanism, but a country whose unmoving bedrock is Higher Laws."

The campaign is not just about abortion, any more than the Scopes trial was just about evolution. Like William Jennings Bryan in the 1920s, Terry and his rescuers believe that they are fighting one of the most brutal manifestations of secular modernity. Terry is convinced that if Operation Rescue does not succeed, "America is not going to make it." But he is confident: "We have an army of people," he insisted, and, as a result of these opera-

tions, "child-killing will fall, child pornography and pornography will follow, euthanasia, infanticide . . . we'll take back the culture."[122] It is a war to
stave off imminent catastrophe and rescue American civilization.

The Reconstruction movement, founded by the Texan economist Gary
North and his father-in-law, Rousas John Rushdoony, is also engaged in a
war against secular humanism, in a more extreme form than that waged by
the Moral Majority. Reconstructionists have abandoned the old premillennial pessimism for a more galvanizing ideology. Like Muslim fundamentalists, North and Rushdoony are principally concerned about the sovereignty
of God. A Christian civilization must be established that will defeat Satan
and usher in the millennial Kingdom. The key concept of Reconstructionism is Dominion. God gave Adam and later Noah the task of subduing the
world. Christians have inherited this mandate and they have the responsibility of imposing Jesus' rule on earth *before* the Second Coming of Christ.
There will be no need, however, for Christians to take action to achieve
this, since God himself will bring the modern state down in a terrible catastrophe. Christians will simply reap the victory that God will effect.

In the meantime, the Reconstructionists are training themselves to take
control when the secular humanist state is destroyed.[123] Their vision is a
complete distortion of Christianity in its abandonment of the ethos of compassion. When the Kingdom comes, there will be no more separation of
church and state; the modern heresy of democracy will be abolished, and
society reorganized on strictly biblical lines. This means that every single
law of the Bible must be put literally into practice. Slavery will be reintro-
duced; there will be no more birth control (since believers must "increase
and multiply"); adulterers, homosexuals, blasphemers, astrologers, and
witches will all be put to death. Children who are persistently disobedient
must also be stoned, as the Bible enjoins. A strictly capitalist economy must
be enforced; socialists and those who incline to the left are sinful. God is
not on the side of the poor. Indeed, as North explains, there is a "tight relationship between wickedness and poverty."[124] Taxes should not be used
in welfare programs, since "subsidizing sluggards is the same as subsidizing evil."[125] The same goes for the Third World, which has brought its
economic problems on its own head because of its addiction to moral per-
versity, paganism, and demonology. Foreign aid is forbidden by the Bible.[126]
While waiting for victory—which, North admits, may be some time off—
Christians must prepare to rebuild society according to God's blueprint and
must support government policies which approximate to these strict biblical
norms.

The Dominion envisaged by North and Rushdoony is totalitarian.
There is no room for any other view or policy, no democratic tolerance for

rival parties, no individual freedom. The chances of this theology's achieving much popularity in the United States are, to be sure, remote; but it has been suggested that in the event of an environmental or major economic catastrophe, an authoritarian state church could replace the liberal polity of the Enlightenment. Christianity, after all, was able to adapt to capitalism, which was alien to many of the teachings of Jesus. It could also be used to back a fascist ideology that, in drastically changed circumstances, might be necessary to maintain public order.[127]

Some of the more conservative Pentecostalists have shown an interest in Reconstruction theology, even though Rushdoony regards Pentecostalism with distaste. Pat Robertson seems to be a transitional figure. He is a Baptist with leanings toward Pentecostalism and revivalism. Like North, he believes that the Second Coming may be far off—a belief which separates him from traditional premillennial fundamentalism.[128] Meanwhile, Christians, Robertson believes, should try to win positions of power to build a society based on biblical norms.[129] He changed the name of his university in Virginia Beach to Regent University; a regent, he explained, is someone "who governs in the absence of a sovereign." The purpose of the college is to prepare its seven hundred students to take over when the Kingdom arrives.[130] Fundamentalism has changed in America since the publication of *The Fundamentals* (1910–15). It has exhibited postmodern, antinomian tendencies on the one hand, and a more hard-line, totalitarian vision on the other.

Fundamentalism is not going to disappear. In America, religion has long shaped opposition to government. Its rise and fall has always been cyclical, and events of the last few years indicate that there is still a state of incipient war between conservatives and liberals which has occasionally become frighteningly explicit. In 1992, Jerry Falwell, who still adheres to the old-style fundamentalism, announced that with the election of Bill Clinton to the presidency, Satan had been let loose in the United States. Clinton, Falwell thundered, was about to destroy the military and the nation by letting "the gays" take over. Executive orders permitting abortion in federally funded clinics, research on fetal tissue, the official endorsement of homosexual rights, were all signs that America "had declared war against God."[131]

In 1993, the war claimed casualties. On February 28, 1993, the Bureau of Alcohol, Tobacco and Firearms stormed David Koresh's Branch Davidian compound in Waco, Texas, because he was said to be stockpiling arms. In fact, though like many Texans the Branch Davidians (an offshoot of the Seventh Day Adventists) had an impressive arsenal, they seemed to have no plans for revolutionary action against the government. The offensive was designed to demonstrate the power and legitimacy of the United States government, but it backfired. It led to the compound's being besieged by the FBI, the burning of the Davidian buildings, and the deaths of eighty men, women, and children. What had actually been demonstrated was the government's ignorance of the sect, its powerlessness before the besieged Davidians, and its tragic inability to control events.

On their side, more extreme Christians are certainly preparing to fight the secular government. Christian Identity, a fascist group, has not been mentioned in this book because it has left fundamentalism far behind, and, indeed, disapproves of fundamentalism. Members of Identity hate the idea of Rapture, which they believe has emasculated American religion: they want to be there to fight the forces of evil during Tribulation. Viciously anti-Semitic, they hate the fundamentalists' support for Zionism, which they regard as a great sin. In their view, the Jews have usurped the title of Chosen People from the Aryan race, and now they have stolen the Holy Land, which should have remained under a British mandate. They do not believe that the wars of the Last Days will be fought in the Middle East, but in America. They predict a new holocaust in which the white race and the United States will be annihilated. They are, therefore, preparing themselves for the catastrophe. They foresee the imminent destruction of the federal government, which they call ZOG (Zionist Occupation Government), which is dominated by Satan and Jews, and dedicated to the destruction of the Aryan nation. Some have formed themselves into militant groups in remote corners of the northwestern United States, where they learn survival techniques, collect guns and ammunition, and prepare for the last war. Some make paramilitary raids on ZOG, killing state officials. Others bomb and set fire to abortion clinics.[132] It is this type of ideology that inspired Timothy McVeigh's bomb attack on the federal building in Oklahoma City on April 19, 1995.

It is difficult to chart the activities and ideals of Christian Identity, which is not a monolithic movement but a constellation of affiliated organizations. Their numbers are small; there are probably no more than 100,000 members, and could be as few as 50,000.[133] But as a trend, Christian Identity is worrying. Like fundamentalists, they have retreated from the world in contempt and fear, and plan to take it over. Like the most extreme types of fundamentalists, members see conspiracy everywhere and cultivate a theology of rage and resentment. But they have outdone the fundamentalists in their overtly fascist ideology, their pure hatred of the United States government, and the extremity of their withdrawal from modern life. No longer concerned with problems of doctrine and biblical inerrancy, the Identity groups want to carve out for themselves a separate Aryan state in America. Christian Identity has developed an ideology of alienation and terror unparalleled in American history. Like Reconstructionism, this loose confederation of Identity communities is a small but disturbing indication of the way religion could be used to articulate helplessness, disappointment, and discontent in the future. The secularist establishment and mainstream denominations may feel that the fundamentalist threat is receding in the United States, but as far as some Christians are concerned the war is still on, the federal government must be destroyed, and the conflict will certainly continue into the twenty-first Christian century.

Religion did not disappear after all, and in some circles it has become more militant than ever. In all three of the monotheistic faiths, fundamentalists have reacted angrily to attempts to privatize or to suppress religion, and have, as they believe, rescued it from oblivion. It has been a hard struggle and in the course of it, the faith has often been distorted; this represents a defeat for religion. But fundamentalism is now part of the modern world. It represents a widespread disappointment, alienation, anxiety, and rage that no government can safely ignore. So far, efforts to deal with fundamentalism have not been very successful; what lessons can we learn from the past that will help us to deal more creatively in the future with the fears that fundamentalism enshrines?

Afterword

WE CANNOT BE RELIGIOUS in the same way as our ancestors in the premodern conservative world, when the myths and rituals of faith helped people to accept limitations that were essential to agrarian civilization. We are now oriented to the future, and those of us who have been shaped by the rationalism of the modern world cannot easily understand the old forms of spirituality. We are not unlike Newton, one of the first people in the Western world to be wholly imbued by the scientific spirit, who found it impossible to understand mythology. However hard we try to embrace conventional religion, we have a natural tendency to see truth as factual, historical, and empirical. Many have become convinced that if faith is to be taken seriously, its myths must be shown to be historical and capable of working practically with all the efficiency that modernity expects. An increasing number of people, especially in Western Europe, which has experienced such tragedy during the twentieth century, have rejected religion. For those who see reason as providing the sole path to truth, this is a principled and honest position. As scientists would be the first to insist, rational *logos* cannot address questions of ultimate meaning that lie beyond the reach of empirical inquiry. Confronted with the genocidal horrors of our century, reason has nothing to say.

Hence, there is a void at the heart of modern culture, which Western people experienced at an early stage of their scientific revolution. Pascal recoiled in dread from the emptiness of the cosmos; Descartes saw the human being as the sole living denizen of an inert universe; Hobbes imagined God retreating from the world, and Nietzsche declared that God was dead: humanity had lost its orientation and was hurtling toward an infinite nothingness. But others have felt emancipated by the loss of faith, and liberated from the restrictions it had always imposed. Sartre, who acknowledged the God-shaped hole in modern consciousness, argued that it was still our duty to reject deity, which negated our freedom. Albert Camus (1913–60) believed that rejecting God would enable men and women to concentrate all their attention and love upon humankind. Others put their faith in the ideals of the Enlightenment, looking forward to a future in which human beings will become more rational and tolerant; they venerate the sacred liberty of the individual instead of a distant, imaginary God. They have created secularist forms of spirituality, which bring them insight, transcendence, and ecstasy, and which have developed their own disciplines of mind and heart.

Nevertheless, a large number of people still want to be religious and have tried to evolve new forms of faith. Fundamentalism is just one of these modern religious experiments, and, as we have seen, it has enjoyed a certain success in putting religion squarely back on the international agenda, but it has often lost sight of some of the most sacred values of the confessional faiths. Fundamentalists have turned the *mythos* of their religion into *logos,* either by insisting that their dogmas are scientifically true, or by transforming their complex mythology into a streamlined ideology. They have thus conflated two complementary sources and styles of knowledge which the people in the premodern world had usually decided it was wise to keep separate. The fundamentalist experience shows the truth of this conservative insight. By insisting that the truths of Christianity are factual and scientifically demonstrable, American Protestant fundamentalists have created a caricature of both religion and science. Those Jews and Muslims who have presented their faith in a reasoned, systematic way to compete with other secular ideologies have also distorted their tradition, narrowing it down to a single point by a process of ruthless selection. As a result, all have neglected the more tolerant, inclusive, and compassionate teachings and have cultivated theologies of rage, resentment, and revenge. On occasion, this has even led a small minority to pervert religion by using it to sanction murder. Even the vast majority of fundamentalists, who are opposed to such acts of terror, tend to be exclusive and condemnatory of those who do not share their views.

But fundamentalist fury reminds us that our modern culture imposes extremely difficult demands on human beings. It has certainly empowered us, opened new worlds, broadened our horizons, and enabled many of us to live happier, healthier lives. Yet it has often dented our self-esteem. At the same time as our rational worldview has proclaimed that humans are the measure of all things, and liberated us from an unseemly dependence upon a supernatural God, it has also revealed our frailty, vulnerability, and lack of dignity. Copernicus unseated us from the center of the universe, and relegated us to a peripheral role. Kant declared that we could never be certain that our ideas corresponded to any reality outside our own heads. Darwin suggested that we were simply animals, and Freud showed that far from being wholly rational creatures, human beings were at the mercy of the powerful, irrational forces of the unconscious, which could be accessed only with great difficulty. This, indeed, was demonstrated by the modern experience. Despite the cult of rationality, modern history has been punctuated by witch-hunts and world wars which have been explosions of unreason. Without the ability to approach the deeper regions of the psyche, which the old myths, liturgies, and mystical practices of the best conservative faith once provided, it seemed that reason sometimes lost its mind in our brave new world. At the end of the twentieth century, the liberal myth that humanity is progressing to an ever more enlightened and tolerant state looks as fantastic as any of the other millennial myths we have considered in this book. Without the constraints of a "higher," mythical truth, reason can on occasion become demonic and commit crimes that are as great as, if not greater than, any of the atrocities perpetrated by fundamentalists.

Modernity has been beneficial, benevolent, and humane, but it has often, especially in its early stages, felt the need to be cruel. This has been especially true in the developing world, which experienced modern Western culture as invasive, imperialistic, and alien. In the Muslim countries we have considered, the modernization process was very different and difficult. In the West, it had been characterized by independence and innovation; in Egypt and Iran, it was accompanied by dependence and imitation, as the Muslim reformers and ideologues were acutely aware. This would alter the tenor of modernity in these countries. If you bake a cake using the wrong ingredients (dried eggs instead of fresh, rice instead of flour) and with incorrect equipment, the end result will not conform to the ideal in the cookbook; it could be delicious, if different, but it could be very nasty indeed. It might be better to use techniques and ingredients that are ready to hand to create a closer approximation to the norm, using local expertise and culinary skill. Islamists such as Afghani, Abdu, Shariati, and Khomeini wanted to use Muslim ingredients to bake their own distinctive and modern cake.

But it has been hard for some Westerners, who no longer think in a religious way, to appreciate this resurgence of faith, especially when it has expressed itself violently and cruelly. Frequently, modern society has become divided into "two nations": secularists and religious living in the same country cannot speak one another's language or see things from the same point of view. What seems sacred and positive in one camp appears demonic and deranged in the other. Secularists and religious both feel profoundly threatened by one another, and when there is a clash of two wholly irreconcilable worldviews, as in the Salman Rushdie affair, the sense of estrangement and alienation is only exacerbated. It is an unhealthy and potentially dangerous situation. Fundamentalism is not going away. In some places it is either going from strength to strength or becoming more extreme. What can the liberal, secular establishment do to build bridges and avert the possibility of future battles?

Suppression and coercion are clearly not the answer. They invariably lead to a backlash and can make fundamentalists or potential fundamentalists more extreme. Protestant fundamentalists in the United States became more reactionary, intransigent, and literal-minded after their humiliation at the Scopes trial. The most extreme forms of Sunni fundamentalism surfaced in Nasser's concentration camps, and the shah's crackdowns helped to inspire the Islamic Revolution. Fundamentalism is an embattled faith; it anticipates imminent annihilation. Not surprisingly, Jewish fundamentalists, be they Zionist or ultra-Orthodox, are still haunted by fears of holocaust and anti-Semitic catastrophe. Repression has bitten deeply into the souls of those who have experienced secularization as aggressive, and has warped their religious vision, making it violent and intolerant in its turn. Fundamentalists see conspiracy everywhere and are sometimes possessed by a rage that seems demonic.

And yet, attempting to exploit fundamentalism for secular, pragmatic ends is also counterproductive. Sadat courted the Muslims of Egypt and wooed the *jamaat al-islamiyyah* to give legitimacy to his regime and build his own power base. Israel supported HAMAS initially, as a way of undermining the PLO. In both cases, the attempt to manipulate and control recoiled tragically and fatally on the secularist state. A more just and objective appraisal of the meaning of these religious movements must be sought.

First, it is important to recognize that these theologies and ideologies are rooted in fear. The desire to define doctrines, erect barriers, establish borders, and segregate the faithful in a sacred enclave where the law is stringently observed springs from that terror of extinction which has made all fundamentalists, at one time or another, believe that the secularists were about to wipe them out. The modern world, which seems so exciting to a liberal, seems Godless, drained of meaning, and even satanic to a fundamentalist. If a patient brought such paranoid, conspiracy-laden, and vengeful fantasies to a therapist, he or she would undoubtedly be diagnosed as disturbed. The premillennial vision, which views some of the most positive institutions of modernity as diabolic, harbors genocidal dreams, and sees humanity as rushing toward a horrific End, is a clear indication of the dread and disappointment that modernity has inspired in many Protestant fundamentalists. We have seen the nihilism that can inform the fundamentalist program. It is impossible to reason such fear away or attempt to eradicate it by coercive measures. A more imaginative response would be to try to appreciate the depth of this neurosis, even if a liberal or a secularist cannot share this dread-ridden perspective.

Second, it is important to realize that these movements are not an archaic throwback to the past; they are modern, innovative, and modernizing. Protestant fundamentalists read the Bible in a literal, rational way that is quite different from the more mystical, allegorical approach of premodern spirituality. Khomeini's theory of Velayat-e Faqih was a shocking and revolutionary overturning of centuries of Shii tradition. Muslim thinkers preached a liberation theology and produced an anti-imperialist ideology that was in tune with other Third World movements of their time. Even ultra-Orthodox Jews, who seemed resolutely to turn their backs upon modern society, found that their *yeshivot* were essentially modern, voluntarist institutions. They adopted a novel stringency in their observance of the Torah and learned to manipulate the political system in a way that brought them more power than any religious Jew had enjoyed for nearly two millennia.

Throughout we have seen that religion has often helped people to adjust to modernity. Shabbateanism, Quakerism, Methodism, and Islamic mysticism helped Jews, Christians, and Muslims prepare for major change, and gave them a context in which they could approach the new ideas. Americans who had no time for the deism of the Founding Fathers of the republic were prepared for the revolutionary struggle by the Great Awakening. Muslims also developed an appreciation for such modern ideals as the separation of religion and politics by means of the dynamic of their own spirituality. Indeed, in Europe, too, secularism and scientific rationality were both at first seen as new ways of being religious. Some of the more recent movements we have considered have also been modernizing. Hasan al-Banna, Shariati, and even Khomeini all sought to bring Muslims to modernity in an Islamic setting that was more familiar to them than the imported ideologies of the West. Only thus could they "return to themselves" and help those who had perforce been left out of the modernizing process to make sense of such institutions as representative government and democratic rule. This was also an attempt to relocate modernity within the ambit of the sacred. Premodern religion had always seen *mythos* and *logos* as complementary. Islamic reformers would site the pragmatic tasks of government within a religious and mystical framework.

This was also part of the fundamentalist rebellion against the hegemony of the secular. It was a way of bringing God back into the political realm from which he had been excluded. In various ways, fundamentalists have rejected the separations of modernity (between church and state, secular and profane) and tried to re-create a lost wholeness. Religious Zionists were "revolting against the revolt" of the secularist Zionists, who had declared their independence of religion. They wanted to have more God and more Torah in the Holy Land than had been possible in the Diaspora. Khomeini and Shariati both insisted that it was impossible to exclude the sacred from politics; Qutb condemned the Godlessness of the secularist regime in Egypt, which he designated *jahili*. Those who had not fully imbibed the secular rationalism of modernity were still aware of the Unseen dimension of existence and wanted it reflected in the polity. They did not see why that should make them less modern, though they tacitly recognized that this would mean a break with some of the old conservative aspects of premodern religion. The fundamentalist reformation of the faith meant that an activism that had hitherto been seen as irreligious was now presented as crucial. Religious Zionists and fundamentalist Christians and Muslims all insisted on the need for dynamism and revolutionary transformation in keeping with the forward thrust and pragmatic drive of modern society.

This battle for God was an attempt to fill the void at the heart of a society based on scientific rationalism. Instead of reviling fundamentalists, the secularist establishment could sometimes have benefited from a long, hard look at some of their countercultures. Shukri Mustafa's communes were a reverse image of Sadat's Open Door policy; the charitable empires created by the Muslim Brothers and the practical measures taken by the members of the *jamaat al-islamiyyah* threw into harsh relief the current government's lack of concern for the poor, a crucial value in Islam. The popularity and power of these movements showed that the people of Egypt still wanted to be religious, despite the secularist trend. So did the cult of Khomeini in Iran: as the confrontation with the regime accelerated, Khomeini took on more and more of the characteristics of the Imams, providing in his own person a Shii alternative to the despotic persona of the shah which was clearly attractive to many of the Iranians. Similarly, the Jewish *yeshivot* provided a contrast to the pragmatic nature of secularist education; in a society which seemed to have cast God and his Law aside, *yeshiva* students studied in order to have an encounter with the divine, not simply to acquire useful information, and made the study of the Torah more central to their lives than ever before. When they created these alternative societies, fundamentalists were demonstrating their disillusion with a culture which could not easily accommodate the spiritual.

Because it was so embattled, this campaign to re-sacralize society became aggressive and distorted. It lacked the compassion which all faiths have insisted is essential to the religious life and to any experience of the numinous. Instead, it preached an ideology of exclusion, hatred, and even violence. But the fundamentalists did not have a monopoly on anger. Their movements had often evolved in a dialectical relationship with an aggressive secularism which showed scant respect for religion and its adherents. Secularists and fundamentalists sometimes seem trapped in an escalating spiral of hostility and recrimination. If fundamentalists must evolve a more compassionate assessment of their enemies in order to be true to their religious traditions, secularists must also be more faithful to the benevolence, tolerance, and respect for humanity which characterizes modern culture at its best, and address themselves more empathetically to the fears, anxieties, and needs which so many of their fundamentalist neighbors experience but which no society can safely ignore.

GLOSSARY

Agudat Israel (Hebrew). "The Union of Israel"; a political party of Orthodox Jews founded in 1912.

Alam al-Mithal (Arabic). "The World of Pure Images"; a realm of the human psyche which is the source of the visionary experience of Muslim mystics and the seat of the creative imagination.

Alim (Arabic). See *ulema*.

Aliyah (Hebrew). An "ascent" to a more exalted mode of being. Zionists used this term for the migration from the *Diaspora (q.v.)* to the Holy Land.

Antichrist. The false prophet whose arrival will herald the Last Days, according to some of the New Testament writers. Antichrist will be a plausible deceiver, who will lead the majority of Christians into apostasy and will be defeated by Christ in the battles foretold in the Book of Revelation.

Ashura (Arabic) "The Tenth"; the tenth day of the month of Muharram, the anniversary of the martyrdom of Husain, grandson of the Prophet Muhammad, at Kerbala in modern Iraq.

Apocalypse "Revelation"; the Greek title of the last book of the New Testament, which describes the vision of the Last Days popularly attributed to St. John. The term has come to apply to the catastrophic events leading up to the Second Coming of Christ and to the end of human history.

Ashkenazic Jews. Central and Eastern European Jewry, usually associated with Germanic and Yiddish culture, in contrast to *Sephardic Jews (q.v.)* of Spanish or Middle Eastern origin.

Avodah (Hebrew). "Work, labor." In biblical times the term applied to the religious service in the Temple.

Awqaf (Arabic). Singular: *waqf.* Pious endowments of income for a religious building or a charitable institution.

Ayatollah. From the Arabic *ayat Allah,* "the sign of God"; an honorific title of a leading *mujtahid (q.v.)* which came into vogue in Iran in the twentieth century.

Baptist Church. A Calvinist denomination that broke away from the mainstream to form an independent sect in England in the 1630s. Believers were baptized as adults when they made a profession of faith. Concerned about religious liberty, some Baptists emigrated to the American colonies in the early seventeenth century.

Batin (Arabic). The "hidden" dimension of existence and of religion which cannot be perceived by the senses or by rational thought, but which is discerned in mystical, intuitive disciplines.

Bazaari (Arabic). A member of the merchant and artisan class of the bazaar.

Bey (Turkish). A commander or general in the Ottoman army.

Bidah (Arabic). Innovation or deviation from customary Islamic practice or belief.

Chalutz (Hebrew). Plural: *chalutzim.* A Zionist pioneer.

Congregationalist Church: Calvinists who assert the autonomy of the local congregation and refuse to accept control by an establishment. Members are bound together by a covenant of loyalty and mutual edification. Persecuted in England, many Congregationalists fled to the Netherlands and the American colonies in the early seventeenth century. The church became especially strong in New England.

Converso (Spanish). Plural: *conversos.* "Convert"; one of the Jews who were forcibly converted to Roman Catholicism in early modern Spain.

Devekut (Hebrew). "Attachment" to God; the perpetual consciousness of the divine which in *Hasidism (q.v.)* is attainable only by the *Zaddik (q.v.).*

Diaspora. The communities of Jews dispersed outside Palestine. Also called the *Galut* (Hebrew Exile).

Divan (Turkish). Literally, "a low couch"; the audience chamber of the sultan or his provincial governors in the Ottoman empire, where justice was administered.

Edah Haredis (Hebrew). The community of ultra-Orthodox *Haredim (q.v.)* in Jerusalem.

Ein Sof (Hebrew). "Without End"; a kabbalistic term for the Godhead, the divine essence, which is inaccessible to humanity but which has revealed itself in creation and in ten successive emanations *(sefiroth),* which adapt the Ultimate to the limited understanding of human beings.

Eschatology. From the Greek, "knowledge of the Last Things"; doctrines concerning the end of history, which include messianism, the Last Judgment, and the final triumph of the faithful.

Falsafah (Arabic). "Philosophy"; an esoteric philosophical movement which tried to reconcile the revealed religion of the Koran with the Greek rationalism of Plato and Aristotle.

Fatwah (Arabic). A formal legal opinion or decision of a religious scholar on a matter of Islamic law.

Faylasuf (Arabic). A practitioner of *Falsafah (q.v.).*

Fedayin (Arabic). Freedom fighters.

Fellahin (Arabic). The Egyptian peasantry.

Fiqh (Arabic). Islamic jurisprudence; the study and application of the body of sacred Islamic law.

Faqih (Arabic). A jurist, a practitioner of *fiqh (q.v.).*

Gaon (Hebrew). A Jewish scholar and religious authority of the first rank.

Gahelet (Hebrew). "Glowing Embers"; the name adopted by the young Orthodox students who became the core group of religious Zionist fundamentalists, basing their ideology on the teachings of Rabbi Zvi Yehuda Kook.

Galut (Hebrew). Exile.

Ghayb (Arabic). The unseen, sacred, or transcendent.

Ghazu (Arabic). Military raids, campaigns.

Ghuluww (Arabic). "Exaggeration"; "extreme" speculations which overstress some aspects of a doctrine, especially in the early Shiah (see *Shii Islam*).

Gush Emunim (Hebrew). "Bloc of the Faithful"; a Zionist pressure group, founded by religious and secularist Jews to promote settlement in the territory occupied by Israel in the June War of 1967.

Habad (Hebrew). An acronym of *hokhmah* (wisdom), *binah* (intelligence), and *daath* (knowledge); the name given to the Hasidic movement founded by Rabbi Shneur Zalman in the late eighteenth century, which afterward settled in Lubavitch, Russia. Hence, the sect is also known as the *Lubavitch Hasidim.*

Hadith (Arabic). Plural: *ahadith.* "Tradition"; documented reports of the teachings and actions of the Prophet Muhammad which do not appear in the Koran, but which were recorded for posterity by his close companions and the members of his family.

Hajj (Arabic). The pilgrimage to Mecca.

Halakhah (Hebrew). The Jewish legal system, based on the 613 divine commandments found in the Torah and on the vast compendium of subsequently developed law and lore in the *Talmud (q.v.)*.

Haredim (Hebrew). Adjective: *haredi*. "The Trembling Ones"; ultra-Orthodox Jews.

Hasidism (Hebrew). A mystical movement founded in the eighteenth century by the Baal Shem Tov.

Haskalah (Hebrew). "Enlightenment"; an intellectual movement pioneered by Moses Mendelssohn in the eighteenth century which attempted to promote the values of the European Enlightenment within Judaism and to integrate Jews into mainstream European culture.

Hijrah (Arabic). "Migration." Originally the term referred to the migration of the Prophet Muhammad and his disciples from Mecca to Medina in 622 CE, the first year of the Islamic calendar. The term has been adopted by Muslim fundamentalists to describe a withdrawal from a society which they deem to have abandoned Islam.

Ijmah (Arabic). The "consensus" of the Muslim community that gives legitimacy to a legal decision.

Ijtihad (Arabic). "Independent Reasoning"; the creative use of reason to apply the *Shariah (q.v.)* to contemporary circumstances. In the fourteenth century, the majority of Muslims decided that "the gates of *ijtihad*" were closed and that scholars must rely on the legal decisions of past authorities instead of upon their own reasoned insights. *Shii Islam (q.v.)*, however, did not close "the gates of *ijtihad*."

Imam (Arabic). "Leader." In mainstream *Islam (q.v.)*, an Imam simply leads the prayers of the Muslim congregation. In *Shii Islam (q.v.)*, the term described those descendants of the Prophet Muhammad who were thought to enshrine the divine wisdom and who alone were the infallible guides of the faithful.

Infitah (Arabic). The policy of "opening up" of the Egyptian economy to the West in 1972.

Irfan (Arabic). The Iranian mystical tradition.

Islah (Arabic). "Reform"; a movement, such as that inspired by Ibn Taymiyyah, to revive the Islamic community by returning to the core values of the Koran and the *Sunnah (q.v.)*.

Islam (Arabic). "Surrender" to the will of God. A Muslim is a man or a woman who has made this existential surrender to the divine and fundamental laws of existence. The majority of Muslims who base their devotion on the *Sunnah (q.v.)* of the Prophet Muhammad are known as Sunnis; Shii Muslims, who have a different orientation, are a minority sect.

Jahiliyyah (Arabic). Adjective: *jahili*. "The Age of Ignorance." Originally, the term applied to the pre-Islamic period in Arabia. Today, Muslim fundamentalists apply it to any society, even a nominally Muslim society, which has, in their view, turned its back upon God and refused to submit to God's sovereignty.

Jamaah al-Islamiyyah (Arabic). Plural: *jamaat*. "Islamic party"; the student Islamist organizations that developed in Egypt during the 1970s.

Janissary (Turkish). "New Troop"; the crack slave infantry corps of the Ottoman empire.

Jihad (Arabic). "Struggle." The term is usually applied to an internal effort to reform bad habits or behavior in the Islamic community or within the individual Muslim. The term is also used more specifically to denote a war waged in the service of religion.

Kabah (Arabic). The cube-shaped shrine in Mecca, the holiest place in the Islamic world.

Kabbalah (Hebrew). The Jewish mystical tradition.

Kawwanot (Hebrew). "Concentrations"; the contemplative disciplines, such as the meditations upon the letters that compose the Divine Name, in Jewish spirituality.

Kehillah (Hebrew). The governing body in one of the Jewish communities in the European *Diaspora* (q.v.).

Kerbala. The plain outside Kufa in Iraq where Husain, the Third Shii *Imam (q.v.)*, grandson of the Prophet Muhammad, was killed by Umayyad troops in 660 CE. Today, Kerbala is one of the holy cities of the Shii Muslims and a place of pilgrimage.

Kibbutz (Hebrew). A Zionist agricultural commune organized on socialist principles.

Knesset (Hebrew). The parliament of the State of Israel.

Kookists. Religious Zionists who adhere to the teachings of Rabbi Zvi Yehuda Kook.

Koran (Arabic). "Recitation"; the divinely inspired scripture which was revealed to the Prophet Muhammad.

Logos (Greek). "Word"; rational, logical, or scientific discourse.

Lubavitch Hasidim. See *Habad.*

Madrasah (Arabic). An Islamic university or seminary, the curriculum of which focuses on religious subjects, especially Islamic law.

Majlis (Arabic). The representative assembly of Iran.

Mamluk (Arabic). "Slave"; the Circassian slave corps which founded a dynasty in the Near East in the thirteenth century but which was defeated by the Ottomans in the early sixteenth century. In Egypt, however, Mamluk commanders retained a de facto control of the country until they were vanquished by Muhammad Ali during the nineteenth century.

Marja-e Taqlid (Arabic). "Model for Imitation"; the title bestowed on the highest ranking *mujtahid (q.v.),* whose rulings are binding on all Shiis who choose to acknowledge his authority. At certain periods there has been a single Marja, and at other times a circle of several *maraji.*

Marrano (Spanish). "Swine"; the term applied to Spanish Jews who were forcibly converted to Christianity, and to their descendants.

Maskilim (Hebrew). Singular: *Maskil.* "Enlightened Ones"; the adherents of the *Haskalah (q.v.).*

Millennium. The thousand-year period of peace and justice that some Christians believe will come into being at the end of human history and will be followed by the Last Judgment. Christians base this belief on a literal interpretation of the predictions of Hebrew prophets and some of the New Testament writers.

Misnagdim (Hebrew). "Opponents." The term was originally used by the Hasidim (see *Hasidism*) to describe their enemies. It now refers to ultra-Orthodox Jews of Lithuanian descent who base their spirituality on Torah study rather than on mystical prayer.

Mufti (Arabic). A consultant in Islamic law.

Mujahidin (Arabic). Holy freedom fighters, who are engaged in a religiously inspired war.

Mujtahid (Arabic). An eminent Shii scholar who is deemed capable of exercising *ijtihad (q.v.)*

Mullah (Arabic). A Muslim functionary appointed to take care of a mosque.

Mythos (Greek). "Myth"; derived, like the words "mystery" and "mysticism," from the Greek *musteion:* to close the eyes or the mouth. A mode of knowledge rooted in silence and intuitive insight which gives meaning to life but which cannot be explained in rational terms. In the premodern world, mythical knowledge was seen as complementary to *logos (q.v.)*

Neo-Orthodox. A Jewish movement founded in the nineteenth century by Rabbi Samuel Raphael Hirsch which attempted to combine traditional Orthodoxy with some of the insights of modernity.

Neturei Karta (Aramaic). "The Guardians of the City"; an ultra-Orthodox Jewish sect which regards Zionism and the secular State of Israel as evil.

Occultation. The Shii doctrine that refers to the concealment of the Twelfth Imam, who is known as the "Hidden Imam," by God during the tenth century. Shiis believe that he will appear shortly before the End of Days to inaugurate a realm of justice.

Open Door Policy. See *infitah.*

Phylacteries. See *tefillin.*

Pillars of Islam. The five obligatory practices of Islam, binding upon all Muslims: the recitation of the Shehada (a brief confession of faith in the unity of God and the prophethood of Muhammad), daily prayer, fasting during the month of Ramadan, almsgiving, and the *hajj (q.v.).*

Postmillennialism. The eschatological belief that Jesus will return *after* Christians have, by their own virtuous efforts, established the *millennium (q.v.)*. At the end of this thousand-year era of peace and righteousness, Jesus will come to earth once again and preside over the Last Judgment.

Premillennialism. The fundamentalist belief that Jesus will have to return to earth *before* the *millennium (q.v.)*. Human society is viewed as so depraved that God is forced to intervene. He will send Jesus Christ to earth and, after he has fought the battles foretold in the Book of Revelation, Jesus will establish his Kingdom and rule the earth for a thousand years. At the end of this period, the Last Judgment will bring human history to a close.

Presbyterianism. A form of Calvinism which originated in Scotland, and is committed to constant reformation, a Bible-based faith, government by elders (Greek: *presbuteroi*) rather than by priests, and the participation of all church members.

Puritans. Members of the late-sixteenth-century Church of England, who originally rose up to express their dissatisfaction with the Elizabethan Settlement of Religion, and wanted a purer form of Protestantism, attacking the "popish" practices of the Anglican Church.

Qadi (Arabic). A judge who administers the *Shariah (q.v.)*.

Rapture. A Christian fundamentalist doctrine which holds that the elect will be spared the horrors of the Last Days and will be "snatched up" into the air with Christ (I Thessalonians 4:17) to await the *millennium (q.v.)*.

Rashidun (Arabic). The four "rightly guided" caliphs, who were the companions and immediate successors of the Prophet Muhammad: Abu Bakr, Umar, Uthman, and Ali ibn Abi Talib. Sunni Muslims (see *Sunni Islam*) regard the *rashidun* as the only rulers who governed in complete accordance with Islamic principles. Shiis (see *Shii Islam*), however, do not recognize the first three *rashidun*, but regard Ali ibn Abi Talib as their first *Imam (q.v.)*.

Rawda (Arabic). The recitation of a dirge lamenting the martyrdom of Husain, the Third Shii *Imam (q.v.)*.

Reconquista (Spanish). A "reconquest" of society by the true faith.

Reform Judaism. A religious movement of the nineteenth century which attempted to rationalize and reinterpret Judaism in the light of Western thought, values, and culture. Today Reform Jews differ principally from the Orthodox in their understanding of revelation, which they regard as progressive and unfolding and therefore allowing for different, changing interpretations of the *Torah (q.v.)*.

Rosh Yeshiva (Hebrew). Plural: *roshey yeshivot*. The head or principal of a *yeshiva (q.v.)*.

Sephardic Jews. Originally the term was used to denote the Jews who were exiled from Spain; later it was extended to refer to Jews of Middle Eastern descent, to distinguish them from the *Ashkenazic Jews (q.v.)*.

Shabbateanism. A Jewish movement of the seventeenth century based on the belief that the Turkish Jewish scholar and mystic Shabbetai Zevi (1626–76) was the Messiah; Shabbateanism finally died out in the early twentieth century.

Shariah (Arabic). "The Path to the Watering Hole"; the body of Islamic sacred laws, derived from the *Koran (q.v.)*, *Sunnah (q.v.)*, and *hadith (q.v.)*. These immutable, divinely inspired laws are held to be the only rightly guided way of life, and regulate every aspect of a Muslim's lifestyle.

Shekhinah (Hebrew). The Divine Presence on earth. In some forms of *Kabbalah (q.v.)*, the Shekhinah is symbolically depicted as a woman tragically separated from *Ein Sof (q.v.)* and exiled with human beings in the material world.

Shii Islam. A minority form of Islam, which does not differ from the majority form, *Sunni Islam*, theologically, but its adherents believe that a descendant of the Prophet Muhammad should lead the Muslim community. Practitioners are called *Shii Muslims* or *Shiis;* they venerate a succession of divinely inspired leaders (see *Imam*), descended from the Prophet through the line of his cousin and son-in-law Ali ibn Abi Talib. The collective term for the movement is the *Shiah*, the "party" of Ali.

Shurah (Arabic). "Consensus"; an Islamic legal principle that requires that the whole community consent, in some way, to a piece of legislation.

Sufi, Sufism. From the Arabic *tasawuuf;* the mystical tradition of *Sunni Islam (q.v.)*.

Sunnah (Arabic). "Custom"; the habits and religious practices of the Prophet Muhammad, which were recorded for posterity by his companions and family and are regarded as the ideal Islamic norm. They have thus been enshrined in Islamic law so that Muslims can approximate closely to the archetypal figure of the Prophet. The term *Sunnah* (adjective: *Sunni*) also applies to the main branch of Islam; see *Sunni Islam.*

Sunni Islam. the majority form of Islam, which bases its devotion on the *Sunnah (q.v.)* of the Prophet Muhammad. Practitioners are called *Sunni Muslims* or *Sunnis.* They do not differ from *Shii Muslims* on matters of belief, but do not require the leader of the Muslim community to be a descendant of the Prophet Muhammad and his son-in-law Ali ibn Abi Talib. The collective term for this form of Islam is the *Sunnah.*

Tajdid (Arabic). "Renewal"; a reform movement that seeks to restore Islam to its purity by returning to the *Koran (q.v.)* and the *Sunnah (q.v.),* rejecting later legislation and practice.

Talmud (Hebrew). "Study, teaching"; the work containing the opinions and statements of the rabbis of Palestine and Babylonia from the first century to the end of the fifth century CE, and their interpreters.

Taqiyyah (Arabic). "Dissimulation"; a protective *Shii* (see *Shii Islam*) doctrine that permitted the believer to conceal his real opinions when threatened by the establishment.

Taqlid (Arabic). "Imitation"; conformity to the authorities of the past, to the existing legal judgments of the four recognized schools of Islamic law, or to the legal decisions of a recognized *faqih* or *mujtahid (qq.v.)*

Tawhid (Arabic). "Making One"; the divine unity which Muslims seek to imitate in their personal and social lives by integrating their institutions and priorities, and by recognizing the overall sovereignty of God.

Taziyeh (Arabic). A Shii passion play depicting the martyrdom of Husain.

Tefillin (Hebrew). Small leather boxes containing the words of the *Shema*: "Hear O Israel! The Lord is God, the Lord is One!" which, in accordance with Deuteronomy 6:4–9, are strapped by Jewish men to the forehead and left arm for weekday morning prayers.

Tikkun (Hebrew). "Restoration"; the redemptive process delineated in kabbalistic spirituality whereby prayers, rituals, and devoted fidelity to the Law will end the exile of the *Shekhinah (q.v.)* and restore the unity of all things with the Godhead.

Torah (Hebrew). "Teaching"; the term refers to the Pentateuch, the first five books of the Jewish scriptures, and to the Law of Moses.

Ulema (Arabic). Singular: *alim.* "Learned Men"; the guardians of legal and religious traditions in Sunni and Shii Islam.

Ummah (Arabic). The Muslim community.

Usuli (Arabic). A school of *Shii Islam (q.v.)* that became predominant in Iran at the end of the eighteenth century. Usulis declared that all Shiis should submit to the legal rulings of a *mujtahid (q.v.)* and emulate his religious behavior, instead of relying on their own judgment.

Velayat-e Faqih (Arabic). "The Mandate of the Jurist"; the theory developed by Ayatollah Ruhollah Khomeini in the early 1970s which argued that a *faqih (q.v.)* should head the state in order to ensure that society conforms wholly to God's will as revealed in the *Shariah (q.v.).* Its widespread acceptance was a revolutionary departure from Shii orthodoxy.

Waqf. See *awqaf.*

Yeshiva (Hebrew). Plural: *yeshivot.* From the verb "to sit"; a Jewish religious academy where students undertake extensive study of the *Talmud (q.v.)* and other rabbinic literature.

Zaddik (Hebrew). "A Righteous Man"; in *Hasidism (q.v.),* a Zaddik is one who has achieved the art of *devekut (q.v.)* and can give his followers access to the divine.

Zahir (Arabic). "Manifest"; the external manifestations of God and the exterior world; also the literal, plain meaning of scripture, as opposed to the *batin (q.v.).*

Zakat (Arabic). "Purity"; the term used for a tax of fixed proportion of income and capital (usually 2.5 percent), which must be paid each year to assist the poor. This is one of the *Pillars of Islam (q.v.)*.

Zimzum (Hebrew). "Withdrawal"; in Lurianic Kabbalah, the Godhead, *Ein Sof (q.v.)*, is depicted as withdrawing into itself to vacate a space which is not-God, thus making room for the material cosmos.

NOTES

Introduction

1. Abdel Salam Sidahared and Anonshiravan Ehteshani (eds.) *Islamic Fundamentalism* (Boulder, Colo, 1996), 4.
2. Martin E. Marty and R. Scott Appleby, "Conclusion: An Interim Report on a Hypothetical Family," *Fundamentalisms Observed* (Chicago and London, 1991), 814–42.
3. Johannes Sloek, *Devotional Language* (trans. Henrik Mossin; Berlin and New York, 1996), 53–96.
4. Mircea Eliade, *Patterns in Comparative Religion* (trans. Rosemary Sheed; London, 1958), 453–55.
5. Sloek, *Devotional Language*, 75–76.
6. Ibid., 73–74; Thomas L. Thompson, *The Bible in History: How Writers Create a Past* (London, 1999), 15–33.
7. Sloek, *Devotional Language*, 50–52, 68–71.
8. Karen Armstrong, *Holy War: The Crusades and Their Impact on Today's World* (London, 1988; New York and London, 1991), 3–75, 147–274.
9. Sloek, *Devotional Language*, 134.

1. Jews: The Precursors (1482–1700)

1. Paul Johnson, *A History of the Jews* (London, 1987), 229; Yirmiyahu Yovel, *Spinoza and Other Heretics. I: The Marrano of Reason* (Princeton, N.J., 1989), 17–18.
2. Johnson, *A History of the Jews*, 230; Friedrich Heer, *The Medieval World 1100–1350* (trans. Janet Sondheimer; London, 1962), 318.
3. Yovel, *The Marrano of Reason*, 17.
4. Johnson, *A History of the Jews*, 217–25.
5. Ibid., 217–25; Haim Maccoby, *Judaism on Trial: Jewish Christian Debates in the Middle Ages* (Princeton, N.J., 1982); Haim Beinart, *Conversos on Trial: The Inquisition in Ciudad Real* (Jerusalem, 1981), 3–6.
6. Johnson, *A History of the Jews*, 225–29.
7. Ibid., 230–31.
8. Gershom Scholem, *Major Trends in Jewish Mysticism* (London, 1955), 246–49.
9. Gershom Scholem, *Sabbatai Sevi, The Mystical Messiah* (London and Princeton, N.J., 1973), 118–19.
10. Ibid., 19.

11. Ibid., 30–45; Scholem, *Major Trends in Jewish Mysticism*, 245–80; Gershom Scholem, "The Messianic Idea in Kabbalism," in Scholem, *The Messianic Idea in Judaism and Other Essays on Jewish Spirituality* (New York, 1971), 43–48.
12. Johannes Sloek, *Devotional Language* (trans. Henrik Mossin; Berlin and New York, 1996), 73–76.
13. Scholem, *Sabbatai Sevi*, 24.
14. Ibid., 23–25; R. J. Werblowsky, "Messianism in Jewish History," in Marc Saperstein (ed.), *Essential Papers in Messianic Movements in Jewish History* (New York and London, 1992), 48.
15. Scholem, *Sabbatai Sevi*, 37–42.
16. Richard L. Rubinstein, *After Auschwitz: Radical Theology and Contemporary Judaism* (Indianapolis, Ind., 1966).
17. R. J. Wenlowsky, "The Safed Revival and Its Aftermath," in Arthur Green (ed.), *Jewish Spirituality*, 2 vols. (London, 1986, 1989), II, 15–19.
18. Gershom Scholem, *On the Kabbalah and Its Symbolism* (New York, 1965), 150.
19. Lawrence Fine, "The Contemplative Practice of Yehudin in Lurianic Kabbalah," in Green (ed.), *Jewish Spirituality* II, 73–78.
20. Ibid., 89–90; Werblowsky, "The Safed Revival and Its Aftermath," 21–24; Louis Jacobs, "The Uplifting of the Sparks in Later Jewish Mysticism," in Green (ed.), *Jewish Spirituality* II, 108–11.
21. Werblowsky, "The Safed Revival and Its Aftermath," 17; Jacob Katz, "Halakah and Kabbalah as Competing Disciplines of Study," in Green (ed.), *Jewish Spirituality* II, 52–53.
22. Yovel, *The Marrano of Reason*, 91, 102.
23. Ibid., 26–27.
24. Y. Baer, *History of the Jews in Christian Spain* (Philadelphia, 1961), 276–7.
25. Yovel, *The Marrano of Reason*, 88–89.
26. Ibid., 93.
27. Fernando de Rojas, *La Celestina*, Act 27.
28. Yovel, *The Marrano of Reason*, 18–19.
29. Ibid., 19–24.
30. Ibid., 54–57.
31. Ibid., 51.
32. Prologue, *Epístola Invecta Contra Prado*, quoted in Yovel, ibid., 51–52.
33. Ibid., 53.
34. Ibid., 75–76.
35. Ibid., 42–51.
36. Ibid., 57–73.
37. Ibid., 4–13, 172–74.
38. Baruch Spinoza, *A Theologico-Political Treatise* (trans. R. H. M. Elwes; New York, 1951), 7.
39. R. M. Silverman, *Baruch Spinoza: Outcast Jew, Universal Sage* (Northwood, U.K., 1995), 154–70.
40. Ibid., 175–91.
41. Yovel, *The Marrano of Reason*, 31–32.
42. David Rudavsky, *Modern Jewish Religious Movements: A History of Emancipation and Adjustments* (New York, 1967), 28–33, 95.
43. Bernard Lewis, *The Jews of Islam* (New York and London, 1982), 24–45.
44. Johnson, *A History of the Jews*, 259.
45. Scholem, *Sabbatai Sevi*, 139.
46. Ibid, 123–38.
47. Ibid, 162.
48. Ibid., 198.
49. Ibid., 204, 206.

50. Ibid., 227.
51. Ibid., 237–38.
52. Ibid., 243–59, 262–67, 370–426.
53. Scholem, *Major Trends in Jewish Mysticism*, 306–07.
54. Scholem, *Sabbatai Sevi*, 367, 403.
55. Ibid., 720–21; 800–801.
56. Ibid., 796–97.
57. Scholem, *Major Trends in Jewish Mysticism*, 312–15.
58. Scholem, *Sabbatai Sevi*, 618–22.
59. Ibid., 622–37; 829–33.
60. Ibid., 840–41.
61. Ibid., 748.
62. Scholem, *Major Trends in Jewish Mysticism*, 300–304.
63. Gershom Scholem, "The Crypto-Jewish Sect of the Donmeh," in Scholem, *The Messianic Idea in Judaism*, 147–66.
64. Saying Number 2152, quoted in Scholem, "Redemption Through Sin," in *The Messianic Idea in Judaism*, 130.
65. Saying Number 1419, in ibid.
66. Ibid., 136–40.

2. Muslims: The Conservative Spirit (1492–1799)

1. Marshall G. S. Hodgson, *The Venture of Islam: Conscience and History in a World Civilization*, 3 vols. (Chicago and London, 1974), II, 334–60.
2. Ibid., III, 14–15.
3. Ibid., II, 406–7.
4. Ibid., III, 107–23.
5. Johannes Sloek, *Devotional Language* (trans. Henrik Mossin; Berlin and New York, 1996), 89–90.
6. Koran 80:11. The text of the Koran used for this book is that of Muhammad Asad, *The Message of the Quran* (Gibraltar, 1980).
7. Koran 35:24–26.
8. Koran 2:100; 13:37; 16:101; 17:41; 17:86.
9. Hodgson, *The Venture of Islam* I, 320–46, 386–89.
10. Ibid., II, 560; III, 113–22. Albert Hourani, *Arabic Thought in the Liberal Age, 1798–1939* (Oxford, 1962), 25–36.
11. John Voll, "Renewal and Reform in Islamic History," in John Esposito (ed.), *Voices of Resurgent Islam* (New York and Oxford, 1983).
12. Majid Fakhry, *A History of Islamic Philosophy* (New York and London, 1970), 350–54; Hodgson, *The Venture of Islam*, II, 470–71.
13. Hodgson, *The Venture of Islam*, I, 383–409, 416–36; II, 194–98; Henri Corbin, *Creative Imagination in the Sufism of Ibn Arabi* (trans. W. Trask; London, 1970), 10–29; 78–79.
14. P. M. Holt, "The Pattern of Egyptian Political History from 1517 to 1798," in P. M. Holt (ed.), *Political and Social Change in Modern Egypt: Historical Studies from the Ottoman Conquest to the United Arab Republic* (London, 1968), 80–82.
15. Ibid., 82–86.
16. Araf Lufti al-Sayyid Marsot, "The Role of the Ulema in Egypt During the Early Nineteenth Century," in Holt (ed.), *Political and Social Change in Modern Egypt*, 264–65.
17. Gemal el-Din Shayyal, "Some Aspects of Intellectual and Social Life in Eighteenth-Century Egypt," in Holt (ed.), *Political and Social Change in Modern Egypt*, 117–23.
18. Araf Lufti al-Sayyid Marsot, "The Ulema of Cairo in the Eighteenth and Nineteenth Cen-

turies," in Niddi R. Keddie (ed.), *Scholars, Saints and Sufis: Muslim Religious Institutions in the Middle East Since 1500* (Berkeley, Los Angeles and London, 1972), 154.

19. Marsot, "The Role of the Ulema During the Early Nineteenth Century," 267–69.
20. Ibid., 270; Daniel Crecelius, "Nonideological Responses of the Egyptian Ulema to Modernization," in Keddie (ed.), *Scholars, Saints and Sufis*, 172.
21. Crecelius, "Nonideological Responses," 167–72.
22. Hodgson, *The Venture of Islam*, III, 126–41, 158–59.
23. Hourani, *Arabic Thought in the Liberal Age*, 41–44.
24. Voll, "Renewal and Reform in Islamic History," 37, 39–42; Hodgson, *The Venture of Islam*, III, 160–61; Hourani, *Arabic Thought in the Liberal Age*, 37–38.
25. R. S. O'Fahey, "Pietism, Fundamentalism and Mysticism: An Alternative View of the 18th and 19th Century Islamic World"; lecture delivered on November 12, 1997, at Northwestern University.
26. Moojan Momen, *An Introduction to Shii Islam: The History and Doctrines of Twelver Shiism* (New Haven, Conn., and London, 1985), 27–33.
27. Magel Baktash, "Taziyeh and Its Philosophy," in Peter J. Chelkowski (ed.), *Tacziyeh, Ritual and Drama in Iran* (New York, 1979), 98–102; Michael J. Fischer, *Iran: From Religious Dispute to Revolution* (Cambridge, Mass., and London, 1980), 19–20; Hamid Algar, "The Oppositional Role of the Ulama in Twentieth Century Iran," in Keddie (ed.) *Scholars, Saints and Sufis*, 233.
28. Momen, *An Introduction to Shii Islam*, 35–38; 46–47.
29. Ibid., 37, 69–70, 145–58; Abdulaziz Abdulhussein Sachedina, *Islamic Messianism: The Idea of the Mahdi in Twelver Shiism* (Albany, 1981), 14–39.
30. Momen, *An Introduction to Shii Islam*, 43–45.
31. Ibn Babuya, "Kamal al-Din," in Momen, *An Introduction to Shii Islam*, 164, 161–90; Sachedina, *Islamic Messianism*, 24–30, 78–112, 150–83.
32. Fischer, *Iran*, 25–26.
33. Sachedina, *Islamic Messianism*, 151–59.
34. Nikki R. Keddie, *Roots of Revolution: An Interpretative History of Modern Iran* (New Haven, Conn., and London, 1981), 10; Sachedina, *Islamic Messianism*, 30.
35. Juan R. Cole, "Imami Jurisprudence and the Role of the Ulema: Mortaza Ansari on Emulating the Supreme Exemplar," in Keddie (ed.), *Scholars, Saints and Sufis*, 36–37; Hodgson, *The Venture of Islam*, II, 323–24, 472–76.
36. Sachedina, *Islamic Messianism*, 110–12.
37. Hodgson, *The Venture of Islam*, III, 22–23, 30–33.
38. The "Twelvers" were distinct from the "Seveners," who recognized the legitimacy of only the first seven Imams and are also known as Ismailis or Fatimids.
39. Momen, *An Introduction to Shii Islam*, 101–09.
40. Hodgson, *The Venture of Islam*, III, 23.
41. Momen, *An Introduction to Shii Islam*, 110–13.
42. Martin Riesebrodt, *Pious Passions: The Emergence of Modern Fundamentalism in the United States and Iran* (trans. Don Reneau; Berkeley, Los Angeles and London, 1993), 102–03.
43. Keddie, *Roots of Revolution*, 16–17.
44. Momen, *An Introduction to Shii Islam*, 114–16.
45. Baktash, "Taziyeh and Its Philosophy," 105.
46. Mary Hegland, "Two Images of Husain: Accommodation and Revolution in an Iranian Village," in Nikki R. Keddie (ed.), *Religion and Politics in Iran: Shiism from Quietism to Revolution* (New Haven, Conn., and London, 1983), 221–25.
47. Hodgson, *The Venture of Islam*, III, 42–46; Mangol Bayat, *Mysticism and Dissent: Socioreligious Thought in Qajar Iran* (Syracuse, N.Y., 1982), 28–47.
48. Hodgson, *The Venture of Islam*, III, 43.
49. Fakhry, *A History of Islamic Philosophy*, 340.

50. Fischer, *Iran*, 239–42.
51. Momen, *An Introduction to Shii Islam*, 117–23, 225; Bayat, *Mysticism and Dissent*, 21–23.
52. Bayat, *Mysticism and Dissent*, 30.
53. Nikki R. Keddie, "Ulema's Power in Modern Iran," in Keddie (ed.), *Scholars, Saints and Sufis*, 223; Momen, *An Introduction to Shii Islam*, 117–18.
54. Keddie, *Roots of Revolution*, 21–22; Momen, *An Introduction to Shii Islam*, 124–26.
55. Keddie, "Ulema's Power in Modern Iran," 226.
56. Momen, *An Introduction to Shii Islam*, 127–28; Cole, "Imami Jurisprudence and the Role of the Ulema," 39–40; Bayat, *Mysticism and Dissent*, 22–23; Hamid Algar, "The Oppositional Role of the Ulema," 234–35.
57. George Annesley, *The Rise of Modern Egypt, A Century and a Half of Egyptian History, 1790–1957* (Durham, U.K., 1994), 4–5.

3. Christians: Brave New World (1492–1870)

1. Robin Briggs, "Embattled Faiths: Religion and Natural Philosophy," in Euan Cameron (ed.), *Early Modern Europe* (Oxford, 1999), 197–205.
2. Marshall G. S. Hodgson, *The Venture of Islam: Conscience and History in a World Civilization*, 3 vols. (Chicago and London, 1974), III, 179–95.
3. Norman Cantor, *The Sacred Chain: A History of the Jews* (New York, 1994; London, 1995), 237–52.
4. Richard Marius, *Martin Luther, the Christian Between God and Death* (Cambridge, Mass., and London, 1999), 73–74, 214–15, 486–87.
5. Alister E. McGrath, *Reformation Thought: An Introduction* (Oxford and New York, 1988), 73–74; *A Life of John Calvin, A Study in the Shaping of Western Culture* (Oxford, 1990), 70.
6. Marius, *Martin Luther*, 101–04, 111, 443.
7. Jaroslav Pelikan, *The Christian Tradition: A History of the Development of Doctrine*, 5 vols. IV, *Reformation of Church and Dogma* (Chicago and London, 1985), 165–67.
8. Joshua Mitchell, *Not By Reason Alone: Religion, History and Identity in Early Modern Political Thought* (Chicago, 1993), 23–30.
9. McGrath, *John Calvin*, 130–32.
10. Richard Tarnas, *The Passion of the Western Mind: Understanding the Ideas That Have Shaped Our World View* (New York and London, 1991), 300.
11. Ibid.
12. Letter to Bentley, December 10, 1692, in Isaac Newton, *The Correspondence of Isaac Newton* (ed. A. H. Hall and L. Tilling; Cambridge, 1959), 223–25.
13. Richard S. Westfall, "The Rise of Science and the Decline of Orthodox Christianity: A Study of Kepler, Descartes and Newton," in David C. Lindberg and Ronald L. Numbers (eds.), *God and Nature: Historical Essays on the Encounter Between Christianity and Science* (Berkeley, Los Angeles, and London, 1986), 231.
14. Ibid., 231–32.
15. Gregory of Nyssa, "Not Three Gods," in Karen Armstrong, *A History of God: The Four Thousand Year Quest in Judaism, Christianity and Islam* (London and New York, 1993), 116–18.
16. Tarnas, *The Passion of the Western Mind*, 300.
17. René Descartes, *Discours de la méthode*, II: 6: 19.
18. Mitchell, *Not By Reason Alone*, 58, 61.
19. Blaise Pascal, *Pensées* (trans. A. J. Krailsheimer; London, 1966), 209.
20. John Locke, *Letter Concerning Toleration* (Indianapolis, Ind., 1955).
21. John Toland, *Christianity Not Mysterious* (1606) in Jaroslav Pelikan, *The Christian Tradi-*

tion, V, *Christian Doctrine and Modern Culture (Since 1700)* (Chicago and London, 1989), 66–69.

22. Ibid., 101.
23. Immanuel Kant, "What Is Enlightenment?" in *On History* (ed. Lewis Beck White; Indianapolis, Ind., 1963), 3.
24. Tarnas, *The Passion of the Western Mind*, 341–48.
25. Immanuel Kant, *Religion Within the Limits of Reason Alone* (1793).
26. Immanuel Kant, *Critique of Practical Reason* (1788).
27. Patrick Masterson, *Atheism and Alienation: A Study of the Philosophic Sources of Contemporary Atheism* (Dublin, 1971), 30.
28. Norman Cohn, *Europe's Inner Demons* (London, 1976).
29. Norman Cohn, *The Pursuit of the Millennium: Revolutionary Millennarians and Mystical Anarchists of the Middle Ages* (London, 1957), 303–18.
30. David S. Lovejoy, *Religious Enthusiasm in the New World: Heresy to Revolution* (Cambridge, Mass., and London, 1985), 67–90.
31. Ibid., 69.
32. Ibid., 112.
33. Pelikan, *Christian Doctrine and Modern Culture*, 118.
34. Jon Butler, *Awash in a Sea of Faith, Christianity and the American People* (Cambridge, Mass., and London, 1990), 36–66.
35. Ibid., 98–128.
36. Lovejoy, *Religious Enthusiasm in the New World*, 113.
37. R. C. Lovelace, "Puritan Spirituality: The Search for a Rightly Reformed Church," in Louis Dupré and Don E. Saliers (eds.), *Christian Spirituality: Post Reformation and Modern* (London and New York, 1989), 313–15.
38. Jonathan Edwards, "A Faithful Narrative of the Surprizing Work of God in Northampton, Connecticut," in Sherwood Eliot Wirt (ed.), *Spiritual Awakening: Classic Writings of the Eighteenth Century to Inspire and Help the Twentieth-Century Reader* (Tring, 1988), 110.
39. Ibid., 113.
40. Ruth H. Bloch, *Visionary Republic: Millennial Themes in American Thought (1756–1800)* (Cambridge, U.K., 1985), 14–15.
41. Ibid., 18–20.
42. Butler, *Awash in a Sea of Faith*, 160.
43. Ibid., 150.
44. *Practical Discourses on the Occasion of the Earthquakes, November 1755* (Boston, 1760), 369–70.
45. *Seven Discourses* (Portsmouth, 1756), 168.
46. Bloch, *Visionary Republic*, 37–58.
47. Ibid., 60–61.
48. Butler, *Awash in a Sea of Faith*, 218–26.
49. Bloch, *Visionary Republic*, 77–81.
50. Ibid., 65–67.
51. Butler, *Awash in a Sea of Faith*, 198.
52. Bloch, *Visionary Republic*, 81–88.
53. *A Valedictory Address to the Young Gentlemen Who Commenced Bachelors of Arts, July 27, 1776* (New Haven, Conn., 1776), 14.
54. Lovejoy, *Religious Enthusiasm in the New World*, 226.
55. Ibid.,
56. Thomas Paine, *Common Sense and the Crisis* (New York, 1975), 59.
57. Bloch, *Visionary Republic*, 55.
58. Ibid., 60–63.
59. Ibid., 29, 31.

60. Butler, *Awash in a Sea of Faith*, 262–65.
61. John F. Wilson, "Religion, Government and Power in the New American Nation," in Mark A. Noll (ed.), *Religion and American Politics: From the Colonial Period to the 1980s* (Oxford and New York, 1990).
62. Butler, *Awash in a Sea of Faith*, 222.
63. Ibid., 216.
64. Timothy Dwight, *The Duty of an American* (New Haven, 1798), 29–30.
65. Butler, *Awash in a Sea of Faith*, 216.
66. Ibid., 219.
67. Henry S. Stout, "Rhetoric and Reality in the Early Republic: The Case of the Federalist Clergy," in Noll (ed.), *Religion and American Politics*, 65–66, 75.
68. Nathan O. Hatch, *The Democratization of American Christianity* (New Haven, Conn., and London, 1989), 22.
69. Ibid., 25–129.
70. Ibid., 68–157.
71. Ibid., 9.
72. Ibid., 36–37, 68–71.
73. Ibid., 115–20.
74. Ibid., 138–39.
75. Ibid., 71.
76. Ibid., 57.
77. Paul Boyer, *When Time Shall Be No More: Prophecy Belief in Modern American Culture* (Cambridge, Mass., and London, 1992), 83–84.
78. Ibid., 83.
79. Ibid., 82.
80. Daniel Walker Howe, "Religion and Politics in the Antebellum North," in Noll (ed.), *Religion and American Politics*, 132–33; George M. Marsden, "Afterword," in ibid., 382–83.
81. Robert P. Swierenga, "Ethno-Religious Political Behavior in the Mid-Nineteenth Century," in Noll (ed.), *Religion and American Politics*, 158; Hatch, *Democratization of American Christianity*, 198–200.
82. Ruth H. Bloch, "Religion and Ideological Change in the American Revolution," in Noll (ed.), *Religion and American Politics*, 55–56.
83. Boyer, *When Time Shall Be No More*, 82.
84. Robert C. Fuller, *Naming the Antichrist: The History of an American Obsession* (Oxford and New York, 1995), 95.
85. Swierenga, "Ethno-Religious Political Behavior," 159–60; Marsden, "Afterword," 283–84.
86. Howe, "Religion and Politics in the Antebellum North," 125–28; Swierenga, "Ethno-Religious Political Behavior," 152–58.
87. Butler, *Awash in a Sea of Faith*, 270.
88. *The Essence of Christianity* (trans. George Eliot; New York, 1957), 33.
89. Karl Marx, "Economic and Philosophical Manuscripts," in *Karl Marx: Early Writings* (trans, and ed. T. B. Borrowmore; London, 1963), 166–67.
90. James R. Moore, "Geologists and Interpreters of Genesis in the Nineteenth Century," in Lindberg and Numbers (eds.), *God and Nature*, 341–43.
91. *Essays and Reviews*, 4th ed. (London, 1861).
92. Owen Chadwick, *The Secularization of the European Mind in the Nineteenth Century* (Cambridge, U.K., 1975), 161–88.
93. Quoted in Peter Gay, *A Godless Jew: Freud, Atheism and the Making of Psychoanalysis* (New Haven, Conn., and London, 1987), 6–7.
94. T. H. Huxley, *Science and Christian Tradition* (New York, 1896), 125.
95. Friedrich Nietzsche, *The Gay Science* (New York, 1974), 181.
96. Ibid.

4. Jews and Muslims Modernize (1700–1870)

1. Paul Johnson, *A History of the Jews* (London, 1987), 309.
2. Yirmanyahu Yovel, *Dark Riddle: Hegel, Nietzsche and the Jews* (Cambridge, U.K., 1998), 3–20, 83–97.
3. "On the Jewish Question," in *Karl Marx: Early Writings* (trans. and ed. T. B. Borrowmore; London, 1963).
4. Benzion Dinur, "The Origins of Hasidism and Its Social and Messianic Foundations," in Gershom David Hundert (ed.), *Essential Papers on Hasidism: Origins to Present* (New York and London, 1991), 86–161.
5. Simon Dubnow, "The Maggid of Miedzyrzecz, His Associates and the Center in Volhynia," in Hundert, *Essential Papers*, 58.
6. Gershom Scholem, "The Neutralization of Messianism in Early Hasidism," in *The Messianic Idea and Other Essays on Jewish Spirituality* (New York, 1971), 189–200; "Devekut or Communion with God," in ibid., 203–37; Louis Jacobs, "The Uplifting of the Sparks in Later Jewish Mysticism," in Arthur Green (ed.), *Jewish Spirituality*, 2 vols. (New York and London, 1986, 1988), II, 116–25; Jacobs, "Hasidic Prayer," in Hundert, *Essential Papers*, 330–48.
7. Benzion Dinur, "The Messianic-Prophetic Role of the Baal Shem Tov," in Marc Saperstein (ed.), *Essential Papers on Messianic Movements and Personalities in Jewish History* (London and New York, 1992), 378–80.
8. Dubnow, "The Maggid of Miedzyrzecz," 65.
9. Ibid., 61.
10. Scholem, "The Neutralization of Messianism in Early Hasidism," 196–98.
11. Louis Jacobs (ed.), *The Jewish Mystics* (London, 1990; New York, 1991), 208–15.
12. The term "Habad" is an acronym formed from the three kabbalistic divine attributes: *Hokhmah* (Wisdom), *Binah* (Intelligence), and *Daat* (Knowledge).
13. Rachel Elior, "HaBaD: The Contemplative Ascent to God," in Green (ed.), *Jewish Spirituality*, II, 158–203.
14. Jacobs, "Hasidic Prayer," 350–55.
15. Jonathan Magonet, *The Explorer's Guide to Judaism* (London, 1998), 11.
16. David Rudavsky, *Modern Jewish Religious Movements: A History of Emancipation and Adjustment*, rev. ed. (New York, 1967), 85.
17. Norman Cantor, *The Sacred Chain, A History of the Jews* (New York, 1994; London, 1995), 236–37.
18. Ibid., 247–48.
19. The Jews of England had been readmitted by Oliver Cromwell and, after the restoration of the monarchy, had by an administrative anomaly been given legal recognition with other "dissenters."
20. Cantor, *The Sacred Chain*, 241–56.
21. Rudavsky, *Modern Jewish Religious Movements*, 157–64.
22. Ibid., 286–87.
23. Ibid., 290.
24. Julius Güttmann, *Philosophies of Judaism, the History of Jewish Philosophy from Biblical Times to Franz Rosenzweig* (London and New York, 1964), 308–51.
25. Rudavsky, *Modern Jewish Religious Movements*, 188, 194–95, 201–04.
26. Ibid., 218–19.
27. Samuel C. Heilman and Menachem Friedman, "Religious Fundamentalism and Religious Jews," in Martin E. Marty and R. Scott Appleby (eds.), *Fundamentalisms Observed* (Chicago and London, 1991), 211–15; Charles Selengut, "By Torah Alone: Yeshiva Fundamentalism in Jewish Life," in Martin E. Marty and R. Scott Appleby (eds.), *Accounting for Fundamen-*

talisms (Chicago and London, 1994), 239–41; Menachem Friedman, "Habad as Messianic Fundamentalism," in ibid., 201.

28. Hayim Soloveitchic, "Migration, Acculturation and the New Role of Texts," in Marty and Appleby (eds.), *Accounting for Fundamentalisms*, 333–34.

29. Rudavsky, *Modern Jewish Religious Movements*, 219–43.

30. Andrew A. Paton, *A History of the Egyptian Revolution*, 2 vols. (Trubner, Germany, 1876), I, 109–11.

31. George Annesley, *The Rise of Modern Egypt: A Century and a Half of Egyptian History* (Durham, U.K., 1994), 7.

32. Gaston Wait (ed. and trans.), *Nicolas Turc, Chronique D'Egypte: 1798–1804* (Cairo, 1950), 78.

33. Youssef M. Choueiri, *Islamic Fundamentalism* (London, 1990), 19.

34. Araf Lutfi al-Sayyid Marsot, "The Ulama of Cairo in the Eighteenth and Nineteenth Centuries," in Nikki R. Keddie, *Scholars, Saints and Sufis: Muslim Religious Institutions in the Middle East Since 1500* (Berkeley, Los Angeles, and London, 1972), 161–62; Daniel Crecelius, "Nonideological Responses of the Egyptian Ulama to Modernization," in ibid., 173–75.

35. Bassam Tibi, *Arab Nationalism, A Critical Enquiry*, 2nd ed. (trans. Marion Farouk Sluglett and Peter Sluglett; London, 1990), 81.

36. Marsot, "The Ulama of Cairo," 162.

37. Annesley, *The Rise of Modern Egypt*, 28–38.

38. Ibid., 51–56.

39. Ibid., 57–59.

40. Ibid., 59–60.

41. Ibid., 62.

42. Marsot, "The Role of the Ulama in Egypt During the Early Nineteenth Century," in P. M. Holt (ed.) *Political and Social Change in Modern Egypt: Historical Studies from the Ottoman Conquest to the United Arab Republic* (London, 1968), 227–28.

43. Annesley, *The Rise of Modern Egypt*, 61.

44. From a survey by Ali Mubarak (1875), in Crecelius, "Nonideological Responses of the Egyptian Ulama," 181–82.

45. Ibid., 180–89; Marsot, "The Role of the Ulama," 278–79.

46. Albert Hourani, *Arabic Thought in the Liberal Age, 1798–1939* (Oxford, 1962), 42–45.

47. Ibid., 46–49.

48. Annesley, *The Rise of Modern Egypt*, 129–41, 152.

49. Ibid., 147.

50. Ibid., 153–55.

51. Gérard de Nerval, *Oeuvres* (ed. Albert Beguin and Jean Richter; Paris, 1952), 895.

52. Michael Gilsenan, *Recognizing Islam: Religion and Society in the Modern Middle East* (London, 1990), 199.

53. Ibid., 198–201.

54. Nikki R. Keddie, *Roots of Revolution: An Interpretive History of Modern Iran* (New Haven, Conn., and London, 1981), 37–38.

55. Ibid., 25, 38–39, 42–43; Keddie, "The Roots of the Ulama's Power in Modern Iran," in Keddie (ed.), *Scholars, Saints and Sufis*, 214–15.

56. Keddie, *Roots of Revolution*, 44–47, 56–63.

57. Juan R. Cole, "Imami Jurisprudence and the Role of the Ulama: Mortaza Ansari on Emulating the Supreme Exemplar," in Keddie (ed.), *Religion and Politics in Iran: Shiism from Quietism to Revolution* (New Haven, Conn., and London, 1983), 41.

58. J. M. Tancoigne, *A Narrative of a Journey into Persia and Residence in Teheran* (trans. William Wright; London, 1820), 196–201.

59. William Beeman, "Cultural Dimensions of Performance Conventions in Iranian Taziyeh," in Peter J. Chelkowski (ed.), *Taziyeh, Ritual and Drama in Iran* (New York, 1979), 26.

60. Michael J. Fischer, *Iran: From Religious Dispute to Revolution* (Cambridge, Mass., and London, 1980), 20, 176.

61. Marshall G. S. Hodgson, *The Venture of Islam: Conscience and History in a World Civilization* 3 vols. (Chicago and London, 1974), III, 155. Mangol Bayat, *Mysticism and Dissent: Socioreligious Thought in Qajar Iran (Syracuse, N.Y., 1982), 37–58.*

62. Bayat, *Mysticism and Dissent,* 60–86.

63. Ibid., 87–91.

64. Ibid., 90–97, 101–09.

65. Ibid., 97–100.

66. Ibid., 110–16.

67. Ibid., 118–25.

68. Ibid., 127–29.

5. Battle Lines (1870–1900)

1. George Steiner, *In Bluebeard's Castle: Some Notes Toward the Re-definition of Culture* (New Haven, Conn., 1971), 17–27.

2. William Blake, *Milton,* Preface.

3. Steiner, *In Bluebeard's Castle,* 23–24.

4. I. F. Clarke, *Voices Prophesying War: Future Wars 1763–3749,* rev. ed. (Oxford and New York, 1992), 37–88.

5. Charles Royster, *The Destructive War: William Tecumseh Sherman, Stonewall Jackson and the Americans* (New York, 1991), 82.

6. Alan T. Nolan, *Lee Considered: General Robert E. Lee and Civil War History* (Chapel Hill, N.C., 1991), 112–33; Charles B. Strozier, *Apocalypse: On the Psychology of Fundamentalism in America* (Boston, 1994), 173–74, 177.

7. Robert C. Fuller, *Naming the Antichrist: The History of an American Obsession* (Oxford and New York, 1995), 111, 148.

8. Paul Boyer, *When Time Shall Be No More: Prophecy Belief in Modern American Culture* (Cambridge, Mass., and London, 1992), 87–90; George M. Marsden, *Fundamentalism and American Culture: The Shaping of Twentieth Century Evangelicalism, 1870–1925* (Oxford and New York, 1980), 50–55; Strozier, *Apocalypse,* 183–85.

9. II Thessalonians 2:3–8.

10. I Thessalonians 4:16.

11. Marsden, *Fundamentalism and American Culture,* 57–63.

12. Ibid., 14–17; Nancy Ammerman, "North American Protestant Fundamentalism," in Martin E. Marty and R. Scott Appleby (eds.), *Fundamentalisms Observed* (Chicago and London, 1991), 8–12.

13. Marsden, *Fundamentalism and American Culture,* 55.

14. Johannes Sloek, *Devotional Language* (trans. Henrik Mossin; Berlin and New York, 1996), 83.

15. Marsden, *Fundamentalism and American Culture,* 110–17.

16. "Inspiration," *Princeton Review* 2, April 11, 1881.

17. Benjamin B. Warfield, *Selected Shorter Writings of Benjamin B. Warfield,* 2 vols. (ed. John B. Meeber; Nutley, N.J., 1902), II, 99–100.

18. Charles Hodge, *What Is Darwinism?* (Princeton, N.J., 1874), 142.

19. Ibid., 60.

20. Ibid., 139.

21. Marsden, *Fundamentalism and American Culture,* 22–25; Fuller, *Naming the Antichrist,* 111–12.

22. Ferenc Morton Szasz, *The Divided Mind of Protestant America, 1880–1930* (University,

Ala., 1982), 16–34, 37–41; Ammerman, "North American Protestant Fundamentalism," 11–12.

23. Mrs. Humphry Ward, *Robert Elsmere* (Lincoln, Neb., 1969), 414.

24. *New York Times,* April 5, 1894.

25. Ibid., February 1, 1897.

26. Ibid., April 18, 1899.

27. *Union Seminary Magazine,* 19, 1907–8.

28. Szasz, *The Divided Mind,* 28, 35–41.

29. Marsden, *Fundamentalism and American Culture,* 30, 78; Boyer, *When Time Shall Be No More,* 93.

30. Szasz, *The Divided Mind,* 75.

31. Ammerman, "North American Protestant Fundamentalism," 12.

32. Fuller, *Naming the Antichrist,* 98–99.

33. Zygmunt Bauman, *Modernity and the Holocaust* (Ithaca, N.Y., 1989), 40–77.

34. Paul Johnson, *A History of the Jews* (London, 1987), 365.

35. Ibid., 380.

36. Menachem Friedman, "Habad as Messianic Fundamentalism," in Martin E. Marty and R. Scott Appleby (eds.), *Accounting for Fundamentalisms* (Chicago and London, 1994), 335–36.

37. Arthur Hertzberg, *The Zionist Idea* (New York, 1969), 106.

38. Aviezer Ravitsky, *Messianism, Zionism, and Jewish Religious Radicalism* (trans. Michael Swirsky and Jonathan Chipman; Chicago and London, 1993), 16–18.

39. Ibid., 22–25, 49.

40. Laurence J. Silberstein, "Religion, Ideology, Modernity: Theoretical Issues in the Study of Jewish Fundamentalism," in Silberstein (ed.), *Jewish Fundamentalism in Comparative Perspective: Religion, Ideology and the Crisis of Modernity* (New York and London, 1993), 13–15.

41. Mangol Bayat, *Mysticism and Dissent: Socioreligious Thought in Qajar Iran* (Syracuse, N.Y., 1982), 133–78.

42. Sad Kitaba, Letter 37, Bayat, *Mysticism and Dissent,* 160.

43. Paharthana Yizirat, in ibid., 161.

44. Bayat, *Mysticism and Dissent,* 44.

45. Quhnikhani yi-Sirat, Bayat, *Mysticism and Dissent,* 161.

46. Bayat, *Mysticism and Dissent,* 174–79.

47. Nikki R. Keddie, *Roots of Revolution: An Interpretive History of Modern Iran* (New York and London, 1981), 66–67.

48. Albert Hourani, *Arabic Thought in the Liberal Age, 1798–1939* (Oxford, 1962), 69–109; Bassam Tibi, *The Crisis of Political Islam: A Pre-Industrial Culture in the Scientific-Technological Age* (Salt Lake City, Utah, 1988), 103–4; Tibi, *Arab Nationalism, A Critical Enquiry,* 2nd. ed. (trans. Marion Farouk Sluglett and Peter Sluglett; London, 1990), 84–88.

49. Hourani, *Arabic Thought in the Liberal Age,* 69.

50. Albert Hourani, *A History of the Arab Peoples* (London, 1991), 304–05.

51. Hourani, *Arabic Thought in the Liberal Age,* 77–78.

52. Ibid., 81.

53. Ibid., 195–97, 245–59; Tibi, *Arab Nationalism,* 99–105.

54. Nikki R. Keddie, *Islamic Response to Imperialism: Political and Religious Writings of Sayyid Jamal al-Din "Al-Afghani"* (Berkeley, 1968); Bayyat, *Mysticism and Dissent,* 134–48; Hourani, *Arabic Thought in the Liberal Age,* 108–92; Majid Fakhry, *A History of Islamic Philosophy* (New York and London, 1970), 372–75.

55. Hourani, *Arabic Thought in the Liberal Age,* 127–28.

56. Tibi, *The Crisis of Political Islam,* 70.

57. Hourani, *Arabic Thought in the Liberal Age,* 123–24.

58. Ibid., 126; Bayat, *Mysticism and Dissent*, 148.
59. Keddie, *Islamic Response to Imperialism*, 187.
60. Tibi, *The Crisis of Political Islam*, 90.
61. Bayat, *Mysticism and Dissent*, 147.
62. Koran 13:11.
63. E. Kedourie, *Afghani and Abduh: An Essay on Religious Unbelief and Political Activism in Modern Islam* (London, 1966), 45.
64. Ernest Renan, *Histoire générale et système comparé des langues semitiques* (ed. H. Pischiari; Paris, 1955), 145–46; Renan, *L'Islamisme et la science* (Paris, 1983).
65. *The Philosophy of Law*, Paragraphs 246, 248.
66. Marshall G. S. Hodgson, *The Venture of Islam: Conscience and History in a World Civilization*, 3 vols. (Chicago and London, 1974), III, 208; Tibi, *The Crisis of Political Islam*, 1–25.
67. Evelyn Baring, Lord Cromer, *Modern Egypt*, 2 vols. (New York, 1908), II, 146–47.
68. Ibid., II, 184.
69. Youssef M. Choueiri, *Islamic Fundamentalism* (London, 1990), 36.
70. Fakhry, *A History of Islamic Philosophy*, 376–81; Tibi, *Arab Nationalism*, 90–93; Hourani, *Arabic Thought in the Liberal Age*, 130–61; Hodgson, *The Venture of Islam*, III, 274–76.
71. Hourani, *Arabic Thought in the Liberal Age*, 131–32.
72. George Annesley, *The Rise of Modern Egypt: A Century and a Half of Egyptian History, 1798–1957*, (Durham, U.K., 1994), 308–09.
73. Hourani, *Arabic Thought in the Liberal Age*, 137.
74. Ibid., 144.
75. Ibid., 137–39.
76. Ibid., 154–55.
77. Leila Ahmed, *Women and Gender in Islam: Historical Roots of a Modern Debate* (New Haven, Conn., and London, 1992), 160.
78. Ibid., 139–40.
79. Ibid., 144–56.
80. Baring, *Modern Egypt*, II, 134, 155, 538–39.
81. Ahmed, *Women and Gender in Islam*, 154.
82. Ibid., 160–61.
83. Ibid., 163–67.

6. Fundamentals (1900–25)

1. W. B. Yeats, "The Second Coming," 3–8.
2. Peter Gay, *A Godless Jew: Freud, Atheism and the Making of Psychoanalysis* (New Haven, Conn., and London, 1987), 39–50.
3. Robert T. Handy, "Protestant Theological Tensions and Political Styles in the Progressive Period," in Mark A. Noll (ed.), *Religion and American Politics: From the Colonial Period to the 1980s* (Oxford and New York, 1990), 282–88.
4. *Christianity and the Social Order* (New York, 1912), 458.
5. Ferenc Morton Szasz, *The Divided Mind of Protestant America, 1880–1930* (University, Ala., 1982), 42–55.
6. Ibid., 56–57.
7. Charles O. Eliot, "The Future of Religion," *Harvard Theological Review* 20, 1909.
8. George M. Marsden, *Fundamentalism and American Culture: The Shaping of Twentieth-Century Evangelicism, 1870–1925* (New York and Oxford, 1980), 117–22.
9. Szasz, *The Divided Mind*, 78–81; Nancy T. Ammerman, "North American Protestant Fundamentalism," in Martin E. Marty and R. Scott Appleby (eds.), *Fundamentalisms Observed* (Chicago and London, 1974), 22.

10. Daniel 11:15; Jeremiah 1:14.

11. Robert C. Fuller, *Naming the Antichrist: The History of an American Obsession* (Oxford and New York, 1995), 115–17; Paul Boyer, *When Time Shall Be No More: Prophecy Belief in Modern American Culture* (Cambridge, Mass., and London, 1992), 101–05; Marsden, *Fundamentalism and American Culture*, 141–44, 150, 157, 207–10.

12. Marsden, *Fundamentalism and American Culture*, 90–92; Fuller, *Naming the Antichrist*, 119. Presbyterians, such as William Jennings Bryan, who was not a premillennialist, tended to be more optimistic about democracy, seeing it as a Calvinist achievement expressing the equality of all human beings before God.

13. Boyer, *When Time Shall Be No More*, 192; Marsden, *Fundamentalism and American Culture*, 154–55.

14. Szasz, *The Divided Mind*, 85.

15. Marsden, *Fundamentalism and American Culture*, 147–48.

16. Szasz, *The Divided Mind*, 86.

17. Marsden, *Fundamentalism and American Culture*, 147–48.

18. *The King's Business*, 19, 1918.

19. "Unprincipled Methods of Postmillennialists," in ibid.

20. Marsden, *Fundamentalism and American Culture*, 147.

21. Ibid., 162.

22. Szasz, *The Divided Mind*, 91.

23. Ibid., 90–91.

24. *The Watchtower Examiner*, July 1920; Fuller, *Naming the Antichrist*, 120.

25. Marsden, *Fundamentalism and American Culture*, 182–83.

26. Ibid., 157–60, 165–75, 180–84; Szasz, *The Divided Mind*, 94–100.

27. Marsden, *Fundamentalism and American Culture*, 171–74.

28. Szasz, *The Divided Mind*, 102.

29. Ammerman, "North American Protestant Fundamentalism," 26; Marsden, *Fundamentalism and American Culture*, 169–83; Ronald L. Numbers, *The Creationists: The Evolution of Scientific Creationism* (Berkeley, Los Angeles, and London, 1992), 41–44, 48–50; Szasz, *The Divided Mind*, 107–18.

30. To J. Baldwin, March 27, 1923, in Numbers, *The Creationists*, 41.

31. Marsden, *Fundamentalism and Modern American Culture*, 184–89; R. Laurence Moore, *Religious Outsiders and the Making of Americans* (Oxford and New York, 1986), 160–63; Szasz, *The Divided Mind*, 117–35; Numbers, *The Creationists*, 98–103.

32. *Union Seminary Magazine* 32 (1922); Szasz, *The Divided Mind*, 110.

33. "The Evolution Trial," *Forum*, 74 (1925).

34. Marsden, *Fundamentalism and Modern American Culture*, 187.

35. Ibid., 187–88.

36. Moore, *Religious Outsiders*, 161–63.

37. Marsden, *Fundamentalism and Modern American Culture*, 217.

38. *The King's Business*, 40, 1922.

39. The Acts of the Apostles, 2:1–6.

40. Joel, 3:1–5.

41. Harvey Cox, *Fire from Heaven: The Rise of Pentecostal Spirituality and the Reshaping of Religion in the Twenty-first Century* (New York, 1995), 48–74.

42. Romans 8:26; Cox, *Fire from Heaven*, 87.

43. Cox, *Fire from Heaven*, 63.

44. Ibid., 76–77.

45. Ibid., 57, 69–71.

46. Ibid., 63.

47. Ibid., 67.

48. Ibid., 81–122.

49. Ibid., 81.
50. "The Aesthetics of Silence," in *A Susan Sontag Reader* (New York, 1982), 195.
51. Ibid.; Cox, *Fire from Heaven*, 91–92.
52. Cox, *Fire from Heaven*, 75.
53. Asher Ginsberg (Ahad Ha-Am), "Slavery in the Midst of Freedom," *Complete Writings* (Jerusalem, 1965), 160.
54. Amos Elon, *The Israelis, Founders and Sons*, rev. ed. (London, 1984), 105, 112.
55. Eliezer Schweid, *The Land of Israel: National Home or Land of Destiny* (trans. Deborah Greniman; New York, 1985), 158.
56. Arthur Hertzberg (ed.), *The Zionist Idea* (New York, 1969), 377.
57. In fact, the Second Zionist Congress made no such declaration, though it did express the secularism of Zionism at this date.
58. "Brooks of the Negev," in Aviezer Ravitsky, *Messianism, Zionism, and Jewish Religious Radicalism* (trans. Michael Swirsky and Jonathan Chipman; Chicago and London, 1993), 95.
59. "On Zion," in Ravitsky, *Messianism*, 89.
60. "Eulogy," in Ravitsky, *Messianism*, 99.
61. "Eder Ha-Yakel," in Ravitsky, *Messianism*, 107.
62. "Orot," in Ravitsky, *Messianism*, 102.
63. Ibid.
64. M. Sotah 9:7.
65. "Orot," in Ravitsky, *Messianism*, 108.
66. Ibid., 104–11.
67. "Arpeli Tohar," in Ravitsky, *Messianism*, 105.
68. "Orot ha Kodesh," in Ravitsky, *Messianism*, 117.
69. Kook, "The War," in Herzberg, *The Zionist Idea*, 423.
70. Bernard Avishai, *The Tragedy of Zionism: Revolution and Democracy in the Land of Israel* (New York, 1985), 94.
71. "Iggerot ha Regati," in Ravitsky, *Messianism*, 120.
72. "Orot," in Ravitsky, *Messianism*, 120.
73. "Iggerot ha Reiyah," in Ravitsky, *Messianism*, 121.
74. Alan L. Mittelman, "Fundamentalism and Political Development: The Case of Agudat Israel," in Laurence J. Silberstein (ed.), *Jewish Fundamentalism in Comparative Perspective: Religion, Ideology, and the Crisis of Modernity* (New York and London, 1993), 225–31.
75. Ibid., 231.
76. Ibid., 234.
77. Ibid., 235.
78. Youssef M. Choueiri, *Islamic Fundamentalism* (London, 1990), 64.
79. Marshall G. S. Hodgson, *The Venture of Islam: Conscience and History in a World Civilization*, 3 vols. (Chicago and London, 1974), III, 171.
80. Albert Hourani, *Arabic Thought in the Liberal Age, 1798–1939* (Oxford, 1962), 170–83.
81. Ibid., 183–89.
82. Ibid., 240–43.
83. Ibid., 224, 230.
84. Ibid., 243–44.
85. Ibid., 242.
86. Azar Tabari, "The Role of the Clergy in Modern Iranian Politics," in Nikki R. Keddie (ed.), *Religion and Politics in Iran: Shiism from Quietism to Revolution* (New Haven, Conn., and London, 1983), 57.
87. Nikki R. Keddie, *Roots of Revolution: An Interpretive History of Modern Iran* (New Haven, Conn., and London, 1981), 72–73.
88. Mangol Bayat, *Mysticism and Dissent; Socioreligious Thought in Qajar Iran* (Syracuse, N.Y., 1982), 184–86.

89. Nikki R. Keddie, "The Roots of the Ulama's Power in Modern Iran," in Keddie (ed.), *Scholars, Saints and Sufis: Muslim Religious Institutions in the Middle East Since 1500* (Berkeley, Los Angeles, and London, 1972), 227.
90. Hamid Algar, "The Oppositional Role of the Ulama in Twentieth-Century Iran," in Keddie (ed.), *Scholars, Saints and Sufis*, 231–34.
91. Ibid., 237–38; Riesebrodt, *Pious Passion: The Emergence of Modern Fundamentalism in the United States and Iran* (trans. Don Reneau; Berkeley, Los Angeles, and London, 1993), 109–10; Tabari, "The Role of the Shii Clergy," 58.
92. Algar, "The Oppositional Role of the Ulama," 238.
93. Ibid., 238–40; Tabari, "The Role of the Clergy," 58–59.
94. Keddie, *Roots of Revolution*, 82.

7. Counterculture (1925–60)

1. George Steiner, *In Bluebeard's Castle: Some Notes Toward the Re-definition of Culture* (New Haven, Conn., 1971), 32.
2. Zygmunt Bauman, *Modernity and the Holocaust* (Ithaca, N.Y., 1989), 77–92.
3. Steiner, *In Bluebeard's Castle*, 47–48.
4. Samuel C. Heilman and Menachem Friedman, "Religious Fundamentalism and Religious Jews," in Martin E. Marty and R. Scott Appleby, *Fundamentalisms Observed* (Chicago and London, 1991), 223.
5. Aviezer Ravitsky, *Messianism, Zionism, and Jewish Religious Radicalism* (trans. Michael Swirsky and Jonathan Chipman, Chicago and London, 1993), 43.
6. Preface to *Va Yoel Moshe*, in Ravitsky, *Messianism*, 65.
7. Ravitsky, *Messianism*, 45.
8. Ibid., 50–51.
9. Ibid., 63–65.
10. Ibid., 54–55.
11. Ibid., 42.
12. Ibid., 53. *Hesed* (love) and *din* (power, stern judgment) are two of the divine emanations in Kabbalah; they need to be balanced carefully against each other, lest God's "stern judgment" overwhelm the world.
13. Karen Armstrong, *Jerusalem, One City, Three Faiths* (London and New York, 1996), 110.
14. J. T. Hagigah, 2:7.
15. Heilman and Friedman, "Religious Fundamentalism and Religious Jews," 226–29; Gerald Cromer, "Withdrawal and Conquest: Two Aspects of the Haredi Response to Modernity," in Laurence J. Silberstein (ed.), *Jewish Fundamentalism in Comparative Perspective: Religion, Ideology, and the Crisis of Modernity* (New York and London, 1993), 166–68; Ravitsky, *Messianism*, 77.
16. Ravitsky, *Messianism*, 67.
17. Ibid., 67.
18. Ibid., 69.
19. Ibid., 71.
20. Heilman and Friedman, "Religious Fundamentalism and Religious Jews," 216–18.
21. Ehud Sprinzak, "Three Models of Religious Violence: The Case of Jewish Fundamentalism in Israel," in Martin E. Marty and R. Scott Appleby (eds.), *Fundamentalisms and the State* (Chicago and London, 1993), 465–69.
22. Ravitsky, *Messianism*, 60.
23. Heilman and Friedman, "Religious Fundamentalism and Religious Jews," 220.
24. Michael Rosenak, "Jewish Fundamentalism in Israeli Education," in Martin E. Marty and R. Scott Appleby (eds.), *Fundamentalisms and Society* (Chicago and London, 1993), 383–84.

25. Mishneh Rav Aaron (Lakewood, 1980), in Hayim Soloveitchic, "Migration, Acculturation and the New Role of Texts," in Martin E. Marty and R. Scott Appleby (eds.), *Accounting for Fundamentalisms* (Chicago and London, 1994), 247.

26. Ibid., 250–51.

27. Ibid., 202.

28. Menachem Friedman, "The Market Model and Religious Radicalism," in Silberstein (ed.), *Jewish Fundamentalism in Comparative Perspective*, 194.

29. Exodus 23:10–11; Leviticus 25:1–7.

30. Heilman and Friedman, "Religious Fundamentalism and Religious Jews," 229–31.

31. Friedman, "The Market Model," 194.

32. Ibid., 197–205.

33. Ibid., 194.

34. Soloveitchic, "Migration, Acculturation and the New Role of Texts," 210, 220–21; Rosenak, "Jewish Fundamentalism in Israeli Education," 382–89.

35. David Hoffman, in Rosenak, "Jewish Fundamentalism in Israeli Education," 385.

36. Ibid., 382.

37. Menachem Friedman, "Habad as Messianic Fundamentalism," in Marty and Appleby (eds.), *Accounting for Fundamentalisms,* 337–41.

38. Ibid., 340–51.

39. Ravitsky, *Messianism,* 186–87.

40. Ibid., 188–92.

41. Nancy T. Ammerman, "North American Protestant Fundamentalism," in Marty and Appleby (eds.), *Fundamentalisms Observed,* 32–33; George M. Marsden, *Fundamentalism and American Culture: The Shaping of Twentieth Century Evangelicalism 1870–1925* (New York and Oxford, 1980), 194.

42. Quentin Schultze, "The Two Faces of Fundamentalist Higher Education," in Marty and Appleby (eds.), *Fundamentalisms and Society,* 499.

43. Melton Wright, *Fortress of Faith: The Story of Bob Jones University* (Greenville, S.C., 1984), 295.

44. Bob Jones II, *Cornbread and Caviare* (Greenville, S.C., 1985), 217.

45. Bulletin: Undergraduate, 1990–91.

46. Schultze, "The Two Faces of Fundamentalist Higher Education," 502.

47. Bob Jones II, *Cornbread and Caviare,* 203–4, 163, 165.

48. R. Laurence Moore, *Religious Outsiders and the Making of Americans* (Oxford and New York, 1986), 116.

49. Robert C. Fuller, *Naming the Antichrist: The History of an American Obsession* (Oxford and New York, 1995), 137–38; Ammerman, "North American Protestant Fundamentalism," 35.

50. Ammerman, "North American Protestant Fundamentalism," 29, 37.

51. Herbert Lockyear, *Cameos of Prophecy: Are These the Last Days?* (Grand Rapids, Mich., 1942), 66, 71.

52. 2 Peter 3:10.

53. Paul Boyer, *When Time Shall Be No More: Prophecy Belief in Modern American Culture* (Cambridge, Mass., and London, 1992), 117–18.

54. *Fundamentalist Journal,* May 1988.

55. Boyer, *When Time Shall Be No More,* 187–89.

56. Zechariah 13:8.

57. John Walvoord, *Israel and Prophecy* (Grand Rapids, Mich., 1962).

58. Richard P. Mitchell, *The Society of the Muslim Brothers* (New York and Oxford, 1969), 1–4.

59. John Esposito, "Islam and Muslim Politics," in Esposito (ed.), *Voices of Resurgent Islam* (New York and Oxford, 1983), 10.

60. Mitchell, *Society of Muslim Brothers,* 4–5.

61. Ibid., 7.

62. Ibid., 6.
63. Ibid., 7, 185–9.
64. Ibid., 14, 232–34.
65. Ibid., 8. This story and speech may be apocryphal, but it gives the flavor of the early Society of Muslim Brothers, founded that night by Banna.
66. Ibid., 9–13, 328.
67. A. Abidi, *Jordan: A Political Study* (London, 1965), 197.
68. Mitchell, *Society of Muslim Brothers*, 260, 308, 224, 226–27.
69. Ibid., 233.
70. Ibid., 236–39.
71. Ibid., 195–98.
72. Ibid., 287.
73. Ibid., 200–04.
74. Ibid., 288–89.
75. Ibid., 274–81.
76. Ibid., 281.
77. Ibid., 235, 240–41.
78. Ibid., 245–53.
79. Ibid., 242.
80. Muhammad al-Ghazzali, in Mitchell, ibid., 229.
81. Mitchell, *Society of Muslim Brothers*, 205–06.
82. Ibid., 206.
83. Marshall G. S. Hodgson, *The Venture of Islam: Conscience and History in a World Civilization*, 3 vols. (Chicago and London, 1974), III, 171.
84. Anwar Sadat, *Revolt on the Nile* (New York, 1957), 142–43.
85. Mitchell, *Society of Muslim Brothers*, 16, 313–18.
86. Ibid., 312.
87. Ibid., 70.
88. Ibid., 319.
89. This allegation was false: after Banna's death, the Society was so badly undermined by internal strife that it would have been incapable of mounting a coup.
90. Ibid., 152–61.
91. Martin Riesebrodt, *Pious Passion: The Emergence of Modern Fundamentalism in the United States and Iran* (trans. Don Reneau; Berkeley, Los Angeles, and London, 1993), 110–13; Nikki R. Keddie, *Roots of Revolution, An Interpretive History of Modern Iran* (New Haven, Conn., and London, 1981), 87–112.
92. Moojan Momen, *An Introduction to Shii Islam: The History and Doctrines of Twelver Shiism* (New Haven, Conn., and London, 1985), 251; Keddie, *Roots of Revolution*, 93–94.
93. Keddie, *Roots of Revolution*, 96–97.
94. Ibid., 95.
95. Ibid., 90, 110.
96. Momen, *An Introduction to Shii Islam*, 226; Riesebrodt, *Pious Passion*, 111–12; Azar Tabari, "The Role of the Shii Clergy in Modern Iranian Politics," in Keddie (ed.), *Religion and Politics: Shiism from Quietism to Revolution* (New Haven, Conn., and London, 1983), 60; Shahrough Akhavi, *Religion and Politics in Contemporary Iran: Clergy-State Relations in the Pahlavi Period* (Albany, N.Y., 1980), 38–40.
97. Tabari, "The Role of the Shii Clergy," 63.
98. Akhavi, *Religion and Politics in Contemporary Iran*, 58–59.
99. Ibid., 27.
100. Tabari, "The Role of the Shii Clergy," 60–64.
101. Yann Richard, "Ayatollah Kashani: Precursor of the Islamic Republic?" in Keddie (ed.), *Religion and Politics*, 101–24.

102. Ibid., 108.
103. Ibid., 107–08.
104. Ibid., 108.
105. Keddie, *Roots of Revolution*, 132–41.
106. Ibid., 142–45.
107. Richard, "Ayatollah Kashani," 118.

8. Mobilization (1960–74)

1. J. L. Talmon, *The Origins of Totalitarian Democracy* (London, 1953).
2. Daniel Crecelius, "Nonideological Responses of the Egyptian Ulama to Modernization," in Nikki R. Keddie (ed.), *Scholars, Saints and Sufis, Muslim Religious Institutions in the Middle East Since 1500* (Berkeley, Los Angeles, and London, 1972), 205–08.
3. Youssef M. Choueiri, *Islamic Fundamentalism* (London, 1990), 92.
4. Charles T. Adams, "Mawdudi and the Islamic State," in John Esposito (ed.), *Voices of Resurgent Islam* (New York and Oxford, 1983); Choueiri, *Islamic Fundamentalism*, 94–139.
5. Adams, "Mawdudi and the Islamic State," 101.
6. Mawdudi, *Islamic Way of Life* (Lahore, 1979), 37.
7. Choueiri, *Islamic Fundamentalism*, 109.
8. Mawdudi, *Jihad in Islam* (Lahore, 1976), 5–6.
9. Adams, "Mawdudi and the Islamic State," 119–20.
10. *Jihad in Islam.*
11. John O. Voll, "Fundamentalism in the Sunni Arab World: Egypt and the Sudan," in Martin E. Marty and R. Scott Appleby (eds.), *Fundamentalisms Observed* (Chicago and London, 1991), 369–74; Yvonne Haddad, "Sayyid Qutb: Ideologue of Islamic Revival," in Esposito (ed.), *Voices of Islamic Revival;* Choueiri, *Islamic Fundamentalism*, 96–151.
12. Haddad, "Sayyid Qutb," 70.
13. Voll, "Fundamentalism in the Sunni Arab World," 369.
14. Haddad, "Sayyid Qutb," 69.
15. Qutb, *Islam and Universal Peace* (Indianapolis, Ind., 1977), 45.
16. *Fi Zilal al-Koran*, I, 556; in Choueiri, *Islamic Fundamentalism*, 122.
17. Ibid., I, 510–11, in Choueiri, ibid., 124.
18. Ibid., III, 1255, in Choueiri, ibid., 131.
19. *Milestones* (Delhi, 1988), 224.
20. *This Religion of Islam* (Gary, Ind., n.d.), 65.
21. Ibid., 65, 38.
22. Haddad, "Sayyid Qutb," 90.
23. Ibid., 130.
24. Ibid., 88–89.
25. *Milestones*, 81.
26. Koran 5:65, 22:40–43, 2:213–15.
27. Koran 49:13.
28. Koran 2:256.
29. *Milestones*, 90.
30. *Fi Zilal al-Koran*, II, 924–25.
31. Ibid., II, 1113, 1132, 1164.
32. Martin Riesebrodt, *Pious Passion: The Emergence of Modern Fundamentalism in the United States and Iran* (Berkeley, Los Angeles, and London, 1993), 116–18; Nikki R. Keddie, *Roots of Revolution: An Interpretive History of Modern Iran* (New Haven, Conn., and London, 1981), 153–83; Mehrzad Borujerdi, *Iranian Intellectuals and the West: The Tormented Triumph of Nativism* (Syracuse, N.Y., 1996), 25–31.

33. Keddie, *Roots of Revolution*, 160–80.
34. Borujerdi, *Iranian Intellectuals*, 27; Choueiri, *Islamic Fundamentalism*, 156.
35. Borujerdi, *Iranian Intellectuals*, 49.
36. Keddie, *Roots of Revolution*, 144.
37. Borujerdi, *Iranian Intellectuals*, 65.
38. Jalal Al-e Ahmad, *Occidentosis: A Plague from the West* (trans. R. Campbell, ed. Hamid Algar; Berkeley, 1984), 34, 37.
39. Borujerdi, *Iranian Intellectuals*, 74–75.
40. Ibid., 72–75.
41. Sharough Akhavi, *Religion and Politics in Contemporary Iran: Clergy-State Relations in the Pahlavi Period* (Albany, N.Y., 1980), 81–83.
42. Riesebrodt, *Pious Passion*, 120–21; Akhavi, *Religion and Politics in Contemporary Iran*, 117–29; Borujerdi, *Iranian Intellectuals*, 81–83.
43. Hamid Algar, "The Oppositional Role of the Ulama in Twentieth-Century Iran," in Keddie (ed.), *Scholars, Saints and Sufis*, 245–46.
44. Hamid Algar, "The Fusion of the Mystical and Political in the Personality and Life of Imam Khomeini": lecture delivered at the School of Oriental and African Studies, London, June 9, 1998.
45. Michael J. Fischer, "Imam Khomeini: Four Levels of Understanding," in Esposito (ed.), *Voices of Resurgent Islam*, 154–56.
46. Keddie, *Roots of Revolution*, 158–59; Moojan Momen, *An Introduction to Shii Islam: The History and Doctrines of Twelver Shiism* (New Haven, Conn., and London, 1985), 254; Algar, "The Oppositional Role of the Ulama," 248.
47. Momen, *Introduction to Shii Islam*, 254.
48. Fischer, "Four Levels of Understanding," 157.
49. Willem M. Floor, "The Revolutionary Character of the Ulama: Wishful Thinking or Reality?" in Nikki R. Keddie (ed.), *Religion and Politics in Iran: Shiism from Quietism to Revolution* (Berkeley, Los Angeles, and London, 1983), Appendix, 97.
50. Akhavi, *Religion and Politics in Contemporary Iran*, 129–31.
51. Algar, "The Oppositional Role of the Ulama," 251.
52. Akhavi, *Religion and Politics in Contemporary Iran*, 138.
53. Keddie, *Roots of Revolution*, 215–59; Sharough Akhavi, "Shariati's Social Thought," in Keddie (ed.), *Religion and Politics*, 145–55; Abdulaziz Sachedina, "Ali Shariati, Ideologue of the Islamic Revolution," in Esposito (ed.), *Voices of Resurgent Islam;* Michael J. Fischer, *Iran: From Religious Dispute to Revolution* (Cambridge, Mass., and London, 1980), 154–67; Borujerdi, *Iranian Intellectuals*, 106–15.
54. Akhavi, *Religion and Politics in Contemporary Iran*, 144.
55. Sachedina, "Ali Shariati," 209–10.
56. Akhavi, "Shariati's Social Thought," 130–31.
57. Sachedina, "Ali Shariati," 198–200.
58. Borujerdi, *Iranian Intellectuals*, 108.
59. Shariati, *Hajj* (Tehran, 1988), 54–56.
60. Akhavi, *Religion and Politics in Contemporary Iran*, 146–49.
61. Shariati, *The Sociology of Islam* (Berkeley, 1979), 72.
62. Sharough Akhavi, "Shariati's Social Thought," in Keddie (ed.), *Religion and Politics*, 132.
63. Marshall G. S. Hodgson, *The Venture of Islam: Conscience and History in a World Civilization*, 3 vols. (Chicago and London, 1974), II, 334–60.
64. Mangol Bayat, *Mysticism and Dissent: Socioreligious Thought in Qajar Iran* (Syracuse, N.Y., 1982), 5–8.
65. Fischer, *Iran*, 154–55.
66. Ali Shariati, *Community and Leadership* (n.p., 1972), 165–66.
67. Sachedina, "Ali Shariati," 203.

68. Akhavi, "Shariati's Social Thought," 134.
69. Akhavi, *Religion and Politics in Contemporary Iran*, 153–54.
70. Akhavi, "Shariati's Social Thought," 144.
71. Sayeed Ruhollah Khomeini, *Islam and Revolution* (trans. and ed. Hamid Algar; Berkeley, 1981), 28.
72. Ibid., 29.
73. Asaf Hussain, *Islamic Iran: Revolution and Counter-Revolution* (London, 1985), 75.
74. Khomeini, *Islam and Revolution*, 374.
75. Fischer, "Four Levels of Understanding," 159.
76. Khomeini, *Islam and Revolution*, 352–53.
77. Michael Rosenak, "Jewish Fundamentalism in Israeli Education," in Martin E. Marty and R. Scott Appleby (eds.), *Fundamentalisms and Society* (Chicago and London, 1993), 392.
78. Ibid., 391.
79. Ibid., 392.
80. Ibid., 395.
81. Gideon Aran, "The Roots of Gush Emunim," *Studies in Contemporary Judaism*, 2, 1986; Aran, "Jewish Religious Zionist Fundamentalism," in Marty and Appleby (eds.), *Fundamentalisms Observed*, 270–71; Aran, "The Father, the Son, and the Holy Land," in R. Scott Appleby (ed.), *Spokesmen for the Despised: Fundamentalist Leaders in the Middle East* (Chicago, 1997), 318–20; Samuel C. Heilman, "Guides of the Faithful, Contemporary Religious Zionist Rabbis," in ibid., 329–30.
82. Interview with *Maariv* (14 Nisan 5723, 1963), in Aviezer Ravitsky, *Messianism, Zionism, and Jewish Religious Radicalism* (trans. Michael Swirsky and Jonathan Chipman; Chicago and London, 1993), 85.
83. Aran, "The Father, the Son and the Holy Land," 310.
84. Ibid., 311.
85. Ian S. Lustick, *For the Land and the Lord: Jewish Fundamentalism in Israel* (New York, 1988), 84.
86. Ravitsky, *Messianism*, 127.
87. Aran, "The Father, the Son and the Holy Land," 310.
88. Ibid., 312.
89. Harold Fisch, *The Zionist Revolution: A New Perspective* (Tel Aviv and London, 1978), 77, 87.
90. Aran, "Jewish Religious Zionist Fundamentalism," 271.
91. Hilkhot Tshava 9:2.
92. Heilman, *Guides of the Faithful*, 357.
93. Ehud Sprinzak, "Three Models of Religious Violence: The Case of Jewish Fundamentalism in Israel," in Martin E. Marty and R. Scott Appleby (eds.), *Fundamentalisms and the State* (Chicago and London, 1993), 472.
94. Aran, "Jewish Religious Zionist Fundamentalism," 277.
95. Uriel Tal, "Foundations of a Political Messianic Tradition in Israel," in Marc Saperstein (ed.), *Essential Papers on Messianic Movements and Personalities in Jewish History* (New York and London, 1992), 495; Ehud Sprinzak, "The Politics, Institutions and Culture of Gush Emunim," in Laurence J. Silberstein (ed.), *Jewish Fundamentalism in Comparative Perspective: Religion, Ideology and the Crisis of Modernity* (New York and London, 1993), 119.
96. Michael Lienesch, *Redeeming America: Piety and Politics in the New Christian Right* (Chapel Hill, N.C., and London, 1995), 1–2.
97. Nancy T. Ammerman, "North American Protestant Fundamentalism," in Marty and Appleby (eds.), *Fundamentalisms Observed*, 39–40; Steve Bruce, *The Rise and Fall of the New Christian Right, Conservative Protestant Politics in America, 1978–88* (Oxford and New York, 1990), 46–47.

98. Nathan O. Hatch, *The Democratization of American Christianity* (New Haven, Conn., and London, 1989), 218.

99. Lienesch, *Redeeming America*, 10.

100. Bruce, *Rise and Fall of the New Christian Right*, 38–40.

101. Ammerman, "North American Protestant Fundamentalism," 40–41; Bruce, *Rise and Fall of the New Christian Right*, 68–69.

102. Ammerman, "North American Protestant Fundamentalism," 42.

103. Susan Rose, "Christian Fundamentalism and Education in the United States," in Marty and Appleby (eds.), *Fundamentalisms and Society*, 455.

104. Ibid., 456–58.

105. Pro-Family Forum, *Is Humanism Molesting Your Child?* (Fort Worth, Tex., 1983).

106. D. Bollier, *Liberty and Justice for Some: defending a free society from the radical right's holy war on democracy* (Washington, D.C., 1982), 100.

107. Tim LaHaye, *The Battle for the Family* (Old Tappan, N.J., 1982), 31–32.

108. Tim LaHaye, *The Battle for the Mind* (Old Tappan, N.J., 1980), 181.

109. John W. Whitehead (with John Conlon), "The Establishment of the Religion of Secular Humanism and Its First Amendment Implications," *Texas Tech Law Review*, 10, 1978.

110. *The Second American Revolution* (Westchester, Ill., 1982), 112.

111. Pat Brooks, *The Return of the Puritans*, 2nd. ed. (Fletcher, N.C., 1979), 14.

112. Ibid., 92–94.

113. Franky Schaeffer, *A Time for Anger: The Myth of Neutrality* (Westchester, Ill., 1982), 122.

114. Rus Walton, *One Nation Under God* (Nashville, Tenn., 1987), 10. Walton's italics.

115. Walton, *FACS! Fundamentals for American Christians* (Nyack, N.Y., 1979), 62.

116. Pat Robertson, *America's Date with Destiny* (Nashville, Tenn., 1986), 68, 73.

117. John Eidsmore, *God and Caesar: Biblical Faith and Political Action* (Westchester, Ill., 1984), 88.

118. John Rushdoony, *This Independent Republic: Studies in the Nature and Meaning of American History* (Nutley, N.J., 1964), 37.

119. Lienesch, *Redeeming America*, 154.

120. *The Battle for the Mind*, 218–19.

121. Hal Lindsey, *The 1980s: Countdown to Armageddon* (Grand Rapids, Mich., 1980), 157.

122. Bruce, *Rise and Fall of the New Christian Right*, 47.

123. Pat Robertson, *The Secret Kingdom* (Nashville, Tenn., 1982), 108–09.

124. Susan Harding, "Contesting Rhetorics in the PTL Scandal," in Silberstein (ed.), *Jewish Fundamentalism in Comparative Perspective*, 63.

125. Bruce, *Rise and Fall of the New Christian Right*, 47–48.

126. Quentin Shultze, "The Two Faces of Fundamentalist Higher Education," in Marty and Appleby (eds.), *Fundamentalisms and Society*, 505.

127. Ibid.

128. Jerry Falwell (with Elmer Towns), *Church Affairs* (Nashville, Tenn., 1971), 41.

9. The Offensive (1974–79)

1. Gideon Aran, "Jewish Zionist Fundamentalism," in Martin E. Marty and R. Scott Appleby (eds.), *Fundamentalisms Observed* (Chicago and London, 1991), 290.

2. Ibid.

3. Ibid.

4. Exodus 19:7.

5. Laurence J. Silberstein, "Religion, Ideology, Modernity: Theoretical Issues in a Study of Jewish Fundamentalism," in Silberstein (ed.), *Jewish Fundamentalism in Comparative Perspective: Religion, Ideology, and the Crisis of Modernity* (New York and London, 1993), 17.

6. Aran, "Jewish Zionist Fundamentalism," 303.

7. Ibid., 312.

8. Robert I. Friedman, *Zealots for Zion: Inside Israel's West Bank Settlement Movement* (New York, 1992), 20.

9. Samuel C. Heilman, "Guides of the Faithful, Contemporary Religious Zionist Rabbis," in R. Scott Appleby (ed.), *Spokesmen for the Despised: Fundamentalist Leaders of the Middle East* (Chicago, 1997), 338.

10. Aran, "Jewish Zionist Fundamentalism," 279; Ehud Sprinzak, "The Politics, Institutions and Culture of Gush Emunim," in Silberstein (ed.), *Jewish Fundamentalism in Comparative Perspective,* 131–32.

11. Aran, "Jewish Zionist Fundamentalism," 280.

12. Ibid., 308.

13. Ibid., 300.

14. Ibid., 315.

15. *Haaretz* (April 14, 1986), in Ian S. Lustick, *For the Land and the Lord: Jewish Fundamentalism in Israel* (New York, 1988), 37.

16. Ibid., 47.

17. Lustick, "Jewish Fundamentalism and the Israeli-Palestinian Impasse," in Silberstein (ed.), *Jewish Fundamentalism in Comparative Perspective,* 141.

18. *Artzai,* 3, 1983, in Lustick, *For the Lord and the Land,* 82–83.

19. Heilman, "Guides of the Faithful," 339.

20. Aran, "Jewish Zionist Fundamentalism," 281.

21. Heilman, "Guides of the Faithful," 341.

22. Friedman, *Zealots for Zion,* 41.

23. Mohamed Heikal, *Autumn of Fury: The Assassination of Sadat* (London, 1984), 36–39.

24. Ibid., 94–96.

25. Gilles Kepel, *The Prophet and Pharaoh: Muslim Extremism in Egypt* (trans. Jon Rothschild; London, 1985), 85; Heikhal, *Autumn of Fury,* 94–97.

26. This had been the teaching of Ali ibn Abi Talib, the fourth of the *rashidun* caliphs venerated by Sunnis, and the First Imam of the Shiah. Asaf Hussain, *Islamic Iran, Revolution and Counter-Revolution* (London, 1985), 55.

27. Kepel, *Prophet and Pharaoh,* 125–26.

28. Rudolph Peters, *Jihad in Classical and Modern Islam, A Reader* (Princeton, N.J., 1996), 153–54.

29. Koran 2:47, 5:64, 78, cf. 61:6, 29:46, 2:129–32.

30. Kepel, *Prophet and Pharaoh,* 113.

31. Ibid., 78–84.

32. Ibid., 72.

33. Ibid., 74–76.

34. Ibid., 76–78.

35. Ibid., 85–86, 89–91.

36. Ibid., 94–99.

37. Ibid., 135–38.

38. Ibid., 152–55.

39. Ibid., 138–39.

40. Ibid., 143–44.

41. Nilufa Göle, *The Forbidden Modern: Civilization and Veiling* (Ann Arbor, Mich., 1996), 135–37.

42. Leila Ahmed, *Women and Gender in Islam: Historical Roots of a Modern Debate* (New Haven, Conn., and London, 1992), 226–28.

43. Ibid., 229–32.

44. Göle, *The Forbidden Modern,* 22.

45. Ahmed, *Women and Gender in Islam*, 220–25.
46. Patrick D. Gaffney, *The Prophet's Pulpit: Islamic Preaching in Contemporary Egypt* (Berkeley, Los Angeles, and London, 1994), 91–112.
47. Ibid., 97–107.
48. Kepel, *Prophet and Pharaoh*, 150–51.
49. William Beeman, "Images of the Great Satan: Representations of the United States in the Iranian Revolution," in Nikki R. Keddie (ed.), *Religion and Politics in Iran: Shiism from Quietism to Revolution* (New Haven, Conn., and London, 1972), 203.
50. Nikki R. Keddie (ed.), *Roots of Revolution: An Interpretive History of Modern Iran* (New Haven, Conn., and London, 1981), 282–83; Mehrzad Borujerdi, *Islamic Intellectuals and the West: The Tormented Triumph of Nativism* (Syracuse, N.Y., 1996), 29–42.
51. Shahrough Akhavi, *Religion and Politics in Contemporary Iran: Clergy-State Relations in the Pahlavi Period* (Albany, N.Y., 1980), 168; Keddie, *Roots of Revolution*, 209–11.
52. Keddie, *Roots of Revolution*, 260.
53. Ibid., 283.
54. Borujerdi, *Iranian Intellectuals*, 50–51.
55. Keddie, *Roots of Revolution*, 242; Michael J. Fischer, *Iran: From Religious Dispute to Revolution* (Cambridge, Mass., and London, 1980), 193.
56. Gary Sick, *All Fall Down: America's Fateful Encounter with Iran* (London, 1985), 30.
57. Koran 7:9–15.
58. Beeman, "Images of the Great Satan," 196.
59. Ibid., 257–73.
60. Ibid., 192.
61. Ibid., 215.
62. Ibid., 216.
63. Keddie, *Roots of Revolution*, 243.
64. Ibid; Fisher, *Iran*, 194.
65. Beeman, "Images of the Great Satan," 198–99.
66. Fischer, *Iran*, 195; Keddie, *Roots of Revolution*, 246–47.
67. Moojan Momen, *An Introduction to Shii Islam: The History and Doctrines of Twelver Shiism* (New Haven, Conn., and London, 1985), 284.
68. Ibid., 288.
69. Fischer, *Iran*, 184.
70. Ibid., 196–97.
71. Keddie, *Roots of Revolution*, 249–50.
72. Fischer, *Iran*, 198–99.
73. Sick, *All Fall Down*, 51; Keddie, *Roots of Revolution*, 250; Fischer, *Iran*, 199. The government claimed that only 122 of the demonstrators had been killed, while 2000 had been injured. Others claimed between 500 and 1000 dead.
74. Sick, *All Fall Down*, 51–52.
75. Fischer, *Iran*, 202.
76. Ibid., 204.
77. Ibid., 205.
78. Ibid. Keddie (*Roots of Revolution*, 252–53) believes that only about one million took part in the demonstration.
79. Momen, *An Introduction to Shii Islam*, 288.
80. Keddie, *Roots of Revolution*, 252–53.
81. Fischer, *Iran*, 207–08.
82. Amir Taheri, *The Spirit of Allah: Khomeini and the Islamic Revolution* (London, 1985), 227.
83. Steve Bruce, *The Rise and Fall of the New Christian Right: Conservative Protestant Politics in America 1978–1988* (Oxford and New York, 1990), 56–65.
84. Ibid., 90.

85. Nancy T. Ammerman, "North American Protestant Fundamentalism," in Marty and Appleby (eds.), *Fundamentalisms Observed*, 46.

86. Bruce, *Rise and Fall of the New Christian Right*, 86–89.

87. Tim LaHaye, *The Battle for the Mind* (Old Tappan, N.J., 1980), 179.

88. Richard A. Vignerie, *The New Right: We're Ready to Lead* (Falls Church, Va., 1981), 126.

89. Susan Harding, "Imagining the Last Days: The Politics of Apocalyptic Language," in Martin E. Marty and R. Scott Appleby (eds.), *Accounting for Fundamentalisms* (Chicago and London, 1994), 70.

90. Paul Boyer, *When Time Shall Be No More: Prophecy and Belief in Modern American Culture* (Cambridge, Mass., and London, 1992), 145.

91. Phyllis Shlafly, *The Power of the Christian Woman* (Cincinnati, Ohio, 1981), 117.

92. Ibid., 30.

93. Beverley LaHaye, *The Restless Woman* (Grand Rapids, Mich., 1984), 54, 126.

94. Tim and Beverley LaHaye, *The Act of Marriage: The Beauty of Sexual Love* (Grand Rapids, Mich., 1976), 285, 173.

95. Tim LaHaye, *Sex Education in the Family* (Grand Rapids, Mich., 1985), 188.

96. Tim LaHaye, *How to Be Happy Though Married* (Wheaton, Ill., 1968), 106.

97. James Robison, *Thank God I'm Free: The James Robison Story* (Nashville, Tenn., 1988), 124.

98. Jerry Falwell, *Listen, America!* (Garden City, N.Y., 1980), 185.

99. Edwin Louis Cole, *Maximized Manhood: A Guide for Family Survival* (Springdale, Pa., 1982), 63.

100. Tim LaHaye, *The Battle for the Family* (Old Tappan, N.J., 1982), 23.

101. Bruce, *Rise and Fall of the New Christian Right*, 95.

102. Ibid., 106–07.

103. A. Crawford, *Thunder on the Right: The New Right and the Politics of Resentment* (New York, 1980), 156–57.

104. A. Weissmann, "Building a Tower of Babel," *Texas Outlook*, Winter, 1982, 13.

10. Defeat? (1979–99)

1. Gary Sick, *All Fall Down: America's Fateful Encounter with Iran* (London, 1985), 165.

2. Hannah Arendt, *On Revolution* (New York, 1963), 18.

3. Shahrough Akhavi, *Religion and Politics in Contemporary Iran: Clergy-State Relations in the Pahlavi Period* (Albany, N.Y., 1980), 172–79; Moojan Momen, *An Introduction to Shii Islam: The History and Doctrines of Twelver Shiism* (New Haven, Conn., and London, 1985), 289–92.

4. Baqer Moin, *Khomeini, Life of the Ayatollah* (London, 1999), 227–28.

5. Sick, *All Fall Down*, 200.

6. Ibid., 231–33, 360.

7. Koran 8:68, 47:5, 24:34, 2:178.

8. Muhammad Zafrullah Khan, *Islam, Its Message for Modern Man* (London, 1962), 182.

9. Michael J. Fischer, *Iran: From Religious Dispute to Revolution* (Cambridge, Mass., and London, 1980), 235.

10. Momen, *An Introduction to Shii Islam*, 293–97.

11. Ibid., 293–95.

12. Gregory Rose, "Velayat-e Faqih and the Recovery of Islamic Identity in the Thought of Ayatollah Khomeini," in Nikki R. Keddie (ed.), *Religion and Politics in Iran: Shiism from Quietism to Revolution* (New Haven, Conn., and London, 1983).

13. Foreign Broadcasting and Information Service (FBIS), October 1, 1979.

14. Khomeini, "The Greater Jihad," in Daniel Brumberg, "Khomeini's Legacy: Islamic Rule

and Islamic Social Justice," in R. Scott Appleby (ed.), *Spokesmen for the Despised: Fundamentalist Leaders of the Middle East* (Chicago, 1997), 35.

15. FBIS, December 24, 1979.
16. Michael J. Fischer, "Imam Khomeini: Four Levels of Understanding," in John Esposito (ed.), *Voices of Resurgent Islam* (New York and Oxford, 1983), 171.
17. FBIS, December 12, 1983.
18. Brumberg, "Khomeini's Legacy," 40.
19. Ibid.
20. Fischer, "Four Levels of Understanding," 169.
21. Homa Katouzian, "Shiism and Islamic Economics: Sadr and Bani Sadr," in Keddie (ed.), *Religion and Politics*, 161–62.
22. See Brumberg, "Khomeini's Legacy," for this version of events.
23. FBIS, February 11 and 12, 1991, in Brumberg, "Khomeini's Legacy," 54.
24. FBIS, March 21, 1981, in ibid., 56.
25. Amir Taheri, *The Spirit of Allah: Khomeini and the Islamic Revolution* (London, 1985), 286.
26. FBIS, October 29, 1980, in Brumberg, "Khomeini's Legacy," 56.
27. FBIS, May 2, 1979, in ibid., 40.
28. Brumberg, "Khomeini's Legacy, 55–56.
29. FBIS, December 24, 1987, in Brumberg, 59.
30. FBIS, January 7, 1988, in ibid., 60.
31. FBIS, January 19, 1998, in ibid., 63.
32. Brumberg, "Khomeini's Legacy," 64–65.
33. FBIS, October 4, 1988, in ibid., 66.
34. Malise Ruthven, *A Satanic Affair: Salman Rushdie and the Rage of Islam* (London, 1990), 29.
35. Brumberg, "Khomeini's Legacy," 67–68.
36. Abdolkarim Sorush, "Three Cultures": Mehrzad Borujerdi, *Iranian Intellectuals and the West: The Tormented Triumph of Nativism* (Syracuse, N.Y., 1996), 162.
37. Farhang Rajaee, "Islam and Modernity," in Martin E. Marty and R. Scott Appleby (eds.), *Fundamentalisms and Society* (Chicago and London, 1993), 113.
38. Farhang Jahanpour, "Abdolkarim Sorush," unpublished paper.
39. *Kiyan*, 5, 1955.
40. Mohamed Heikal, *Autumn of Fury: The Assassination of Sadat* (London, 1984 ed.), 230.
41. Ibid., 118–19.
42. Ibid., 241–42.
43. Koran 57:16.
44. Johannes J. G. Jansen, *The Neglected Duty: The Creed of Sadat's Assassins and Islamic Resurgence in the Middle East* (New York and London, 1988), 162.
45. Ibid., 183–84.
46. Koran 2: 216.
47. Koran 9:5.
48. Jansen, *Neglected Duty*, 195.
49. Ibid., 167–82.
50. Ibid., 167.
51. Ibid., 169.
52. Ibid., 199.
53. Ibid., 200.
54. Ibid., 192–93.
55. Koran 9:4.
56. Jansen, *Neglected Duty*, 90, 198.
57. Ibid., 200.
58. Ibid., 201–02.

59. Ibid., 49–88.
60. Ibid., 60, 71.
61. Patrick D. Gaffney, _The Prophet's Pulpit: Islamic Preaching in Contemporary Egypt_ (Berkeley, Los Angeles, and London, 1994), 260.
62. Andrea B. Rugh, "Reshaping Personal Relations in Egypt," in Marty and Appleby (eds.), _Fundamentalisms and Society_, 152, 168–70.
63. Gaffney, _The Prophet's Pulpit_, 260–61.
64. Rugh, "Reshaping Personal Relations in Egypt," 153–62.
65. Gaffney, _The Prophet's Pulpit_, 262–64.
66. Ibid., 261–62.
67. Steve Negus, "Carnage at Luxor," _Middle East International_, November 21, 1997.
68. "Kuntres Misayon," in Aviezer Ravitsky, _Messianism, Zionism and Jewish Religious Radicalism_ (trans. Michael Swirsky and Jonathan Chipman; Chicago and London, 1993), 69.
69. Ha Homah, in ibid., 68.
70. Ibid., 151–59; Charles Selengut, "By Torah Alone: Yeshiva Fundamentalism in Jewish Life," in Martin E. Marty and R. Scott Appleby (eds.), _Accounting for Fundamentalisms_ (Chicago and London, 1994), 257–58.
71. Ravitsky, _Messianism_, 148–50.
72. Ibid., 164.
73. Samuel C. Heilman and Menachem Friedman, "Religious Fundamentalism and Religious Jews," in Martin E. Marty and R. Scott Appleby (eds), _Fundamentalisms Observed_ (Chicago and London, 1991), 243–50.
74. Ravitsky, _Messianism_, 178.
75. Heilman and Friedman, "Religious Fundamentalism and Religious Jews," 254.
76. Ibid., 253; Selengut, "By Torah Alone," 236.
77. Gideon Aran, "Jewish Zionist Fundamentalism," in Marty and Appleby (eds.), _Fundamentalisms Observed_, 294–95.
78. Ibid., 293.
79. Samuel C. Heilman, "Guides of the Faithful: Contemporary Religious Zionist Rabbis," in Appleby (ed.), _Spokesmen for the Despised_, 345.
80. Ibid.
81. Leviticus 19:33–34.
82. Shabbat 31A.
83. Exodus 23:23–33; Joshua 6:17–21, 8:20–29, 11:21–25.
84. "The Messianic Legacy," _Morasha_ 9; Ian S. Lustick, _For the Land and the Lord: Jewish Fundamentalism in Israel_ (New York, 1988), 75–76.
85. I Samuel 15:3.
86. _Bat Kol_, February 26, 1980.
87. "The Right to Hate," _Nekudah_, 15; Ehud Sprinzak, "The Politics, Institutions and Culture of Gush Emunim," in Laurence J. Silberstein (ed.), _Jewish Fundamentalism in Comparative Perspective: Religion, Ideology, and the Crisis of Modernity_ (New York and London, 1993), 127.
88. Ehud Sprinzak, _The Ascendance of Israel's Far Right_ (Oxford and New York, 1991), 97.
89. Ibid., 94–95.
90. Aran, "Jewish Zionist Fundamentalism," 267–68.
91. Ravitsky, _Messianism_, 133–34; Sprinzak, _Ascendance of Israel's Far Right_, 96.
92. Sprinzak, _Ascendance of Israel's Far Right_, 97–98.
93. Ibid., 220.
94. Raphael Mergui and Philippe Simonnot, _Israel's Ayatollahs: Meir Kahane and the Far Right in Israel_ (London, 1987), 45.
95. Ibid.

96. Sprinzak, *Ascendance of Israel's Far Right*, 223–25.

97. Ibid., 221.

98. Sprinzak, "Three Models of Religious Violence: The Case of Jewish Fundamentalism in Israel," in Martin E. Marty and R. Scott Appleby (eds.), *Fundamentalisms and the State* (Chicago and London, 1993), 479.

99. Ibid., 480.

100. Beverley Milton-Edwards, *Islamic Politics in Palestine* (London and New York, 1996), 73–116.

101. Ibid., 116–23.

102. Ibid., 149.

103. Ibid., 184–85.

104. Ibid., 186.

105. Heilman, "Guides of the Faithful," 352–53.

106. Ibid., 354.

107. Amos Oz, *In the Land of Israel* (trans. Maurice Goldberg-Bartura; London, 1983), 6, 9.

108. Quoted by Charles Liebman, "Jewish Fundamentalism and the Israeli Polity," in Marty and Appleby (eds.), *Fundamentalisms and Society*, 79.

109. Robert Wuthnow, "Quid Obscurum: The Changing Terrain of Church-State Relations," in Mark A. Noll (ed.), *Religion and American Politics: From the Colonial Period to the 1980s*, (Oxford and New York, 1990), 14.

110. Robert Wuthnow and Matthew P. Lawson, "Sources of Christian Fundamentalism in the United States," in Marty and Appleby (eds.), *Accounting for Fundamentalisms*, 20.

111. Ibid., 26–27.

112. Steve Bruce, *The Rise and Fall of the New Christian Right: Conservative Protestant Politics in America 1978–88* (Oxford and New York, 1990), 143.

113. Susan Harding, "Contesting Rhetorics in the PTL Scandal," in Silberstein (ed.), *Jewish Fundamentalism in Comparative Perspective*.

114. Ibid., 67.

115. Bruce, *Rise and Fall of the New Christian Right*, 144.

116. Lawrence Wright, *Saints and Sinners* (New York, 1993), 81–82.

117. Ibid., 82.

118. Ibid., 72–73.

119. Ibid., 79.

120. Bruce, *Rise and Fall of the New Christian Right*, 144–45, 193.

121. Faye Ginsburg, "Saving America's Souls: Operation Rescue's Crusade Against Abortion," in Marty and Appleby (eds.), *Fundamentalisms and the State*, 557.

122. Ibid., 568.

123. Nancy T. Ammerman, "North American Protestant Fundamentalism," in Marty and Appleby (eds.), *Fundamentalisms Observed*, 49–53; Michael Lienesch, *Redeeming America: Piety and Politics in the New Christian Right* (Chapel Hill, N.C., and London, 1995), 226.

124. Gary North, *In the Shadow of Plenty: The Biblical Blueprint for Welfare* (Fort Worth, Tex., 1986), xiii.

125. Ibid., 55.

126. North, *The Sinai Strategy: Economics and the Ten Commandments* (Tyler, Tex., 1986), 213–14.

127. Jeremy Rifkin and Ted Howard, *The Emerging Order: God in the Age of Scarcity* (New York, 1979), 239.

128. Harvey Cox, *Fire from Heaven: The Rise of Pentecostal Spirituality and the Reshaping of Religion in the Twenty-first Century* (New York, 1995), 287–88.

129. Lienesch, *Redeeming America*, 228.

130. Cox, *Fire from Heaven*, 290.

131. Susan Harding, "Imagining the Last Days: The Politics of Apocalyptic Language," in Marty and Appleby (eds.), *Accounting for Fundamentalisms*, 75.

132. Michael Barkun, *Religion and the Racist Right: The Origins of the Christian Identity Movement* (Chapel Hill, N.C., 1994).

133. Ibid., 107, 109.

BIBLIOGRAPHY

Abidi, A. *Jordan: A Political Study*. London, 1965.

Ahlstrom, Sydney E. *A Religious History of the American People*. Garden City, N.Y., 1972.

Ahmed, Akbar S. *Postmodernism and Islam, Predicament and Promise*. London and New York, 1972.

Ahmed, Leila. *Women and Gender in Islam: Historical Roots of a Modern Debate*. New Haven, Conn., and London, 1992.

Akhavi, Shahrough. *Religion and Politics in Contemporary Iran: Clergy-State Relations in the Pahlavi Period*. Albany, N.Y., 1980.

———. "Shariati's Social Thought." In Nikki R. Keddie (ed.), *Religion and Politics in Iran: Shiism from Quietism to Revolution*. New Haven, Conn., and London, 1983.

Alatus, Syed H. *Intellectuals in Developing Societies*. London, 1977.

Al-e Ahmad, Jalal. *Occidentosis: A Plague from the West*. Trans. R. Campbell. Ed. Hamid Algar. Berkeley, 1984.

Algar, Hamid. *Religion and State in Iran, 1785–1906*. Berkeley, 1969.

———. "The Oppositional Role of the Ulama in Twentieth-Century Iran." In Nikki R. Keddie (ed.), *Scholars, Saints and Sufis, Muslim Religious Institutions in the Middle East Since 1500*. Berkeley, Los Angeles, and London, 1972.

———. *Mirza Malkum Khan, A Biographical Study of Iranian Modernism*. Berkeley, 1973.

Altmann, Alexander. *Moses Mendelssohn: A Biographical Study*. University, Ala., 1973.

———. *Essays in Jewish Intellectual History*. Hanover, N.Y., 1981.

Amir-Moezzi, Mohammed Ali. *The Divine Guide in Early Shiism: The Sources of Esotericism in Islam*. Trans. David Streight. Albany, N.Y., 1994.

Ammerman, Nancy T. *Bible Believers: Fundamentalists in the Modern World*. New Brunswick, N.J., 1987.

———. "North American Protestant Fundamentalism." In Martin E. Marty and R. Scott Appleby (eds.), *Fundamentalisms Observed*. Chicago and London, 1991.

Andrews, Samuel J. *Christianity and Anti-Christianity in Their Final Conflict*. Chicago, 1937.

Annesley, George. *The Rise of Modern Egypt: A Century and a Half of Egyptian History, 1798–1957*. Durham, UK, 1994.

Appleby, R. Scott (ed.). *Spokesmen for the Despised: Fundamentalist Leaders of the Middle East*. Chicago, 1997.

Aran, Gideon. "The Roots of Gush Emunim," *Studies in Contemporary Jewry* 2, 1986.

———. "Jewish Zionist Fundamentalism." In Martin E. Marty and R. Scott Appleby (eds.), *Fundamentalisms Observed*. Chicago and London, 1991.

————. "The Father, the Son and the Holy Land, The Spiritual Authorities of Jewish-Zionist Fundamentalism in Israel," in R. Scott Appleby (ed.), _Spokesmen for the Despised: Fundamentalist Leaders of the Middle East_. Chicago, 1997.

Arendt, Hannah. _The Origins of Totalitarianism_. New York, 1958.

————. _On Revolution_. New York, 1963.

Avineri, Schlomo. _The Making of Modern Zionism: The Intellectual Origins of the Jewish State_. London, 1981.

Avishai, Bernard. _The Tragedy of Zionism: Revolution and Democracy in the Land of Israel_. New York, 1985.

Baer, Y. _History of the Jews in Christian Spain_. Philadelphia, 1961.

Baker, George W., and Dwight W. Chapman (eds.). _Men and Society in Disaster_. New York, 1902.

Bakker, Jim (with Robert Paul Lamb). _Move That Mountain!_ Plainfield, N.J., 1976.

Bakker, Tammy (with Cliff Dudley). _I Gotta Be Me_. Harrison, Ark., 1978.

———— (with Cliff Dudley). _Run to the Roar_. Harrison, Ark., 1980.

Baktash, Magel. "Ta'ziyeh and Its Philosophy." In Peter J. Chelkowski (ed.), _Ta'ziyeh: Ritual and Drama in Iran_. New York, 1979.

Baring, Evelyn, Lord Cromer. _Modern Egypt_. 2 vols. New York, 1908.

Barkett, Larry. _Your Finances in Changing Times_. Chicago, 1975.

Barkun, Michael. _Disaster and the Millennium_. New Haven and London, 1974.

————. "Divided Apocalypse: Thinking About the End in Contemporary America," _Soundings_ 66: 3, 1983.

————. _Religion and the Racist Right: The Origins of the Christian Identity Movement_. Chapel Hill, N.C., 1994.

Baron, Salo Wittmayer. _A Social and Religious History of the Jews_. 16 vols. New York, 1952.

Barr, James. _Fundamentalism_. Philadelphia, 1978.

Bateson, M. C., J. W. Clinton, J. B. M. Kassarjian, H. Safavi, and M. Soraya. "Safavy Batin: A Study of the Iranian Ideal Character Types." In L. Carl Brown and Norman Itzkowitz (eds.), _Psychological Dimensions of Near Eastern Studies_. Princeton, N.J., 1977.

Bauman, Zygmunt. _Modernity and the Holocaust_. Ithaca, N.Y., 1989.

Bayat, Mangol. _Mysticism and Dissent: Socioreligious Thought in Qajar Iran_. Syracuse, N.Y., 1982.

Beeman, William. "Cultural Dimensions of Performance Conventions in Iranian Ta'ziyeh." In Peter J. Chelkowski (ed.), _Ta'ziyeh: Ritual and Drama in Iran_. New York, 1979.

————. "Images of the Great Satan: Representations of the United States in the Iranian Revolution." In Nikki R. Keddie (ed.), _Religion and Politics in Iran: Shiism from Quietism to Revolution_. New Haven, Conn., and London, 1983.

Beinart, Haim. _Conversos on Trial: The Inquisition in Ciudad Real_. Jerusalem, 1981.

Bellah, Robert N., and Phillip E. Hammond. _Varieties of Civil Religion_. San Francisco, 1980.

Berger, Peter L. _The Social Reality of Religion_. London, 1969.

Berthoff, Rowland, and John M. Murrin. "Feudalism, Communalism, and the Yeoman Freeholder: The American Revolution Considered as a Social Accident." In Stephen G. Kurtz and James H. Hutson (eds.), _Essays on the American Revolution_. Chapel Hill, N.C., 1973.

Bloch, Ruth H. _Visionary Republic: Millennial Themes in American Thought, 1756–1800_. Cambridge, U.K., 1985.

————. "Religion and Ideological Change in the American Revolution." In Mark A. Noll (ed.), _Religion and American Politics: From the Colonial Period to the 1980s_. Oxford and New York, 1990.

Bloom, Harold. _The American Religion: The Emergence of the Post-Christian Nation_. New York, 1992.

Bollier, D., _Liberty and Justice for Some: defending a free society from the radical right's holy war on democracy_. Washington, D.C., 1982.

Bonomi, Patricia U. *Under the Cope of Heaven: Religion, Society and Politics in Colonial America.* New York and Oxford, 1986.

Boone, Kathleen C. *The Bible Tells Them So: The Discourse of Protestant Fundamentalism.* London, 1990.

Borujerdi, Mehrzad. *Iranian Intellectuals and the West: The Tormented Triumph of Nativism.* Syracuse, N.Y., 1996.

Bossy, John. *Christianity and the West, 1400–1700.* Oxford and New York, 1985.

Boyer, Paul. *When Time Shall Be No More: Prophecy and Belief in Modern American Culture.* Cambridge, Mass., and London, 1992.

Briggs, Robin. "Embattled Faiths: Religion and Natural Philosophy." In Euan Cameron (ed.), *Early Modern Europe.* Oxford, 1999.

Brinton, Crane. *The Anatomy of Revolution.* New York, 1950.

Brookes, James. *Maranatha, or The Lord Cometh.* New York, 1889.

Brooks, Pat. *The Return of the Puritan.*, 2nd ed. Fletcher, N.C., 1979.

Brown, Jerry Wayne. *The Rise of Biblical Criticism in America, 1800–1870: The New England Scholars.* Middletown, Conn., 1969.

Brown, L. Carl, and Norman Itzkowitz (eds.). *Psychological Dimensions of Near Eastern Studies.* Princeton, N.J., 1977.

Browne, E. G. "The Babis of Persia," *Journal of the Royal Asiatic Society* 21, 1889.

———. *A Year Amongst the Persians.* Cambridge, U.K., 1927.

Bruce, Steve. *The Rise and Fall of the New Christian Right: Conservative Protestant Politics in America 1978–1988.* Oxford and New York, 1990.

Brumberg, Daniel. "Khomeini's Legacy: Islamic Rule and Islamic Social Justice." In R. Scott Appleby (ed.), *Spokesmen for the Despised: Fundamentalist Leaders of the Middle East.* Chicago, 1997.

Buber, Martin. *Jewish Mysticism and the Legend of Baal Shem.* London, 1932.

———. *Hasidism and Modern Man.* New York, 1958.

Buckley, Michael J. *At the Origins of Modern Atheism.* New Haven, Conn., and London, 1987.

Bull, Hedly. *The Anarchic Society: A Study of Order in World Politics.* New York, 1977.

Butler, Jon. *Awash in a Sea of Faith, Christianizing the American People.* Cambridge, Mass., and London, 1990.

Cameron, Euan (ed.). *Early Modern Europe.* Oxford, U.K., 1999.

Cantor, Norman. *The Sacred Chain: A History of the Jews.* New York, 1994; London, 1995.

Caplan, Lionel (ed.). *Studies in Religious Fundamentalism.* Albany, N.Y., 1987.

Cassirer, Ernst. *The Philosophy of Enlightenment.* 4 vols. Trans. F. C. A. Koelin and J. T. Peregrove. Princeton, N.J., 1951.

Chadwick, Owen. *The Victorian Church.* 2 vols. London, 1970.

———. *The Secularization of the European Mind in the Nineteenth Century.* Cambridge, U.K., 1975.

Chelkowski, Peter J. (ed.). *Ta'ziyeh: Ritual and Drama in Iran.* New York, 1979.

Chilton, David. *Paradise Restored: A Biblical Theology of Dominion.* Fort Worth, Tex., 1985.

Choueiri, Youssef M. *Islamic Fundamentalism.* London, 1990.

Clarke, I. F. *Voices Prophesying War: Future Wars 1763–3749.* 2nd ed. Oxford and New York, 1992.

Clifford, James A., and G. E. Marcus (eds.). *Writing Culture: The Poetics and Politics of Ethnography.* Berkeley and London, 1986.

Cohn, Norman. *The Pursuit of the Millennium: Revolutionary Millennarians and Mystical Anarchists of the Middle Ages.* London, 1957.

———. *Europe's Inner Demons.* London, 1976.

———. *Cosmos, Chaos and the World to Come: The Ancient Roots of Apocalyptic Faith.* New Haven, Conn., and London, 1993.

Cole, Edwin Louis. *Maximized Manhood: A Guide for Family Survival.* Springdale, Pa., 1982.

Cole, Juan R. "Imami Jurisprudence and the Role of the Ulama: Mortaza Ansari on Emulating the Supreme Exemplar." In Nikki R. Keddie (ed.), *Religion and Politics in Iran: Shiism from Quietism to Revolution*. New Haven, Conn., and London, 1983.

Colwell, Stephen. *The Position of Christianity in the United States, in Its Relations with Our Political Institutions and Especially with Reference to Religious Instruction in the Public Schools*. New York, 1853.

Cooper, John, Ronald L. Nettler, and Mohamed Mahmoud (eds.). *Islam and Modernity: Muslim Intellectuals Respond*. London and New York, 1998.

Corbin, Henri. *Creative Imagination in the Sufism of Ibn Arabi*. Trans. W. Trask. London, 1970.

Cox, Harvey. *The Secular City: A Celebration of Its Liberties and an Invitation to Its Disciplines*. New York, 1965.

———. *Fire from Heaven: The Rise of Pentecostal Spirituality and the Reshaping of Religion in the Twenty-first Century*. New York, 1995.

Crecelius, Daniel. "Nonideological Responses of the Egyptian Ulama to Modernization." In Nikki R. Keddie (ed.), *Scholars, Saints and Sufis: Muslim Religious Institutions in the Middle East Since 1500*. Berkeley, Los Angeles, and London, 1972.

Cromartie, Michael (ed.). *No Longer Exiles: The Religious New Right in American Politics*. Washington, D.C., 1993.

Cromer, Gerald. "Withdrawal and Conquest: Two Aspects of the Haredi Response to Modernity." In Laurence J. Silberstein (ed.), *Jewish Fundamentalism in Comparative Perspective: Religion, Ideology, and the Crisis of Modernity* (New York and London, 1993).

Cuddihy, John Murray. *The Ordeal of Civility: Freud, Marx, Lévi-Strauss and the Jewish Struggle with Modernity*. Boston, 1974.

Darby, John N. *The Hopes of the Church of God in Connexion with the Destiny of the Jews and the Nations as Revealed in Prophecy*. 2nd ed. London, 1842.

———. *Lectures on the Second Coming*. Repr. London, 1909.

Davis, Joyce M. *Between Jihad and Salaam: Profiles in Islam*. New York, 1997.

Delumeau, Jean. *Catholicism Between Luther and Voltaire: A New View of the Counter Reformation*. London and Philadelphia, 1977.

De Nerval, Gérard. *Oeuvres*. Eds. Albert Beguin and Jean Richter. Paris, 1952.

De Vos, Richard. *Believe!*. Old Tappan, N.J., 1976.

Dinur, Benzion. "The Origins of Hasidism and Its Social and Messianic Foundations." In Gershon David Hundert (ed.), *Essential Papers on Hasidism, Origins to Present*. New York and London, 1991.

———. "The Messianic-Prophetic Role of the Baal Shem Tov." In Marc Saperstein (ed.), *Essential Papers on Messianic Movements and Personalities in Jewish History*. New York and London, 1992.

Djaït, Hichem. *Europe and Islam: Cultures and Modernity*. Berkeley, 1985.

Dobson, Ed, and Ed Hindson. *The Seduction of Power*. Old Tappan, N.J., 1988.

Dobson, James. *Dare to Discipline*. New York, 1977.

Donovan, John B. *Pat Robertson: The Authorized Biography*. New York, 1988.

Douglas, Mary, and Steven Tipton (eds.). *Religion and America: Spiritual Life in a Secular Age*. Boston, 1982.

Dreshner, S. H. *The Zaddik*. New York, Toronto, and London, 1960.

Dubnow, Simon. "The Beginnings: The Baal Shem Tov (Besht) and the Center in Podolia." In Gershon David Hundert (ed.), *Essential Papers on Hasidism, Origins to Present*. New York and London, 1991.

———. "The Maggid of Miedzyrzecz, His Associates and the Center in Volhynia." In Gershon David Hundert (ed.), *Essential Papers on Hasidism, Origins to Present*. New York and London, 1991.

Duby, Georges. *L'an Mil*. Paris, 1980.

Dupré, Louis, and Don E. Saliers (eds.). *Christian Spirituality: Post Reformation and Modern.* New York and London, 1989.

Duprée, A. Hunter. *Asa Gray 1810–1888.* Cambridge, Mass., 1959.

————. "Christianity and the Scientific Community in the Age of Darwin." In David C. Lindberg and Ronald L. Numbers, *God and Nature: Historical Essays on the Encounter between Christianity and Science.* Berkeley, Los Angeles, and London, 1986.

Durkheim, Emile. *The Elementary Forms of the Religious Life.* New York, 1961.

————. *Sociology and Philosophy.* New York, 1974.

Durraq, A. *L'Egypte sous le Regne de Barsbay 1422–1438.* Damascus, 1961.

Dwight, Timothy. *A Valedictory Address to the Young Gentlemen Who Commenced Bachelors of Arts, July 25th, 1776.* New Haven, Conn., 1776.

————. *The Duty of an American.* New Haven, Conn., 1798.

————. *A Discourse in Two Parts.* Boston, 1813.

Edwards, Jonathan. *The Works of the Rev. Jonathan Edwards.* Ed. E. Hickman. 2 vols. London, 1865.

Ehrenreich, Barbara. *Blood Rites: Origins and History of the Passions of War.* New York, 1997.

Eidsmore, John. *God and Caesar: Biblical Faith and Political Action.* Westchester, Ill., 1984.

Eisen, A. M. "Strategies of Modern Jewish Faith" in Arthur Green (ed.), *Jewish Spirituality,* Vol. II. London, 1988.

Eliade, Mircea. *The Myth of the Eternal Return, or Cosmos and History.* Trans. Willard J. Trask. Princeton, N.J., 1954.

————. *Patterns of Comparative Religion.* Trans. Rosemary Sheed. London, 1958.

————. *The Sacred and the Profane.* Trans. Willard J. Trask. New York, 1959.

————. *Images and Symbols: Studies in Religious Symbolism.* Trans. Philip Mairet. Princeton, N.J., 1991.

Elior, Rachel. "HaBaD: The Contemplative Ascent to God." In Arthur Green (ed.), *Jewish Spirituality.* Vol. II. London, 1988.

Eliot, Charles O. "The Future of Religion," *Harvard Theological Review* (2), 1909.

Elon, Amos. *The Israelis: Founders and Sons.* Rev. ed. London, 1984.

Enayat, Hamid. "The Politics of Iranology." *Iranian Studies,* 1973, 6.I.

Esposito, John. *Islam, The Straight Path.* Rev. ed. New York and Oxford, 1988.

————. *The Islamic Threat: Myth or Reality.* New York and Oxford, 1995.

———— (ed.). *Voices of Resurgent Islam.* New York and Oxford, 1983.

————, with John L. Donohue (eds.). *Islam in Transition: Muslim Perspectives.* New York and Oxford, 1982.

Ettinger, Shmuel. "The Hasidic Movement—Reality and Ideals." In Gershom David Hundert (ed.), *Essential Papers on Hasidism, Origins to Present.* New York and London, 1991.

Evenett, H. O. *The Spirit of the Counter-Reformation.* Cambridge, U.K., 1968.

Fakhry, Majid. *A History of Islamic Philosophy.* New York and London, 1970.

Falwell, Jerry. *Listen America!.* Garden City, N.Y., 1980.

————. *Strength for the Journey: An Autobiography.* New York, 1987.

————, with Ed Dobson and Ed Hindson, eds.). *The Fundamentalist Phenomenon: The Resurgence of Conservative Christianity.* Garden City, N.Y., 1981.

————, with Elmer Towns. *Church Affairs.* Nashville, Tenn., 1971.

Febvre, Lucien. *The Problem of Unbelief in the Sixteenth Century.* Trans. Beatrice Gottlieb. Cambridge, Mass., 1982.

Festinger, Leon. *A Theory of Cognitive Dissonance.* Stanford, Calif., 1957.

Feuerbach, Ludwig. *The Essence of Christianity.* Trans. George Eliot. New York, 1957.

Fine, Lawrence. "The Contemplative Practice of Yehudim in Lurianic Kabbalah." In Arthur Green (ed.), *Jewish Spirituality.* Vol. II. London, 1988.

Finney, Charles Grandison. *Lectures on Revivals of Religion.* Ed. William G. McLaughlin. Cambridge, Mass., 1960.

Fisch, Harold. *The Zionist Revolution: A New Perspective.* Tel Aviv and London, 1978.

Fischer, Michael J. *Iran: From Religious Dispute to Revolution.* Cambridge, Mass., and London, 1980.

———. "Imam Khomeini: Four Levels of Understanding." In John Esposito (ed.), *Voices of Resurgent Islam.* New York and Oxford, 1983.

Floor, Willem M. "The Revolutionary Character of the Ulama: Wishful Thinking or Reality?" In Nikki R. Keddie (ed.), *Religion and Politics in Islam: Shiism from Quietism to Revolution.* New Haven, Conn., and London, 1983.

Focillon, Henri. *L'An Mille.* Paris, 1952.

Foster, Lawrence. *Religion and Sexuality: Three American Communal Experiments in the Nineteenth Century.* Oxford and New York, 1981.

Foucault, Michel. *Language, Counter-Meaning, Practice: Selected Essays and Interviews.* Ed. Donald F. Benchard. Ithaca, N.Y., 1977.

———. *Power/Knowledge: Selected Interviews and Other Writings.* Ed. Colin Gordon. New York, 1980.

Fox, George. *The Journal of George Fox.* Ed. J. L. Nickalls. Cambridge, U.K., 1911.

Friedman, Menachem. "The Market Model and Religious Radicalism." In Laurence J. Silberstein (ed.), *Jewish Fundamentalism in Comparative Perspective: Religion, Ideology and the Crisis of Modernity.* New York and London, 1993.

———. "Habad as Messianic Fundamentalism." In Martin E. Marty and R. Scott Appleby (eds.), *Accounting for Fundamentalisms.* Chicago and London, 1994.

Friedman, Robert I. *Zealots for Zion: Inside Israel's West Bank Settlement Movement.* New York, 1992.

Fuller, Robert C. *Naming the Antichrist: The History of an American Obsession.* Oxford and New York, 1995.

Gaffney, Patrick D. *The Prophet's Pulpit: Islamic Preaching in Contemporary Egypt.* Berkeley, Los Angeles, and London, 1994.

Gay, Peter. *The Enlightenment: An Interpretation.* 2 vols. New York, 1966.

———. *A Godless Jew: Freud, Atheism and the Making of Psychoanalysis.* New Haven, Conn., and London, 1987.

Geertz, Clifford. *Local Knowledge.* New York, 1983.

———. *Postmodernism, Reason and Religion.* London and New York, 1992.

Gibb, H. A. R., and H. Bowen. *Islamic Society and the West.* London, 1957.

Gilsenan, Michael. *Recognizing Islam: Religion and Society in the Modern Middle East.* London, 1990.

Ginsberg, Asher (Ahad Ha-Am). *Complete Writings.* Jerusalem, 1965.

Ginsburg, Faye. "Saving America's Souls: Operation Rescue's Crusade Against Abortion." In Martin E. Marty and R. Scott Appleby (eds.), *Fundamentalisms and the State.* Chicago and London, 1993.

Göle, Nilufa. *The Forbidden Modern: Civilization and Veiling.* Ann Arbor, Mich., 1996.

Goodwyn, Lawrence. *The Populist Movement: A Short History of the Agrarian Revolt in America.* New York, 1978.

Grant, George. *The Dispossessed: Homelessness in America.* Fort Worth, Tex., 1986.

———. *In the Shadow of Plenty: The Biblical Blueprint for Welfare.* Fort Worth, Tex., 1986.

———. *The Changing of the Guard: Biblical Blueprints for Political Action.* Fort Worth, Tex., 1987.

———. *Bringing In the Sheaves: Transforming Poverty into Productivity.* Brentwood, Tex., 1988.

Green, Arthur (ed.). *Jewish Spirituality.* 2 vols. London, 1986, 1988.

Güttmann, Julius. *Philosophies of Judaism: The History of Jewish Philosophy from Biblical Times to Franz Rosenzweig.* London and New York, 1964.

Haddad, Yvonne. "Sayyid Qutb: Ideologue of Islamic Revival." In John Esposito (ed.), *Voices of Resurgent Islam.* New York and Oxford, 1983.

Haldeman, Isaac M. *The Signs of the Times.* New York, 1912.

Hall, David D. (ed.). *The Antinomian Controversy, 1636–1638: A Documentary History.* Middletown, Conn., 1968.

Hall, Stuart. "Significance, Representation, Ideology," *Critical Studies in Mass Communication* 2:2, 1985.

Halliday, Fred. *Islam and the Myth of Confrontation: Religion and Politics in the Middle East.* London and New York, 1996.

HAMAS, *The Covenant of the Islamic Resistance Movement.* Jerusalem, 1988.

Hambrick-Stowe, Charles. "Puritan Spirituality in America." In Louis Dupré and Don E. Saliers (eds.), *Christian Spirituality: Post Reformation and Modern.* New York and London, 1989.

Hammond, Phillip E. (ed.). *The Sacred in a Secular Age: Toward Revision in the Scientific Study of Religion.* Berkeley, 1985.

———. *The Protestant Presence in Twentieth–Century America: Religion and Political Culture.* Albany, N.Y., 1992.

Hanan, Denis, and H. Aldersworth (eds.). *British-Israel Truth.* 14th ed. London, 1932.

Handy, Robert T. "Protestant Theological Tensions and Political Styles in the Progressive Period." In Mark A. Noll (ed.), *Religion and American Politics: From the Colonial Period to the 1980s.* Oxford and New York, 1990.

Hanna, Sami, and George H. Gardner (eds.). *Arab Socialism: A Documentary Survey* Leiden, Netherlands, 1969.

Harding, Susan. "Contesting Rhetorics in the PTL Scandal." In J. Silberstein (ed.), *Jewish Fundamentalism in Comparative Perspective: Religion, Ideology, and the Crisis of Modernity.* New York and London, 1993.

———. "Imagining the Last Days: The Politics of Apocalyptic Language." In Martin E. Marty and R. Scott Appleby (eds.), *Accounting for Fundamentalisms.* Chicago and London, 1994.

Hatch, Nathan O. *The Democratization of American Christianity.* New Haven, Conn., and London, 1989.

Hegland, Mary. "Two Images of Husain: Accommodation and Revolution in an Iranian Village." In Nikki R. Keddie (ed.), *Religion and Politics in Iran: Shiism from Quietism to Revolution.* New Haven, Conn., and London, 1983.

Heikal, Mohamed. *Autumn of Fury: The Assassination of Sadat.* London, 1984.

Heilman, Samuel. *Defenders of the Faith: Inside Ultra-Orthodox Jewry.* New York, 1992.

———. "Quiescent and Active Fundamentalisms: The Jewish Cases." In Martin E. Marty and R. Scott Appleby (eds.), *Accounting for Fundamentalisms.* Chicago and London, 1994.

———. "Guides of the Faithful: Contemporary Religious Zionist Rabbis." In R. Scott Appleby (ed.), *Spokesmen for the Despised: Fundamentalist Leaders of the Middle East.* Chicago, 1997.

——— (with Menachem Friedman). "Religious Fundamentalism and Religious Jews." In Martin E. Marty and R. Scott Appleby (eds.), *Fundamentalisms Observed.* Chicago and London, 1991.

Heimert, Alan. *Religion and the American Mind: From the Great Awakening to the Revolution.* Cambridge, Mass., 1968.

Helms, Jesse. *When Free Men Shall Stand.* Grand Rapids, Mich., 1976.

Herberg, Will. *Protestant, Catholic, Jew.* Garden City, N.Y., 1955.

Hertzberg, Arthur. *The Zionist Idea.* New York, 1969.

Hill, Donna. *Joseph Smith, The First Mormon.* Garden City, N.Y., 1977.

Hobbes, Thomas. *Leviathan.* Ed. Michael Oakeshott. New York, 1962.

Hodge, Charles. *What Is Darwinism?* Princeton, N.J., 1874.

Hodgson, Marshall G. S. *The Venture of Islam: Conscience and History in a World Civilization.* 3 vols. Chicago and London, 1974.

Hoffer, Eric. *The True Believer: Thoughts on the Nature of Mass Movements.* New York and Evanston, Ill., 1951.

Hofstadter, Richard. *Anti-Intellectualism in American Life*. New York, 1962.
———. *The Paranoid Strain in American Politics*. New York, 1965.
Holt, P. M. (ed.). *Political and Social Change in Modern Egypt: Historical Studies from the Ottoman Conquest to the United Arab Republic*. London, 1968.
———. "The Pattern of Egyptian Political History from 1517 to 1798." In ibid.
Hoogland, Eric. "Social Origins of the Revolutionary Clergy." In Nikki R. Keddie and E. Hoogland (eds.), *The Iranian Revolution and the Islamic Republic*. Syracuse, N.Y., 1986.
Hourani, Albert. *Arabic Thought in the Liberal Age, 1798–1939*. Oxford, 1962.
———. *A History of the Arab Peoples*. London, 1991.
Hudson, Bradford B. "Anxiety Response to the Unfamiliar." *The Journal of Social Issues* 10:3, 1954.
Hundert, Gershom David (ed.). *Essential Papers on Hasidism, Origins to Present*. New York and London, 1991.
Hunter, J. D. *Evangelicalism, The Coming Generation*. Chicago, 1987.
Hussain, Asaf. *Islamic Iran: Revolution and Counter-Revolution*. London, 1985.
Huxley, T. H.. *Science and Christian Tradition*. New York, 1896.
Jacobs, Louis. *Hasidic Prayer*. New York, 1973.
———. "The Uplifting of the Sparks in Later Jewish Mysticism." In Arthur Green (ed.), *Jewish Spirituality*, Vol. II. London, 1988.
———. "Hasidic Prayer." In Gershom David Hundert (ed.), *Essential Papers on Hasidism: Origins to Present*. New York and London, 1991.
——— (ed.). *The Jewish Mystics*. London, 1990; New York, 1996.
Jansen, Johannes J. G. *The Neglected Duty: The Creed of Sadat's Assassins and Islamic Resurgence in the Middle East*. New York and London, 1988.
Johnson, Paul. *A History of the Jews*. London, 1987.
Jones, Bob, II. *Cornbread and Caviare*. Greenville, S.C., 1985.
Jones, Richard F. *Ancients and Moderns: A Study in the Rise of the Scientific Movement in Seventeenth-Century England*. Berkeley, 1965.
Kamen, Henry. *The Spanish Inquisition: An Historical Revision*. London, 1997.
Kant, Immanuel. *Critique of Practical Reason and Other Writings*. Ed. Lewis Beck White. Indianapolis, Ind., 1963.
———. *On History*. Ed. Lewis Beck White. Indianapolis, Ind., 1963.
Kaplan, Laurence (ed.). *Fundamentalism in Comparative Perspective*. Amherst, 1992.
Karam, Azza M. *Women, Islamism and the State: Contemporary Feminism in Egypt*. London and New York, 1998.
Katouzian, Homa. "Shiism and Islamic Economics: Sadr and Bani Sadr." In Nikki R. Keddie (ed.), *Religion and Politics in Iran: Shiism from Quietism to Revolution*. New Haven, Conn., and London, 1983.
Katz, Jacob. "Halakah and Kabbalah as Competing Disciplines in Study." In Arthur Green (ed.). *Jewish Spirituality*. Vol II. London, 1988.
———. "Israel and the Messiah." In Marc Saperstein (ed.), *Essential Papers on Messianic Movements and Personalities in Jewish History*. New York and London, 1992.
Kautsky, John H. (ed.). *Political Change in Underdeveloped Countries*. 7th ed. New York, 1967.
Keddie, Nikki R. *Islamic Response to Imperialism: Political and Religious Writings of Sayyid Jamal ad-Din "al-Afghani"*. Berkeley, 1968.
———. *Roots of Revolution: An Interpretive History of Modern Iran*. New Haven, Conn., and London, 1981.
——— (ed.). *Scholars, Saints and Sufis: Muslim Religious Institutions in the Middle East Since 1500*. Berkeley, Los Angeles, and London, 1972.
——— (ed.). *Religion and Politics in Iran: Shiism from Quietism to Revolution*. New Haven, Conn., and London, 1983.

————, with Beth Baron (eds.). *Women in Middle Eastern History: Shifting Boundaries in Sex and Gender*. New Haven, Conn., and London, 1991.

————, with Eric Hoogland (eds.). *The Iranian Revolution and the Islamic Republic*. Syracuse, N.Y., 1986.

————. "The Roots of the Ulama's Power in Modern Iran." In Keddie (ed.), *Scholars, Saints and Sufis*.

Kedourie, E. *Afghani and Abduh: An Essay on Religious Unbelief and Political Activism in Modern Islam*. London, 1966.

————, with S. Haim (eds.). *Zionism and Arabism in Palestine and Israel*. London, 1982.

Kepel, Gilles. *The Prophet and Pharaoh: Muslim Extremism in Egypt*. Trans. Jon Rothschild. London, 1985.

————. *The Revenge of God: The Resurgence of Islam, Christianity and Judaism in the Modern World*. Trans. Alan Braley. Cambridge, U.K. 1994.

Khan, Muhammad Zafrulla. *Islam, Its Meaning for Modern Man*. London, 1962.

Khomeini, Sayeed Ruhollah. *Islam and Revolution*. Trans. and ed. Hamid Algar. Berkeley, 1981.

Kilpatrick, F. P. "Problems of Perception in Extreme Situations," *Human Organization* 16, Summer, 1957.

Köbben, A. J. F. "Prophetic Movements as an Expression of Social Protest," *International Archives of Ethnography* 49, part I, 1960.

Kook, Abraham Isaac. *The Essential Writings of Abraham Isaac Kook*. Ed. and trans. Ben Zion Bokser. Warwick, N.Y., 1988.

Kuhn, Thomas S. *The Structure of Scientific Revolutions*. 2nd ed. Chicago, 1970.

Lacleu, Ernesto (ed.). *The Making of Political Identities*. London and New York, 1994.

LaHaye, Beverley. *The Spirit-Controlled Woman*. Eugene, Or., 1976.

————. *I Am a Woman by God's Design*. Old Tappan, N.J., 1980.

————. *The Restless Woman*. Grand Rapids, Mich., 1984.

LaHaye, Tim. *How to Be Happy Though Married*. Wheaton, Ill., 1968.

————. *Understanding the Male Temperament*. Eugene, Or., 1977.

————. *The Battle for the Mind*. Old Tappan, N.J., 1980.

————. *The Battle for the Family*. Old Tappan, N.J., 1982.

————. *Sex Education in the Family*. Grand Rapids, Mich., 1985.

———— (with Beverley LaHaye). *The Act of Marriage: The Beauty of Sexual Love*. Grand Rapids, Mich., 1976.

Lambton, Ann K. S. "A Reconsideration of the Position of the *Marja al-taqlid* and the Religious Institutions," *Studia Islamica* 20, 1964.

Langdon, Samuel. *Government Corrupted by Vice and Recovered by Righteousness*. Watertown, Mass., 1775.

Lawrence, Bruce B. *Defenders of God: The Fundamentalist Revolt Against the Modern Age*. London and New York, 1990.

Lea, H. C. *A History of the Inquisition in Spain*. 4 vols. New York, 1906–07.

Leone, Mark. *Roots of Modern Mormonism*. Cambridge, Mass., 1979.

Lewis, Bernard. *The Jews of Islam*. New York and London, 1982.

Liebman, Charles. *Deceptive Images*. New Brunswick, N.J., 1988.

————. "Jewish Fundamentalism and the Israeli Polity." In Martin E. Marty and R. Scott Appleby (eds.), *Fundamentalisms and Society*. Chicago and London, 1993.

Lienesch, Michael. *Redeeming America: Piety and Politics in the New Christian Right*. Chapel Hill, N.C., and London, 1995.

Lindberg, David, and Ronald L. Numbers (eds.). *God and Nature: Historical Essays on the Encounter Between Christianity and Science*. Berkeley, Los Angeles, and London, 1986.

Lindsey, Hal. *The Late Great Planet Earth*. Grand Rapids, Mich., 1970.

————. *The 1980s: Countdown to Armegeddon*. Grand Rapids, Mich., 1980.

Locke, John. *A Letter Concerning Toleration*. Indianapolis, Ind., 1955.

————. *The Reasonableness of Christianity.* Ed. George W. Ewing. Washington D.C., 1965.

————. *Two Treatises of Government.* Ed. Peter Laslett. Cambridge, U.K. 1988.

Lockyear, Herbert. *Cameos of Prophecy: Are These the Last Days?* Grand Rapids, Mich., 1942.

Louth, Andrew. *Discovering the Mystery: An Essay on the Nature of Theology.* Oxford, 1983.

Lovejoy, David S. *Religious Enthusiasm in the New World: Heresy to Revolution.* Cambridge, Mass., and London, 1985.

Lovelace, R. C. "Puritan Spirituality: The Search for a Rightly Reformed Church." In Louis Dupré and Don E. Saliers (eds.), *Christian Spirituality: Post Reformation and Modern.* New York and London, 1989.

Lowenthal, David. *The Past Is a Foreign Country.* Cambridge, U.K., 1965.

Lustick, Ian S. *For the Land and the Lord: Jewish Fundamentalism in Israel.* New York, 1988.

————. "Jewish Fundamentalism and the Israeli-Palestinian Impasse." In Laurence J. Silberstein (ed.), *Jewish Fundamentalism in Comparative Perspective: Religion, Ideology, and the Crisis of Modernity.* New York and London, 1993.

Lyotard, Jean-François. *The Postmodern Condition.* Manchester, U.K., 1986.

Maccoby, Haim (ed. and trans.). *Judaism on Trial: Jewish Christian Disputations in the Middle Ages.* Princeton, N.J., 1982.

MacQuarrie, John. *Thinking About God.* London, 1975.

————. *In Search of Deity: An Essay in Dialectical Theism.* London, 1980.

Magonet, Jonathan. *The Explorer's Guide to Judaism.* London, 1998.

Mahler, Raphael. *Hasidism and the Jewish Enlightenment: Their Confrontation in Galicia and Poland in the First Half of the Nineteenth Century.* Trans. Aaron Klein and Jenny Machlowitz Klein. Philadelphia, New York, and Jerusalem, 1985.

Marius, Richard. *Martin Luther, the Christian Between God and Death.* Cambridge, Mass., and London, 1999.

Marsden, George M. *Fundamentalism and American Culture: The Shaping of Twentieth-Century Evangelicalism, 1870–1925.* New York and Oxford, 1980.

————. "The Religious Right: A Historical Overview." In Michael Cromartie (ed.), *No Longer Exiles: The Religious New Right in American Politics.* Washington, D.C., 1993.

Marshall, Peter, and David Manual. *The Light and the Glory.* Old Tappan, N.J., 1977.

Marsot, Araf Lutfi al-Sayyid. "The Role of the Ulema in Egypt During the Early Nineteenth Century." In P. M. Holt (ed.), *Political and Social Change in Modern Egypt: Historical Studies from the Ottoman Conquest to the United Arab Republic.* London, 1968.

————. "The Ulama of Cairo in the Eighteenth and Nineteenth Centuries." In Nikki R. Keddie (ed.), *Scholars, Saints and Sufis: Muslim Religious Institutions in the Middle East Since 1500.* Berkeley, Los Angeles, and London, 1972.

Marty, Martin E., and R. Scott Appleby (eds.). *Fundamentalisms Observed.* Chicago and London, 1991.

————. *Fundamentalisms and Society.* Chicago and London, 1993.

————. *Fundamentalisms and the State.* Chicago and London, 1993.

————. *Accounting for Fundamentalisms.* Chicago and London, 1994.

————. *Fundamentalisms Comprehended.* Chicago and London, 1995.

Marx, Karl. *Karl Marx: Early Writings.* Trans. T. B. Bottomore. London, 1963.

Masterson, Patrick. *Atheism and Alienation: A Study of the Philosophic Sources of Contemporary Atheism.* Dublin, 1971.

Matin-Asgari, Afshin. "Abdolkarim Sorush and the Secularization of Islamic Thought in Iran," *Iranian Studies* 30, 1997.

Mawdudi, Abul Ala. *Islamic Law and Constitution.* Lahore, 1967.

————. *Jihad in Islam.* Lahore, 1976.

————. *The Economic Problem of Man and Its Islamic Solution.* Lahore, 1978.

————. *Islamic Way of Life.* Lahore, 1979.

Mayhew, Jonathan. *Practical Discourses Delivered on the Occasion of the Earthquakes in November 1755.* Boston, 1760.

McClelland, J. S. *A History of Western Political Thought.* London, 1996.

McGrath, Alister E. *The Intellectual Origins of the European Reformation.* Oxford and New York, 1987.

———. *Reformation Thought: An Introduction.* Oxford and New York, 1988.

———. *A Life of John Calvin: A Study in the Shaping of Western Culture.* Oxford, 1990.

McLoughlin, William G. *Revivals, Awakenings and Reform.* Chicago, 1978.

Mead, Sidney. *The Nation with the Soul of a Church.* New York, 1975.

Mergui, Raphael, and Philippe Simonnot. *Israel's Ayatollahs: Meir Kahane and the Far Right in Israel.* London, 1987.

Miller, Perry. *The New England Mind. from Colony to Province.* Cambridge, Mass., 1953.

———. *Errand into the Wilderness.* Cambridge Mass., 1956.

Milton-Edwards, Beverley. *Islamic Politics in Palestine.* London and New York, 1996.

Mitchell, Joshua. *Not by Reason Alone: Religion, History and Identity in Early Modern Political Thought.* Chicago, 1993.

Mitchell, Richard P. *The Society of the Muslim Brothers.* London, 1969.

Mittleman, Alan L. "Fundamentalism and Political Development: The Case of Agudat Yisrael." In Laurence J. Silberstein (ed.), *Jewish Fundamentalism in Comparative Perspective: Religion, Ideology, and the Crisis of Modernity.* New York and London, 1993.

Moin, Baqer. *Khomeini: Life of the Ayatollah.* London, 1999.

Momen, Moojan. *An Introduction to Shii Islam: The History and Doctrines of Twelver Shiism.* New Haven, Conn., and London, 1985.

Moore, James R. "Geologists and Interpreters of Genesis in the Nineteenth Century." In David C. Lindberg and Ronald L. Numbers (eds.), *God and Nature: Historical Essays on the Encounter Between Christianity and Science.* Berkeley, Los Angeles and London, 1986.

Moore, R. Laurence. *Religious Outsiders and the Making of Americans.* Oxford and New York, 1986.

Mottahedeh, Roy. *The Mantle of the Prophet: Religion and Politics in Iran.* London, 1985.

Murrin, John M. "Religion and Politics in America from the First Settlements to the Civil War." In Mark A. Noll (ed.), *Religion and American Politics: From the Colonial Period to the 1980s.* Oxford and New York, 1990.

Nash, Ron. *Poverty and Wealth: The Christian Debate Over Capitalism.* Westchester, Ill., 1986.

Negus, Steve. "Carnage at Luxor." *Middle East International,* November 21, 1997.

Newton, Isaac. *The Correspondence of Isaac Newton.* Eds. A. R. Hall and L. Tilling. Cambridge, 1959.

Nieburg, H. L. "Agonistic—Rituals of Conflict." *The Annuals* 391, September, 1970.

Nietzsche, Friedrich. *The Gay Science.* New York, 1974.

Nolan, Alan T. *Lee Considered: General Robert E. Lee and Civil War History.* Chapel Hill, N.C., 1991.

Noll, Mark A. (ed.). *Religion and American Politics: From the Colonial Period to the 1980s.* Oxford and New York, 1990.

North, Gary. *Unconditional Surrender: God's Program for Victory.* Tyler, Tex., 1981.

———. *Honest Money.* Fort Worth, Tex., 1986.

———. *The Sinai Strategy: Economics and the Ten Commandments.* Tyler, Tex., 1986.

———. *In the Shadow of Plenty: The Biblical Blueprint for Welfare.* Fort Worth, Tex., 1986.

———. *Inherit the Earth: Biblical Blueprints for Economics.* Fort Worth, Tex., 1987.

———. *Is the World Running Down? Crisis in the Christian Worldview.* Tyler, Tex., 1988.

Numbers, Ronald L. *The Creationists: The Evolution of Scientific Creationism.* Berkeley and Los Angeles, 1992.

———, with Jonathan M. Butler (eds.). *The Disappointed: Millerism and Millennarianism in the Nineteenth Century.* Bloomington, Ind., 1987.

O'Fahey, R. S. "Pietism, Fundamentalism and Mysticism: An Alternative View of the Eighteenth-and Nineteenth-Century Islamic World." Lecture delivered at Northwestern University, November 12, 1997.

Otis, George. *God, Money and You.* Van Nuys, Calif., 1975.

Otto, Rudolf. *The Idea of the Holy: An Inquiry into the Non-Rational Factor in the Idea of the Divine and Its Relation to the Rational.* Trans. John W. Harvey. Oxford, 1923.

Outler, Albert C. *John Wesley.* Oxford and New York, 1964.

Oz, Amos. *In the Land of Israel.* Trans. Maurice Goldberg-Bartura. London, 1983.

Paine, Thomas. *Common Sense and the Crisis.* New York, 1975.

Parsons, Jonathan. *Seven Discourses.* Portsmouth, N.H., 1756.

Partner, Peter. *God of Battles: Holy Wars of Christianity and Islam.* London, 1997.

Pascal, Blaise. *Pensées.* Trans. and ed. A. J. Krailsheimer. London, 1966.

Paton, Andrew A. *A History of the Egyptian Revolution.* 2 vols. Trubner, Germany, 1876.

Pelikan, Jaroslav. *The Christian Tradition: A History of the Development of Doctrine.* 5 vols. IV: *Reformation of Church and Dogma,* Chicago and London, 1985. V: *Christian Doctrine and Modern Culture (Since 1700),* Chicago and London, 1989.

Peters, Rudolph. *Jihad in Classical and Modern Islam. A Reader.* Princeton, N.J., 1996.

Plath, David (ed.). *Aware of Utopia.* Urbana, Ill., 1971.

Qutb, Sayyid. *Islam and Universal Peace.* Indianapolis, Ind., 1977.

———. *Fi Zilal al-Koran.* 6 vols. Beirut, 1981.

———. *Milestones.* Delhi, 1988.

———. *This Religion of Islam.* Gary, Ind., n.d.

Rahman, Fazlur. *The Philosophy of Mulla Sadra.* Albany, N.Y., 1975.

———. *Islam.* Chicago, 1979.

———. *Islam and Modernity: Transformation of an Intellectual Tradition.* Chicago, 1982.

Raitt, Jill, with Bernard McGinn and John Meyendorff (eds.). *Christian Spirituality: High Middle Ages and Reformation.* New York, 1988; London, 1989.

Rajaee, Farhang. "Islam and Modernity." In Martin E. Marty and R. Scott Appleby (eds.), *Fundamentalisms and Society.* Chicago and London, 1993.

Rauschenbusch, Walter. *Christianity and the Social Crisis.* New York, 1907.

———. *Christianity and the Social Order.* New York, 1912.

Ravitsky, Aviezer. *Messianism, Zionism, and Jewish Religious Radicalism.* Trans. Michael Swirsky and Jonathan Chipman. Chicago and London, 1993.

Renan, Ernest. *Histoire générale et système comparé des langues semitiques.* Ed. H. Pischiari. Paris, 1955.

———. *L'Islamisme et la science.* Paris, 1883.

Richard, Yann. "Ayatollah Kashani: Precursor of the Islamic Republic?" In Nikki R. Keddie (ed.), *Religion and Politics in Iran: Shiism from Quietism to Revolution.* New Haven, Conn., and London, 1983.

Riesebrodt, Martin. *Pious Passion: The Emergence of Modern Fundamentalism in the United States and Iran.* Trans. Don Reneau. Berkeley, Los Angeles, and London, 1993.

Rifkin, Jeremy, and Ted Howard. *The Emerging Order: God in the Age of Scarcity.* New York, 1979.

Robertson, Pat. *The Secret Kingdom.* Nashville, Tenn., 1982.

———. *America's Dates with Destiny.* Nashville, Tenn., 1986.

———. *The New Millennium.* Dallas, Tex., 1990.

———. *The New World Order.* Dallas, Tex., 1991.

———. with Jamie Buckingham. *Shout It from the Housetops.* Plainfield, N.J., 1972.

Robertson, Roland, and JoAnn Chirico. "Humanity, Globalization and Worldwide Religious Resurgence: A Theoretical Exploration," *Sociological Analysis* 46, 1985.

Robison, James. *Thank God I'm Free: The James Robison Story.* Nashville, Tenn., 1988.

Rose, Gregory. "Velayat-e Faqih and the Recovery of the Islamic Identity in the Thought of

Ayatollah Khomeini." In Nikki R. Keddie (ed.), *Religion and Politics in Iran: Shiism from Quietism to Revolution*. New Haven, Conn., 1983.

Rose, Susan. "Christian Fundamentalism and Education in the United States." In Martin E. Marty and R. Scott Appleby (eds.), *Fundamentalisms and Society*. Chicago and London, 1993.

Rosenak, Michael. "Jewish Fundamentalism in Israeli Education." In Martin E. Marty and R. Scott Appleby (eds.), *Fundamentalisms and Society*. Chicago and London, 1993.

Ross, Andrew (ed.). *Universal Abandon: The Politics of Postmodernism*. Minneapolis, Minn., 1988.

Royster, Charles. *The Destructive War: William Tecumseh Sherman, Stonewall Jackson, and the Americans*. New York, 1991.

Rubinstein, Richard. *After Auschwitz: Radical Theology and Contemporary Judaism*. Indianapolis, Ind., 1966.

———. *The Coming of History*. New York, 1978.

Rudavsky, David. *Modern Jewish Religious Movements: A History of Emancipation and Adjustment*. Rev. ed. New York, 1967.

Rugh, Andrea B. "Reshaping Personal Relations In Egypt." In Martin E. Marty and R. Scott Appleby (eds.), *Fundamentalisms and Society*. Chicago and London, 1993.

Rushdoony, R. J. *This Independent Republic: Studies in the Nature and Meaning of American History*. Nutley, N.J., 1964.

———. *Thy Kingdom Come: Studies in Daniel and Revelation*. Fairfax, Va., 1978.

———. *Politics of Guilt and Pity*. Fairfax, Va., 1978.

———. *God's Plan for Victory: The Meaning of Post-Millennialism*. Fairfax, Va., 1980.

Rutherford, Jonathan (ed.). *Identity, Community, Culture Difference*. London, 1990.

Ruthven, Malise. *A Satanic Affair: Salman Rushdie and the Rage of Islam*. London, 1990.

Sachedina, Abdulaziz Abdulhussein. *Islamic Messianism: The Idea of the Mahdi in Twelver Shiism*. Albany, N.Y., 1981.

———. "Ali Shariati: Ideologue of the Iranian Revolution." In John Esposito (ed.), *Voices of Resurgent Islam*. New York and Oxford, 1983.

Sacks, Jonathan. *The Persistence of Faith: Religion, Morality and Society in a Secular Age*. London, 1991.

Sadat, Anwar. *Revolt on the Nile*. New York, 1957.

Said, Edward W. *Orientalism: Western Conceptions of Orient*. New York, 1978.

Sandeen, Ernest. *The Roots of Fundamentalism*. Chicago, 1970.

Saperstein, Marc (ed.). *Essential Papers on Messianic Movements and Personalities in Jewish History*. New York and London, 1992.

Schaeffer, Franky. *A Time for Anger: The Myth of Neutrality*. Westchester, Ill., 1982.

Schlafly, Phyllis. *The Power of the Christian Woman*. Cincinnati, 1981.

Scholem, Gershom. *Major Trends in Jewish Mysticism*. London, 1955.

———. *On the Kabbalah and Its Symbolism*. New York, 1965.

———. *The Messianic Idea in Judaism and Other Essays on Jewish Spirituality*. New York, 1971.

———. *Sabbatai Sevi, the Mystical Messiah, 1626–1676*. London and Princeton, N.J., 1973.

Schultze, Quentin. "The Two Faces of Fundamentalist Higher Education." In Martin E. Marty and R. Scott Appleby (eds.), *Fundamentalisms and Society*. Chicago and London, 1993.

Schweid, Eliezer. *The Land of Israel: National Home or Land of Destiny*. Trans. Deborah Greniman. New York, 1985.

Scofield, C. I. *The Scofield Reference Bible*. New York and Oxford, 1917.

———. *Addresses on Prophecy*. New York, n.d.

Selengut, Charles. "By Torah Alone: Yeshiva Fundamentalism in Jewish Life." In Martin E. Marty and R. Scott Appleby (eds.), *Accounting for Fundamentalisms*. Chicago and London, 1994.

Shariati, Ali. *Community and Leadership.* (n.p) 1972.

———. *The Sociology of Islam.* Berkeley, 1979.

———. *Hajj.* Tehran, 1988.

Shayyal, Gamal el-Din. "Some Aspects of Intellectual and Social Life in Eighteenth-Century Egypt." In P. M. Holt (ed.), *Political and Social Change in Modern Egypt: Historical Studies from the Ottoman Conquest to the United Arab Republic.* London, 1968.

Shriver, Peggy L. "The Paradox of an Inclusiveness-That-Divides," *Christian Century,* January 21, 1984.

Sick, Gary. *All Fall Down: America's Fateful Encounter with Iran.* London, 1985.

Sidahared, Abdel Salam, and Anonshiravan Ehteshani (eds.). *Islamic Fundamentalism.* Boulder, Colo., 1996.

Silberstein, Laurence J. (ed.). *Jewish Fundamentalism in Comparative Perspective: Religion, Ideology, and the Crisis of Modernity.* New York and London, 1993.

———. "Religion, Ideology, Modernity: Theoretical Issues in a Study of Jewish Fundamentalism." In ibid.

Silverman, R. M. *Baruch Spinoza: Outcast Jew, Universal Sage.* Northwood, U.K. 1995.

Sloek, Johannes. *Devotional Language.* Trans. Henrik Mossin. Berlin and New York, 1996.

Smart, Ninian. *Beyond Ideology: Religion and the Future of Western Civilization.* London, 1981.

Smith, Wilfred Cantwell. *Islam in Modern History.* Princeton and London, 1957.

———. *Belief and History.* Charlottesville, Va., 1977.

———. *Faith and Belief.* Princeton, N.J., 1979.

Soloveitchic, Hayim. "Migration, Acculturation, and the New Role of Texts." In Martin E. Marty and R. Scott Appleby (eds.), *Accounting for Fundamentalisms.* Chicago and London, 1994.

Sontag, Susan. *A Susan Sontag Reader.* New York, 1982.

Spinoza, Baruch. *A Theologico-Political Treatise.* Trans. R. H. M. Elwes. New York, 1951.

Sprinzak, Ehud. *The Ascendance of Israel's Radical Right.* Oxford and New York, 1991.

———. "The Politics, Institutions and Culture of Gush Emunim." In Laurence J. Silberstein (ed.), *Jewish Fundamentalism in Comparative Perspective: Religion, Ideology, and the Crisis of Modernity.* New York and London, 1993.

———. "Three Models of Religious Violence: The Case of Jewish Fundamentalism in Israel." In Martin E. Marty and R. Scott Appleby (eds.), *Fundamentalisms and the State.* Chicago and London, 1993.

Stampp, Kenneth. *The Imperilled Union: Essays on the Background of the Civil War.* New York, 1980.

Steiner, George. *In Bluebeard's Castle: Some Notes Toward the Re-definition of Culture.* New Haven, Conn., 1971.

Stout, Harry S. "Rhetoric and Reality in the Early Republic: The Case of the Federalist Clergy." In Mark A. Noll (ed.), *Religion and American Politics: From the Colonial Period to the 1980s.* Oxford and New York, 1990.

Strauss, Leo. *Spinoza's Critique of Reason.* New York, 1982.

Strozier, Charles B. *Apocalypse: On the Psychology of Fundamentalism in America.* Boston, 1994.

Swierenga, Robert P. "Ethno-religious Political Behavior in the Mid-Nineteenth Century." In Mark A. Noll (ed.), *Religion and American Politics: From the Colonial Period to the 1980s.* Oxford and New York, 1990.

Szasz, Ferenc Morton. *The Divided Mind of Protestant America, 1880–1930.* University, Ala., 1982.

Tabari, Azar. "The Role of the Shii Clergy in Modern Iranian Politics." In Nikki R. Keddie (ed.), *Religion and Politics in Iran: Shiism from Quietism to Revolution.* New Haven, Conn., and London, 1983.

Taheri, Amir. *The Spirit of Allah: Khomeini and the Islamic Revolution.* London, 1985.

Tal, Uriel. "Foundations of a Political Messianic Trend in Israel." In Marc Saperstein (ed.),

Essential Papers on Messianic Movements and Personalities in Jewish History. New York and London, 1992.

Talmon, J. L. *The Origins of Totalitarian Democracy*. London, 1953.

Tancoigne, J. M. *A Narrative of a Journey into Persia and Residence in Tehran*. Trans. William Wright. London, 1820.

Tarnas, Richard. *The Passion of the Western Mind: Understanding the Ideas That Have Shaped Our World View*. New York and London, 1991.

Terdiman, Richard. *Discourse/Counter-Discourse*. Ithaca, N.Y., 1985.

Thaiss, Guster. "Religious Symbolism and Social Change." In Nikki R. Keddie, *Scholars, Saints and Sufis: Muslim Religious Institutions in the Middle East Since 1500*. Berkeley, Los Angeles, and London, 1972.

Thompson, Thomas L. *The Bible in History: How Writers Create a Past*. London, 1999.

Tibi, Bassam. *The Crisis of Political Islam: A Pre-Industrial Culture in the Scientific-Technological Age*. Salt Lake City, Utah, 1988.

———. *Arab Nationalism, A Critical Enquiry*. Trans. Marion Farouk Sluglett and Peter Sluglett. 2nd ed. London, 1990.

Tuveson, Ernest Lee. *Millennium and Utopia: A Study in the Background of the Idea of Progress*. New York, 1964.

———. *Redeemer Nation*. Chicago, 1968.

Viguerie, Richard A. *The New Right: We're Ready to Lead*. Falls Church, Va., 1981.

Voll, John. *Islam: Continuity and Change in the Modern World*. Boulder, Colo., 1982.

———. "Renewal and Reform in Islamic History." In John Esposito (ed.), *Voices of Resurgent Islam*. New York and Oxford, 1983.

———. "Fundamentalism in the Sunni Arab World: Egypt and the Sudan." In Martin E. Marty and R. Scott Appleby (eds.), *Fundamentalisms Observed*. Chicago and London, 1991.

Walton, Rus. *FACS! Fundamentals for American Christians*. Nyack, N.Y., 1979.

———. *One Nation Under God*. Nashville, Tenn., 1987.

———. *Biblical Solutions to Contemporary Problems: A Handbook*. Brentwood, Tenn., 1988.

Walvoord, John. *Israel and Prophecy*. Grand Rapids, Mich., 1962.

———. *Armageddon, Oil and the Middle East Crisis*. Grand Rapids, Mich., 1990.

Ward, Mrs. Humphry. *Robert Elsmere*. Lincoln, Neb., 1969 edn.)

Warfield, Benjamin B. *Selected Shorter Writings of Benjamin B. Warfield*. 2 vols. Ed. John E. Meeber. Nutley, N.J., 1902.

Weber, Max. *The Protestant Ethic and the Spirit of Capitalism*. New York, 1958.

Weber, Timothy. *Living in the Shadow of the Second Coming: American Premillennialism, 1875–1982*. Grand Rapids, Mich., 1983.

Weit, Gaston, ed. and trans. *Nicolas Turc, Chronique d'Egypte, 1798–1804*. Cairo, 1950.

Wells, H. G.. *The War of the Worlds*. London, 1898.

———. *Anticipations*. London, 1902.

Werblowsky, R. J. Zvi. "The Safed Revival and Its Aftermath." In Arthur Green (ed.), *Jewish Spirituality*. Vol. II. London, 1988.

———. "Messianism in Jewish History." In Marc Saperstein (ed.), *Essential Papers on Messianic Movements and Personalities in Jewish History*. New York and London, 1992.

Westfall, Richard S. "The Rise of Science and Decline of Orthodox Christianity: A Study of Kepler, Descartes and Newton." In David C. Lindberg and Ronald L. Numbers (eds.), *God and Nature: Historical Essays on the Encounter between Christianity and Science*. Berkeley, Los Angeles, and London, 1986.

Whitehead, John W. *The Second American Revolution*. Westchester, Ill., 1982.

———. *The Stealing of America*. Westchester, Ill., 1983.

———. *An American Dream*. Westchester, Ill., 1987.

———, with John Conlon. "The Establishment of the Religion of Secular Humanism and Its First Amendment Implications." *Texas Tech Law Review* 10, 1978.

Willems, Emilio. *Followers of the New Faith.* Nashville, Tenn., 1967.

Williams, G. H. *The Radical Revolution.* Philadelphia, 1962.

Wilson, John F. "Religion, Government and Power in the New American Nation." In Mark A. Noll (ed.), *Religion and American Politics: From the Colonial Period to the 1980s.* Oxford and New York, 1990.

Wirt, Sherwood Eliot (ed.). *Spiritual Awakening: Classic Writings of the Eighteenth Century. Devotions to Inspire and Help the Twentieth-Century Reader.* Tring, U.K, 1988.

Wolfenstein, Martha. *Disaster: A Psychological Essay.* Glencoe, Ill., 1957.

Wood, Gordon S. *The Creation of the American Republic.* Chapel Hill, N.C., 1969.

Wright, Lawrence. *Saints and Sinners.* New York, 1993.

Wright, Melton. *Fortress of Faith: The Story of Bob Jones University.* Greenville, S.C., 1984.

Wuthnow, Robert, and Matthew P. Lawson. "Religious Movements and Counter Movements in North America." In James Beckford (ed.), *New Religious Movements and Rapid Social Change.* Paris, 1987.

———. "Quid Obscurum: The Changing Terrain of Church-State Relations." In Mark A. Noll (ed.), *Religion and American Politics: From the Colonial Period to the 1980s* (Oxford and New York, 1990).

———. "Sources of Christian Fundamentalism in the United States." In Martin E. Marty and R. Scott Appleby (eds.), *Accounting for Fundamentalisms.* Chicago and London, 1994.

Yovel, Yirmiyahu. *Spinoza and Other Heretics.* 2 vols. I: *The Marrano of Reason;* II: *The Adventures of Immanence.* Princeton, N.J., 1989.

———. *Dark Riddle: Hegel, Nietzsche, and the Jews.* Cambridge, U.K., 1998.

ACKNOWLEDGMENTS

As always, I must express heartfelt thanks to my literary agents, Felicity Bryan, Peter Ginsberg, and Andrew Nurnburg, and to my editors, Jane Garrett, Michael Fishwick, and Robbert Amerlaan. Their encouragement, enthusiasm, and devoted work on my behalf over the years have been quite indispensable, as well as a source of joy. I am also most grateful to the production team at Knopf for their skilled, patient work: Melvin Rosenthal (production editor), Anthea Lingeman (designer), Claire Bradley Ong (production manager), and Archie Ferguson, who designed the jacket.

I must also express my gratitude to Michele Topham and Carole Robinson in Felicity Bryan's office, for their constant help and their calm support in moments of crisis; to John Esposito, who invited me to the Center for Muslim-Christian Understanding at Georgetown University in Washington, D.C. (giving me access to its rich resources and the expertise of every single one of its members), and, with his wife, Jeanette, lavished such generous hospitality upon me. Thanks also to Rosie Tollemache, who acted as my assistant for three glorious months, before leaving to have her baby, Lizzie, and to Henrik Mossin, my Danish translator, for introducing me to the work of Johannes Sloek. Finally, a big thank you to Kate Jones and John Tackaberry for their friendship in moments of despair and for the many beautifully cooked meals that supplemented my dismal diet during the long months of writing.

INDEX